BUSINESS LAW

For the Students of B.Com. (Pass & Hons.), CA, CS and Other Equivalent Examinations

BUSINESS LAW

For the Students of BCom (Pass & Honours), CA, CS and Other Equivalent Examinations

R.S.N. PILLAI
M.A. M.Com., LLB
Prof. & Head of the Department of Commerce
Arignar Anna College, Aramboly
Kanyakumari

BAGAVATHI
M.A., M.Com.
240, Chidambaranager
Nagercoil
Kanyakumari

S. Chand And Company Limited
(ISO 9001 Certified Company)

S. Chand And Company Limited

(ISO 9001 Certified Company)

Head Office: D-92, Sector–2, Noida – 201301, U.P. (India), Ph. 91-120-4682700

Registered Office: A-27, 2nd Floor, Mohan Co-operative Industrial Estate, New Delhi – 110 044, Phone: 011-49731800

www.**schandpublishing.com**; e-mail: **info@schandpublishing.com**

Marketing Offices:

Chennai : Ph: 23632120; chennai@schandpublishing.com
Guwahati : Ph: 2738811, 2735640; guwahati@schandpublishing.com
Hyderabad : Ph: 40186018; hyderabad@schandpublishing.com
Jalandhar : Ph: 4645630; jalandhar@schandpublishing.com
Kolkata : Ph: 23357458, 23353914; kolkata@schandpublishing.com
Lucknow : Ph: 4003633; lucknow@schandpublishing.com
Mumbai : Ph: 25000297; mumbai@schandpublishing.com
Patna : Ph: 2260011; patna@schandpublishing.com

© S. Chand And Company Limited, 1999

All rights reserved. No part of this publication may be reproduced or copied in any material form (including photocopying or storing it in any medium in form of graphics, electronic or mechanical means and whether or not transient or incidental to some other use of this publication) without written permission of the copyright owner. Any breach of this will entail legal action and prosecution without further notice.

Jurisdiction: *All disputes with respect to this publication shall be subject to the jurisdiction of the Courts, Tribunals and Forums of New Delhi, India only.*

First Edition 1999
Subsequent Editions and Reprints 2000, 2001, 2002, 2003, 2004, 2005, 2006, 2007 (Twice), 2008, 2009 (Twice), 2010
Third Revised Edition 2010; Reprints 2011, 2014 (Twice), 2015, 2016, 2017 (Twice), 2018, 2019 (Twice), 2020, 2021, 2022 (Thrice)

Reprint 2024 (Twice)

ISBN: 978-81-219-1927-2 **Product Code:** H8BUL48GLAW10ENAC10R

PRINTED IN INDIA

By Vikas Publishing House Private Limited, Plot 20/4, Site-IV, Industrial Area Sahibabad, Ghaziabad – 201 010 and Published by S. Chand And Company Limited, A-27, 2nd Floor, Mohan Co-operative Industrial Estate, New Delhi – 110 044.

PREFACE TO THE THIRD REVISED EDITION

We are encouraged by the widespread response from students, teachers and colleagues to the previous edition of the book — **Business Law**. In this revised and updated edition, the text has undergone an exhaustive revision and a substantial value addition.

The book has been written in a simple language and lucid style. Obsolete materials have been deleted and new concepts and information have been incorporated wherever found necessary. The whole book has been thoroughly revised and enlarged: many vital points have been added. The whole book is in the form of capsule model and unnecessary explanations have been removed. The present book is an asset to the student-community.

Vital points have been given in Boxes so that students can easily identify and memorise them. We have received appreciation letters from Kashmir to Kanyakumari, regarding the fruitful benefits filled in the Boxes. Really, they are the best tonics to teachers and students.

The book has been revised in the light of the comments and suggestions from a large number of our friends and readers for which we are really grateful to them.

The book could not be authored without the support and professional contribution from colleagues and teacher-friends. The feedback from friends has enabled us to remove all types of omissions. We express our deep gratitude to the students and teachers for their continuous response to the book — Business Law, since 1999.

We are thankful to the Management Team and the Editorial Department of S. Chand & Company Ltd. for all help and support in the publication of this book.

We are fully confident that the book would prove useful to the students of Commerce and Law. Suggestions for further improvement of the book are welcome and shall be gratefully acknowledged.

Kanyakumari
(Cell No. 9994045593, 9566367303)

R.S.N. Pillai
Bagavathi

Disclaimer : While the authors of this book have made every effort to avoid any mistake or omission and have used their skill, expertise and knowledge to the best of their capacity to provide accurate and updated information. The author and S. Chand does not give any representation or warranty with respect to the accuracy or completeness of the contents of this publication and are selling this publication on the condition and understanding that they shall not be made liable in any manner whatsoever. S.Chand and the author expressly disclaim all and any liability/responsibility to any person, whether a purchaser or reader of this publication or not, in respect of anything and everything forming part of the contents of this publication. S. Chand shall not be responsible for any errors, omissions or damages arising out of the use of the information contained in this publication. Further, the appearance of the personal name, location, place and incidence, if any; in the illustrations used herein is purely coincidental and work of imagination. Thus the same should in no manner be termed as defamatory to any individual.

PREFACE TO THE FIRST EDITION

The object of this book BUSINESS LAW is to set out the basic principles of Mercantile Law simply and clearly. An attempt has been made to present the concepts as briefly and concisely as possible without sacrificing essential features. Leading cases have been provided for illustration. Section numbers of the relevant Statutes have been given in order to facilitate reference. Vital points have been given in boxes so that students may easily identify and memorise them.

The book is specially designed to meet the needs of the students of B.Com., C.A., MBA, etc. of Indian Universities. It is hoped that all those genuinely interested in mastering Mercantile Law will find this book quite useful.

We are extremely thankful to Mr. Rajendra Kumar Gupta, Managing Director and Mr. Ravindra Kumar Gupta Director of M/s S. Chand and Company, New Delhi for bringing out this book in a short span of time. Suggestions for improvement of this book are most welcome and they will be incorporated in subsequent editions.

Nagercoil.
May, 1999

R.S.N. Pillai
Bagavathi

CONTENTS

THE INDIAN CONTRACT ACT, 1872

SPECIAL CONTRACT

THE SALE OF GOODS ACT, 1930

THE INDIAN PARTNERSHIP ACT, 1932

THE NEGOTIABLE INSTRUMENT ACT, 1881

THE CARRIAGE OF GOODS ACT

THE INSOLVENCY ACT

THE ARBITRATION ACT

LAW OF INSURANCE

TABLE OF CASES

THE INDIAN CONTRACT ACT, 1872

CHAPTER I

Introduction

AT A GLANCE

EVOLUTION

Freedom is the birth right of man and he derives utmost pleasure in its exercise. Slavery is the greatest of evils that he has to fight against. However, absolute individual freedom can exist at best in the world of ideas only, unless one, like Robinson Crusoe, gets an opportunity to live on a lonely island cut off from the rest of humanity. For, man is a social animal and has to surrender a part of his freedom to the society that in turn ensures him safety, security and peace. Society lays down rules of conduct for common good, sometimes at the expense of the individual.

The term "Society" is used to mean a community or a group of persons, living in any region, who are united together by some common bond. In early stages of history, society was unorganised, and commerce and trade had not developed. The rights of individuals were not recognised. But with the growth of civilization people became gradually aware of their own rights. They began to demand and fight for their rights. Redress was sought for wrongs committed. Individuals and groups began to resist oppression and injustice. Rulers were forced to submit themselves to public opinion. The individual had to be given his due, as he learnt to assert his rights. In the end society could not but recognize certain rights. Society began to take deterrent measures against wrongdoers and provide remedy to the injured ones. However, the party that was proved to be stronger was very often considered to be on the right and decision was in favour of the stronger party. Might often dictated the laws.

It is often found that law changes with a change in the society. Law is a body of rules that are used for regulating the conduct of the members of a society, and every society frames these rules according to its needs. Thus, as soon as the people start thinking that their needs are different from those of earlier times, they will consider changing their rules also. Todays' society is pluralistic as its members come from different races or tribes, communities and nations and follow different religious persuasions and have linguistic preferences. This march of the society from uniformity to plurality has brought about a clear measure of changes connected with the different factors that together constitute law and legal systems. It became the bounden duty of the society and the State to administer laws impartially and maintain peace and order.

As the State tended to become more and more powerful and even autocratic, more protection was required for individuals. Revolutions, like the French Revolution, brought about changes in the system of Government and gave new directions to the development of law. Law was periodically refashioned to meet the new problems created by social conditions. In good old days, the matters were decided on the basis of customs prevalent in society, but with the development of society, the customs gradually diminished, and legislative Acts and precedents became the main source of law.

Law and society are very closely related. Law aims at bringing about and maintaining peace and order in the society. The purpose of law is the administration of justice. Law is the body of precepts in accordance with which justice is administrated by the authority of the State. Justice is one of the noblest of ideals and is never fully realized. The primary purpose of law is to keep peace in society. Unless peace is attained and maintained a society cannot survive.

Every system of law must carry sanctions or punishments for violation of rules. Legally, a set of rules alone is not sufficient, unless:

(*a*) it is enforced by the State,
(*b*) it has its source in Sovereign Authority,
(*c*) it is accompanied by sanctions,
(*d*) it has a command and compel a course of conduct,
(*e*) it attempts to achieve security and uniformity in its application.

NEED FOR LAW

The existence of law is necessary for maintaining of peace and order in the society. In the absence of law, no person will recognise the rights of others. Life cannot be lived peace-fully and business cannot be carried out smoothly without law to regulate the conduct of people and to protect their property and contract rights. Life and business would soon become a matter of the survival not only of the fittest but also of the most ruthless, in the absence of law. Take the example of a game. A game cannot be played satisfactorily without rules to govern the players.

As a human being, every person comes into contact with others in different capacities; for instances, with sellers as a buyer, with companies as a shareholder, with traders as a purchaser of things, with insurers as assured, with government as a taxpayer, citizen or employee etc. In all such dealings, a person is expected to observe certain sets of rules which govern each other. It follows that some knowledge of law is necessary for every person. As a matter of tact, an individual is confronted, almost daily, with situations that demand certain knowledge of law, in the absence of which he may suffer on account of legal actions against him. There is a well-known maxim known as "*ignorantia juris non excusat*" which means that "ignorance of law is no excuse". One should know the law to which he is subject because *ignorance of law is no excuse.*

Example: If Mr. A is caught travelling in a train without ticket, *he cannot plead* that he was not aware of the rule regarding the purchase of ticket and therefore, Mr. A may be excused.

Example: If Mr. B is caught driving car without driving license, *he cannot plead* that he was not aware of the traffic rules regarding the obtaining of a driving license and therefore, he may be excused. Thus a person cannot escape liability on the ground of ignorance of law. However, this does not mean that every member of society must learn every branch of law. The requirement is that he must know something about rules and regulations by which he is governed, and the general principles of law of the land. The term 'law' denotes rules and principles either enforced by an authority or self-imposed by the members of a society to control and regulate people's behaviour with a view to securing justice, peaceful life and social security.

DEFINITION OF LAW

Law, as it is, is the command of the Sovereign. Law in its legal sense, as distinguished from other uses of the term, means those principles and rules that govern and regulate social conduct and the observance of which can be enforced in courts. A few definitions of law are given below:

1. "Law is that portion of the established habit and thought of mankind which has gained distinct and formal recognition in the shape of uniform rules backed by the authority and power of the Government" **— Woodrow Wilson**
2. "Law is a rule of civil conduct, prescribed by the supreme power of a State, commanding what is right and prohibiting what is wrong" **— Blackstone**
3. "Law is a rule of external human action enforced by the sovereign political authority". **— Holland**
4. Law is a rule of conduct imposed and enforced by the sovereign." **— Austin**

The State makes law. Violation of State law involves a penalty which is enforced by the Government through the sovereign power of the State. Whatever is not enforceable is not law. Laws of State are applicable to all without exception in identical circumstances.

It is neither desirable nor feasible to control all kinds of activities of people through a uniform set of rules and principles. Civilised societies, therefore, provide and enforce different sets of rules and guiding principles for different kinds of social behaviour. Therefore, there are several branches of law—Civil Law, Constitutional Law, International Law, Industrial and Mercantile Law. In this book, we shall confine our discussion to Mercantile or Commercial Law, as it exists in India.

MERCANTILE LAW

Mercantile law, also known as Commercial Law or Business Law, is that branch of law which governs and regulates trade and commerce. According to Slater, "the phrase Mercantile law or Commercial law, is generally used to denote that portion of the law which deals with the rights and obligations arising out of transactions between mercantile persons". Mercantile law, as a matter of fact, is one of the important branches of Civil law. It cannot be regarded as a separate branch of law. A mercantile person is one who enters into business transactions and he may be an individual, an association of persons, such as partnership or company.

SCOPE

With the increasing complexities of the modern business world, the scope of Mercantile Law has enormously widened. It is generally understood to include the laws relating to contracts, sales of goods, partnerships, companies, negotiable instruments, insurance, insolvency, carriage of goods, arbitration etc. The term Mercantile Law is used to denote that branch of law which deals with the rights and obligations arising out of mercantile transactions between mercantile persons. It should be noted that Business law is not altogether distinct and separate from other branches of law. In its application, recourse is often taken to other pieces of legislation. Laws as such are all interrelated. It is only a matter of convenience that legislation is classified into Business law, Labour law etc.

SOURCES OF MERCANTILE LAW

Indian Mercantile Law is largely based on the English Mercantile Law. However, necessary modifications have been made to provide for the local customs or usages of trade as necessitated by the peculiar conditions prevailing in India. It is important to note that in the absence of any specific law or custom or usage on a particular point, the rules of English Common Law are still applied by the courts in India. The important sources of Mercantile Law in India may be discussed under the following heads:

1. English Mercantile Law
   (*a*) The English Common Law
   (*b*) Principles of Equity
   (*c*) Law Merchant
2. Precedents
3. Indian Statute Law
4. Local Customs and Usages.

1. *English Mercantile Law*

Indian Mercantile Law is largely based on English Mercantile Law. In order, therefore, to trace the origin of the legal principles governing commercial transactions in India, it becomes necessary to know the sources of English Mercantile Law. These sources are :

(*a*) *The English Common Law*

The term "Common Law" is used to denote the case law based upon English customs, usages and traditions which were developed over centuries by the English Courts. Group life creates customs. When these customs become established to a reasonable extent each member of society is justified in assuming that every other member of the society will respect them and will act in conformity with them. Customs and usages which were evolved, recognised and adopted as rules of conduct by the English community, acquired the name of Common Law. When they became common over a wide area, when found expression in the judicial pronouncements, they became legal principles of law. The court by its decision, laid down a principle, based upon a custom or convenience, and they created a precedent which would provide guidance in similar future controversies. This is also referred to as "Unwritten Law" and it is not contained in any act of the legislature.

(*b*) *Principles of Equity*

English law of equity is another guideline for Indian courts. It is that branch of English Law which is based on principles of equity, justice and good conscience. It is also an unwritten law and developed separately from the Common Law. It grew as a system of law supplementary to the Common Law. In a sense, equity made up the deficiencies of the Common Law, especially where the Common Law worked harshly. The decisions of these courts became precedents for the subsequent cases. It may be noted that the law based on equity was flexible as compared to the Common Law.

(*c*) *Law Merchant or Lex Mercatoria*

One of the most important sources of English Mercantile Law is the Law Merchant or Lex Mercatoria based on customs usages, prevalent among merchants and traders. Initially, it was not recognised by the courts. But later on, in the beginning of the 17th century, the King's courts i.e., Common Law Courts began to recognise the rules of Law Merchant, which then became a part of Common Law. The fixed and stereotyped English Common Law was of little use for the settlement of disputes among merchants. The Law Merchant was developed with the progress of trade and commerce in England. In order to obtain quick relief and to protect them against lawlessness, there sprang up, among the merchants and traders a number of customs and usages for the conduct of their business dealings. The traders established their own tribunals consisting mainly of the merchants themselves. The rules pronounced by these tribunals became the law popularly known as the Law Merchant or Lex Mercatoria, which was an independent law till it was accepted and recognised by the Common Law Courts.

2. *Precedents* (Past Judicial Decisions of Courts)

The past judicial decisions of courts, referred to as Precedents, are an important source of law. They are binding on all courts having jurisdiction lower to that of the court which gave the judgment. That is, in India, the Supreme Court is the highest court, and its decisions have binding force on all courts subordinate to it. It is based on the principle that what has been decided in the earlier case is binding in a similar case, unless there is a change in the circumstances of the case.

3. *Indian Statute Law* (Act of Indian Legislature)

The legislature is the main source of law in modern times. In India, the Central and State legislatures possess law making powers and have exercised their powers extensively. It will be interesting to know that the bulk of the Indian Mercantile Law is the Statute Law, which in turn is largely based on the English Law. Where there is no specific provision on any particular point, the Common Law of England is applied by the Indian Courts. The important Acts passed by the Indian legislature are the Indian Contract Act 1872, the Negotiable Instruments Act 1881, the Sales of Goods Act 1930, The Indian Partnership Act 1932, the Companies Act 1956 etc.

4. *Local Customs and Usages*

The customs and usages of particular trades are important source of Indian Mercantile Law. They play an important role in regulating business dealings and guide the courts in deciding disputes arising out of mercantile transactions, but such a custom or usage must be widely known, certain and reasonable and must not be opposed to any legislative enactment. When the custom is accepted by a court and is incorporated in a judicial decision, it becomes a legally recognised custom.

THEORETICAL QUESTIONS

1. Define the term "Law". State the object of law and need for its knowledge.
2. What are the sources of Commercial Law in India?
3. What is the scope of Mercantile Law?
4. What are precedents?
5. Define Lex Mercatoria.

II

CHAPTER

Nature and Kinds of Contracts

(Section 1–2)

AT A GLANCE

- Introduction
- Definition of Contract
- Obligation
- Consensus Ad Idem
- Nature of the Act
- Elements of Valid Contract
- Classification of Contract
- Legal Validity
- Mode of Creation
- Performance
- Theoretical Questions
- Multiple Choice Questions
- Answers

INTRODUCTION

The law of contracts forms the oldest branch of the law relating to business transactions. It affects every person in one way or the other, as all of us enter into some kind of contract everyday. The law of contracts is applicable not only to the business community but also to others. Everyone of us enters into a number of contracts almost every day. When a person takes a seat in a bus or deposits his luggage in a railway clock room or entrusts his car to the mechanic for repairs etc., he enters into a contract, though he may not be aware of this fact. Such contracts create legal rights and obligations. The law of contracts is primarily concerned with self-imposed obligations. The parties to a contract do enjoy freedom of contract and the rights and duties created by them can be enforced even though the terms of the contract are harsh or unfair to one party. When people entered into a contract they made a piece of private law binding on each other and beneficial to themselves and in a wider sense to the community at large. The parties to a contract, in a sense, make the law for themselves. It does not lay down a number of rights and duties which the law will enforce, it consists rather of a number of limiting principles, subject to which the parties may create rights and duties for themselves which the law will uphold. Thus we can say that the parties to a contract, in a sense, make the law for themselves. When contracts were entered into freely and voluntarily they would be held enforceable by courts of justice. The law of contract determines the circumstances under which a promise or an agreement shall be legally binding on the person making it. It also provides the remedies which are available in a court of law against a person who fails to fulfil his contract and other conditions, under which the remedies are available. Legally enforceable promises are termed contracts. The object and function of law of contract is to see that, as far as it is possible, expectations created by promises of the parties are fulfilled and obligations prescribed by the agreement of the parties are enforced.

The law relating to contracts in India is contained in the Indian Contract Act 1872. The Act came into force on the first day of September 1872. It is not an exhaustive code containing the entire law of contracts. The Act as it now stands contains the general principles of Contract, Contract of Indemnity, suretyship, Bailment and Agency. Other branches of contract are now governed by other Acts such as the Partnership Act, the Negotiable Act, the Sales of Goods Act etc. Within the limiting principles laid down in the Indian Contract Act 1872, the parties may create rights and duties between themselves. Such rights and duties created must not be unlawful and must not infringe the legal principles. The Indian Contract Act may be divided into two parts :

Section 1 to 75 deals with the general principles of the Law of Contract.

Section 124 to 238 deals with special types of contracts such as,

(*a*) Contract of Indemnity and guarantee (Sec. 124 to 147)

(*b*) Contract of Bailment and Pledge (Sec. 148 to 181)

(*c*) Contract of Agency (Sec. 182 to 238)

DEFINITION OF CONTRACT

An agreement which creates legal obligations is a contract. The obligation is an undertaking to do or abstain from doing some definite act or acts. Section 2(h) of the Indian Contract Act 1872 defines a contract as follows :

"An agreement enforceable by law is a contract."

In other words, an agreement which can be enforced in a court of law is known as a contract. Thus a contract consists of the two elements : (1) An agreement and (2) the agreement must be enforceable by law.

First, there must be an agreement. Secondly, such an agreement must be enforceable by law. The Contract Act is the law of those agreements which create legal obligations. It will be enforceable if it is coupled with obligations. Thus contract is a combination of the two ideas of agreement and obligation. An obligation is the legal duty to do or abstain from doing what one has promised to do or abstain from doing.

The term agreement is defined in Section 2(e) of the Indian Contract Act which reads as under :

"Every promise and every set of promises, forming consideration for each other, is an agreement."

Sec. 2(b) defines promise as "A proposal when accepted, becomes a promise". Thus an agreement is an accepted proposal. We can easily conclude from the above mentioned provisions that an agreement consists of an offer or proposal from one party and its acceptance by the other. In other words :

Agreement = Offer + Acceptance

Agreement means a promise. It is created when a person makes an offer to another person and that other person signifies his assent or accepts it.

OBLIGATION

Obligation is a legal tie which imposes upon determinate person or persons the necessity of doing or abstaining from doing a definite act or acts. Obligations are also said to be varied; such as social obligations, obligations arising out of torts, obligations arising out of compromise decree, obligations arising out of quasi-contracts etc.

CONSENSUS AD IDEM

Consensus ad idem means identity of mind. Two or more persons are said to consent with each other when they agree upon the same thing in the same sense. Mentally, two or more persons must have identical intention in order to agree upon any subject matter for the purpose of making an agreement.

However, there are some agreements which are not enforceable in a law court. Such agreements do not give rise to contractual obligations and are not contracts. An agreement of purely social or domestic nature is not a contract.

> **Example : Balfour V Balfour (1919)**
>
> A husband and wife were residents in Ceylon, where husband was employed. They went to England on nine months leave. At the end of the time the husband had to return alone as the wife was advised to remain in England because of illness. The husband promised to send her a maintenance allowance of £ 30 a month until she returned to Ceylon. The husband failed to pay the amount. The wife sued for the allowance. It was held that there was no binding contract. She could not recover as it was a social agreement and parties did not intend to create any legal relations.

In everyday life a number of social and domestic arrangements are entered into and in these cases the parties usually do not intend to create legal relations between themselves. For example, a promise to lunch together at a friend's house or to attend a social function or to play a cricket match etc. When the two parties enter into an agreement, their intention must be to create legal relationship between them. If there is no such intention on the part of the parties, there is no contract between them.

The law of contract is not the law of those agreements which do not create legal obligations. In other words, the law of contract is not concerned with those agreements where the parties do not have the intention to create legal obligations. In social, domestic, moral or religious agreements, the usual presumption is that the parties do not intend to create legal obligations.

> **Example :** A invites B to a dinner. B accepts the invitation but fails to turn up. Here, A cannot sue B for damages because the parties to this agreement do not intend to create legal obligations.

The law of contract is applicable not only to business but also to all daytoday personal dealings. In fact, each one of us enter into a number of contracts from sunrise to sunset.

> **Examples:** (*i*) When you purchase a newspaper or milk, you enter into a contract with the vendor.
>
> (*ii*) A polished B's shoes without being asked by B to do so. B does not make any attempt to stop A from polishing the shoes. B is bound to pay because B has accepted A's implied offer by conduct, that is, by not stopping A from polishing the shoes.

NATURE OF THE ACT

The basic features or nature of the Indian Contract Act 1872 may be discussed, in brief, under the following heads :

1. Enforcement of the Act

The Act came into force on 1st September 1872. The Act is not retrospective in operation and does not apply to contracts entered into before it came into force. The Act applies to the whole of India except the State of Jammu and Kashmir.

2. It lays down the principles, not the rights and duties of the parties

The Sections 1 to 75 of the Contract Act lay down general principles relating to the formation, novation, alteration, performance and discharge of contracts. It does not lay down the rights and duties of the parties to a contract. The Act contains certain principles of law of contracts within which the parties are allowed to create their own legal rights and obligations under a contract. The parties are free to make their own terms and conditions of a contract subject to the provisions of the law of the land.

It does not lay down a number of rights and duties which the law will enforce; it consists rather of a number of limiting principles, subject to which the law will uphold. The parties to a contract, in a sense, make the law for themselves.

Thus a contract is made in accordance with the provisions of the Contract Act but the legal rights and obligations between the parties created by a contract are enforceable by action against the party in default.

3. The Act is not complete and exhaustive

The Contract Act does not profess to be a complete and exhaustive code dealing with the law of contracts. The Act contains certain general principles of the law of contracts alongwith the laws as some special contracts, that is, quasi-contract, indemnity, guarantee, bailment, pledge and agency. It does not incorporate law relating to all kinds of contracts. For example, the laws relating to sale of goods, partnerships, negotiable instruments, insurance etc. have not been incorporated in it. Separate Acts have been enacted to deal with such special contracts.

Further-more, where the cases are not covered either by the Contract Act or by any other special enactment relating to the contract, the provisions of Hindu Law to Hindus and Mahomedan Law to Mahomedans are applied. In the same way, it is also permissible to apply the established English principles of law in such a way as not to be inconsistent with justice, equity and good conscience.

The preamble to the Contract Act also states that this Act defines and amends only certain parts of the law relating to contracts. Therefore, all the Statutes, Acts and Regulations not amended or repealed, remain unaffected by the provisions of this Act. Again any usage or custom of trade, not inconsistent with the provisions of this Act, also remains unaffected.

Thus, all the laws, and customs of trade, not inconsistent with the provisions of the Contract Act remain unaffected and are allowed to prevail and applied where there is no express provision in the Contract Act.

4. It creates right in personam

Right has been defined as a capacity to control the other with the assent and assistance of the State. There are two types of rights available to a person : (*i*) right in personam or jus in personam; and (*ii*) right in rem or jus in rem. "The right in personam" means a right against a particular person or persons. "The right in rem" implies a right available to a person against the whole world. The rights created by a contract are purely personal in nature and only enforceable by action against the party in default.

Examples :

(*a*) Mr. A sells his scooter to Mr. B for Rs. 8,000. Mr. A has a right to recover the price of the scooter from Mr. B. The right of A is a right in personam, that is, against a particular person B. This is jus in personam.

(*b*) Mr. A buys a bike and becomes the owner of the bike. Mr. B has a right to have quiet possession of the bike and enjoy it against the whole world. Nobody, in the world, can disturb in his such a right. The right of Mr. A is jus in rem, that is the right against the whole world.

ESSENTIAL ELEMENTS OF A VALID CONTRACT

According to Section 10 of the Act lay down the essentials of a valid contract. According to the section, "All agreements are contracts if they are made by the free consent of the parties competent to contract, for a lawful consideration and with a lawful object, and are not hereby expressly declared to be void". Contracts are agreements, but all agreements need not be contracts. The term 'agreements' is, thus, much wider than the term 'contract'. An agreement becomes enforceable by law when it fulfils certain conditions. These conditions, which may be called the essential elements of a contract, are :

1. Offer and Acceptance
2. Intention to create legal relations
3. Lawful Consideration
4. Capacity of parties
5. Free and genuine consent
6. Lawful object
7. Agreement not declared void
8. Certainty and possibility of performance
9. Legal formalities.

These essential elements are explained briefly. Again all the above points will be discussed in detail in separate chapters.

1. *Offer and Acceptance*

An agreement is the foundation of a contract. An agreement is the result of an offer and its acceptance. An agreement comes into existence by acceptance of an offer. In an agreement there must be atleast two parties, one of them making the offer and the other accepting it. Acceptance must be in accordance with the terms and conditions of the proposal. An acceptance to be valid must be absolute and unqualified and in accordance with the exact terms of the offer. A proposal, when accepted becomes a promise. (See chapter III)

The person making the offer is known as 'offerer', 'proposer' or 'promisor'. The person to whom the offer is made is known as 'offeree' or 'proposee' or 'promisee'.

> **Example :** A proposes to sell his car to B for Rs. 50,000 and B conveys his acceptance. The agreement comes into existence.

2. *Intention to Create Legal Relations*

There must be an intention (among the parties) that the agreement shall result in or create legal relations. An obligation is the legal duty to do or abstain from doing a definite act or acts. If the parties do not intend to create legal obligations, there is no contract between them. An agreement which gives rise to a moral or social obligation is not contract. Promise in the case of social engagements is generally without an intention to create legal relationship. Thus an agreement to go for a movie, to play a game, to go for a walk etc. cannot be enforced in a court of law. Such an agreement, therefore, cannot be considered to be a contract. (See chapter VII).

> **Example :** I invited you for a dinner. You accepted the invitation. It is a social agreement. If I fail to serve you, you cannot go to Courts of Law for enforcing the agreement. Similarly, if you fail to attend the dinner, I cannot go to Court of Law for enforcing the agreement.

3. *Lawful Consideration*

The agreement must be supported by lawful consideration on both sides. Each party to the agreement must give or promise something and receive something or a promise in return. Consideration is the price for which the promise of the other is sought. (See Chapter VII).

> **Example :** If A offers to sell his scooter to B for Rs. 10,000 and B accepts the offer, then for A Rs. 10,000 is the consideration and for B the scooter is the consideration.

4. *Capacity of Parties*

The parties to an agreement must be competent to a contract, otherwise it cannot be enforced by a Court of Law. Minors, Lunatics, Drunkards, Idiots, Alien enemy, Convicts etc. are incompetent to contract. Under section 11 of the act, "Every person is competent to contract who is of the age of majority according to the law to which he is subject, and who is of sound mind, and is not disqualified from contracting by any law to which he is subject" (See Chapter V).

5. *Free and Genuine Consent*

The consent of the parties to the agreement must be free and genuine. The consent of the parties should not be obtained by misrepresentation, fraud, undue influence, coercion or mistake. If the consent is obtained by any of these flaws, then the contract is not valid. (See Chapter VI).

6. *Lawful Object*

The object for which the agreement has been entered must not be illegal or immoral or opposed to public policy. That is, the object of the agreement must be lawful and not one of which the law disapproves. (Chapter VII).

7. *Agreement not Declared Void*

The agreements must not have been expressly declared to be void by any law in force in the country. If certain agreements are expressly declared to be void by the law of the country, then such agreements if entered into, shall not be enforceable by Courts of Law. Under Indian Contract Act, there are five categories of agreements which are expressly declared to be void. They are : (See Chapter VIII).

1. Agreement in restraint to marriage (Sec. 26)
2. Agreement in restraint of trade (Sec. 27)
3. Agreement in restraint of proceedings (Sec. 28)
4. Agreements having uncertain meaning (Sec. 29)
5. Wagering agreement (Sec. 30).

8. *Certainty and Possibility of Performance*

Agreements to form valid contracts must be certain. If it is vague and it is not possible to ascertain its meaning, it cannot be enforced. The performance of an agreement must be possible. An agreement to do an impossible act is not valid. (See Chapter IX).

9. *Legal Formalities*

A contract may be oral or in writing. If, however, a particular type of contract is required by law to be in writing, it must comply with the necessary formalities as to writing, registration and attestation, if necessary. If these legal formalities are not carried out, then the contract is not enforceable at law.

The Indian Contract Act contains rules regarding each of the elements mentioned above. These rules are discussed in the subsequent chapters.

Essentials of a Valid Contract

1. There must be an *offer* and its *acceptance.*
2. The consent of the parties must be *free and genuine.*
3. The parties must intend to *create legal relationship.*
4. The parties must be *competent to contract.*
5. There must be *lawful consideration* on both sides.
6. There must be *lawful object.*
7. The agreement *not declared void* or *illegal.*
8. The terms of a contract should be *clear.*
9. The performance must *not be impossible.*
10. *Legal formalities*, if any.

Before dealing with the various essentials of a valid contract, one by one, it will be appropriate to discuss the classification of contract, because we shall be using the terms like, voidable contract, void contract, void agreement etc., very often in the course of our discussion.

CLASSIFICATION OF CONTRACTS

Contracts may be classified into the following three main categories :

I. ***According to enforceability i.e., legal validity***
   (1) Valid Contract
   (2) Void Agreement
   (3) Void Contract
   (4) Voidable Contract
   (5) Illegal Agreement
   (6) Unenforceable Contract

II. ***According to formation i.e., mode of creation***
   (1) Express Contract
   (2) Implied Contract
   (3) Quasi Contract

III. ***According to performance***
   (1) Executed Contract
   (2) Executory Contract
   (3) Unilateral Contract
   (4) Bilateral Contract

I. Classification According to Legal Validity

(i) Valid Contract : A contract which satisfies all the legal requirements laid down in Sec. 10 of the Act, is known as a valid contract. A valid contract is an agreement which is binding and enforceable at law.

(ii) Void Agreement : "An agreement not enforceable by law is said to be void". (Sec. 2 (g)). A void agreement has no legal effect. It confers no rights on any person and creates no obligations. Such an agreement is without any legal effect abinitio (from the very beginning).

Example : An agreement with a minor, for instance, is void from the beginning. The same is true of agreements in restraint of marriage, in restraint of trade, uncertain agreement etc.

(iii) Void Contract : A void contract is that which is not enforceable by law. Sec. 2 (j) of the Act lays down that "A contract which ceases to be enforceable by law becomes void when it ceases to be enforceable". A contract which is enforceable by law at the time it was made. But later on if it becomes legally unenforceable due to some reasons, it is called void contract.

Example : A promised to marry B. Later on B died. In this case, the contract becomes void on the death of B.

(iv) Voidable Contract : "An agreement which is enforceable by law at the option of one or more of the parties thereon, but not at the option of the other or others, is a voidable contract". Sec. 2 (i) A voidable contract is one which is enforceable by law at the option of one of the parties. Until it is avoided or rescinded by the party entitled to do so by exercising his option in that behalf, it is a valid contract. Such a contract is voidable at the option of the aggrieved party i.e., the party whose consent was so caused. (Sec. 19 and 19 A). In such cases where the consent is not free, the party whose consent is so caused becomes the aggrieved party who can either affirm the contract or set aside or rescind it. This right of recession should, however, be exercised within reasonable time and before the third party acquires rights under the contract.

Example : A agreed to sell his car to B for Rs. 50,000. The consent was obtained by use of force. The contract is voidable at the option of A. A can put an end to this contract, if he so decides.

(v) *Illegal Agreement :* An agreement is illegal and void if its object or consideration :
(*a*) is forbidden by law,
or (*b*) is of such a nature that, if permitted, it would defeat the provisions of any law;
or (*c*) is fraudulent;
or (*d*) involves or implies injury to the person or property of another;
or (*e*) the court regards it as immoral, or opposed to public policy (Sec. 23).
Thus an agreement to commit murder, robbery etc.

(*vi*) *Unenforceable Contract :* The unenforceable contracts are those which cannot be enforced in a Court of Law because of some technical defects. In certain cases, there are special provisions of law which require some formalities to be fulfilled, e.g., there are special provisions which provide that a contract must be in writing, or it must be registered, or it must be properly stamped or it must be attested etc. If such formalities are not properly observed, the contract cannot be enforced in a Court of Law. Such contracts can be enforced if the technical defect is removed.

II. Classification According to Formation i.e., Mode of Creation

(*i*) *Express Contract :* Sec. 9 provides that "In so far as the proposal or acceptance of any promise is made in words the promise is said to be express". An express promise will result in an express contract. When such contract is formed, there is no difficulty in understanding the rights and obligations of the parties.

Example : A writes a letter to B that he offers to sell his car for Rs. 60,000 and B in reply informs A that he accepts the offer. This is an express contract.

(*ii*) *Implied Contract :* Sec. 9 further states "In so far as such proposal or acceptance is made otherwise than in words, the promise is said to be implied". Such contract comes into existence on account of act or conduct of the parties.

Example : Mr. X went to a restaurant and took a cup of coffee.

In this, there is an implied contract that he will pay for the cup of coffee, even though he makes no express promise to do so.

(*iii*) *Quasi Contract :* There are certain dealings which are not contracts strictly, though the parties act as if there is a contract. In fact, it is an obligation which the law creates in the absence of any agreement. It rests on the ground of equity that "a person shall not be allowed to enrich himself unjustly at the expense of another.

Thus, a finder of lost goods is under an obligation to find out the true owner and return the goods.

Example : Mr. X supplied Y, a lunatic, with necessaries suitable to his conditions in life. In this case, X is entitled to be reimbursed from Y's estate.

III. Classification According to Performance

(*i*) *Executed Contract :* When both the parties have completely performed their respective obligations, under the contract, the contract is said to be executed. That is, it is a contract where under the terms of a contract nothing remains to be done by either the party. For instance, in case of cash sales, the contract is executed at once.

(*ii*) *Executory Contract :* In this contract the obligations of the parties are to be performed at a later time. When both the parties have not performed their respective obligations under the contract, the contract is said to be executory.

Example : Mr. A agrees to sell his bus to B for a certain amount. Delivery and payment are to be made in the month following. The contract is said to be executory.

Suppose, A delivered the bus to B, but B has not paid the amount, the contract is still executory because B is still under obligation to pay the price. As such, the contract as a whole is executory one, though it is partly executed and partly executory.

(*iii*) ***Unilateral Contract :*** In certain contracts one party has to fulfil his obligations, whereas the other party has already performed his obligations. Such a contract is called "unilateral" or "one sided contract" or "contract with executed consideration". Thus in case of unilateral contract the obligation is outstanding only against one of the parties at the time of formation of contract.

Example : Mr. A has lost his son. He offers by advertisement a reward of Rs. 50,000 to any person, who will bring his son safely to home. Mr. B who comes across the advertisement, finds the boy and bring him before A. As soon as B does this act, the contract comes into existence. Now only A has to perform his obligation by paying Rs. 50,000 to B, because B had already performed his part of obligation by finding the boy.

(*iv*) ***Bilateral Contract :*** Bilateral contract is one in which the obligation on the part of both the parties to the contract are outstanding at the time of formation of the contract. In such contracts, promise on one side is exchanged for a promise on the other. Thus, bilateral contracts are similar to executory contracts, and are also known as contracts with executory consideration.

Example : Mr. A promised to paint B's house for a sum of Rs. 500. It is a bilateral contract as there is exchange of promises and obligations of both the parties are outstanding at the time of formation of the contract.

Classification of contracts in the English Law

In English law, contracts are classified into (*a*) Formal Contracts and (*b*) Simple Contracts.

Formal Contracts

English Contract Act recognizes formal contracts. Validity of these contracts depends upon their form and they are valid even without consideration. They are of two types :

(*i*) Contracts under Seal, and

(*ii*) Contracts of Record

Contracts under seal are in writing and signed by the parties to them. The following contracts should be under seal, otherwise they will not be valid :

(*a*) Contracts without consideration :

(*b*) Lease of land for period of more than three years;

(*c*) Contracts by corporations; and

(*d*) Contracts with British Shipping

Contracts of Records include the court judgements and recognisances. Obligations in such cases arise out of court judgements and not under contracts.

Simple Contracts

All contracts other than the formal ones are called simple contracts or parol contracts. They may be made : (*i*) Orally, (*ii*) in writing or (*iii*) implied by conduct.

THEORETICAL QUESTIONS

1. Define the term Contract. (*B.Com. Delhi*)
2. What are the essentials of a Valid Contract? (*B.Com. Delhi*)
3. "All contracts are agreements, but all agreements are not contracts" Discuss. (*B.Com. M.S.*)
4. "The parties to a contract, in a sense, make the law for themselves" Comment. (*B.Com. Kerala*)
5. "In commercial and business agreements, the presumption is that the parties intend to create legal relations". Comment. (*B.Com. Hons. Delhi*)
6. "The law of contracts is not the whole law of agreements nor is it the whole law of obligations". Discuss. (*B.Com. Bombay*)
7. Is the law of contracts the whole law of obligations. (*B.Com. Hons. Delhi*)

8. Write short notes on :

(*a*) Valid Contract (*b*) Voidable Contract

(*c*) Executed Contract (*d*) Void contract

(*e*) Unenforceable Contract. (*B.Com. Madras*)

MULTIPLE CHOICE QUESTIONS

I. Choose correct option for each of the following:

(1) Law of Contract in India is contained in :

(*a*) The Indian Contract Act 1872. (*b*) The Indian Contract Act 1972.

(*c*) The Indian Contract Act 1930. (*d*) The Indian Contract Act 1932.

(2) The Indian Contract Act applies to :

(*a*) Whole of India except the State of Jammu and Kashmir.

(*b*) Whole of India including the State of Jammu and Kashmir.

(*c*) Whole of India except Goa, Daman, Diu.

(*d*) Whole of India including Goa, Daman Diu.

(3) The Indian Contract Act came into force on :

(*a*) 1st September 1972. (*b*) 1st July 1932.

(*c*) 1st September 1872. (*d*) 1st July 1930.

(4) The Indian Contract Act contains :

(*a*) 75 Sections. (*b*) 124 Sections.

(*c*) 1 to 238 sections except Sections 76 to 123. (*d*) 238 Sections.

(5) The Indian Contract Act enacted in the year:

(*a*) 1972. (*b*) 1872.

(*c*) 1857. (*d*) 1957.

(6) A contract creates:

(*a*) Jus in personam. (*b*) Jus in rem.

(*c*) Both (*a*) and (*b*) (*d*) Neither (*a*) nor (*b*).

(7) Which of the following statement is true :

(*a*) An agreement enforceable by law is a contract.

(*b*) An agreement is an accepted proposal.

(*c*) Both (*a*) and (*b*). (*d*) None of these.

(8) A jus in personam means a right against :

(*a*) A specific person. (*b*) The public at large.

(*c*) A specific thing. (*d*) None of these.

(9) Usage or customs of the trade applies to a contract where:

(*a*) It is reasonable. (*b*) It is legal.

(*c*) It is universal. (*d*) The Contract Act does not expressly provide for.

(10) A contract gives rise to the :

(*a*) Rights against the whole world.

(*b*) Rights against a business firm.

(*c*) Rights of a party against another party to the contract.

(*d*) Rights against a particular person.

(11) An agreement is valid :

(*a*) which creates legal and social obligations of the parties.

(*b*) which creates rights of a party.

(*c*) which is written on a piece of paper and signed by the parties.

(*d*) which creates legally binding rights and obligations of the parties to it.

(12) A contract is one which :

(*a*) creates and defines obligations of the parties to it.

(*b*) creates only business obligations of the parties to it.

(*c*) creates legally binding relations between the parties to it.

(*d*) creates legal and social obligations of the parties to it.

(13) An agreement means :

(*a*) a group of promises.

(*b*) every promise and every set of promise forming consideration for each other.

(*c*) expression of willingness to do something.

(*d*) an assurance to make an agreement in future.

(14) A commercial agreement may stipulate that it :

(*a*) will not be enforceable by law.

(*b*) will not create legal relations between the parties.

(*c*) will not be subject to jurisdiction of any law Court.

(*d*) either (*a*) or (*b*) or (*c*) or all of the above.

(15) Every agreement :

(*a*) creates social obligations.

(*b*) creates moral obligations.

(*c*) creates legal obligations.

(*d*) may or may not create legal obligations.

(16) In social agreements usual presumption is :

(*a*) that parties do not intend to create social relations.

(*b*) that parties intend to perform them.

(*c*) that parties do not intend to make legal and social relations.

(*d*) that the parties do not intend to create legal relations between them.

(17) An agreement comes into existence :

(*a*) when an offer is made.

(*b*) when offers are exchanged between the parties.

(*c*) when offeree signifies his assent to the offeror.

(*d*) when the offeree accepts an offer with some of its conditions.

(18) A contract creates :

(*a*) rights and obligations of the parties to it.

(*b*) obligations of the parties to it.

(*c*) mutual understanding between the parties to it.

(*d*) mutual lawful rights and obligations of the parties to it.

(19) A contract is valid one :

(*a*) if it is certain in some respects.

(*b*) if its meaning and terms are certain or capable of being made certain.

(*c*) if it has certain valid conditions.

(*d*) if it is to be performed at a certain date at the desire of a party.

(20) In a commercial contract usual presumption is :

(*a*) that the parties have no intention to create legal relations.

(*b*) that the parties would create legal relations in future.

(*c*) that the parties have intention to create legal relations.

(*d*) that the parties are at discretion to treat the contract as valid or void.

(21) A contract needs to have :

(*a*) any one of the essentials of a contract.

(*b*) all the essentials of a contract except consideration.

(*c*) all the essentials of a contract simultaneously at the time of making and enforcing it.

(*d*) all the essentials of a contract when it is made.

(22) The term contract has been defined under :

(*a*) sec. 2(h) of the General Contract Act, 1872.

(*b*) sec. 2(h) of the Common Contract Act, 1872.

(*c*) sec. 2(h) of the Indian Contract Act, 1872.

(*d*) sec. 2(h) of the Uniform Contract Act of India, 1872.

(23) An agreement is :

(*a*) enforceable by law if it meets the requirements of the law of the land.

(*b*) enforceable by law if any one party to it wants.

(*c*) enforceable against the law.

(*d*) enforceable by law if it is made by competent parties.

(24) A contract needs to be written, registered and signed by parties and witnessed :

(*a*) if the parties desire so. (*b*) if the Contract Act directs so.

(*c*) if the law governing the contract requires so. (*d*) if the consideration in the contract is very small.

(25) All agreements are valid :

(*a*) if they are made by persons competent to contract.

(*b*) if they are made by the free consent of the parties.

(*c*) if they are made for lawful objects.

(*d*) if they are made in accordance with the law of contracts.

(26) All commercial agreements :

(*a*) are legally binding.

(*b*) are not legally binding.

(*c*) are legally binding if made in accordance with the provisions of the law.

(*d*) are legally binding even if no party intends so.

(27) All contracts are agreements but all agreements are not contracts because :

(*a*) all agreements are not commercial contracts.

(*b*) all agreements do not have all the essentials of a valid contract at the time of enforcement of the agreement.

(*c*) all agreement do not have all the essentials of a valid contract both at the time of formation and enforcement of the contract.

(*d*) all agreements are personal and domestic contracts.

(28) A contract comes into existence by :

(*a*) Proposal + Assent to the proposal + Enforceability by law.

(*b*) Proposal + Acceptance of some conditions by the offeree + Other essentials of a contract.

(*c*) Promise + Consideration + Free consent of the parties.

(*d*) Agreement + Consideration + Certainty.

(29) A contract to contract in future is :

(*a*) valid contract. (*b*) no contract.

(*c*) void agreement. (*d*) illegal agreement.

(30) A contract is an agreement :

(*a*) not against the interest of public.

(*b*) not against the interest of any individual.

(*c*) not against the law of the land.
(*d*) which complies all the principles of law of contracts.

(31) A contract with the Government must be :
(*a*) written on stamp paper.
(*b*) written and registered.
(*c*) written.
(*d*) written, stamped and registered.

(32) Every promise and every set of promises, forming consideration for each other is :
(*a*) a contract.
(*b*) agreement.
(*c*) reciprocal promise.
(*d*) none of the above.

(33) A contract is a combination of :
(*a*) agreement and consideration.
(*b*) agreement and free consent.
(*c*) agreement and enforceability.
(d) agreement and competence of parties.

(34) The maximum number of parties in a contract may be :
(*a*) two.
(*b*) infinite.
(*c*) four.
(*d*) three.

(35) A void agreement :
(*a*) is null and void.
(*b*) is not enforceable by law.
(*c*) does not create legal obligations.
(*d*) all of the above.

(36) A void contract arises when :
(*a*) the parties are incompetent to contract.
(*b*) there is absence of free consent.
(*c*) impossibility of performance of contract arises.
(*d*) consideration fails.

(37) In a voidable contract, the aggrieved party has a right of :
(*a*) rescission of the contract.
(*b*) restitution.
(*c*) both (*a*) and (*b*) above.
(*d*) neither (*a*) nor (*b*).

(38) A valid contract :
(*a*) is always enforceable.
(*b*) can not become void agreement subsequently.
(*c*) may cease to be enforceable and become void contract.
(*d*) either (*a*) or (*c*).

(39) A voidable contract is one :
(*a*) which is voidable at the option of parties to the contract.
(*b*) which is voidable at the option of any one party to the contract.
(*c*) which is voidable at the option of the aggrieved party to the contract.
(*d*) which is voidable with the mutual consent of the parties the contract.

(40) A void agreement is :
(*a*) void from beginning.
(*b*) void subsequently.
(*c*) void due to change in law.
(*d*) void because party wants so.

(41) An agreement enforceable by law at the option of one party but not of the other party is called :
(*a*) void contract.
(*b*) voidable contract.
(*c*) unlawful agreement.
(*d*) void agreement.

(42) A contract is voidable for the want of :
(*a*) consideration.
(*b*) free consent.
(*c*) capacity to contract.
(*d*) all of the above.

(43) In a void agreement :

(*a*) a party may be incompetent to contract.
(*b*) consideration is missing.
(*c*) absence of free consent.
(*d*) both (*a*) and (*b*) above.

(44) A void agreement is one :

(*a*) which does not have any value in the eye of law.
(*b*) which is enforceable by law.
(*c*) which is unenforceable due to certain technical defects in it.
(*d*) which is against the interest of the other party.

(45) Void contract is one :

(*a*) which is voidable in the beginning but becomes void subsequently.
(*b*) which is valid at the time of its formation but becomes voidable subsequently.
(*c*) which is valid at the time of its formation but becomes void subsequently.
(*d*) which is unenforceable in the beginning but becomes illegal subsequently.

(46) A void agreement :

(*a*) is illegal.
(*b*) is unenforceable by law.
(*c*) violates legal procedure.
(*d*) is against the interest of an individual.

(47) A voidable contract :

(*a*) may be enforced.
(*b*) cannot be enforced.
(*c*) may be illegal.
(*d*) is partly legal and partly illegal.

(48) A void contract :

(*a*) is void from beginning.
(*b*) becomes void when it ceases to be enforceable.
(*c*) is void when aggrieved party wants to avoid.
(*d*) when law treats it void.

(49) Contractual obligations are created by :

(*a*) Contracts.
(*b*) status of a person.
(*c*) quasi-contract.
(*d*) all of the above.

(50) A quasi-contract is :

(*a*) made by the parties.
(*b*) unlawful.
(*c*) imposed upon the parties by the law.
(*d*) not a valid contract in the eye of law.

ANSWERS

1. (*a*)	**2.** (*a*)	**3.** (*c*)	**4.** (*c*)	**5.** (*b*)	**6.** (*a*)	**7.** (*c*)	**8.** (*a*)	**9.** (*d*)	**10.** (*c*)
11. (*d*)	**12.** (*c*)	**13.** (*b*)	**14.** (*d*)	**15.** (*c*)	**16.** (*d*)	**17.** (*c*)	**18.** (*d*)	**19.** (*b*)	**20.** (*c*)
21. (*c*)	**22.** (*c*)	**23.** (*a*)	**24.** (*c*)	**25.** (*d*)	**26.** (*c*)	**27.** (*c*)	**28.** (*a*)	**29.** (*b*)	**30.** (*d*)
31. (*c*)	**32.** (*b*)	**33.** (*c*)	**34.** (*b*)	**35.** (*c*)	**36.** (*c*)	**37.** (*c*)	**38.** (*d*)	**39.** (*c*)	**40.** (*a*)
41. (*b*)	**42.** (*b*)	**43.** (*d*)	**44.** (*a*)	**45.** (*c*)	**46.** (*b*)	**47.** (*a*)	**48.** (*b*)	**49.** (*a*)	**50.** (*c*)

CHAPTER

Offer and Acceptance

(Section 3–9)

AT A GLANCE

- Offer or Proposal
- Elements
- How an Offer is made?
- Types of offers
- Essentials of Valid Offer
- Acceptance
- Essentials of Valid Acceptance
- Communication of Offer and Acceptance
- Revocation of Offer
- Revocation of Acceptance
- Theoretical Questions
- Multiple Choice Questions
- Practical Problems
- Answers.

While discussing the essential elements of a valid contract in the preceding chapter, we observed that as a first step in making of a contract, there must be a *lawful offer* by one party and a *lawful acceptance* of the offer by the other party. Thus A says to B, "will you buy my car for Rs. 80,000?". This is an offer. If B says "Yes", the offer is accepted and a contract is formed.

OFFER OR PROPOSAL

The term offer or proposal is defined in Sec. 2(a) of the Indian Contract Act, which reads as under :

"When one person signifies to another his willingness to do or to abstain from doing anything with a view to obtaining the assent of that other to such act or abstinence, he is said to make a proposal".

The person making the proposal or offer is called *proposer, offeror* or *promisor*. The person to whom the offer or proposal is made is called the *proposee* or *offeree*. When the offeree accepts the offer, he is called *promisee* or *acceptor*. An offer is synonymous with proposal. An offer has two parties.

(*a*) A promise by the offeror to do or to abstain from doing anything, and

(*b*) A request by the offeror to the offeree to do or to abstain from doing something in return.

The essential elements of offer are :

1. There can be no proposal by a person to himself. That is, there must be atleast two parties — Offerer and Offeree or Acceptor.
2. An offer is simply a request by the offerer to the offeree.
3. A proposal may be positive or negative.
4. A proposal must be made to obtain assent of the offeree.

HOW AN OFFER IS MADE

Sec. 3 of the Act gives us the manner in which an offer may be made. Further Sec. 9 of the Act states. "In so far as the proposal or acceptance of any promise is made in words, the promise is said to be *express*. In so far such proposal or acceptance is made otherwise than in words, the promise is said to be *implied*".

Thus an offer can be made by any act which has the effect of communicating it to another person. An offer may be (*a*) Express Offer or (*b*) Implied Offer.

(*i*) EXPRESS OFFER

An offer which is made by words, written or spoken, is called an express offer.

Examples : (1) A says to B, "Will you purchase my scooter for Rs. 8,000?" This is an express offer.

(2) A writes a letter to B offering to sell his car for Rs. 60,000 to him. This is an express offer.

(*ii*) IMPLIED OFFER

An offer which is expressed by conduct, is called implied offer. In simple words, it is inferred from the conduct of the person or the circumstances of the particular case.

Example : KSRTC runs special buses on a particular route. There is an implied offer from KSRTC to carry the passengers on the route who are prepared to pay the specified fare. This is an implied offer.

On the basis of offeree, there are two types of offers : (*i*) Specific Offer and (*ii*) General Offer.

(*i*) SPECIFIC OFFER

A specific offer is one which is made to a definite person or particular group of persons. A specific offer can be accepted only by that definite person or that particular group of persons to whom it has been made.

Examples : (1) Mr. A makes an offer to B to sell his car for Rs. 50,000. The offer has been made to a definite person, *i.e.*, B. And B alone can accept it. This is a specific offer.

(*ii*) GENERAL OFFER

A general offer is one which is not made to a definite person, but to the world at large or public in general. A general offer can be accepted by any person by fulfilling the terms of the offer.

Example :

Carlill Vs. Carbolic Smoke Ball Company (1893).

In the above case, the Carbolic Smoke Ball Company issued an advertisement in which the Company offered to pay £ 100 to any person who contracts influenza, after having used their smoke balls three times daily for two weeks, according to the printed directions. It was also added that £ 1000 are deposited with the Alliance Bank showing the sincerity of the Company. One Mrs. Carlill used the smoke balls according to the printed directions. But she subsequently suffered from influenza. She sued the Company for the promised reward, and it was held that the Company was liable to the reward. Thus the case is important as it lays down the following principles.

1. An offer may be made to the general public in which case it can be accepted by any particular individual.
2. It was not a mere advertising puff and the deposit in the bank showed the sincerity in the promise.
3. It was argued that a notification of the acceptance should have been made to the Company. But on this point, it was held that in such cases "the performance of the conditions is the acceptance of the offer".
4. An advertisement need not always be a mere invitation to offer but may in certain circumstances amount to an offer.

On the basis of nature of offer, an offer may be : (*i*) Cross Offer, (*ii*) Counter-Offer and (*iii*) Standing Offer.

(*i*) CROSS OFFER

When two person make identical offers, that is, similar in terms, conditions etc., to each other, without having knowledge of each other's offer, are known as cross offers. Such offers do not constitute a contract even though both the parties intend to do or not to do the same thing. It is also important to note that one's offer cannot be treated as acceptance of other's offer. When one of the parties accepts the offer of the other party, contract comes into existence.

> **Example :** A, by a letter, offered to sell his car to B for Rs. 50,000. Without knowing about A's offer. B also by a letter, offered to buy A's car for Rs. 50,000. Both the offers crossed each other in post. Here, the offers are cross offers, and thus, no binding contract will come into existence.

(*ii*) COUNTER OFFER

When an offer is accepted on the terms and conditions other than set out by the offerer, it is not an acceptance but a counter offer. A counter offer is, in fact, not only a rejection of the original offer but is also a new offer by the original offeree.

> **Example :** *Hyde Vs. Wrench* (1840)
>
> It was held that a counter-offer would amount to a rejection of the original offer. On 6th June, the defendant offered to sell an estate to the plaintiff for £ 1,000. On 8th June, the plaintiff made a reply offering to purchase it for £ 950. It was refused by the defendant on 27th June. Then, on 29th June, the plaintiff wrote that he was prepared to pay £ 1,000. It was held that the Plaintiff's letter expressing his willingness to purchase for £ 950 was not an acceptance. It was a counter-offer which terminated the original offer. It was not afterwards possible to revive the proposal of the defendant by tendering an acceptance of it.

(*iii*) STANDING OFFER

An offer which is allowed to remain open for acceptance over a period of time, is known as a standing, open or continuing offer. For example, an offer to supply 500 bags of rice from 1st January to 30th June, in accordance with the orders which may be placed from time to time, is a standing offer.

ESSENTIALS AND LEGAL RULES FOR A VALID OFFER

The following are the legal rules for a valid offer :

1. *The offer must be communicated to the other party*

An offer is effective only when it is communicated to the offeree. A person cannot accept an offer unless he knows of the existence of the offer. Until the offer is made known to the offeree, there can be no acceptance and no contract. An offer is completed only when it has been communicated to the offeree. An offer accepted without its knowledge, does not confer any legal rights on the acceptor. According to Sec. 4 of the Act, "The communication of a proposal is complete when it comes to the knowledge of the person to whom it is made.

> **Example :** *Lalman Shukla Vs. Gauri Dutt (1913).*
>
> The defendant sent the plaintiff who was in his service in search of his missing nephew. Later on the defendant announced that anybody, who discovered the missing boy would be given a reward of Rs. 501. The plaintiff discovered the boy without knowing the reward. When the plaintiff came to know about the reward, he brought an action against the defendant to recover the same. His suit was dismissed on the ground that he could not accept the offer, unless he had knowledge of it.

2. *The Terms of the Offer must be Definite and Clear*

The terms of an offer should be definite and certain and not vague or ambiguous. Anson says "The law requires the parties to make their own contract : it will not make a contract for them out of terms which are indefinite or illusory". Further Sec. 29 of the Act lays down "Agreements, the meaning of which is not certain, or capable of being made certain, are void". The offer must be reasonably definite and requires nothing to complete it except acceptance.

Examples : (1) *Montreal Gas Co. Vs. Vasey (1900).*

The plaintiff relied on a clause that if the company were satisfied with him as a customer the company would "favourably consider an application for renewal of the contract". The court held that there was nothing in these words to create legal obligation.

(2) *Taylor Vs. Portington (1855)*

X Purchased a horse from Y and promised to buy another, if the first one proves lucky. X refused to buy the second horse. Y could not enforce the agreement it being loose and vague.

(3) A offered to sell his car to B for Rs. 40,000 or Rs. 45,000. There is nothing to show which of the two prices was to be given. This offer cannot be accepted as it is not clear. Thus, no contract will result from this offer.

3. *The Offer must be Capable of Creating Legal Relationship*

If the offer does not intend to give rise to legal consequences, it is not a valid offer in the eye of law. An offer must be such that when accepted it will result in a valid contract. The offer must be one which is capable of creating a legal relationship. A social party or an invitation to play cards is not a legal relationship. Generally speaking, in the case of agreements regulating social relations, it is natural inference that the parties do not intend to create legal relations, while in the case of agreements, regulating business relations, the inference is that the parties intend to create legal relations.

Examples : (1) *Balfour Vs. Balfour (1919)* (See Chapter II)

The agreement was only an arrangement between husband and wife, and the parties never intended to make a bargain.

(2) Rose and Frank Co. Vs. Crompton & Bros Ltd. (1925)

Sometimes the parties to a business transaction may deliberately state that they do not intend to enter into any legal relationship. The plaintiffs, an American firm, were the constituted selling agents in North America for the defendant, an English Company under a written agreement. It contained the following clause : "This arrangement is not entered into nor is this memorandum written, as a formal or legal agreement, and shall not be subject to legal jurisdiction in the Law Courts". It was held that the agreement was not legally binding contract. The intention of the parties as expressed in the written document was respected by the court.

4. *The Offer must be Made with a View to Obtain Acceptance*

When a person is making an offer it means that he is making it with a view to obtain the consent of the offeree. Sec. 2 (a) of the Act lays down, "When one person signifies to another his willingness to do or to abstain from doing anything, with a view to obtaining the assent of that other to such act or abstinence, he is said to make a proposal." The terms of an offer should be clear so that there is no confusion whether it is a valid offer or a mere statement of intention. A declaration by a person that he intends to do something gives no right of action to another.

An offer must be distinguished from an "*invitation to receive offer*" or as it is sometimes expressed in judicial language as "*invitation to treat*". If an advertisement is made by a company that it has stock of books to sell or houses to let, there is no offer to be bound by any contract.

Such advertisements are "*offers to negotiate*" or "*offers to receive offers*" or "*offers to chaffer*". Advertisements are generally assumed to constitute "*invitations to trade*". The trader merely indicates that he is willing to consider an offer made by a buyer on these terms. That is, he is inviting an offer and not making one.

Catalogue and Price List : A catalogue or a price list of a shopkeeper is not an offer. It is only an invitation to receive offer from his customers. The trader merely indicates that he is willing to consider an offer made by a buyer on the terms. That is, he is inviting an offer and not making one. A shopkeeper cannot be compelled to sell his goods as per the printed price. Thus the buyer only gives an offer, which may or may not be accepted by the shopkeeper.

Declaration of Intention : Sometimes, a person declares that he has the intention to do something and this does not amount to an offer. Such a declaration only means that an offer will be made or invited in future.

Advertisement : Newspaper advertisements inviting applications for a job or inviting tenders for some work is not an offer. It is only an invitation to make offers. Applicants who reply to the advertisement are the offerers.

Following are other example of invitation to make an offer :

(1) Goods exhibited with price on a label stuck to them in showcase.
(2) Menu card in a restaurant.
(3) Prospectus of a company inviting public to subscribe for shares or debentures.
(4) An advertisement inviting applications for situation or a post.
(5) An advertisement for sale of goods by auction.
(6) Railway timetable, etc.

Examples :

(1) *Harris Vs. Nickerson (1873)*

In this case an auction sale was advertised whereupon the plaintiff travelled a distance to attend the sale with a view to buy the article. On his arrival he found that the sale was cancelled on which he sued the auctioneer for breach of contract on the ground that the advertisement was an offer made to the public which he accepted by travelling. The court held that the advertisement was merely a declaration of intention and that there could not be an acceptance.

(2) Pharmaceutical Society Vs. Boots Cash Chemists (1953)

Where a shopkeeper displays goods in a shop window, or even puts them out on shelves in a self-service store, that is to be construed as an invitation to treat and not as an offer to sell. When a customer picks up an article in a self-service store and takes it to the cashier's desk to pay for it, his action cannot be said to be an acceptance of an offer to sell but is an offer to buy which the shopkeeper may or may not accept.

5. *An Offer may be Positive or Negative :*

Sec. 2 (a) reads as under :

"When one person signifies his willingness to do or abstain from doing something..."

Thus, an offer may be to do something or not to do something. An offer to do something, is a positive offer. And an offer not to do something, is negative offer.

6. *The Offer should not Contain any term the Non-compliance of which Amounts to Acceptance:*

Thus an offeror cannot say that if acceptance is not communicated upto a certain date, the offer would be presumed to have been accepted. If the offeree does not reply, there is no contract, because no obligation to reply can be imposed on him, on the grounds of justice.

7. *Special Terms and Conditions of the Offer be Communicated :*

If the acceptor or the promisee had no knowledge of special terms, before or at the time of the contract, they are not binding upon the acceptor.

Example : *Henderson Vs. Stevenson (1875)*

The plaintiff purchased a ticket from a steamship company. On the face of it the words, "From Dublin to Whitehaven" were written. On the back there were some conditions exonerating the company from liability for loss or injury to the passenger or his luggage. The plaintiff had no knowledge of this condition. His luggage was lost. In a suit claiming damages for the loss, it was held that the plaintiff was not debarred by the condition of which he had no knowledge.

If the acceptor or the promisee had the knowledge or may be presumed to have the knowledge because a reasonably sufficient notice has been given to him by suitable words on the document of special terms, before or at the time of the contract, the terms are binding upon the acceptor whether he has read them or not is immaterial.

Example : *Parker Vs. South Eastern Railway Co. (1877).*

A passenger deposited a bag in the cloakroom at a Railway Station. The acknowledgment receipt given to him bore, on the face of it, the words "See back". One of the conditions printed on the back limited the liability of the Railways for any package to £ 10. The bag was lost, and passenger claimed £ 24 S 10, its value, pleading that he had not read the conditions on the back of the receipt. Held, the passenger was bound by the conditions printed on the back as the company gave reasonable notice on the face of the receipt as to the conditions at the back of the document.

8. *Two Identical Cross-Offers do not Result in a Contract*

When two parties make identical offers to each other, in ignorance of each other's offer, the offers are cross-offers. Cross-offers do not constitute acceptance of one's offer by the other and as such there is no completed agreement.

Example : *Tinn Vs. Hoffmann (1873).*

The defendant wrote to the plaintiff offering to sell a certain quantity of iron at a particular price. The same day the plaintiff wrote to the defendant offering to buy the same quantity of iron at the same price. Unknown to each other the letters crossed in post. The plaintiff claimed that there was a contract. It was held that mere cross-offers made in ignorance of each other would not create a contract.

Essentials of a Valid Offer

1. It must be made with a view to obtain acceptance.
2. It must be intended to create legal relations.
3. The terms of the offer must be definite and certain.
4. The offer must be communicated to the offeree.
5. An offer may be express or implied.
6. It must be distinguished from "Invitation to offer" or "declaration of intention".
7. The special terms of the offer must be communicated.
8. The offer should not contain any terms the non-compliance of which amounts to acceptance.
9. Two identical cross-offers do not result in a contract.
10. An offer may be general or specific.

Agreement to Agree in Future

Agreement to make a future contract does not create any obligation. Therefore, a contract cannot be made to make another contract. If the parties have not agreed upon the terms of their contract but have made an agreement to agree in future, there is no contract. Subsequently, agreement to agree in future becomes contradictory. Such agreement is not possible as the conditions for future cannot be decided.

ACCEPTANCE

Sec. 2 (b) defines acceptance as "When one person to whom the proposal is made signifies his assent thereto, the proposal is said to be accepted. A *proposal*, when accepted becomes a *promise*".

Who can Accept?

An offer can be accepted only by the person or persons for whom the offer is intended. An offer made to a particular person can only be accepted by him because he is the only person intended to accept. But, an offer made to the *world at large* can be accepted by any person whatsoever. To constitute a valid acceptance the assent must be communicated to the offeror.

Example : *Boulton Vs. Jones (1857).*

Mr. A sold his business to his manager B without disclosing the fact to his customers. C, a customer, who had a running account with A, sent an order for the supply of goods to A by name. B received the order and executed the same. It was held that there was no contract between B and C because C never made any offer to B.

In the suit by the plaintiff against the defendant for the price of the goods, it was held that Jones was not liable, since Boulton knew that the offer was not addressed to him.

Essentials and Legal Rules for a Valid Acceptance :

The acceptance of an offer to be legally effective must satisfy the following requirements:

1. *Acceptance must be Absolute and Unqualified* (Sec. 7 (1))

In order to be legally effective it must be an absolute and unqualified acceptance of all the terms of the offer. Even the slightest deviation from the terms of the offer makes the acceptance invalid. Acceptance should be in toto and without any condition. Thus an acceptance with a variation is no acceptance. A qualified or a conditional acceptance is no acceptance at all. In fact, it is only counter-offer. A counter-offer puts an end to the original offer and it cannot be revived by subsequent acceptance.

Example : *Hyde Vs. Wrench (1840).*

The defendant offered to sell his farm to the plaintiff for £ 1000. Plaintiff made a reply offering to purchase it for £ 950. It was refused by the defendant. Then, the plaintiff wrote that he was prepared to pay £ 1000. It was held that the plaintiff's letter expressing his willingness to purchase for £ 950 was not an acceptance. The court held that the offer to buy at £ 950 in response to the offer to sell for £ 1000 was only a counter-offer, which amounted to rejection of the original offer and it was not possible to revive the original offer. Hence, there was no contract between the parties.

2. *Acceptance must be Communicated to the Offeror*

The acceptance is completed only when it has been communicated to the offeror. Until the acceptance is communicated it does not create any legal relations. A mere mental acceptance is no acceptance. A mere mental acceptance means that the offeree is assenting to an offer in his mind only and has not communicated it to the offeror.

Example : *Brogden Vs. Metropolitan Railway Co. (1877).*

A draft agreement relating to the supply of coal was sent to the manager of a Railway Company for his acceptance. The manager wrote the word "approved" and put the draft in the drawer of his table intending to send it to the Company's solicitor for a formal contract to be drawn up. By some oversight the document remained in the drawer. Held, there is no contract.

3. *The Acceptance must be in the Prescribed Manner*

Where the offeror prescribes a particular mode of acceptance then the acceptor should follow that mode. However, where acceptance is not made in the prescribed mode, the proposer may, within a reasonable time after the acceptance is communicated to him, insist that his proposal shall be accepted in the prescribed mode, and not otherwise. But if he fails to do so, he accepts the defective acceptance.

In case no mode of acceptance is prescribed by the proposer, then the acceptance must be according to some usual and reasonable mode.

4. *The Acceptance must be in Response to Offer*

There can be no acceptance without offer. Acceptance cannot precede offer. For example: no allotment of shares in a company can be made unless the allottee has applied for them beforehand. As such, acceptance should follow the offer and no precede it.

5. *The Acceptance must be by the Offeree*

An offer can be accepted only by the person or persons to whom it is made. A valid contract arises only if acceptance is communicated by a person who has the authority to accept. If it is communicated by any unauthorised person, it will not create any legal relationship.

> **Example :** *Powel Vs. Lee (1908).*
>
> Mr. A applied for the post of a Headmaster in a school. He was selected by the appointing authorities. But the decision of his appointment was not communicated to him. One of the members of the appointing committee informed him of his appointment. But this member was not authorised to communicate the decision. He communicated the decision in his individual capacity. Subsequently, the appointing authority cancelled his selection. Mr. A brought a legal action for breach of contract. His action was rejected by the court and it was observed, that "there must be notice of acceptance from the contracting party in some way. Information from an unauthorised person is as insufficient as overhearing from behind the door."

6. *The Acceptance must be given before the Offer Lapses or is Revoked*

To be legally effective acceptance must be given within the specified time limit, if any, and no time is stipulated, acceptance must be given within a reasonable time. The term, reasonable time depends upon the facts and circumstances of each case.

> **Example :** *Ramsgate Victoria Hotel (Co. Vs. Montefiore* (1866))
>
> The defendant applied for shares in the plaintiff company in June. The allotment (acceptance) of shares was made in late November. Defendant refused to take shares. His refusal to accept the shares led to the dispute. It was held that he was not bound to accept the shares as the allotment of shares was not within reasonable time.

7. *Acceptance may be Express or Implied*

An acceptance, which is expressed by words, written or spoken, is called express acceptance. The acceptance, which is expressed by conduct, is called an implied acceptance.

> **Essentials of a Valid Acceptance**
>
> 1. It must be *absolute and unqualified.*
> 2. It must be *communicated to the offeror.*
> 3. It must be in the *prescribed manner.*
> 4. It must be made within *reasonable time.*
> 5. It must be by the *offeree.*
> 6. It must be in *response to offer.*
> 7. It must be made *before the offer lapses.*
> 8. It cannot be implied *from silence.*

COMMUNICATION OF OFFER AND ACCEPTANCE

Communication of Offer

An offer can be communicated by any act or omission of the offeror by which he intends to communicate it (Sec. 3). The offer can be communicated in any way which has the effects of laying before the offeree, the offeror's willingness to do or abstain from doing something.

The communication of an offer is complete when it comes to the knowledge of the person to whom it is made (Sec. 4). When an offer is made by post, its communication will be complete when the letter containing the offer reaches the offeree.

> **Example :** Mr. A offers by a letter to sell his house to B at a certain price. The communication of the offer is complete when B receives the letter.

Communication of Acceptance

The acceptance can be communicated by any act or omission of the acceptor by which he intends to communicate it or by any act or omission which has the effect of communicating it (Sec. 3).

The communication of an acceptance is complete as against the proposer when it is put in a course of transmission to him so as to be out of the power of the acceptor. As against the acceptor the communication of an acceptance is complete when it comes to the knowledge of the proposer.

The completion of communication of acceptance has two aspects, viz.,

(*i*) as against the proposer, and

(*ii*) as against the acceptor.

The communications of acceptance is complete :

(*i*) *as against the proposer*, when it is put into a course of transmission to him, so as to be out of the power of the person who makes it;

(*ii*) *as against the acceptor*, when it comes to the knowledge of the proposer.

> **Example :** A proposes, by a letter to sell his house to B at a certain price. B accepts A's proposal by a letter sent by post. The communication of acceptance is complete.
>
> (*i*) *as against A* when the letter is posted;
>
> (*ii*) *as against B*, when the letter is received by A.

REVOCATION OF AN OFFER

Section 6 has described the modes in which an offer lapses. An offer comes to an end, and is no longer open to acceptance under the following circumstances :

1. *By Notice :* An offer may be revoked any time before acceptance but not afterwards. An offer lapses when a notice of revocation has been given any time before its acceptance is complete as against the offeror.

2. *By lapse of time :* When the proposer prescribes a time within which the proposal must be accepted, the proposal lapses as soon as the time expires.

3. *After expiry of reasonable time :* If no time has been prescribed, the proposal lapses after the expiry of a reasonable time. What is reasonable time will depend on the circumstances of the case.

4. *By Death or Insanity :* The offer lapses by death or insanity of the offeror provided that the offeree comes to know about it before acceptance.

5. *By non-fulfillment of conditions :* If the offeree fails to fulfil a condition precedent to acceptance, the offer lapses.

6. *By Counter-offer :* An offer also lapses, if a counter-offer is made to it.

7. *By rejection by offeree* : When offeree rejects the offer, it comes to an end. Similarly, a proposal once refused is dead and cannot be revived by its subsequent acceptance.

REVOCATION OF ACCEPTANCE

"An acceptance may be revoked at any time before the communication of the acceptance is complete as against the acceptor but not afterwards" (Sec. 5). In fact, revocation of acceptance amounts to withdrawal of the acceptance to a proposal by the offeree himself.

> **Example :** A proposes, by a letter sent by post, to sell his house to B. B accepts the proposal by a letter sent by post. B may revoke his acceptance any time before the letter communicating it reaches A but not afterwards.

According to English law, an acceptance once complete cannot be revoked. Acceptance is necessarily irrevocable for it is acceptance that binds both the parties. Anson has said, "Acceptance is to offer what a lighted match is to a train of gunpowder. It produces something which cannot be recalled or undone". Therefore, when the acceptance is effected properly the offer ceases to be an offer and it becomes an enforceable contract.

Rules Relating to Offer and Acceptance Made over Telephone

Offer and acceptance can be communicated through the telephone. The rules regarding offer and acceptance as well as their communication by telephone or telex are the same as for the contract made by the mutual meeting of the parties. The contract is formed as soon as the offer is accepted but the offeree must make it sure that his acceptance is received by the offeror, otherwise there will be no contract, as communication of acceptance is not complete. If telephone abruptly goes dead during conversation, the acceptor must dial again to confirm that the words of acceptance were duly heard by the offeror.

When Communication is not Necessary

In certain cases, however, communication of acceptance is not necessary. The proposer may prescribe a particular mode of acceptance. Then the acceptor has to do is to follow that mode. Announcement to pay reward for discovering a lost thing is an offer of this kind. Again, the offeror may have acquiesced in a certain conduct on the part of the offeree as equivalent to acceptance. (Carlill Vs. Carbolic Smoke Ball Co.).

THEORETICAL QUESTIONS

1. Define the term 'offer' *(B. Com. M.S.)*

2. Explain the legal rules regarding a valid offer.

3. "An invitation to offer is not an offer". Comment. *(B. Com. Madurai)*

4. Distinguish between an offer and an invitation to offer. *(B. Com. Delhi)*

5. Define acceptance, and state the legal rules governing valid acceptance.

6. What are the circumstance in which an offer is terminated. *(B. Com. Calcutta)*

7. Acceptance must be absolute, and must correspond with the terms of the offer. Discuss with suitable illustrations. *(B. Com. Calcutta)*

8. "An acceptance to be valid must be communicated. Explain *(B. Com. Madras)*

9. What do you mean by counter-offer. *(B. Com. Mysore)*

10. What is a general offer *(B. Com. Calicut)*

11. There cannot be a contract to make a contract. *(B. Com. Mysore)*

MULTIPLE CHOICE QUESTIONS

CHOOSE CORRECT OPTION FOR EACH OF THE FOLLOWING :

1. An offer is :

(*a*) a suggestion by one person to another.
(*b*) expression of willingness by a person to another to do something in order to obtain assent of the other person.
(*c*) communication of willingness of a person to another person.
(*d*) an intention of a person to do or to abstain from doing an act.

2. A proposal when accepted becomes a :

(*a*) Promise. (*b*) Contract.
(*c*) Offer. (*d*) Acceptance.

3. Cross offers by two parties to each other :

(*a*) amount to acceptance of one's offer by the other.
(*b*) do not amount to acceptance of one's offer by the other.
(*c*) amount to an agreement.
(*d*) amount to a contract.

4. An offer which can be accepted by anyone is called:

(*a*) a specific offer. (*b*) a general offer.
(*c*) a standing offer. (*d*) a cross offer.

5. When the offeree offers to qualified acceptance of the offer subject to modifications and variations he is said to have made a :

(*a*) Standing, open or Continuing offer. (*b*) Counter Offer.
(*c*) Cross Offers. (*d*) Special Offer.

6. A counter offer means :

(*a*) conditional acceptance to an offer.
(*b*) identical offers made by two parties to each other in ignorance.
(*c*) rejection of offer.
(*d*) both (*a*) and (*c*) above.

7. When offer is made to a definite person, it is known as :

(*a*) General Offer. (*b*) Cross Offer.
(*c*) Counter Offer. (*d*) Special Offer.

8. A valid offer must :

(*a*) be to do or to abstain from doing something.
(*b*) be made with an intention to create legal relations.
(*c*) be communicated before acceptance.
(*d*) all of the above.

9. A valid offer may lapse by :

(*a*) cross offer. (*b*) counter offer.
(*c*) expiry of time limit of offer. (*d*) both (*b*) and (*c*)

10. A cross-offer means :

(*a*) sending identical offers by two parties to each other in ignorance.
(*b*) conditional acceptance.
(*c*) an offer made to public at large.
(*d*) all of the above.

11. A general offer is one which is made :

(*a*) by *A* to *B*. (*b*) by A to all the residents of his colony.
(*c*) by A to all the students of his college. (*d*) both (*b*) and (*c*) above.

12. An offer may lapse by :

(*a*) Revocation. (*b*) Counteroffer.
(*c*) Rejection of Offer by Offeree. (*d*) All of these.

13. In case of illegal agreements, the collateral agreements are:

(*a*) Valid. (*b*) Void.

(*c*) Voidable. (*d*) None of these.

14. A promise is :

(*a*) a valid offer. (*b*) a contract.

(*c*) an accepted offer. (*d*) a valid agreement.

15. When a proposal is accepted, it becomes :

(*a*) promise. (*b*) contract.

(*c*) legal promise. (*d*) tentative agreement.

16. A proposal can be accepted :

(*a*) by sending a letter of acceptance. (*b*) by fulfilling conditions of the offer.

(*c*) by doing the act as desired by the offeror. (*d*) in any of the above ways.

17. A person to whom proposal is made is called :

(*a*) promisee. (*b*) acceptor.

(*c*) offeree. (*d*) promisor.

18. When a person signifies his assent to a proposal made to him, the proposal is said to have been :

(*a*) agreed to make a contract. (*b*) accepted.

(*c*) provisionally agreed. (*d*) created contract.

19. Acceptance to be valid must :

(*a*) be absolute. (*b*) be unqualified.

(*c*) both be absolute and unqualified. (*d*) fulfill all of the above and also other conditions.

20. On acceptance of a proposal, it becomes :

(*a*) promise. (*b*) contract.

(*c*) provisional agreement. (*d*) none of the above.

21. On acceptance of a proposal, the person making the proposal becomes :

(*a*) promisee. (*b*) promisor.

(*c*) proposer. (*d*) acceptor.

22. Where a contract is made by post, the place of contract is :

(*a*) the place from where the offer is made. (*b*) the place where the offer is received.

(*c*) the place where letter of acceptance is posted. (*d*) the place where the offeror resides.

23. A proposal is revoked :

(*a*) when a notice of revocation of offer is served to the offeree before his acceptance.

(*b*) when the subject matter of offer is destroyed before acceptance.

(*c*) when the offeree has knowledge of death of the offerer.

(*d*) in all of the above cases.

24. Acceptance means :

(*a*) accepting the offer with some of its conditions.

(*b*) accepting the offer with all the conditions of offer except some.

(*c*) accepting the offer by disclosing conditions of the acceptor.

(*d*) accepting the offer with all the conditions of the offer.

25. An express offer means :

(*a*) an offer made by letter. (*b*) an offer made by telephone.

(*c*) an offer made by e-mail. (*d*) all of the above.

26. An implied offer means an offer made :

(*a*) by spoken words. (*b*) by SMS on cell phone.

(*c*) by body language or actions. (*d*) both (*a*) and (*c*)

27. Standing offer means :

(*a*) Offer allowed to remain open for acceptance over a period of time.

(*b*) Offer made to the public in general.

(*c*) When the offeree offers to qualified acceptance of the offer.

(*d*) Offer made to a definite person.

28. Acceptance can be revoked :

(*a*) at any time when the acceptor thinks fit.

(*b*) at any time before the offerer receives the communication of acceptance.

(*c*) at any time when the idea of acceptance comes to the mind of the offeree.

(*d*) at any time stated in (*a*) and (*c*) above.

29. An agreement enforceable by law is a :

(*a*) Promise (*b*) Contract.

(*c*) Obligation. (d) Lawful promise.

30. Communication of acceptance is complete as against the acceptor :

(*a*) when it comes to the knowledge of the offerer.

(*b*) when it is put in to the course of transmission by the acceptor.

(*c*) when it is communicated to the acceptor that the acceptance has reached to the offerer.

(*d*) when the letter of acceptance is dropped in a letter box.

31. The communication of offer is complete :

(*a*) when it is put into the course of transmission.

(*b*) when it comes to the knowledge of the person to whom it is made.

(*c*) when it is sent to the person to whom it is made.

(*d*) in all the above cases.

32. Communication of acceptance is complete as against the proposer :

(*a*) when it comes to the knowledge of the offerer.

(*b*) when it is put in to the course of transmission to him so as to be out of power of the acceptor to withdraw it.

(*c*) when the acceptance reaches to the proposer.

(*d*) in all the above cases.

33. A person may give his acceptance to an offer :

(*a*) after receiving the offer in writing. (*b*) before receiving the offer.

(*c*) after having the knowledge of the offer. (*d*) after expiry of the time of offer.

34. A offers to sell his car on internet, it is :

(*a*) express offer. (*b*) implied offer.

(*c*) particular offer. (*d*) no offer.

35. An advertisement to pay reward to anyone who traces the missing boy of the advertiser is:

(*a*) an express offer. (*b*) an implied offer.

(*c*) a general offer. (*d*) None of these.

36. A prospectus issued by a company for subscription of its shares and debentures is :

(*a*) an express offer to sell the shares/debentures. (*b*) an implied offer to sell the shares/debentures.

(*c*) a general offer to sell the shares/debentures. (*d*) an invitation to make an offer to buy.

37. A promisee is a person :

(*a*) who makes a proposal.
(*b*) who accepts a proposal.
(*c*) who receives a proposal.
(*d*) who thinks to accept a proposal.

38. Acceptance to an offer may be given by :

(*a*) adding conditions.
(*b*) accepting conditions of the offer.
(*c*) accepting consideration sent by the offer.
(*d*) both (*b*) and (*c*).

39. An acceptance is valid :

(*a*) when offeree adds his conditions with acceptance.
(*b*) when offeree accepts all the conditions of the offer.
(*c*) when it is not against the interest of any person.
(*d*) when acceptance is caused by coercion.

40. Acceptance to an offer may be given by :

(*a*) any person.
(*b*) competent person.
(*c*) authorised person.
(*d*) both by (*b*) and (*c*).

41. Display of goods in the shop for sale with price tags in BAZAR where self service system is there is:

(*a*) an express offer to sell the goods.
(*b*) an implied offer to sell the goods.
(*c*) a general offer to sell the goods.
(*d*) an invitation to make an offer to buy.

42. On approval of tender to supply specific quantity of certain goods during a specific period, it becomes:

(*a*) an agreement.
(*b*) a contract.
(*c*) a standing offer.
(*d*) None of these.

43. A void agreement is one which is :

(*a*) Valid but not enforceable.
(*b*) Enforceable at the option of both the parties.
(*c*) Enforceable at the option of one party.
(*d*) Not enforceable in a court of law.

44. X, by a letter dated 4th Jan. 2009 offers to sell his house to Y for Rs. 20 lakhs. The letter reaches Y on 6th Jan., who posts his acceptance on 7th Jan. which reaches A on 9th Jan. Here, the communication of offer is complete on :

(*a*) 4th Jan. 2009.
(*b*) 6th Jan.
(*c*) 7th Jan.
(*d*) 9th Jan.

45. If X sends a telegram on 6th Feb. revoking his offer, and his telegram reaches Y before the letter of the acceptance is posted. Is revocation of offer valid?

(*a*) It is valid.
(*b*) It is invalid.
(*c*) It is uncertain.
(*d*) None of the above.

ANSWERS

1. (*b*)	2. (*a*)	3. (*b*)	4. (*b*)	5. (*b*)	6. (*a*)	7. (*d*)	8. (*d*)	9. (*d*)	10. (*a*)
11. (*d*)	12. (*d*)	13. (*b*)	14. (*c*)	15. (*a*)	16. (*d*)	17. (*c*)	18. (*b*)	19. (*d*)	20. (*a*)
21. (*b*)	22. (*c*)	23. (*d*)	24. (*d*)	25. (*d*)	26. (*c*)	27. (*a*)	28. (*b*)	29. (*b*)	30. (*a*)
31. (*b*)	32. (*b*)	33. (*c*)	34. (*a*)	35. (*c*)	36. (*d*)	37. (*b*)	38. (*d*)	39. (*b*)	40. (*d*)
41. (*d*)	42. (*c*)	43. (*d*)	44. (*b*)	45. (*a*)					

PRACTICAL PROBLEMS

1. A offers to sell his cycle to B for Rs. 1,000. B offers to buy it for Rs. 750. A refuses to sell. B then says to A, "I accept your offer and shall purchase the cycle for Rs. 1, 000. "Is A bound to sell the cycle to B for Rs. 1,000. *(AIMA)*
   (**Ans.** A is not bound to sell the cycle. B's acceptance is a counter-offer)
2. Mr. P sees a rare book displayed in a shop. It is labelled "First Edition Rs. 50. P enters the shop and puts Rs. 50 on the counter and asks for the book. The bookseller refuses to sell saying that the real price of the book was Rs. 100 and that it had been marked as Rs. 50 by mistake. Is the bookseller bound to sell the book for Rs. 50.
   (**Ans.** A display of book in a shop amounts to a mere invitation to an offer, and not offer itself. The shopkeeper can refuse to sell the book).

IV

CHAPTER

Consideration

(Sections 2(d), 10, 23–25)

AT A GLANCE

INTRODUCTION

Consideration is one of the most important essentials of a valid contract. In simplest terms, consideration is what a promisor demands as the price for his promise. Consideration is "which for what" – something that a person gives for something he receives.

In *Currie Vs. Misa* (1875), consideration was defined as "a valuable consideration in the sense of the law may consist either in some right, interest, profit or benefit accruing to one party, or some forbearance, detriment, loss or responsibility given, suffered or undertaken by the other."

In simple words, the consideration is the price of the promise. This term is used in the sense of *quid-pro-quo i.e.*, something in return. This *something* may be some benefit, right, interest or profit or it may also be some forbearance, detriment, loss or responsibility upon the other party.

Section 2 (d) of the Indian Contract Act defines consideration as follows : "When at the desire of the promisor, the promisee or any other person has done or abstained from doing, or does or abstains from doing, or promises to do or to abstain from doing something, such act or abstinence or promise is called a consideration for the promise".

The analysis of this legal definition shows that followings are the essential parts of the consideration :

(*a*) The consideration is an act, or abstinence.

(*b*) Such act, or abstinence should be done at the desire of the promisor.

(*c*) Such act or abstinence may be done by the promisee or any other person.

(*d*) Such act or abstinence is either already executed, or is in the process of execution or may still executory.

The meaning of consideration becomes clear from the following examples :

Examples: (1) A agrees to sell a house to B for Rs. 1,00,000. For A's promise, the consideration is Rs. 1,00,000. For B's promise, the consideration is the house.

(2) A agrees to sell his scooter to B for Rs. 8,000. In this case, B's promise to pay the amount of Rs. 8,000 is the consideration for A's promise to sell the scooter. And A's promise to sell the scooter is the consideration for B's promise to pay the amount of Rs. 8,000.

(3) A promises to maintain B's child and B promises to pay A Rs. 1,000 per month for the purpose. Here the promise of each party is the consideration for the promise of the other party.

(4) A engages B as a clerk in his office for Rs. 2,000 a month. The monthly wage is the consideration received by B; the services of B constitute the consideration received by A.

Abdul Azeez Vs. Masum Ali (1914)

In this case, a person wanted to build a mosque. He approached the donors who promised substantial sum by way of donation before a particular period. When the person to whom the promises were made, was not given the donation, he filed a suit. The Court held that neither there was benefit to the promisor (donors), nor liability for the promisee or donee. The donee also did not incur any liability. Hence, there was no benefit for the donors or detriment to the donee. So, the suit was dismissed.

Keder Nath Vs. Gauri Mohamed (1886)

In this case, a building promoter desired to construct a Town Hall in the city of Howrah. Here also several persons promised to donate sizable amounts. The promoter incurred liability from out of his pocket, on the strength of the promise made by the donors. He filed a suit when the donors failed to pay the money. The court held that the liability incurred by the donee (plaintiff) is sufficient consideration for the promise to donate by the defendant donors. Suit was decreed. So, liability incurred in pursuance of promise is always enforceable.

Essentials and legal Rules for a Valid Consideration

Essentials of consideration or the legal rules in respect of consideration to an agreement are as under :

1. ***The Consideration must move at the desire of the Promisor :***

Indian Contract Act says that an act or abstinence, which forms consideration for the promise, must be done or promised to be done according to the desire of the promisor. That is, an act shall not be a good consideration for a promise unless it is done at the desire of the promisor. Thus acts done or services rendered voluntarily, or at the desire of third party, will not amount to valid consideration so as to support a contract.

Examples : Mr. A sees B's house on fire and helps in extinguishing it. *B* did not ask for his help. Thus A cannot demand payment for his services.

Durga Prasad Vs. Baldeo (1880)

The plaintiff constructed a market at the request of the District Collector. The defendants, who occupied the shops, promised to pay the plaintiff a commission on articles sold through shops, in consideration of the plaintiff having spent money on the construction of the market. In a suit by the plaintiff for the recovery of commission, it was held that the promise was not supported by consideration. Held, the agreement was void being without consideration as plaintiff did not construct the shops at the desire of defendant, but at the desire of the District collector.

2. ***The Consideration may move from the promisee or any other person***

Promisee is the person to whom the promise is made. Under the Indian Law, consideration may move from the promisee or any other person. It means a person can sue on contract, even if the consideration for the promise moved from a third party. While under the English Law, consideration must move from the promisee only.

Example : *Chinnayya Vs. Ramayya* (1881)

In the case, A, an old lady, by a deed of gift, made over certain property to her daughter R, with a direction that the daughter should pay an annuity to A's brother C, as has been done by A. Accordingly, on the same day, R, the daughter, executed a writing in favour of her maternal uncle C agreeing to pay the annuity. Afterwards she declined to fulfil her promise saying that no consideration had moved from her maternal uncle *i.e.*, the promisee. It was held that the words "the promisee or any other person" in Sec. 2 (d) clearly show that a stranger to the consideration may maintain a suit. Hence the maternal uncle, though a stranger to the consideration was entitled to maintain the suit.

But the English Law is entirely different. According to English Law consideration must necessarily move from the promisee. The party who wishes to enforce a contract must be able to show that he himself has furnished consideration for the promise of the other party.

3. *The Consideration may be past, Present or Future*

Sec. 2 (d) defining consideration clearly makes it clear that it may be past, present or future, as it states "........has done or abstained from doing (*past*), or does or abstains from doing (*present*) or promises to do or abstain from doing (*future*) something ......". Thus :

(*a*) *Past Consideration :* A past consideration is something wholly done, forborne or suffered before the making of the agreement. This is, present promise is based on the consideration already taken place.

Example : A found B's purse and gave it to him. B promised to give Rs. 100 as a reward. Here for B's promise, the act of A in finding B's purse is the past consideration.

(*b*) *Present consideration* (Executed). Consideration which moves simultaneously with the promise is called present consideration. Cash sales provide an excellent example of the present consideration.

Example : A receives Rs. 50,000 in cash from B in return of his car which he promises to deliver to B. It is present consideration for the promise to deliver the car.

(*c*) Future consideration (Executory) When the consideration from one party to the other is to pass subsequently to the making of the contract, it will be future consideration.

Example : A agreed to sell his car after two weeks at an agreed price. B agreed to pay the price on delivery. Here, as the amount and the car are to be transferred in future, therefore, the consideration is future for both the parties.

4. *The Consideration need not be Adequate*

Consideration is something in return. This *something in return* need not, necessarily be equal in value with *something given*. The consideration need not be adequate to the promise for the validity of an agreement. The law only insists on the presence of consideration and not on the adequacy of it. It leaves the people free to make their own bargains. Inadequate consideration does not render a contract void. The law requires that contract should be supported by consideration. The adequacy of the consideration is for the parties to consider at the time of making the agreement, and not for the court when it is sought to be enforced.

Sec 25, explanation 2 provides that "An agreement to which the consent of the party is freely given is not void merely because the consideration is inadequate; but the inadequacy of the consideration may be taken into account by the court in determining the question whether the consent of the promisor was freely given."

Example : A agreed to sell his car worth Rs. 40,000 for Rs. 25,000 to B. A's consent to the agreement was freely given. The consideration, though inadequate will not affect the validity of the contract.

5. *The Consideration must be Real and not Illusory*

Although consideration need not be adequate to the promise, it should be competent, real and valuable in the eyes of the law. It should not be unreal or illusory. Where consideration is physically impossible, illegal or illusory, it is not real and, therefore, shall not be a valid consideration.

Example : If A promises to put life in the dead body of B's son for Rs. 50,000, the agreement is void because of the physical impossibility of the performance.

6. *The Consideration must be Lawful*

The consideration to a promise must be lawful. The consideration to an agreement is unlawful if :

(1) It is forbidden by law; or
(2) It is of such a nature that, if permitted, it would defeat the provisions of any law; or
(3) It is fraudulent; or
(4) It involves or implies injury to a person or property of another; or
(5) The court regards it as immoral or opposed to public policy. Every agreement of which the consideration is unlawful is void.

7. *The Consideration must be Something which the Promisor is not already Bound to do*

A person may be bound to do something by law. Consideration should be more than what the promisee is bound to do either according to law or on the basis of contract. Where a person, who by his official status or by the operation of law is under public duty to act, the discharging of that duty cannot be regarded as consideration. In fact, performance of existing obligation is no consideration for a promise.

Examples (1) : *Collins Vs. Godefroy* (1831)

In this case, the plaintiff received a summon to appear at a trial as a witness on behalf of defendant. The defendant promised him a sum of money for the troubles taken. Any person receiving the summons to attend the court is legally bound to give evidence in court. Therefore, it was held that there was no consideration for the promise.

(2) *Ramchander Chintaman Vs. Kalu Raju* (1877)

In this case, there was a promise to pay to the vakil an additional sum, if the suit was successful. Held; The promise was void being without consideration as the vakil was already under the obligation to do the best to make the suit successful under his prior contract. Therefore, there was no consideration for the subsequent promise.

(3) *England Vs. Davidson* (1840)

The defendant offered a reward to anyone who should give information leading to the conviction of a thief. The plaintiff, a police constable gave such information. It was contended that the plaintiff being a police constable was bound to procure the arrest of criminals and there was no consideration for the promise. The plea was rejected and it was held that as the services rendered were outside the scope of his ordinary duties, it would be sufficient consideration. The acts done in excess of the duty will constitute consideration.

8. *The Consideration may be either Positive or Negative*

The consideration may be a promise to do something or abstain from doing something. That is, consideration may be an act to do or not to do something – positive or negative.

Examples : (1) A requested B to sell certain goods on credit. B agreed to do so provided C will give guarantee for the payment of price of goods supplied to A by B. C guaranteed the payment of the price. Here selling of goods by B to A is the consideration for C's promise to guarantee the payment. This is a positive consideration.

(2) *Debi Radha Rani Vs. Ram Dass* (1941)

A wife is ready to sue her husband for maintenance allowance. On husband's agreeing to pay her a monthly allowance by way of maintenance, she forbears to sue. Held, the wife's forbearance to sue amounts to consideration for husband's agreement for payment of maintenance allowance.

Stranger to Consideration and Stranger to Contract

If consideration is furnished not by the promisee but by a third person, the promisee becomes a stranger to consideration. Similarly, a person, who is not a party to a contract cannot claim rights, even though the contract is for his benefit. And such a person is known as stranger to contract.

The term privity of consideration is a doctrine which means stranger to the consideration or consideration given by any other person than the promisee. Under the English Law, the consideration must be furnished by the promisee only. If it is furnished by any other person, the promisee becomes a stranger to the consideration and, therefore, he cannot enforce the promise. It means a stranger to consideration in a contract cannot sue on the contract. The validity of privity of consideration, according to the Indian contract law, it is not necessary that the consideration should be furnished by the promisee. That is, a stranger to consideration, in a contract, has the right to sue. However, doctrine of privity of contract is applicable in India also. This means a stranger to a contract cannot sue. In this regard both Indian and English Law are the same, *i.e.*, under both, a stranger to a contract cannot sue as the legal effect of a contract is confined to the contracting parties only.

Exceptions to the Rule of Privity of Contract

The rule "A stranger to a contract cannot sue", is subject to the following exceptions :

1. *Beneficiaries in the case of trust*

An agreement to create a trust can be enforced by the beneficiary. Under such a contract, a benefit is given to a person who is not a party to the contract. However, stranger must be clearly designated as a beneficiary and the trust or charge in his favour must also be of some specific property.

Examples : (*i*) *Amirullah Vs. Central Government* (1959)

It was pointed out that the addressee of an insured article is the beneficiary under the contract between the sender and the Central Government who is liable for compensation under Post Office Act, for non-delivery. A trust of movable property is deemed to be declared by the sender from the fact that he addressed the insured cover as deliverable to the addressee. A constructive trust having been created in favour of the addressee, he is entitled to have the benefit as against the trustee, the Central Government through the Post Office, and sue it.

(*ii*) *Khwaja Muhmmad Vs. Hussaini Begum* (1909)

H sued her father-in-law K to recover Rs. 15,000 being the arrears of allowance called *Kharcha-i-Pandan* (Betal box expenses) *i.e.*, pin money payable to her by K under an agreement made between K and H's father in consideration of H's marriage to K's son D. Both H and D were minors at the date of marriage. The Privy Council held the promise be enforceable by H.

2. *Marriage Settlement, Partition and other Family Arrangement*

Where a provision is made in a partition or family arrangement for maintenance or marriage expenses of female members, such members, though not parties to the agreement, can sue on the contract.

Examples : (*i*) *Shuppu Ammal Vs. Subramaniyan* (1910)

Two brothers, on a partition of joint properties, agreed to invest in equal shares a certain sum of money for the maintenance of their mother. Held, she was entitled to require her sons to make the investment.

(*ii*) *Daropti Vs. Jaspat Rai* (1905)

A, ill-treated his wife, B. She left him because of his cruelty. A entered into an agreement with B's father to treat her properly. He further agreed to pay monthly allowance to his wife, if he failed to treat her properly. Subsequently, B was again ill-treated by A and was driven out of the house. She was held entitled to enforce the promise made by A to her father, though she was not a party to it.

3. *Acknowledgment of Liability*

Sometimes one of the parties to contract acknowledges the payment to a third party or otherwise constitutes himself as an agent of the third party. And that party acknowledges the payment to the third person or constitutes himself as an agent of that third person, then the third person can recover the amount from such party.

Examples : *Surjan Vs. Nanat* (1940)

A receives some money from B to be paid over to C and he admits of this receipt to C. C can recover this amount from A who shall be regarded as the agent of C.

(*ii*) *Kshirod Behari Dutt Vs. Man Gobinda Panda* (1933)

There was an agreement between A, a tenant and B, a sub-tenant, under which B was paying the rent directly to the landlord. After some time, B stopped paying the rent to the landlord, and the rent fell in arrear. It was held that the landlord was entitled to recover the unpaid rent from B.

4. *Contracts through Agent*

Where a contract is entered into by an agent, the principal can sue on it.

5. Assignee of a Contract

Under certain circumstances a party to a contract can transfer his rights under the contract to third party. A holder in due course of a negotiable instrument is a holder who has obtained the negotiable instruments in good faith and for valuable consideration. He may sue the prior parties to the negotiable instrument.

Rules Regarding Consideration

1. Consideration must move at the desire of the promisor.
2. Consideration may move from the promisee or any other person.
3. Consideration may be past, present or future.
4. Consideration need not be adequate.
5. Consideration must be real and not illusory.
6. Consideration must be lawful.
7. Discharging of a pre-existing obligation is not consideration.
8. Consideration may be either positive or negative.

"No Consideration No Contract" Exceptions to the Rule

General rule of law is that an agreement without consideration is void. Sec. 25 deals with exceptions to this rule where a contract, even though without consideration, is enforceable. They are as follows :

1. ***Natural Love and Affection***

Sec. 25 (1) of the Indian Contract Act, which reads as under : "An agreement without consideration is void, unless it is expressed in writing and registered under the law for the time being in force for the registration of documents and is made on account of natural love and affection between parties standing in near relation to each other."

The following conditions must be satisfied for the application of this exception :

(*i*) The agreement is made by a written document.

(*ii*) The document is registered according to the law relating to registration in force at the time.

(*iii*) The agreement is made on account of natural love and affection.

(*iv*) The parties to the agreement stand in a near relation to each other.

> **Example :** *Rajlukhy Debee Vs. Bhootnath* (1900)
>
> An agreement entered into by a husband with his wife, during quarrels and disagreement, whereby the husband promised to give some property to the wife. The agreement is void because, under the circumstances, there is no natural love and affection between the parties.

2. ***Voluntary Compensation***

A promise made without any consideration is valid if, "it is a promise to compensate wholly or in part, a person who has already voluntarily done something for the promisor, or something which the promisor was legally compellable to do"

In other words, a promise to pay for past voluntary services is binding even though it is without consideration. The following conditions must be satisfied for the application of this exception :

(*a*) The services should have been rendered voluntarily.

(*b*) The services should have been done for the promisor.

> **Example :** A found B's purse and gave it to him. B promised to give Rs. 100 as reward. This is a valid contract.

3. ***Time Barred Debt***

(Sec. 25 (3)) A promise by a debtor to pay a time-barred debt is enforceable that it is made in writing and is signed by the debtor or his agent generally or specifically authorised in that behalf. The promise may be to pay whole or part of the debt. Here it may be mentioned that a debt becomes time-barred if it is not claimed for a period of three years from the date it becomes due.

> **Example :** D owes C Rs. 1,000 but the debt is barred by the Limitation Act. D signs a written promise to pay C Rs. 500 on account of the debt. This is a contract.

4. ***Agency (Sec. 185)***

No consideration is required between the principal and agent to create an agency.

5. ***Completed Gift***

Explanation 1, to Sec. 25 states that "Nothing in this Section shall affect the validity, as between the donor and the donee, of any gift actually made".

THEORETICAL QUESTIONS

1. Define consideration. What are the essentials of a valid consideration? *(B.Com. Delhi)*
2. "Insufficiency of consideration is immaterial; but an agreement without consideration is void. Comment. *(B.Com. Madras)*
3. Define consideration. "An agreement without consideration is void". Are there any exceptions to the rule? If so, explain them. *(B.Com. Delhi)*
4. Distinguish between a stranger to consideration and a stranger to contract? *(B.Com. Mysore)*
5. No consideration No contract. Examine critically. *(B.Com. Kerala)*
6. "Stranger to a consideration cannot sue." Are there any exceptions to this rule? *(B.Com. M.S.)*
7. Consider the doctrine of privity of contract and give an account of the exceptions to the doctrine. *(B.Com. Madras)*
8. "The legal effects of a contract are confined to the contracting parties". Comment. *(B.Com. M.S.)*
9. Consideration need not be adequate but it must have some value in the eyes of law."*(B.Com. Delhi)*
10. "Past consideration is a good consideration". Comment. *(B.Com. Kerala)*
11. "Consideration may be past, present or future" Explain with examples. *(B.Com. Madras)*
12. What are the differences between Indian Law and English Law as regards consideration?

MULTIPLE CHOICE QUESTIONS

Choose correct option for each of the following :

1. Consideration means:

(*a*) doing or abstaining from doing something at the desire of the promisor.
(*b*) doing or abstaining from doing something voluntarily.
(*c*) doing or abstaining from doing something which the promisee is already under a duty to do.
(*d*) all of the above.

2. Consideration may be given :

(*a*) by the promisor. (*b*) by the promisee only.
(*c*) by the promisee or any other person on his behalf.
(*d*) by promisor or any other person.

3. Consideration must be :

(*a*) at the desire of the promisee. (*b*) at the desire of the promisor.
(*c*) at the desire of the acceptor. (*d*) at the desire of the offeree.

4. Consideration is :

(*a*) something in return. (*b*) something of value.
(*c*) something invaluable. (*d*) doing something voluntarily.

5. Consideration can be :

(*a*) past not the future. (*b*) past, present and future.
(*c*) present but not future. (*d*) past and future.

6. Consideration :

(*a*) need not be adequate. (*b*) need not be real.
(*c*) need not have monetary value. (*d*) need not be certain.

7. According to the legal provisions :

(*a*) a contract without consideration is not void.
(*b*) a stranger to contract can not sue but a stranger to consideration can sue.
(*c*) consideration in a contract must be at the desire of the promisee.
(*d*) a stranger to contract can sue but a stranger to consideration can not sue.

8. Consideration in a contract :

(*a*) may move from the promisee or any other person.
(*b*) may not move from a stranger.
(*c*) may not be measurable in terms of money.
(*d*) may not be past.

9. Consideration may be :

(*a*) an act.
(*b*) abstinence from doing an act.
(*c*) a promise.
(*d*) all of the above.

10. Consideration in a contract :

(*a*) may be any thing.
(*b*) may be nothing.
(*c*) must be at the desire of the promisor.
(*d*) may be illusory.

11. Inadequacy of consideration :

(*a*) never affects the validity of the contract.
(*b*) affect the validity of the contract.
(*c*) renders the contract unlawful.
(*d*) does not affect the validity of the contract but the Court may take into consideration when a party alleges that his consent was not free.

12. Valid consideration may also be :

(*a*) forbearance to sue.
(*b*) compromise of a pending suit.
(*c*) composition with creditors.
(*d*) any of the above.

13. According to the provisions of the Contract Act :

(*a*) A contract without consideration is valid if the parties making it, are near friends.
(*b*) A contract to indemnify services rendered in the past is void.
(*c*) A contract to pay time-barred debt is void.
(*d*) All of the above statements are wrong.

14. A contract without consideration is :

(*a*) if the near relatives do not make the contract in writing.
(*b*) if any person verbally agrees to pay his time-barred debts.
(*c*) where near relatives make an agreement to resolve a family dispute and the agreement is written and registered.
(*d*) in all of the above cases.

15. A contract without consideration is valid :

(*a*) where near relatives make an agreement to resolve a family dispute and the agreement is written and registered.
(*b*) where a debtor makes a written agreement to pay his time barred debt.
(*c*) where a person agrees to compensate a person for his services rendered in the past at his request.
(*d*) in all of the above cases.

16. A promise to compensate the other for his services rendered in the past is valid :

(*a*) if he rendered services voluntarily.
(*b*) if he rendered at the request of the promisor.
(*c*) if he voluntarily rendered services which the promisor was legally liable to do.
(*d*) either (*a*) or (*c*) above.

17. An assignee being a stranger to a contract :

(*a*) can sue.
(*b*) cannot sue.
(*c*) none of these.

18. A promise to compensate, wholly or in part, a person who has already voluntarily done something for the promise is :

(*a*) enforceable.
(*b*) not enforceable.
(*c*) void.
(*d*) voidable.

19. Compromise of disputed claims :

(*a*) is a good consideration for a contract.
(*b*) is not a good consideration for a contract.
(*c*) results in a void agreement.
(*d*) is not permitted by law.

20. An agreement made without consideration is :

(*a*) valid.
(*b*) voidable.
(*c*) illegal.
(*d*) void.

ANSWERS

1. (*a*)	**2.** (*c*)	**3.** (*b*)	**4.** (*a*)	**5.** (*b*)	**6.** (*a*)	**7.** (*b*)	**8.** (*a*)	**9.** (*d*)	**10.** (*c*)
11. (*d*)	**12.** (*d*)	**13.** (*d*)	**14.** (*d*)	**15.** (*b*)	**16.** (*d*)	**17.** (*a*)	**18.** (*a*)	**19.** (*a*)	**20.** (*d*)

PRACTICAL PROBLEMS

1. Mr. A promises to donate Rs. 5,000 towards the repairs of a Church. Mr. A does not pay the sum. Can the Trustees recover the promised amount from A :

(*a*) if they have not incurred any liability on the faith of A's promise.

(*b*) if they have incurred any liability on the faith of A's promise.

Answer : (or decision)

(*a*) The Trustees cannot recover the promised amount. It was held that since nothing was done on the faith of the promise, there was a no consideration in this case and therefore, the defendant was not liable to pay the promised amount.

(*b*) The Trustees can recover the promised amount. The agreement is valid because it was supported by consideration in the form of a detriment to the trustees who had incurred liability on the faith of the promise made by A. (Refer Kedar Nath Vs. Gauri Mohamed).

2. A, a client promises to pay B, his advocate Rs. 5,000 in addition to his fees if he succeeds. A succeeds but refuses to pay Rs. 5,000. Can B recover from A ?

B cannot recover the amount, A promises to pay the additional sum was without any consideration. The consideration must be something which the promiser is not already bound to do. Here, B was bound to render the best service under the original contract. (Refer: Ramchandra Chintaman Vs. Kalu Raju).

V

CHAPTER

Contractual Capacity

(Sections 10–12)

AT A GLANCE

INTRODUCTION

Section 10 of the Indian Contract Act requires the parties to be competent to make a valid contract. Sec. 10 states, "All agreements are contracts, if they are made by the free consent of the parties competent to contract." Thus, the question arises, what is the competency to make a contract? The "capacity to contract" means the competence *i.e.*, capability of the parties to enter into a valid contract.

CAPACITY TO CONTRACT

The term "capacity to contract" is defined in Sec. 11 of the Indian contract Act which reads as under :

"Every person is competent to contract *who is of the age of the majority according to the law to which he is subject*, and *who is of sound mind*, and *is not disqualified from contracting by any law to which he is subject.*"

In other words, all persons are competent to make contracts except the following :

1. Minors.
2. Persons of unsound mind.
3. Persons disqualified by any law to which they are subject.

MINOR

A minor is a person who has not attained the age of majority. For the purposes of entering into contract, "the age of majority" is eighteen years. The term minor is explained in Section 3 of the Indian Majority Act. 1875, which reads as under :

"A minor is a person who has not completed eighteen years of age".

In the following two cases, a person becomes major on completion of 21 years:

(*a*) Where a guardian of a minor's person or property has been appointed under the Guardians and Wards Act 1890, and

(*b*) Where the superintendence of minor's property is assumed by a court of wards.

The age of majority is to be determined according to the law to which the minor is subject. In England, for all purposes, a minor is a person who is under the age of eighteen years.

According to Sec. 3 of the Indian Majority Act 1875, a person attains majority as under :

(*i*) Where a guardian of a minor's person or property is appointed under the Guardian and Wards Act 1890	(*i*) On completion of 21 years
(*ii*) Where minor's property has passed under the superintendence of the court of wards	(*ii*) On completion of 21 years
(*iii*) In all other cases	(*iii*) On completion of 18 years

Law Relating to Minor

Infancy is said to be a disability, but in practice it is really protection granted by the Law Courts. It has been rightly observed : "The law protects their (infants') persons; preserves their rights and estates, excuseth their laches, and assists them in their pleadings; the judges are their Counsellors, the Jury are their servants and Law is their guardian".

Sec. 11 of the Act does expressly say anything about the nature of a minor's agreement and the legal effect of such an agreement. It is, therefore, necessary to fall back upon the judicial pronouncements by Courts of Law. Till the historic judgement in Mohri bibee Vs. Dharmdas Ghose (1903) Courts of Law in India were not unanimous regarding the nature of a minor's agreement whether it is void or voidable. The controversy was finally resolved by the Privy Council in Mahori Bibee Vs. Dharmdas Ghose (1903).

Mohri Bibee Vs. Dharmdas Ghose (1903)

In this case, a minor had executed a mortgage for the sum of Rs. 20,000 out of which the lender had paid the minor only Rs. 8,000. The minor then filed a suit for setting aside the mortgage. It was contended that as the contract was voidable and the minor was now repudiating it the amount of Rs. 8,000 actually paid to the minor must be refunded under Section 65 of the Indian Contract Act. The Privy Council pointed out that as the minor's contract was absolutely void no question of refunding money could arise in these circumstances. Money advanced to a minor cannot be recovered. Thus, from this it is clear that minor's agreement is void *ab-initio i.e.*, not existent from the very beginning, and is, therefore, absolutely void and devoid of any consequences.

Minor's agreement

The law regarding minor's agreements may be summed up as under ;

1. *An Agreement with a Minor is Void Ab-initio*

Law acts as the guardian of minors and protect their rights because they don't possess the capacity to judge what is good and what is bad for them. Thus, agreement with a minor is void ab-initio, *i.e.*, absolutely void and not merely voidable. An agreement with a minor does not create any legal rights and obligations between the concerned parties.

According to Sec. 65 of the Contract Act "when a contract becomes void any person who has received any advantage under such contract, is bound to restore it, or make compensation for it." The Privy Council rejected the argument and held that the minor's contract was *ab initio void* and no question of refunding any money could arise in such circumstances.

2. *The Rule of Estoppel does not Apply to a Minor*

The rule of estoppel does not apply to a minor i.e., minor is not estopped from pleading his infancy in order to avoid a contract, even if he has entered into an agreement by falsely representing that he was of full age. In other words, where an infant represents fraudulently or otherwise that he is of age and thereby induces another to enter into a contract with him, then in an action found on the contract, the infant is not estopped from setting up infancy.

> **Example :** In *Vaikuntarama Pillai Vs. Authimoolam Chettiar* (1915), the Madras High Court has held that as there is a clear statutory provision that a minor being incompetent to contract is incapable of incurring any liability for any debt, the law of estoppel cannot overrule this provision to make him liable. If estoppel is permitted against the minor, then it would be against his interest. The unscrupulous businessmen would exploit the minor by obtaining a statement from the minor to the effect that the minor represented himself as the major. However, "the plea of minority can always be used as a *shield* but not as a *sword.*"

3. *No Restitution Except in Certain Cases*

A minor cannot be ordered to make compensation for a benefit obtained under a void agreement, because Sections 64 and 65 of the Contract Act, which deal with restitution, apply only to contracts between competent parties and are not applicable to a case where there is not and could not have been any contract at all. Thus, when the minor receives the benefits of money, he may be compelled to restore the same. This is based on the principle that he, who seeks equity, must do equity. In this regard the following observations of Allahabad High Court are worth noting :

"Where persons, who are in fact under age, induce others to purchase property from them, they are liable in equity to make restitution to the purchaser for the benefits they have obtained, before they can recover possession of the property sold."

> **Example :** *Leslie Vs. Sheill* (1914)
>
> This case explains the doctrine of restitution. In this case, the defendant, a minor, falsely misrepresented himself to be a major, and obtained two loans of £ 200 each from the plaintiffs, who were money-lenders. He failed to repay the amount. The plaintiffs brought an action to recover £ 475, being the principal amount of loan and interest thereon. It was held by the Court of Appeal that the money could not be recovered. If that were allowed that would amount to enforcing the agreement to repay the loan, which is void under the Infants' Relief Act 1874.

4. *Minor's Liability for Necessaries*

Minor is liable for '*necessaries*' supplied or '*necessary services*' rendered to him or his minor dependents. In other words, if a person supplies necessaries to a person who is incapable of entering into a contract or to anyone whom such incapable person is legally bound to support, then he can claim reimbursement from the property of such incapable person. *For such contracts he cannot be held liable personally. His property or estate alone will be liable.*

Minor is said to be an individual who is not mentally matured. He can be deceived easily because he is an innocent person. Thus, the aim of the law is to protect him. "Things necessary are those without which an individual cannot reasonably exist." They cannot include luxuries or costly or unnecessary articles. The law says any agreement made with a minor for supply of food, clothing and shelter are essential and therefore they are necessaries. The term "necessary" has to be interpreted with reference to the status and standard of life led by minors.

However, the following cases have already been decided by the courts in connection with "necessaries."

Example : (*i*) *Nash Vs. Inman* (1908) : Inman, an infant undergraduate in Cambridge bought eleven fancy waistcoats from Nash. He was at the time adequately provided with clothing. Held, the waistcoats were not necessary and the price could not be recovered.

Example : (*ii*) *Kunwarlal Vs. Surajmal* (1963) : It has been held that the house given to a minor on rent for living and continuing his studies is deemed to be supply of necessaries suited to the minor's condition in life, and the rent for the house can be recovered.

Example : (*iii*) *Sham Charan Mal Vs. Chowdary Debya Singh* (1894)

In this case, money was advanced to a minor for defending himself in certain criminal proceedings against him. The minor executed a bond in respect of his loan. He used this amount for the purpose of his defence. It was held that the amount borrowed was in connection with his personal liberty and it comes within the term "necessaries" of Sec. 68 of the Contract Act.

Example : (*iv*) *Ryder Vs. Wombwell* (1868)

In this case, the defendant, a minor with an income of £ 500 a year, bought from the plaintiff a pair of crystal, ruby and diamond solitaires and an antique goblet in silver gilt. In a suit for the price, these articles were held to be not necessaries.

Example : (*v*) *Kedar Nath Vs. Ajudhia Prasad* (1883)

The money advanced to save minor's property from sale in execution of a decree. It was held that this loan was for necessaries.

5. *Minor's Liability in Tort*

The infant is liable for his tort, *i.e.* a wrong, unless the tort is in reality a breach of contract. The tort must be separate from and independent of contract otherwise many contracts would be enforced on minors in an indirect manner. For example, an infant hired a horse for riding and injured it by over-riding. Here the infant had committed a tort, i.e., negligence in the performance of the contract. It was held that "If an infant in the course of doing what he is entitled to do under the contract is guilty of negligence, he cannot be made liable in tort if he is not liable on the contract" for "you cannot convert a contract into a tort to enable you to sue an infant". In another case an infant hired a horse expressly for riding and not for jumping and then he lent it to a friend who jumped the horse and killed it. Here "what was done by the infant was not an abuse of the contract, but was the doing of an act which he was expressly forbidden by the owner to do with the animal", and, therefore, the infant was held liable for the tort.

6. *No Specific Performance*

Since an agreement by a minor is absolutely void, the court will never direct "specific performance" of such an agreement by him. But a contract entered into, on behalf of a minor, by his guardian or by the manager of his estate, is binding on the minor and can be specifically enforced by or against the minor provided : (*a*) the contract is within the authority of the guardian or manager, and (*b*) it is for the benefit of the minor.

7. *No. Ratification*

The term 'ratification' may be defined as the act of confirming or approving. The doctrine of 'no ratification' implies that an agreement made by a minor (during the period of minority) cannot be confirmed by him on attaining majority. This is so because minor's agreement is void ab-initio and, therefore, cannot be made valid by ratification.

Example : *Arumugan Vs. Duraisinga* (1914)

Where a minor borrowed a sum of money by executing a simple pronote for it and after attaining majority, executed a second pronote in respect of the original loan plus interest thereon, a suit upon the second pronote was not maintainable.

8. ***A Minor can be a Beneficiary***

Incompetency of a minor to enter into contract means incompetency to bind himself by a contract. There is nothing which debars him from becoming a beneficiary, *e.g.*, payee, an endorsee or a promisee in a contract. Such contracts can be enforced at his option, but not at the option of the other party. Thus, the law does not regard him as incompetent for accepting a benefit.

In *Shrafat Ali Vs. Noor Mohd.* (1924). The Rangoon High Court held that a minor may enforce a promissory note executed in his favour. A minor may become a promisee.

9. ***Partnership by Minor***

The partnership of partners results from their agreement. A minor, being incompetent to enter into a contract, cannot be a partner in the firm. However, he may be admitted only to the benefits of the firm. This provision is contained in Section 30 (1) of the Indian Partnership Act. 1932, which reads as under :

> "A person who is a minor, according to the law to which he is subject may not be a partner in a firm, but with the consent of all the partners for time being, he may be admitted to the benefits of partnership."

10. ***A Minor can be an Agent***

An agent is merely a connecting link between his principal and third person. Therefore, a minor can be appointed as an agent. But he will not be personally liable for any of his acts. Sec. 184 of the Indian Contract Act reads as under :

> "As between the principal and third persons any person may become an agent, but no person who is not of the age of majority and of sound mind can became an agent so as to be responsible to his principal".

11. ***Minor can be a Shareholder***

A minor can hold fully paid up shares of a company. He cannot hold partly paid-up shares as he cannot be held liable for calls. Since membership of a company arises on the basis of a contract, a minor cannot be a member of a company. A minor, being incompetent to contract, cannot be a shareholder of the company. A company can also refuse to register transfer or transmission of shares in favour of a minor unless the shares arc fully paid.

12. ***A Minor cannot be Declared Insolvent***

A minor cannot be adjudicated an insolvent, for, he is incapable of contracting debts. Even for necessaries supplied to him, he is not personally liable, only his property is liable.

13. ***Minor cannot be a Surety***

A minor cannot be a surety as he is not liable to pay or compensate anything under a contract.

14. ***Position of Minor's Parents***

Minor's contracts do not impose any liability on his parents even if the contracts are for necessaries. The parents or the guardians of the minor may pay money borrowed by him just out of moral obligations. But the parents or guardians can be held liable when the minor child is acting as an agent of his parents or guardians.

15. ***Contracts of Apprenticeship and Service***

A contract of apprenticeship is valid and binding upon a minor because such a contract is protected by the Apprentices Act 1961, provided the case falls within the terms of that Act. The Act inter alia, provides that the minor must not be less than fourteen years of age and the contract must be entered into on behalf of the minor by his guardian. The Act was passed, with a view to enabling children to learn trades, crafts and employments, by which, when they come to full age, they may gain a livelihood. A contract of service is not binding by or against a minor.

Minor Under the English Law

Under the English Law, an infant (equivalent of minor under the Indian Law) is a person who is below 18 years of age. Contracts entered into by an infant fall into one of the following classes:

1. *Void Contracts*

All contracts, whether by speciality or by simple contract, entered into by infants for the repayment of money lent or to be lent, or for the payment of goods supplied or to be supplied (other than contracts for necessaries), and all accounts stated with infants, are absolute void. (Infants Relief Act 1874).

2. *Infant's Voidable Contracts*

When an infant enters into a contract of a continuing obligation, the contract cannot be enforced against him during infancy. But after he attains majority, the contract is binding on him unless he repudiates it within a reasonable time. Examples of these contracts are : tenancy agreements, partnership agreements, agreement to take shares (which are not fully paid) and marriage settlements.

3. *Contracts binding on the infant*

An infant is bound by contracts for (*a*) necessaries, and (*b*) education, training or beneficial service.

4. *Contracts Enforceable by the Infant but not Against him*

All Contracts, other than void, voidable or binding contracts, of an infant are unenforceable against him, either during or after infancy. But the infant can enforce such contracts.

Position of Minor's Agreement

1. An agreement with a minor is void ab-initio.
2. The rule estoppel does not apply to a minor.
3. No restitution except in certain cases.
4. A minor's estate is liable for necessaries supplied.
5. A minor is generally liable for a tort.
6. Court never orders specific performance of his agreement.
7. His agreement cannot be ratified on his attaining majority.
8. A minor can be a promisee or beneficiary.
9. A minor can be a partner, to the benefits of partnership.
10. A minor can be an agent.
11. A minor can be a shareholder.
12. A minor cannot be declared insolvent.
13. A minor can not be a surety.
14. A contract of apprenticeship is binding on him.
15. A contract of service is not binding.
16. A minor is always allowed to plead minority.

PERSONS OF UNSOUND MIND

In order to be competent to contract a person must be of sound mind (Sec. 11)

What is a sound mind?

Sec. 12 of the Indian Contract Act reads as follows :

"A person is said to be of sound mind for the purpose of making a contract if, at the time when he makes it, he is capable of understanding it and of forming a rational judgement as to its effect upon his interests".

The section further states that :

(*i*) "A person who is usually of unsound mind, but occasionally of sound mind, may make a contract when he is of sound mind." Thus a patient in a lunatic asylum who is at intervals of sound mind, may contract during those intervals.

(*ii*) "A person who is usually of sound mind, but occasionally of unsound mind, may not make a contract when he is of unsound mind." Thus, a sane man, who is delirious from fever or who is so drunk that he cannot understand the terms of a contract or form a rational judgement as to its effect on his interests, cannot contract whilst such delirium or drunkenness lasts. Thus, from the examples, soundness of mind of a person depends on two facts :

(*i*) Capacity to understand the nature and the terms of the contract.

(*ii*) Ability to form a rational judgement as to its effect on a person's interests.

Thus a person who does not satisfy these conditions, is of unsound mind and is incapable of entering into a valid agreement. The agreement made by persons of unsound mind, like that of minors, are also absolutely void. The reason for the same is that a valid agreement requires the assent of two sound mind. Sec. 11 of the Indian Contract Act specifically declares that persons of unsound mind are incompetent to enter into an agreement. If any person relies on the unsoundness of mind of the other person, he must prove it to the satisfaction of the court.

Legal position of the persons of unsound mind, has been discussed as under :

Idiots

An idiot is a person who has completely lost his mental faculties of thinking. Idiocy is a congenital defect caused by lack of development of the brain. He is incapable of entering into a contract and, therefore, a contract with an idiot is void.

Example : *Inder Singh Vs. Parmeshwardhari Singh* (1957)

A sold his property worth about Rs. 25,000 for Rs. 7,000. His mother proved that he was a congenital idiot, incapable of understanding the transaction. Held that the sale was void.

Lunatics

Lunatic is a person whose mental faculties of thinking are deranged *i.e.*, disordered due to some mental strain or some other reasons. However, the mental powers of such person may not be completely lost. A lunatic differs from an idiot in as much as the latter is hopelessly mad, *i.e.*, of unsound mind and has no lucid intervals, whereas a lunatic has lucid intervals during which he is perfectly sane. If, therefore, a contract is entered into with a lunatic during his lucid interval, *i.e.*, when he was perfectly sane, it is binding on him and his estate would be liable; otherwise the contract is bad.

Drunken or Delirious Person

Drunkard is a person who is under the influence of drinks or drugs. Drunkenness produces temporary incapacity, till the drunkard is under the effect of intoxication. If a person is so drunk, intoxicated or delirious from fever as to be incapable of understanding the nature and effect of an agreement or to form a rational judgement as to its effect on his interest, his condition is similar to that of a lunatic and on the same grounds as in the case of person of unsound mind he cannot enter into valid contracts whilst such delirium or drunkenness lasts.

There may be mental decay or senile mind due to old age or poor health. When such person is not capable of understanding the contract and its effect upon his interests, he cannot enter into contract. Similarly, hypnotism produces temporary incapacity till a person is under the effect of artificial induced sleep.

Effects of Agreements Made by Persons of Unsound Mind

An agreement entered into by a person of unsound mind is treated on the same footing as that of minor's and, therefore, an agreement by a person of unsound mind is absolutely void and inoperative as against him but he can derive benefit under it.

PERSONS DISQUALIFIED BY LAW

The following persons, who are disqualified by the law to which they are subject, are not competent to enter into a contract :

1. *Alien Enemies*

All persons other than Indian citizens are aliens. An alien is a person who is a foreigner to the land. He may be either an 'alien friend' or an 'alien enemy'. An alien (citizen of a foreign country) living in India can enter into contracts with citizens of India during peace time only, and that too subject to any restrictions imposed by the Government in that respect. On the declaration of a war between his country and India, he becomes an alien enemy and cannot enter into contracts. "Alien friend can contract but an alien enemy can't contract". Contracts entered into before the declaration of the war stand suspended and cannot be performed during the course of war, of course, they can be revived after the war is over provided they have not already become time-barred.

2. *Foreign Sovereigns and Ambassadors*

Foreign sovereigns and accredited representatives of a foreign state or ambassadors enjoy special privilege, by which they cannot be sued in Indian courts. However, they can, if they choose, enter into contracts and can enforce such contracts in Indian courts. Ex-kings are not entitled to this privilege and, therefore, can be sued in Indian courts just as ordinary citizens. In India, under Section 86 of the Civil Procedure Code previous sanction of the Central Government is to be obtained, for suing the rulers of foreign states, ambassadors and envoys.

3. *Convicts*

A convict is a person, who is sentenced by a competent court to the death sentence or imprisonment. A convict cannot enter into a valid contract while undergoing sentence, nor can sue. His incompetency is over, when the period of his sentence is over or he is pardoned. Thus, the competency right to make a contract or sue is only suspended during the course of his sentence and is not lost. Whenever he is freed, he regains such rights.

4. *Insolvents*

When a person is declared an insolvent, his property vests in the Receiver or Official Assignee. And the insolvent is deprived of his power to deal with the property. Therefore, he cannot enter into a contract relating to his property. However, this disqualification of an insolvent is removed when the court passes an order of discharge.

5. *Married Women*

Law has not made any distinction regarding contractual capacity of males and females. A woman, whether married or unmarried, enjoys the same contractual capacity as a man. Whatever property a woman possesses, she has absolute ownership over it. She is free to deal with her personal property in the way she likes. Her husband is not at all responsible for her contracts.

6. *Professional Persons*

It is only in England, where the barristers cannot sue their clients for their professional fees. In

India, no such rule exists. In India, every barrister, who has got himself enrolled as an advocate of an Indian High Court can sue his clients for his fees. Under Indian Bar Council Act 1927 enrolment of an advocate is necessary before he can practise.

7. ***Corporations and Companies***

Joint stock companies and a corporations incorporated under an Act passed by Parliament or State legislature are artificial persons created by law. A joint stock company cannot enter into contracts which are beyond its powers conferred upon it by its Memorandum of Association. Similarly a corporation cannot enter into contracts outside the powers conferred on it by the special Act under which the corporation was incorporated. These artificial persons cannot enter into contracts of marriage.

THEORETICAL QUESTIONS

1. Define the term 'capacity to contract'. State the law relating to the competence of the parties giving suitable examples. *(B.Com. Madurai)*
2. An agreement with a minor is absolutely void in India. Discuss. *(B.Com. Madras)*
3. What do you understand by competency of parties? State the position of a minor in detail. *(B.Com. Bombay)*
4. What is the legal effect of a minor's misrepresentation of his age while entering into an agreement? *(B.Com. Delhi)*
5. What is the effect of agreements entered into by persons of unsound mind? *(B.Com. Kerala)*
6. What do you understand by 'necessaries' supplied to a minor? *(B.Com. Madurai)*
7. Discuss the legal position of a minor as (*a*) a promisor, (*b*) a promisee and (*c*) an agent. *(B.Com. Madurai)*
8. Who are the persons incompetent to make a contract by status? *(B.Com. Madras)*
9. What is meant by 'sound mind'? *(MBA, Madras)*
10. What are necessaries? When is a minor liable on a contract for necessaries? *(B.Com. MS)*

MULTIPLE CHOICE QUESTIONS

Choose correct option for each of the following :

1. **Minor's agreement is :**
   (*a*) void from beginning. (*b*) voidable.
   (*c*) void when Court declares it void. (*d*) valid.
2. **An agreement with minor :**
   (*a*) is always void. (*b*) sometimes void.
   (*c*) is valid if made for supply of necessaries of life.
   (*d*) is valid if made with consent of the Court.
3. **Which of the following persons do not fall under the category of persons of unsound mind ?**
   (*a*) alien. (*b*) idiot.
   (*c*) lunatics. (*d*) drunken persons.
4. **All persons are capable of contracting :**
   (*a*) if they are major as per the law.
   (*b*) if they are of sound mind.
   (*c*) if they are not disqualified by any other law of the land to which they are subject.
   (*d*) if they fulfill all the above conditions.

5. Minor can be :

(*a*) a partner in a firm.
(*b*) an agent.
(*c*) a principal of his agent.
(*d*) all of the above.

6. A minor can :

(*a*) ratify his agreement after attaining majority.
(*b*) be directed by the Court for specific performance of the contract.
(*c*) always plead his minority.
(*d*) be held liable for cheques issued by him.

7. The age of majority of a person whose property has been placed under the superintendence of a Court of wards is :

(*a*) 15 years.
(*b*) 18 years.
(*c*) 21 years.
(*d*) 22 years.

8. Minor's agreement is void but the minor can enforce the agreement against the other major party :

(*a*) if he is a promisee in the agreement.
(*b*) if he is a promisor in the agreement.
(*c*) if he is a promisee in the agreement and he has performed his part of promise under the agreement.
(*d*) if the Court has no objection.

9. Capacity to contract means :

(*a*) the parties are financially sound to make contracts.
(*b*) the parties are physically able and willing to make contracts.
(*c*) the parties are legally competent to enter into contracts.
(*d*) all of the above.

10. A minor can be :

(*a*) drawer of a cheque.
(*b*) payee of a cheque.
(*c*) acceptor of bill of exchange.
(*d*) surety.

11. A minor can be held personally liable :

(*a*) for cheques issued by him.
(*b*) for promises made by him with other joint promisors.
(*c*) for guarantee given by him.
(*d*) for none of the above.

12. This is true :

(*a*) that law presumes that every person is competent to contract unless otherwise proved.
(*b*) that a minor can make contract for necessaries of life.
(*c*) that a person of unsound mind can enter into family contracts.
(*d*) that a wife can always make valid business contracts and bind her husband.

13. Agreement made by a person of unsound mind is :

(*a*) voidable.
(*b*) void.
(*c*) unlawful.
(*d*) sometimes void and sometimes valid.

14. These two persons can enter into a valid contract :

(*a*) one minor and a major person.
(*b*) one minor and a person who is usually of sound mind.
(*c*) husband and wife.
(*d*) one major person and an insolvent person.

15. A person usually of sound mind but occasionally of unsound mind :

(*a*) can always enter into contract.

(*b*) can enter into contract when he looks to be of sound mind.

(*c*) can never enter into contract.

(*d*) cannot enter into contract when he is of unsound mind.

16. A person who is usually of unsound mind but occasionally of sound mind :

(*a*) can enter into contract when he is of unsound mind.

(*b*) can never enter into contract.

(*c*) can sometimes enter into contract.

(*d*) can enter into contract when he is of sound mind.

17. For necessaries supplied to a minor or his dependents :

(*a*) A minor is personally liable. (*b*) Guardian of a minor is personally liable.

(*c*) Claim can be made against minor's property. (*d*) None of these.

18. A contract by an idiot is :

(*a*) voidable. (*b*) invalid.

(*c*) enforceable. (*d*) void ab-initio.

19. Flaw in capacity may arise from :

(*a*) want of consideration. (*b*) illegality of object.

(*c*) unsoundness of mind. (*d*) uncertainty of object.

20. On attaining majority, an agreement with a minor :

(*a*) can be ratified. (*b*) becomes void.

(*c*) cannot be ratified. (*d*) becomes valid.

ANSWERS

1. (*a*)	**2.** (*a*)	**3.** (*a*)	**4.** (*d*)	**5.** (*b*)	**6.** (*c*)	**7.** (*c*)	**8.** (*c*)	**9.** (*c*)	**10.** (*b*)
11. (*d*)	**12.** (*b*)	**13.** (*b*)	**14.** (*c*)	**15.** (*d*)	**16.** (*d*)	**17.** (*c*)	**18.** (*d*)	**19.** (*c*)	**20.** (*c*)

PRACTICAL PROBLEMS

1. A sold his house to B and received a token advance. The registration of the sale deed could not be done because A was a minor. B filed a suit for the recovery of his advance. Is the suit maintainable? (*B.Com. Madurai*)

(No. An agreement with a minor is void)

2. A, a minor, borrows Rs. 10,000 and executes a pronote for the amount in favour of B. After attaining the majority, A executes another pronote in settlement of the first pronote. Will B succeed in recovering money from A? Give reasons in support of your answer. (*B.Com. Osmania*)

(No. B will not succeed in recovering money from A. The contract is void, *abinitio*. Ratification by a minor, of a contract, on attaining majority is not allowed).

VI

CHAPTER

Free Consent

(Sections 10, 13–22)

INTRODUCTION

According to Sec. 10, 'free consent' of all parties to an agreement is one of the essential elements of a valid contract. The consent of the parties means that there is perfect identity of mind of both the parties *i.e.*, there is no misunderstanding between the parties regarding the subject-matter of the contract. For enforceability of an agreement, it is not only necessary that the parties to the agreement should have given consent but their consent should also be free.

Consent

The term 'consent' is defined in Sec. 13 of the Indian Contract Act, which reads as under :

"Two or more persons are said to consent when they agree upon the same thing in the same sense".

'Consent' means that the parties should have the identity of mind, *i.e.*, the parties must understand the subject-matter of the contract in the same sense. Thus consent involves identity of minds or consensus *ad-idem i.e.*, agreeing upon the same thing in the same sense. When there is no consent, there is no contract. When parties enter into an agreement concerning a particular person or thing, but each has a different person or thing in mind then there is no consent of the parties and no contract comes into existence between them.

Example : A had two cars, one is of green colour and the other is white. A offered to sell his green car to B for Rs. 50,000. B accepted the offer believing it to be for the white one. In this case, no contract arises between A and B as there is no real consent of the parties.

FREE CONSENT

Free consent defined in Section 14 reads as follows: Consent is said to be free when it is not caused by:

(1) coercion, as defined in Section 15 or
(2) undue influence, as defined in Section 16, or
(3) fraud, as defined in Section 17, or
(4) misrepresentation, as defined in Section 18, or
(5) mistake, subject to provisions of Sections 20, 21 and 22.

When a consent is caused by mistake of both the parties, then the agreement is void. It will, therefore, be observed that consent under the first four circumstances *i.e.*, under coercion, undue influence, fraud and misrepresentation, makes the contract voidable, while consent under mistake of both the parties makes the agreement void. See the chart below:

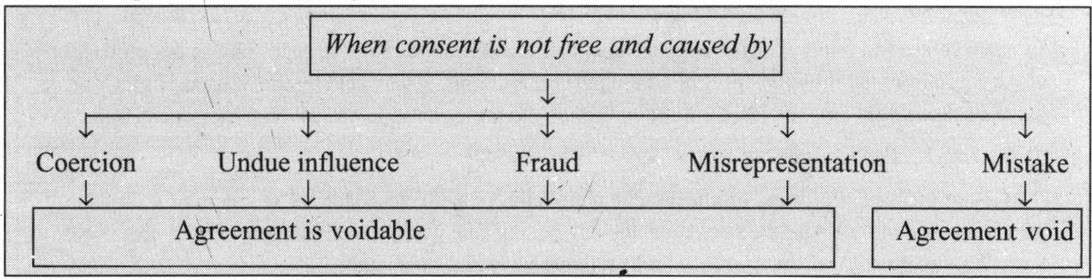

"If consent is caused by *coercion* or *undue influence* or *fraud* or *misrepresentation*, the consent is not free. If the consent is caused by *mistake*, there is no consent at all". "When there is no consent, there is no contract."

Consent is said to be so caused when it would not have been given but the existence of such coercion, undue influence, fraud, misrepresentation or mistake.

In fact, where there is no consensus *ad idem*, there is no common intention or meeting of minds of the parties, and as such no contract comes into existence. In the absence of 'free consent' the contract may turn out to be either voidable or void depending upon the nature of the flaw in consent.

When the consent is 'not free' then the contract is voidable at the option of the party whose consent is not free. But in cases of 'no consent, no contract will come into existence, it will be void ab initio.

COERCION

Coercion means forcibly compelling a person to enter into a contract. Coercion is threat or force used by one party against the other for making him to enter into an agreement.

Sec. 15 of the Act defines :

"Coercion" is the committing or threatening to commit, any act forbidden by the Indian Penal Code, or the unlawful detaining, or threatening to detain, any property, to the prejudice of any person whatever, with the intention of causing any person to enter into an agreement."

Coercion implies a committing or threatening to commit some act which is contrary to law. According to the above definition of coercion, it may be in any of the following acts :

(1) To commit an act forbidden by the Indian Penal code; or
(2) The threat to commit an act forbidden by the Indian Penal Code; or
(3) Unlawful detention of any property; or
(4) The threat to unlawful detention of any property.

However, it is necessary that

(*i*) The act, amounting to coercion, must have been done with the intention of causing any person to enter into an agreement. and (*ii*) It does not matter, whether the Indian Penal Code is or is not in force at the place where coercion is employed.

Examples : (1) *Renganayakamma Vs. Alwar Chetty* (1889)

A young widow of 13 years was forced to agree to adopt a boy to her husband under the threats of preventing the dead body of her husband from being removed for cremation. The widow adopted the boy and subsequently applied for cancellation of the adoption. Because her consent was not free but induced by coercion. It was held that coercion was employed as any person who obstructed a dead body from being removed would be guilty of an offence under Sec. 197 of the Indian Penal Code.

(2) *Muthiah Chettiar Vs. Karuppen Chetty* (1927)

An agent refused to hand over the account books of a business to the new agent unless the principal released him from liability in respect of all the past transactions. It was held by the Madras High Court that the release deed was avoidable at the option of the principal as it was given under coercion.

(3) *Bansraj Vs. the Secretary of State* (1939)

The Government gave a threat of attachment against the property of A, for the recovery of a fine due from B, the son of A, A paid the fine. Held, the payment of fine was induced by coercion and, therefore, A was entitled to recover the money paid to remove wrongful attachment.

Threat to File a Suit

To threaten a criminal or civil prosecution does not constitute coercion because it is not an act forbidden by the Indian Penal Code. But a threat to file a suit on a false charge constitutes coercion, for such an act is forbidden by the Indian Penal Code.

Threat to Commit Suicide

Sometimes, by threat to commit suicide, a person obtains the consent of the other. The doubt arises because suicide though forbidden by the Indian Panel code is for obvious reasons not punishable. A dead person cannot be punished. But, since Section 15 declares that committing or threatening to commit suicide should obviously be so regarded (suicide being forbidden).

Example : *Chikkam Ammiraju Vs. Chikkam Seshamma* (1918)

In this case a person, by threat to commit suicide, induced his wife and son to execute a release deed in favour of his brother in respect of certain properties which they claimed as their own. The transaction was set aside on the grounds of coercion. It was stated by the majority of judges that though 'a threat to commit suicide' was not punishable under the Indian Penal Code, it must be deemed to be forbidden by that Code, as 'an attempt to commit suicide' was punishable under Sec. 309 of that Code. Their Lordships observed : "The term 'any act forbidden by the Indian Penal Code' is wider than the term 'punishable by the Indian Penal Code'. Simply because a man escapes punishment, it does not follow that the act is not forbidden by the Penal Code. For example, a lunatic or a minor may not be punished. This does not show that their criminal acts are not forbidden by the Penal Code."

Burden of Proof

The burden of proving that the consent was obtained by coercion, lies upon the person who wants to avoid the contract on the ground of coercion. He will have to prove that he would never have entered into the contract if the coercion had not been directed against him.

Effect of Coercion

The effect of coercion is that it makes the contract voidable at the option of the party whose consent is obtained by coercion, that is, such party can put an end to the contract if he so chooses. The burden of proof that coercion was used lies on the party who wants to set aside the contract on the plea of coercion. The effect of coercion is emphasised in Sections 19 and 72 of Indian contract Act.'

Section 19 states : "when consent to an agreement is caused by coercion, the agreement is a contract voidable at the option of the party whose consent was so caused."

Section 72 states : "A person to whom money has been paid or anything delivered under coercion, must repay or return it."

Duress

In the English Law, the near equivalent of the term 'coercion' is 'duress'. The term coercion in India covers much wider field than duress in England. Duress has been defined as causing, or threatening to cause, bodily violence or imprisonment, with a view to obtain the consent of the other party to the contract. In short, for duress the act or threat must be aimed at the life or liberty of the other party to the contract or the members of his family. A threat destroy or detain property will not amount to 'duress'.

Duress Differs from Coercion on the Following Points

1. Coercion can be employed by any person whereas duress can be employed only against the other party to the contract or the members of his family.
2. Coercion may be employed by any person, not necessarily by the promisee. Duress can be employed only by the party to the contract or his agent.
3. Coercion is wider in its scope and includes unlawful detention of goods also. Duress, on the other hand, does not include unlawful detention of goods. Only bodily violence or imprisonment is duress.

UNDUE INFLUENCE

The term 'undue influence' means the unfair use of one's superior power in order to obtain the consent of a person who is in a weaker position. In certain cases, the parties to an agreement are so related to each other that one of them is in a position to dominate the will of the other. Sometimes a party is compelled to enter into an agreement against his will because of an unfair persuasion by the other party. The term 'undue influence' is defined in Sec. 16 of the Indian Contract Act :

Sec. 16 (1) "A contract is said to be induced by 'undue influence' where, (*i*) the relations subsisting between the parties are such that one of the parties is in a position to dominate the will of the other, and (*ii*) uses the position to obtain an unfair advantage over the other."

The phrase **"in a position to dominate the will of the other"** is clarified by the same Section, under sub-section (2) thus :

Section 16 (2) "A person is deemed to be in a position to dominate the will of another :

(*a*) "Where he holds a real or apparent authority over the other"

Example : Relationship between master and servant

Relationship between police officer and accused.

(*b*) "Where he stands in a fiduciary relation to the other".

Fiduciary relation means a relation of mutual trust and confidence.

Example: Relationship between father and son

Relationship between doctor and patient

Relationship between trustee and beneficiary etc.

(*c*) "Where he makes a contract with a person whose mental capacity is temporarily or permanently affected by reason of age, illness or mental or bodily distress etc."

Example : Old illiterate persons.

Thus, there are the following three ingredients of undue influence :

(*a*) That the relations subsisting between the parties are such that one of the parties is in a position to dominate the will of the other :

(*b*) That the dominant party obtains an unfair advantage over the other : and

(*c*) That the dominant party uses its dominant position to obtain that unfair advantage.

Examples : (1) X having advanced a sum to his son Y during his minority: upon Y being major, X using his parental influence gets a bond signed for higher amount. It is a case of undue influence.

(2) A, a man enfeebled by disease or age is induced by B's influence over him as his medical attendant to agree to pay B an unreasonable sum for his professional service. B employs undue influence (Fiduciary position).

(3) A, a spendthrift and a weak-minded, just comes of age, conveys a share of his family estate to his father-in-law for a nominal consideration. Undue influence is presumed to have been exercised.

Relationships which Raise a Presumption of Undue Influence

Some relationships are such in nature that they raise a presumption of undue influence, *viz.*,

(*a*) Parent and child
(*b*) Father and son
(*c*) Guardian and ward
(*d*) Trustee and beneficiary
(*e*) Doctor and patient
(*f*) Teacher and student
(*g*) Religious adviser and disciple, etc.

There is, however, no presumption of undue influence in the following cases :

(*a*) Husband and wife (not being parda-nashin)
(*b*) Creditor and debtor
(*c*) Landlord and tenant

In these cases undue influence shall have to be proved.

PRESUMPTION OF UNDUE INFLUENCE

Undue influence is presumed to exist in three cases, viz., (*i*) when one party is holding real and apparent authority over the other, (*ii*) where there is fiduciary relationship between the parties and (*iii*) where the contracts are made with the persons in mental distress, it is presumed that one party is in a position to dominate the will of the other. Apart from these, following are the cases which indicate the presumption of undue influence :

1. *Unconscionable Transactions*

Unfair or unreasonable bargains belong to the category of 'unconscionable transactions'. These are such transactions where as between two contracting parties, one is in a dominant position and makes an exorbitant profit of the other's distress. In such cases, the law presumes that the consent must have been obtained by undue influence. The burden is shifted to the stronger party to prove that the consent of the other party is freely given. This provision is contained in Section 16 (3) of the Indian Contract Act, which reads as under :

"Where a person who is in a position to dominate the will of another, enters into a contract with him, and the transaction appears, on the face of it or in the evidence adduced, to be unconscionable, the burden of proving that such contract was not induced by undue influence shall lies upon the person in a position to dominate the will of other"

2. *Pardanashin Woman*

Pardanashin women are women who live in complete seclusion by reason of the custom and practice of the community to which they belong. Pardanashin women are a special class of persons who, by Indian Law have been presumed to be ordinarily incapable of managing their affairs. Therefore, their transactions are also treated in a different footing. The principles to be applied to transactions with pardanashin women are not merely on the ground of undue influence but also on the wider basis of equity and good conscience. In case of sales, mortgages, gifts, release or the execution of any other document effected by a pardanashin woman, it is not enough to show that the transaction or deed was explained to her it must be further shown affirmatively that the same was fully understood by her. The burden of proving these will be on those who support the transaction or deed.

Example : *Rani Annapurni Vs. Swaminathan* (1910)

A poor Hindu widow borrowed Rs. 1,500 from a money lender at 100 per cent per annum rate of interest for the purpose of enabling her to establish her right to maintenance. It lies on the money-lender to prove that there was no undue influence.

Example : *Inche Noriah Vs. Shaik Omar* (1929)

A Malay woman of great age and wholly illiterate executed a gift deed in favour of her nephew. The respondent managed the whole of her affairs, including her domestic affairs. In an action to set aside the deed on the ground that the relation between the parties at the time when the deed was executed was such as to raise a presumption of undue influence against the respondent. Held that "the facts proved by the respondent are not sufficient to rebut the presumption of undue influence which is raised by the relationship proved to have been in existence between the parties".

Example : *Smt. Takri Devi Vs. Smt. Rama Dogra* (1984)

It was held that an old illiterate woman gifted her valuable immovable property to her advocate. It was held that the relationship was fiduciary and that it could be presumed that the advocate was in a position to dominate the will of the woman and as the transaction appeared to be unconscionable, the court in the circumstances of the case further held that the gift deed was the result of undue influence by the donee advocate.

Effect of Undue Influence (19 A)

The effect of undue influence is that it makes the contract voidable at the option of the party whose consent is obtained by undue influence i.e., such party can put an end to the contract, if he so chooses. Further Sec. 19A reads as follows :

"When consent to an agreement is caused by undue influence, the agreement is a contract voidable at the option of the party where consent was so caused."

"Any such contract may be set aside either absolutely, or, if the party who was entitled to avoid it has received any benefit thereunder, upon such terms and conditions as the court may seem just"

Burden of Proof

Sometimes a contract is challenged in a Court of Law on the ground of undue influence, then it is the duty of the weaker party to prove that his consent was obtained by undue influence. The plaintiff has to establish the following two points :

(*i*) The superior party was in a position to dominate his will, and

(*ii*) The superior party actually used his influence to obtain his consent to the contract.

The suit is, generally, filed by the weaker party to avoid the contract. Therefore, the burden of proving undue influence is on the plaintiff, who files a suit in a Court of Law.

Examples : *Sethani Vs. Bhanna* (1993)

A sale deed of her property was executed by an old, blind, illiterate and tribal women in favour of the respondent, on whom she was totally dependent. There was no evidence of consideration having passed at the time of sale or the respondent having proved the absence of undue influence. The respondent was held and bound to return the advantage obtained by him in this case.

Rukmini Vs. Krishnan Nair (1985)

In this case an old lady of 70, who had a paralytic stroke was made to execute a gift dead without the contents of deed being made known to her. It was held that the burden of proof was on the donee to show that there was no undue influence.

Shrimati Vs. Sudhakar Bhatkar (1988)

The plaintiff was an illiterate lady, managing her properties. The defendant was living in a part of the house, owned by the plaintiff as a tenant. He treated the plaintiff as his mother. He persuaded to gift her property to him, which she did. The gift deed was registered in his favour.

It was held that more persuasion by the plaintiff to the defendant to gift the property did not mean undue influence. There was nothing to show that he was able to dominate her will. The transaction was held to be valid as there was no undue influence in this case.

Mannu Singh Vs. Umadat Pande (1890)

The plaintiff, an-aged Hindu, executed a deed or gift in respect of the whole of his property in favour of the defendant, who was plaintiff's spiritual adviser. The only reason for the gift was his desire to secure benefits to his soul in the next world. Soon after the execution of the said deed, the plaintiff applied for cancellation of the same by a suit brought by him under Sec. 39 of the Specific Relief Act 1877.

Sec. 111 of Indian Evidence Act 1872 was applied to this situation, according to which, in case of a person being in a position of active confidence, the burden of proof lies on such a person who enjoys such a confidence. It was held that because of the fiduciary relationship between the parties, and the absurdity of the reason given by the plaintiff in the gift deed for executing the gift deed, and in view of the provision contained in Sec, 111 of Indian Evidence Act, the defendant must prove the absence of undue influence. Since he has failed to prove the same, the plaintiff is entitled to obtain the cancellation of the deed.

Lakshmi Amma Vs. Telengala Narayana Bhatta (1970)

The executant of a deed of settlement was a person of advanced age and was suffering from diabetes and other ailments and whose physical and mental condition was very weak. He executed a deed settling his entire property in favour of one of his grandsons to the exclusion of his own issues and other grandchildren. He did not make any provision for the residence of his wife in the said residential house and also debarred himself from dealing with the property in his lifetime. He subsequently applied for the cancellation of the deed on account of undue influence. It was held by the Supreme Court, reversing the decision of the Kerala High Court, that the facts and circumstances raised a grave suspicion as to the genuineness of the execution of the document, and it was for the grandson, who is the settlee of the property, to show that the said deed had been executed voluntarily and without any external pressure or influence.

Rebutting the Presumption

The presumptions of undue influence can be rebutted by showing that :

(*i*) Full disclosure of facts was made by the influencing party to the party alleged to have been influenced at the time of entering into the contract.

(*ii*) The price was adequate.

(*iii*) The weaker party was in receipt of independent advice before making the consent or it was the free exercise of independent will. Thus presumption of undue influence can be rebutted.

COMPARISON BETWEEN COERCION AND UNDUE INFLUENCE

Points of difference between coercion and undue influence are :

(1) Definition : Coercion as defined under section 15 of Indian Contract Act, 1872 is an act *based upon the use of physical force, punishable* under Indian Penal Code: while undue influence as defined under Section 16, is an act *based upon the use of moral force, which is not punishable.*

(2) Parties : Coercion can be employed by any person even by a stranger to the contract: while undue influence is employed by any of the parties to the contract.

(3) Relationship of the Parties : In coercion, *the parties need not have any relationship* in between themselves : while in case of undue influence, the parties to the contract must have a *fiduciary relationship*, by which one of them becomes in a position to dominate the will of the other.

(4) Dominance of one party : In coercion, *none of the parties has dominating position to dominate the will of the other party*, while in undue influence *one of the parties has the position to dominate the will of the other.*

(5) Rights : In coercion, *the aggrieved party has a right to avoid the contract, but has to restore the benefits to the other party*, if he has received such benefits : while in undue influence, *contracts may be set aside in full by the aggrieved party* or on the terms and conditions by the court, as it may decide.

(6) Onus : In coercion, *the aggrieved party has to prove the exercise of coercion by the other party*, while in undue influence, the aggrieved party *has to prove the existence of fiduciary relationship. The other party has also to prove that the contract was not induced by undue influence and no undue benefit has been obtained.*

(7) Punishment : Coercion is an act punishable under Indian Penal Code, while undue influence is *not punishable* under it.

FRAUD

The term fraud may be defined as an intentional, deliberate or wilful misstatement of facts which are material for the formation of a contract. It includes all acts committed by a person with a view to deceive another person. To deceive means to induce a man to believe that a thing is true which is false. The important requirement of fraud is that the misstatement of facts must be made by one party with an intention to deceive the other.

Definition

According to Section 17 of the Indian contract Act : "Fraud" means and includes any of the following acts committed by a party to a contract or with his connivance, or by his agent, with intent to deceive another party thereto or his agent, or to induce him to enter into the contract :

1. the suggestion as to a fact, of that which is not true by one who does not believe it to be true;
2. the active concealment of a fact by one having knowledge or belief of the fact;
3. a promise made without any intention of performing it;
4. any other act fitted to deceive;
5. any such act or omission as the law specially declares to be fraudulent.

Explanation : Mere silence as to facts likely to affect the willingness of a person to enter into a contract is not fraud, unless the circumstances of the case are such that, regard being had to them, it is the duty of the person keeping silence to speak, or unless his silence is, in itself, equivalent to speech.

The following illustrations are appended to the section :

(*a*) A sells, by auction, to B, a horse which A knows to be unsound. A says nothing to B about the horse's unsoundness. This is not fraud in A.

(*b*) B is A's daughter and has just come to age. Here, the relation between the parties would make it A's duty to tell B if the horse is unsound.

(*c*) B says to A, "If you do not deny it, I shall assume that the horse is sound". A says nothing. Here A's silence is equivalent to speech.

(*d*) A and B, being traders, enter upon a contract. A has private information of a change in prices which would affect B's willingness to proceed with the contract. A is not bound to inform B.

Essentials of Fraud

On analysis of the above definition, 'fraud' means and includes any of the following acts :

1. *Making a False Suggestion as to a Fact*

To constitute fraud there must be an assertion of something false within the knowledge of the party asserting it. That is, to constitute fraud, there must be a false representation or a statement by a party to a contract who knows that the suggestion is false. There must be intention to deceive the other party or the intention to induce him to enter a contract.

Example : *Peek Vs. Gurney (1873)*

The prospectus of a company did not refer to the existence of a document disclosing liabilities. This gave the impression that the company was prosperous. If the existence of the document had been disclosed the impression would have been quite different. Held, non-disclosure amounted to fraud and any one who purchased shares on the faith of this prospectus could avoid the contract.

2. *Active Concealment of a Fact*

A person making a false statement is not guilty of fraud if he honestly believes in its truthfulness. The fraudulent act must have been made with the knowledge of its falsity (*i.e.*, without belief in its truth). It must be remembered that active concealment does not mean non-disclosure of material fact, since the explanation to Sec. 17 clearly says that silence is not fraud except under certain circumstances. Mere non-disclosure of fact is not fraud, where there is no duty to disclose.

Essentials of Fraud

1. Making a false suggestion as to a fact.
2. Active concealment of a fact.
3. A promise without intention to perform.
4. Any act fitted to deceive.
5. Representation of fact to deceive.
6. The party, subjected to fraud, suffered loss.

Example : *Derry Vs. Peek* (1889)

The directors of a Tramway Company issued a prospectus stating that they had the right to run tram cars with steam power instead of with horses as before. In fact, the Act incorporating the company provided that such power might be used with the sanction of the Board of Trade. But, the Board of Trade refused to give permission and the company had to be wound up. A shareholder sued the directors for damages for fraud. The House of Lords held that the directors were not liable in fraud because they honestly believed what they said in the prospectus to be true.

3. *A Promise Made without any Intention of Performing It*

If a man while entering into a contract has no intention to perform his promise, there is fraud on his part.

> **Example :** Purchase of goods without any intention of paying for them.

4. *Any other Act Fitted to Deceive*

A deceit which does not deceive is not fraud. All surprise, trick, cunning, dissembling and other unfair way that is used to cheat anyone is considered fraud. The expression 'act fitted to deceive' means any act which is done with obvious intention of committing fraud.

> **Example :** *Horsefall Vs. Thomas* (1862)
> A brought a cannon of B. B knew the cannon had a defect which rendered it worthless, and so puts a metal plug to conceal the defect. A accepted the cannon without examining it. The cannon burst, when used. Held, there was no fraud because A would have bought it even if no deceptive plug had been put. He was not in fact deceived by it.

5. *Any such Act or Omission as the Law Specially Declared to be Fraudulent*

Sec. 17 (5) refers to the provisions in certain acts which make it obligatory to disclose relevant facts. Thus under Sec. 55 of the Transfer of Property Act, the seller of immovable property is bound to disclose to the buyer all material facts. Failure to do so amounts to fraud.

6. *The Party Subjected to Fraud must have Suffered some Loss*

It is a common rule of law that there is no fraud without damages. As such 'fraud without damage' does not give rise to an action of deceit.

Silence as Fraud

Explanation to Section 17 of the Act states that :

"Mere silence as to facts likely to affect the willingness of a person to enter into a contract is not fraud, unless the circumstances of the case are such that, regard being had to them, it is the duty of the person keeping silence to speak, or unless his silence is, in itself, equivalent to speech."

In other words, the silence amounts to fraud in the following cases :

1. *Duty to Speak*

Mere silence amounts to fraud when the person keeping silent, is under duty to speak. The duty to speak arises when one party reposes trust and confidence in the other. The duty to speak exists where the parties stand in a fiduciary relationship. For example, father and son, guardian and ward etc. Duty to disclose also arises when one of the parties has absolutely no means of discovering the truth, and as such, has to depend upon the other party to the contract. Contract of insurance, contract of family arrangement, contracts for the sale of land, contract in which fiduciary relationship exist, etc. are example of contracts of 'utmost good faith'. Contracts of this character are called contracts uberrimae fidei..

> **Example :** A sells by auction to B a horse which A knows to be unsound. B is A's daughter and has just come of age. Here the relation between the parties would make it A's duty to tell B if the horse is unsound.

2. *Silence is Equivalent to Speak*

Where the circumstances are such that 'Silence is in itself equivalent to speech.' Thus, where A says to B, "If you do not deny it, I shall assume that the horse is sound". A says nothing. Here A's silence is equivalent to speech.

Half Truth : A person may keep silent. But if he speaks, he is duty bound to disclose the whole truth. A person may become guilty of fraud by non-disclosure if he voluntarily discloses something and then stops half the way. If the party keeping silent, volunteers to disclose a state of facts partly, as a result of which the undisclosed part renders the disclosed part false.

Example : *King Vs. Kylsant* (1932)

The prospectus issued by a company disclosed that his company had paid dividends every year between 1921 and 1927. The statement was true. However, during these years, the company had incurred heavy trading losses. The dividends were paid out only out of the secret reserve. No disclosure was made of these losses. It was held that the prospectus was false and the directors who knew that it was false, were held guilty of fraud.

Change of Circumstances : A statement was true at the time when it was made. But when it is actually acted upon by the other party, it may become false due to the change of circumstances. In such cases, it is the duty of the person, who made the statement, to communicate the change of circumstances.

Example : *Rajagopala Iyer Vs. The South Indian Rubber Works* (1942)

The prospectus of a company contained a statement that certain persons are the directors of the company. This statement was true when made. On the basis of this statement, certain persons applied for the allotment of shares. But before the allotment took place, some directors retired from the company. This change was not communicated to the applicants of shares. It was held that they were entitled to avoid the allotment.

CONTRACTS "UBERRIMAE FIDEI"

Uberrimae fidei contracts are contracts where law imposes upon the parties the duty of making a full disclosure of all material facts. In such contracts, if one of the parties has any information concerning the subject matter of the transaction which is likely to affect the willingness of the other party to enter into the transaction, he is bound to disclose the information.

The following contracts come within the class of uberrimae fidei contracts:

1. *Contracts of Insurance*

All contracts of insurance are *contracts of utmost good faith i.e. contracts of uberrimae fidei.* It is, therefore, necessary for the person taking out a policy to disclose all material facts which are known to him. The insurer is entitled to be put in possession of all material information possessed by the insured. Failure to fulfil this obligation renders the contract voidable at the option of the insurer.

Example : *London Assurance Vs. Mensel* (1879)

The plaintiff brought an action against the defendant to set aside an agreement for insurance, alleging that it was the duty of the defendant to have informed them that his life had been refused by several companies, that such fact was a very material fact in a contract of life assurance and that they would not have entertained the defendant's proposal had he informed them that his life had been refused by other companies.

Example : *Sarojam Vs. LIC of India* (1986)

The assured was suffering from a serious heart ailment not only when the proposal for the insurance of his life was made, but also for several years prior to that. The assured gave false answers to the questions in the proposal form so as to conceal his ailment and induced the LIC to accept the proposal. He died of heart ailment within a few months, after the date of policy. It was held that in view of the false answers to the questions given by the assured in the proposal form, the contract of insurance was vitiated and the LIC was, therefore entitled to repudiate the policy and decline the payment of claim thereunder.

2. *Fiduciary Relationship*

If the parties to a contract stand in fiduciary relationship, the relationship requires fullest disclosure by the party in whom confidence is reposed. The relationship between a trustee and beneficiary, guardian and ward, agent and principal, solicitor and client etc. fall under this category.

3. *Contracts for the sale of immovable property*

Under Sec. 55(1) (a) of the Transfer of Property Act, the seller is bound "to disclose to the buyer any material defect in the property or in the seller's title thereto of which the seller is, and the buyer is not, aware, and which the buyer could not with ordinary care discover."

Example : *Akhtar Jahan Begam Vs. Hazarilal* (1927)

A sold some property to B stating in the sale deed that he would not be liable to B if he suffered any loss owing to A's defective title. A had, earlier to this transaction, sold this property to somebody else, but did not inform B about it. It was held that A had committed fraud and the contract was voidable at the option of B.

4. *Contracts to take shares*

A contract to take shares in a company is usually made on the faith of the statements made by the promoters in the prospectus. Now the Companies Act requires that a lot of details must be given in the prospectus. The list covers most of the representations and non-disclosures that may mislead an applicant for shares. Even apart from such statutory provision it is long settled that the promoters must show the utmost good faith in the preliminaries to an issue of shares.

5. *Family Settlement*

A contract of family arrangement is one of utmost good faith. Hence, when members of a family make arrangements for the settlement of the family property, every member of the family must disclose all material facts within his knowledge, and which might affect the judgement of the others in entering into a compromise. The arrangement will not be binding on those members who are kept in the dark due to concealment of material facts by the other members.

6. *Partnership Contracts*

At the time of formation of a partnership, a person who induces another to become a member of the partnership must disclose every fact within his knowledge which is likely to affect the consent of the other party to become a partner. Once the partnership is formed the parties stand in the confidential relation of principal and agent. Each partner is bound to disclose to the others all material facts and to exercise the utmost good faith in all that relates to the common business. Each one participating in the actual business must do so to the greatest common advantage of all.

7. *Contracts of Marriage*

Every party in a marriage contract is under a duty to disclose all the material facts.

CONSEQUENCES OF FRAUD

Sec. 19 of the Indian Contract Act states :

"When consent to an agreement is caused by fraud, the agreement is a contract voidable at the option of the party whose consent was so caused.".

In other words, a party who has been induced to enter into an agreement by fraud has the following remedies open to him :

1. He can avoid the performance of the contract.

2. He can insist that the contract shall be performed and that he shall be put in the position in which he would have been if the representation made had been true.

Example : A fraudulently informs B that A's estate is free from encumbrance. B thereupon buys the estate. The estate is subject to a mortgage. B may avoid the contract or may insist on its being carried out and the mortgage debt repaid by A.

3. The aggrieved party can sue for damages. Fraud is a civil wrong or tort; hence compensation is payable.

Example : *Kiran Bala Vs. Bhaire Prasad Srivastava* (1982)

The first marriage of the appellant, Kiran Bala, had been annulled on the ground that she was of unsound mind at the time of that marriage. She was married to the respondent, Bhaire Prasad Srivastava, the second time. The facts of the annulment of the first marriage on the ground that she was an idiot, and also that she was under treatment for mental ailment were not disclosed to the bridegroom either by the girl or her parents. It was held that it was not the duty of the bridegroom to find out these facts, but it was the duty of the girl or her parents not to conceal these facts. Consent of the bridegroom was held to have been obtained by fraud, and the second marriage of the appellant with the respondent was, therefore, annulled by a decree or nullity under Sec. 12(1)(c) of Hindu Marriage Act.

LOSS OF RIGHT OF RESCISSION

When a contract is induced by fraud, it is voidable at the option of the party whose consent was so caused. He has the option either to rescind the contract or to affirm it. But his right of rescission is lost in the following cases :

1. *By Affirmation*

If after becoming aware of his right to rescind, the aggrieved party affirms the transaction either by express words or by an act which shows an intention to affirm it, the right of rescission is lost. For example, if a person, who has purchased shares on the faith of a misleading prospectus, subsequently becomes aware of its falsity, but accepts dividends paid to him, he will not be permitted to avoid the contract.

2. *Lapse of Time*

After the fraud is discovered by the aggrieved party, the contract must be rescinded within a reasonable time. If the contract is not rescinded within the reasonable time, this right is lost. The reasonable time is an important factor which depends upon the facts and circumstances of each case.

3. *Restitution not Possible*

If the party seeking rescission is not in a position to restore the benefits he may have obtained under the contract, example, where the subject-matter of the contract has been consumed or destroyed, the right to rescind the contract be exercised.

4. *Right of Third Parties*

Sometimes, the third party acquires the right in the subject-matter of the contract in good faith, without any knowledge of fraud between the other two parties. And the third party pays the due consideration for acquiring the rights. In such cases, the aggrieved party loses the right to rescind the contract.

Example : *Phillips Vs. Brooks Ltd.* (1919)

'A' by fraud, obtained certain goods from 'B'. And sold the same to 'C' who purchased them in good faith. In this case, B's right to rescind the contract with A is lost, as the third party C has acquired interest in the subject-matter in good faith.

MISREPRESENTATION

Representation is a statement or assertion, made by one party to the another before or at the time of contract, regarding some fact relating to it. Misrepresentation is a false statement which the person making it honestly believes to be true or which does not know to be false. In other words, a representation which is false or misleading is known as misrepresentation. A false representation may be made by a person either (*a*) innocently or (*b*) intentionally, (*i.e.*, wilfully or deliberately). Again a false statement is made innocently *i.e.*, without any intention of deceiving the other party, it is called misrepresentation. But, if the false statement is made intentionally, *i.e.*, to deceive the other party, it is called fraud. The term misrepresentation is defined by Sec. 18 of the Indian Contract Act as under :

(Sec. 18) "Misrepresentation means and includes :

1. The positive assertion, in a manner not warranted by the information of the person making it, of that which is not true, though he believes it to be true;

2. any breach of duty which without an intent to deceive, gains an advantage to the person committing it, or any one claiming under him, by misleading another to his prejudice or to the prejudice of anyone claiming under him;

3. causing, however, innocently a party to an agreement to make a mistake as to the substance of the thing which is the subject of the agreement."

Thus misrepresentation may occur in any one of the following acts:

1. *Unwarranted Assertion*

The positive assertion, in a manner not warranted by the information of the person making it, of that which is not true, though he believes it to be true. The term 'warranted statement' may be defined as a statement made on the basis of information received from a trustworthy source. Whereas the term 'unwarranted statement' means a statement made on the basis of information received from untrustworthy source. When a person makes a positive statement that a fact is true when his information does not warrant it to be so, though he believes it to be true, this act amounts to misrepresentation.

> **Example :** A learns from B that C would be director of a company to be formed. A tells this to D in order to induce him to purchase shares of that company and D does so. This is misrepresentation by A, though he believed in the truthness of the statement and there was no intention to deceive, as the information was derived not from C but from B and was mere hearsay.

2. *Breach of Duty*

Breach of duty which brings an advantage to the person committing it by misleading the other to his prejudice. This clause covers those cases where a statement when made was true but subsequently before it was acted upon, it became false to the knowledge of the person making it. In such a case, the person making the statement comes under an obligation to disclose the change in circumstances to the other party, otherwise he will be guilty of misrepresentation.

> **Example :** *Bannerman Vs. White* (1861)
>
> The defendant agreed to buy hops from the plaintiff on the understanding that no sulphur has been used in their growth. The plaintiff made a representation that no sulphur had been used in the cultivation of hops and the defendant made it clear that he would not buy if sulphur has been used. In fact, sulphur had been used on five out of three hundred acres and this was forgotten by the plaintiff when he made the representation that no sulphur had been used. The court held that the assurance was intended to be a term in the contract and, in a sense a condition, without which the contract would not have proceeded with. Hence, the contract could be avoided on the ground of innocent misrepresentation, although the representation was not fraudulent.

3. *Innocent Mistake*

According to Sec. 18 (3), if a party to an agreement induces the other party, although innocently, to commit a mistake as to the nature or quality of the subject-matter of the agreement, he becomes guilty of misrepresentation.

> **Example :** *The Oceanic Steam Navigation Co. Vs. Soonderdas Dhurumsey* (1890)
>
> The defendants chartered a ship from the plaintiff Co. The ship was described in the charter party, and the plaintiff company represented that the tonnage of the ship was not more than 2,800. It later turned out that the registered tonnage was 3,045 tonnes. The defendant refused to accept the ship in fulfillment of the charter. In a suit by the plaintiff company, it was held that the defendants were entitled to avoid the charter party because of the misrepresentation as to the tonnage.
>
> **Example :** *Johnson Vs. Crowe* (1874)

The defendant agreed to sell and deliver a boiler to the plaintiff at Rajghat. At the time of entering into the agreement, the plaintiff made the representation that there was a road all the way to carry the boiler. The representation was innocent. In fact, there was a suspension bridge on the way and the bridge was not strong enough to bear the weight of the boiler. When the defendant came to know of the fact, he abstained from delivering the boiler. In a suit by the plaintiff, it was held that the agreement was voidable at the option of the defendant.

Essentials of Misrepresentation

A misrepresentation would be relevant, if it satisfies the following requirements, in brief :

1. It must be false, but the person who made it honestly believes it to be true.
2. It must relate to the material facts of the contracts.
3. It must have been made without any intention to deceive the other party.
4. The other party must have believed in it and acted upon.
5. It must induce the other party to make a contract.
6. It must have been made before conclusion of the contract.
7. It may be caused by representing half truth.
8. It must subsequently become false.

Effect of Misrepresentation

In the case of misrepresentation by the other party, the aggrieved party can :

1. avoid or rescind the contract; or

2. accept the contract but insist that he shall be placed in the position in which he would have been, if the misrepresentation had been true.

Misrepresentation does not entitle the aggrieved party to claim damages.

Distinction between Misrepresentation and Fraud

The following are the points of difference between the two:

1. In the case of misrepresentation, there is no *intention to deceive* the other party to the contract. In the case of fraud, there is the *intention to deceive.*

2. Misrepresentation is *not an act punishable* by the Indian Penal Code. Hence, it is not an offence. However, in certain cases, fraud can become *a criminal act punishable* under Indian Penal Code.

3. Misrepresentation is an *innocent wrong*. The person making the false statement believe it to be true. The fraud is *intentional or wilful wrong*. The person making the false statement does not believe it to be true.

4. In case of misrepresentation, *the aggrieved party cannot avoid the contract, if he has the means to discover the truth with ordinary prudence.* But in case of fraud, the *contract is voidable even though the aggrieved party has the means of discovering the truth with ordinary prudence.*

5. Although, generally, silence is not fraud, in the case of contracts of utmost good faith and those involving fiduciary relation, *silence can become fraud.* But, *silence cannot become an action of misrepresentation.*

Losing the Right of Rescission

The right of rescission is lost in the following cases :

1. *By Lapse of time :* If the misrepresentation is discovered by the aggrieved party, the contract must be rescinded within a reasonable time. But if the contract is not rescinded within the reasonable time, this right is lost.

2. *By affirmation:* After becoming aware of the right to rescind, the aggrieved party affirms the contract (express or implied).

3. *Third party acquires the right in the subject-matter:* Sometimes, a third party acquires the rights in the subject-matter of the contract in good faith, without the knowledge of the misrepresentation between the parties. In such cases, the aggrieved party loses the right to rescind the contract.

MISTAKE

A contract which is otherwise valid, may sometimes become vitiated owing to mistake which affects the consenting minds of the parties to it. Mistakes may be defined as an erroneous belief concerning something. In other words, the term "mistake" may be defined as an incorrect belief which leads one party to misunderstand the other. The mistakes take place where the concerned parties are not fully aware of the terms of the agreement, and they take the terms in a different sense. An agreement is valid as a contract only when the parties agree upon the same thing in the same sense.

Classification

Sections 20, 21 and 22 of the Act deal with the legal effect of mistake without defining the term :

Sec. 20 lays down that, "Where both the parties to an agreement are under a mistake as to a matter of fact essential to the agreement, the agreement is void."

Sec. 21 lays down that, "A contract is not voidable because it was caused by a mistake as to any law in force in India : but a mistake as to a law not in force in India has the same effect as a mistake of fact."

Sec. 22 states that "A contract is not voidable merely because it was caused by one of the parties to it being under a mistake as to a matter of fact."

There are many types of mistakes. But the following are important from the subject point of views :

The mistake may be: (*i*) *Mistake of facts* and (*ii*) *Mistake of law.*

Mistakes of fact may be : (*i*) *Bilateral mistakes*, and (*ii*) *Unilateral Mistake.*

Bilateral Mistake

'Bilateral mistake' may be defined as a mistake in which both the parties to an agreement are confused about the facts which are essential to the agreement. Sec. 20 provides "Where both parties to an agreement are under a mistake as to a matter of fact essential to the agreement, the agreement is void". The following two conditions must be fulfilled for application of Sec. 20 :

1. Both the parties must be under a mistake.
2. The mistake must relate to a matter of fact, essential to the agreement.

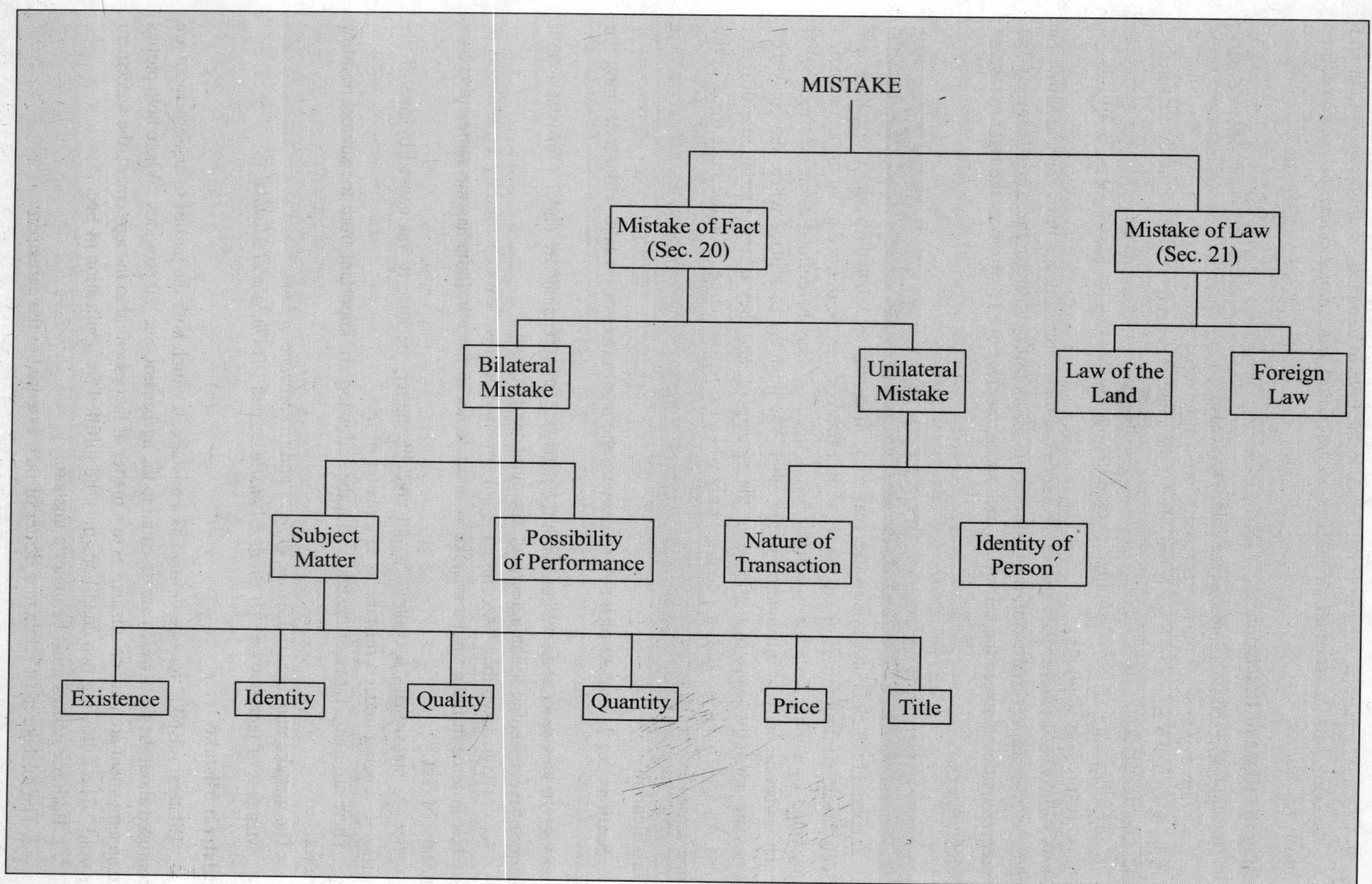
MISTAKE
Mistake of Fact (Sec. 20)
Mistake of Law (Sec. 21)
Bilateral Mistake
Unilateral Mistake
Law of the Land
Foreign Law
Subject Matter
Possibility of Performance
Nature of Transaction
Identity of Person
Existence
Identity
Quality
Quantity
Price
Title

Bilateral mistakes are of two types :

(*i*) Bilateral mistakes as to the subject-matter.

(*ii*) Bilateral mistakes as to possibility of performance.

(*i*) ***Bilateral Mistake as to the Subject-matter***

The identity and nature of subject-matter of an agreement is an essential to every agreement. The bilateral mistake about the subject-matter renders the agreement void. The following are the mistakes about the subject-matter.

(*a*) *Mistake as to the existence of the subject matter :*

If both the parties believe the subject-matter of the contracts to be in existence, which in fact, is not in existence at the time of contract, the contract is void.

Example : *Couturier Vs. Hastie* (1856)

The agreement was with regard to the sale of a cargo of corn supposed at the time of contract to be in transit from Salonica to England. But unknown to both parties that the cargo had become fermented and had already been sold at an intermediate port. Neither of the parties was aware of this fact at the time of the contract. The House of Lords held that the buyer was not liable to pay for the corn as the contract was vitiated by mistake.

(*b*) *Mistake as to identity of the subject-matter*

Where two parties intend to contract, and the first party intends to contract with regard to one thing while the second intends another thing, there is no agreement. That is where the parties agree upon different things, i.e., one meaning one thing and the other meaning another, the contract is void.

Example : *Raffles Vs. Wichelhaus* (1864)

The defendant agreed to buy certain goods from the plaintiff to arrive from Mumbai through a ship named "Peerless". There were two ships with the name Peerless sailed from Mumbai, one in October and the other in December. The defendant meant the earlier one and the plaintiff the later. The plaintiff sued for breach of contract, as the defendant refused to take delivery. The agreement was held to be void as there was no true consent of the parties.

(*c*) *Mistake as to Quality of the Subject-Matter*

If there is a mutual mistake of both the parties as to the quality of the subject-matter, i.e., if the subject-matter is something essentially different, from what the parties believed it to be, the agreement is void.

Example : *Smith Vs. Hughes* (1871)

When the plaintiff offered to sell and exhibited a sample of oats without mentioning anything about their age, the defendant said. "I am always a buyer of good oats". After agreeing to buy oats the defendant found, when a portion was delivered, that they were not old oats but new. Consequently, he refused to accept them and contended that the contract was void for mistake. Held, that the two minds were not ad idem as to the age of oats; they certainly were ad idem as to the sale and purchase of them. The court held that the contract was binding.

Strictly speaking it is the mistake as to substance of the subject-matter going to the very root of contract and affecting the whole consideration which makes it void and not the mistake as to quality. For, the principle of caveat emptor (let the buyer beware) clearly states that there is no implied warrant or condition as to the quality or fitness for any particular purpose of goods supplied under a contract of sale and the buyer must be held to have taken the risk that the goods sold might prove defective or might in some way be different from that which the parties believed it to be, in the absence of any misrepresentation or guarantee by the seller.

Example : *Lead Vs. International Galleries* (1950)

The plaintiff brought an action for the recovery of the price paid by him to defendant for a picture which they both mistakenly believed to be a painting by Constable. The picture without this quality was essentially different from what the parties believed to be. The court said, "There was no mistake at all about the subject-matter of the sale. It was a specific picture "Salisbury Cathedral". The parties were agreed on the same terms on the same subject-matter and that was sufficient to make a contract".

(*d*) *Mistake as to the Quantity of the Subject-matter*

If both the parties are acting under a mistake as to the quantity of the subject-matter, the agreement is void.

Example : *Henkel Vs. Pape* (1870)

The defendant enquired about the price of rifles from plaintiff stating that he may buy as many as 50. Plaintiff quoted the price. After enquiring about the price of rifles, ordered by telegram for three rifles. The telegraph clerk transcribed the message as "Send the rifles". Plaintiff despatched 50 rifles. Defendant accepted only three and returned 47. Plaintiff filed a suit for damages for non-acceptance of 47 rifles. It was held that there was no contract as although the mistake was caused by the negligence of a third party. Of course, defendant must pay the price of 3 rifles accepted by him.

(*e*) *Mistake as to Price of the Subject-matter*

If there is a mutual mistake as to the price of the subject-matter, the agreement is void.

Example : *Webster Vs. Cecil* (1861)

W offered to purchase certain plots of land belonging to C at £ 2,000. C rejected the offer. Later on C wrote a letter offering to sell the plots to W for "£ 1,200". His real intention was to make an offer for "£ 2,100". W accepted the offer made. Held, W was not entitled to enforce the contract as he knew that the "offer" was made by C under mistake.

(*f*) *Mistake as to Title of the Subject-matter*

Where the parties believe that the seller is the owner of the thing which he purports to sell, but in fact, he has no title to it, the contract is void on the ground of mistake. That is, if the seller is selling a thing which he is not entitled to sell, and both the parties are acting under a mistake, the contract is void.

Example : *Cooper Vs. Phibbs* (1867)

A agreed to take a lease of a fishery (occupation of fishing) from B. Unknown to both the parties the fishery actually belonged to A. It was held that the agreement was void.

(*ii*) ***Bilateral Mistakes as to the Possibility of Performance***

Consent is nullified, if both the parties believe that the contract is capable of being performed, when in fact, it is not the case. The contract in such a case is void on the ground of impossibility. Impossibility may be : (*a*) Physical (*b*) Legal.

(*a*) *Physical Impossibility*

It is when the performance of the contract becomes physically impossible.

Example : *Griffith Vs. Braymer* (1903)

A contract for the hire of a room was made for witnessing the coronation procession of Edward VII. Unknown to both the parties, the procession had already been cancelled. This agreement was held to be void. In this case, the performance of the agreement was impossible as the purpose for which the room was hired had been defeated. And both the parties were mistaken about the fact of impossibility of performance.

Example : *Galloway Vs. Galloway* (1914)

The plaintiff and the defendant, believing themselves to be lawfully married, entered into a separation agreement by which the defendant agreed to pay a certain amount to the plaintiff. They were not, in fact, validly married. In an action by the plaintiff for the arrears of the payment, it was held that the agreement was void as there was a mutual mistake of fact which was material to the existence of the contract.

(*b*) *Legal Impossibility*

A contract is void if it provides that something shall be done which cannot, as a matter of law, be done.

Effect of Bilateral Mistake

In case of bilateral mistake of the essential fact renders the contract void ab-initio. Sec. 20 provides :

"Where both the parties to an agreement are under a mistake as to a matter of fact essential to an agreement, the agreement is void". Such an agreement is void and cannot be enforced at the option of either party to the contract. Thus, an agreement entered into under a bilateral mistake of fact is without any legal effect.

Unilateral Mistake

The term 'unilateral mistake' may be defined as a mistake in which only one of the parties to an agreement is confused about the facts which are essential to the agreement. Sec. 22 provides that:

"a contract is not voidable merely because it was caused by one of the parties to it being under a mistake as to a matter of fact". Accordingly, unilateral mistake is not a valid ground for avoiding the contract. A person is bound by an agreement to which he has expressed a clear assent unless the unilateral mistake is caused by misrepresentation or fraud.

If anyone due to his own negligence or lack of reasonable care does not ascertain what he is contracting about, he must blame himself and cannot avoid the contract. A mistake by one of the parties does not generally affect the validity of a contract.

Example : *A.A. Singh Vs. Union of India* (1970)

Where the government sold by auction the right of fishery and the plaintiff offered the highest bid thinking that the right was sold for three years, when in fact, it was for one year only, he could not avoid the contract because it was his unilateral mistake caused by his negligence. He ought to have ascertained the tenure of fishery before bidding at the auction.

Example : *Bell Vs. Lever Brothers Ltd.* (1932)

There are a number of cases in which the observations show that a mistake as to quality will not generally avoid the contract. In Bell Vs. Lever Brothers Ltd., Lord Atkin gave the following example : "A buys B's horse; he thinks the horse is sound and he pays the price of a sound horse; he would certainly not have bought the horse if he had known, as the fact is that the horse is unsound. If B has made no representation as to soundness and has not contracted that the horse is sound, A is bound and cannot recover the price".

In the following cases, where the consent is given by a party under a mistake which is so fundamental as goes to the root of the agreement and has the effect of nullifying consent, no contract will arise even though there is a unilateral mistake only.

1. *Mistake as to the Identity of the Party*

Mistake as to the identity of the party makes a contract void, only when the intention was to enter into a contract with a particular person other than the person with whom the contract has been entered into. For example, where A intends to enter into an agreement only with B, but enters into an agreement with C, believing him to be B. In this case there is a mistake about the identity of the contracting party and agreement will be void if A intended to contract with B only.

Example : *Cundy Vs. Lindsay & Co.* (1878)

One Blenkarn, knowing that Blenkiron & Co. were the reputed customers of Lindsay & Co., ordered some goods from Lindsay & Co. by imitating the signature of Blenkiron. These goods were then sold to Cundy, an innocent purchaser. In a suit by Lendsay against Cundy for recovery of goods, it was held that as Lindsay never intended to contract with Blenkarn, there was no contract between them and as such even an innocent purchaser of the goods from Blenkarn did not get a good title, and must return them or pay their price.

Example : *Lake Vs. Simmons* (1927)

A woman, by falsely representing to a firm of jewellers that she was the wife of a certain Baron, obtained two pearl necklaces on the pretext of showing them to her husband with a view to buying at the agreed price. The woman then sold the necklaces to an innocent buyer. It was held that there was no contract between the jewellers and the woman and, therefore, the buyer must return the necklaces to the jewellers. Though the woman got the physical possession of the necklaces, there was no mental assent, as the jewellers intended to deal with her but quite a different person, namely, the wife of the Baron.

2. *Mistake as to the Nature of the Transaction*

A contract is void when one of the parties to it does not intend to enter into it, but through the fault of another and without any fault of his own, makes a mistake as to the nature of the contract.

Example : *Foster Vs. Mackinnon* (1869)

A placed a document before B an old man. A falsely told B that it was an ordinary guarantee and induced him to sign the document. B signed the document on the belief that it was a mere guarantee. In fact the document was a bill of exchange which was later endorsed by B to C. C filed as suit against A on the basis of the bill of exchange. It was held that A was not liable for the bill as he never intended to sign the bill of exchange. He was deceived not merely for the legal effect, but also for the very nature of the document.

Effect of Unilateral Mistake

It should be borne in mind that in the aforesaid type of mistakes, even if one party's consent is induced by misrepresentation of another, the contract is not merely voidable but is entirely void and third party would acquire no rights.

Mistake of Law

Mistake of law may be of the following types :

1. Mistake of law of the land
2. Mistake of foreign law.

1. ***Mistake of law of the land***

Everyone is deemed to be conversant with the law of his country, and hence the maxim "ignorance of law is no excuse" *i.e.*, ignorantia juris non excusant. Everyone is presumed to have the knowledge of the law of the land. One cannot get relief on the ground that he had done a particular act in the ignorance of the law. Sec. 21 reads as "A contract is not voidable because it was caused by a mistake as to any law in force in India".

> **Example :** A and B make a contract grounded on the erroneous belief that a particular debt is barred by Indian Law of Limitation; the contract is not voidable.

2. ***Mistake of Foreign Law***

The above maxim that "ignorance of law is no excuse" applies only to the law of the country and not to foreign law. The mistake of foreign law is to be treated as a mistake of fact. Sec. 21 reads, "A mistake as to a law not in force in India has the same effect as a mistake of fact."

THEORETICAL QUESTIONS

1. What is meant by 'Free consent' ? Illustrate your answer. *(B.Com. MS)*
2. Define consent. When is consent said to be free? *(B.Com. Madurai)*
3. Define the term 'coercion' as used in Indian Contract Act. What are the essentials for a coercion? *(B.Com. Kerala)*
4. "An agreement requires meeting of the minds". Comment. *(B.Com. Modern)*
5. What is undue influence? Differentiate between undue influence and coercion.
6. Define fraud. Differentiate fraud and misrepresentation. *(B.Com. MS)*
7. What is misrepresentation? *(B.Com. MS)*
8. Mere silence as to facts is not fraud. Comment.
9. Explain clearly the meaning of misrepresentation. What are the consequences of misrepresentation in a contract? *(CA)*
10. "A deceit which does not deceive is no fraud". Illustrate your answer.
11. A contract caused by mistake is void. Explain. *(B.Com. Bombay)*
12. What do you understand by bilateral mistake of fact? How does the bilateral mistake affect the validity of the contract? *(B.Com. Madurai)*
13. Explain "Ignorance of law is no excuse". *(B.Com. MS)*
14. "Two or more persons are said to consent when they agree upon the same thing in the same sense. Explain this statement. *(B.Com Madurai)*
15. What do you understand by unilateral mistake of fact? *(B.Com Madurai)*
16. "A threat to commit an act forbidden by the Indian Penal Code amounts to coercion". Explain and illustrate this statement. Does a threat to commit suicide amount to coercion? If yes, how would you justify that a threat to commit suicide is forbidden by Indian Penal Code?
17. Under what circumstances a contract said to be induced by undue influence? State the comparison between coercion and undue influence.
18. "A deceit which does not deceive is no fraud". Examine this statement giving suitable examples.
19. What are the defences available to a person against whom undue influence is alleged?
20. A contract induced by undue influence is voidable. Discuss.

MULTIPLE CHOICE QUESTIONS

Choose correct option for each of the following :

1. **Consent means parties agreeing on :**
   (*a*) the terms of contract.
   (*b*) some thing about a contract.
   (*c*) the same thing in the same sense.
   (*d*) the method of performance of contract.
2. **Two persons are said to consent :**
   (*a*) when they agree on their own things clearly.
   (*b*) when they agree upon the same thing in their own way.
   (*c*) when they agree upon the same thing in the same sense.
   (*d*) when they agree to do something.
3. **Consent means :**
   (*a*) consensus *proxima.*
   (*b*) consensus *ad item.*
   (*c*) consensus in general.
   (*d*) consensus on causes.

4. **Free consent means :**
   (*a*) parties agreeing on the same thing in the same sense.
   (*b*) parties agree to do some thing.
   (*c*) parties willfully agree on the same thing in the same sense.
   (*d*) either (*a*) or (*b*)

5. **Consent means :**
   (*a*) general consent.
   (*b*) meeting of minds on the same thing in the same sense.
   (*c*) meeting of minds on different things.
   (*d*) free consent.

6. **Enforceable agreement is one :**
   (*a*) which is made by two parties.
   (*b*) which is made by competent parties.
   (*c*) which is made by free consent of the parties.
   (*d*) which fulfils all the above conditions as well as other conditions required by law.

7. **When the consent to an agreement is caused by undue influence, the contract is:**
   (*a*) Valid. (*b*) Voidable.
   (*c*) Void. (*d*) Illegal.

8. **Undue influence can be exercised by :**
   (*a*) a stranger to the contract. (*b*) a dominating party to the contract.
   (*c*) none of these. (*d*) a week party to the contract.

9. **Moral pressure is involved in the case of :**
   (*a*) Coercion. (*b*) Misrepresentation.
   (*c*) Undue Influence. (*d*) Fraud.

10. **Where one party is in a position to dominate the will of another and uses his superior position to obtain the consent of a weaker party, the consent is said to be obtained by :**
    (*a*) coercion. (*b*) fraud.
    (*c*) undue influence. (*d*) misrepresentation.

11. **An agreement is void if consent is caused by :**
    (*a*) coercion. (*b*) misrepresentation.
    (*c*) mistake as to material fact. (*d*) all the above.

12. **A contract is said to have been made without free consent when it is caused by :**
    (*a*) mistake of fact. (*b*) coercion.
    (*c*) unilateral mistake of one of the parties. (*d*) mistake of law.

13. **X threatens to kill *Y* if he does not agree to sell his scooter to him for Rs. 2,000 only. Here *Y*'s consent is obtained by :**
    (*a*) undue influence. (*b*) coercion.
    (*c*) fraud. (*d*) none of these.

14. **Where an agreement is reached without the consent of all the parties, the agreement is :**
    (*a*) void. (*b*) voidable.
    (*c*) valid. (*d*) either (*b*) or (*c*).

15. **A contract is said to be made without consent when the contract is caused by :**
    (*a*) coercion. (*b*) undue influence.
    (*c*) fraud. (*d*) bilateral mistake of fact.

16. **A when consent to a contract is caused by coercion, the contract is :**
    (*a*) void. (*b*) voidable.
    (*c*) illegal. (*d*) both (*a*) and (*c*)

17. When a contract is caused by the coercion, aggrieved party may :

(*a*) avoid the contract. (*b*) demand restitution.
(*c*) treat the contract illegal. (*d*) claim both (*a*) and (*b*).

18. Coercion means :

(*a*) committing any act forbidden by I.P.C. to take revenge from the party.
(*b*) detaining property of another in order to enjoy the property.
(*c*) threatening to unlawful detaining of property of another with an intention of causing him to make a contract.
(*d*) threatening a debtor to sue by the money lender.

19. When a contract is caused by coercion, the burden of proving that the consent was obtained by coercion, lies on :

(*a*) the person who wants to avoid the contract. (*b*) party alleged coercion.
(*c*) the persons witnessing the use of coercion. (*d*) none.

20. The act amount to coercion is :

(*a*) threat to sue a debtor by the money lender. (*b*) threat to strike by employees.
(*c*) threat to suicide. (*d*) threat to detain property under mortgage.

21. *X* agrees to sell his car worth Rs. 2,00,000 to *Y* for Rs 30,000 only, and *X*'s consent was obtained by coercion. Here, the agreement is :

(*a*) void. (*b*) voidable.
(*c*) valid. (d) unlawful.

22. Undue influence involves :

(*a*) Use of physical pressure.
(*b*) Use of position to obtain an unfair advantage over the other.
(*c*) none of these.
(*d*) A Threat.

23. Coercion in a contract may proceed from :

(*a*) the party to the contract.
(*b*) any other person who is a stranger to the contract.
(*c*) the government.
(*d*) (*a*) or (*b*) above.

24. As per the Indian Contract Act, a person is said to have committed fraud :

(*a*) when he makes a false statement as to facts relating to a contract and he himself believes it to be true.
(*b*) when he makes a false statement as to facts relating to a contract and he himself does not believe it to be true.
(*c*) when he innocently makes a false statement as to facts relating to a contract and he himself believes it to be true.
(*d*) in case of (*a*) and (*c*) above.

25. A contract caused by undue influence may be :

(*a*) voidable. (*b*) absolutely rescinded by the court.
(*c*) conditionally rescinded by the Court (*d*) all of the above.

26. When consent to a contract is caused by undue influence, the contract is :

(*a*) void. (*b*) voidable.
(*c*) valid. (*d*) illegal.

27. Where a contract is made without free consent of the parties, the contract is :

(*a*) void. (*b*) voidable.
(*c*) lawful. (*d*) illegal.

28. Fraud means :

(*a*) a false representation of fact made innocently with a view to deceive the other party.
(*b*) a false representation of fact made wilfully without any intention to receive the other party.
(*c*) a false representation of fact made wilfully with a view to deceive the other party.
(*d*) none of these.

29. When the consent to an agreement is obtained by coercion, the agreement is voidable at the option of :
(*a*) either party to the agreement.
(*b*) a party whose consent was so obtained.
(*c*) a party who obtained the consent.
(*d*) none of these.

30. Where the consent of both the parties is given by mistake, the contract is :
(*a*) void.
(*b*) valid.
(*c*) voidable.
(*d*) illegal.

31. A contract made by mistake about the Indian Law, is
(*a*) void.
(*b*) valid.
(*c*) voidable.
(*d*) illegal.

ANSWERS

1. (*c*)	**2.** (*c*)	**3.** (*b*)	**4.** (*c*)	**5.** (*b*)	**6.** (*c*)	**7.** (*b*)	**8.** (*b*)	**9.** (*c*)	**10.** (*c*)
11. (*c*)	**12.** (*b*)	**13.** (*b*)	**14.** (*a*)	**15.** (*d*)	**16.** (*b*)	**17.** (*d*)	**18.** (*c*)	**19.** (*a*)	**20.** (*c*)
21. (*b*)	**22.** (*b*)	**23.** (*d*)	**24.** (*a*)	**25.** (*d*)	**26.** (*b*)	**27.** (*b*)	**28.** (*c*)	**29.** (*b*)	**30.** (*a*)
31. (*a*)									

PRACTICAL PROBLEMS

1. Peter by way of misrepresentation leads Deepak erroneously to believe that 100 quintals of indigo are made annually at Peter's factory. Deepak examines the accounts of the factory and finds that only 50 quintals of indigo have been made. Afterwards, Deepak buys the factory. Deepak now wants to avoid the contract on the ground of misrepresentation. Advise him giving the reasons. (*CA*)
(No. Deepak cannot avoid the contract)
2. The manager of a cinema theatre gave instructions that no tickets were to be sold to R. R, knowing this, asked his friend to buy a ticket for him. With this ticket R went to the theatre but was refused admission. He filed a suit for damages for breach of contract against the theatre. Would he succeed? Decide giving the provision of the Indian contract Act in this regard. (*CA*)
(R would not succeed. Sec. 22. Refer Cundy Vs Lindsay)
3. X sells a horse to Y for Rs. 1,200, but unknown to both parties at the time of the transaction, the horse was dead. Discuss the rights and liabilities of X and Y. Would it make any difference to your answer if the horse was seriously ill at the time of transaction and died within a few hours after the transaction? (*CA*)
(Agreement is void. Sec. 20)
4. Ram's son absconded from home. He sent his servant in search of the boy. When the servant had left, Ram, by handbills, offered to pay Rs. 500 to anybody discovering the boy. The servant came to know of this offer only when he had already traced the missing child. He, however, brought an action to recover the reward. Will he succeed in his attempt? Give reasons. (*CA*)
(No. Refer Lalman Vs. Guri Dutt)
5. M, an old man of poor sight endorses a bill of exchange for Rs. 5,000 thinking that it was a guarantee. Is M liable to pay the amount?
(M is not liable to pay the amount) (*B.Com. Madurai*)

VII

CHAPTER

Legality of Object and Consideration

(Sections 23–24)

AT A GLANCE

INTRODUCTION

The law has sought to impose limitations on the freedom of contract by declaring certain agreements to be void and certain others, both unlawful and void. Presence of consideration is not only enough for the validity of a contract but the consideration or object must also be lawful. If the object of an agreement is the performances of an unlawful act, the agreement is unenforceable. Sec. 10 lays down that all agreements are contracts if made for lawful consideration with a lawful object.

Further Section 23 declares what kinds of consideration and objects are not lawful. The words 'object' and 'consideration' are not used in the same sense. For example, where money is borrowed for the purpose of marriage, the consideration for the contract is loan and object is marriage. That is, the word 'object' means 'purpose'.

DEFINITION

According to Sec. 23, "the consideration or object of an agreement is lawful unless; it is forbidden by law; or

is of such a nature that, if permitted, it would defeat the provisions of any law; or is fraudulent; or

involves or implies injury to the person or property of another; or

the court regards it as immoral, or opposed to public policy.

In each of these cases, the consideration or object of an agreement is said to be unlawful. Every agreement of which the object or consideration is unlawful is void."

The following illustrations appended to Sec. 23 of the Act, clearly indicate that the consideration and object are not the same.

Illustrations :

(*a*) *A* agrees to sell his house to *B* for Rs. 10,000. Here *B*'s promise to pay the sum of Rs. 10,000 is the consideration for *A*'s promise to sell the house, and *A*'s promise to sell the house is the consideration for *B*'s promise to pay Rs. 10,000. These are lawful considerations.

(*b*) *A* promises to pay *B* 1,000 rupees at the end of six months if *C*, who owes the sum to *B* fails to pay it. *B* promises, to grant time to *C*, accordingly. Here the promise of each party is the consideration for the promise of the other party, and they are lawful considerations.

(*c*) *A* promises, for a certain sum paid to him by *B* to make good to *B* the value of his ship if it is wrecked on a certain voyage. Here, *A*'s promise is the consideration for *B*'s payment, and *B*'s payment is the consideration for *A*'s promise and these are lawful considerations.

(*d*) *A* promises to maintain *B*'s child, and *B* promises to pay 1,000 rupees yearly for the purpose. Here, the promise of each party is the consideration for the promise of the other party. They are lawful considerations.

(*e*) *A*, *B* and *C* enter into an agreement for the division among them of gains acquired, or to be acquired, by fraud, the agreement is void, as its object is unlawful.

(*f*) *A* promises to obtain for *B* an employment in the public service, and *B* promises to pay 1,000 rupees to *A*. The agreement is void, as the consideration for it is unlawful.

(*g*) *A*, being agent for a landed proprietor, agrees for money, without the knowledge of his principal, to obtain for *B* a lease of land belonging to his principal. The agreement between *A* and *B* is void, as it implies a fraud by concealment by *A*, on his principal.

(*h*) *A* promises *B* to drop a prosecution which he has instituted against *B* for robbery, and *B* promises to restore the value of the things taken. The agreement is void, as its object is unlawful.

(*i*) *A*'s estate is sold for arrears of revenue under the provisions of an Act of the Legislature, by which the defaulter is prohibited from purchasing the estate. *B*, upon an understanding with *A*, becomes the purchaser, and agrees to convey the estate to *A*, upon receiving from him the price which *B* has paid. The agreement is void, as it renders the transaction in effect, a purchase by the defaulter, and would so defeat the object of the law.

(*j*) *A*, who is *B*'s mukhtar, promises to exercise his influence, as such with *B* in favour of *C* and *C* promises to pay 1,000 rupees to *A*. The agreement is void because it is immoral.

(*k*) *A* agrees to let her daughter to hire to *B* for concubinage. The agreement is void, because it is immoral, though the letting may not be punishable under the Indian Penal Code.

An agreement will not be enforceable if its object or the consideration is unlawful. According to Sec. 23 of the Act, the consideration and the object of an agreement are unlawful in the following cases:

1. If it is forbidden by law.
2. If it would defeat the provisions of any law.
3. If it is fraudulent.
4. If it causes injury to the person or property of another.
5. If the court regards it as immoral.
6. If the court regards it as opposed to public policy.

1. *If it is Forbidden by Law*

If the object or the consideration of an agreement is the doing of an act forbidden by law, the agreement is void. An act or an undertaking is forbidden by law :

(*i*) when it is punishable by the criminal law of the country, or

(*ii*) when it is prohibited by special legislation derived from the legislature.

Example : A promises B to drop a prosecution which he has instituted against B for robbery, and B promises to restore the value of the things taken. The agreement is void, as its object is unlawful.

Example : *Sreenevasa Rao Vs. Raja Ram Mohan* (1952)
A loan granted to the guardian of a minor to enable him to celebrate the minor's marriage in contravention of the Child Marriage Restraint Act 1929 is illegal and cannot be recovered back.

2. ***If it is of such a Nature that, if Permitted, it would Defeat the Provisions of any Law***

This clause refers to cases where the object or consideration of an agreement is of such a nature that, though not directly forbidden by law, it would indirectly lend to a violation of law, whether enacted or otherwise (Hindu and Mohammedan Laws).

> **Example :** *Alexander Vs. Rayson* (1936)
> P let a flat to R at a rent of £ 1,200 a year. To reduce the Municipal tax he entered two agreements with R. One, by which the rent was stated to be £ 450 and other by which R agreed to pay £ 750 for services in connection with the flat. In a suit filed against R to recover £ 750, it was held that the agreement was made to defraud the municipal authority and was void and P cannot recover the money.

3. ***If it is Fraudulent***

An agreement entered into between parties with a fraudulent purpose is unlawful within the meaning of Section 23 and hence void.

> **Example :** A being agent for landed proprietor, agrees for money, without the knowledge of his principal, to obtain for B a lease of land belonging to his principal. The agreement between A and B is void, as it implies a fraud by concealment by A, on his principal.

4. ***If it Involves or Implies Injury to the Person or Property of Another***

If the object of an agreement is to cause injury to the person or property of another, it is void, being unlawful agreement.

> **Example :** *Ram Sarup Vs. Bansi Mandar* (1915)
> A debtor who owed Rs. 100 executed a bond by which he was required to put forth manual labour until the amount was repaid, and in the case of default, he had to pay exorbitant interest. The court held that, "such a condition is indistinguishable from slavery" and, as such, the contract involved injury to the person of the debtor.

5. ***If the Court Regards it as Immoral***

An agreement whose object or consideration is immoral, is illegal and, therefore, void. It is generally stated that contracts *contra bonos mores*, *i.e.* contrary to good morals are void. An agreement is unlawful for immorality in either of the following cases :

(*i*) case of sexual immorality, *e.g.*, illicit cohabitation or prostitution; or

(*ii*) furtherance of sexual immorality *e.g.*, financial help to a prostitute for improving her trade.

> **Example :** *Upfill Vs. Wright* (1911)
> The plaintiff sued for the rent of a flat let to the defendant with the knowledge that she was the keep mistress of a person who used to visit her there. The court held that as the flat was let for an immoral purpose the plaintiff could not recover.

6. ***If the Court Regards it as Opposed to Public Policy***

Sec. 23 refers to contracts in which the consideration or object of an agreement is unlawful as "the court regards it as opposed to public policy". "Public policy" has not been defined in the Act. It is left to the court to regard whether in the circumstances of a particular case the object or consideration is opposed to public policy. In doing so the courts have always been following the rules of Common law as established by decided cases.

In simple words, public policy may be defined as that policy of the law which prevents the enforceability of agreements that are injurious to the society. An agreement is said to be opposed to public policy when it is against public interest. The term is not capable of exact definition. This is a wider term and it is difficult to determine its limits with any degree of exactness. Public policy is that principle of law which holds that no citizen can lawfully do that which is injurious to the public or is against the interest of the society or the state. Broadly speaking, an agreement which tends to promote corruption or injustice or immorality is said to be opposed to public policy.

DOCTRINE OF PUBLIC POLICY

An agreement is said to be opposed to public policy, when it hurts the public welfare. It is a rule of law that no person shall do anything which is not for the good of the community. It is a tough task to define public policy as it is a complex term. Public policy is defined as "that principle of law which holds that no subject can lawfully do that which has a tendency to be injurious to the public, or against the public good – which may be termed the policy of the law or public policy in relation to the law. However, in different case laws it has been held that public policy is a vague, unlimited and elastic term. However, "the flexibility of the doctrine of public policy is potentially dangerous. It could provide a judge with an excuse for invalidating any contract, which he violently disliked.

Public policy is an illusive concept. It has been described as an untrustworthy guide, uncertain one, unruly horse etc., and, therefore, the doctrine of public policy is generally governed by precedents. "The doctrine of public policy is a very unruly horse, and when once you get astride it, you never know where it will carry you".

The following are some of the commonly accepted heads of public policy:

1. ***Agreements of Trading with Alien Enemy***

An agreement made with an alien enemy in times of war, if it helps or aids the economy of the enemy country will be opposed to public policy and so unlawful. The contracts which have been entered into before the outbreak of war, are either suspended or dissolved.

2. ***Agreements Interfering with the Course of Justice***

When an offence has been committed, the guilty party must be prosecuted and any agreement which seeks to prevent the prosecution of such a person is opposed to public policy and is void. An agreement the object of which is to interfere with the course of justice, *e.g.*, an agreement not to disclose misconduct to the other interested party or an agreement to influence a judge to induce him to decide the case in a party's favour, is obviously opposed to public policy and is void. In civil cases, compromises and settlements are not only allowed but also are encouraged. The law also allows compromise agreements in respect of compoundable offences. An agreement to refer present or future disputes to arbitration is a valid agreement.

3. ***Agreement for Stifling Prosecution***

Public interest requires that criminals should be prosecuted and punished. Contracts for stifling prosecution are a common type of contracts opposed to public policy. Lord Westbury has said, "you shall not make a trade of a felony. If you are aware that a crime has been committed, you shall not convert that crime into a source of profit or benefit to yourself."

> **Example :** A, knowing that B has committed a murder, obtains a promise from B to pay him (A) Rs. 10,000, in consideration of not exposing B, there is a case of stifling prosecution and the agreement is illegal and void.

4. ***Agreements for the Sale of Public Offices and Titles***

Traffic by way of sale in public offices and appointment obviously tends to the prejudice of the public service by interfering with the selection of the best qualified persons. Such sales, are, therefore, unlawful and void.

5. *Agreements of Maintenance and Champerty*

In England agreements of maintenance and champerty are void on the ground of their being opposed to public policy.

When a person agrees to help another by money or otherwise in litigation in which he is not himself interested, it is called maintenance. When a person helps another in litigation in exchange of a promise to handover a portion of the fruits of the litigation, if any, it is called champerty. In India, the maintenance and champertous agreements are not absolutely void. If an agreement is fair and is made the *bona fide* object of assisting a person, it will be valid. Similarly, a fair agreement to supply funds to a person to carry on a suit in consideration of having a fair share or property, if recovered, is not opposed to public policy. Agreements which appear to be made for purposes of gambling in litigation and for injuring or oppressing others by encouraging unholy litigation would not be enforced under Indian Law also. Each case is to depend upon the facts of the case and the nature of the terms of the contract.

6. *Agreements in Restraint of Marriage*

According to Section 26 of the Contract Act "every agreement in restraint of the marriage of any person, other than a minor, is void." Marriage is the fundamental right of every person. Therefore, an agreement in restraint of this fundamental right of a person is opposed to public policy and void.

> **Example :** A promised to marry none else except B, and in default pay her a fixed amount. A married someone else and B sued A for the recovery of the sum. Held, the contract was in restraint of marriage, and as such void.

7. *Marriage Brokerage Agreement*

It is the interest of society that reckless or unsuitable marriage should be prevented and third parties are not allowed to make money by bringing about matrimonial unions. Agreements to procure marriages for reward are void on the ground that marriage ought to proceed, from the free and voluntary decision of the parties. English law holds it bad or void not for the sake of the particular persons but for the public that marriages may be on a proper foundation.

In India, however, marriages are in most cases negotiated by the parents of the parties and the custom of appointing agents or brokers for finding out a suitable match is well established. Therefore, there is some difference of opinion on the question whether the English rule regarding marriage brokerage contracts should be applied here.

Further, an agreement of dowry *i.e.*, to pay money to the parents of the bride or the bridegroom in consideration of their agreeing to the contract of marriage is also illegal and cannot be enforced. But such an agreement is illegal in respect of payment only, the validity of the marriage is not affected.

8. *Agreements Interfering with Parental Duties*

The father and the mother are the natural guardians of a minor child. According to law the father is the guardian of his minor child, after the father, the right of guardianship vests in the mother. This right cannot be bartered away by any agreement. Any agreement which is inconsistent with the duties arising out of such guardianship is void as being opposed to public policy.

> **Example :** *Atma Ram Vs. Banku Mal* (1930)
>
> For monetary consideration. A agrees to place his daughter at the disposal of B to be married as B likes. The agreement is illegal and void as it would interfere with A's parental duty to select a husband in the best interest of the girl.

9. *Agreements in Restraint of Trade*

According to Sec. 27, "every agreement by which anyone is restrained from exercising a lawful profession, trade or business of any kind, is to that extent void". An agreement which prevents a person from carrying on any lawful business is void. The public policy requires that every man shall be at liberty to work for himself and shall not be at liberty to deprive himself of the fruit of his labour, skill or talent, by any contract that he enters into.

Agreements Opposed to Public Policy

1. Agreements of trading with enemy.
2. Agreements interfering with course of justice.
3. Agreements in restraints of legal proceedings.
4. Agreements for stifling prosecution.
5. Agreements of maintenance and champerty.
6. Agreements to oust the jurisdiction of courts.
7. Agreements varying periods of limitation.
8. Traffic in public offices and titles.
9. Agreements to influence elections to public office.
10. Agreements to create interest opposed to duty.
11. Agreements to create monopolies.
12. Agreements to restrain parental rights.
13. Agreements restraining personal freedom.
14. Agreements restraining marriage.
15. Marriage brokerage agreements.
16. Agreements to defraud creditors.
17. Agreements in restraint of trade.
18. Agreements interfering with marital duties.
19. Agreements waiving illegality or immorality.
20. Agreements not to bid.

Exception to the principle *"An agreement in restraint to trade is void"*, are discussed below:

(A) *Sale of Goodwill*

One who sells the goodwill of a business may agree with the buyer to refrain from carrying on a similar business so long as the buyer carries on a like business therein. Thus the seller of goodwill may be restrained from carrying on :

(*a*) a similar business;
(*b*) within specified local limits;
(*c*) so long as the buyer or his representative in the title carries on the like business; and
(*d*) provided, the restraint is reasonable in point of time and place.

(B) *Agreements of Partners*

The Indian Partnership Act 1932, has also laid down certain exceptions to the rule that "All agreement in restraint of trade are void" These exceptions are :

(a) As a Partner in the Firm : Under Section 11 (2) of the Indian Partnership Act, 'A partner shall not carry on business other than that of the firm, while he is a partner'.

(b) As on Outgoing Partner : Under Section 36 (2) of the Indian Partnership Act, "An outgoing partner may agree with his partners not to carry on a business similar to that of the firm within a specified period or within specified local limits.

(*c*) *In case of Dissolution of the Firm :* Under Section 54 of the Indian partnership Act, "Partners may, upon or in anticipation of the Dissolution of the firm, make an agreement that some or all of them will not carry on a business similar to that of the firm within a specified period or within specified local limits.

(*d*) *In case of Sale of Goodwill of the Firm :* Section 55 (3) of the Indian Partnership Act states, "Any partner may, upon the sale of goodwill of the firm, make an agreement with the buyer that such partner will not carry on any business similar to that of the firm within a specified period or within specified local limits."

However, the restriction must be reasonable and specify the local limits and the period for which it will remain in force.

(C) *Trade Combination*

An agreement between different firms in the nature of a trade combination in order to maintain a price level and to avoid underselling is not illegal. Such combinations are often desirable in the interest of trade itself and also for the promotion of public interest. Thus, an agreement between manufacturers or traders not to sell their goods below a certain price, to pool profits and to divide the business and profits in certain proportion does not amount to restraint of trade, and is perfectly valid.

> **Example :** *Fraser & Co. Vs. Bombay Ice Co.* (1904)
>
> Certain ice manufacturers entered into agreement not to sell ice below a certain minimum price. The agreement was held to be valid.

AGREEMENTS UNLAWFUL IN PART

We have noted that when the consideration or the object is unlawful, the agreement is void. Sec. 24 explains the position in cases when only a part of the consideration or object are unlawful, as follows :

According to Sec. 24, "Agreement void, if consideration and objects unlawful in part, if any part of single consideration for one or more objects, or any one or any part of any one of several considerations for a single object, is unlawful, the agreement is void."

When there are two sets of distinct promises, and when the void part of the agreement can be properly separated from the rest, the latter does not become invalid.

Thus, we can study the above provision in the following heads :

(1) *When lawful part can be separated from the unlawful part :*

If a part of the consideration or the object which is unlawful can be separated from the lawful part, the Court will enforce that part which is lawful. (Sec. 24)

> **Example :** A appoints B as a supervisor to lock after his legal and illegal business for a salary of Rs. 10,000, being Rs. 4,000 for doing legal works and Rs. 6,000 for doing illegal works. The parts of consideration can be severable, the former is enforceable and the later is not.

(2) *When lawful and unlawful parts cannot be separated*

Where the lawful and unlawful parts of consideration of object cannot be separated the whole agreement is boid (Sec. 24)

(3) *Reciprocal promise, one is legal and the other is illegal*

When there is reciprocal promises, first to do a legal thing and secondly to do an illegal thing. The first set of promise is a contract but the second is void. (Sec. 57)

Example : *Alice Marry Hill Vs. William Clarke* (1905)

The plaintiff, a married woman, agreed to live in adultery with the defendant and also agreed to serve him as his house-keeper. In return, the defendant agreed to pay the plaintiff a single consolidated remuneration of Rs. 4,000 per month. It was held that because the lawful part could not be severed from the unlawful one, the whole of the agreement was void.

(D) *Service Contracts*

Agreements of service often contains a clause by which the employee is prohibited from working anywhere else during the term of the agreement. For example, a doctor employed in a hospital may be debarred from private practice. Such negative stipulations in service contracts are not considered to be in restraint of trade and are, therefore, valid.

10. *Agreements Restricting Personal Liberty*

An agreement which restricts the personal liberty of an individual is void as being opposed to public policy.

11. *Agreements Varying Periods of Limitation*

Agreements curtailing or extending the periods of limitations prescribed by the Law of Limitation are void as their subject is to defeat the provisions of Law.

12. *Agreements to Influence Elections to Public Office*

An agreement with voters to procure their votes for monetary consideration or with the third persons to influence voters are void being opposed to public policy.

13. *Agreements to Create Monopolies*

Since monopoly is opposed to public policy, an agreement to create a monopoly is void.

14. *Agreements to Defraud Creditors*

Agreements to defraud creditors or any revenue authority are void being opposed to public policy.

15. *Agreements Interfering Marital Duties*

An agreement interfering with marital duties is void.

16. *Agreements not to bid*

An agreement not to bid against one another is unlawful if the object is to defraud a third person or a decree holder.

17. *Waiver of Illegality*

Agreements which seek to waive an illegality or immorality are void.

THEORETICAL QUESTIONS

1. What do you understand by the legality of object and consideration? State the essentials for lawful object and consideration.
2. "All agreements are contract if they are made for lawful consideration with lawful object". Explain with suitable examples.
3. Explain the term 'Public Policy' and state the agreements opposed to public policy. Explain any three agreements opposed to public policy. *(B.Com. Bangalore)*
4. Under what circumstances is the object or consideration of a contract deemed unlawful? Illustrate with examples. *(B.Com M.S.)*
5. When is an agreement said to be against public policy? Give five examples of agreements which are against public policy. *(B.Com. Calcultta)*
6. A promise to give money to induce B to give false evidence. B gives false evidence but A refused to give money. Is A bound to pay the money to B.
   (No. The agreement is illegal)

MULTIPLE CHOICE QUESTIONS

I. Choose correct option for each of the following :

1. **Consideration or object of an agreement is unlawful :**
   (*a*) if it is prohibited by law. (*b*) if Court regards it immoral.
   (*c*) if it is fraudulent. (*d*) in all of the above cases.
2. **An agreement the object or consideration of which is unlawful, is**
   (*a*) Void. (*b*) Voidable.
   (*c*) Valid. (*d*) Contingent.
3. **A and B agree that A shall pay Rs. 10 lakh for which B shall deliver to A either rice or smuggled gold :**
   (*a*) the whole agreement is void. (*b*) the agreement to deliver rice is valid.
   (*c*) the whole agreement illegal. (*d*) both (*a*) and (*c*) above.
4. **A and B agree that A shall sell B a house for Rs. 10 lakh but if B uses it as a gambling house, he shall pay A Rs. 50 lakh :**
   (*a*) the whole agreement is unlawful and void.
   (*b*) the first promise is legal and enforceable.
   (*c*) the whole agreement is valid because selling a house is not unlawful.
   (*d*) either (*a*) or (*c*) above.
5. **An agreement which is harmful to social and economic welfare or any other interest of the public, if it :**
   (*a*) defeats the provisions of law. (*b*) is against public policy.
   (*c*) is fraudulent. (*d*) is forbidden by law.
6. **An agreement in restraint of marriage is valid in case of following persons.**
   (*a*) Minors. (*b*) Married.
   (*c*) Educated. (*d*) None of these.
7. **If the object or consideration of an agreement is unlawful in part :**
   (*a*) the whole agreement is unlawful and void.
   (*b*) only unlawful part is void.
   (*c*) only lawful part is enforceable if it can be severed from the unlawful part.
   (*d*) whole agreement is voidable.
8. **An agreement in restraint of marriage, *i.e.*, which prevents a person from marrying, is**
   (*a*) valid. (*b*) void.
   (*c*) voidable. (d) contingent.
9. **A, a banker lends money to a prostitute for the purchase of a car for the use of her occupation. The banker :**
   (*a*) cannot recover the loan, because the loan was given for promotion of immoral activity.
   (*b*) can recover the loan because it was for the purchase of a car.
   (*c*) cannot recover the loan because it is forbidden by law.
   (*d*) can seize the car and recover the loan by selling it.
10. **Champerty is an agreement whereby one party :**
    (*a*) having no interest in suit, agrees to assist another to maintain suit.
    (*b*) agrees to assist another in recovering property and in turn is to share in the proceeds of the action.
    (*c*) none of these.
11. **Every agreement in restraint of marriage is void :**
    (*a*) In case of marriage of any person.

(*b*) In case of marriage of a person other than minor.

(*c*) In case of marriage of a minor person.

(*d*) none of these.

12. Any agreement with unlawful object or consideration is :

(*a*) void. (*b*) voidable.

(*c*) valid. (*d*) illegal.

13. A person enters into agreement whereby he is bound to do something which is against his public or professional duty. The agreement is :

(*a*) void on the ground of public policy. (*b*) valid.

(*c*) illegal. (*d*) voidable.

14. An agreement, which prevent a person from carrying a lawful business, is :

(*a*) Valid. (*b*) Voidable.

(*c*) Void. (*d*) Contingent.

15. The collateral transactions to an illegal agreement are:

(*a*) illegal (*b*) voidable.

(*c*) valid. (*d*) none of the above.

16. An agreement made with an alien enemy is :

(*a*) unlawful on the ground of public policy.

(*b*) unlawful because it become difficult to be performed.

(*c*) valid.

(*d*) voidable.

17. Illegal Agreements are :

(*a*) void-ab-initio. (*b*) voidable.

(*c*) valid. (*d*) none of these.

18. The consideration or object of an agreement is considered unlawful, if it is :

(*a*) forbidden by law. (*b*) immoral.

(*c*) fraudulent. (*d*) all of these.

19. If one of the several considerations or objects of an agreement is unlawful the agreement is :

(*a*) valid so far as the agreement relate to other consideration or objects.

(*b*) voidable so far as the agreement relate to unlawful consideration or objects.

(*c*) void.

(*d*) none of these.

20. Ram and Gopi enter into an agreement for the division between them the profits to be acquired by them by fraud. The agreement is :

(*a*) illegal. (*b*) unlawful and void.

(*c*) voidable. (*e*) immoral but valid.

ANSWERS

1. (*c*)	**2.** (*a*)	**3.** (*b*)	**4.** (*b*)	**5.** (*b*)	**6.** (*a*)	**7.** (*c*)	**8.** (*b*)	**9.** (*a*)	**10.** (*b*)
11. (*b*)	**12.** (*a*)	**13.** (*a*)	**14.** (*c*)	**15.** (*a*)	**16.** (*a*)	**17.** (*a*)	**18.** (*d*)	**19.** (*c*)	**20.** (*b*)

CHAPTER

Void Agreements

(Sections 26–30)

AT A GLANCE

INTRODUCTION

According to Sec. 2 (g) "An agreement not enforceable by law is said to be void". Thus a void agreement does not give rise to any legal consequences and is void *ab-initio*. A void agreement does not create any legal rights and obligations. The courts will enforce only those agreements which fulfil the conditions of enforceability as laid down in Sec. 10 of the Indian Contract Act. An agreement, though it might have all the essentials of a valid contract, must not have been expressly declared void by any law in force in the country. The contract Act has specifically declared certain agreements as void.

Difference between Void Agreement and Void Contract

Void Agreement	*Void Contract*
1. A void agreement is one which is not enforceable at law and does not give rise to any legal consequence.	1. Void contract is one which is valid when formation, it becomes enforceable because of one reason or the other.
2. It is void *ab-initio* (from the very beginning) and no contract comes into existence at all.	2. A contract which is enforceable by law, may sometimes cease to be enforceable subsequently,, for such reasons as impossibility or illegality.
3. A void agreement is never valid.	3. A void contract is valid till it ceases to be valid contract.

VOID AGREEMENTS

An agreement can be void because of mistake, lack of consideration, want of capacity etc. A list of such agreements is given below :

1. Agreements by persons who are not competent to contract (Sec. 11).
2. Agreements made under a bilateral mistake of fact (Sec. 20).
3 Agreement with unlawful consideration and object (Sec. 23).
4. Agreements of which the consideration or object is unlawful, in part (Sec. 24).
5. Agreements without consideration (Sec. 25).

The last essential of a valid contract as declared by Sec. 10 is that it must not be one which expressly declared' to be void by the Act. Therefore, there arises a question as to what are expressly declared void Agreements. The following Agreements have been declared to be void by the Indian Contract Act.

6. Agreements in restraint of marriage (Sec. 26).
7. Agreements in restraint of trade (Sec. 27).
8. Agreements in restraint of legal proceedings (Sec. 28).
9. Uncertain Agreements (Sec. 29).
10. Agreements by way of wager (Sec. 30).
11. Agreements contingent on impossible events (Sec. 36).
12. Reciprocal promises to things legal, and also other things illegal (Sec. 57).

Agreements 1 to 8 have already been discussed in earlier chapters. In this chapter, we shall discuss the remaining agreements and legal provisions relating to void agreements.

9. ***Uncertain Agreements*** (Sec. 29)

"Agreements, meaning of which is not certain, or capable of being made, are void" (Sec. 29). Agreements with uncertain meaning is void. Through Sec. 29, the law aims to ensure that the parties to a contract should be aware of the precise nature and scope of their mutual rights and obligations under the contract. Thus, if the words used by the parties are vague or indefinite, the law will not enforce the agreement.

Illustrations (appended to Sec. 29)

Examples (*a*) A agrees to sell to B "a hundred tons of oil". There is nothing whatever to show what kind of oil was intended. The agreement is void for uncertainty.

(*b*) A agrees to sell to B one hundred tons of oil of a specified description, known as an article of commerce. There is no uncertainty here to make the agreement void.

(*c*) A, who is a dealer of coconut oil only, agrees to sell to B. "one hundred tons of oil". The nature of A's trade affords an indication of the meaning of the words and A has entered into a contract for the sale of one hundred tons of coconut oil.

(*d*) A agrees to sell to B "all the grains in my granary at Ramnagar". There is no uncertainty here to make the agreement void.

(*e*) A agrees to sell to B "one thousand mounds of rice at a price to be fixed by C". As the price is capable of being made certain there is no uncertainty here to make the agreement void.

(*f*) A agrees to sell to B "my white horse for Rs. 500 or Rs. 1,000". There is nothing to show which of the two prices was to be given. The agreement is void.

Further, an agreement "to enter into an agreement in future" is void for uncertainty unless all the terms of the proposed agreement are agreed expressly or impliedly.

10. ***Agreements by Way of Wager*** (Sec. 30)

Sec. 30 states "Agreements by way of wager are void; and no suit shall be brought for recovering anything alleged to be won on any wager or, entrusted to any person to abide the result of any game or other uncertain event on which any wager is made."

A wager means a bet. The subject-matter of bet may be anything. It is a game of chance, in which the event of either gain or loss, is wholly dependant on an uncertain event. In other words, "wagering agreements" or "wager" may be defined as an agreement in which one person agrees to pay certain amount of money (*i.e.*, stake money) to the other person on the happening or non-happening of a specified uncertain event. The wagering agreements are void. A wagering agreement is one in which the winner gains at the expense of the loser, the outcome being determined largely by chance. Thus,

where A and B mutually agree that if it rains today A will pay B Rs. 100 and if it does not rain B will pay A Rs. 100: or where C and D enter into an agreement that on tossing up a coin, if it falls head upwards C will pay D Rs. 100 and if it falls tail upwards D will pay C Rs. 100: there is wagering agreement.

To quote justice Hawkins "A wagering contract is one by which two persons professing to hold opposite views touching the issue of a future uncertain event mutually agree that, dependent upon the determination of the event, one shall win from the other, and that other shall pay or handover to him, a sum of money or other stake; neither of the contracting parties having any other interest in that contract than the sum of stake he will so win or lose, there being no other real consideration for the making of such contract by either of the parties. It is essential to a wagering contract that each party may under it either win or lose, whether he will win or lose being dependent on the issue of the event, and, therefore, remaining uncertain until that issue is known. If either of the parties may win but cannot lose, or may lose but cannot win, it is not a wagering contract".

It is important to note that the contracting parties should not have any interest in the contract other than the amount which they will win or lose.

> **Example :** A and B enter into an agreement that if it rains on Sunday, A will pay Rs. 100 to B. And if it does not rain on Sunday, B will pay Rs. 100 to A. This is a wagering agreement.

Essential Features of a Wager

Following are the tests or essentials of a wagering contracts :

1. *Two Parties*

An important feature of a wager is that there should be two persons or two groups of parties, either of whom is capable of winning or losing.

2. *Uncertain Events*

It is an important element of a wagering agreement that it must be dependent upon a uncertain event, *i.e.*, the agreement must be conditional on the determination of an uncertain event. A wager generally contemplates a future event, but it may also relate to a past event provided the parties are not aware of its result or the time of its happening.

3. *Each Party must Stand Either to Win or Lose*

It is another essential element of the wagering agreement that each party to the agreement must stand to win or lose. In other words, upon the conclusion of the agreement, one party has to win while the other to lose. Thus, in wagering agreement there has to be mutuality in the sense that the gain of one party would be loss of the other on the happening or non-happening of the uncertain event.

If one of the parties alone is to win but cannot lose, or he may lose but cannot win, or he can neither win nor lose, the agreement is not a wager.

> **Example :** *Babasaheb Vs. Rajaram* (1931)
>
> Two wrestlers agreed to enter into a wrestling competition subject to the condition that the person who failed to appear on the day fixed for the match should forfeit Rs. 500 to the other party, and that if the competition took place, the winner should receive Rs. 1,125 out of the gate collections. The

defendant having failed to turn up, the plaintiff sued him for the recovery of Rs. 500. Rejecting the arguments of the defendant that the contract was a wager, the Court held that the amount was recoverable on the ground that, "the stakes did not come of the pockets of the parties but had to be paid from the gate money provided by the public."

4. *Stake or Bet must the only Interest*

Neither party should have any interest in the happening or non-happening of the event other than the sum or stake he will win or lose. Thus, an agreement is not a wager if the party to whom money is promised on the occurrence of an event has an 'interest' in its non-occurrence. If either of the parties has any proprietary interest in the subject-matter of the agreement, the same ceases to be a wagering agreement, but becomes enforceable as a contract. It is on this basis that we distinguish between a wagering agreement and a contract of insurance.

5. *A Promise to Pay Money or Money's Worth*

The parties must agree to pay money or money's worth on the happening or non-happening of the uncertain event.

Effects of Wagering Agreements

Sec. 30 of the Act clearly lays down that all wagering contracts are void. Wagering is equal to gambling. As a matter of fact, though a wagering agreement is void and unenforceable, but it is not forbidden by law.

Example : *Gherulal Parakh Vs. Mahadeodas Maiye* (1959)

The appellant and the respondent entered into a partnership to carry on wagering contracts with two firms of Hapur. They agreed to make the contracts in the name of the respondent on behalf of the firms and to divide the profit and loss resulting from the transaction in equal shares. The respondent entered into such contracts. The net result of these contracts was a loss. Since the respondent had to pay the full amount due to the merchant at Hapur, he wanted the appellant to bear his share of the loss. Since the appellant denied his liability, the firm was dissolved and the respondent sued the appellant.

The Court held that, "Though a wager is void and unenforceable, it is not forbidden by law and, therefore, the object of a collateral agreement is not unlawful under Section 23 of the Contract Act and partnership being an agreement within the meaning of Section 23, it is not unlawful, though its object is to carry on wagering transactions. We, therefore, hold that in the present case the partnership is not unlawful within the meaning of Section 23 of the Act. "Accordingly, while a wagering agreement cannot be enforced between immediate parties, collateral transactions are enforceable.

In the State of Maharashtra and Gujarat wagering agreements are, by a local statute, not only void but also illegal.

In the case of void agreements, collateral agreements, *i.e.*, agreements which are subsidiary or incidental to the main agreement, are valid. Therefore, though wagering are void, transactions collateral to such agreements are valid.

Example : A borrows Rs. 500 from B to pay to C, to whom B has lost a bet. Contract between A and B is valid.

Exceptions in the Wagering Agreements

Exception to section 30 "This section shall not be deemed to render unlawful a subscription or contribution, or agreement to subscribe or contribute, made or entered into for or towards any plate, prize or sum of money, of the value or amount of five hundred rupees or upwards, to be awarded to the winner or winners of any horse-race".

1. *Commercial Transaction*

Agreements for sale and purchase of any commodity or share market transactions, in which there is a genuine intention to do legitimate business *i.e.*, to give and take delivery of goods or shares, are not wagering agreements. If there is no such genuine intention and parties only want to gamble on the rise or fall of the market by paying or receiving the differences in prices only, the transaction would be wagering agreement and, therefore, void. "In order to constitute a wagering contract, neither party should intend to perform the contract itself, but only to pay the difference."

2. *Horse Racing Competition*

An agreement to contribute to the payment of a prize of the value of Rs. 500 or upwards to the winners of a horse race, is valid. This is statutory exception laid down in Sec. 30 of the Contract Act.

3. *Prize Competitions*

Sometimes, the skill plays a substantial part for the successful solution of certain competitions, for example, cross-words competitions, picture puzzles, athletic competitions etc. Prizes are awarded according to the merits of the solution. Prize competitions which are games of skill, are not wagers. Thus, an agreement to enter into a wrestling contest in which the winner was to be rewarded by the entire sale proceeds of tickets, was held not to be wagering contract.

5. *Contract of Insurance*

A contract of insurance is a contract between the insured on the one side and the underwriter or the insurance company on the other, by which the latter, in consideration of a payment called the premium paid by the former, undertakes to indemnify the insured against any loss arising from a contingency upto the sum agreed upon. A contract of insurance whether of life, fire, accident, margins etc., is not a wager, though its performance depends upon an uncertain event.

Comparison between Wagering Agreement and Contract of Insurance

Contract of Insurance	*Wagering Agreement*
1. It is valid and can be enforced in court of law.	1. It is void, under Sec. 30 without any legal effect.
2. Contracts of insurance are regarded as beneficial to the public.	2. Wagering agreements do not serve any useful purpose.
3. Contracts of insurance are based on scientific and actuarial calculation of risk.	3. Wagering agreements are gamble without any scientific calculation of risk.
4. The holder of an insurance policy must have an insurable interest in the event upon which the insurance money becomes payable. Contracts are entered into to protect an interest.	4. In a wagering agreement there is no interest to protect and the parties bet exclusively because they can thereby make some easy money.
5. It is a contract of indemnity. Because, the underlying idea of the contract is to indemnify the insured person *i.e.* to compensate him for the loss suffered by him. However, the life insurance contracts are not the contracts of indemnity.	5. It is not a contract of indemnity because the amount to be paid to the winner is not paid as a compensation of loss.
6. The amount which is to be paid to the insured person is not fixed. Only the actual lose suffered by him is to be compensated. However, in case of life insurance, the amount may be treated as fixed.	6. The amount is fixed which is to be paid to the winner on the conclusion of the uncertain event.

11. ***Agreement for Impossible Events*** (Sec. 36)

Sec. 36 lays down that, "Contingent agreements to do or not to do anything if an impossible event happens, are void, whether the impossibility of the event is known or not to the parties to the agreement at the time when it is made."

Examples : (1) A agrees to pay B Rs. 1,000 if two straight lines should enclose a space. The agreements is void.

(2) A agrees to pay B Rs. 1,000 if B will marry A's daughter C. C was dead at the time of the agreement. The agreement is void.

According to Sec. 56, "An agreement to do an act impossible in itself is void."

(3) A agrees with B to discover treasure by magic. The agreement is void.

(4) A and B contract to marry each other. Before the time fixed for the marriage, A goes mad. The contract become void.

12. ***Reciprocal Promise to do Thing Legal, and also other Things Illegal***

Sec. 57 lays down "Where persons reciprocally promise, first, to do certain things which are legal, and secondly, under specified circumstances, to do certain other things which are illegal, the first set of promises is a contract, but the second is a void agreement.

Example : A and B agree that A shall sell B a house for Rs. 10,000 but that, if B uses it as a gambling house, he shall pay A Rs. 50,000 for it.

The first set of reciprocal promises namely, to sell the house and pay Rs. 10,000 for it, is a contract. The second set is for an unlawful object namely, that B may use the house as a gambling house, and is a void agreement.

THEORETICAL QUESTIONS

1. What do you understand by void agreements? *(B.Com., Kerala)*
2. What are the various agreements which have been expressly declared to be void by the Indian Contract Act?
3. What do you understand by wagering agreement? *(B.Com., MS)*
4. What are the essentials of a wagering agreement? *(B.Com., Chennai)*
5. "A wagering agreement is void and unenforceable, but it is not forbidden by law". Critically examine the statement with suitable examples.
6. What tests would you apply to determine if, or not, an agreement is by way of wager?
7. Insurance contracts are basically wagering agreements, Comment. *(B.Com., Madurai)*
8. Distinguish between a wagering agreement and insurance contract.
9. A promises B in consideration of Rs. 10,000, never to marry throughout life. Is this valid contract? **(Ans** : No)
10. A lends money to B to enable him to pay off the loss which he sustained in a wagering transaction with C. Can A recover the money lent by him? **(Ans** : A can recover)

MULTIPLE CHOICE QUESTIONS

I. Choose correct option for each of the following :

1. **An agreement by which any party to it is restricted absolutely from enforcing his right under a contract is :**

   (*a*) valid. (*b*) void.
   (*c*) voidable. (*d*) lawful.

2. A restraint by trade combination is valid if it :

(*a*) is not in restraint of trade.

(*b*) is in the interest of its member as well as in the public interest.

(*c*) does not create monopoly.

(*d*) fulfils all of the above conditions.

3. A husband and wife agreed that on husband's marrying another girl, the first wife would get a right of divorce. The restriction on the husband is :

(*a*) valid. (*b*) invalid.

(*c*) void. (*d*) illegal.

4. A person buying goodwill of a business may impose a restriction on the seller that he will not carry on :

(*a*) any business in the specified local limits. (*b*) similar business with in the specified local limits.

(*c*) similar business in any part of the world. (*d*) both (*b*) and (*c*) above.

5. An agreement, the meaning of which is not certain or capable of being made certain is :

(*a*) illegal. (*b*) void.

(*c*) valid. (*d*) unlawful.

6. An agreement not to a sue in a law Court but to refer the dispute for arbitration is :

(*a*) valid. (*b*) void.

(*c*) illegal. (*d*) restriction on legal right.

7. An agreement, the meaning of which is not certain but capable of being made certain is :

(*a*) valid. (*b*) voidable.

(*c*) void. (*d*) unlawful.

8. The partnership deed providing that no partner of the firm shall carry on any business other than that of the firm while he is a partner. This restriction is :

(*a*) valid. (*b*) void.

(*c*) illegal. (*d*) unenforceable.

9. A void agreement :

(*a*) is unlawful and illegal. (*b*) is unenforceable by law.

(*c*) violates legal procedure. (*d*) both (*a*) and (*c*).

10. Athletic competitions are valid because they are :

(*a*) games of skill. (*b*) games of muscle power.

(*c*) games of luck. (*d*) all of the above.

11. Where the partners of a firm agree that none of them will carry on any business other than that of the firm, the agreement is :

(*a*) valid. (*b*) voidable.

(*c*) void. (*d*) unlawful.

12. Agreements expressly declared to be void are :

(*a*) agreements in restraint of trade. (*b*) agreement in restraint marriage.

(*c*) wagering agreements. (*d*) all of the above.

13. When the goodwill of the firm is sold after dissolution, a partner :

(*a*) may not carry on any competing business with that of the firm.

(*b*) may carry on any competing business with that of the firm.

(*c*) may not carry on any business with in the specified local limits.

(*d*) all of the above.

14. Agreement involving awards of Rs. 500 or more to the winners of horse race is :

(*a*) void. (*b*) not unlawful.
(*c*) voidable. (*d*) illegal.

15. An agreement in restraint of marriage is valid if it imposes restriction on :

(*a*) minor. (*b*) major unmarried.
(*c*) major married. (*d*) all the above.

16. Valid restriction on an employee is that :

(*a*) he will not serve anybody else during the period of employment.
(*b*) he will have to serve the employer at least for a period of three years.
(*c*) he will not resign from his job at least for three years.
(*d*) above (*b*) and (*c*).

17. An agreement in restraint of marriage, that is, which prevents a person from marrying, is :

(*a*) valid. (*b*) void.
(*c*) voidable. (*d*) contingent.

18. An agreement, which prevents a person from carrying a lawful business, is :

(*a*) valid. (*b*) voidable.
(*c*) void. (*d*) contingent.

19. An agreement is restraint of trade is void only if the restraint imposed is :

(*a*) complete. (*b*) conditional.
(*c*) partial. (*d*) any of these.

20. An agreement to pay money or money's worth on the happening or non-happening of a specified uncertain event is :

(*a*) wagering agreement. (*b*) quasi contract.
(*c*) contingent contract. (*d*) uncertain agreement.

ANSWERS

1. (*b*)	**2.** (*d*)	**3.** (*a*)	**4.** (*b*)	**5.** (*b*)	**6.** (*a*)	**7.** (*a*)	**8.** (*a*)	**9.** (*b*)	**10.** (*a*)
11. (*a*)	**12.** (*d*)	**13.** (*b*)	**14.** (*b*)	**15.** (*a*)	**16.** (*a*)	**17.** (*b*)	**18.** (*c*)	**19.** (*d*)	**20.** (*a*)

CHAPTER

Contingent Contract

(Sections 31–36)

AT A GLANCE

- Definition
- Collateral Events
- Characteristics of Contingent Contract
- Rules Regarding Contingent Contract
- Contingent Contract Vs. Wagering Agreement
- Theoretical Questions
- Multiple Choice Questions.

DEFINITION

Section 31 of the Indian Contract Act defines a Contingent Contract as: "A contingent contract is a contract to do or not to do something, if some event, *collateral* to such contract does or does not happen". Thus it is a contract, the performance of which is *dependent* upon, the happening or non-happening of an uncertain event, *collateral* to such contract.

Example: A contracts to pay B Rs. 10,000 if B's house is burnt.

This is a contingent contract.

It is a contract in which the performance becomes due, only upon the happening of some event which may or may not happen.

A promise is 'absolute' or 'unconditional' when the promisor undertakes to perform it in any event. A promise is 'conditional' when performance is due only if an event, collateral to the contract, does or does not happen. Contingent means conditional and the condition is of uncertain nature. A contract, for example, to pay a sum of money on the expiry of a fixed time or on the death of a person is not a contingent contract because these events are of a certain nature. But a contract to pay a certain sum of money on the destruction of a house by earthquake is a contingent contract, because that contingency may or may not happen.

Contracts of insurance, guarantee and indemnity are examples of contingent contracts. In simple words, the performance of a contingent contract becomes due only upon happening or non-happening of some future uncertain event: it is a conditional contract.

COLLATERAL EVENT

According to Pollock and Mulla, a 'collateral event' means an event which is "neither a performance directly promised as part of the contract, nor the whole of the consideration for a promise". Thus, where A contracts to pay Rs. 100 to B for white-washing his house on the terms that no payment shall be made till the completion of the work, it is not a contingent contract, because the event (B's completing the work) is not collateral to the contract, but is itself a reciprocal promise or is the very thing contracted for, and is thus an integral part of the contract. Similarly, a contract for the sale of goods wherein the seller agrees to give delivery of goods after a week provided the purchaser makes the payment within two days, is an absolute contract and not a contingent contract, because the event (making payment by the buyer) is an integral part of the contract (a condition precedent) and not collateral to the contract.

But a contract, whereby A promises to pay B Rs. 10,000 if B's house is burnt, is a contingent contract because the liability of A arises only when B's house is burnt. This is an event collateral to the main contract because the burning of B's house is not the performance required from B under the contract nor is it the consideration obtained from B. It is an independent event.

In simple words, the collateral event is one which does not form part of consideration of the contract, and is independent of it. For example, A contracts to pay Rs. 50,000 to B, a contractor, for constructing a building, provided the construction is approved by an architect. It is a contingent contract because the consideration of the promise to pay Rs. 50,000, is the construction of the building, and the event, namely, approval by an architect, is a collateral event, which is independent of the consideration, and it is on the happening of this collateral event that the contract shall be enforced.

CHARACTERISTICS OF CONTINGENT CONTRACT

There are three essential characteristics of a contingent contract, *viz.* :

1. Its performance depends upon the uncertainty of happening or non-happening in future of some event. It is this dependence on a future event which distinguishes a contingent contract from other contracts.
2. The event must be collateral, *i.e.*, incidental to the contract.
3. The contingent event should not be mere will of the promisor.

RULES REGARDING PERFORMANCE OF CONTINGENT CONTRACTS

The rules regarding the performance of contingent contracts, as contained in Section 32 to 36 of the Contract Act, are given below :

1. *The Happening of a Future Uncertain Event*

According to Sec. 32, "Contingent contracts to do or not to do anything, if an uncertain future event happens, cannot be enforced by law unless and until that event has happened. If the event becomes impossible, such contracts become void."

Examples: (1) A makes a contract with B to buy B's horse if A survives C. This contract cannot be enforced by law unless and until C dies in A's life time.

(2) A makes a contract with B to sell a horse to B at a specified price, if C to whom the horse has been offered, refuses to buy him. The contract cannot be enforced by law unless and until C refuses to buy the horse.

(3) A contracts to pay B a sum of money when B marries C. C dies without being married to B. The contract become void.

A contingent contract dependent on the happening of future uncertain event can be enforced only when that event has happened. If the event becomes impossible then such contract becomes void, and thus cannot be enforced by law.

2. *The Non-happening of an Uncertain Future Event*

According to Sec. 33, "Contingent contracts to do or not to do anything if any uncertain future event does not happen, can be enforced when the happening of that event becomes impossible and not before."

> **Example :** A agrees to pay B a sum of money if a certain ship does not return. The ship is sunk. The contract can be enforced when the ship sinks. Because when the ship sinks the event becomes impossible as the ship can never return.

Thus enforceability depends upon the impossibility of the contingent event. Until the event becomes impossible, the contract cannot be enforced.

3. *When Event to be Deemed Impossible*

According to Sec. 34, "If the future event on which a contract is contingent is the way in which a person will act at an unspecified time, the event shall be considered to become impossible when such person does anything which renders it impossible that he should so act within any definite time, or otherwise than under further contingencies".

> **Example :** A agrees to pay B a sum of money if B marries C. C marries D. The marriage of B to C must now be considered impossible, although it is possible that D may die and that C may afterwards marry B.

If the uncertain event is the future conduct of a third party, such event shall be considered impossible if that person does any act due to which the contract cannot be enforced in any definite time.

4. *The Happening of an Event within Fixed Time*

According to first para of Sec. 35, "Contingent contracts to do or not to do anything if a specified uncertain event happens within a fixed time become void if at the expiration of the time fixed, such event has not happened, or if, before the time fixed such event becomes impossible."

> **Example :** A promises to pay B a sum of money if a certain ship returns within a year. The contract may be enforced if the ship returns within the year and becomes void if the ship is burnt within the year.

In other words, if a person has undertaken to perform something within a fixed time provided an event happens, he is bound to perform his promise if the event happens within the fixed time. If the time fixed elapses and the event does not happen, or the event becomes impossible before the time fixed, the contract becomes void.

5. *The Non-happening of an Event within a Fixed Time*

According to second para of Sec. 35, "Contingent contracts to do or not to do anything if a specified uncertain event does not happen within a fixed time may be enforced by law when the time fixed has expired and such event has not happened, or, before the time fixed has expired, if it becomes certain that such event will not happen."

> **Example :** A promises to pay B a sum of money if a certain ship does not return within a year. The contract may be enforced if the ship does not return within the year, or is burnt within the year.

If a promise is to be performed within a fixed time provided an event does not happen, such a promise may be enforced if the event does not happen, within the fixed time or the time expires without the event happening.

6. *Impossible Events*

According to Sec. 36, "Contingent agreements to do or not to do anything if an impossible event happens, are void, whether the impossibility of the event is known or not to the parties, to the agreement at the time when it is made".

Examples: (1) A agrees to pay B Rs. 1,000 if two straight lines should enclose a space. The agreement is void.
(2) A agrees to pay B Rs. 1,000 if B will marry A's daughter C. C was dead at the time of the agreement. The agreement is void.

Difference between Contingent Contract and Wagering Agreement

The main points of distinction between the two are as under :

Contingent Contract	*Wagering Agreement*
1. It is perfectly valid and can be enforced in a Court of Law.	1. It is absolutely void and cannot be enforced in a Court of Law.
2. In this case, there may not be reciprocal promises.	2. In this case, there are reciprocal promises.
3. In this case, parties are interested in the subject-matter of the contract.	3. The parties have no other interest in the subject-matter except for the sum or stake they will win or lose.
4. A contingent contract is not of a wagering nature.	4. A wagering agreement is essentially of a contingent nature.
5. In this case, the future uncertain event is merely collateral or incidental.	5. In this case,, the uncertain event is the only determining factor.

THEORETICAL QUESTIONS

1. What do you understand by a contingent contract? (*B.Com. Delhi*)
2. What are the characteristics of a contingent contract? (*B.Com. Kerala*)
3. Distinguish between a contingent contract and a wagering agreement. (*B.Com. Chennai*)
4. A agrees to construct a building for Rs. 1 lakh on the terms that no payment shall be made till the completion of the work. Is this contingent contract?
   (**Ans. :** This is not a contingent contract)
5. A agrees to sell land to B at a price to be fixed by C. C refuses to fix the price. Is the contract enforceable?
   (**Ans.** The contract is unenforceable)
6. Discuss the law relating to the enforcement of contingent contracts. (*M.Com. MS*)
7. What elements are essential to make a contract a contingent one? (*M.Com. Jabalpur*)

MULTIPLE CHOICE QUESTIONS

1. Choose correct option for each of the following :

1. **A contingent contract is:**
   (*a*) Void. (*b*) valid.
   (*c*) voidable. (*d*) illegal.
2. **A contingent contract dependent on the happening of future uncertain event can be enforced when the event :**
   (*a*) happens. (*b*) does not happen.
   (*c*) become impossible. (*d*) all of these.

3. An agreement to do an impossible act is :
(*a*) void. (*b*) voidable.
(*c*) illegal. (*d*) enforceable.

4. Contracts of insurance are :
(*a*) Uncertain agreements. (*b*) contingent agreements.
(*c*) wagering agreements. (*d*) none of these.

5. X contracts to pay Y Rs. 1,00,000 of Y's house is burnt. This is a :
(*a*) wagering agreement. (*b*) voidable.
(*c*) void agreement. (*d*) contingent contract.

6. An uncertain agreement is :
(*a*) illegal. (*b*) valid.
(*c*) void. (*d*) voidable.

7. A contingent contract may be :
(*a*) void from beginning.
(*b*) void subsequently when event becomes impossible to happen.
(*c*) voidable. (*d*) unlawful.

8. A contract contingent upon non-happening of an event within fixed time, the contract may be enforced :
(*a*) if it becomes certain that the event will not happen.
(*b*) if the event happens within the time fixed.
(*c*) when the parties decide.
(*d*) when a third party decides.

9. A agrees to pay Rs. 1,000 to B if a certain ship returns within a year. However, the ship sinks within the year. So contract becomes :
(*a*) valid. (*b*) void.
(*c*) voidable. (*d*) illegal.

10. The following contracts are contingent contracts :
(*a*) contract of insurance. (*b*) contract of guarantee.
(*c*) contract to deliver goods on receipt from the factory.
(*d*) both (*a*) and (*b*).

11. A contract to do or to abstain from doing a certain thing on the happening of an event :
(*a*) cannot be enforced. (*b*) can be enforced when the event has happened.
(*c*) can be enforced at any time. (*d*) cannot be lawful.

12. A contract is not contingent contract :
(*a*) if the event is bound to happen. (*b*) if the promisor has control over the event.
(*c*) if the event is a part of the promise of the contract.
(*d*) in all of the above cases.

13. If the performance of contingent contract depends upon happening of some event and the happening of that event becomes impossible if the contract becomes :
(*a*) voidable. (*b*) void.
(*c*) illegal. (*d*) both (*a*) and (*c*).

14. A contract based on happening or non-happening of some event which is collateral to contract is called :
(*a*) wagering contract. (*b*) contingent contract.
(*c*) uncertain contract. (*d*) illegal contract.

15. A contingent contract based upon the happening of future event within a fixed time, the contract can be :
(*a*) enforced even if the event does not take place within the fixed time.
(*b*) enforced if the event happens within the fixed time.
(*c*) enforced even if the event happens after the expiry of fixed time.
(*d*) enforced at any time.

ANSWERS

1. (*b*) **2.** (*a*) **3.** (*a*) **4.** (*b*) **5.** (*d*) **6.** (*c*) **7.** (*b*) **8.** (*a*) **9.** (*b*) **10.** (*d*)
11. (*b*) **12.** (*d*) **13.** (*b*) **14.** (*b*) **15.** (*b*)

X

CHAPTER

Performance of Contract

(Sections 37–67)

AT A GLANCE

- Introduction
- Actual Performance
- Attempted Performance
- Essentials of Valid Tender
- Effect of refusal
- Persons who should perform the Contract
- Who can demand performance
- Performance of Joint Promises
- Devolution of Joint promises
- Time and Place of Performance
- Time as the Essence of Contract
- Performance of Reciprocal Promise
- Kinds of Reciprocal Promise
- Rules of Reciprocal Promise
- Appropriation of payments
- Contracts which need not be performed
- Assignment of contracts
- Theoretical Questions
- Multiple Choice Questions.

INTRODUCTION

Performance of contract means fulfillment of legal obligations created by the contract. That is, performance of contract means fulfilling of their respective legal obligations created under the contract by both the promisor and the promisee. When a contract is duly performed by both the parties, the contract comes to a happy ending. If the parties to a contract have done what they had undertaken to do as per the terms of the contract, they become free from any further liability. Performance by all the parties of the respective obligations is the normal and natural mode of discharging or terminating a contract. According to Section 37 of the Act,

"The parties to a contract must either (*a*) perform, or (*b*) offer to perform, their respective promises, unless (*c*) such performance is dispensed with or (*d*) excused under the provisions of this Act, or any other law."

Accordingly, the contracting parties are bound to perform their respective obligations unless the performance is dispensed with or excused under the provisions of the Contract Act or of any other law. The phrase, "perform or offer to perform" (words used in the Sec. 37) provides for two modes of performance — *Actual performance* or *Attempted Performance.*

ACTUAL PERFORMANCE

When a party has done, what he had undertaken to do and nothing is left, the promise is said to be performed. The contract is completely terminated when both the parties perform the exact thing which each has agreed to do under the contract. When a party to a contract does what he had undertaken to do under the contract, he is said to have actually performed his obligation to the contract — actual performance. Then, it becomes the duty of the other party to do what he had agreed to do under the contract. If only one party performs his promise, he alone is discharged and he acquires a right to take action against the other party for the performance of his obligation.

Attempted Performance (or Tender) or (Offer of Performance)

Attempted performance is also know as offer of performance or tender. A contract need not be actually performed. A valid offer of performance is considered to be performance itself. Sometimes, the party who is bound to perform a promise under a contract is ready and willing to perform it at the proper time and place. This willingness of the party is known as "Attempted Performance" or "Offer to perform" or "Tender". As such, if the offer is not accepted by the other party to the contract, the obligation of the party making the tender is extinguished, and he is not liable for non-performance; although his rights still continue. According to Sec. 38 of the Act, "Where a promisor has made an offer of performance to the promisee, and the offer has not been accepted, the promisor is not responsible for non-performance, nor does he thereby lose his rights under the contract". If a valid tender of performance is rejected by the promisee, then the promisor is excused from further performance. The promisor can also bring an action against the promise for breach of the contract. Thus, a valid tender of performance is equivalent to performance.

ESSENTIALS OF VALID TENDER

A tender, to be legally valid, must fulfil the following conditions (Sec. 38):

1. *It must be Unconditional*

A tender coupled with a condition is no tender. Valid tender of performance must be an unconditional one. That is, an unconditional tender is one which is in accordance with the terms of the contract.

2. *It must be Made at a Proper Time and Place*

A tender before or after the due date or at a place other than agreed upon is not a valid tender. If the place is not mentioned, the rule is that the debtor must find the creditor; Where no time is fixed then it is valid to make the tender within reasonable time. What is proper time and place is a question of fact depending on the circumstances of each case.

> **Example :** A owes B Rs. 500 payable on 1st October with interest. B offers to pay the principal amount with interest up to September 1st. It is not a valid tender as it is not made at the agreed time.

3. *It should be in Respect of the Whole Obligation*

An offer to perform a promise in part is not a valid tender. The tender must be whole and not of the part. If a debtor offers to pay only the principal amount and not the interest, the tender is not valid. Part payment or part delivery of the goods contracted for, is not a valid tender.

4. *It must Provide Reasonable Opportunity*

If the tender relates to delivery of goods, it must give reasonable opportunity to the promisee for inspection of goods so that he may be sure that the goods tendered are of agreed description. A tender of goods, when the other party cannot inspect the goods, is not a valid tender.

> **Example :** (Appended to Sec. 38). A contracts to deliver to B at his warehouse, on the 1st March, 100 bales of cotton of a particular quality. In order to make an offer of performance, A must bring the cotton to B's warehouse on the appointed day under such circumstances that B may have a reasonable opportunity of satisfying himself that the thing offered is cotton of the quality contracted for and that there are 100 bales.

5. *It must be in the Proper Form*

A tender of money must be in the legal tender money and not in any foreign currency. A person is not bound to accept a cheque. But a payment by a cheque is valid tender if the person to whom it is made is ready and willing to accept it.

6. *It must be Made to a Proper Person*

A valid tender must be made to a proper person, *i.e.*, the promisee or his authorised agent. A tender of performance made to a stranger or a third party is not a valid tender.

> **Example :** A agreed to supply certain goods to B on 1st June. On the particular day, A supplied the goods to C, a friend of B. It is not a valid tender.

7. *The Person Making a Tender must be Able and Willing to Perform his Obligation*

It must be made by a person who is in a position and is willing to perform the promise. A tender by a minor or idiot is not valid tender. If the tender is of cash payment, actual cash must be available for ready payment. A party cannot be said to be able and willing if he has neither possession nor control over the goods, he had promised to supply.

8. *It may be to one of the Joint Promisees*

An offer to one of several joint promisees is a valid offer of performance as if it is an offer to all of them. A tender can be legally made to even one of the joint promisees. For example, a payment made to a partner is deemed to be a payment to the partnership firm.

Tender or attempted performances is of two types : (*i*) tender of goods and (*ii*) tender of money.

Essentials of a Valid Tender

1. It must be unconditional.
2. It must be made at proper time and place.
3. It should be in respect of the whole obligation.
4. It must provide a reasonable opportunity of inspection.
5. It must be made to a proper person.
6. It must be in proper form.
7. It must be made to one of the several joint promisees.
8. It must be by a person who is able to perform the whole promise.
9. Tender of money, must be in legal tender money.

Effect of Refusal of Correct Tender

Sec. 38 lays down, "Where a promisor has made an offer of performance to the promisee, and the offer has not been accepted, the promisor is not responsible for non-performance, nor does he thereby lose his rights under the contract." It has been clearly stated the effect of refusal to a correct tender. In case of a valid tender of goods, refusal by the person to whom it is made discharges the person by whom it is made from liability. Where the seller in a contract for the sale of goods satisfies all the requirements of the contract as to delivery of the goods but the buyer refuses to accept the goods, he is discharged by such a tender of performance. Similarly, where a debtor makes a valid tender of money, but the creditor refuses to accept it, the debtor is not discharged from making the payment. Thus the effect of a refusal of a tender are:

(*A*) Promisor becomes free from his responsibilities to the contract, and

(*B*) His rights against the promisee as per the contract continue.

Effect of Refusal of a Party to Perform Promise Wholly

Sec. 39 lays down, "When a party to contract has refused to perform, or disabled himself from performing his promise in its entirely, the promisee may put an end to the contract, unless he has signified, by words or conduct, his acquiescence in its continuance".

Example : (Appended to this section): A, a singer, enters into a contract with B, the manager of a theatre, to sing at his theatre two nights in every week, during the next two months, and B engages to pay her Rs. 100 for each night's performance. On the sixth night A wilfully absents herself from the theatre. B is at liberty to put an end to the contract.

Example : (Appended to this section) : A, singer, enters into a contract with B, the manager of a theatre, to sing at his theatre two nights in every week during the next two months, and B engages to pay her at the rate of Rs. 100 for each night. On the sixth night A willfully absents herself. With the assent of B, A sings on seventh night. B has signified his acquiescence of the continuance of the contract, and cannot now put an end to it, but is entitled to compensation for the damage sustained by him through A's failure to sing on the sixth night.

PERSONS WHO SHOULD PERFORM THE CONTRACT

1. *The Promisor Himself*

According to Para 1 of Sec. 40, "If it appears from the nature of the case that it was the intention of the parties to any contract that any promise contained in it should be performed himself, such promise must be performed by the promisor." It means that the promises depending upon the personal skill or diligence or upon personal consideration between the parties, must be performed by the promisor himself. A personal contract, in which the personality of the promisor is a vital element, should be performed by the promisor personally. For example, contract to sing, to paint, to dance, to act etc. In such cases, if the promisor dies, such contracts come to end.

Example : A promises to paint a picture for B. A must perform this promise personally.

2. *The Agent*

According to Para 2 of the Sec. 40, "In other cases, the promisor or his representatives may employ a competent person to perform it." The contracts which do not involve any personal skill or consideration, can also be performed by an agent appointed by the promisor.

Example : A promises to pay B a sum of money. A may perform this promise, either by personally paying the money to B or by causing it to be paid to B by another; and, if A dies before the time appointed for payment, his representatives must perform the promise or employ some proper person to do so.

3. *The Legal Representative*

In the cases not involving personal skill or volition, the legal representatives of a deceased promisor are bound to perform the contract. (Sec. 37, Para 2). If the promisor dies before the performance, his legal representative become liable to perform the contract. On the death of a person, the benefits and burdens of his contracts pass to the legal representatives as part of his estate. But, at the same time, contracts, which involve the use of personal skill or are founded on personal considerations, cannot be performed by the legal representatives because such contracts come to an end on the death of the promisor.

Example : A promises to deliver goods to B on a particular day on payment of Rs. 1,000. A dies before that day. A's representatives are bound to deliver the goods to B and B is bound to pay Rs. 1,000 to A's representatives.

Example : A promises to paint a picture for B before a certain day. A dies before the particular day. The contract cannot be enforced either by A's representative or by B.

4. *The Third Person*

Sec. 41 states "When a promisee accepts performance of the promise from the third person, he cannot afterwards enforce it against the promisor.

5. *The Joint Promisors*

In case of joint promisors, a promisee may compel one or more of the joint promisors in the absence of a contract to the contrary.

Who can Demand Performance

1. It is only the promisee who can demand performance of the promise under a contract. It makes no difference whether the promise is for the benefit of the promisee or any other person.

2. Under certain cases a stranger to the contract can enforce the contract. Examples, trust, assignee etc.

3. The legal representative can enforce performance of the contract upon the other party or their legal representatives.

Example : A promises B to pay Rs. 1,000 to C. A does not pay the amount to C. C cannot take action against A. It is only B who can enforce this promise against A.

PERFORMANCE OF JOINT PROMISES

When two or more persons enter into an agreement with one or more persons, a twofold problem arises, *viz.*, who is liable to perform the promise under such a contract; and who can demand such performance? Joint promise means two or more persons may enter into a joint agreement with one or more persons.

Suppose, A and B jointly promise to pay Rs. 1,000 to X and Y. In such cases, the question arises who is liable to perform the contract and who can demand performance? The rules regarding devolution of joint liabilities and the rights of joint promisors are contained in Section 42 to 45 of the Indian Contract Act. These rules are discussed here under :

Devolution of Joint Liabilities

1. When one or more person have made a joint promise, all such persons must fulfil the promise unless a contrary intention appears by the contract. (Sec. 42).

2. Upon the death of anyone of them his legal representatives must jointly with the surviving promisors fulfil the promise. On the death of all the promisors, the representatives of all of them must jointly fulfil the promise. (Sec. 42)

3. When two or more persons make a joint promise, the promisee is entitled, in the absence of express agreement to the contrary, to compel any one or more of such joint promisors to perform the whole of the promise (Para 1 of Sec. 43).

4. In case of death of original debtor, if the debt falls upon a number of heirs, promisee must bring the suit against all heirs collectively, because the liability is only joint and not several in case of co-heirs. Co-heirs are not joint promisors.

5. Each promisor may compel contribution. Each of two or more joint promisors may compel every other promisor to contribute equally with himself to the performance of the promise unless a contrary intention appears from the contract (Para 2 of Sec. 43).

6. If anyone of the joint promisors makes a default in making the contribution, if any, the remaining joint promisors must bear the lose arising from such default in equal shares (Section 43, Para 3).

Examples : (*a*) A, B and C jointly promise to pay D Rs. 3,000. D may compel either A or B or C to pay him Rs. 3,000.

(*b*) A, B and C jointly promise to pay D the sum of Rs. 3,000. C is compelled to pay the whole. A is insolvent but his assets are sufficient to pay one-half of his debts. C is entitled to receive Rs. 500 from A's estate and Rs. 1,250 from B.

(*c*) A, B and C are under a joint promise to pay D Rs. 3,000. C is unable to pay anything and A is compelled to pay the whole. A is entitled to receive Rs. 1,500 from B.

(*d*) A, B and C are under a joint promise to pay D Rs. 3,000, A and B being only sureties for C. C fails to pay. A and B are compelled to pay the whole sum. They are entitled to recover it from C.

Devaluation of Joint Rights (Sec. 45)

1. When a person has made a promise to several persons, then unless a contrary intention appears from the contract, the right to claim performance rests between him and them during their life time.

2. When one of the promisees dies, the right to claim performance rests with his legal representatives jointly with the surviving promisees.

3. When all the promisees die, the right to claim performance rests with their legal representatives jointly.

Example : (Appended to Sec. 45). A, in consideration of Rs. 5,000 lent to him by B and C, promises B and C jointly to repay them that sum with interest on a day specified. B dies. The right to claim performance rests with B's representative jointly with C during C's life and after the death of C with the representatives of B and C jointly.

Time and Place for Performance

So far as the time and place of performance of a contract is concerned, it must be agreed upon by the parties to the contract themselves. Sections 46 to 50 lay down rules in this regard. These rules are :

1. *Performance within a Reasonable Time* (Sec. 46)

Section 46 states that, "Where by the contract, a promisor is to perform his promise without application by the promisee, and no time for performance is specified, the engagement must be performed within a reasonable time."

The question "what is a reasonable time" in each particular case, is a question of fact. Sometimes, the time for performance is not specified in the contract, and the promisor himself has to perform the promise without being asked by the promisee. In such cases, the promise must be performed within a reasonable time.

2. *Performance of the Promise where the time is Specified* (Sec. 47)

"When a promise is to be performed on a certain day, and the promisor has undertaken to perform it without application by the promisee, the promisor may perform it at any time during the usual hours of business on such day and at the place at which the promise ought to be performed." (Sec 47).

Example : A promises to deliver goods at B's warehouse on the first January. On that day A brings the goods to B's warehouse, but after the usual hours for closing and they are not received. A has not performed his promise.

3. *Application for Performance to be at Proper Time and Place* (Sec. 48)

"When a promise is to be performed on a certain day, and promisor has not undertaken to perform it without application by the promisee, it is the duty of the promisee to apply for performance at a proper place and within usual hours of business." (Sec. 48)

4. *To Appoint a Reasonable Place for Performance* (Sec. 49)

"When a promise is to be performed without application by the promisee, and no place is fixed for the performance of it, it is the duty of the promisor to apply to the promisee to appoint a reasonable place for the performance of the promise and to perform it at such place." (Sec. 49)

> **Example :** A undertakes to deliver a thousand mounds of jute to B on a fixed day. A must apply to B to appoint a reasonable place for the purpose of receiving it, and must deliver it to him at such place.

5. *Performance as Prescribed by the Promisee* (Sec. 50)

"The performance of any promise may be made in any manner, or at any time which the promisee prescribes or sanctions." (Sec 50).

> **Example :** A owes B Rs. 2,000. B accepts A's cycle valuing Rs. 500 in reduction of the debt. The delivery of cycle will amount to a part payment of the debt.

TIME AS THE ESSENCE OF THE CONTRACT

"The time as the essence of the contract" means that the time is an essential element, and the concerned parties must perform their promise within specified time. This gives the other party a right to expect that it shall be performed that time. But if the promisor fails to do so, the question arises whether the contract becomes voidable at the option of the promisee? To determine whether time is the essence, it is necessary to look into the nature of the contract and the intention of the parties to it.

In commercial transactions, time regarding the delivery of goods is, ordinarily, the essence of the contract. In other words, in a contract of sale or purchase of goods, the time of delivery and payment are considered to be of the essence of the contract. In the case of contract of sale or purchase of immovable property, the time is not considered to be of essence of the contract.

In the following cases, the time is generally considered to be of the essence of the contract.

1. Where the parties have expressly agreed to treat the time as the essence of the contract.
2. Where the delay in performing the contract operates as an injury to the party.
3. Where the nature and necessity of the contract requires the time to be the essence of the contract.

The question, whether time is the essence of the contract or not, is to be decided. Though it depends upon the facts and circumstances in the case, the Indian Contract Act lays down the following provisions in this regard.

1. *When Time is the Essence of the Contract*

"When a party to a contract promises to do a certain thing at or before a specified time, or certain things at or before specified times, and fails to do any such thing at or before the specified time, or contract, or so much of it as has not been performed, becomes voidable at the option of the promisee, if the intention of parties was that time should be of the essence of the contract." Thus, the innocent party may put an end to the contract if he so chooses. (Sec. 55, Para 1) An intention to make time as the essence of the contract must be expressed in a clear language.

> **Example :** A promised to deliver goods to B on 1st Jan. But he failed to deliver the goods by that time. The contract was voidable at the option of B.

2. *When Time is not the Essence of the Contract*

"If it was not the intention of the parties that time should be of the essence of the contract, the contract does not become voidable by the failure to do such thing at or before the specified time; but the promisee is entitled to compensation from the promisor for any loss occasioned to him by such failure." (Sec. 55, Para 2). Where the time is not of the essence of the contract and the promisor fails to perform it within the specified time, the promisee is not entitled to avoid the contract.

Example : *Hitkari Motors Vs. Attar Singh* (1962)

In a contract for the purchase of chassis for a diesel truck to be supplied within 2 months time, was held to be of the essence of the contract.

3. *When Performance is Accepted at a Time other than Agreed Upon*

"If in case of a contract voidable on account of the promisor's failure to perform his promise at the time agreed, the promisee accepts performance of such promise at any time other than agreed, the promisee cannot claim compensation for any loss occasioned by the non-performance of the promise at the time agreed, unless, at the time of such acceptance, he gives notice to the promisor of his intention to do so". (Sec. 55 Para 3). When time is the essence of the contract, the promisee accepts the performance of the promise after the fixed time, he cannot claim compensation for any loss caused to him by the non-performance of the promise at the agreed time.

PERFORMANCE OF RECIPROCAL PROMISE

Under Section 2 (*f*), "Promises which form the consideration or a part of consideration for each other are called reciprocal promises." In the case of bilateral contracts, each party is not only the promisor but the promisee also, since one of them gives a promise in exchange for the other. A promise against a promise is a good consideration. An agreement may consist of either (*a*) a promise supported by consideration given, or (*b*) a promise supported by another promise. In the latter case, when an agreement is supported by another promise, it will be a reciprocal promise. Thus, in reciprocal promises each party gives a promise for a promise. Reciprocal promises are of the following types :

1. *Mutual and Concurrent* (Simultaneous Reciprocal Promise) (Sec. 51)

"When a contract consists of reciprocal promises to be simultaneously performed no promise need perform his promise unless the promisee is ready and willing to perform his reciprocal promise."

Examples : (1) All cash sales are examples of simultaneous or concurrent promises, as delivery of goods and payment of price take place simultaneously.

(2) A and B contract that A shall deliver goods to B and paid for by B on delivery. Here, A need not deliver the goods unless A is ready and willing to pay for the goods on delivery. Similarly, B need not pay for the goods unless A is ready and willing to deliver them on payment.

2. *Mutual and Independent* (Sec. 52)

"Where the order in which reciprocal promises are to be performed is expressly fixed by the contract they shall be performed in that order; and, where the order is not expressly fixed by the contract, they shall be performed in that order which the nature of the transaction requires."

Example : A and B contract that A shall build a house for B at a fixed price. A's promise to build the house must be performed before B's promise to pay for it.

Example : A and B contract that A shall make over his stock-in-trade to B at a fixed price, and B promises to give security for the payment of money. A's promise need not be performed until the security is given, for the nature of the transaction requires that A should have security, before he delivers up his stock.

3. *Conditional and Dependent* (Sec. 54)

"When a contract consists of reciprocal promises, such that one of them cannot be performed or that its performance cannot be claimed till the other has been performed, and the promisor of the promise last mentioned fails to perform it, such promisor cannot claim the performance of the reciprocal promise and must make compensation to the other party to the contract for any loss which such other party may sustain by the non-performance of the contract."

Example : A promises to construct B's house, provided that B supplies cement and bricks. This will be a conditional and dependent promise. Here, A need not perform the promise if B fails to supply cement and bricks.

Rules Regarding Performance of Reciprocal Promise

1. Section 51 states, "When a contract consists of reciprocal promises to be performed simultaneously, no promisor need to perform his promise unless the promisee is ready and willing to perform his reciprocal promise."

Example : (1) A and B contracted that A shall deliver certain goods to B to be paid for by B on delivery. In this case, the promises are mutual and concurrent and must be performed simultaneously.

(2) Section 52 states, "Where the order in which reciprocal promises are to be performed, is expressly fixed by the contract, they must be performed in that order; and where the order is not expressly fixed by the contract, they must be fixed in the order which the nature of the transaction requires."

Example : A, a furniture-maker contracted B to make certain furniture for him, provided B agreed to supply necessary timber. B failed to supply timber. Here, A need not make furniture and B cannot claim the performance. Besides, B is bound to make compensation to A for any loss caused to A by the non-performance.

3. According to Sec. 53, "When a contract contains reciprocal promises and one party to the contract prevents the other from performing his promise, the contract becomes voidable at the option of the party so prevented; and he is entitled to compensation from the other party for any loss which he may sustain in consequence of the non-performance of the contract."

Example : A and B contract that B shall execute certain works for A for a thousand rupees, B is ready and willing to execute the work accordingly but A prevents him from doing so. The contract is voidable at the option of B, and if he elects to rescind it, he is entitled to recover from A compensation for any loss which he has incurred by its non-performance.

4. "Where the nature of reciprocal promises is such that one of them cannot be performed till the other party has performed his promise then if the latter fails to perform it, he cannot claim the performance of the promise from the other. In such a case, he must make compensation to the other party to the contract for any loss which such other party may sustain by the non-performance of the contract." (Sec. 54).

Example : A promises B to sell him one hundred bales of merchandise, to be delivered next day, and B promises A to pay for them within a month. A does not deliver according to his promise. B's promise to pay need not be performed, and A must make compensation.

5. If time is the essence in a mutual contract and the promise is not performed at the time prescribed by the promisee, the other party may assume that the contract is terminated (Sec. 55).

6. Any reciprocal agreement to do an act, performance of which is impossible since beginning, is void under Sec. 56.

7. Where persons reciprocally promise, firstly, to do certain things which are legal, and secondly, under specified circumstances, to do certain other things which are illegal, the first set of promises is a contract, but the second is a void agreement.

8. In the case of an alternative promise, one branch of which is a legal and the other illegal, the legal branch alone can be enforced.

Example : A and B agree that A shall pay B Rs. 1,000, for which B shall afterwards deliver to A either rice or smuggled opium. This is a valid contract to deliver rice and a void agreement as to the opium.

Appropriation of Payments (Secs. 59 to 61)

Appropriation of payments means application of payments. When a debtor, who owes several debts to the same creditor, makes a payment which is insufficient to satisfy the whole indebtedness, the question arises, as to which of the debts the payment to be applied. The rule in Clayton's case is, "*Quiequid solvitur secundum modum solventis*", *i.e.*, whatever paid is paid or is to be applied according to the mode laid down by the payer. Thus according to this maxim, when a debtor makes a payment, he may appropriate it to any debt he pleases, and the creditor must apply it accordingly. In India the rule in Clayton's case has been following subject to the provision of the Indian Contract Act 1872. The rule in Clayton's case was stated as : "If a man owes another two debts upon distinct causes, and pays him a sum of money, the payer has a right to say, to which account, the money so paid is to be appropriated."

The rules regarding appropriation of payments are contained in Sections 59 to 61. These rules are :

1. *Appropriation by Debtor* (Sec. 59)

"Where a debtor, owing several distinct debts to one person, makes a payment to him, either express intimation, or under circumstances implying that the payment is to be applied to the discharge of some particular debt, the payment, if accepted, must be applied accordingly."

Examples : (*a*) A owes B, among other debts, Rs. 1,000 upon a promissory note which falls due on the Ist June. He owes B no other debt of that amount. On Ist June A pays to B Rs. 1,000. The payment is to be applied to the discharge of the promissory note.

(*b*) A owes to B, among other debts, the sum of Rs. 567. B writes to A and demands payment of this sum. A sends to B Rs. 567. This payment is to be applied to the discharge of the debt of which B had demanded payment.

2. *Appropriation by Creditor* (Sec. 60)

"Where the debtor has omitted to intimate and there are no other circumstances indicating to which debt payment is to be applied, the creditor may apply it at his discretion to any lawful debt actually due and payable to him by the debtor, even time-barred debt." But it cannot be applied to a disputed debt.

3. *Appropriation by Law* (Sec. 61)

"Where neither party makes any appropriation, the payment shall be applied in discharge of the debt in order of time, whether they are or are not barred by the law in force for the time being as to the limitation of suits. If the debts are equal standing payment shall be applied in discharge of each proportionately."

Example : A owes B three loans — (1) Rs. 100 on 1st Jan. (2) Rs. 200 on 1st Feb. and (3) Rs. 150 on 1st March. If he pays Rs. 350, the payment shall be appropriated towards the first and second loans in full and the rest Rs. 50 towards the third one.

4. *Appropriation towards Interest*

Sometimes, the debtor makes part payment without stating whether it is towards interest or principal. In such cases, the general rule is that the payment must first be adjusted towards interest and the balance towards the principal amount.

5. *Appropriation in Order of Receipts and Payments*

The laid down in Clayton's case, which is applicable in case of a current or running account without break, is that, unless there is a contrary intention, the items on the credit side of an account must be appropriated against the items on the debit side of the account in order of date.

Contracts which Need not be Performed

1. "If the parties to a contract agree to substitute a new contract for it, or to rescind or alter it, the original contract need not be performed." (Sec. 62).

> **Example :** A owes money to B under a contract. It is agreed between A, B and C that B shall thenceforth accept C as his debtor instead of A. The old debt of A to B is at an end, a new debt from C to B has been contracted.

2. "Every promisee may dispense with or remit, wholly or in part, the performance of the promise made to him, or may extend the time for such performance, or may accept instead of it any satisfaction which he thinks fit." (Sec. 63).

> **Examples :** (1) A promises to paint a picture for B. B afterwards forbids him to do so. A is no longer bound to perform the promise.
>
> (2) A owes B Rs. 5,000. C pays to B Rs. 1,000 and B accepts them in satisfaction of claim on A. This payment is a discharge of the whole claim.

3. According to Sec. 64, when a voidable contract is rescinded, the other party need not perform his promise.

> **Example :** A pays B Rs. 1,000 in consideration of B's promise to marry C, A's daughter. C is dead at the time of the promise. The agreement is void, but B must repay A the sum of Rs. 1,000.

4. "If any promisee neglects or refuse to afford the promisor reasonable facilities for the performance of his promise, the promisor is excused by such neglect or refusal as to any non-performance caused thereby." (Sec. 67).

> **Example :** A contracts with B to repair B's house. B neglects or refuses to point out to A the places in which his house requires repair. Here, A is excused for the non-performance of the contract, if it is caused by such neglect or refusal.

Assignment of Contracts

Transfer of liabilities and rights under a contract to a third party, is known as assignment of contract. Thus, in the case of an assignment, the original party or parties to the contract drop out and others take its place. To assign means to transfer. The assignment of contracts may be by : (1) the act of parties or (2) the operation of law.

1. *Assignment by the Act of parties*

(A) *Assignment of Contractual Liabilities :* This is subject to the following rules :

(*i*) Under Section 40, contracts involving personal ability of skill or any other personal qualification cannot be assigned, for example, painting of a picture by a painter, acting in a film by the actor engaged. Thus, it is the state where one party cannot delegate the act of performance to another.

(*ii*) A promisor cannot assign his liabilities under a contract. In other words, a promisee cannot be compelled to accept a third person to perform the promise.

> **Example :** A owes Rs. 100 to B and B owes the same amount to C. B cannot ask C to recover from A unless there is another contract between A and C for the purpose.

(B) *Assignment of Contractual Rights :* This is subject to the following rules :

(*i*) The rights and benefits under a contract cannot be assigned, if they are of personal nature.

> **Example :** A owes B Rs. 100. The creditor can transfer the right of recovery to C from A. It will be a valid assignment being of a personal nature.

(*ii*) An actionable claim can be assigned only by an instrument in writing. Notice of such assignment must also be given to the debtor.

2. *Assignment by Operation of Law*

This may take place in any one of the two circumstances :

(*i*) *Death :* Upon the death of a party to the contract his rights and liabilities under the contract are assigned to his heirs and legal representatives. But when the personal skill and abilities are involved the contractual relations are put to an end by the death of the promisor.

(*ii*) *Insolvency :* In case of a party to the contract being declared insolvent, his rights and liabilities under the contract are assigned to the Official Receiver or Assignee, as the case may be.

THEORETICAL QUESTIONS

1. What do you understand by the term 'performance of contract'? (*B.Com. MS*)
2. What do you understand by the term 'tender of performance'? (*B.Com. Kerala*)
3. State the persons by whom the contract should be performed. In what circumstances the performance by a third party is effective?
4. What are the essentials of a valid tender? (*B.Com. Delhi*)
5. State briefly the provisions of the Contract Act relating to the devolution of joint rights and liabilities. (*B.Com. Kolkata*)
6. What are reciprocal promises? (*B.Com. MS*)
7. When is the time deemed to be the essence of the contract in the performance of contracts. Discuss. (*B.Com. Chennai*)
8. What rules govern the appropriation of payment by a debtor who makes payment of one of several debts owed by him to the creditor? (*CAIIB*)
9. State and discuss the circumstances under which contracts need not be performed.
10. What are reciprocal promises? (*B.Com. Bhopal*)
11. What is meant by assignment of a contract? (*B.Com. Madras*)
12. What do you understand by appropriation of payments? State the provisions of Indian Contract Act which govern the appropriation of payments made by a debtor. (*M.Com. MS*)
13. State the rules for the performance of legal and illegal reciprocal promises. (*M.Com. Jabalpur*)
14. Discuss in detail the rules relating to the time and place for performance of a contract. (*M.Com. Kerala*)
15. What are the liabilities of a joint promisor under a contract? (*M.Com. MS*)

MULTIPLE CHOICE QUESTIONS

I. Choose correct option for each of the following :

1. A tender of performance is valid, if it is :

(*a*) unconditionally. (*b*) by an able and willing person.
(*c*) for whole obligation. (*d*) all of the above.

2. Performance of contract means :

(*a*) fulfilling all the obligations by a party.
(*b*) fulfilling all the obligations by the promisor.
(*c*) performing all the promises and fulfilling all the obligations by all the parties.
(*d*) both (*a*) and (*b*).

3. Suppose the time fixed for performance of the contract has expired but the time is not essential. What is the remedy of the promisee in the circumstances?

(*a*) Can rescind the contract. (*b*) No remedy available.
(*c*) To claim compensation (*d*) Can't be determined.

4. An attempted performance discharges the promisor from his liability :

(*a*) to deliver the goods. (*b*) to pay the price.
(*c*) to pay any damages. (*d*) above (*a*) and (*c*).

5. Promises which form the consideration or part of the consideration for each other are called:

(*a*) Joint Promises. (*b*) Independent Promises.
(*c*) Reciprocal Promises. (*d*) None of these.

6. X, Y and Z jointly promised to pay Rs. 1 lakh to A. X dies before payment of the amount. The promise :

(*a*) becomes void.
(*b*) must be performed by both Y and Z.
(*c*) must be performed by Y, Z and X's legal representatives.
(*d*) becomes voidable.

7. In case one of the joint promisors is compelled to perform a promise, he can :

(*a*) compel any other joint promisor to contribute equally.
(*b*) compel all the other joint promisors to contribute equally unless a contrary intention appears from the contract.
(*c*) compel all but one of the joint promisors to contribute equally.
(*d*) compel none of the joint promisors.

8. A promise can be performed by :

(*a*) promisor. (*b*) representative.
(*c*) third party. (*d*) by any of the above.

9. Tender of performance means :

(*a*) tender for supply of goods. (*b*) offering performance of promise under a contract.
(*c*) attempted performance. (*d*) actual performance.

10. A contract must be performed by the promisor himself :

(*a*) if the promisee wants so. (*b*) if the contract involves personal skill.
(*c*) if representative refuses to perform. (*d*) in all the above cases.

11. When a valid tender of goods is rejected, the promisor :

(*a*) is not liable for non-performance of contract.
(*b*) is discharged from his obligation under the contract.
(*c*) does not lose his right under the contract.
(*d*) is entitled to all of the above.

12. Where the performance of a promise by one party depends on the prior performance of promise by the other party, such reciprocal promises fall under the category of :

(*a*) Mutual and concurrent. (*b*) Mutual and independent.
(*c*) Conditional and dependent. (*d*) Both (*a*) and (*b*).

13. Sale of goods for cash is an example of :

(*a*) mutual and independent promises. (*b*) mutual and dependent promises.
(*c*) mutual and concurrent promises. (*d*) conditional and dependent promises.

14. In which case the promisor must apply for the performance :

(*a*) where no time for performance is specified and the promise is to be performed without demand by the promisee.
(*b*) where no place for performance is specified and the promise is to be performed without demand by the promisees.
(*c*) where time for performance is specified and the promise is to be performed without demand by the promisee.
(*d*) none of these.

15. A promisee can accept performance of a promise :

(*a*) from the promisor himself. (*b*) from the agent of the promisor.
(*c*) from a third party. (*d*) from any of the above.

16. When a valid tender of goods is not accepted, it is called :

(*a*) actual performance. (*b*) attempted performance.
(*c*) no performance. (*d*) discharge of contract.

17. The performance of a promise is not required :

(*a*) when parties substitute a new contract.
(*b*) when performance becomes difficult.
(*c*) when the promisee rejects a tender of performance.
(*d*) under (*a*) and (*c*).

18. Personal actions dies with the person. This rule means that the promise must be performed by:

(*a*) the promisor himself.
(*b*) the legal representatives of the promisor.
(*c*) the agent of the promisor.
(*d*) any other person.

19. In case of a joint promise, generally a promisee may compel for performance of the promise to :

(*a*) any one of the joint promisors.
(*b*) all the joint promisors.
(*c*) all but one joint promisor.
(*d*) (*a*) or (*b*) or (*c*) above .

20. When two or more persons have made a joint promise, then unless a contrary intention appears from the contract, all such persons must fulfil promise :

(*a*) jointly.
(*b*) jointly and severally.
(*c*) severally.
(*d*) jointly or severally.

21. A and B fix 15th September as date of performance of a contract but A failed to perform it. However, they never intended to treat the time as an essence of the contract. B can :

(*a*) rescind the contract.
(*b*) claim damages for non-performance.
(*c*) cannot claim damages for non-performance.
(*d*) both (*a*) and (*c*) above.

22. In case all joint promises are alive, the performance of the contract may be demanded by :

(*a*) all the promisees jointly.
(*b*) any one or more of joint promisees.
(*c*) none of these.

23. In commercial transactions, time is considered to be of the essence of the contract, and if the party fails to perform the contract within specified time, the contract becomes :

(*a*) voidable at the option of the other party.
(*b*) void and cannot be enforced.
(*c*) illegal for non-compliance of legal terms.
(*d*) enforceable in higher court only.

24. Where one of the joint promisors makes a default in contributing his share :

(*a*) the other joint promisors are not liable to bear the loss arising from such default.
(*b*) the other joint promisors must bear the loss arising from such default equally.
(*c*) the other joint promisors need not agree to share the loss equally.
(*d*) the contract becomes void.

25. When after the formation of a valid contract, an event happens which makes the performance of contract impossible, then the contract becomes :

(*a*) void.
(*b*) valid.
(*c*) voidable.
(*d*) illegal.

26. Where time is the essence of the contract and the promisor fails to perform his promise in time, the contract becomes :

(*a*) Illegal.
(*b*) Voidable.
(*c*) Void.
(*d*) None of these.

27. In which case time is considered to be essence of contract :

(*a*) where the parties have expressly agreed to treat the time as the essence of the contract.
(*b*) where the non-performance at the specified time operates as an injury to the party.
(*c*) where the nature and necessity of the contract requires the performance of the contract within the specified time.
(*d*) All of above.

28. In case all joint promisors are alive, the performance of the contract may be demanded from :

(*a*) all the promisors jointly.
(*b*) any one or more of joint promisors.
(*c*) none of these.

29. Owning to a strike in the factory of X he is not able to supply the goods to Y as per the terms of the agreement. The agreement in such a case :
(*a*) is discharged. (*b*) becomes void.
(*c*) is not discharged. (*d*) is voidable at the option of X.

30. X who owes Rs. 20,000 to Y dies leaving an estate of Rs. 5000. The legal representatives of X are :
(*a*) liable for Rs. 20,000. (*b*) not liable at all.
(*c*) liable for Rs. 5,000. (*d*) liable for Rs. 2,000.

31. The promises which are to be performed simultaneously are called :
(*a*) Mutual and Independent. (*b*) Mutual and Concurrent.
(*c*) Mutual and Dependent. (*d*) None of these.

32. Where neither party makes any appropriation, the money received must be applied:
(*a*) first towards principal and then towards interest.
(*b*) first towards interest and then towards principal.
(*c*) equally towards principal and interest.
(*d*) in the ratio of principal and interest.

33. Where debt to be discharged is not indicated by the debtor, the creditor:
(*a*) can apply the payment to any lawful debt other than time barred debt.
(*b*) can apply the payment to any lawful debt other than time barred debt and disputed debt.
(*c*) can apply the payment to any lawful debt other than disputed debt.
(*d*) none of these.

34. Assignment by operation of law takes place:
(*a*) only in case of death of any party. (*b*) only in case of insolvency of any party.
(*c*) in case of death/insolvency of any party. (*d*) none of these.

35. In which commercial contracts, time is not considered to be the essence of a contract :
(*a*) Time fixed for the delivery of goods. (*b*) Time fixed for the payment of the price.
(*c*) (*a*) and (*b*). (*d*) none of these.

36. When a contract contain reciprocal promises and one party to the contract prevents the other from performing his promise, the contract becomes :
(*a*) illegal. (*b*) voidable.
(*c*) void. (*d*) none of these.

37. Actionable claims can :
(*a*) never be assigned. (*b*) always be assigned by an instrument in writing.
(*c*) none of these. (*d*) always be assigned orally.

38. When a party to a contract transfers his contractual rights to another, it is :
(*a*) rescission of contract. (*b*) discharge of contract.
(*c*) waiver of contract. (*d*) assignment of contract.

39. Notice of assignment of actionable claims :
(*a*) need not be given to the debtor. (*b*) may be given to the debtor.
(*c*) must be given to the creditor. (*d*) must be given to the debtor.

40. Each party is a promisor and a promisee in case of :
(*a*) past consideration. (*b*) every contract.
(*c*) present consideration. (*d*) reciprocal promises.

ANSWERS

1. (*d*)	**2.** (*c*)	**3.** (*c*)	**4.** (*d*)	**5.** (*c*)	**6.** (*c*)	**7.** (*b*)	**8.** (*d*)	**9.** (*b*)	**10.** (*b*)
11. (*b*)	**12.** (*c*)	**13.** (*c*)	**14.** (*b*)	**15.** (*d*)	**16.** (*b*)	**17.** (*d*)	**18.** (*a*)	**19.** (*d*)	**20.** (*a*)
21. (*b*)	**22.** (*a*)	**23.** (*a*)	**24.** (*b*)	**25.** (*a*)	**26.** (*b*)	**27.** (*d*)	**28.** (*a*)	**29.** (*c*)	**30.** (*c*)
31. (*b*)	**32.** (*b*)	**33.** (*c*)	**34.** (*c*)	**35.** (*b*)	**36.** (*b*)	**37.** (*b*)	**38.** (*d*)	**39.** (*d*)	**40.** (*d*)

XI

CHAPTER

Quasi Contract
(Sections 68–72)

AT A GLANCE

- Introduction
- Meaning
- Basis of Quasi-contracts
- Features
- Quasi-contract Vs. Contract
- Types of Quasi Contracts
- Claims for Necessaries Supplied
- Payment by an interested Person
- Benefits of Non-gratuitous Act
- Finder of Goods
- Money paid or things Delivered by Mistake
- Theoretical Questions
- Multiple Choice Questions.

INTRODUCTION

We have discussed that a contract can be enforced only when it has the essential elements of contracts, *viz.*, offer and acceptance, free consent, lawful object and consideration and capacity of the parties to contract. A contract is the result of an agreement enforceable by law. However, in certain cases the law creates and enforces legal rights and obligations when no real contract exists. That is, under certain circumstances obligations resembling those created by a contract are imposed by law although the parties have never entered into a contract. For example, A, trader leaves certain goods at B's shop by mistake. B treats the goods as his own. But he is bound to return them to A. This kind of contractual relations are known as *quasi contracts*. They are also called *implied contracts* or *constructive contracts* under the English Law. Indian Contract Act deals with them as "*certain relations resembling those created by contracts*". In Roman Law they are called *obligatio quasi ex contractu*.

MEANING

Winfield has defined the terms as "liability not exclusively referable to any other head of the law, imposed upon a particular person to pay money to another particular person on the ground of unjust benefit". It is a special relationship between two persons analogous to contract rather than to tort with a resultant duty to pay money and an underlying aim of making restitution for a benefit unjustly received. It does not arise from any agreement of the parties concerned, but is imposed by the law, so that in this respect a quasi contract resembles a tort. It is a right available against a particular person and in that respect it resembles a contractual right.

Similarly, in an American case, *Miller Vs. Schloss*,

observed that "A quasi or constructive contract rests upon the equitable principle that a person shall not be allowed to enrich himself unjustly at the expense of another. In truth, it is not a contract at all. It is obligation which the law creates, in the absence of any agreement, when and because the acts of the parties or others have placed in the possession of one person money, or its equivalent, under such circumstances that in equity and good conscience he ought not to retain it, and which *ex acquo ot bono* belongs to another. Duty, and not a promise or agreement or intention of the person sought to be charged, define it".

As a matter of fact, "quasi contract" is not a contract in the strict sense of the term because there is no real contract in existence. Though the Indian Contract Act 1872 does not define quasi-contracts, it calls them relations resembling those of contracts. Quasi contract may be defined as "a transaction in which there is no contract between the parties; the law creates certain rights and obligations between them which are similar to those created by a contract.

BASIS OF QUASI CONTRACTS

Quasi-contract is a kind of contract by which one party is bound to pay money in consideration of something done or suffered by the other party. These contracts are based on the maxim, "*nemo debet locu platari ex liena justua*" *i.e.*, no man must grow rich out of another person's cost. Again quasi contract is to prevent unjust enrichment, or unjust benefit, *i.e.*, no one should grow rich out of another person's loss. According to Sec. 73, a suit for damages for the breach of the contract can be filed in the case of a quasi contract in the same way as in the case of a completed contract.

Features of a Quasi-contract

The salient characteristics or features of a quasi-contract, in brief, are as under :

1. It is *imposed by law* and does not arise from any contract.
2. It is not a true contract but an *obligation imposed by law.*
3. It arises from a duty of a party and *not by promise of any party.*
4. It always gives rise to *right in personam*, not in rem.
5. It rests on the *principle of equity* that a person should not be allowed unjustly to enrich himself at the expense of another.
6. The right under it is always *a right to money*, generally, though not always, to a liquidated sum of money.
7. A suit for *its breach may be filed* in the same way as in the case of a complete contract.

Distinction between Quasi-Contract and Contract

Basis of Distinction	*Quasi-Contract*	*Contract*
1. Obligation	Obligation is imposed by law	Obligation is mutually created by the parties.
2. Essentials of Contract	It does not possess all the essentials of a contract	It possess all the essentials of a contract
3. Basis	It is found upon the principle of equity	It is founded upon the law of contract
4. Formation	The law imposes upon the parties.	It is intentionally formed by the parties.

Types of Quasi Contracts

The different types of quasi contractual obligations which the Indian Contract Act deals with are contained in Sections 68 to 72. They are :

1. Claim for necessaries supplied (Sec. 68)

2. Reimbursement of money, due by another (Sec. 69)
3. Liability to pay for non-gratuitous Act (Sec. 70)
4. Responsibilities of finder of goods (Sec. 71)
5. Money paid or things delivered by mistake or under coercion (Sec. 72)

1. *Claim for Necessaries Supplied* (Sec. 68)

"If a person, incapable of entering into a contract or anyone whom he is legally bound to support, is supplied by another person with necessaries suited to his condition in life, the person who has furnished such supplies is entitled to be reimbursed from the property of such incapable person." (Sec. 68).

> **Examples :** (1) A supplies B, a lunatic, with necessaries suitable to his condition in life. A is entitled to be reimbursed from B's property.
>
> (2) A supplies the wife and children of B, a lunatic, with necessaries suitable to their conditions in life. A is entitled to be reimbursed from B's property.

This Section covers the case of necessaries supplied to a person incapable of contracting, say, a minor, lunatic etc., and to persons whom the incapable person is bound to support, say his wife and minor children. However, following points should be noted :

(*i*) The goods supplied must be necessaries. What will constitute necessaries shall vary from person to person depending upon the social status he enjoys.

(*ii*) It is only the property of the incapable person that shall be liable. He cannot be held liable personally. Thus, where he does not own any property, nothing shall be payable.

2. *Payment by an Interested Person* (Sec. 69)

According to Section 69 of the Act, "A person who is interested in the payment of money which another is bound by law to pay, and who, therefore, pays it, is entitled to be reimbursed by the other".

> **Example :** B holds land in Bengal, on a lease granted by A, the Zamindar. The revenue payable by A to the government being in arrear, his land is advertised for sale by the Government. Under the revenue law, the consequence of such sale will be annulment of B's lease. But to prevent the sale and the consequent annulment of his own lease, pays to the Government the sum due from A. A is bound to make good to B the amount so paid.

The applicability of this Section is subject to the following conditions :

(*i*) The defendant should be bound by law to pay.

(*ii*) The plaintiff should be interested in making the payment in order to protect his own interest and the payment should not be voluntary one.

(*iii*) The payment must not be such as the plaintiff himself was bound to pay.

> **Example :** *Tulsa kunwar Vs. Jageshar Prasad* (1901)
>
> X's goods were wrongfully attached in order to realise arrears of Government revenue due by Y. X pays the amount to save the goods from sale. X is entitled to recover the money from Y.
>
> **Example :** *Brooks Wharf Vs. Goodman Brothers* (1937)
>
> The defendants warehoused certain goods which they had imported from Russia, with the plaintiffs. The goods were stolen. Under the law, the customs duty on the goods could be recovered either from the owners of the goods or from the warehouseman. The warehouseman, that is the plaintiffs were called upon to pay the customs duty which the owners of the goods, that is, the defendants were bound by law to pay. The plaintiffs claimed the amount of the duty paid by them from the defendants. It was held that they were entitled to recover the same.

3. *Benefit of Non-gratuitous Act* (Sec. 70)

According to Section 70, "Where a person lawfully does anything for another person, or delivers anything to him not intending to do so gratuitously, and such other person enjoys the benefit thereof, the latter is bound to make compensation to the former in respect of, or to restore, the thing so done or delivered."

Examples : (1) A, a tradesman, leaves goods at B's house by mistake. B treats the goods as his own. He is bound to pay A for them.

(2) A saves C's property from fire. A is not entitled to compensation from C, if the circumstances show that he intended to act gratuitously.

For application of this Section, the following conditions must be fulfilled :

(*i*) The thing must have been done lawfully.

(*ii*) The person doing the act must not have intended to do it gratuitously, and

(*iii*) The person for whom the act is done, must have enjoyed the benefit of the act.

Example : *Damodar Mudaliar Vs. Secretary for State of India* (1894)

The Government carried out repairs to an irrigation tank, owned by the Government jointly with a zamindar. Government sued the zamindar for contribution in respect of expenses incurred for repairs. It was held that Government in carrying out the repairs had acted lawfully and had not intended to carry them out gratuitously and that the zamindar who enjoyed the benefit of the repairs was liable to pay compensation.

4. *Responsibilities of Finder of Goods* (Sec. 71)

According to Section 71, "A person who finds goods belonging to another and takes them into his custody, is subject to the same responsibility as a bailee." Thus an agreement is also implied by law between the owner and finder of the goods and the latter is deemed to be a bailee. This obligation is imposed on the basis of quasi contract. A finder of goods is bound to take as much care of goods found as a man of ordinary prudence would take of his own goods under similar circumstances.

Responsibilities of Finder of Goods : (1) He is bound to take as much care of the goods as a man of ordinary prudence does under the same circumstances.

(2) He has to take all necessary measures to trace the true owner, otherwise he will be guilty of wrongful conversion of property.

(3) The property will vest in the finder, till the true owner is found out.

(4) He can retain the goods against the whole world except the true owner.

Rights of Finder of Goods : 1. He is entitled to receive from the true owner, all expenses incurred by him for preserving the goods or finding the true owner.

2. The finder has the right to sell the goods in the following cases :

(*a*) Where the thing found is in danger of perishing or losing the greater part of their value.

(*b*) Where the owner cannot, with reasonable diligence, be found out.

(*c*) Where the owner is found out, but he refuses to pay the lawful charges to the finder.

(*d*) Where the lawful charges of the finder, in respect of the thing found, amount to two-third of the value of the thing found.

NB : The rights and duties of a bailee shall be discussed in detail under chapter 'Bailment and Pledge'.

5. *Money Paid or Things Delivered by Mistake or under Coercion* (Sec. 72)

According to Section 72, "A person to whom money has been paid, or anything delivered, by mistake or under coercion, must repay or return it." Payment by mistake under this section must refer to a payment which was not legally due.

Examples : (1) A and B jointly owe Rs. 100 to C. A alone pays the amount to C and B not knowing this fact, pays Rs. 100 to C. C is bound to repay the amount to B.

(2) A railway company, refuses to deliver certain goods to the consignee, except upon the payment of an illegal charges for carriage. The consignee pays the sum charged in order to obtain the goods. He is entitled to recover so much of the charge as was illegally excessive.

(3) *Hollins Vs. Fowler* H picked up a diamond on the floor of F's shop and handed over to F to keep it till the owner appeared. In spite of the best efforts the true owner could not be searched. After some time H tendered to F the lawful expenses incurred by him for finding the true owner and asked him (F) to hand over the diamond to H. F refused. It was held that F must return the diamond to H as H was entitled to retain it against the whole world except the true owner.

Example : *Kotrabasappa Vs. The Indian Bank* (1987)

The defendant was constituent of the plaintiff bank having his account there. The plaintiff bank received a telegraphic transfer advice and the confirmation telegram from one of its branches for crediting the defendant's account with a sum of Rs. one lakh. Instead of crediting the account of the defendant with that sum once, the bank by mistake and oversight credited his account with Rs. one lakh twice. The defendant withdrew this money each time. It was held that the defendant had utilised the additional sum of Rs. one lakh wrongly credited to his account by mistake, he was, therefore, bound to return that amount with interest.

THEORETICAL QUESTIONS

1. Define quasi contracts. State the circumstances in which quasi contractual obligations arise.
2. Discuss the provisions of Indian Contract Act 1872 relating to quasi contract. *(B.Com. Delhi)*
3. Quasi contracts are based on the maxim '*nemo debet locuplatari exliena justua*'. Explain the same with suitable examples. *(B.Com. MS)*
4. State the legal position of a finder of goods. *(B.Com. Kolkata)*
5. A quasi contract is not a contract at all. It is an obligation which the law creates. Discuss. *(B.Com. MS)*
6. State the difference between contract and quasi contract. *(M.Com. Jabalpur)*

MULTIPLE CHOICE QUESTIONS

I. Choose correct option for each of the following :

1. A Quasi-contract is also known as :
(*a*) Contract implied in law. (*b*) implied contract.
(*c*) unintentional contract. (*d*) both (*a*) and (*c*).

2. A Quasi-contract is :
(*a*) not made by the parties. (*b*) the result of application of principle of equity.
(*c*) is imposed by law. (*d*) all of the above.

3. The right under Quasi-contract is available against :
(*a*) specific person(s) only. (*b*) specific person and the whole world.
(*c*) the whole world . (*d*) none of these.

4. A Quasi Contract :
(a) is a contract. (*b*) has only a legal obligation.
(*c*) is an agreement. (*d*) is none of these.

5. A Quasi-contract is :
(*a*) implied by the act or conduct of the parties. (*b*) implied by law.
(*c*) intentionally made. (*d*) both (*a*) and (*c*).

6. Quasi-contract arises from :
(*a*) Contract by the parties. (*b*) Principle of equity.
(*c*) Laws of the land. (*d*) Status of persons.

7. A quasi-contract is :
(*a*) not a real contract.
(*b*) not a contract having all the essentials of valid contract.
(*c*) a contract imposed by law on the parties.
(*d*) all of the above.

8. A Quasi-contract is :
(*a*) contract imposed by law.
(*b*) deemed contract.
(*c*) not a real contract.
(*d*) both (*a*) and (c).

9. A person who makes payment of money on behalf of another is entitled to be reimbursed :
(*a*) when the person making the payment has interest in making the payment.
(*b*) when the person on whose behalf he pays the money is bound by law to pay.
(*c*) when the person receiving the payment is legally entitled to receive.
(*d*) when all the above conditions are satisfied.

10. A minor has been supplied necessaries on credit :
(*a*) He is not liable.
(*b*) His estate is liable.
(*c*) He is personally liable.
(*d*) He is not personally liable.

11. A person enjoying the benefits of lawful non-gratuitous acts of another person, he :
(*a*) is bound to pay the another.
(*b*) is not bound to pay another.
(*c*) that another person can not claim.
(*d*) above both (*b*) and (*c*).

12. A Quasi-contract arises from :
(*a*) the intention to create legal relations.
(*b*) compliance of all legal formalities.
(*c*) a true contract.
(*d*) the principle of natural justice.

13. Sometimes, a person finds certain goods belonging to some other persons. In such a case, the finder
(*a*) becomes the owner of the goods and can use them.
(*b*) is under a duty to trace the true owner and return the goods.
(*c*) can sell the perishable goods if true owner cannot be found.
(*d*) both (*b*) and (*c*).

14. Sometimes, a party is entitled to claim compensation in proportion to the work done by him. It is possible by a suit for :
(*a*) damages.
(*b*) quantum meruit.
(*c*) injunction.
(*d*) None of these.

15. The basis of quasi contractual relations' is the :
(*a*) existence of a valid contract between the parties.
(*b*) prevention of unjust enrichment at the expense of others.
(*c*) Provisions contained in Section 10 of the Contract Act.
(*d*) Existence of a voidable contract between the parties.

16. Quantum meruit means :
(*a*) a non-gratutious promise
(*b*) as much as is earned
(*c*) an implied promise.
(*d*) as much as is paid.

17. A finder of goods has the same responsibility as a :
(*a*) bailee.
(*b*) next best owner.
(c) real owner.
(*d*) bailor.

18. When an agreement is discovered to be void, any person who has received any advantage under such agreement.
(*a*) is bound to restore it.
(*b*) may retain it.
(c) is not bound to return it.

19. The obligation under Quasi-Contract is :
(*a*) imposed by law.
(*b*) created by the consent of parties to agreement.
(*c*) none of these.

20. Money advanced for the purchase of necessaries supplied to a person who is incapable of contracting is recoverable from :
(*a*) that person
(*b*) none of these.
(*c*) the property of such person.

ANSWERS

1. (*d*)	**2.** (*d*)	**3.** (*a*)	**4.** (*b*)	**5.** (*b*)	**6.** (*b*)	**7.** (*d*)	**8.** (*d*)	**9.** (*d*)	**10.** (*b*)
11. (*a*)	**12.** (*d*)	**13.** (*d*)	**14.** (*b*)	**15.** (*b*)	**16.** (*b*)	**17.** (*a*)	**18.** (*a*)	**19.** (*a*)	**20.** (*c*)

CHAPTER

Discharge of Contracts

AT A GLANCE

INTRODUCTION

When the rights and obligations arising out of a contract are extinguished, the contract is said to be discharged or terminated. Thus the discharge of a contract means that the parties are no more liable under the contract.

VARIOUS MODES OF DISCHARGE

Following are the various modes in which a contract may be discharged :

1. By Performance
2. By Agreement
3. By Impossibility of Performance
4. By Lapse of Time
5. By Operation of Law
6. By Breach of Contract

Discharge of a contract means termination of contractual relations between the parties to a contract. A contract is said to be discharged when the rights and obligations of the parties under the contract come to an end.

1. *Discharge by Performance of Contract*

Performance is the usual mode of discharge of a contract. The contract is said to be discharged when parties to a contract, perform their respective obligation which they have agreed to do. That is, when the parties to a contract fulfil their obligations arising out of the contract within the time and in the manner prescribed, the contract is said to have been discharged by performance. This topic has already been discussed in detail in the chapter X (Performance of Contract). However, they are repeated here.

A contract can be discharged by performance in any of the following ways :

(A) ***By Actual Performance :***

A contract is said to be discharged by actual performance when the parties to the contract perform their promises in accordance with the terms of the contract.

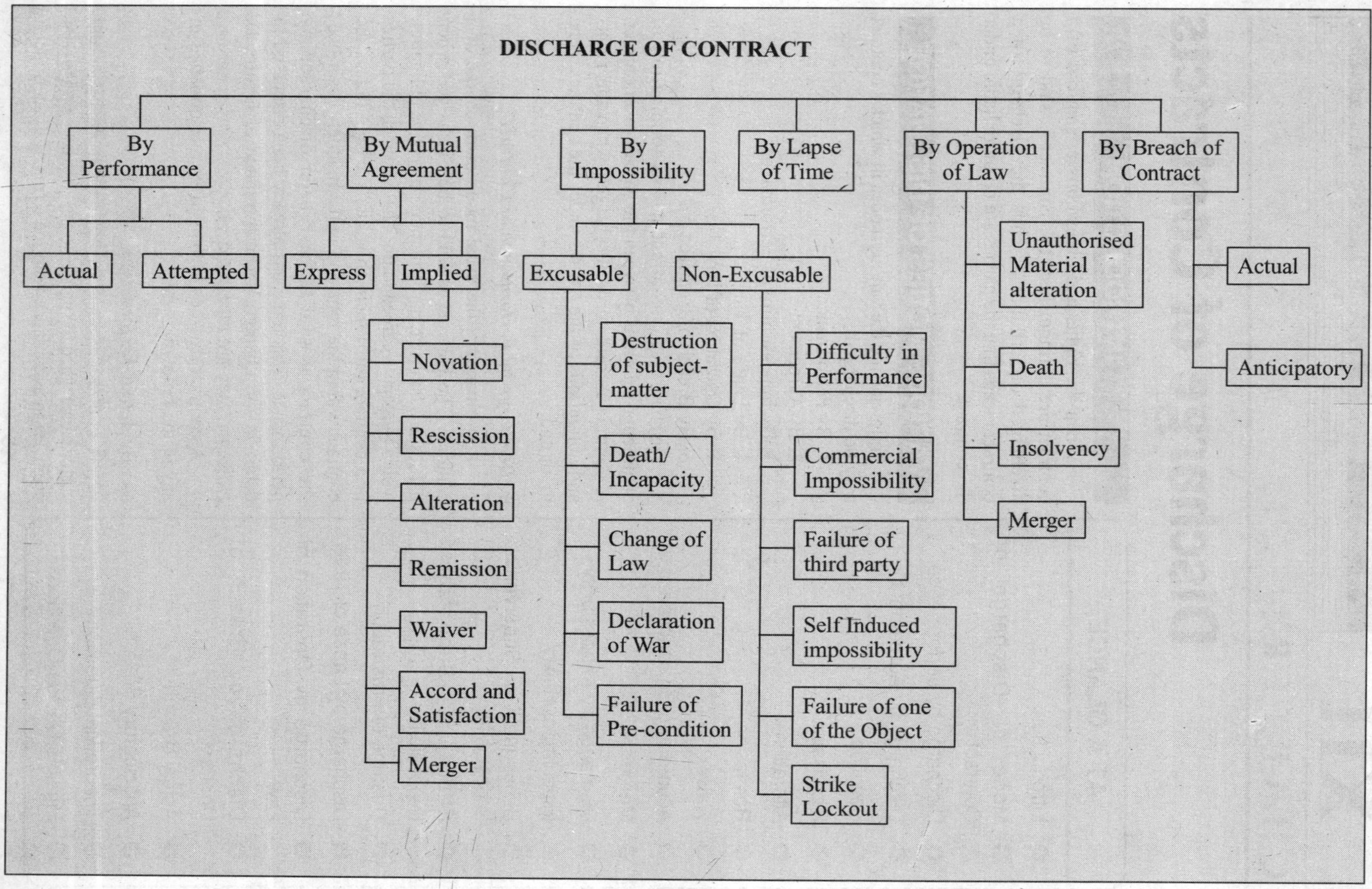
DISCHARGE OF CONTRACT
By Performance
Actual
Attempted
By Mutual Agreement
Express
Implied
Novation
Rescission
Alteration
Remission
Waiver
Accord and Satisfaction
Merger
By Impossibility
Excusable
Destruction of subject-matter
Death/ Incapacity
Change of Law
Declaration of War
Failure of Pre-condition
Non-Excusable
Difficulty in Performance
Commercial Impossibility
Failure of third party
Self Induced impossibility
Failure of one of the Object
Strike Lockout
By Lapse of Time
By Operation of Law
Unauthorised Material alteration
Death
Insolvency
Merger
By Breach of Contract
Actual
Anticipatory

(3) ***By Attempted Performance or Tender***

A contract is said to be discharged by attempted performance when the promisor has made an offer of performance to the promisee but it has not been accepted by the promisee.

2. *Discharge by Agreement*

A contract may discharged by mutual agreement of the concerned parties. The rights and obligations created by an agreement can be discharged without their performance by means of another agreement between the parties which provides for the extinguishment of the earlier rights and obligations. As a contract is created by an agreement, in the same way, it can be discharged by an agreement, *i.e.*, by further consent to another contract. The consent may either be (*i*) Express or (*ii*) Implied.

(*i*) *Express Consent at the Time of Formation of Contract*

Example : A sells a machine to B on approval with the condition that if the machine does not work efficiently, B can return it within one week. B may return the machine within one week if the machine does not give satisfaction. Consent to return the machine is given to B at the time of the formation of the contract.

(*ii*) *Express Consent Subsequent to Formation of Contract*

Sections 62 and 63 deal with the express consent to contract :

"If the parties to a contract agree to substitute a new contract for it, or rescind or alter it, the original contract need not be performed." (Section 62).

"Every promisee may dispense with or remit, wholly or in part, the performance of the promise made to him, or may extend the time for such performance, or may accept instead of it any satisfaction which he thinks fit." (Section 63).

In other words, the original contract is discharged when the parties enter into a fresh contract in place of original contract. And the following are the important methods for the discharge of a contract by a fresh contract :

(1) Novation
(2) Rescission
(3) Alteration
(4) Remission
(5) Waiver
(6) Accord and Satisfaction
(7) Merger.

(1) ***Novation***

The term 'Novation' means substitution of a new contract for the existing one. The new contract may be between the same parties or between different parties. In other words, it is a transaction by which, with the consent of all parties concerned, the old contract is cancelled and substituted by a new contract. Discharge of the old contract is the consideration for the new contract. Novation implies a fresh contract in place of the old one. The new contract should be valid and enforceable. The novation may be of the following two types :

(*a*) *Novation Involving Change of Parties*

In this type, the parties to the contract are changed but the contract remains the same. The usual and most common form of novation is substituting a new debtor in place of an old one with the consent of the creditor.

Example : A is indebted to B and B to C. By mutual agreement B's debt to C and A's debt to B is cancelled and C accepts A as his debtor. This is novation.

(*b*) *Novation without changes of Parties*

Substitution of a contract may take place even without change of parties. That is, sometimes the concerned parties to a contract agree to substitute the existing contract for a new contract. In such situations the original contract is discharged and need not be performed.

Example : A owes B Rs. 10,000. A enters into an agreement with B and gives B a mortgage of his (A's) estate for Rs. 5,000 in place of the debt of Rs. 10,000. This is new contract and extinguishes the old.

Rules regarding '*Novation*' are as follows :

(*i*) Novation must be done before the expiry of the time of performance of the original contract.

(*ii*) It is possible only by mutual consent of the parties and may not be compulsory.

(*iii*) New contract replacing the old one must be capable of legal enforcement.

(*iv*) It must substitute the present contract. An agreement to substitute a contract in future will not be novation.

(*v*) As a result of novation, old contract is totally discharged and law does not entertain any action based upon the terms of the old contract.

Moreover, the new contract must also be valid and enforceable. If the new contract is not enforceable, the parties remain bound by the original contract.

Example : A owes B Rs. 1,000 under a contract, B owes C Rs. 1,000, B orders A to credit C with Rs. 1,000 in his books, but C does not assent to the arrangement. B still owes C Rs. 1,000 and no new contract has been entered into.

(2) ***Rescission***

Rescission means cancellation of the contract. While novation results in a new contract in place of the old one, rescission is the cancellation of the original contract. A contract may be discharged, before the date of performance, by agreement between the parties to the effect that it shall no longer bind them. Such an agreement amounts to "rescission" or cancellation of the contract, the consideration for mutual promises being the abandonment by the respective parties to their rights under the contract. An agreement of rescission releases the parties from their obligations arising out of the contract. A contract can be rescinded in any of the following ways :

Example : A promises to supply certain goods to B on a certain day. Before the actual date of performance A and B mutually agree that the contract will not be performed. The contract is rescinded.

Rescission may take place in any of the following modes:

(*i*) *By Mutual Consent*. Parties may enter into a simple agreement to rescind the contract before its breach.

(*ii*) *By the Aggrieved Party :* When any of the parties has committed a breach of contract, the aggrieved party can rescind the contract without, in any way, affecting the right to compensation from the breach of contract.

(*iii*) *By the Party whose Consent is not Free :* In case of a voidable contract, the party whose consent is not free, may rescind the contract, if it so desires.

(*iv*) *Non-performance till a long Time :* Where none of the parties has performed its part for a long time and no other party has objected against it, the contract may be taken as rescinded.

Rescission may either be total or partial. Former is the discharge of the whole contract, while the latter is the variation of the original contract either by :

(*a*) Rescinding some of the terms of the contract; or

(*b*) Substituting new terms for the ones which are rescinded; or

(*c*) Adding new terms without rescinding any of the terms of the original contract.

(3) *Alteration*

Alteration means a change in one or more of the material terms of the contract. The alteration is valid when it is made with the consent of all the parties. An alteration may either be material or immaterial. If a material alteration in a written contract is done by mutual consent, the original contract is discharged by alteration and the new contract in its altered form takes its place. A material alteration is one which alters the legal effect of the contract, for example, a change in the amount of money to be paid, the rate of interest, or the names of the parties. Immaterial alteration, for example, correcting a clerical error in figures or the spelling of a name, etc. has no effect on the validity of the contract and does not amount to alteration in the technical sense. If the parties mutually agree to change certain terms of the contract, it has the effect of terminating the original contract.

Although novation and alteration appear to be the same since, in both the cases, the terms of the contract are substantially *varied*, in the case of novation, there may be a change of the parties while in the case of alteration, the parties remain the same.

> **Example :** A enters into a contract with B for the supply of a machine at his warehouse on 1st February. Later both A and B agree to postpone the date of delivery to 1st March. This change amounts to alteration of the contract.

(4) *Remission*

Remission may be defined "as the acceptance of a lesser sum than what was contracted for or a lesser fulfillment of the promise made". According to Section 63 of the Act, "Every promisee may dispense with or remit, wholly or in part, the performance of the promise made to him, or may extend the time for such performance, or may accept instead of it any satisfaction which he thinks fit." It is a unilateral act of the promises discharging the obligation of the other party, either partly or wholly. Thus a contract may be discharged by remission of performance or extension of time or by the acceptance of any other satisfaction by the promisee.

> **Examples :** (1) A owes B Rs. 5,000. A pays to B who accepts in satisfaction of the whole debt Rs. 2,000 paid at the time and place at which the Rs. 5,000 were payable. The whole debt is discharged.
>
> (2) A owes B Rs. 5,000. C pays to B Rs. 1,000 and B accepts them in satisfaction of claim on A. This payment is a discharge whole claim.

Here the law differs from the English Law because in English Law every release must be either by deed or supported by consideration, whereas our Indian Law does not require consideration or a new agreement to support a remission of performance.

> **Example :** *Kapur Chand Godha Vs. Mir Nawab Himayat Ali Khan* (1963)
>
> In this case, the defendant was liable to pay Rs. 27 lakhs. His estate was taken over by a committee to administer it. The committee offered to pay Rs. 20 lakhs to the creditor in full satisfaction and he accepted the offer. But afterwards the creditor sued the debtor for the balance of Rs. 7 lakhs. The Supreme Court held the case is covered by Sec. 63 and he is not entitled to sue.

(5) *Waiver*

Waiver means the abandonment of a right which a person is entitled to. That is, waiver means abandoning the rights. Where a party waives his right under the contract, the other party is released of his obligations. A waiver is nothing unless it amounts to a release. To constitute a waiver neither an agreement nor consideration is necessary.

> **Example :** A agrees to repair the car of B. B later on forbids A to repair the car. A is no longer bound to perform the promise. Thus, the contract is terminated by waiver.

(6) *Merger*

Merger takes place when an inferior right accruing to a party, under a contract merges into a superior right accruing to the same party either under the same or the other contract. In such cases, the inferior rights merge into the superior rights. And on merger the inferior rights vanish and are not required to be enforced.

> **Example :** A purchases a house, which he was having on lease. His right as a lessee will merge into his right as an owner, as right of a lessee is inferior to the right of an owner.

(7) *Accord and Satisfaction*

These two terms are used in English Law. The term 'accord' may be defined as the promise to accept less amount than what is due under the contract. Satisfaction means the payment or fulfillment of the lesser obligation. Under the English Law, the old contract is discharged when the accord is followed by satisfaction. An accord is unenforceable, but an accord accompanied by satisfaction is valid and thereby discharges the obligation under the old contract. The old contract is discharged only when the less sum is actually paid and accepted by the promisee, *i.e.*, there must be actual performance of the new promise and its acceptance by the other party.

> **Example :** A owes B Rs. 1,000. B agrees to accept Rs. 500 in full satisfaction. This agreement is an accord and cannot be enforced. But when Rs. 500 are actually paid to B who accepts them in full satisfaction of his claim of Rs. 1,000, it is a valid discharge.

3. *Discharge by Impossibility of Performance*

A contract is discharged if its performance becomes impossible. In other words, there is no question of discharge of a contract which is entered into to perform something that is obviously impossible. For instance, an agreement to discover treasure by magic. In such cases, there is no contract to terminate. The impossibility in these cases is inherent in the transactions. Such a contract is void *ab-initio*. The impossibility of performance may be of two types :

(A) Initial Impossibility
(B) Subsequent Impossibility

(A) *Initial Impossibility* (Pre-contractual Impossibility)

It is the impossibility which exists at the time of formation of a contract. If an agreement contemplates doing something which is absolutely impossible, the same becomes void *ab initio*. The rule is based on the following two maxims :

(*a*) *Lex non cogit ad impossibilia est, i.e.*, the law does not recognise what is impossible; and
(*b*) *Impossibilium nulla obligatio est, i.e.*, what is impossible does not create an obligation.

1st para of Section 56 of the Indian Contract Act reads as under :

"An agreement to do an act impossible in itself, is void".

Thus parties are discharged as a void agreement does not create any rights and obligations on the contracting parties. The fact of impossibility may be (*i*) known to the parties or (*ii*) unknown to the parties. In both the cases the agreement is void.

If the initial impossibility is known to the promisor alone, he must pay compensation to the promisee for any loss which the promisee may suffer on account of non-performance of the contract. Para 3 of the Section 56 of the Indian Contract Act lays down :

"When one person has promised to do something, which he knew or with reasonable diligence, might have known, and which the promisee did not know to be impossible or unlawful, such promisor must make compensation to such promisee for any loss which such promisee sustains through the non-performance of the promise."

> **Example :** A contracts to marry B, being already married to C, and being forbidden by the law to which he is subject to practice polygamy. A must make compensation to B for the loss caused to her by the non-performance of his promise.

(B) *Subsequent (or Supervening) Impossibility*

Impossibility which arises subsequent to the formation of contract is known as subsequent or supervening impossibility. A contract, which at the time it was entered into, was capable of being performed may subsequently become impossible to perform or unlawful. Para 2 of Section 56 lays down that :

"A Contract to do an act which after the contract is made, becomes impossible, or, by reason of some event which the promisor could not prevent, unlawful becomes void when the act becomes impossible or unlawful."

> **Example :** A, contracts to take in cargo for B at a foreign port, A's Government afterwards declares war against the country in which the port is situated. The contract becomes void when war is declared.

A contract becomes void on the ground of subsequent impossibility only if the following conditions are satisfied:

(*i*) The act should have become impossible.

(*ii*) The impossibility should have been caused by circumstances which were beyond the control of the concerned parties.

(*iii*) The impossibility should not be self-induced by the promisor or due to his negligence.

Case where the doctrine of Supervening Impossibility Applies

Supervening impossibility may occur in many ways, some of which are explained below:

(1) *Destruction of Subject Matter*

When the subject-matter of a contract, subsequent to its formation, is destroyed, without the fault of the promisor or promisee, the contract is discharged. In the case, Taylor Vs. Caldwell (1863). Blackburn observed as follows: "In contracts in which the performance depends on the continued existence of a given person or thing, a condition is implied that the impossibility of performance arising from the perishing of the person or thing shall excuse the performance."

> **Examples :** (1) *Taylor Vs. Caldwell* (1863)
>
> A music hall was let for a series of concerts on certain days. The hall was burnt down before the date of the first concert. The contract becomes void.
>
> (2) *V.L. Narasu Vs. P.S.V Iyer* (1953)

There was an agreement between the owner of a theatre and a producer, to exhibit a picture. The municipal authority issued an order to demolish the theatre because it was unsafe. The owner of the theatre has no knowledge of the defective and unsafe nature of the building. In this case it was held that continued existence of the theatre was a fundamental basis of the contract and the demolition of the theatre discharged the contract because of supervening impossibility.

(2) *Death or Personal Incapacity*

A promise may become physically incapable of performance by reason of the death or incapacity of some person whose continued life and health are necessary for the performance of the contract. Such impossibility discharges the promisor from liability.

Example : *Robinson Vs. Davison* (1871)

An artist undertook to sing at a theatre on a particular day. On the day in question, the defendant was unable to perform owing to illness. It was held that the artist was not liable to damages.

(3) *Change of Law*

A contract is discharged by impossibility of performance by the subsequent change in the law. The parties are also excused from performing their obligations if the performance of the contract becomes impossible by delegated legislation of powers under an Act or delegated legislation. Impossibility created by law is a valid excuse for non-performance.

Example : *Re Shipton, Anderson & Co.* (1915)

A agreed to sell to B a specific quantity of wheat lying in his godown. Before the delivery could be made, the godown was sealed by the Government and it requisitioned the whole quantity of wheat under statutory powers. It was held that the contract is discharged as the delivery of the wheat became impossible.

(4) *Declaration of War*

A contract entered into before the commencement of war remains suspended during the war. However, such a contract may be revived and may be enforced at the end of the war. If the performance of the contract goes to help the enemy, it becomes void.

Example : A contracts to take in cargo for B at a foreign port. A's Government afterwards declares war against the country in which the port is situated. The contract becomes void when the war is declared.

(5) *Failure of Pre-condition*

When certain things necessary for performance cease to exist the contract becomes void on the ground of impossibility. If a contract depends on the occurrence of an event, which does not in fact happen the contract is discharged.

Example : *Krell Vs. Henry* (1903)

A contract was to hire a flat for viewing the coronation procession of the king. The procession had to be cancelled on account of king's illness. In a suit for the recovery of the rent, it was held that the contract become impossible of performance and that the hirer need not pay the rent.

Cases not Covered by Supervening Impossibility

"He who agrees to do an act must do it or pay damages for not doing it" is the general rule of the law of contract. Some of the circumstances in which a contract is not discharged on the ground of subsequent impossibility are stated below :

(1) *Difficulty of Performance*

A contract is not discharged by reason of the fact that the performance is more difficult, more expensive or more burdensome or less profitable than the parties anticipated. Difficulty does not excuse performance.

Example : *Blackburn Bobbin Co. Vs. Allen & Sons* (1918)

A sold B a certain quantity of Finland timber to be supplied between July and September. Before any timber was supplied war broke out in the month of August and transport was disorganised so that A could not bring any timber from Finland. It was held that the difficulty in getting the timber from Finland did not excuse A from performance.

(2) *Commercial Impossibility*

The impossibility contemplated in Section 56 is a physical and legal impossibility and not a commercial impossibility. Commercial impossibility means that the situation has so changed that if the contract is performed, it will result in a loss to the promisor. Such a situation may arise on account of higher price of raw materials, increase in wages, increase in taxes etc. Commercial impossibility does not discharge a contract.

> **Example :** *Karl Ettlinger Vs. Chagandas & Co.* (1915)
>
> The defendant agreed to supply goods to the plaintiff, to be sent from Bombay to Antwerp. Owing to the outbreak of war before the shipment there was a sharp increase in the shipping rates. When the defendant contended frustration, it was held that the increase in freight rates did not excuse performance.

(3) *Failure of a Third Party*

The doctrine of supervening impossibility does not cover cases where the contract could not be performed because of the impossibility created by the failure of a third person on whose work the promisor relied.

> **Example :** *Ganga Saran Vs. Ram Charan R Gopal* (1952)
>
> The respondent agreed to supply to the appellant 61 bales of cloth to be manufactured by the New Victoria Mills, Kanpur, "as soon as they are supplied to him by the said Mill". In a suit for damages for non-delivery of goods the defendant pleaded impossibility on the ground that the goods were not supplied to him by the Mill. Held, that the words "as soon as they are supplied to him by the Mill" simply indicate the process of delivery and did not convey the meaning that the delivery was contingent on their being supplied by the Mill. Hence the case did not fall within the provisions of Sections 32 and 56 as the default was due to the fault of the defendant.

(4) *Self Induced Impossibility*

When the impossibility is due to the default of the contracting party himself, Section 56 would not apply. In such cases, the contract is not discharged on the ground of frustration. That is, a contract is not discharged in case of self-induced impossibility.

(5) *Failure of one of the Several Objects*

When a contract is entered into for several objects, failure of one of the objects does not terminate the contract. That is, when the contract is for multiple objects, failure of any one or more of them does not make the contract discharged.

> **Example :** *Herne Bay Steamboat Co. Vs. Hutton* (1903)
>
> X agreed to let out a boat to Y for the purpose of viewing a naval review to be held on the occasion of the Coronation of Edward VII and to cruise round the fleet. Owing to the King's illness the naval review was abandoned but the fleet was assembled and the beat could have been used to cruise round the fleet. Held the contract was not terminated.

(6) *Strikes, Lockouts and Civil Disturbances :*

These events do not discharge a party from performing his part of the contract unless there is a clause in the contract providing that in such cases the contract is not to be performed or that the time of performance is to be extended.

> **Example :** *Jacobs Vs. Credit Lyonnais* (1884)
>
> A agreed to supply B certain goods to be produced in Algeria. The goods could not be produced because of riots and civil disturbances in that country. Held, there was no excuse for non-performance of the contract.

THE EFFECTS OF SUPERVENING IMPOSSIBILITY

(1) Contract becomes Void

According to Para 1 of Section 56, "an agreement to do an act impossible in itself is void.".

According to Para 2 of Section 56, "A contract to do an act which after the contract is made, becomes impossible, or, by reason of some event which the promisor could not prevent, unlawful becomes void when the act becomes impossible or unlawful.

(2) Benefits to be Restored

Section 65 provides that "When an agreement is discovered to be void or when a contract becomes void, any person who has received any advantage under such agreement or contract is bound to restore it, or to make compensation for it, to the person from whom he received it."

(3) Compensation for Non-performance

Section 56, Para 3 provides that "When one person has promised to do something, which he knew or with reasonable diligence might have known, and which the promisee did not know to be impossible or unlawful, such promisor must make compensation to such promisee for any loss which such promisee sustains through the non-performance of the promise."

> **Example :** A pays B Rs. 1,000 in consideration of B's promising to marry C, A's daughter. C dies before marriage. B must repay A Rs. 1,000.

Doctrine of Frustration

In England before 1863 it was the law that everyone was absolutely bound to perform any obligation which he had undertaken to perform and could not claim to be excused on the ground that the performance subsequently became impossible. Even today in many cases the following observation is kept in view :

"When the party by his own contract creates a duty or charge upon himself, he is bound to make it good, if he may, notwithstanding any accident by inevitable necessity, because he might have provided against it by his contract." (Paradine Vs. Jane).

> **Example :** *Paradine Vs. Jane* (1647)
>
> A person J got a lease of land from P on a rental basis, Then a German Prince seized the land and it was not possible for J to use it. The landlord P sued for rent. The Court held that J must carry out all the terms on the contract including the payment of rent.

However, the parties may, be express or implied provisions in the contract, excuse one or both of them from performing their respective obligations under the contract, on the fulfilment of a condition or on the occurrence of an event. So from the contract it may be interpreted by the courts as containing such a provision by implication. This principle was first introduced by the court in the case of Taylor Vs. Caldwell (1863).

> *Taylor Vs. Caldwell* (1863)
>
> In this case, the defendant agreed to let a music hall for series of concerts. Before the day of performance, the music hall was destroyed by fire without the fault of either party. It was held that on the destruction of the music hall the contract became void as its performance depended upon the continued existence of the music hall. The court observed that the contract was subject to an implied condition that the parties shall be excused from performance, before breach, the performance becomes impossible from the perishing of thing without default of the parties. The performance of the contract had become physically impossible because of the destruction of the subject-matter (music hall) of contract.

The term 'frustration' is the concept used in English Law which is the parallel concept of supervening impossibility. When the common object of a contract can no longer be carried out, the court may declare the contract to be at an end. This is known as 'Doctrine of Frustration'. Anson says : "Most legal systems make provision for the discharge of a contract where, subsequent to its formation, a change of circumstances renders the contract legally or physically impossible of performance."

The following observation of Supreme Court is worth noting in this regard :

"The view that Section 56 applies only to cases of physical impossibility and that where this section is not applicable recourse can be had to principles of English Law on the subject, is not correct. Section 56 lays down a rule of positive law and does not leave the matter to be determined according to the intention of the parties. The impossibility contemplated is not confined to something not humanly possible. If the performance of contract becomes impracticable or useless having regard to the object and purpose the parties had in view, then it must be held that performance of the contract had become impossible. But the supervening events should take away the basis of the contract and it should be of such a character that it strikes at the root of the contract"

Example : *Satyabrate Ghose Vs. Mugneeram Bangur & Co.* (1954)

An agreement was entered into for the sale of land subject to the condition that the seller would do some development work on the land. Before the work could be completed the land was requisitioned by the Government for war purposes. Held, the contract was not frustrated.

The Supreme Court held that, "In our opinion, the events which have happened here cannot be said to have made the performance of the contract impossible and the contract has not been frustrated at all" by making the observation that, "when there is no time limit whatsoever in the contract, nor even an understanding between the parties on that point, and when during the war the parties could naturally anticipate restrictions of various kinds, which would make the carrying on of these operations more tardy and difficult than in times of peace, we do not think that the order of requisition affected the fundamental basis upon which the Government rested or struck at the roots of the adventure.

4. Discharge by Lapse of Time

A contract is discharged by lapse of time. The Limitation Act 1940 lays down that in case of breach of a contract legal action should be taken within a specified period. If it is not performed and if no action is taken by the promisee in the Court of Law within the specified period, he is debarred from enforcing the contract. Lapse of time terminates a contract. The period of limitation for simple contract is three years. If the three years expire and creditors fails to file a suit to recover his amount, the debtor is discharged from his liability.

5. Discharge by Operation of Law

Following are the circumstances under which the law regards the contract as discharged :

(1) *Unauthorised Material Alteration*

A material alteration made in a written document or contract by one party without the consent of the other, will make the whole contract void. An alteration which is not material or which is authorised will not affect the validity of the contract. A material alteration is one which changes, in a significant manner, the legal identity or character of the contract or the right and liabilities of the parties to the contract. The effect of making such an alteration is exactly the same as that of cancelling the contract. Both parties will be discharged from their respective obligations.

(2) *Death*

Death of the promisor results in termination of the contract in cases involving personal skill or ability. In other cases, the rights and liabilities of the deceased person pass on to the legal representatives.

(3) *Insolvency*

A contract is discharged by the insolvency of one of the parties to it when an Insolvency Court passes an "order of discharge" exonerating the insolvent from liabilities on debts incurred prior to his adjudication.

(4) *Merger*

This has been explained in page 130.

6. Discharge by Breach of Contract

The 'breach of contract' means the failure of a party to perform his obligations. The party who fails to perform his obligations, is said to have committed a breach of contract. Breach is also a method of discharge of a contract. A breach of a contract discharges the aggrieved party from performing his obligations. Breach of contract may either be (*i*) Actual Breach of Contract or (*ii*) Anticipatory Breach of Contract.

(*i*) *Actual Breach of Contract*

Actual breach may take place (*a*) at the time when the performance is due, or (*b*) during the performance of the contract.

(*a*) *Actual Breach of Contract, at the Time when the Performance is Due*

Actual breach of contract occurs at the time when the performance is due, when one party fails or refuses to perform his obligation under the contract. For example, where on the appointed day the seller does not deliver the goods or the buyer refuses to accept the delivery. If the time was the essence of the contract, the failure to perform the contract within the specified time results in breach of the contract. And if the time was not the essence of the contract, the other party may accept performance and claim compensation for delayed performance. This point has been discussed in previous chapter.

Example : A agrees to deliver 5 bags of sugar to B on 1st July, but fails to do so on that date, he is said to have committed a breach of contract. Similarly, on 1st July A tenders the sugar but B, for no valid reason, refuses to accept them, B becomes guilty of breach.

(*b*) *Actual Breach during the Performance of the Contract*

It occurs when one party fails or refuses to perform the obligation under the contract during the performance of the contract. It is an actual breach of contract during its performance. Refusal of performance may be express or implied. This type of breach of contract occurs in the case of instalment contracts such as, sale of goods, delivery by installments, payment by instalments etc.

Example : *Cort Vs. Ambergate Railway Co.* (1851)

The plaintiff contracted to supply to the defendant Co. 3,900 tons of railway chairs at a certain price. After 1,787 tons had been delivered the company told him that no more will be required. This is a breach of contract by the company.

(*ii*) *Anticipatory Breach of Contract*

It occurs when a party repudiates his obligation under the contract before the time for performance arrives. It is a declaration by one party of his intention not to perform his obligation under the contract. In other words, a refusal by the promisor to perform his part of the contract, before the due date of performance is known as the anticipatory breach of contract.

Section 39 of Indian Contract Act lays down "When a party to the contract (*i*) has refused to perform or (*ii*) disabled himself from performing the contract, (*iii*) in its entirety, the promisee may put an end to the contract, (*iv*) unless he had signified by words or conduct, his acquiescence in its continuance."

In simple words, when the promisor, prior to the due date of performance, altogether refuses to perform his obligations under the contract or disables himself from doing so, there occurs a breach of contract.

The promisee can choose one of the following rights :

(*a*) He can treat the contract as broken and put an end to it on that ground. In such a case he is entitled to claim damages against the other party as on breach of the whole agreement.

(*b*) He is at liberty to keep the contract alive, accept performance of it if made by the other party and claim damages for the part not performed. This is called waiving the breach or acquiescing in the continuance of the contract even after its breach by the other side.

Examples : A, a singer, enters into a contract with B, the manager of a theatre, to sing at his theatre two nights in every week during the next two months, and B engages to pay her Rs. 100 for each night's performance. On the sixth night A wilfully absents herself from the theatre. B is at liberty to put an end to the contract.

Example : A, singer, enters into a contract with B, the manager of a theatre, to sing at his theatre two nights, every week during the next two months, and B engages to pay her at the rate of Rs. 100 for each night. On the sixth night A wilfully absents herself. With the assent of B, A sings on the seventh night. B has signified his acquiescence in the continuance of the contract and cannot now put an end to it but he is entitled to compensation for the damage sustained by him through A's failure to sing on the sixth night.

The anticipatory breach may take place either by express refusal to perform the contract or by some act of the promisor, which makes the performance impossible. In other words, it may be (*i*) express or (*ii*) implied anticipatory breach.

(*i*) *Express Repudiation or Renunciation :* It takes place when one party renunciates his liability under the contract expressly, before the performance becomes due.

Example : A agreed to supply certain goods to B on 1st January. But before this date, A expressly informed B that he would not supply the goods to him. This is an anticipatory breach of contract by express refusal to perform it.

(*ii*) *Implied Repudiation or by Creating Impossibility :* A promisor may before the time of performance arrives, by doing some act, make the performance of the contract impossible. It discharges the contract.

Example : A agreed to marry B. But before the agreed date of marriage, A married C. This is anticipatory breach of contract by A's conduct which has made the performance impossible.

Consequence of Anticipatory Breach

When anticipatory breach occurs, the aggrieved party can take the following steps :

(*i*) He can treat the contract as discharged, so that he is no longer bound by any obligations under the contract; and

(*ii*) He can immediately adopt the legal remedies available to him for breach of contract, *viz.*, file a suit for damages or specific performance or injunction.

Examples : (1) *Avery Vs. Bowden* (1856)

B chartered A's ship agreeing to load cargo within 45 days. However, on arrival of the ship, B showed his inability to load cargo. A however, did not treat the repudiation as immediate breach of contract and chose to wait till 45 days, Before expiry of 45 days, war broke out which rendered performance illegal. It was held that A could not succeed as contract had ended by frustration and not by breach.

(2) *Hochester Vs. De La Tour* (1853)

The defendant agreed on 12th April, to employ the plaintiff as his courier and to accompany him upon a tour. The employment was to commence on Ist June. On 11th May, he wrote to the plaintiff that he had changed his mind, and hence, would not require a courier. The plaintiff sued for damages before 1st June and succeeded. Lord Campbell observed that, "it cannot be laid down as a universal rule that, whereby an agreement an act is to be done on a future day, no action can be brought for a breach of the agreement till the day for doing the act has arrived".

(3) *Frost Vs. Knight* (1872)

The defendant promised to marry the plaintiff upon his father's death; but during his father life time he renounced the contract. Held, the plaintiff was entitled to sue without waiting the father's death.

THEORETICAL QUESTIONS

1. What do you mean by discharge of contract? Discuss the various modes by which it may be discharged.
2. What do you understand by impossibility of performance?
3. Impossibility of performance is, as a rule not an excuse for non-performance of a contract. Discuss.
4. Distinguish between actual breach and anticipatory breach of contract.
5. Discuss the effect of supervening impossibility on the performance of a contract.
6. What is discharge by frustration?
7. Explain the position of aggrieved party in case of anticipatory breach of contract.
8. What do you understand by novation? What is the difference between alteration and novation?
9. Discuss the doctrine of frustration and its applicability with reference to the provisions of Indian Contract Act.
10. When does a contract terminate by operation of law?
11. Discuss the 'novation' and 'rescission' as a mode of discharge of contract giving suitable examples. What is the difference between the two. (*M.Com. Delhi*)
12. What do you understand by breach of contract? Discuss in detail giving suitable examples. (*M.Com. Agra*)
13. Explain the position of aggrieved party in case of anticipatory breach of contract. (*M.Com. MS*)
14. What do you understand by the doctrine of quantum meruit? State the cases in which a claim for quantum meruit arises. (*M.Com. Delhi*)
15. Does an impossibility which arises subsequent to the formation of a contract excuse the promisor from performing the contract in all cases?

MULTIPLE CHOICE QUESTIONS

I. Choose correct option for each of the following :

1. **A contract is discharged :**
   (*a*) when all the parties perform their promises.
   (*b*) when performance of contract becomes impossible.
   (*c*) when one party makes a breach of contract.
   (*d*) in all of the above cases.
2. **A contract is said to be discharged by rescission :**
   (*a*) when parties to a contract are changed.
   (*b*) when terms of a contract are altered.
   (*c*) when an aggrieved party exercises his option to avoid the contract.
   (*d*) when a party to a contract waives his rights under the contract.
3. **Discharge of Contract means :**
   (*a*) Performing the promise by a party.
   (*b*) discharge of obligations under a contract by a party.
   (*c*) discharge or performance of obligations under a contract by a party to it.
   (*d*) performing or extinguishing obligations under a contract by all the parties.

4. A party stands discharged from his liability under a contract :
(*a*) when the party performs the promise.
(*b*) when other party waives his rights.
(*c*) when the party dies and the contract involves personal skill.
(*d*) in all of the above cases.

5. When a party to a contract refuses to perform the contract before the date of performance, it is called :
(*a*) actual breach of contract.
(*b*) express breach of contract.
(*c*) anticipatory breach of contract.
(*d*) frustration of contract.

6. A contract is discharged by alteration :
(*a*) when a new contract is substituted for the existing one.
(*b*) when one or more of the terms of contract are changed.
(*c*) when a party waives his rights under the contract.
(*d*) when a party rescinds the contract.

7. A contract is discharged by remission :
(*a*) when a party waives all his rights under a contract.
(*b*) when a party cancels an existing contract.
(*c*) when a party accepts lesser performance in discharge of a whole obligation.
(*d*) when a party makes novation of a contract..

8. A contract is discharged by impossibility of performance :
(*a*) when impossibility existed at the time of formation of contract.
(*b*) when impossibility arises after making a contract.
(*c*) when impossibility of performance was known to both the parties at the time of making the contract.
(*d*) both (*a*) and (*c*).

9. A contract is said to have been frustrated :
(*a*) when subject-matter of the contract is destroyed after making the contract.
(*b*) when some commercial hardship arises.
(*c*) when workers go on strike.
(*d*) when the performance of contract becomes very difficult.

10. Where a contract could not be performed because of the default by a third person on whose work the promisor relied, it :
(*a*) is not discharged.
(*b*) becomes void.
(*c*) is discharged.
(*d*) becomes voidable.

11. Agreement does not become void where initial impossibility is :
(*a*) known to both the parties.
(*b*) to promisor only.
(*c*) unknown to both the parties.
(*d*) none of these.

12. Impossibility which does not exist at the time of making the contract but which arises subsequently after the formation of the contract is called :
(*a*) Initial Impossibility.
(*b*) Supervening Impossibility.
(*c*) None of these.

13. A contract is discharged by breach when a party to a contract :
(*a*) refuses to perform his promise.
(*b*) fails to perform his promise.
(*c*) disables himself from performing his part of the promise.
(*d*) does any of the above.

14. In case of anticipatory breach of contract, the aggrieved party has the option :
(*a*) to treat the contract as discharged.
(*b*) to treat the contract as breached and file a suit against the party for breach of contract.
(*c*) to treat the contract alive and wait for performance till the agreed date of performance.
(*d*) either (*b*) or (*c*) above.

15. A contract is discharged by novation :
(*a*) when a new contract is substituted in place of an existing one.
(*b*) when an existing contract is rescinded.
(*c*) when some of the conditions of the contract are changed.
(*d*) when all the parties to the contract are changed.

16. Acceptance by the promisee of a lesser fulfillment of the promise made is called:
(*a*) Alteration. (*b*) Rescission.
(*c*) Waiver. (*d*) Remission.

17. Where the performance of a contract becomes subsequently impossible or unlawful, the contract becomes:
(*a*) Illegal. (*b*) Voidable.
(*c*) Void. (*d*) None of these.

18. In case the goods are sold on credit, a debt is discharged by lapse of time if debt is not recovered within :
(*a*) 3 years from the date of grant of credit. (*b*) 3 years from the date of expiry of credit period.
(*c*) 12 years from the date of expiry of credit period.
(*d*) none of these.

19. A contract has become more difficult to performance due to some uncontemplated events or delays. The contract :
(*a*) is discharged. (*b*) becomes void.
(*c*) is not discharged. (*d*) becomes voidable.

20. Mr. X lends Rs 10,000 to Mr. Y. He later tells Y that he need not repay the amount, the contract is discharged by :
(*a*) breach. (*b*) novation.
(*c*) waiver. (*d*) performance.

21. X undertakes to paint a picture for Y. He dies before he paints the picture. The contract :
(*a*) is discharged by death.
(*b*) becomes voidable at the option of Y.
(*c*) becomes voidable at the option of the legal representatives of X.
(*d*) will have to be performed by the legal representatives of X.

22. A creditor agrees with his debtor and a third party to accept that third party as his debtor. The contract is discharged by :
(*a*) performance. (*b*) waiver.
(*c*) rescission. (*d*) alteration.

23. If an agreement contains an undertaking to perform an impossibility, the agreement is :
(*a*) void ab *initio*. (*b*) void.
(*c*) voidable at the option of the plaintiff. (*d*) illegal.

24. An agreement to do an act impossible in itself :
(*a*) is void. (*b*) is voidable.
(*c*) is void *ab initio*. (*d*) becomes void when impossibility is discovered.

25. Discharge of contract by anticipatory breach of contract takes place :
(*a*) when the performance is due.
(*b*) before the performance is due.
(*c*) when any party has performed a part of the contract and then refuses or fails to perform the remaining part of the contract.
(*d*) none of these.

ANSWERS

1. (*d*) **2.** (*c*) **3.** (*d*) **4.** (*d*) **5.** (*c*) **6.** (*b*) **7.** (*c*) **8.** (*b*) **9.** (*a*) **10.** (*a*)
11. (*b*) **12.** (*c*) **13.** (*d*) **14.** (*d*) **15.** (*a*) **16.** (*d*) **17.** (*c*) **18.** (*b*) **19.** (*c*) **20.** (*c*)
21. (*a*) **22.** (*b*) **23.** (*a*) **24.** (*a*) **25.** (*b*)

CHAPTER

Remedies for Breach of Contract

(Sections 73–75)

AT A GLANCE

- Introduction
- Suit for Rescission
- Suit for Damages
- Kinds of Damages
- Rules regarding Damages
- Liquidated Damage and Penalty
- English Law on Penalty
- Indian Law
- Stipulation Regarding payment of Interest
- Suit upon Quantum Meruit
- Suit for Specific Performance
- Suit for Injunction
- Theoretical Questions
- Multiple Choice Questions.

INTRODUCTION

Parties to a lawful contract are expected to perform their respective promises. When one of the parties refuses to perform his promise, he is said to have committed *a breach of the contract*. Whenever there is breach of contract, the injured or the aggrieved party is entitled to bring an action for damages. A right of action is conferred upon the party injured. In some circumstances, the breach not only gives rise to a cause of action but will also discharge the injured party from performance of his part of the agreement. In case of breach, the aggrieved or injured party has one or more of the following remedies :

I. Suit for Rescission
II. Suit for Damages
III. Suit upon Quantum Meruit
IV. Suit for Specific Performance
V. Suit for Injunction

I. SUIT FOR RESCISSION

Rescission means setting aside or cancelling. In other words, the term 'rescission' may be defined as the cancellation of the contract. When a contract is broken by one party, the other party may treat the breach as discharge and refuse to perform his part of the contract, *i.e.*, putting an end to the contract. On the rescission of the contract, the aggrieved or injured party is discharged from all the obligations under the contract.

> **Example :** A promises B to sell his car for Rs. 60,000 on certain date. B agreed to pay the price on receipt of the car. A refused to sell his car to B. B need not pay the price.

According to Section 75 of the Indian Contract Act, "A person who rightly rescinds a contract is entitled to compensation for any damage which he has sustained through the non-fulfillment of the contract."

Example : A, a singer, contracts with B, the manager of a theatre, to sing at his theatre, for two nights in every week during the next two months, and B engages to pay her Rs. 100 for each night's performance. On the sixth night A wilfully absents herself from the theatre, and B in consequence, rescinds the contract. B is entitled to claim compensation for the damage which he has sustained through the non-fulfillment of the contract.

Section 66 of the Contract Act provides that such rescission may be communicated in the same manner as the communication of revocation of a proposal. A party on rescinding a contract is bound to restore the advantage he has received under the contract.

Power of the Court (Section 27 of the Specific Relief Act 1963)

When is Rescission Granted?

The court may grant rescission of the contract :

(*a*) Where the contract is voidable or terminable by the plaintiff;

(*b*) Where the contract is unlawful for causes apparent on its face and the defendant is more to blame than the plaintiff.

When is Rescission Refused?

The court may refuse to grant rescission of the contract :

(*a*) Where the plaintiff has expressly or impliedly ratified the contract; or

(*b*) Where owing to the change of circumstances, the parties cannot be restored to their original positions; or

(*c*) Where third parties have, during the subsistence of the contract acquired rights in good faith and for value; or

(*d*) Where only a part of the contract is sought to be rescinded and such part is not severable from the rest of the contract.

II. SUIT FOR DAMAGES

The damages are a monetary compensation allowed to the injured party for the loss or injury suffered by him as a result of the breach of contract. In the event of a breach of contract, the other party earns certain rights including the right to claim damages or loss arising therefrom. The object of awarding is to put the aggrieved party in the same position, has the contract been performed. The term 'damages' is used to mean compensation in money as a substitute for the promised performance. The fundamental principle underlying damages is not punishment but compensation. Damages are to be awarded for losses which naturally arose from the breach. The law of contract does not seek to punish the guilty. The guilty party is liable to pay damages to the aggrieved party. The court will compel the party in breach to make good the loss by paying to the other party.

KINDS OF DAMAGES

Damages are of the following kinds :

(1) Ordinary or General or Compensatory Damages

(2) Special Damages

(3) Exemplary or Punitive or Vindictive Damages

(4) Nominal Damages

1. ***Ordinary or General or Compensatory Damages***

Ordinary damages are those which naturally arose in the usual course of things from such breach. Damages, awarded to compensate the injured party for the actual amount of loss suffered by him consequent upon the breach, are known as general damages. General damages are usually assessed on the basis of actual loss. The measure of ordinary damage is the difference between the contract price and market price at the date of breach.

Example : A contracts to deliver 100 bags of rice at Rs. 1,000 a bag on a future date. On the due date he refuses to deliver. The price on that day is Rs. 1,100 per bag. The measure of damages is the difference between the market price on the date of breach and the contract price *i.e.*, Rs. 10,000 (100 × Rs. 100).

In a contract of sale of goods, the damages are measured equal to the profits *i.e.*, the difference between the contract price and market price of such goods on the date of breach. Section 73 provides that compensation for any remote or indirect loss or damage by reason of breach shall not be claimable.

Example : A contracts to sell and deliver 500 bales of cotton to B on a fixed day. A knows nothing of B's mode of business. A breaks his promise, and B having no cotton, is obliged to close his mill. A is not responsible to B for the loss caused to B by the closing of the mill. (However, B can claim damages for the breach of contract. He cannot claim the loss of profit caused by the closing of the mill because it cannot be considered to have been in contemplation of both the parties when they made the contract and thus is a remote consequence of the breach).

2. *Special Damages*

Special damages are those resulting from a breach of contract under some special or unusual circumstances. These damages constitute the indirect loss suffered by the injured party due to the breach of contract. These are the damages which parties knew, when they made the contract, as likely to arise from the breach of the contract. When there are certain special or extraordinary circumstances present and their existence is communicated to the promisor, the non-performance of the promise entitles to the promisee to not only the ordinary damages but also special damages that may result therefrom. It is important to note that notice to this effect must have been given to the other party. If he had no knowledge, he is not answerable. Subsequent knowledge of special circumstances will not create any special liability on the guilty party.

Example : A builder, contracts to erect and finish a house by first of January, in order that B may give possession of it at that time to C, to whom B has contracted to let it. A is informed of the contract between B and C. A builds the house so badly that, before the first January, it falls down and has to be rebuilt by B, who, in consequence, loses the rent which he was to have received from C and is obliged to make compensation to C for the breach of his contract. A must make compensation to B for the cost of *rebuilding* the house, for *the rent lost*, and for *the compensation made to* C.

3. *Exemplary or Punitive or Vindictive Damages*

These are such damages which are awarded by way of compensation for the loss suffered and not by way of punishment. Exemplary damages are granted for injured feeling, sufferings etc. Where courts take into account the feelings of the aggrieved party, exemplary damages may be ordered. Exemplary damages have no place in the law of contract and are not recoverable for a breach of contract. But there are two exceptions :

(*a*) *Breach of a contract to marry* : In this case the amount of the damages will depend upon the extent of injury to the party's feelings, one may be ruined, other may not mind so much.

(*b*) *Dishonour of a cheque by a banker when there are sufficient funds to the credit of the customer* : In this case the rule of ascertaining damages is, "the smaller the cheque, the greater the damage". Of course, the actual amount of damages will differ according to the status of the party.

4. *Nominal Damages*

These are the damages which are very small in amount. In some cases there may be a breach of contract but no material loss would have been caused thereby. Thus nominal damages are awarded only for the name sake. Nominal damages are awarded simply to recognise the right of the party to claim damages of the breach of the contract even though the party suffered no loss.

Rules Regarding Damages

According to Section 73 of the Indian Contract Act, "When a contract has been broken, the party who suffers by such branch is entitled to receive from the party who has broken the contract, compensation for any loss or damage caused to him thereby, which naturally arose in the usual course of thing from such breach, or which the parties knew, when they made the contract, to be likely to result from the breach of it".

"Such compensation is not to be given for any remote and indirect loss or damage sustained by reason of the breach".

The leading case of Hadley Vs. Baxendale, which is said to be the foundation of modern law of damages in England and India. Section 73 of the Indian Contract Act dealing with the principles regarding the measures of damages is based on the decision given in Hadley Vs. Baxendale. The fact of the case is as follows :

Hadley Vs. Baxendale (1854)

The plaintiffs were engaged in milling business at Gloucester. The mill was stopped owing to the breakage of a crank shaft, which was the only one they had. They ordered a replacement from a firm Greenwich. The engineers at Greenwich asked for the defective shaft to be sent to them as a pattern to make a new one. The shaft was entrusted to the defendant, a common carriers, for taking it to a manufacturer at Greenwich to be used as a model for the manufacture of a new one. The defendant was informed that it must be delivered immediately. There was a delay due to negligence on the part of the carriers and in consequence, the plaintiffs received the new shaft only after a long delay. During the interval, the mill remained idle and the plaintiffs lost the profits which might have been made if the factory was working.

The plaintiffs bought a suit for damages not only for the delay in the delivery of shaft but also for the loss of profits suffered by the mill for not having been worked. Held that plaintiffs were entitled only to ordinary damages. And the defendant was not liable for the loss of profits caused by the stoppage of the mill during the period of additional delay due to defendant's negligence as defendant was not told the existence of special circumstance.

In this case, the following observations of Justice Alderson are worth noting :

"When two parties have made a contract which one of them has broken, the damages which the other party ought to receive in respect of such breach of contract should be such as may fairly and reasonably be considered either arising naturally, *i.e.*, according to the usual course of things, from such breach of contract itself, or such as may reasonably be supposed to have been in the contemplation of both at the time they made the contract, as the probable result of the breach of it."

On the basis of the decision, the following two rules were laid down :

(*a*) The damages which arise naturally in the usual course, from the breach itself, *i.e.*, the general damages, are recoverable.

(*b*) The damages which arise due to unusual circumstances (special damages) are recoverable only if the special circumstance are brought to the knowledge of the defaulting party.

Example : *Madras Railway Co. Vs. Govinda Ram* (1898)

Govinda Ram was a tailor and he delivered a sewing machine and a cloth bundle to the defendant company to be carried to a place where he expected to carry on his business and make large profits on the occasion of a festival to be held at that place. Owing to the fault of the defendant's servants, there was a delay in transit and the goods were not delivered till after the conclusion of the festival. The plaintiff claimed as damages the expenses of staying there and the loss of profits which he would have earned at the festival. It was held that the damages claimed were too remote. Moreover, the special circumstances were not brought to the knowledge of the Railway Company.

Explanation to Section 73 provides that, "In estimating the loss or damage arising from a breach of contract, the means which existed of remedying the inconvenience caused by non-performance of the contract must be taken into account" The principles regarding the measure of damages is based on the decision given in *Hadley Vs. Baxendale.*

The rules may now be summarised as follows :

1. *General Damages*

A party who suffers by breach of a contract is entitled to only such damages which arise naturally in the usual course of things as a result of such breach. Rest of the damages will be deemed to be a remote consequence and are not recoverable.

> **Example :** A agreed to sell B two bales of cotton at Rs. 1,000 per bale, the delivery to be given on 15th January. A failed to give delivery. The remedy for B would be to claim the difference between the market price and the contract price for the same quality of cotton in case the market price is higher than the contract price.

2. *Special Damages*

Special damages are recoverable only if the special circumstances were brought to the notice of the defaulting party. That is, where a party claims special damage for any loss sustained he must prove that the other party knew at the time of the making of the contract that special loss was likely to result from the breach of the contract.

> **Example :** *Pinnock Bros. Vs. Lewis & Peat Ltd.* (1923)
>
> P bought from L some copra cake. P sold the cake to B, who sold it to various dealers who in turn sold it to farmers, who used it for feeding cattle. The copra cake was poisonous and the cattle fed on it died. The various buyers filed suits against P and obtained damages. P claimed from L damages and costs he had to pay. Held, as it was within the contemplation of the parties that the copra cake was to be used for feeding cattle. L was liable to pay damages.

3. Remote Damages

The second para of Section 73 states that "Such compensation is not to be given for any remote and indirect loss or damage sustained by reason of the breach". The remote or indirect damages are not due to natural and probable consequences of the breach of the contract. In other words, these are the damages which arise indirectly from the breach. The injured party is not entitled to any remote or indirect loss.

> **Example :** *Hobbs Vs. London & S.W. Railway Co.* (1875)
>
> Mr. Hobbs and family travelled from Hampden to Wimbledon. But the train went in wrong direction and the family had to get down at a place, where there was no conveyance and no place to stay. The result that they had to walk home several miles at midnight on drizzling night. Mrs. Hobbs got ill. Mr. Hobbs filed a suit (*i*) for damages for inconvenience and (*ii*) also damages for wife's illness. The court awarded damages in respect of the first claim. But the second claim did not arise in the usual course of things and was too remote a consequence.

4. *Restitution and Compensation*

Damages are paid as restitution and compensation and not as punishment. In fact through damages, efforts are made to put the party back into the same position as if the contract had been performed. In other words, "If a contract is broken, law will endeavour, so far as money can do it, to place the injured party in the same position as if the contract had been performed".

> **Example :** In a contract of sale of goods, the damages are measured equal to the profits, *i.e.*, the difference between the contract price and market price of such goods on the date of breach.

5. *Mitigation of Loss*

The injured party has to take all reasonable steps to minimise the loss caused by the breach. Explanation to Section 73 of the Indian Contract Act reads as under :

"In estimating the loss or damage arising from a breach of contract, the means which existed of remedying the inconvenience caused by the non-performance of the contract must be taken into account".

The loss caused by the breach must be kept to the minimum. The damages which results due to the negligence of the aggrieved party, are not recoverable.

> **Example :** *Neki Vs. Prabhu*
>
> The plaintiff took a shop on lease and paid an advance. The defendant could not give him possession and the plaintiff chose to do no business for 8 months though there were other shops available in the vicinity. Held, he was entitled only to a refund of his advance, and nothing more, as he had failed in his duty to minimise the loss by not taking another shop in the neighbourhood.

6. *Nominal Damages*

Nominal damages are small amounts awarded by the court when the aggrieved party cannot prove any substantial loss suffered by him. These are neither awarded by way of compensation to the aggrieved party nor by way of punishment to the guilty party. For instance if the contract price is Rs. 10 and after a breach the party obtained the goods from the market also for Rs. 10, he may get only nominal damages for his worries and inconvenience.

7. *Actual Loss (Actual Damages)*

Ordinarily, the aggrieved party is entitled to recovery by way of compensation, only the actual loss suffered by him.

In a breach of contract for the sale of goods, the damages payable would be the difference between the contract price and the market price at the date the breach takes place.

8. *Vindictive or Exemplary Damages*

Vindictive or exemplary damages are not usually awarded for breach of contract except in case of breach of contract of marriage or wrongful refusal by the bank to honour the customer's cheque. Such damages are awarded by way of lesson to the wrongdoer.

9. *Liquidated Damage*

When the parties to a contract mutually agree that in the event of a breach the one shall pay to the other a specified sum of money, called liquidated damage. When such an amount has been mentioned in the contract, under Sec. 74 of the Indian Contract Act, the injured party is entitled to get reasonable compensation not exceeding the amount mentioned.

> **Example :** A contract with B to pay B Rs. 1,000 if he fails to pay B Rs. 500 on a given day. A fails to pay B Rs. 500 on that day. B is entitled to recover from A such compensation not exceeding Rs. 1,000 as the Court considers reasonable.

10. *Damages in Quasi Contracts*

According to Section 73, para 3, "When an obligation resembling those created by contract has been incurred and has not been discharged, any person injured by the failure to discharge it is entitled to receive the same compensation from the party in default, as if such person had contracted to discharge it and had broken his contract."

Explanation : "In estimating the loss or damage arising from a breach of contract, the means which existed of remedying the inconvenience caused by the non-performance of the contract must be taken into account". (Refer Chapter – Quasi Contract)

11. ***Difficulty of Assessment***

Difficulty in calculating damages is no ground for refusing damages. The court must make an assessment of loss and pass a decree for it.

> **Example :** *Chaplin Vs. Hicks* (1911)
>
> H organised a beauty competition in which 50 ladies were to be selected by votes of the readers of certain newspapers. H would select 12 out of the 50 and secured theatrical jobs for them. C was one of the 50 and by H's breach of contract, C was prevented from being present when the final selection was made. It was held that C was entitled to damages even though it was difficult to calculate them. The fact that damages are difficult to assess does not prevent the injured party from recovering them.

Some other types of Damages :

(*a*) *Damages for Loss of Reputation*

Generally, such damages are not recoverable. An exception to this rule arises in case of a banker, who wrongfully refuses to honour a customer's cheques. If the customer is a businessman, he can recover damages in respect of any loss to his business reputation by such breach.

(*b*) *Cost of Decree*

The aggrieved party is entitled, in addition to the damages, to get the cost of getting the decree for damages. However, the cost of suit for damages is at the discretion of the court.

(*c*) *Damages from Carriers*

Damages can be claimed from the carriers even without notice for deterioration caused to goods by delay in transit.

Some Illustrations appended to Section 73 :

> **Examples :** (1) A hires B's ship to go to Bombay, and there takes on board, on the first January, a cargo which A is to provide and to bring it to Calcutta, the freight to be paid when earned. B's ship does not go to Bombay, but A has opportunities of procuring suitable conveyance for the cargo upon terms as advantageous as those on which he had chartered the ship. A avails himself of those opportunities, but is put to trouble and expense in doing so. A is entitled to receive compensation from B in respect of such trouble and expense.
>
> (2) A contracts to buy B's ship for Rs. 60,000, but breaks his promise. A must pay to B, by way of compensation, the excess, if any, of the contract price other than the price which B can obtain for the ship at the time of the breach of promise.
>
> (3) A, the owner of a boat, contracts with B to take a cargo of jute to Mirzapur, for sale at that place, starting on a specified day. The boat, owing to some unavoidable cause, does not start at the time appointed, whereby the arrival of cargo at Mirzapur is delayed beyond the time when it would have arrived if the boat had sailed according to contract. After that date, and before the arrival of cargo, the price of jute falls. The measure of the compensation payable to B by A is the difference between the price which B could have obtained for the cargo at Mirzapur at the time when it would have arrived if forwarded in due course and its market price at the time when it actually arrived.
>
> (4) A contracts to repair B's house in a certain manner, and receives payment in advance. A repairs the house but not according to contract. B is entitled to recover from A the cost of making the repairs conform to the contract.
>
> (5) A contracts to let his ship to B for a year, from 1st January, for a certain price. Freights rise, and on the 1st January, the hire obtainable for the ship is higher than the contract price. A breaks his promise. He must pay to B, by way of compensation, a sum equal to the difference between the contract price and the price for which B could hire a similar ship for a year on and from the 1st January.
>
> (6) A contracts to supply B with a certain quantity of iron at a fixed price, being a higher price than that for which A could procure and deliver the iron. B wrongfully refuses to receive the iron. B must pay to A, by way of compensation, the difference between the contract price of the iron and the sum for which A could have obtained and delivered it.

(7) A delivers to B, a common carrier, a machine, to be conveyed without delay, to A's mill, informing B that his mill is stopped for want of the machine. B unreasonably delays the delivery of the machine, and A, in consequence, losses a profitable contract with the Government. A is entitled to receive from B, by way of compensation, the average amount of profit which would have been made by the working of the mill during the time that delivery of it was delayed, but not the loss sustained through the loss of the Government contract.

(8) A contracts to pay a sum of money to B on a day specified. A does not pay the money on that day; B in consequence of not receiving the money on that day, is unable to pay his debts, and is totally ruined. A is not liable to make good to B anything except the principal sum he contracted to pay, together with interest upto the day of payment.

Liquidated Damages and Penalty

A contract sometimes mentions that in case of breach of contract, a particular sum is payable by the party committing the breach. The sum so stipulated or agreed upon, may either be liquidated damage or penalty.

Liquidated damage is a sum fixed or ascertained by the parties to the contract, which is a fair and genuine pre-estimate of the probable loss that might occur as a result of breach of contract. Thus, liquidated damages are an assessment of loss, which in the opinion of the parties, will occur due to breach. Such damages are effective and recoverable by the aggrieved party from the other.

Penalty is the sum mentioned in the contract at the time of its formation which is disproportionate to the damage likely to occur as a result of the breach of the contract. Penalty is fixed with a view to getting the contract performed, but it has no concern with the probable loss likely to occur to the parties due to the breach of the contract.

Thus the liquidated damages are the fair assessment of the amount which will compensate the aggrieved party for the loss suffered due to breach of the contract. Whereas, the penalty is not a fair assessment of the loss for breach. It is fixed with a view to prevent the party from committing the breach of the contract, that is, to compel the other party to perform the contract.

There is a distinction between penalty and liquidated damages under English Law. Indian Law makes no distinction between the two.

English Law on Penalty and Liquidated Damages

According to English Law, the amount of money payable is interpreted either as liquidated damage or as a penalty.

The amount fixed is considered to be a penalty if it is not based upon a reasonable calculation of actual loss but is fixed by way of punishment and as a threat. It is named so high that it operates as a threat and is laid down with intention to secure performance. It is disproportionate to the damages likely to accrue as a result of breach. It is greater than the genuine estimate of loss which the injured party may suffer. Penalty is a sum payable in terrorem.

In the case of liquidated damages the amount is fixed by the parties at the time of formation of the contract on the basis of reasonable and fair calculation after making a genuine pre-estimate of loss.

In case of liquidated damages, English courts allow only the amount stipulated, never more or less even though it is shown that the actual loss is different from the amount mentioned. Penalty clauses, however, are treated as invalid. The court allows only reasonable compensation by way of damages.

Example : *Dunlop Pneumatic Tyre Co. Vs. new Garage Motor Co.* (1915)

The appellants sold tyres and tubes, to the respondents who contracted not to resell them, at a price below the manufacturer' list price. The respondents further agreed to pay £ 5 by way of liquidated damages for every breach of this agreement. They sold tyres and tubes at less than the list price. The House of Lords held that the sum fixed was a pre-estimate of the damage and not a penalty.

INDIAN LAW

As noted, in English Law, liquidated damages are enforceable but penalty cannot be claimed. In India, there is no such distinction recognised between penalty and liquidated damages. Section 74 of the Indian Contract states:

"When a contract has been broken, if a sum is named in the contract as the amount to be paid in case of such breach, or if the contract contains any other stipulation by way of penalty, the party complaining of the breach is entitled, whether or not actual damage or loss is proved to have been caused thereby, to receive from the party who has broken the contract reasonable compensation not exceeding the amount so named or, as the case may be, the penalty stipulated for". If the parties have fixed what the damages will be, the courts will never allow more. But the court may allow less. A decree is to be passed only for reasonable compensation, not exceeding the sum named by the parties.

Some illustrations appended to Section 74.

Examples : (1) A contracts with B, that if A practises as a Chartered Accountant in Delhi, he will pay B Rs. 2,000. A practises as a Chartered Accountant in Delhi, B is entitled to such compensation not exceeding Rs. 2,000 as the Court considers reasonable.

(2) A, who owes money to B, a money-lender, undertakes to repay him by delivering to him 10 mounds of grain on a certain date, and stipulates that, in the event of his not delivering the stipulated amount by the stipulated date, he shall be liable to deliver 20 mounds. This is stipulation by way of penalty, and B is only entitled to reasonable compensation in case of breach.

(3) A undertakes to repay B a loan of Rs. 1,000 by five monthly installments with a stipulation that, in default of payment of any installments, the whole shall become due. This stipulation is not by way of any penalty, and the contract may be enforced according to its terms.

(4) A borrows Rs. 100 from B, and gives him a bond for Rs. 200 payable by five yearly installments of Rs. 40, with a stipulation that in default of payment of instalment, the whole shall become due. This is stipulation by way of penalty.

STIPULATION REGARDING PAYMENT OF INTEREST

According to the first explanation to Section 74 of the Indian Contract Act provides that "A stipulation for increased interest, from the date of default may be a stipulation by way of penalty".

Example : (*Appended to the Section*)

A gives B a bond for repayment of Rs. 1,000 with interest at 12% per annum at the end of six months, with the stipulation that in case of default interest will be payable at the rate of 75% per annum from the date of default. This is a stipulation by way of penalty and B is only entitled to recover from A such compensation as the court considers reasonable.

The following rules may be noted in connection with payment of interest :

1. A stipulation for increased interest from the date of default shall be a stipulation by way of penalty if the rate of interest is abnormally high. (See the above example).
2. Where there is a stipulation to pay increased interest from the date of bond and not merely from the date of default, it is always considered as penalty.
3. A stipulation to pay compound interest at a higher rate on default is to be considered a penalty.
4. An agreement to pay a particular rate of interest with a stipulation that a reduced rate will be acceptable if paid punctually is not a stipulation by way of penalty.
5. The sum stipulated is considered as penalty if it is greater than the borrowed sum to be paid.

III. Suit Upon Quantum Meruit

The phrase 'Quantum Meruit' means "payment in proportion to the amount of work done" or "reasonable value of work done". A person can, under certain circumstances, claim payment for work done or goods supplied without any contract and in cases where the original contract has terminated by breach of contract by one party or has become void for some reason. This is known as the Doctrine of Quantum Meruit. This doctrine is applied where there is no express promise to definite remuneration to a person.

CLAIM FOR QUANTUM MERUIT ARISES IN THE FOLLOWING CASES

1. *When a Contract is Found to be Void*

Section 65 lays down that when a contract is discovered to be unenforceable for some technical reason, any person who has done something under the contract, is entitled to reasonable compensation.

> **Example :** *Craven Ellis Vs. Canons Ltd.* (1936)
>
> C was employed as managing director of a company by the board of directors of the company under written contract. The contract was found to be void because the directors who constituted the board were unqualified. C actually worked as a managing director for some time. It was held that he was entitled to remuneration on the basis of quantum meruit.

2. *When Something is Done without any Intention to do so Gratuitously*

This has been explained under Quasi contracts

3. *When one Party Abandons or Refuses to Perform the Contract*

Sometimes, a party performs a part of the contract, but abandons it without completing, or refuses to perform the remaining part. In such cases, the compensation for the work done may be recovered on the basis of quantum meruit.

> **Example :** *Planche Vs. Colburn* (1831)
>
> P was required by C to write a story for a children's magazine, and the story would be published serially. After P had written a few chapters and delivered them to C, the publication of the magazine was stopped by C. It was held that P could recover remuneration proportionate to his work from C.

4. *When a Contract is Divisible*

When a contract is divisible, and the party not in default has enjoyed the benefit of the part performance, the party in default may sue on quantum meruit.

> **Example :** A contracts with B to deliver to him 250 mounds of rice before the 1st May. A delivers 130 mounds only before that day, and none after. B retained 130 mounds of rice. He is bound to pay A for them.

5. *When an Indivisible Contract is Performed Badly*

When an indivisible contract for a lump sum is completely performed but badly, the person who has performed the contract can claim the lump sum; but the other party can make a deduction for bad work.

> **Example :** *Hoeing Vs. Isaacs* (1952)
>
> P agreed to decorate D's flat for a lump sum of £ 750, certain requirements having been laid down. P did the work but D complained of faulty workmanship. It cost D £ 204 to remedy defect. Held, P could recover from D £ 750 less £ 204.

IV. Suit for Specific Performance

Specific performance means the actual carrying out of the contract as agreed. Where damages are not an adequate remedy for breach of the contract, the court may direct the party in breach to carry out his promise according to the terms of the contract. This is called "Specific Performance" of the contract. Specific performance of the contract cannot be claimed as a matter of right. Rules regarding the granting of this relief are contained in the Specific Relief Act.

Some of the cases in which specific performance of the contract may be enforced are as follows :

(*a*) Where monetary consideration is not an adequate remedy for the breach of a contract;

(*b*) Where there exists no standard for ascertaining the actual damage caused by the non-performance of the act;

(*c*) When it is probable that compensation in money on non-performance of the contract cannot be obtained.

Specific performance is not granted in the following cases, when :

(*a*) Damages are an adequate remedy;

(*b*) The contract is not certain;

(*c*) The contract is inequitable to either party;

(*d*) The contract is of revocable nature;

(*e*) The contract is made by the trustee in breach of trust;

(*f*) The contract is of personal nature (contract to marry)

(*g*) The contract made by a company *ultra vires* of its memorandum of Association; and

(*h*) The court cannot supervise its carrying out.

V. Suit for Injunction

'Injunction' is an order of a court restraining a person from doing a particular act. It is a mode of securing the specific performance of the negative terms of the contract. That is, it is order of the court restraining a person from doing something which he promised not to do. This type of order is generally issued in cases where the compensation in terms of money is not an adequate relief. Thus, injunction is a preventive relief. It is appropriate in case of 'anticipatory breach of contract.'

Example : *Metropolitan Electrical Supply Co. Vs. Ginder* (1901).

G agreed to take the whole of his electricity from a certain company. The agreement was interpreted as a promise not to buy electricity from any other company. He was, therefore, restrained by an injunction from buying electricity from any other company.

THEORETICAL QUESTIONS

1. What are the remedies available to an aggrieved party in case of breach of contract?
2. State the rules governing the assessment of damages for breach of contract in the light of the decision in Hadley Vs. Baxandale.
3. Distinguish between liquidated damages and penalty.
4. What is meant by breach of contract? What are the remedies available to an aggrieved party on the breach of contract.
5. Examine critically the rule in Hadley Vs. Baxandale.
6. When do a claim on quantum meruit arise?
7. Under what circumstances is a party entitled to specific performance?
8. What is meant by injunction?
9. What are liquidated damages?
10. Explain the principles governing the assessment of damages for breach of contract. (*M.Com. Bhopal*)
11. Discuss the legal position regarding award of damages for breach of contract. (*M.Com. MS*)
12. "If a contract is broken, the law will endeavour so far as money can do it, to place the injured party in the same positions as if the contract has been performed." Discuss. (*M.Com. Mumbai*)

MULTIPLE CHOICE QUESTIONS

I. Choose correct option for each of the following :

1. **An aggrieved party can claim ordinary damages :**
   (*a*) when he has suffered damages by breach of contract.
   (*b*) when the damages has arisen in the usual course of things by breach of contract.
   (*c*) when there is a possibility of damages in the usual course of things.
   (*d*) in the case of (*a*) and (*b*) above.
2. **The aggrieved party may claim damages for breach of contract :**
   (*a*) ordinary damages. (*b*) special damages.
   (*c*) remote and indirect damages. (*d*) both (*a*) and (*b*) above.
3. **Breach of contract occurs :**
   (*a*) when any one party to the contract fails or refuses to perform his obligations under the contract.
   (*b*) when any one party disables himself from performing his part of his contract.
   (*c*) when any one party makes the performance of the contract impossible by his own acts.
   (*d*) in any one of the above cases.
4. **In case of breach of contract, the aggrieved party may avail the remedies of :**
   (*a*) rescission of contract. (*b*) novation of the contract.
   (*c*) claiming damages. (*d*) both (*a*) and (*c*) above.
5. **Special damages can be claimed by the aggrieved party :**
   (*a*) where he has brought to the notice of the other party the special circumstances of the case at the time of contract.
   (*b*) where he has brought to the notice of the other party the special circumstances of the case at any time before the breach of the contract.
   (*c*) where he presumed that the other party has knowledge of special circumstances of the case.
   (*d*) in all the above cases.
6. **Anticipatory breach of a contract takes place :**
   (*a*) during the performance of the contract. (*b*) at the time when the performance is due.
   (*c*) before the performance is due. (*d*) at the time when the contract is entered into.
7. **An aggrieved party may not use the right of rescission of a contract :**
   (*a*) when third party has acquired rights in good faith before rescission of the contract.
   (*b*) when he has ratified contract.
   (*c*) when a party seeks rescission of a part of a contract.
   (*d*) in all of the above cases.
8. **The court may grant rescission where the contract is :**
   (*a*) voidable at the option of the plaintiff. (*b*) void.
   (*c*) unenforceable. (*d*) illegal.
9. **In case of anticipatory breach, the aggrieved party may treat the contract :**
   (*a*) as discharged and bring an immediate action for damages.
   (*b*) as operative and wait till the time for performance arrives.
   (*c*) exercise option either (*a*) or (*b*).
   (*d*) only option (a) is available.
10. **While measuring the damages for breach of contract, the aggrieved party is required to prove :**
    (*a*) that he has suffered loss due to the breach of contract.
    (*b*) he has taken all reasonable steps to minimise the loss.
    (*c*) he has informed the other party the possibility of loss.
    (*d*) both (*a*) and (*b*) above.
11. **The court may enforce specific performance of contract :**
    (*a*) when no standard for measuring actual damages exists.
    (*b*) when the monetary compensation can not be considered as adequate.

(*c*) when the specific performance of the contract runs into minute details.
(*d*) in the cases (*a*) and (*b*) above.

12. The claim on the basis of doctrine of "quantum meruit" may arise :
(*a*) when the contract is terminated by breach.
(*b*) when something has been done non-gratuitously.
(*c*) when the contract is divisible.
(*d*) in all of the above cases.

13. It is true with regard to the claim of damages :
(*a*) that usually damages actually suffered are allowed.
(*b*) that sometimes Court may award nominal damages.
(*c*) that smaller the amount of cheque dishonoured, the greater the loss of reputation.
(*d*) all of the above.

14. In case of an anticipatory breach of the contract, the aggrieved party :
(*a*) must rescind the contract and claim damages for breach of contract without waiting until the due date for performance.
(*b*) must treat the contract as operative and wait till the due date for performance and claim damages if the promise still remains under-formed.
(*c*) both (*a*) and (*b*).
(*d*) none of these.

15. In case of anticipatory breach of contract, if the promisee decides not to rescind the contract, the contract shall remain alive for the benefit of :
(*a*) promisor only.
(*b*) both the promisor and aggrieved party.
(*c*) none of these.
(*d*) aggrieved party only.

16. In case of actual breach of a contract, where the time is essence of contract, the contract becomes:
(*a*) illegal.
(*b*) voidable.
(*c*) void.
(*d*) none of these.

17. When prior to the due date of performance, the promisor absolutely refuses to perform the contract, it is known as :
(*a*) abandonment of contract.
(*b*) actual breach of contract.
(*c*) remission of contract.
(*d*) anticipatory breach of contract.

18. In case of actual breach of a contract if performance beyond stipulated tie is accepted :
(*a*) the promisee can not claim compensation even if he gives notice of his intention to do so.
(*b*) the promisee can claim compensation even if he does not give notice of his intention to do so.
(*c*) the promisee can claim compensation if he gives notice of his intention to do so.
(*d*) none of these.

19. Penalty is :
(*a*) a fair and genuine pre-estimate of the damages likely to result due to breach.
(*b*) a sum disproportionate to the damages likely to result due to breach.
(*c*) nor specified at the time of formation of contract.
(*d*) not enforceable in India.

20. The damages which can be awarded even if the aggrieved party has not suffered any loss, are called :
(*a*) Ordinary Damages.
(*b*) Exemplary Damages.
(*c*) Special Damages.
(*d*) Nominal Damages.

21. In case of breach of contract, the aggrieved party is entitled to claim :
(*a*) Liquidated damages or Penalty whichever is higher.
(*b*) Actual compensation or Penalty whichever is higher.
(*c*) Actual compensation or Liquidated Damages whichever is higher.
(*d*) Reasonable compensation not exceeding the specified sum.

22. The special damages, *i.e.*, the damages which arise due to some special or unusual circumstances:

(*a*) Are not recoverable altogether.
(*b*) Are illegal being punitive in nature.
(*c*) Cannot be claimed as a matter of right.
(*d*) Can be claimed as a matter of right.

23. Specific performance may be ordered by the Court when

(*a*) the contract is voidable.
(*b*) damages are an adequate remedy.
(*c*) damages are not an adequate remedy.
(*d*) the contract is uncertain.

24. Suit for specific performance means :

(*a*) demanding the court's direction to the defaulting party to carry out the promise according to the term of the contract.
(*b*) demanding court in order prohibiting a person to do a particulars act.
(*c*) none of these.

25. The damages which can be claimed only when the special circumstances are communicated to the promisor are called :

(*a*) Ordinary Damages.
(*b*) Exemplary Damages.
(*c*) Special Damages.
(*d*) Nominal Damages.

26. The foundation of modern law of damages was laid down in:

(*a*) *Tinn* v. *Hoffman.*
(*b*) *Hadley v. Baxendale.*
(*c*) *Taylor v. Caidwell.*
(*d*) *Addis v. Gramophone Co.*

27. The measure of damages in case of breach of a contract is the difference between the :

(*a*) Contract price and the market price at the date of breach.
(*b*) Contract price and the maximum market price during the term of the contract.
(*c*) Contract price and the price at which the plaintiff might have sold the goods.
(*d*) Contract price and the price fixed by Court.

28. In case of breach of contract, which of the following remedy is available to the aggrieved party?

(*a*) Suit for rescission.
(*b*) Suit for specific performance.
(*c*) Suit for damages.
(*d*) All of these.

29. Suit for Injunction means :

(*a*) demanding the court's direction to the defaulting party to carry out the promise according to the term of the contract.
(*b*) demanding court in order prohibiting a person to do a particular act.
(*c*) none of these.

30. In case of a wrongful dishonour of a cheque by a banker having sufficient funds to the credit of the customer, the Court may award :

(*a*) ordinary damages.
(*b*) exemplary damages.
(*c*) nominal damages.
(*d*) contemptuous damages.

ANSWERS

1. (*d*)	**2.** (*d*)	**3.** (*d*)	**4.** (*d*)	**5.** (*a*)	**6.** (*c*)	**7.** (*d*)	**8.** (*a*)	**9.** (*c*)	**10.** (*d*)
11. (*d*)	**12.** (*d*)	**13.** (*d*)	**14.** (*d*)	**15.** (*b*)	**16.** (*b*)	**17.** (*d*)	**18.** (*c*)	**19.** (*b*)	**20.** (*d*)
21. (*d*)	**22.** (*c*)	**23.** (*c*)	**24.** (*a*)	**25.** (*c*)	**26.** (*b*)	**27.** (*a*)	**28.** (*d*)	**29.** (*b*)	**30.** (*b*)

SPECIAL CONTRACTS

CHAPTER

Contract of Indemnity and Guarantee

(Sections 124–147)

AT A GLANCE

- Introduction
- Contract of Indemnity
- English Law Relating to Indemnity
- Essentials of a Valid Contract of Indemnity
- Right of Indemnity Holder
- Right of Indemnifier
- Contract of Guarantee
- Essentials
- Invalid Guarantee
- Contract of Indemnity Vs. Contract of Guarantee
- Kinds of Guarantee
- Revocation of Continuing Guarantee
- Surety's Liability
- Rights of Surety
- Right against Creditor
- Right against Debtor
- Right against co-sureties
- Discharge of Surety from Liability
- Theoretical Questions
- Multiple Choice Questions.

INTRODUCTION

The contract of indemnity and guarantee are the special kinds of contracts. They are species of general contract. As such, the principles of the general law of contract are applicable to them. Therefore, they must have all the essentials of a valid contract, for example, consideration, competency of the parties, lawful object etc. However, the special legal provisions relating to these contracts are contained in Sections 124 to 147 of the Indian Contract Act, besides the general principles.

CONTRACT OF INDEMNITY

To indemnify means to compensate or make good the loss. The contract of indemnity is entered into with the object of protecting the promisee against anticipated loss. The contingency upon which the whole contract of indemnity depends is the happening of loss. Section 124 of the Indian Contract Act defines a contract of indemnity thus:

"A contract by which one party promises to save the other from loss caused to him by the conduct of the promisor himself or by the conduct of any other person, is called a contract of indemnity." (Sec. 124).

> **Example :** (Appended to this section), A contracts to indemnify B against the consequence of any proceedings which C may take against B in respect of a certain sum of Rs. 200. This is a contract of indemnity.

In simple words, a contract of indemnity is a contract in which one person promises to protect or compensate the other for the loss suffered by him due to the conduct of the promisor or any other person. In the above example, A is the '*indemnifier*' and B is the '*indemnified.*' In other words, a person who promises to make good the loss, that is, the promisor is called the *indemnifier* and the person whose loss is to be made good, that is, the promisee is called the *indemnity-holder* or the person who is *indemnified.*

A contract of indemnity has two parties, *viz.*, the promisor or the indemnifier and the promisee or the indemnified or the indemnity-holder. The object of contract of indemnity is essentially to protect the promisee from the anticipated (future) loss.

The definition of contract of indemnity, as given in Section 124, is not exhaustive. This section includes :

(*a*) Only express promises to indemnify, and

(*b*) Only those cases where the loss arises from the conduct of the promisor or of any other person.

The section does not include:

(*a*) Implied promises to indemnify,

(*b*) Cases where loss arises from accidents and events not depending on the conduct of the promisor or any other person.

ENGLISH LAW RELATING TO INDEMNITY

Further, as per the Section 124, the loss must have been occasioned either by the conduct of the promisor himself or by the conduct of any other person. Thus, loss occasioned by the conduct of the promisee or an Act of God is not covered. If this strict view were to be accepted, a large number of insurance transactions shall not be covered under a contract of indemnity. Although the definition of indemnity, according to the Indian law is restrictive in scope when compared to the English definition, courts of law in India have followed the English law relating to indemnity. According to the English law, a contract of indemnity means "a promise to save another harmless from loss caused as a result of a transaction entered into at the instance of the promisor". English law on indeminity is wider. English law includes promises to save another harmless from the loss not only from the conduct of the promisor or third person, but also from loss caused by events or accidents like death, disability, destruction by fire, cyclone etc. Therefore, the English definition of the contracts of indemnity is exhaustive and that is why Indian courts accept it.

Example : *Gajanan Moreshwar Vs. Moreshwar Madan* (1942)

In this case, the Bombay High Court observed that "Sections 124 and 125 of the Indian Contract Act are not exhaustive of the law of indemnity and courts here would apply the same principles that the courts in England do."

ESSENTIALS OF A VALID CONTRACT OF INDEMNITY

The analyses of the definition of contract of indemnity, the following are the essentials for a valid contract of indemnity:

(1) The contract of indemnity must contain all the essentials of valid contract – competency of the parties, free consent, consideration, legality of the object etc.

(2) It is a contract between two parties. One person promises to save the other from any loss, which he may suffer.

(3) The loss may be caused by the conduct of the promisor himself or any other person.

(4) The contract of indemnity may be express or implied.

An express promise is one where a person promises in express terms to compensate the other from the loss. That is, an express contract is by words or by writing.

Example : Policy of insurance is a good example for express contract of indemnity.

An implied promise is one where the conduct of the promisor shows that he promised to indemnify the other party against the loss suffered by him. That is, implied contract of indemnity may be inferred from the circumstances of the case and also from the relationship of the parties.

For instance :

(1) As a general rule, Section 69 of the Contract Act provides that a person who is interested in the payment of money which another is bound by law to pay and who, therefore, pays it, is entitled to be reimbursed by the other.

(2) By virtue of Section 222 of the Indian Contract Act, "the employer of an agent is bound to indemnify him against the consequences of all lawful acts done by such agent in exercise of the authority conferred upon him".

(3) On the sale of shares in a company the transferee is bound to indemnify the transferor against future calls, whether made by the company or by the liquidator.

Rights of Indemnity-holder (Indemnified) (Sec. 125)

The promisee in a contract of indemnity, acting within the scope of his authority, is entitled to recover from the promisor :

(1) All damages which he may be compelled to pay in any suit in respect of any matter to which the promise to indemnify applies. [Sec. 125 (1)]

(2) All costs which he may be compelled to pay in any such suit if, in bringing or defending it, he did not contravene the orders of the promisor, and acted as it would have been prudent for him to act in the absence of any contract of indemnity, or if the promisor authorised him to bring or defend the suit. [Sec. 125 (2)].

(3) All sums which he may have paid under the terms of any compromise of any such suit, if the compromise was not contrary to the orders of the promisor, and was one which it would have been prudent for the promisee to make in the absence of any contract of indemnity, or if the promisor authorised him to compromise the suit. (Sec. 125 (3))

An indemnity-holder shall be entitled to all these rights provided he acts within the scope of his authority and the compromise must not be contrary to the orders of the indemnifier.

Rights of Indemnifier (promisor)

The Act makes no mention of the rights of an indemnifier. It has been held, however, that his rights, in such cases are similar to the rights of a surety, under Section 141 of the Indian Contract Act. That is, the rights of the promisor are virtually the same as those of the surety in a contract of guarantee.

COMMENCEMENT OF INDEMNIFIER'S LIABILITY

Regarding the commencement of the liability of the indemnifier, the Act is silent. There have been diversified views held regarding the time of commencement of the indemnifier's liability. There is difference of opinion among the different High Courts. Some of the High Courts, example Bombay, Nagpur etc., have held that the indemnifier can be made liable only when the indemnity-holder has incurred an actual loss, *i.e.*, discharged the liability : while other High Courts, example, Calcutta, Allahabad, Madras, Patna etc., have held that the indemnified can compel the indemnifier to make good his loss even before he has actually discharged his liability. In a case Osman Jalal & Sons Vs. Gopal (1919), Calcutta court observed, "Indemnity is not given by repayment after payment. Indemnity requires that the party to be indemnified shall never be called upon to pay". A similar observation was made, in Liverpool Insurance Company's case, "to indemnify does not merely mean to reimburse in respect of moneys paid, but to save from loss in respect of the liability against which the indemnity has been given. If it be held that payment is a condition precedent to recovery, the contract may be of little value to the person to be indemnified, who may be unable to meet the claim in the first instance".

The liability of the indemnifier commences as soon as the liability of the indemnity-holder becomes absolute.

CONTRACT OF GUARANTEE

According to Section 126, "a contract of guarantee" is a contract to perform the promise, or discharge the liability, of a third person in case of his default." A guarantee may be either oral or written.

> **Example :** A gives a loan of Rs. 1,000 to B and C promises to A that if B does not repay the loan, he will pay. This is a contract of guarantee. In this example :
>
> A is the creditor
>
> B is the principal debtors
>
> C is the surety (guarantor)
>
> The person to whom the guarantee is given is called the *creditor*.
>
> The person who gives the guarantee is called the *surety*.
>
> The person for whom the guarantee is given is called the *principal debtor*.
>
> **Example :** A and B go into a shop. A says to the shopkeeper, "Let him (B) have the goods, I will see you paid". This is a contract of indemnity. If he says, "If B does not pay you, I will pay". It is a guarantee.

Thus in a contract of indemnity, there are two parties – indemnifier and indemnified. In case of guarantee, there are three parties – the principal debtor, the creditor and the surety.

In a contract of guarantee there are three separate agreements :

One between the principal debtor and the creditor.

The second between the creditor and the surety, and

the third between the surety and the principal debtor.

The contract between the surety and the principal debtor is that of an indemnity, and by which the principal debtor requests the surety to act as such, and impliedly promises to indemnify the surety, in case surety is called upon by the creditor to pay off the debt, due by the principal debtor.

In English law, a guarantee is defined as a promise made by one person to another to be collaterally answerable for the debt, default or miscarriage of a third person and must be evidenced in writing. Guarantee may be oral or written. Under English law, the contract of guarantee is required to be evidenced by writing of any sort. Under Indian law a contract of guarantee may be tacit or implied and may be inferred from the course of conduct of the parties concerned.

ESSENTIALS OF A CONTRACT OF GUARANTEE

The following conditions are to be fulfilled for a contract of guarantee :

(1) A contract of guarantee must satisfy all the essential elements of a valid contracts, such as there must be lawful consideration and object, there must be free consent etc.

(2) There must be atleast three parties : (1) Surety (guarantor), (2) Principal Debtor, (3) Creditor. All the Parties must join the contract.

(3) A contract of guarantee pre-supposes the existence of a liability enforceable at law. It is of the essence of a contract of guarantee that there should be a liability, existing or future, enforceable at law.

(4) There are two types of liability *viz.*, (1) primary liability and (2) secondary liability. The primary liability is on the principal debtor. And the surety has secondary liability. Surety becomes liable only when principal debtor fails to perform his promise.

(5) It is an undertaking to perform the promise of other on his failure to do so. That is, the surety undertakes to perform the promise of the principal debtor in the event of latter's failure to perform his promise.

(6) A contract of guarantee may be oral or written. The contract may be express or even implied from the conduct of the parties. Under English Law, the contract of guarantee must be in writing and signed by the party who offers guarantee.

(7) A contract of guarantee, like every other contract, must satisfy all the essential elements of a valid contract. However, special features are to be noticed with reference to consideration and capacity to contract.

(*a*) Section 127 of the Act clearly provides that "Anything done, or any promise made, for the benefit of the principal debtor may be a sufficient consideration to the surety for giving the guarantee". Here, the consideration received by the principal debtor is taken to be sufficient consideration for the surety. It is not necessary that there should be direct consideration between the surety and creditor. However, past consideration is no consideration for a contract of guarantees. But "a contract of guarantee without consideration is void."

Examples : (1) B requests A to sell and deliver to him goods on credit. A agrees to do so, provided C will guarantee the payment of the price of the goods. C promises to guarantee the payment in consideration of A's promise to deliver the goods. This is a sufficient consideration for C's promise.

(2) A sells and delivers goods to B. C afterwards requests A to forbear to sue B for the debt for a year, and promises if he does so, C will pay for them in default of payment by B. A agrees to forbear as requested. This is sufficient consideration for C's promise.

(3) A sells and delivers goods to B. C afterwards, without consideration, agrees to pay for them in default of B. The agreement is void.

(*b*) Parties to a contract of guarantee must be competent to contract. However, the incapacity of the principal debtor does not affect the validity of a contract of guarantee. The creditor and the surety must be competent to enter into a valid contract. In case, the principal debtor is a minor, the surety is regarded as a principal debtor and is personally liable to pay the debt, though the principal is not liable. (Kashiba Vs. Sripat) It was observed that the contract between the surety and the creditor is not collateral but independent and the surety is held liable as principal debtor. The Bombay High court considered the question in Manju Vs. Shivappa and held that "if a minor could not default, the liability of the guarantor, being secondary, does not arise at all". Similar decision has been given by Madras High court in Edavan Nambiar Vs. Moolaki Raman (1957).

INVALID GUARANTEE

A contract of guarantee is invalid in the following cases :

1. *Misrepresentation*

According to Section 142, "any guarantee which has been obtained by means of misrepresentation made by the creditor, or with his knowledge and assent, concerning a material part of the transaction, is invalid." Though a suretyship is not a contract *uberrimae fidei*, law requires that the surety shall be entitled to know so much as to be aware of the nature of the transaction for which he is making himself responsible.

2. *Concealment*

According to Section 143, "Any guarantee which the creditor has obtained by means of keeping silence to material circumstances is invalid." The expression keeping silence clearly implies intentional concealment as distinguished from mere non-disclosure. It must in fact amount to a misrepresentation of what the surety is undertaking. Where a guarantee is given for fidelity of an employee the employer must disclose any previous misconduct of the employee in his office or which he is aware. The creditor should disclose to the surety the facts which are likely to affect the surety's liability.

Examples : (1) A engages B as clerk to collect money for him. B fails to account for some of his receipts, and A, in consequence, calls upon him to furnish security for his duly accounting. C gives his guarantee for B's duly accounting does not acquaint C with B's previous conduct. B afterwards makes default. The guarantee is invalid.

(2) A guarantees to C payment for iron to be supplied by him to B to the amount of 2,000 tons. B and C have privately agreed that B should pay five rupees per ton beyond the market price, such excess to be applied in liquidation of an old debt. This agreement is concealed from A. A is not liable as a surety.

3. *Not Joining by Co-surety*

According to Section 144, "where a person gives a guarantee upon a contract that a creditor shall not act upon it until another person has joined in it as co-surety, the guarantee is not valid if that other person does not join." The surety is discharged from his liability.

COMPARISON BETWEEN CONTRACT OF INDEMNITY AND CONTRACT OF GUARANTEE

The following are the points of distinction between the two :

Contract of Indemnity	*Contract of Guarantee*
1. There are two parties – the Indemnifier and the Indemnity holder.	1. There are three parties – the Creditor the principal Debtor and the Surety.
2. The liability of the indemnifier is primary.	2. The liability of the Principal Debtor is primary. The liability of the Surety is secondary, that is,, the surety is liable only if the principal debtor fails.
3. There is only one contract *i.e.*, between indemnifier and indemnified.	3. There are three contracts *i.e.*, first between the creditor and the principal debtor,, second between the creditor and the surety and third between the surety and the principal debtor.
4. Indemnifier need not act on the request of the indemnified.	4. Surety gives guarantee on the request of the principal debtor.
5. The liability of indemnifier arises on the happening of a contingent event.	5. There is an existing debt or duty, the performance of which is guaranteed by the surety.
6. An indemnifier cannot sue a third party for loss in his own name because there is no privity of contract. He can do so only if there is an assignment in his favour.	6. A surety on discharging the debt due by the principal debtor, can take action against the principal debtor for his own recovery.
7. It is for reimbursement of loss.	7. It is for the security of the creditor for ensuring his payment.
8. The promisor has some interest in the transaction, apart from indemnity.	8. The surety gets nothing substantial for his promise. He is not connected with the contract except by means of the promise to pay the debt.

KINDS OF GUARANTEE

A guarantee may usually be given for :

(1) The repayment of a debt;

(2) The repayment of the price of goods sold on credit; and

(3) Good conduct or honesty of a person employed with a particular person.

Guarantee may either be retrospective or prospective. The former is given for an existing debt while the latter is given for some future agreement. Mainly, there are two types of contract of guarantee. They are (1) Simple (specific) guarantee and (2) continuing guarantee.

Simple or Specific Guarantee

Simple guarantee is one in which guarantee is given for a single specific debt or transaction. It comes to an end as soon as the liability under that transaction ends. A specific guarantee once given is irrevocable.

Continuing Guarantee

According to Section 129, "A guarantee which extends to a series of transactions is called a continuing guarantee". It is a guarantee which is given for a series of transactions of continuing nature. It is not confined to single transaction. It is like a standing offer which is accepted by the creditor every time a subsequent transaction take place. Whether a guarantee is continuing or not depends on the language of the guarantee, the subject-matter and the surrounding circumstances.

Examples : (1) A, in consideration that B will employ C in collecting the rent of B's Zamindari, promises B to be responsible, to the amount of Rs. 5,000, for the due collection and payment by C of those rents. This is a continuing guarantee.

(2) A guarantees payment to B a tea-dealer to the amount of £ 100, for any tea he may from time to time supply to C. B supplies C with tea to the above value of £ 100 and C pays B for it. Afterwards B supplies C with the tea to the value of £ 200. C fails to pay. The guarantee given by A was a continuing guarantee, and he is accordingly liable to B to the extent of £ 100.

(3) A guarantees payment to B of the price of five sacks of flour, to be delivered by B to C and to be paid for in a month. B delivers five sacks to C, C pays for them. Afterwards B delivers four sacks to C which C does not pay for. The guarantee given by A was not a continuing guarantee, and accordingly he is not liable for the price of the four sacks.

REVOCATION OF CONTINUING GUARANTEE

A continuing guarantee may be revoked as regards future transactions under the following circumstances :

(1) *By Notice*

"A continuing guarantee may, at any time, be revoked by the surety as to future transactions by notice to the creditor" (Sec. 130). The liability of surety ceases from the date of his service of notice upon the creditor. However, surety remains liable for the transactions entered into by him before giving the notice.

(2) *By Death of Surety*

"The death of the surety operates, in the absence of any contract to the contrary, as revocation of continuing guarantee, so far as regards future transactions" (Sec. 131). The estate of the surety is liable for all transactions entered into prior to death of the surety unless there was a contract to the contrary. However, his estate shall not be liable for the transactions entered into after his death, even if the creditor has no notice of the death.

Examples : (1) A, in consideration of B's discounting, at A's request, bills of exchange for C, guarantees B, for twelve months, the due payment of áll such bills to the extent of Rs. 5,000. B discounts bills for C to the extent of Rs. 2,000. Afterwards, at the end of three months, A revokes the guarantee. This revocation discharges A from all liability to B, for any subsequent discount. But A is liable to B for Rs. 2,000 on default of C.

(2) A guarantees to B to the extent of Rs. 10,000, that C shall pay all the bills that B shall draw upon him. B draws upon C. C accepts the bill. A gives notice of revocation. C dishonours the bill at maturity. A is liable upon his guarantee.

SURETY'S LIABILITIES

The extent of the surety's liabilities are discussed below :

(1) Section 128 dealing with the surety's liability states that, "The liability of the surety is co-extensive with that of the principal debtor, unless it is otherwise provided by the contract". The term "co-extensive with that of the principal debtor" shows the quantum of the surety's liability. It means that a surety is liable for what a principal debtor is liable. That is, the liability of the surety will be neither more nor be less than that of the principal debtor, unless there is a contract to the contrary. However, by a special contract, it may be made less than that of the principal debtor but never greater.

Example : A guarantees to B the payment of a bill of exchange by C, the acceptor. The bill is dishonoured by C. A is liable not only for thé amount of the bill but also for any interest and charges which may have become due on it.

(2) The liability of the surety is only secondary, collateral or contingent. His liability arises only on default by the principal debtor. The surety's liability arises immediately on the default of the principal debtor unless there is an express provision in the contract that the creditor must in the first instance proceed against the principal debtor or must give a notice of default to the surety. If the contract is silent, notice of the default is not necessary to bring an action against the surety. The creditor may file a suit against the surety without suing the principal debtors. If the surety becomes insolvent before default by the principal debtor, the creditor cannot prove against the surety's receiver in insolvency.

(3) Surety is liable only when principal debtor does not pay. The liability of the surety is secondary, the primary liability being that of the principal debtor. The surety cannot be called upon to pay unless the principal debtor has committed the default. Besides, the creditor cannot ask the surety for performance, unless he himself has performed a part of the contract. Thus, surety is considered with favour both at law and equity. For this reason, the surety is sometimes called a favoured debtor.

(4) A discharge of the principal debtor by operation of law (example, insolvency) does not discharge the surety.

(5) The liability of a surety does not come to an end upon the death of the principal debtor.

(6) Where a creditor holds securities from the principal debtor for his debt, the creditor need not first resort to these securities before suing the surety, unless otherwise agreed.

(7) We understand that surety is liable for the whole amount for which the principal debtor is liable. However, the surety may, by special agreement, limit his liability to a fixed amount. In such case, surety's liability will not be more than the amount fixed by him.

Rights of Surety

The rights of a surety can be discussed under the following three heads :

1. Against the creditor.
2. Against the principal debtor.
3. Against the co-sureties.

A. Rights of a Surety against the Creditor

(1) *Right to benefit of creditor's securities*

According to Section 141 of the Act, "A surety is entitled to the benefit of every security which the creditor has against the principal debtor at the time when the contract for suretyship is entered into, whether the surety knows of the existence of such security or not; and if the creditor losses or, without the consent of the surety, parts with such security, the surety is discharged to the extent of the value of the security." The surety is entitled to all the securities which the creditor was holding at the time of contract of guarantee. The surety can claim the securities from the creditor on the discharge of full liability of the principal-debtor which has been guaranteed by the surety. The surety, however, is not entitled to the benefit to the benefit of any security subsequently given.

(2) *Right of Subrogation*

According to Section 140, "Where a guaranteed debt has become due, on default of the principal debtor to perform a guaranteed duty has taken place, the surety, upon payment or performance of all that he is liable for, is invested with all the rights which the creditor had against the principal debtor." Such a right of the surety which the law vests in him, is known as the right of subrogation. Thus, if the creditor has the right to stop goods in transit or has a seller's lien, the surety, on payment of all he is liable for, will be entitled to exercises these rights.

Right to File Quia Timet Action

(3) The surety has a right at any time after the guaranteed debt has become due and before he is called upon to pay, to require the creditor to sue for and recover the guaranteed debt. This is called the right to *quia timet* action. However, he must undertake to indemnify the creditor for the risk, delay and expenses which he may incur by so doing.

(4) In the case of fidelity guarantees like guarantee of conduct, honesty etc. of the principal debtor, the surety can call upon the creditor or the employer to dismiss the employee whose honesty he has guaranteed, in the event of proved dishonesty of the servant and thus further loss can be avoided.

Right to Set off

(5) The surety is also entitled to the benefit of any set-off or counter claim, which the principal debtor might possess against the creditor in respect of the same transaction.

Examples : (1) C advances to B, his tenant Rs. 2,000 on the guarantee of A. C has also a further security for the Rs. 2,000 by a mortgage of B's furniture. C cancels the mortgage. B becomes insolvent and C sues A on his guarantee. A is discharged from liability to the amount of the value of the furniture.

(2) C, a creditor whose advance to B is secured by a decree, receives also a guarantee for that advance from A. C afterwards takes B's goods in execution under the decree, and then, without the knowledge of A, withdraws, the execution. A is discharged.

(3) A, as surety for B, makes a bond jointly with B to C, to secure a loan from C to B. Afterwards, C obtains from B a further security for the same debt. Subsequently, C gives up the further security. A is not discharged.

B. Right against the Principal Debtor

1. *Right of Subrogation*

When the surety has paid the guaranteed debt on the default of the principal debtor, the surety steps into the shoes of the creditor and will be able to exercise as against the principal debtor all these rights and remedies which could be exercised by the creditor. In other words, the surety is subrogated to all rights which the creditor had against the principal debtor.

2. *Right to be Indemnity*

According to Section 145, "In every contract of guarantee there is an implied promise by the principal debtor to indemnify the surety; and the surety is entitled to recover from the principal debtor whatever sum he has rightfully paid under the guarantee, but no sums which he has paid wrongfully." The right occurs only on payment of all that the surety is liable under the guarantee.

Examples : (1) B is indebted to C and A is surety for the debt. C demands payment from A and on his refusal sues him for the amount. A defends the suit, having reasonable grounds for doing so, but is compelled to pay the amount of debt with costs. He can recover from B the amount paid by him for costs, as well as the principal debt.

(2) C lends B a sum of money, and A on the request of B accepts a bill of exchange drawn by B upon A to secure the amount. C, the holder of the bill demands payment of it from A, and, on A's refusal to pay, sues him upon the bill. A, not having reasonable grounds for so doing, defends the suit, and has to pay the amount of the bill and costs. He can recover from B the amount of the bill, but not the sum paid for costs, as there was no real ground for defending the action.

(3) A guarantees to C, to the extent of Rs. 2,000, payment for rice to be supplied by C to B. C supplies to B rice to a less amount than Rs. 2,000 but obtains from A payment of the sum of Rs. 2,000 in respect of the rice supplied. A cannot recover from B more than the price of the rice actually supplied.

C. Rights against co-sureties

When a debt is guaranteed by two or more sureties, they are called co-sureties. In such a case all the co-sureties are liable to contribute towards the payment of the guaranteed debt as per the agreement among them.

1. *Right to Contribution*

According to Section 146, "Where two or more persons are co-sureties for the same debt or duty, either jointly or severally and whether under the same or different contracts, and whether with or without the knowledge of each other, the co-sureties, in the absence of any contract to the contrary, are liable, as between themselves, to pay each an equal share of the whole debt or of that part of it which remains unpaid by the principal debtor." When a surety paid more than his share of the debt or a decree has been passed against him for more than his share, he has a right of contribution from the other sureties who are equally bound to pay with them.

Examples : (1) A, B and C are sureties to D for the sum of Rs. 3,000 lent to E. E makes default in payment. A, B and C are liable, as between themselves to pay Rs. 1,000 each.

(2) A, B and C are sureties to D for the sum of Rs. 1,000, lent to E and there is a contract between A, B and C that A is to be responsible to the extent of one quarter, B to the extent of one quarter and C to the extent of one half. E makes default in payment. As between the sureties, A is liable to pay Rs. 250, B Rs. 250 and C Rs. 500.

2. *Bound in Different Sums*

According to Section 147, "Co-sureties who are bound in different sums are liable to pay equally as for as the limits of their respective obligations permit." Therefore, the liability when apportioned equally will be subject to the maximum each one has guaranteed.

Examples : A, B and C, as sureties for D, enter into three several bonds, each in different penalty, namely, A in the penalty of Rs. 10,000, B in that of Rs. 20,000, C in that of Rs. 40,000 conditioned for D's duly accounting to E. D makes default to the extent of Rs. 30,000, A, B and C are liable to pay Rs. 10,000.

(*a*) If D makes default to the extent of Rs. 40,000, A is liable to pay Rs. 10,000 (his maximum limit of liability) and B and C Rs. 15,000 each.

(*b*) If D makes default to the extent of Rs. 60,000, then A is liable to pay Rs. 10,000, B Rs. 20,000 and C Rs. 30,000, and

(*c*) If D makes default to the extent of Rs. 70,000, then A, B and C have to pay each the full penalty of his bond.

DISCHARGE OF SURETY FROM LIABILITY

A surety is to be discharged when his liability comes to an end. Circumstances in which a surety is discharged are discussed as follows :

1. *Notice of Revocation* (Sec. 130)

A guarantee may be specific guarantee or continuing guarantee. A specific guarantee once given is irrevocable. Section 130 of the Indian Contract Act provides that "a Continuing guarantee may at any time be revoked by the surety, as the future transactions, by notice to the creditor". However, surety remain liable for transactions entered into prior to the notice.

2. *Death of Surety* (Sec. 131)

Section 131 of the Act provides, "The death of the surety operates, in the absence of any contract to the contrary, as revocation of continuing guarantee, so far as regard to future transactions".

3. *Novation* (Sec. 62)

Novation means the substitution of a new contract either between the same parties or different parties for the old one. Thus novation of a contract of guarantee discharges it.

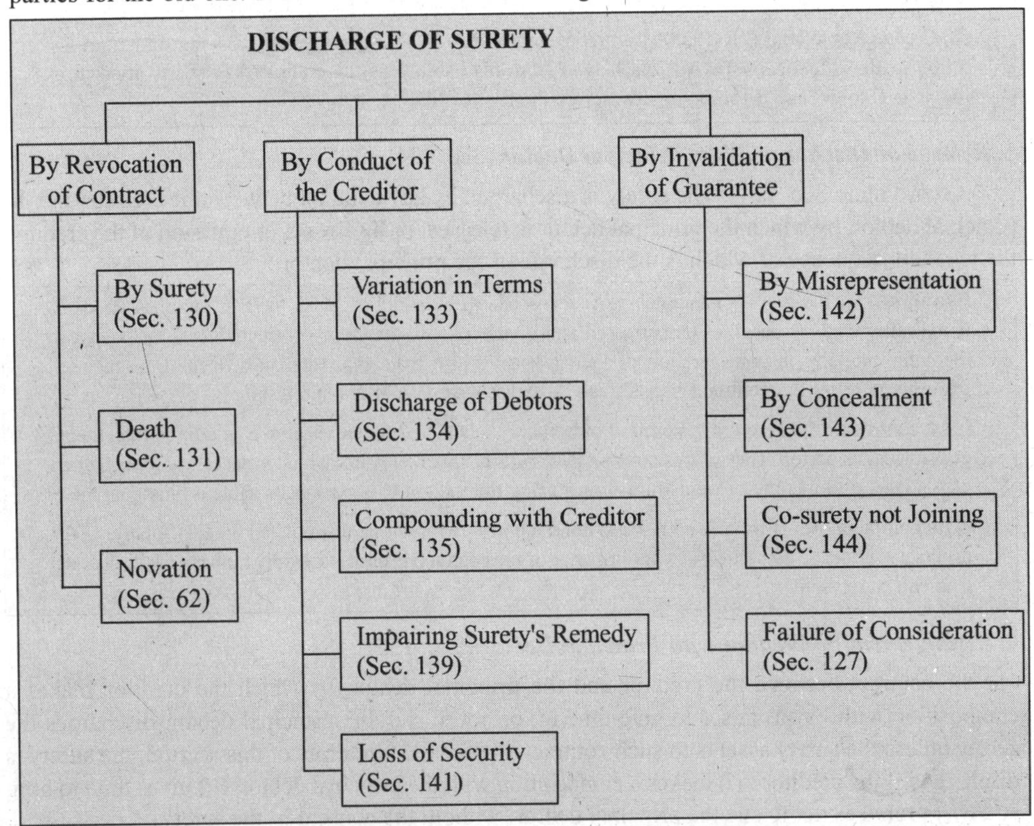

4. *Variance in Terms of Contract* (Sec. 133)

According to Section 133 of the Act, "Any variance, made without surety's consent, in the terms of contract between the principal debtor and the creditor, discharges the surety as to the transactions subsequent to the variance."

Examples : (1) A becomes surety to C for B's conduct as a manager in C's bank. Afterwards, B and C contract, without A's consent, that B's salary shall be raised, and that he shall become liable for one-fourth of the losses on overdrafts. B allows a customer to overdraw, and the bank losses a sum of money. A is discharged from his suretyship by the variance made without his consent and is not liable to make good this loss.

(2) A guarantees C against the misconduct of B in an office to which B is appointed by C, and of which the duties are defined by an Act of the Legislature. By a subsequent Act the nature of the office is materially altered. Afterwards, B misconducts himself. A is discharged by the change from future liability under his guarantee, though the misconduct of B is in respect of a duty not affected by the later Act.

(3) C agrees to appoint B as his clerk to sell goods at a yearly salary, upon A's becoming surety to C for B's duly accounting for moneys received by him as such clerk. Afterwards, without A's knowledge or consent, C and B agree that B should be paid by a commission on the goods sold by him and not by a fixed salary. A is not liable for subsequent misconduct of B.

(4) A gives to C a continuing guarantee to the extent of Rs. 3,000 for any oil supplied by C to B on credit. Afterwards B becomes embarrassed, and, without the knowledge of A, B and C contract that C shall continue to supply B with oil for ready money, and that the payment shall be applied to the then existing debts between B and C. A is not liable on his guarantee for any goods supplied after this new arrangement.

(5) C contracts to lend B Rs. 5,000 on first March. A guarantees repayment, C pays the amount of Rs. 5,000 to B on first January. A is discharged from his liability, as the contract has been varied in as much as C might sue B for the money before the first of March.

5. *Release or Discharge of the Principal Debtor* (Sec. 134)

According to Sec. 134, "The surety is discharged by any contract between the creditor and the principal debtor, by which the principal debtor is released, or by any act or omission of the creditor, the legal consequence of which is the discharge of the principal debtor."

Examples : (1) A gives a guarantee to C for goods to be supplied by C to B. C supplies goods to B and afterwards B becomes embarrassed and contracts with the creditors (including C) to assign to them his property in consideration of their releasing him from their demands. Here B is released from his debt by the contract with C, and A is discharged from his suretyship.

(2) A contracts with B to grow a crop of indigo on A's land and to deliver it to B at a fixed rate, and C guarantees A's performance of this contract, B diverts a stream of water which is necessary for irrigation of A's land, and thereby prevents him from raising the indigo. C is no longer liable on his guarantee.

(3) A contracts with B for a fixed price to build a house for B within a stipulated time, B supplying the necessary timber. C guarantees A's performance of the contract. B omits to supply timber. C is discharged from his suretyship.

6. *Arrangement by Creditor with Principal Debtor* (Sec. 135)

"A contract between the creditor and the principal debtor, by which the creditor makes a composition with, or promises to give time to, or not to sue, the principal debtor, discharges the surety unless the surety assents to such contract." (Sec. 135) In terms of this section, the surety is discharged if the creditor : (*i*) makes a composition with the principal debtor, (*ii*) gives time to him, and (*iii*) promises not to sue the principal debtor, without the consent of the surety.

In the following cases, the surety is not discharged:

(*a*) According to Section 136, "When a contract to give time to the principal debtor is made by the creditor with a third person and not with the principal debtor, the surety is not discharged.

> **Example :** C, the holder of an overdue bill of exchange drawn by A as surety for B, and accepted by B, contracts with M to give time to B. A is not discharged.

(*b*) According to Section 137, "Mere forbearance on the part of the creditor to sue the principal debtor, or to enforce any other remedy against him, does not, in the absence of any provision in the guarantee to the contrary, discharge the surety.

> **Example :** B owes to C a debt guaranteed by A. The debt becomes payable. C does not sue B for a year after the debt has become payable. A is not discharged from the suretyship.

(*c*) According to Section 138, "Where there are co-sureties, a release by the creditor of one of them does not discharge the others, neither does it free the surety so released from his responsibility to the other sureties.

7. *Impairing Surety's Remedy*

According to Section 139, "If the creditor does any act which is inconsistent with the rights of the surety, or omits to do any act which his duty to the surety requires him to do, and the eventual remedy of the surety himself against the principal debtor is thereby impaired, the surety is discharged.

> **Examples :** (1) B contracts to build a ship for C for a given sum, to be paid by installments as the work reaches certain stages. A becomes surety to C for B's due performance of the contract. C, without the knowledge of A, prepays to B the last two installments. A is discharged, by this prepayment.
>
> (2) C lends money to B on the security of a joint and several promissory note made in C's favour by B, and by A, as surety for B, together with a bill of sale of B's furniture, which gives power to C to sell the furniture, and apply the proceeds in discharge of the note. Subsequently, C sells the furniture, but owing to his misconduct and wilful negligence, only a small price is realised. A is discharged from liability on the note.
>
> (3) A puts M as apprentice to B, and gives a guarantee to B for M's fidelity. B promises on his part that he will, atleast once in a month, see M make up the cash. B omits to see this done, as promised, and M embezzles. A is not liable to B on his guarantee.

8. *Loss of Security* (Sec. 141)

Section 141 provides, "A surety is entitled to the benefit of every security which the creditor has against the principal debtor at the time when the contract of suretyship is entered into, whether the surety knows of the existence of such security or not; and, if the creditor loses or, without the consent of the surety, parts with such security, the surety is discharged to the extent of the value of the security." The word "loss" here means loss because of carelessness or negligence. Thus if the security is lost due to an act of God or enemies of the state or unavoidable accident, the surety would not be discharged.

> **Examples :** (1) C advances to B, his tenant, Rs. 2,000 on the guarantee of A. C has also a further security for the Rs. 2,000 by a mortgage of B's furniture. C cancels the mortgage. B becomes insolvent and C sues A on his guarantee. A is discharged from liability to the amount of the value of the furniture.
>
> (2) C, a creditor whose advance to B is secured by a decree, receives also guarantee for that advance from A. C afterwards, takes B's goods in execution under the decree, and then, without the knowledge of A, withdraws, the execution. A is discharged.
>
> (3) A, as surety for B, makes a bond jointly with B to C, to secure a loan from C to B. Afterwards, C obtains from B a further security for the same debt. Subsequently, C gives up further security. A is not discharged.

9. *Misrepresentation* (Sec. 142)

Explained above

10. *Concealment* (Sec. 143)

Explained above

11. *Failure of Co-surety to Join* (Sec. 144)

"Where a person gives a guarantee upon a contract that the creditor shall not act upon it until another person has joined in it as co-surety, the guarantee is not valid if that other person does not join." (Sec. 144).

12. *Lack of Essential Elements*

A contract of guarantee like any other contract must have all the essential elements of a valid contract – competent parties, consideration etc. If it lacks any of the essentials, the contract becomes void and the surety is discharged.

Discharge of Surety

1. By notice of revocation (130)
2. By death of surety (131)
3. By novation (62)
4. By variation in terms of contract (133)
5. By release of principal debtor (134)
6. By compounding by creditor with principal debtor (135)
7. By impairing surety's remedy (139)
8. By loss of security (141)
9. By misrepresentation (142)
10. By concealment (143)
11. By failure of co-surety to join (144)
12. By failure of consideration (127)

THEORETICAL QUESTIONS

1. What is "Contract of Indemnity" What are the rights of indemnity holder? *(B.Com. M.S.)*
2. Define the "Contract of Indemnity". Distinguish it from a Contract of Guarantee. State the rights of an indemnity holder when sued. *(B.Com. Madurai)*
3. Define a contract of Guarantee. What are the essentials of a Contract of Guarantee?
4. What are the various kinds of a guarantee? Define a continuing guarantee.
5. "A surety is a favoured debtor" Discuss.
6. State the nature and extent of surety's liability. How and in what circumstances the surety is discharged from his liability?
7. "The liability of a surety is secondary; it is co-extensive with that of the principal debtor". Elucidate. *(AIMA)*
8. Explain the situations which make the contract of surety invalid and thereby surety is discharged.
9. "Between co-sureties there is equity of burden and benefit". Comment. *(B.Com. Delhi)*
10. When a surety is discharged from liability. *(CA)*
11. Briefly discuss the rights of a surety against :
    (*a*) Creditor (*b*) Principal debtor and (*c*) Co-sureties.
12. What is the nature of surety's liability?

MULTIPLE CHOICE QUESTIONS

1. In a contract of guarantee, a parson who promises to discharge another's liability, is known as:

(*a*) principal Debtor. (*b*) Creditor.
(*c*) surety. (*d*) indemnified.

2. The party who gives the indemnity is known as :

(*a*) indemnity-holder (*b*) surety.
(*c*) indemnifier. (*d*) principal debtor.

3. A surety is discharged from liability by :

(*a*) materiel alteration in terms. (*b*) revocation notice by surety.
(*c*) discharge of principal by creditor. (*d*) all of these.

4. A guarantee given for minor's debt is :

(*a*) valid. (*b*) voidable.
(*c*) void. (*d*) illegal.

5. The liability of a surety arises, when the

(*a*) principal debtor commits default in payment.
(*b*) creditor fails to recover anything from principal debtor.
(*c*) court directs him to pay.
(*d*) surety is reimbursed by debtor.

6. The liability of the indemnifier to compensate the indemnity-holder commences when :

(*a*) indemnity-holder has suffered actual loss. (*b*) liability of indemnity-holder becomes certain.
(*c*) he is called upon to pay. (*d*) he fixed the date for the same.

7. A contract in which a person promises to discharge liability of another person in case of default by such person, is known as a :

(*a*) quasi-contract. (*b*) contract of guarantee.
(*c*) contract of indemnity. (*d*) none of these.

8. A contract of indemnity is a :

(*a*) contingent contract. (*b*) wagering contract.
(*c*) quasi-contract. (*d*) void agreement.

9. Any variance made without surety's consent in the terms of the contract of guarantee discharges the surety :

(*a*) as to transaction prior to variance. (*b*) as to transactions subsequent to variance.
(*c*) as to all transactions. (*d*) from his liability under the guarantee.

10. The right of subrogation in a contract of guarantee is available to the :

(*a*) creditor. (*b*) principal debtor.
(*c*) surety. (*d*) indemnifier.

ANSWERS

1. (*c*) **2.** (*c*) **3.** (*d*) **4.** (*a*) **5.** (*a*) **6.** (*b*) **7.** (*b*) **8.** (*a*) **9.** (*b*) **10.** (*c*)

CHAPTER

Contract of Bailment and Pledge

(Sections 148–181)

AT A GLANCE

INTRODUCTION

A bailment is the delivery of goods by a person to another for definite purpose, on the condition that after the purpose is accomplished, the goods have to be returned. Common examples of bailment are hiring of goods, furniture or cycle etc., delivering of cloth to a tailor for making suit, delivering a car or scooter for repairs, depositing luggage in cloak room, delivering dresses to a dry cleaners etc.

According to Section 148 of the Indian Contract Act, "A bailment is the delivery of goods by one person to another for some purpose, upon a contract that they shall, when the purpose is accomplished, be returned or otherwise disposed of according to the directions of the person delivering them".

The person delivering the goods is called the BAILOR. The person to whom they are delivered is called the BAILEE. The transaction is called BAILMENT.

Bailment means 'to deliver' or 'to hand over'. Bailment signifies a contract resulting from delivery. It involves change of possession and not transfer of ownership. It implies a sort of relationship in which the personal property of one person, temporarily, goes into the possession of another person. Custody of goods without possession does not constitute bailment. For example, a servant.

According to Halsbury a bailment is "a delivery of personal chattels in trust on a contract, express or implied, that the trust shall be duly executed, and the chattels re-delivered, in either their original or altered form, as soon as the time of use for, or condition on which they were bailed, shall have elapsed or been performed."

ESSENTIALS OF BAILMENT

Section 148 of the Act explains the characteristics of bailment. They are as under :

1. *Contract*

Bailment is based upon a contract between bailor and bailee. The agreement is that the goods are to be returned when the purpose is fulfilled. The condition is that the goods should be returned either in their original form or in altered form. For example, where a watch is delivered to a watch repairer for repairs, it is agreed that it will be returned after repairs. The agreement may be express or implied.

2. *Delivery of Goods*

Bailment involves change of possession. It necessarily involves a temporary delivery of possession of goods by bailor to bailee for some specific purpose is the most important. The ownership of the goods is retained by the bailor. Possession should be distinguished from mere custody. Mere custody without possession does not create bailment. For example, a domestic servant or a guest.

Example : *Kaliaperumal Vs. Visalakshi* (1938)

A lady employed a goldsmith for the purpose of melting old jewelry and making new jewels. Every evening she used to receive the half-made jewels from the goldsmith and put them into a box which was left in a room in the goldsmith's house, of which she retained the key. On one night they were stolen. Held, there was a redelivery of the jewels to the lady and they were not in the possession of the goldsmith when stolen. No negligence on the part of the goldsmith was proved. Therefore, the goldsmith was not liable for the loss of jewelry.

Ultzen Vs. Nicols (1894)

It was pointed out in this case, that, "One who has custody without possession, like a servant, or a guest using his host's goods is not a bailee."

In this case, the plaintiff entered the defendant's restaurant to dine. His coat was taken by a waiter and hung on hook behind the plaintiff. While the plaintiff was dining, his coat was stolen. In a suit by the plaintiff, it was held that the proprietor of the restaurant was liable for the loss.

The waiter, in this case, had taken possession of the coat and selected the place himself for its safe-keeping. He did not act as a servant under instructions from the owner to collect the coat and keep it in a particular place. Hence, the owner of the restaurant had become the bailee.

On the other hand, in Deyong Vs. Shenburn (1946), it was held that an actor who left his clothes in his dressing room, did not constitute the theatre owners bailees of the clothes.

How is Delivery Made?

According to Section 149 of the Act, "the delivery to the bailee may be made by doing anything which has the effect of putting the goods in the possession of the intended bailee or of any person authorised to hold them on his behalf." Delivery of goods may be *actual* or *constructive*. The actual delivery means the delivery when the bailor hands over the physical possession of the goods to the bailee. For example, delivery of car for repairs. Constructive delivery or symbolic delivery, on the other hand, does not involve handing over the physical possession, but something is done which has the effect of putting the goods in the possession of bailee. For example, delivery of Railway Receipt amounts to delivery of goods, that is, here there is no actual transfer of goods. But something is done *i.e.*, handing over the Railway Receipt has the effect of putting the goods in the possession of bailee. Explanation to Section 148 states that "If a person already in possession of the goods of another contracts to hold them as a bailee, he thereby becomes the bailee, and the owner becomes the bailor of such goods although they may not have been delivered by way of bailment".

3. *Specific Purpose*

When goods are delivered by mistake without any purpose, there is no bailment within the meaning of Section 148. Delivery of goods must be for some specific purpose. The bailee is bound to return the goods as soon as the purpose is accomplished or otherwise disposed off according to the directions of the bailor.

4. *Return of Goods*

Bailment is made for some purpose and after the accomplishment of the purpose, the goods should be returned to the bailor or to somebody according to the directions of the bailor, either in their original form or in an altered form.

The bailment is concerned with only movable goods. Money is not included in movable goods. A deposit of money into the bank does not constitute a bailment because there is no obligation to return the identical money. Deposit of GP Notes, pronotes etc. with a bank for safe custody is treated as bailment.

In short, essentials of bailment are

(1) A delivery of (2) goods (3) by one person called the bailor (4) to another person called the bailee (5) for a specific purpose and (6) upon a contract (condition) that the goods shall be returned in specie either in their original or in an altered from or (7) otherwise disposed of according to the direction of the bailor.

Differences between Sale and Bailment, in brief, are given below :

(1) In a sale, the ownership in goods is transferred from seller to buyer : while in bailment, there is transfer of possession only and no ownership is transferred to bailee.

(2) In a sale, there is no return of goods from buyer to seller. But in bailment, the bailee returns the goods to the bailor.

(3) The buyer can use the goods in any way he likes : but in bailment, the bailee can use the goods only according to the directions of the bailor.

(4) In a sale, the consideration for a sale is the price in terms of money. In bailment, the consideration is an understanding to return the goods after the purpose is accomplished.

Kinds of Bailment

Bailment may be classified on the basis of (*i*) Benefit and (*ii*) Reward.

KINDS ON THE BASIS OF BENEFIT

On the basis of benefits, bailment may be classified into three types :

(A) ***Bailment for the Exclusive Benefit of Bailor :*** It may be in the case of safe custody, where goods are delivered to a neighbour or someone else for safe custody without any charge, while the bailor (owner) goes away.

(B) ***Bailment for the Exclusive Benefit of Bailee :*** It may be in the case of a delivery of a thing to someone else for his use without any charge, for example, delivery of scooter to a friend to go somewhere.

(C) ***Bailment for Mutual Benefit :*** In this type of bailment delivery of goods is done with some consideration, for example, delivering a scooter to a mechanic for repairs.

KINDS ON THE BASIS OF REWARD

On the basis of reward, bailment is classified into two :

(A) ***Gratuitous Bailment.*** It is one in which neither the bailor nor the bailee is entitled to any remuneration, for example, A gives his book to B for reading.

(B) ***Non-gratuitous Bailment.*** It is a bailment for some charges. Either the bailor or the bailee is entitled to a remuneration, for example, cycle let out for hire, or cycle given for repairing etc.

DISTINCTION BETWEEN GRATUITOUS AND NON-GRATUITOUS BAILMENT

The following are the points of difference between the two :

(1) Consideration. In case of gratuitous bailment no consideration passes between the bailor and the bailee. In ease of non-gratuitous bailment either the bailor or the bailee is entitled to remuneration.

(2) Duty to disclose defects in goods bailed. If bailment is gratuitous, it is the duty of the bailor to disclose to the bailee known faults in goods bailed, while in case of non-gratuitous the bailor is responsible for damages occurred to the bailee due to defect in goods even if he himself was not aware of the existence of such defect in goods bailed.

(3) Repayment of necessary expenses. In case of a gratuitous bailment, it is the duty of the bailor to meet the bailee's necessary expenses incurred for the purpose of bailment. However, in case of non-gratuitous bailment the bailor has no duty to for such expenses.

(4) Premature termination. If a gratuitous bailment is made for a specified time or purpose, and the bailor compels the return of the thing bailed even before the expiry of the time. A non-gratuitous bailor has no right to terminate the bailment before the expiry of the specified period or completion of the specified purpose.

(5) Termination on death. A gratuitous bailment is terminated by the death either of the bailor or of the bailee, but a non-gratuitous bailment is not so terminated.

CONSIDERATION

Bailment is based upon a contract between the bailor and the bailee. It becomes necessary to discover consideration supporting the contract, if the bailment is gratuitous – "for the exclusive benefit of the bailor or for the exclusive benefit of the bailee". "The detriment suffered by the bailor in parting with the possession of the goods is sufficient consideration to support the promise on the part of the bailee to return the goods."

DUTIES OF BAILOR

1. *To Disclose the Faults in the Goods Bailed*

Section 150 provides "The bailor is bound to disclose to the bailee the faults in the goods bailed, of which the bailor is aware and which materially interfere with the use of them, or expose the bailee to extraordinary risks; and, if he does not make such disclosure, he is responsible for damage arising to the bailee directly from such faults.

If the goods are bailed for hire, the bailor is responsible for such damage, whether he was or was not aware of the existence of such faults in the goods bailed."

Duties of a bailor to disclose faults in the goods are different for gratuitous and non-gratuitous bailors. A gratuitous bailor is a bailor who lends his goods to the bailee without any charge. A gratuitous bailor is bound to disclose to the bailee all those defects of which he is aware and which expose the bailee to extraordinary risk. Failure to make such disclosure will make the bailor liable for damages arising to the bailee directly from such faults. Gratuitous bailor will not be liable for the defects which are not within his knowledge. (Section 150 First para).

Example : A lends a horse which he knows to be vicious to B. He does not disclose the fact that the horse is vicious. The horse runs away, B is thrown and injured. A is responsible to B for damage sustained.

A non-gratuitous bailor is a bailor who lends his goods to the bailee for charges *i.e.*, he is the bailor for reward. The duty of a bailor for reward is much greater. The bailor must see that the goods which he gives on hire are safe. The non-gratuitous bailor is liable for all damages which are caused due to the faults in the goods to the bailee irrespective of the fact whether the faults were known to him or not (Section 150 Para 2). It is the duty of the bailor to supply goods as fit for the purpose for which they are hired.

Example : A hires a carriage of B. The carriage is unsafe, though B is not aware of it, and A is injured, B is responsible to A for the injury.

2. *Repay Necessary Expenses* (Sec. 158)

According to Section 158, "Where, by the conditions of the bailment, the goods are to be kept or to be carried, or to have work done upon them by the bailee for the bailor, and the bailee is to receive no remuneration, the bailor shall repay to the bailee the necessary expenses incurred by him for the purpose of bailment." Thus, in the case of gratuitous bailment, the bailor has to repay to the bailee all the necessary expenses incurred by him for the purpose of bailment. In the case of non-gratuitous bailment, the bailor is held responsible to bear only extra-ordinary expenses.

Example : If a horse is lent for journey, the expenses of feeding the horse would be borne by the bailee (ordinary expense). But if the horse becomes sick and expenses have been incurred for its recovery, the bailor should have to pay it (extraordinary expenses).

3. *To Indemnify the Bailee* (Sec. 159)

If the borrower is compelled to return goods, in the case of gratuitous bailment, before the specified time and suffers loss which exceeds the benefit derived by him, the bailor's duty is to indemnify the borrower for such loss.

4. *Responsibility for any Loss due to Defect in Title* (Sec. 164)

"The bailor is responsible to the bailee for any loss which the bailee may sustain by reason that the bailor was not entitled to make the bailment, or to receive back the goods, or to give directions, respecting them."

Duties of Bailor

1. To disclose known defects
2. To bear expenses (gratuitous)
3. To bear extra-ordinary expenses. (Non-gratuitous)
4. To receive back the goods
5. To indemnify the bailee

5. *To Receive back the Goods*

When the bailee returns the goods after the purpose is fulfilled or the time is expired, it is the duty of the bailor to receive back the goods. In case, the bailor refuses to receive back the goods, he is liable to pay compensation to the bailee who incurs expenses in maintaining the same.

DUTIES OF BAILEE

1. *To Take Reasonable Care of the Goods Bailed* (Sec. 151)

According to Section 151, "In all cases of bailment the bailee is bound to take as much care of the goods bailed to him as a man of ordinary prudence would, under similar circumstances, take of his own goods of the same bulk, quality and value as the goods bailed."

Further Section 152 states, "The bailee, in the absence of any special contract, is not responsible for the loss, destruction or deterioration of the thing bailed, if he has taken the amount of care of it described in Section 151".

Coldman Vs. Hill (1919)

In this case, some cattle belonging to the plaintiff were left with the defendant for grazing. Without any negligence on the part of the defendant, the cattle were stolen. The defendant did not inform the plaintiff or the police. He did not also put forth any efforts to recover them thinking that it would be useless to do so.

In a suit by the plaintiff, it was held that the defendant was liable for the loss, unless he could prove that, even if he had reported the loss, the cattle could not have been recovered. Thus, the duties of the bailee do not come to an end when the goods are lost or stolen. It is his duty not only to prove that there was no negligence on his part, but should also show that he used reasonable care to assist in their recovery.

2. *Not to Make Unauthorised Use of Goods Bailed* (Sec. 154)

"If the bailee makes any use of the goods bailed, which is not according to the conditions of the bailment, he is liable to make compensation to the bailor for any damage arising to the goods from or during such use of them".

Examples : (1) A lends a horse to B for his own riding only. B allows C, member of his family, to ride the horse. C rides with care, but the horse accidently falls and is injured. B is liable to make compensation to A for the injury done to the horse.

(2) A hires a horse in Calcutta from B expressly to march to Banaras. A rides with due care, but marches to Cuttack instead. The horse accidently falls and is injured. A is liable to make compensation to B for the injury to the horse.

3. *Not to Mix the Goods Bailed with his Own Goods* (Secs. 155, 156 and 157)

The bailee should not mix the goods bailed with his own goods. If he mixes, the following rules apply :

(*a*) "If the bailee, with the consent of the bailor, mixes the goods of the bailor with his own goods, the bailor and the bailee shall have an interest, in proportion to their respective shares, in the mixture thus produced" (Sec. 155).

Example : A bails one bag of sugar to B. B with the consent of A, mixes A's sugar with three bags of his own. Here A and B have interest in the mixture in proportion of 1 : 3.

(*b*) "If the bailee, without the consent of the bailor mixes the goods of the bailor with his own goods, and the goods can be separated or divided, the property in the goods remains in the parties respectively : but the bailee is bound to bear the expenses of separation or division, and any damage arising from the mixture" (Sec. 156).

Example : A bails 100 bales of cotton marked with a particular mark to B. B without A's consent mixes the 100 bales with other bales of his own bearing a different mark. A is entitled to have his 100 bales returned and B is bound to bear all the expenses incurred in the separation of the bales and any other incidental damages.

(*c*) "If the bailee, without the consent of the bailor, mixes the goods of the bailor with his own goods, in such a manner that it is impossible to separate the goods bailed from the other goods and deliver them back, the bailor is entitled to be compensated by the bailee for the loss of the goods" (Sec. 157).

> **Example :** A bails a barrel of cape flour worth Rs. 45 to B. B without A's consent mixes the flour with country flour of his own, worth only Rs. 25 a barrel. B must compensate A for the loss of his flour.

4. *To Return the Goods Bailed* (Sec. 160)

According to Section 160, "It is the duty of the bailee to return, or deliver, according to the bailor's directions, the goods bailed, without demand, as soon as the time for which they were bailed has expired, or the purpose for which they were bailed has been accomplished." Again according to Section 165, "Where there are several joint bailors, the bailee may return the goods to any one of the joint owners."

According to Section 161, "If, by the default of the bailee, the goods are not returned, delivered or tendered at the proper time, he is responsible to the bailor for any loss, destruction or deterioration of the goods from that time".

> **Example :** *Shaw & Co. Vs. Symmons & Sons* (1917)
>
> A delivered certain books to B to be bound and return within reasonable time. B could not complete the job within reasonable time. The books were subsequently burnt in an accidental fire in B's premises. B was held liable in damages for the loss of the books and the plea that the fire was accidental or an act of God was of no avail.

5. *To Return Increase or Profit Accrued*

According to Section 163, "In the absence of any contract to contrary, the bailee is bound to deliver to the bailor, or according to his directions, any increase or profit which may have accrued from the goods bailed".

> **Example :** A leaves a cow in the custody of B to be taken care of. The cow has a calf. B is bound to deliver the calf as well as the cow to A.

6. *Not to Set up an Adverse Title*

Under section 117 of the Indian Evidence Act, the bailee holds the goods on behalf of and for the bailor, he cannot deny the title of the bailor. It is the duty of the bailee to return the goods only to the bailor even though any third person is claiming title over them.

Duties of Bailee

1. To take care of goods bailed
2. Not to make unauthorised use
3. To return the goods bailed
4. Not to mix the goods with his own.
5. To deliver accretion to goods
6. Not to set up adverse title.

RIGHTS OF BAILOR

Rights of a bailor are almost the same as the duties of a bailee. These rights are summarised as follows :

1. *Right to sue*

The bailor has a right to sue the bailee for the enforcement of the bailee's duties and liabilities.

2. *Right to Terminate the Bailment* (Sec. 153)

Section 153 states that "A contract of bailment is voidable at the option of the bailor, if the bailee does any act with regard to the goods bailed, inconsistent with the conditions of the bailment."

Example : A lends to B for hire a horse for his own riding. B drives the horse in his carriage. A can terminate the bailment.

3. *Unauthorised use by the Bailee* (Sec. 154)

Section 154 states, "If the bailee makes any use of the goods bailed, which is not according to the conditions of the bailment, he is liable to make compensation to the bailor for any damage arising to the goods from or during such use of them."

Example : A lends a horse to B for his own riding only. B allows C, a member of his family to ride the horse. C rides with care, but the horse accidentally falls and is injured. B is liable to make compensation to A for the injury does to the horse.

4. *Right against Mixture of Goods Bailed* (Sections 155, 156 and 157)

For details, see the duties of a bailee (given above)

5. *Right to Demand Return of Goods* (Sec. 159)

In case of gratuitous bailment the bailor can, at any time, exercise his option to terminate the contract and take back the goods bailed.

6. *He is Entitled to Claim Damages*

Bailor can claim damages for loss, destruction or deterioration of the goods bailed, owing to bailee's negligence.

7. *Right to Claim Increase in Value or Profits* (Sec. 163)

The bailor is entitled to get any increase or profit from the goods bailed.

8. *Suit against Wrongdoer* (Sec. 180)

The bailor can sue a third person who wrongfully deprives the bailee of the use of the goods, or does them any injury.

9. *Share in the Compensation Received* (Sec. 181)

Compensation in any suit, under sec. 180, received shall be apportioned between bailor and bailee, in accordance with their respective interest.

Rights of Bailor

1. Claim damage against bailee's negligence
2. Right of termination
3. Claim for damages against unauthorised use
4. Compensation for unauthorised mix
5. Entitled to get back the goods
6. To enforce duties of bailee
7. Right to claim accretion to goods
8. Right to sue against wrongdoers

Rights of Bailee

The duties of the bailor are the rights of the bailee. However, to recapitulate, the bailee has the following rights against bailor :

1. A bailee is entitled to claim damages for any loss caused to him from the undisclosed faults in the goods bailed. (Sec. 150)

2. In case of gratuitous bailment, bailee is entitled to recover from bailor all necessary expenses incurred by him for bailment (Sec. 158) : and of the extraordinary expenses in case of non-gratuitous bailment.
3. Right to indemnify, in case of gratuitous bailment, against premature termination of the contract by the bailor for any loss sustained. (Sec. 159)
4. A bailee is entitled to claim any loss sustained by him because of non-entitlement or defective entitlement of the bailor on goods bailed.
5. If a third person claims the ownership of the goods bailed, the bailee can ask the court to decide the ownership and can withhold the delivery to the bailor.
6. If a third person wrongfully deprives the bailee of the use or possession of the goods bailed to him, he has the right to bring an action against such third party (Sec. 180)
7. According to Section 165, in case of several joint bailors, the bailee can deliver the goods back to one of them without the consent of all.
8. Bailee enjoys the right of lien (Sec. 170 and 171)
   Bailee's lien, discussed separately, in this chapter.

RIGHTS OF BAILOR AND BAILEE AGAINST WRONGDOERS

1. *Right to Sue :* (Section 167)

If a person, other than the bailor, claims the goods bailed, he may apply to the courts to stop delivery of the goods bailed and to decide the title to the goods.

2. *Suit by Bailor or Bailee against Wrongdoer :* (Section 180)

If a third party wrongfully deprives the bailee of the use of the goods bailed or does them any injury, the bailee is entitled to use all such remedies as the owner of the goods might have used. Either the bailee or the bailor may file a suit against the third party in such cases.

3. *Apportionment of relief or compensation obtained by such suit :* (Section 181)

Whatever is obtained by way of relief or compensation in any such suits shall, as between the bailor and the bailee be dealt with according to their respective interests.

Bailee's Lien

"Lien is a right available to a person to retain that which is in his possession and which belongs to another, until the demands of the person in possession are satisfied". Thus, lien is available to a person who has in his possession, the goods belonging to another entitling him to retain such goods till the debts due to him are paid. Once the possession is lost, lien is also lost. This right is sometimes know as possessory lien.

Examples : (1) A delivers a rough diamond to B, a jeweller, to be cut and polished which is accordingly done. B is entitled to retain the stone till he is paid for the services he has rendered.

(2) A gives cloth to B, tailor to make into a coat. B promises A to deliver the coat as soon as it is finished, and to give A three months' credit for the price. B is not entitled to retain the coat until he is paid.

Lien is of two types : (*i*) Particular Lien and (*ii*) General Lien.

(*i*) Particular Lien

Particular or specific lien means the right to retain the particular goods until claims arising on those goods are satisfied. Section 170 confers the right of particular lien upon a bailee and provides, "Where the bailee has, in accordance with the purpose of the bailment, rendered any service involving the exercise of labour or skill in respect of the goods bailed, he has, in the absence of a contract to the contrary, a right to retain such goods until he receives the remuneration for the services he has rendered in respect of them."

Particular lien is available under the following conditions :

1. The goods must be in the possession of bailee. If the possession is lost, the lien is also lost.

2. The bailee must have rendered some services involving the exercise of labour and skill in respect of goods bailed so as to confer additional value on the article.

3. The services must have been performed in full in accordance with the directions of the bailor, within the agreed time or a reasonable time.

4. The bailee can exercise this lien provided there is no contract to contrary.

5. The bailee must have rendered some service in relation to the thing bailed and must be entitled to some remuneration for it, which must have been paid.

6. The bailee retain only such goods on which he has expended labour or skill.

If all the above mentioned conditions are satisfied, the bailee can exercise his right of particular lien until he is paid for his services.

Skinner Vs. Jager (1863)

In this case, the plaintiff delivered an organ for repair to the defendant. The defendant promised to repair it for Rs. 100. Subsequently, he refused to repair it for Rs. 100, and wanted to retain the organ for the work done on it. It was held that the defendant could not retain the organ, and nothing could be demanded as there was an express contract for the work to be done in its entirety.

(*ii*) General Lien

It means the right to retain goods not only for demands arising out of the goods retained but for a general balance of accounts in favour of certain persons. That is, this right entitles a person to retain possession of any goods belonging to another for any amount due to him whether in respect of those goods or any other goods. According to Section 171, "Bankers, factors, wharfingers, attorneys of High Court, and policy brokers may in the absence of a contract to the contrary retain, as security for a general balance of amount, any goods bailed to them; but no other person have a right to retain, as a security for such balance, goods bailed to them unless there is an express contract to that effect."

General lien is a privilege and is given only to certain kinds of bailee, *viz.*, (1) Bankers, (2) Factors, (3) Wharfingers, (4) Attorneys of High Court and (5) Policy brokers. Any of these persons can exercise general lien against any goods under their possession in respect of any sum legally due on a general balance of account.

Particular Lien and General Lien distinguished :

Particular Lien	*General Lien*
1. Particular lien can be exercised by all bailees.	1. General lien can be exercised only by bankers, factors, wharfingers, attorneys and policy brokers.
2. Particular lien is available on those things only on which some skill or labour has been used or money incurred.	2. General lien is available on all the goods bailed.
3. It can be used for the remuneration of services rendered on anything.	3. General lien is used for any balance of account.

Termination of Lien

A lien may be extinguished by any of the following ways :

1. A gratuitous bailment is terminated by the death of either the bailor or the bailee (Sec. 162).

2. In case, the bailment is for a specific purpose, it terminates as soon as the purpose is accomplished (Sec. 148).

3. When the bailment is for a stipulated period, it comes to an end on the expiry of the specified period (Sec. 148).

4. If the bailee does any act, with regard to the goods bailed, which is inconsistent with the terms of the bailment, the bailment terminates (Sec. 153).

5. A lien is lost by surrender of possession of goods.

6. Lien is terminated when the debt is satisfied.

Finder of Lost Goods

A person who finds goods belonging to another and takes them into custody is called a finder of lost goods. A person, who finds goods belonging to the other, is not bound to take them into his custody or take charge of it. But if he picks them up or take charge of the goods, he becomes the bailee of those goods. Section 71 of the Act, clearly states that a person who finds goods belonging to another and takes them into his custody, is subject to the same responsibilities as a bailee.

Duties of a Finder of Lost Goods

His duties are the same as those of a bailee. In brief, the following are the duties of a finder of lost goods.

(*a*) He must take reasonable care of the goods found (Sec. 151).

(*b*) He must try to find out the true owner of the goods. If he fails, he will be liable as a trespasser or a thief.

(*c*) He must not mix up the goods with his own goods.

(*d*) He should not use the goods found for his own purpose.

Rights of the Finder of Goods

1. The finder has the right of lien over the goods for his expenses.

As such he can retain the goods against the owner, until he receives compensation for trouble and expenses for preserving the goods and finding out the owner. But he has no right to sue the owner for any compensation.

2. In case the owner has offered any specific reward for the return of goods, the finder may sue for such reward and he may retain the goods until such reward is paid.

3. A finder has the right to retain possession of the goods against the whole world, except the true owner.

4. According to Section 169 of the Act, the finder of goods may sell if :

(*a*) the owner cannot, with reasonable diligence be found, or

(*b*) he refuses, upon demand, to pay the lawful charges of the finder, or

(*c*) the thing is in danger of perishing or of losing the greater part of its value, or

(*d*) the lawful charges of the finder, in respect of the thing found, amount to two-thirds of its value.

Pledge or Pawn

Pledge or pawn is a special kind of bailment where a thing is delivered as security for the repayment of a debt. According to Section 172 of the Contract Act, "The bailment of goods as security for payment of a debt or for performance of a promise, is called pledge. The bailor in this case is called the pawnor. The bailee is called the pawnee". The following are the two parties to a pledge :

(*a*) Pawnor or pledger means the person who delivers the goods.

(*b*) Pawnee or Pledgee means the person to whom the goods are delivered as security.

> **Example :** A borrows Rs. 5,000 from B and keeps his scooter as security for repayment of the debt. This kind of bailment of property is called a pledge or pawn. Here A is the pawnor and B the pawnee.

Essentials of Pledge

Essentials of a valid pledge are as follows :

1. The goods must be delivered by borrower to the lender as a security for repayment of debt or for performance of a promise.
2. The possession of the goods passes from one person to the other person and not the ownership.
3. Pledge can be of only movable goods – documents of title, shares, valuables etc. Immovable properties cannot be pledged.
4. The goods, pledged with the pawnee, to be returned on receipt of his full dues.

Duties of Pawnor

1. It is the duty of the pawnor to repay the loan taken from the pawnee within the time and in the manner specified in the contract.
2. He has to compensate the pawnee for any extraordinary expenses incurred by him.
3. Default or risk, if any, in the goods pledged, should be known to pawnee.

Rights of Pawnor

1. The pawnor has the right to take back the goods pledged provided that he has paid the whole of the amount of debt alongwith any interest or charges thereon, to the pawnee.
2. The duties of the pawnee are the rights of the pawnor. Therefore, the pawnor can enforce by suit all the duties of the pawnee (enumerated below).
3. Usually a time may be stipulated for the payment of the debt, or performance of the promise, for which the pledge is made. If the pawnor makes default in payment of the debt or performance of the promise at the stipulated time he may redeem the goods pledged at any subsequent time before the actual sale is made. But on exercising such right of redemption the pawnor must pay any expenses which might have arisen from his default (Sec. 177).

Duties of Pawnee

The duties of pawnee are similar to bailee. However, his duties, in brief, are given below :

1. He has to take reasonable care of the goods pledged.
2. He is not permitted any unauthorised use of the goods pledged.
3. He has to return the pledged goods on the payment of debt.
4. He should not do any act in violation of the terms of the contract.
5. He should not mix the goods pledged with his own goods.
6. Any accruals to the goods pledged belong to the pledgor and should be delivered accordingly.

RIGHTS OF PAWNEE

1. *Right of Retainer* (Sec. 173)

The pawnee may retain the goods for :

(*a*) payment of the debt or the performance of the promise;
(*b*) interest on the debt;
(*c*) All necessary expenses incurred by him in respect of the possession or for the preservation of the goods pledged. (Sec. 173). Pawnee's right of retention is that of a particular lien.

2. *Right of Retainer for Subsequent Advances* (Sec. 174)

If the pawnee lends money to the same pawnor subsequent to the pledge, the right of the retainer over the pledged goods extends to subsequent advances also (Sec. 174).

3. *Right to Extraordinary Expenses* (Sec. 175)

The pawnee is entitled to receive from the pawnor extraordinary expenses incurred by him for the preservation of the goods pledged (Sec. 175).

4. *Right in case of Default by Pawnor* (Sec. 176)

Where the pawnor makes a default in payment of the debt or in the performance of the promise under the contract of pledge, the pawnee will have the following rights :

(*a*) He can file a suit against the pawnor for the debt.

(*b*) He can retain the goods pledged as a collateral security.

(*c*) He may sue for the sale of goods or the realization of his amount due.

(*d*) He can sell the goods pledged after giving the pawnor a reasonable notice of the sale.

(*e*) He can recover any deficiency arising on the sale of the goods by him from the pawnor. But surplus, if any, shall be given to the pawnor (Sec. 176).

5. *Right against the True Owner, when the Pawnor's Title is Defective*

When the pawnor has obtained possession of the goods pledged by him under voidable contract but the contract has not been rescinded at the time of the pledge, the pawnee acquires a good title to the goods, provided he acted in good faith and without notice of the pawnor's defect of title (Sec. 178 A).

Pledge and Lien Distinguished

Pledge	*Lien*
1. Pledge is created by contract between the parties.	1. In most cases, lien is created by law.
2. Goods are bailed as a promise.	2. Lien is only a right to retain.
3. It gives right to sell.	3. It gives no right to sell.
4. It is terminated on returning the goods pledged.	4. The right of lien is lost with the loss of the possession of goods.
5. Pawnee has the right to enforce his claim against pawnor.	5. A lien holder cannot sue to enforce his claim. It is merely a passive and possessory right.

Bailment and Pledge Compared

Similarities

1. In both, delivery of goods is important.
2. In both, possession of goods alone is transferred and the ownership is retained by owner.
3. Both are created by agreement between the parties.
4. In both, moveable goods are the subject matter.
5. In both, the goods are returned on the fulfillment of purpose.

Bailment and Pledge distinguished :

Pledge	*Bailment*
1. Goods are pledged as a security.	1. Goods are bailed for carrying out specific purpose.
2. In case of default, the pawnee may retain the goods. He can sell the goods.	2. The bailee can retain the goods bailed but he cannot sell it.
3. Pawnee has no right to use the goods.	3. Bailee may use the goods bailed as per the terms of the contract.

Pledge and Mortgage Distinguished :

Pledge	*Mortgage*
1. Moveable property is the subject matter.	1. Immovable property is the subject matter.
2. A pawnee is not allowed to use the goods pledged.	2. Mortgagee has the right to use the property mortgaged.
3. Delivery of possession is essential.	3. The property in goods passes to the mortgagee though their possession remain with the mortgagor.
4. Only one loan can be taken at a time on the pledge of the same goods.	4. On a mortgage of asset more than one loan can be taken.
5. A pledgee cannot impose the right of foreclosure on the goods pledged with the exception of exercising his right to sell on giving notice to the pledger.	5. In mortgage, a mortgagee can do so under certain circumstances.

PLEDGE BY NON-OWNERS

It is a general rule that it is only the owner who can make a valid pledge. No one can convey a better title than what he had, is applicable to bailment and pledge. But, Sections 178, 178 A and 179 of the Indian Contract Act provides certain circumstances in which the pledge made by a non-owner or a co-owner is also valid. In the following cases, a non-owner can make a valid pledge.

1. *Pledge by Mercantile Agent*

According to Section 178, pledge by a mercantile agent, who is not authorised by the owner of goods, will be valid, if the following conditions are fulfilled :

(*a*) The mercantile agent is in possession of goods or document of title to the goods;
(*b*) Such possession is with the consent of the owner;
(*c*) He acts in the ordinary course of business while making the pledge.
(*d*) The pawnee acts in good faith, and
(*e*) The pawnee has no notice of the pawnor's defective title.

2. *Pledge by Seller or Buyer in Possession after Sale*

According to Section 30 of Sales of Goods Act, a seller left in possession of goods after sale and a buyer, who obtains possession of goods with the consent of the seller before sale, can create a valid pledge provided that the pawnee acts in good faith and has no notice of the previous sale of goods to the buyer or of the lien of the seller over the goods.

3. *Pledge by a Person in Possession under a Voidable Contract*

Where a person obtains possession of goods under a voidable contract, the pledge created by him will be valid, subject to the following conditions :

(*a*) The contract has not been rescinded before the contract of pledge.
(*b*) The pawnee acts in good faith, and
(*c*) The pawnee has no notice of the pawnor's defect of title (Sec. 178 A).

4. *Pledge by Person having Limited Interest* (Sec. 179)

Where a person pledges the goods, in which he has only a limited interest, the pledge is valid to the extent of that interest.

Example : A finds a cycle on the road and gets it repaired for Rs. 100 and pledges it with B for Rs. 200. The real owner can get the cycle on payment of Rs. 100.

5. *Pledge by Co-owners in Possession*

One of the several joint owners of the goods in possession thereof, with the consent of the other co-owners, may create a valid pledge of the goods.

THEORETICAL QUESTIONS

1. What are the duties of a bailee? What rights does he enjoy under contract of bailment? *(B.Com. M.S.)*
2. Define a Contract of bailment. What are its essentials? *(B.Com. Madurai)*
3. Explain bailee's particular lien and bailee's general lien. *(B.Com.)*
4. What is lien? How does particular lien differ from general lien? *(B.Com. Madras)*
5. What are the rights of a bailor against a bailee when the latter mixes his own goods with him? *(B.Com. Kerala)*
6. Define pledge. What are the essentials of a valid pledge? *(B.Com. Mad)*
7. Discuss the rights and obligations of a finder of goods. *(B.Com. M.S.)*
8. Distinguish between pledge and bailment.
9. Explain the rights of pawnee.
10. Distinguish between gratuitous and non-gratuitous bailment. *(CA)*
11. When will a pledge made by a non-owner of goods becomes valid?
12. "The position of a finder of goods is exactly that of a bailee in the case of a deposit." Comment and discuss.

OBJECTIVE TYPE QUESTIONS

Multiple Choice Questions

1. A bailee has :

(*a*) a right of particular lien over the goods bailed.
(*b*) a right of general lien.
(*c*) a right of both particular and general lien.
(*d*) no lien at all over the goods bailed.

2. The position of the finder of lost goods is that of a :

(*a*) bailor. (*b*) bailee.
(*c*) surety. (*d*) principal debtor.

3. A gratuitous bailee is liable for defects in the goods bailed :

(*a*) even if he is not aware of them. (*b*) only if he is aware of them.
(*e*) in all cases.

4. A who purchases certain goods from B by a misrepresentation pledges them with C. The pledge is :

(*a*) valid. (*b*) void.
(*c*) voidable. (*d*) invalid.

5. A gratuitous bailment is one which is :

(*a*) supported by consideration. (*b*) not supported by consideration.
(*c*) not enforceable by law. (*d*) void.

6. The delivery of goods by one person to another as security for the repayment of a debt, is known as :

(*a*) Bailment. (*b*) Hypothecation.
(*c*) pledge. (*d*) mortgage.

7. Creation of security on the immovable property for securing the repayment of the loan, is known as:
(*a*) bailment. (*b*) pledge.
(*c*) hypothecation. (*d*) mortgage.

8. The delivery of goods by one person to another for some specific purpose, is known as :
(*a*) bailment. (*b*) hypothecation.
(*c*) pledge. (*d*) Mortgage.

9. The bailment of goods can be made by its owner of :
(*a*) immovable goods. (*b*) movable goods.
(*c*) both of these. (*d*) none of these.

10. A lent his bike to his friend, for two days without any charges. It is a :
(*a*) hypothecation. (*b*) non-gratuitous bailment.
(*c*) gratuitous bailment. (*d*) beneficial bailment.

ANSWERS

1. (*a*) **2.** (*b*) **3.** (*b*) **4.** (*a*) **5.** (*b*) **6.** (*c*) **7.** (*d*) **8.** (*a*) **9.** (*b*) **10.** (*c*)

CHAPTER

Contract of Agency

(Sections 182–238)

AT A GLANCE

INTRODUCTION

Modern business is becoming complex day by day. Due to vast expansion of the modern business, it is not possible for a person to carry on all the business transactions himself. Thus circumstances require a businessman to depend upon another persons to transact his business. A businessman must necessarily depend on others for the efficient running of the business. He must delegate some of his powers to another. The another person who acts on behalf of a businessman is known as *an agent*. The person to whom such act is done, or who is so represented is called *the principal*. The contract which creates the relationship of principal and agent is called *an agency.* Thus, A appoint B to sell his cars on his (A's) behalf. A is the principal. B is his agent. The relationship between A and B is called *agency.*

Section 182 of the Act defines that "an agent is a person employed to do any act for another, or to represent another in dealings with third person. The person for whom such act is done, or who is so represented, is called the principal."

The function of an agent is to bring about contractual relations between the principal and the third parties. The acts of the agent bind his principal to third persons. Similarly the acts of the agent also give right to third persons against the principal. The function of an agent is to bring his principal into contractual relationship with third parties. Thus, the agent is merely a contracting link between the principal and the third parties. The agent has the power to make the principal answerable to the third parties for his conduct. So every person who acts for another is not an agent. In this regard, the observations of Justice Ramaswamy are worth-noting :

"In legal phraseology, every person who acts for another is not an agent. A domestic servant renders to his master a personal service; a person may till another's field or work in his shop or factory or mine or may be employed upon his roads or ways. In none of these capacities, he is an agent and he is not acting for another in dealings with third persons. It is only when he acts as a representative of the other in business negotiations, that is to say, in the creation, modifications or termination of contractual obligations between that other and third persons, that he is an agent. Representative character and derivative authority may briefly be said to be the distinguishing features of an agent."

RULES OF AGENCY

The above mentioned facts indicate that there are two important rules of agency (test of agency) *viz.*:

(1) Agency exists whenever a person can bind another by acts done on his behalf. That is, when acted upon by the agent, it connects the principal with third persons. The principal acquires rights and liabilities and the agent drops out and ceases to be a party to the contract. The agent acts only as a "conduit pipe". The acts of the agent are considered the acts of his principal. Section 226 provides that "Contracts entered into through an agent, and obligations arising from acts done by an agent, may be enforced in the same manner, and will have the same legal consequences, as if the contracts had been entered into and the acts done by the principal in person."

Examples : (1) A buys goods from B, knowing that he is an agent for their sale, but not knowing who is the principal. B's principal is the person entitled to claim from A price of the goods, and A cannot in a suit by the principal, set-off against that claim a debt due to himself from B.

(2) A, being B's agent, with authority to receive money on his behalf, receives from C a sum of money due to B. C is discharged of his obligation to pay the sum in question to B.

2. Whatever a person can lawfully do himself, he may also do the same through an agent. In other words, "*Qui facit per alium facit per se*" is the principle of agency, which means, "He who does through another does by himself. This rule is subject to certain exceptions, for example, contracts involving personal services or skill, such as marriage, singing, painting etc. A wife is not the agent of the husband except under special circumstances and for special purposes. Similarly, a guardian is not an agent of a minor.

Agent distinguished from other relations :

Agent	*Servant*
1. An agent is authorised to act on behalf of his principal and has power to create legal relations between the principal and third persons.	1. A servant has no representative character. He has no authority to make contract on behalf of his master.
2. An agent is not subject to the direct control and supervision of the principal.	2. A servant acts under the direct control and supervision of his employer.
3. An agent may work for several principals.	3. A whole time servant serves only one master.
4. The principal directs an agent "as to what is to be done".	4. The master has the right to direct not only "what work is to be done" but also "how the work is to be done".
5. An agent may be paid by way of commission on the basis of work done.	5. A servant is paid by way of salary or wages.
6. The principal is liable for only those acts of his agent which are done within the scope of authority and is not liable for those acts of the agent which are done outside the scope of such authority.	6. An employer is liable for the wrongful acts of the servant, if such acts are committed in the course of employment.

Agent	Independent Contractor
1. An agent represents his principal and has the authority to create contractual relationship between his principal and third parties.	1. An independent contractor does not represent his employer. And no authority to create contractual relationship between his master and third parties.
2. An agent is not personally liable in ordinary cases.	2. Independent contractor is personally liable for all acts done by him.
3. The question of authority arises in case of agency.	3. The question of authority does not arise in the case of independent contractor.
4. An agent is bound to act in the matter of agency subject to the directions and control of his principal.	4. An independent contractor undertakes to perform a certain specified work,, the manner and means of performance being left to his discretion.

Agent	Bailee
1. An agent may not have possession of any goods or property of the principal.	1. A bailee has possession of goods of the bailor.
2. An agent has authority to contract on behalf of his principal.	2. A bailee does not have such authority.

Who can appoint an Agent? (Who may be a principal)

According to Section 183, "Any person who is of the age of majority according to the law to which he is subject, and who is of sound mind, may employ an agent." Thus, it is essential that a principal must have contractual capacity. A minor or a person of unsound mind cannot be a principal. The agent is employed mainly to bring about a contractual relationship between the principal and third persons. Hence the principal and the third persons must be capable of entering into a contract. The contract of agency is based upon the maxim; *Qui facit per facit per se*" that is, he who does through another does by himself.

WHO MAY BE AN AGENT

Section 184 lays down that "As between the principal and third persons any person may become an agent, but no person who is not of the age of majority and of sound mind can become an agent, so as to be responsible to his principal according to the provisions in that behalf." An agent is a connecting link or a "conduit pipe" between the principal and third party. It is immaterial whether or not the agent is legally competent to contract. There is no bar to the appointment of a minor as an agent. Thus even a minor or a person of unsound mind can be appointed as agent. But personally such a person is not responsible to the principal like an adult agent. It is so because the act of the agent is the act of the principal. Therefore, the principal is liable to third persons for the acts of a minor agent. However, it may be noted that such an incompetent agent shall not be liable to the principal. And the principal cannot recover any compensation from an incompetent agent for losses caused by misconduct or unauthorised acts of such agent. However, in the interest of the principal that the agent should have contractual capacity.

ESSENTIALS OF AGENCY

1. ***The Principal must be Competent to Enter into a Valid Contract***

Section 183 clearly states that any person who is major and of sound mind can employ an agent. An incompetent person *i.e.*, a minor or lunatic, cannot appoint an agent because they cannot act as principal.

2. ***Any Person may Become an Agent*** (Sec. 184)

The agent need not be competent to contract. Even a person having no contractual capacity, for example, a minor or a person of unsound mind, may become an agent. An agent brings about a contractual relationship between his principal and third persons and, therefore, his contractual capacity is immaterial. Incompetent persons can be appointed as agents only at the risk of the principal himself.

3. ***There should be an Agreement between the Principal and the Agent***

The agreement may be express or implied. (Discussed below).

4. ***The agent must act in Representative Capacity***

"The essence of the matter is that the principal authorised the agent to represent or act for him in bringing the principal into contractual relationship with a third person."

5. According to Section 185, "no consideration is required for the creation of a valid agency relationship."

CREATION OF AN AGENCY

The relationship of principal and agent may be created in the following ways :

1. ***Agency by Express agreement*** (Section 187)

The authority of an agent may be expressed or implied (Sec. 186).

A contract of agency may be created by express words, written or oral. Normally, the authority given by a principal to his agent is express authority, enabling the agent to bind the principal by acts done within the scope of that authority. Generally, a written agreement is the power of attorney executed on a stamped paper in favour of the agent. The power of attorney is a document which gives an authority or power to a person to act, on behalf of the principal in accordance with the terms and conditions mentioned in it. A power of attorney may be general or special (particular). A general power of attorney authorises an agent to do all things on behalf of the principal *i.e.*, to act generally in the business of agency. A special or particular power of attorney is one which authorises an agent to do a single act.

2. ***Agency by Implied Agreement***

According to Sec. 187, "An authority is said to be implied when it is to be inferred from the circumstances of the case; and things spoken or written, or the ordinary course of dealing, may be accounted circumstances of the case". Implied agency arises when there is no express agreement appointing a person as agent. Implied agency arises from the conduct, situation or relationship of parties. That is, authority to act as agent can be inferred from the nature of business, the circumstances of the case, the conduct of the principal or the course of dealing between the parties.

Example : A owns a shop in Serampur, living himself in Calcutta, and visiting the shop occasionally. The shop is managed by B, and he is in the habit of ordering goods from C in the name of A for the purpose of the shop, and of paying for them out of A's funds with A's knowledge. B has an implied authority from A to order goods from C in the name of A for the purposes of the shop.

Partners, wives etc., are usually regarded as agents by implications of their relationship. Implied agency may be of the following type :

A. Agency by Estoppel

Estoppel means to prevent a person from denying a fact. When a person has by his conduct or statements induced others to believe that a certain person is his agent, he is estopped from subsequently denying it. Section 237, lays down that "when an agent has, without authority, done acts or incurred obligations to third persons on behalf of his principal, the principal is bound by such acts or obligations, if he has by his words or conduct induced such third persons to believe that such acts and obligations were within the scope of the agent's authority." Lord Halsbury says, "Estoppel arises when you are precluded from denying the truth of anything which you have represented as a fact, although it is not a fact."

Examples : (1) A consigns goods to B for sale, and gives him instructions not to sell under a fixed price. C, being ignorant of A's instructions enters into a contract with B to buy the goods at a lower price than the reserved price. A is bound by the contract.

(2) A entrusts B with negotiable instruments endorsed in blank. B sells them to C in violation of private orders from A. The sale is good.

B. Agency by Holding Out

Agency by holding out is a branch of the agency by estoppel. Here an 'agency by holding out' requires some affirmative or positive act or conduct by the principal to establish agency subsequently. Thus, A, who is a domestic servant of B, generally purchase goods on credit from C and pays them regularly. C can assume that A is B's implied agent. Subsequently A uses B's authority to purchase goods for his own use. C files a suit against B to recover the cost of the goods which were actually consumed by A. In this case, B is bound by his prior conduct in holding out that A was his agent. C can recover the price from B. Similarly if a husband recognises and takes upon himself the liability in respect of his wife's past dealings with tradesmen, he holds her out to be his agent and to have his authority to contract on his behalf even for articles of luxury.

C. Agency by Necessity

Generally the authority given by a principal to his agent is an express authority enabling the agent to bind the principal by acts done within the scope of that authority. But in certain circumstances the law confers an authority in one person to act as agent for another without requiring the consent of the principal. Sometimes extraordinary circumstances require that a person who is not really an agent should act as an agent of another. Bowstead has rightly observed : "An agency by necessity is conferred by law in certain cases, where a person is faced with an emergency in which the property or interests of another are imminent danger, and it becomes necessary in order to preserve the property or interests, to act before the instructions of the owner can be obtained. The law assumes the consent of the owner to the creation of the relationship of principal and agent".

Example : *G.N. Railway Vs. Swaffield* (1874)

Where a horse sent by rail was not taken delivery of by the owner, the station master had to feed the horse. It was held that the station master became an agent of necessity and the owner liable for the charges incurred by him.

The following conditions must be satisfied for the agency of necessity :

(*i*) It must be impossible to get the principal's instructions.

(*ii*) The course taken must be the only practicable one in the circumstances.

(*iii*) The agent of necessity must act honestly in the interests of all parties concerned.

(*iv*) There must be real emergency and necessity to act on behalf of principal.

Agency of necessity may arise in any of the following circumstances :

(*a*) Where the agent exceeds his authority, bonafide, in an emergency.

(*b*) Where the carrier of goods acting as a bailee, does anything to protect or preserve the goods, in an emergency.

(*c*) Where a husband improperly leaves his wife without providing proper means for her subsistence.

Example : *Sims & Co. Vs. Midland Railway Co.* (1913)

A quantity of butter was consigned with the defendant railway Company. It was delayed in transit due to strike. The butter being perishable the company sold them. The sale was held binding on the owner. The sale was justified by the necessities of the case. It was also not practicable to get instructions from the owner. The doctrine of necessity applies when there is real emergency.

Munro Vs. Willmott (1948)

Willmott allowed Munro to keep her motor car in his yard for a short time. But the car remained for several years. This caused inconvenience in the garage. When Munro could not be contacted, he sold the car. It was held that the sale was not binding on the owner as there was no emergency which required the sale of the car.

Debenham Vs. Mellon (1880)

The defendant was the manager of a hotel where the wife also acted as a manager. Though they lived together in the same hotel, they did not have any domestic establishment of their own. The wife bought some clothes from a tradesman who demanded payment from the husband. It was held that the husband was not liable as there was no domestic establishment.

3. *Agency by Operation of Law*

An agency is also constituted by operation of law. For example, a partner is the agent of the firm and the act of the partner to carry on the business of the firm in the usual way binds the firm and its partners. Similarly, promoter of a new company is its agent.

4. *Agency by Ratification*

Ratification means subsequent acceptance by the principal in respect of an act done by the agent without authority. In other words, ratification means the subsequent adoption and acceptance of an act originally done without authority or instructions. Ratification is an approval of a previous act or contract. For example, A buys certain goods on behalf of B. B did not appoint A as his agent. B may, upon hearing of the transaction, accept or reject it. If B accepts it, the act is ratified and A becomes his agent with retrospective effect. On ratification, the principal is bound by the acts already done on his behalf. Section 196 of the Act provides, "Where acts done by one person on behalf of another but without his knowledge or authority, he may elect to ratify or to disown such acts. If he ratify them, the same effects will follow as if they had been performed by his authority." In such cases, a valid agency is created by ratification. It is also known as "*expost facto agency*". An agent who possesses limited authority, but exceeds his authority, may bind the principal, if his act done in excess of the authority if later ratified by the principal.

Ratification has got retrospective effect. That is, the agency comes into existence from the moment the agent acted and not from the time when the principal ratified. This is in accordance with the maxim: *omins ratihabitio retrotrahitur et priori mandato aequiparatur* (every ratification has a retrospective effect and is equal to a previous mandate).

> **Example :** *Bolton Parters Vs. Lambert* (1881)
>
> The managing director of a company, purporting to be an agent of the company but without its authority, accepted an offer by the defendant for the purchase of some sugar works belonging to them. The defendant then revoked his offer, but the company ratified the manager's acceptance. The defendant was held bound by the contract. If the acceptance was conditioned, the agent saying "subject to ratification", then the revocation would be valid if made before ratification.

Essentials of Valid Ratification

Ratification becomes valid only if the following conditions are satisfied :

1. *The Agent must Act on Behalf of the Principal*

An agent must contract as an agent. That is, if a person acts in his own name, which does not indicate any agency relationship, his act cannot be ratified. When an act is done on behalf of the ratifier, such act can be ratified by him. But a person entering into a contract in his own name cannot later shift it on to a third party. An undisclosed principal cannot step in and ratify acts done by a third person. The person who has the right to ratify is the person in whose name or on whose behalf the contract was entered into. A person cannot ratify an act unless it was purported to be done on his behalf.

> **Example :** *Keighley Maxsted & Co.Vs. Durant* (1901)
>
> A corn merchant was authorised by the appellant company to buy wheat on a joint account for himself and the company at a certain price. He failed to buy at the agreed price, but later contracted with Durant to buy wheat from him at a higher price. This was without authority from the appellants. Though he intended to buy for the company, he contracted in his own name and did not disclose the agency. Later his act was ratified by the company but the company failed to take delivery due to fall in price of wheat. Durant sued the company for breach of the contract. Action brought for breach of contract failed on the ground that the agent contracted in his own name, therefore, his act was not open to anybody's ratification. Thus any ratification made by the company was ineffective.

2. *The Principal must be in Existence at the Time of Contract*

Another condition to ratification is that the principal claiming the ratification must have been in existence on the day the act sought to be ratified was done. That is, the principal must have been in existence at the time when the act was done. This is because rights and obligations cannot attach to a non-existent person. For example, a company after incorporation cannot ratify an act done by its promoter on its behalf before incorporation as the company was not in existence when the act was done.

3. *The Principal must have Contractual Capacity*

The principal must be competent to contract both at the time of original contract and at the time of ratification. For example, a company cannot ratify the acts done in its name before its incorporation.

4. *The Principal must have Full Knowledge of Material Facts*

The ratification must be made with the full knowledge of all the material facts. Section 198 states that "No valid ratification can be made by a person whose knowledge of facts of the case is materially defective".

5. *Whole Transaction must be Ratified*

A person cannot ratify a part of the transaction which is beneficial to him and reject the rest.

There cannot be partial ratification and partial rejection. When a person ratifies the part of the transaction, it is treated as the whole transaction (Sec. 199).

6. *Ratification must be made within Reasonable Time*

The ratification becomes valid only if it is made within a reasonable time after the act to be ratified is done. However, where time to ratify is limited, ratification must be done before the time has expired.

7. *Act to be Ratified should not be Void or Illegal*

Ratification can be made only of valid and lawful acts. An act which is void from the very beginning cannot be ratified. But a voidable contract may be ratified because it is not void from the very beginning.

8. *Ratification must not Injure a Third Person*

Any act which would become injurious to others by ratification, cannot be ratified. Section 200 states, ratification cannot be made so as to subject a third party to damages or terminate any right or interest of a third person.

Examples : (1) A not being authorised thereto by B, demands on behalf of B, the delivery of a chattel, the property of B, from C, who is in possession of it. This demand cannot be ratified by B, so as to make C liable for damages for his refusal to deliver.

(2) A holds a lease from B, terminable on three months' notice. C, an unauthorised person, gives notice of termination to A. The notice cannot be ratified by B, so as to be binding on A.

9. *Ratification may be Express or Implied*

According to Section 197, "Ratification may be expressed or may be implied in the conduct of the person on whose behalf the acts are done.

Examples : (1) A, without authority, buys goods for B. Afterwards B sells them to C on his own account. B's conduct implies a ratification of the purchase made for him by A.

(2) A, without B's authority lends B's money to C. Afterwards B accepts interest on the money from C. B's conduct implies a ratification of the loan.

Ratification must be communicated to the other party. Ratification of acts not within the principal's authority is ineffective. A contract between the principal and the third party comes into existence not from the date of ratification, but from the date when the agent first contracted. However, this rule is not applicable where the agent accepts the offer "subject to ratification". In such cases the contract comes into existence from the date of ratification or approval by the principal. An offer can be withdrawn before such ratification.

IMPLIED AUTHORITY BETWEEN HUSBAND AND WIFE (WIFE AS THE AGENT)

Between husband and wife, the authority may be express or implied or that of necessity. As a general rule, husband can be held liable only for what he has expressly or impliedly sanctioned. Wife has an implied authority by necessity to pledge her husband's credit under the following circumstances :

(*a*) When she is living with her husband;

(*b*) The wife is living separate and claiming maintenance;

(*c*) The wife pledges her husband's credit to a reasonable extent and in reasonable manner for ordinary household expenses;

(*d*) Wife can pledge her husband's credit only for necessaries.

Ultimately, it depends on circumstances of each case whether the wife can pledge her husband's credit. The wife has no implied authority, under the following circumstances :

(*a*) To borrow money to pay her previous debts;

(*b*) When husband has expressly forbidden his wife to pledge his credit;

(*c*) He had given sufficient money to his wife for purchasing necessaries;

(*d*) Where the wife lives apart under no justifiable circumstances.

Essentials for a valid Ratification

1. Agent must act on behalf of the principal.
2. The principal must be alive at the time of the contract.
3. The principal must be competent to contract.
4. Ratification must be done with full knowledge of the principal.
5. Ratification must not be for the parts but for the whole transaction.
6. Ratification must be done within reasonable time.
7. The act to be ratified should be lawful.
8. Ratification must be communicated to concerned party.
9. Ratification should not injure a third person.
10. Ratification may be express or implied.

KINDS OF AGENTS

According to the extent of their authority, agents may be classified into three categories and they are :

(A) *General Agent :* General agent is one who represents the principal in all matters concerning a particular business. He is appointed mostly by general power of attorney. The authority of a general agent is continuous until it is terminated.

(B) *Special Agent :* Special agent is one who is appointed for a particular purpose. He has limited authority. He represents the principal in some particular transaction. His authority ends no sooner the particular act is performed.

(C) *Universal Agent :* A universal agent is one who is authorised to transact all the business of his principal of every kind and to do all the acts which the principal can lawfully do and can delegate.

Another classification, is on the basis of the nature of work performed, into Mercantile and Non-mercantile agents. A mercantile (Commercial) agents may assume any of the following forms:

(*a*) *Broker :* A broker makes contracts in the name of his principal and not on his own name. He is an agent. He is primarily employed to negotiate between two parties. He is usually employed for sale of goods. He has no possession of goods to be sold as in the case of factor. Unlike a factor he is not entrusted with the custody and apparent ownership of the goods, but he is a mere negotiator to effect business. He is paid commission for his services.

(*b*) *Factor :* A factor is a mercantile agent to whom the possession of the goods is given for the purpose of selling the same. He has authority to sell in his own name. He has got discretionary powers to enter into contracts of sale with third parties. He has a general lien on the goods of his principal for all charges and expenses due from the principal.

(*c*) *Commission Agent :* A commission agent is a mercantile agent who buys and sells the goods on behalf of his principal and receives commission for his labour. He may or may not be in actual possession of goods. His position is similar to that of a broker. He buys or sells goods on behalf of his principal on the most favourable terms. He is paid commission for his services.

(*d*) *Del Credere Agent :* He is an agent who guarantees the solvency of the buyer. He occupies the position of a guarantor as well as an agent. A del credere agent is not dropped out after establishing the link between the principal and the third person. If the other party fails to pay the price or otherwise causes damage to the principal, the del credere agent must pay compensation to the principal.

Non-mercantile agents : They include advocates, insurance agent, solicitor, guardian, wife etc.

The rights and duties of the agent and the principal *inter se* may depend mainly upon the terms of the contract. However, agent and principal stand in a mutual relationship and, therefore, owe a number of duties and assume rights against each other. They are discussed as under.

DUTIES OF AN AGENT TOWARDS THE PRINCIPAL

An agent has the following duties towards the principal :

1. *Duty in Conducting Principal's Business* (Sec. 211)

Section 211 states that "An agent is bound to conduct the business of his principal according to the directions given by the principal, or in the absence of any directions, according to the custom which prevails, in doing business of the same kind at the place where the agent conducts such business. When the agent acts otherwise, if any loss be sustained he must make it good to his principal, and if any profit accrues, he must account for it." It is the duty of an agent to work for his principal as per his instructions. If the principal has not given any directions, then it is the duty of the agent to follow the custom prevailing in the same kind of business at the place where the agent conducts business.

Examples : (1) A, an agent engaged in carrying on for B, a business, in which it is the custom to invest from time to time, at interest, the money which may be in hand omits to make such investments. A must make good to B the interest usually obtained by such investment.

(2) B, a broker, in whose business it is not the custom to sell on credit, sells goods of A on credit to C whose credit at the time was very high. C, before payment, becomes insolvent. B must make good the loss to A.

(3) *Lilley Vs. Doubleday* (1881)

The defendant, an agent, was instructed to keep the goods at a particular warehouse. The defendant warehoused a portion of the goods at another place, where the goods were destroyed by fire, without any negligence on the part of the defendant. The agent was held liable for the loss because any departure from instruction makes the agent liable.

2. *Use of Ordinary Skill and Diligence* (Sec. 212)

Section 212 states, "An agent is bound to conduct the business of the agency with as much skill as is generally possessed by persons engaged in similar business unless the principal has notice of his want of skill. The agent is always bound to act with reasonable diligence, and to use such skill as he possesses; and to make compensation to his principal in respect of the direct consequences of his own neglect, want of skill or misconduct, but not in respect of loss or damages which are indirectly or remotely caused by such neglect, want of skill or misconduct." Illustrations appended to this section are as follows :

Examples : (1) A, an agent for the sale of goods, having authority to sell on credit, sell to B on credit, without making the proper and usual enquiries as to the solvency of B.B, at the time of such sale, is insolvent. A must make compensation to his principal in respect of any loss thereby sustained.

(2) A, an insurance broker, employed by B, to effect an insurance on a ship, omits to see that the usual clauses are inserted in the policy. The ship is afterwards lost. In consequence of the omission of the clauses nothing can be recovered from the underwriters. A is bound to make good the loss to B.

(3) A, a merchant in Calcutta has an agent B, in London to whom a sum of money is paid on A's account, with orders to remit. B retains the money for a considerable time. A, in consequence of not receiving the money, becomes insolvent. B is liable for the money and interest from the day on which it ought to have been paid, according to the rate, and for any further direct loss — as example by variation of rate of exchange but not further.

(4) A, a merchant in England, directs B, his agent at Bombay who accepts the agency, to send him 100 bales of cotton by a certain ship. B, having it in his power to send the cotton, omits to do so. The ship arrived safely in England. Soon after her arrival, the price of cotton rises. B is bound to make good to A, the profit which he might have made by the 100 bales of cotton at the time the ship arrived, but not any profit he might have made by the subsequent rise.

Pannalal Jankidas Vs. Mohanlal (1950)

In this case, the agent who was directed to insure the goods against fire, did not comply with the directions. The goods were subsequently destroyed owing to an explosion in the Bombay docks. Even if the goods had been insured, such a loss was recoverable since the explosion would have been an excepted peril. But, according to an ordinance promulgated by the Bombay Government, full compensation could be claimed for loss of goods insured against fire, and only half the value of the goods, in case they were not insured. Since the principal in this case got only half the value of the goods, he hold the agent liable for the other half. The contention of the agent that the loss was too remote, was rejected by the Supreme Court which held that the loss was the direct result of the agent's negligence.

3. *Duty to Render Accounts* (Sec. 213)

Sec. 213 states that "An agent is bound to render proper accounts to his principal on demand." It is the duty of an agent to keep true and correct account of all transactions.

4. *To get Directions of Principal* (Sec. 214)

According to Section 214, "It is the duty of an agent in the case of difficulty, to use all reasonable diligence in communicating with the principal, and is seeking to obtain his instructions." But in case of emergency where there is no time to communicate with the principal, the agent may act in good faith without consulting the principal.

5. *Duty not to Deal on his Own Account* (Sec. 215)

According to Sec. 215, "If an agent deals on his own account in the business of the agency without first obtaining the consent of his principal and acquainting him with all material circumstances which have come to his own knowledge on the subject, the principal may repudiate the transaction, if the case shows either that any material fact has been dishonestly concealed from him by the agent, or that the dealings of the agent have been disadvantageous to him." The agent has a duty to avoid conflict of interest between the agent and the principal.

Examples : (1) A directs B to sell A's estate. B buys the estate for himself in the name of C. A on discovering that B has bought the estate for himself, may repudiate the sale, if he can show that B has dishonestly concealed any material fact, or that the sale has been disadvantageous to him.

(2) A directs B to sell A's estate. B on looking over the estate before selling it, finds a mine on the

estate which is unknown to A, B informs A that he wishes to buy the estate for himself, but conceals the discovery of the mine. A allows B to buy in ignorance of the existence of the mine. A, on discovering that B knew of the mine at the time he bought the estate, may either repudiate or adopt the sale at his option.

6. *Duty not to Make Secret Profits* (Sec. 216)

Section 216 states that "If an agent, without the knowledge of his principal, deals in the business of the agency on his own account, instead of on account of his principal, the principal is entitled to claim from the agent any benefit which may have resulted to him from the transaction."

Example : A directs B, his agent, to buy a certain house for him. B tells A it cannot be bought, and buys the house himself, A may, on discovering that B has bought the house, compel him to sell it to A at the price he gave for it.

Example : *Costa Rica Co. Vs. Forwood* (1901)

Similarly, in this case, it was observed that "If a person, while holding a fiduciary position and acting in that capacity makes a profit without fully disclosing his interest to those persons towards whom he stands in such a position, he must account to them for that profit."

7. *Duty to Pay Sums Received for Principal* (Sec. 218)

Section 218 states that the agent is bound to pay to his principal all sums received on his account after deducting therefrom his dues on account of remuneration and expenses.

8. *Not to Delegate* (Sec. 190)

According to Section 190 that an agent cannot delegate his authority or employ another to perform acts which he has expressly or impliedly undertaken to perform personally. Ordinarily, an agent cannot further delegate the authority which has been delegated to him by his principal.

9. *Duty to Protect the Interest of the Principal* (Sec. 209)

According to Section 209, "When an agency is terminated by the principal dying or becoming of unsound mind, the agent is bound to take on behalf of the representatives of his late principal, all reasonable steps for the protection and preservation of the interests entrusted to him."

10. *Adverse Title*

The agent must not set up his own title or the title of third parties to the goods received by him from the principal.

11. *Naming an Agent for Principal* (Sec. 195)

Section 195 states that in selecting an agent for his principal, an agent is bound to exercise the same amount of discretion as a man of ordinary prudence would exercise in his own case: if he does this he is not responsible to the principal for the acts or negligence of the agent so selected.

Example : A instructs B, a merchant to buy a ship for him. B employs a ship surveyor of good reputation to choose a ship for A. The surveyor makes the choice negligently and the ship turns out to be unworthy and is lost. B is not, but the surveyor is responsible to A.

12. *Liable for Acts of Sub-agent* (Secs. 192 and 193)

Where the sub-agent is appointed by the agent without authority, the agent is responsible both to the principal and the third party.

Duties of an Agent

1. To conduct the business of agency according to instructions.
2. To follow customs in the absence of instructions.
3. To carry out the business with skill and diligence.
4. To render proper accounts to the principal.
5. To communicate with the principal, in case of difficulty.
6. To pay sums to the principal received for him.
7. To protect and preserve the interest of the principal.
8. Not to deal on his own account.
9. Not to make unauthorised profit from agency.
10. Not to use information obtained in the course of business against the principal.
11. Not to delegate authority.
12. Not to set up adverse title.

RIGHTS OF AN AGENT

Following are the rights of an agent :

1. *Right to Retain Money* (Sec. 127)

Sec. 127 lays down that "An agent may retain, out of any sums received on account of the principal in the business of the agency, all moneys due to himself in respect of advances made or expenses properly incurred by him conducting such business and also such remuneration as may be payable to him for acting as agent."

2. *Right to Receive Remuneration* (Sec. 219)

Sec. 219 lays down that "In the absence of any special contract, payment for the performance of any act is not due to the agent until the completion of such act, but an agent may detain moneys received by him on account of goods sold, although the whole of the goods consigned to him for the sale may not have been sold, or although the sale may not be actually complete." The agent is entitled to remuneration when the work is completed except in the case of sale of goods and where there is an agreement to the contrary.

Example : *Sheikh Farid Baksh Vs. Hargulal Singh* (1937)

An agent was appointed to introduce a customer, who is willing to purchase B's property. The agent introduced one customer, C, who was willing to purchase the property. The sale was settled and earnest money paid. But the sale could not be completed due to C's inability to find money. It was held that the agent was entitled to his commission.

3. *Effect of Misconduct* (Sec. 220)

"An agent who is guilty of misconduct in the business of the agency is not entitled to any remuneration in respect of that part of the business which he has misconducted." (Sec. 220). An agent who misconducts is also liable to compensate his principal.

Examples : (1) A employs B to recover Rs. 1,00,000 from C and to lay it out on good security. B recovers the amount and lays Rs. 90,000 on good security, but lays out Rs. 10,000 on security which he ought to have known to be bad, whereby A loses Rs. 2,000. B is entitled to remuneration for recovering the Rs. 1,00,000 and for investing Rs. 90,000. He is not entitled to any remuneration for investing the Rs. 10,000 and he must make good the Rs. 2,000 to A.

(2) A employs B to recover Rs. 1,000 from C; through B's misconduct the money is not recovered. B is entitled to no remuneration for his services and must make good the loss.

4. *Right of Lien* (Sec. 221)

Section 221 lays down that "In the absence of any contract to the contrary, an agent is entitled to retain goods, papers and other property, whether movable or immovable, of the principal received by him, until the amount due to himself for compensation, disbursements and services in respect of the same has been paid or accounted for to him". The agent can only retain the goods. He has no power to sell them.

5. *Right to be Indemnified against Consequence of Lawful Acts* (Sec. 222)

Section 222 lays down that "The employer to an agent is bound to indemnify him against the consequences of all lawful acts done by such agent in exercise of the authority conferred upon him."

> **Example :** B, at Singapur under instructions from A of Calcutta, contracts with C to deliver certain goods to him. A does not send the goods to B, and C sues B for breach of contracts. B informs A of the suit, and A authorises him to defend the suit. B defends the suit, and is compelled to pay damages and costs and incurs expenses. A is liable to B for such damages, costs and expenses.
>
> **Example :** B, a broker at Calcutta, by the orders of A, merchant there, contracts with C for the purchase of 10 casks of oil for A. Afterwards A refuses to receive the oil, and C sues B. B informs A, who repudiates the contract altogether. B defends but unsuccessfully, and has to pay damages and costs and incur expenses. A liable to B for such damages, costs and expenses.

6. *Right to be Indemnified against Consequences of Acts done in Good Faith* (Sec. 223)

Section 223 lays down that "Where one person employs another to do an act, and the agent does the act in good faith, the employer is liable to indemnify the agent against the consequences of that act, though it causes an injury to the rights of third person."

> **Examples :** (1) (appended to Sec. 223)
>
> A, a decree holder and entitled to execution of B's goods, requires the officer of the court to seize certain goods, representing them to be the goods of B. The officer seizes the goods, and is sued by C, the true owner of the goods. A is liable to indemnify the officer for the sum which he is compelled to pay to C in consequences of obeying A's directions.
>
> (2) B, at the request of A, sells goods in the possession of A, but which A had no right to dispose of. B does not know this and hands over the proceeds of the sale to A. Afterwards C, the true owner of the goods, sues B and recovers the value of the goods and costs. A is liable to indemnify B for what he has been compelled to pay to C and for B's own expenses.

7. *Right to Compensation* (Sec. 225)

Section 225 lays down that "The principal must make compensation to his agent in respect of injury caused to such agent by the principal's neglect or want of skill."

> **Example :** A employs B as a bricklayer in building a house and puts up the scaffolding himself. The scaffolding is unskillfully put and B is in consequence hurt. A must make compensation to B.

8. *To do Lawful Acts* (Sec. 188)

According to Sec. 188 "An agent having authority to do an act has the authority to do every lawful thing which is necessary in order to do such act."

> **Example :** A is employed by B, residing in London, to recover at Bombay a debt due to B, A may adopt any legal process necessary for the purpose of recovering the debt, and may give a valid discharge for the same.

9. *In Emergency* (Sec. 189)

Sec. 189 lays down that "An agent has authority, in an emergency, to do all such acts for the purpose of protecting his principal from loss as would be done by a person of ordinary prudence, in his own case, under similar circumstances."

Examples : (1) (appended to Sec. 189). An agent for sale may have goods repaired if it be necessary.

(2) A consigns provisions to B at Calcutta, with directions to send them immediately to C at Cuttack. B may sell the provisions at Calcutta, if they will not bear journey to Cuttack without spoiling.

10. *Right of Stoppage of Goods*

An agent has the right of stoppage of goods in transit if he has bought goods either with his own money or by incurring a personal liability for the price and the principal has become insolvent.

Rights of Agent

1. To receive remuneration agreed upon.
2. To retain principal's money due to himself.
3. To be indemnified against lawful acts.
4. To be indemnified against consequences of acts done in good faith.
5. Right of lien on the possession of goods.
6. To stop goods in transit.
7. To claim compensation for injury by the principal's negligence.
8. To protect principal's property from loss.
9. To be liable for his misconduct.
10. To claim compensation for premature termination of agency.

DUTIES OF PRINCIPAL

Duties of the principal towards his agent are the rights of the agent against the principal. The following are the duties, in brief :

1. *Agent to be indemnified* (Sec. 222)

"The employer of an agent is bound to indemnify him against the consequences of all lawful acts done by such agent in exercise of the authority conferred upon him." (Sec. 222).

2. *Against Consequences of the Acts done in Good Faith* (Sec. 223)

"Where one person employs another to do an act, and the agent does the act in good faith, the employer is liable to indemnify the agent against the consequences of that act, though it causes an injury to the right persons." (Sec. 223).

3. *Non-liability of Employer of Agent to do a Criminal Act* (Sec. 224)

According to Sec. 224, "Where one person employs another to do an act which is criminal, the employer is not liable to the agent either upon the expenses or an implied promise, to indemnify him against the consequences of that act."

Example : A employs B to beat C, and agrees to indemnify him against all consequence of the acts. B thereupon beats C and has to pay damages to C for so doing. A is not liable to indemnify B for those damages.

4. *Duty to Indemnify the Loss for Principal's Neglect* (Sec. 225)

According to Sec. 225, "The principal must make compensation to his agent in respect of injury caused to such agent by the principal's neglect or want of skill."

---

*Scaffolding = A temporary stage or platform for workmen.

Example : A employs B as a bricklayer in building a house and puts up the *scaffolding himself. The scaffolding is unskillfully put up, and B is in consequence hurt. A must make compensation to B.

5. *To Pay Remuneration and Dues*

It is the duty of the principal to pay the agent all of his dues, remuneration, commission etc., and also to reimburse all advance and expenses incurred by him in exercise of his authority.

RIGHTS OF THE PRINCIPAL

The rights of a principal are indirectly the duties of an agent. The duties of an agent have been discussed. However, the rights of the principal are given below : (in brief).

1. The principal is entitled to enforce all the duties of the agent. This is because agent's duties are the principal's right.

2. He may repudiate the transaction if it shows either that any material fact has been dishonestly concealed from him by the agent or that the dealings of the agent have been disadvantageous to him. (Sec. 215).

3. If an agent, without the knowledge of the principal, deals in the business of the agency on his own account instead of an account of his principal, the principal is entitled to claim from the agent any benefit which may have resulted to him from the transaction. (Sec. 216).

4. He is entitled to compensation for any loss or any profit accruing, owing to departure from instructions. (Sec. 211).

5. The principal is entitled to demand proper accounts from the agent. (Sec. 213).

6. The principal is entitled to compensation in respect of the direct consequences of the agent's negligence, want of skill or misconduct. (Sec. 212).

7. The principal has the right to refuse remuneration if the agent is guilty of misconduct. (Sec. 220).

8. "Where acts are done by one person on behalf of another, but without his knowledge or authority, he may elect to ratify or to disown such acts. If he ratifies them, the same effects will follow as if they had been performed by his authority." (Sec. 196).

9. The principal may revoke the authority given to his agent at any time before the authority has been exercised so as to bind the principal (Sec. 203).

10. The principal has the right to give instruction in cases of difficulty when contacted by the agent. (Sec. 214).

AGENT'S AUTHORITY

Authority of an agent means his capacity or power to bind the principal with the third parties. The principal is bound by the acts of his agent done by him within the scope of his authority. Sec. 226 of the Indian Contract Act provides that "Contracts entered into through an agent, and obligations arising from acts done by an agent, may be enforced in the same manner, and will have the same legal consequences, as if the contracts had been entered into and the acts done by the principal in person."

Examples : (1) A buys goods from B, knowing that he is an agent for their sale, but not knowing who is the principal. B's principal is the person entitled to claim from A price of the goods, and A cannot in a suit by the principal, set-off against that claim a debt due to himself from B.

(2) A, being B's agent, with authority to receive money on his behalf, receives from C a sum of money due to B. C is discharged of his obligation to pay the sum in question to B. The authority of the agent to bind the principal may be :

(*i*) Actual or Real authority or (*ii*) Ostensible or Apparent authority.

(*i*) *Actual or Real Authority* : Actual authority of an agent is the authority conferred on him by the principal. Sec. 186 states that "The authority of an agent may be express or implied". An authority is said to be express when it is given by words spoken or written. Further, according to Sec. 187. "An authority is said to be implied when it is to be inferred from the circumstances of the case; and things spoken or written or the ordinary course of dealing may be accounted circumstances of the case."

Further according to Sec. 188 Para 1, "An agent, having an authority to do an act, has authority to do every lawful thing which is necessary in order to do such act." Sec. 188 Para 2 states, "An agent, having an authority to carry on a business, has authority to do every lawful thing necessary for the purpose, or usually done in the course of conducting such business."

> **Examples :** (1) A is employed by B, residing in London, to recover at Bombay a debt due to B. A may adopt any legal process necessary for the purpose of recovering the debt, and may give a valid discharge for the same.
>
> (2) A appoints B as his agent to carry on his business of a ship-builder. B may purchase timber and other materials and hire workmen for the purpose of carrying on the business.

***(ii) Ostensible Authority* :** Ostensible or apparent authority is the authority of an agent as it appears to others. It happens when the principal creates an appearance which reasonably leads another to believe that his agent has some authority. If a principal creates an appearance that reasonably leads another to believe that his agent has the authority to make contracts for him, he cannot deny this authority when a third party relies upon this appearance by making a contract with that agent. The following statement from Smith and Watt's Mercantile Law clarifies the concept of ostensible authority.

"Implied authority is real authority, the exercise of which is binding not only as between the principal and the third party, but also between the principal and agent. It differs only from an express authority in that it is conferred by no express words, but is to be gathered from surrounding circumstances. The term 'ostensible authority' on the other hand, denotes no authority at all. It is a phrase conveniently used to describe the position which arises when one person clothed another, or allowed him to assume an appearance of authority to act on his behalf, without actually giving him any authority either express or implied, by which appearance of authority a third party is misled into believing that a real authority exists."

Agent's Authority in an Emergency

According to Sec. 189, "An agent has authority, in an emergency, to do all such acts for the purpose of protecting his principal from loss as would be done by a person of ordinary prudence, in his own case, under similar circumstances."

> **Examples :** (1) An agent for sale may have goods repaired if it be necessary.
>
> (2) A consigns provisions to B at Calcutta, with directions to send them immediately to C at Cuttack. B may sell the provisions at Calcutta, if they will not bear the journey to Cuttack without spoiling.

PRINCIPAL'S LIABILITY FOR THE ACTS OF THE AGENT

An agent acting on behalf of the principal, creates liability of the principal to third parties as it is the general rule of agency. An agent acting within the scope of his authority, binds the principal. The position of the principal in relation to third parties under contracts made by agent may be discussed under the following heads :

(A) Where the agent contracts for a named principal.

(B) Where the agent contracts for an unnamed principal.

(C) Where the agent contracts for an undisclosed principal.

A. Agent Acting for a Named Principal

(1) *When the Agent Acts within the Scope of his Authority* (Sec. 226)

Acts of the agent are the acts of the principal. Sec. 226 states that, "Contracts entered into through an agent, and obligations arising from acts done by an agent, may be enforced in the same manner, and will have the same legal consequences, as if the contracts had been entered into and the acts done by the principal in person."

> **Examples :** (1) A buys goods from B, knowing that he is an agent for their sale, but not knowing who is the principal. B's principal is the person entitled to claim from A price of the goods, and A cannot in a suit by the principal, set-off against that claim a debt due to himself from B.
>
> (2) A, being B's agent, with authority to receive money on his behalf, receives from C a sum of money due to B. C is discharged of his obligation to pay the sum in question to B.

(2) *Acts of an Agent beyond his Authority* (Sec. 227)

(*a*) *Where Authority can be Separated* : Section 227 states that "When an agent does more than he is authorized to do, and when the part of what he does which is within his authority, can be separated, from the part which is beyond his authority, so much only of what he does as is within his authority is binding as between him and his principal." The principal is not bound by unauthorised acts of his agent.

> **Example :** A being owner of a ship and cargo authorises B to procure an insurance for Rs. 4,000 on the ship. B procures a policy for Rs. 4,000 on the ship and another for the like sum on the cargo. A is bound to pay the premium for the policy on the ship, but not the premium for policy on the cargo.

(*b*) *Where authority cannot be separated :* Section 228 states that "Where an agent does more than he is authorised to do, and what he does beyond the scope of his authority cannot be separated from what is within it, the principal is not bound to recognise the transaction." He is in such a case entitled to repudiate the whole transaction.

> **Example :** A authorises B to buy 500 sheeps for him. B buys 500 sheeps and 200 lambs for a sum of Rs. 6,000. A may repudiate the whole transaction.

(*c*) *Notice given to agent as notice to principal :* Section 229 states that "Any notice given to or information obtained by the agent, provided it be given or obtained in the course of the business transacted by him for the principal, shall, as between the principal and third parties, have the same legal consequences as if it had been given to or obtained by the principal." This means that the knowledge of the agent is the knowledge of the principal.

> **Examples :** (1) (appended to Sec. 229) A is employed by B to buy from C certain goods, of which C is the apparent owner, and buys them accordingly. In the course of the treaty for the sale, A learns that the goods, really belonged to D, but B is ignorant of that fact. B is not entitled to set off a debt owing to him from C against the price of the goods.
>
> (2) A is employed by B to buy from C goods of which C is the apparent owner. A was, before he was so employed, a servant of C, and then learnt that the goods really belonged to D, but B is ignorant of the fact. In spite of the knowledge of his agent, B may set-off against the price of the goods a debt owing to him from C.

(*d*) *Principal's Liability for Unauthorised Acts of the Agent:* Section 237 states that "When an agent has, without authority, done acts or incurred obligations to third persons on behalf of his principal, the principal is bound by such acts or obligation if he has by his words or conduct induced such third persons to believe that such acts and obligations were within the scope of the agent's authority." The liability of the principal is based on the doctrine of estoppel and not on any real authority. The liability of the principal under Section 237 is not based on any real authority but is by estoppel.

Example : A consigns goods to B for sale, and gives him instructions not to sell under a fixed price. C, being ignorant of B's instructions enters into a contract with B to buy the goods at a lower than the reserved price. A is bound by the contract.

(*e*) *Misrepresentation or Fraud by the Agent* (Sec. 238) : If in ordinary conduct of agency the agent has committed some fraud or has made some misrepresentation, it is presumed that the fraud or misrepresentation has been committed by the principal and, therefore, the principal will be liable to the third parties for such fraud or misrepresentation. But if the fraud or misrepresentation committed by the agent is for the act beyond the agent's authority, the principal will not be liable. (Sec. 238).

Example : A, being B's agent for the sale of goods induces C to buy them by a misrepresentation, which he was not authorised by B. The contract is voidable, as between B and C, at the option of C.

B. Where Agent Acting for Unnamed Principal

Where an agent expressly contracts disclosing his representative character, but without disclosing the identity of his principal, the principal is said to be unnamed. In such cases, the principal is bound by the contracts made on his behalf. That is, the rights and liabilities of the principal are the same as if the principal were named. However, such acts must be within the scope of agent's authority and the unnamed principal must be in existence at the time of contract. If however, the agent declines to disclose the identity of the principal, he will become personally liable on the contract entered into by him.

C. Agent Acting for Undisclosed Principal

The doctrine of undisclosed principal comes into play when an agent, though having authority to contract on behalf of another, makes the contract apparently on his own name without disclosing the fact of agency, or without disclosing the identity of the principal though the fact of agency is disclosed. An agent may enter into a contract with a person without disclosing the name of the principal. Sections 231 and 232 deal with the rights of the parties in cases where the principal are not disclosed. They are as follows :

(1) If an agent makes a contract with a person to whom the fact of agency is not known, the principal may require the performance of the contract (Sec. 231).

(2) The third party contracting with the agent has, as against the principal, the same rights as he would have had as against the agent if the agent had been the principal (Sec. 231).

(3) If the principal discloses himself before the contract is completed, the other contracting party will have the option to refuse to fulfil the contract. For this he should show that, if he had known who the principal in the contract was, or if he had known that the agent was not a principal, he would not have entered into the contract (Sec. 231).

(4) If the principal requires the performance of the contract, he can obtain it only subject to the rights and obligations subsisting between the agent and the other party to the contract (Sec. 232).

(5) Further, as provided by Sec. 233, in cases where the agent is personally liable, a person dealing with him may hold either him or his principal, or both of them liable.

Personal Liability of Agent

1. Where principal is a foreigner.
2. Where the agent acts for undisclosed principal.
3. Where the agent makes himself expressly liable.
4. Where the principal cannot sue (*e.g.* : Minor).
5. Where agency is coupled with special interest.
6. When agent acts for a non-existing principal.
7. Where trade or custom makes the agent liable.
8. Where agent acts, receives or pays money by fraud or by mistake.
9. Where an agent acts beyond his authority.
10. Where the agent signs negotiable instruments in his own name.
11. When the agent appoints sub-agent without authority.
12. Where the agent is an unauthorised one.

LIABILITY OF PRETENDED AGENT

A pretended agent is a person who represents himself to be an agent of another, when in fact he has no authority from him whatsoever. That is, he is a person who is falsely representing himself to be an authorised agent of another person. Sec. 235 states that "A person untruly representing himself to be the authorised agent of another, and thereby inducing a third person to deal with him as such agent, is liable if his alleged employer does not ratify his acts, to make compensation to the other in respect of any loss or damage which he has incurred by so dealing." But if the principal ratifies the act of the agent, then he will not be personally liable.

It must be noted that although the pretended agent is liable to make compensation to the other contracting party, but he has no right to proceed against that party for the performance of the contract (Sec. 236).

AGENT WHEN PERSONALLY LIABLE?

Sec. 230 of the Contract Act clearly states that "In the absence of any contract to that effect, an agent cannot personally enforce contracts entered into by him on behalf of his principal, nor is he personally bound by them." We have already discussed that an agent is merely a connecting link between his principal and the third party. However, if an agent undertakes personal liability, then he may be held liable for such contracts. In the following cases, an agent can be held personally liable :

1. *The Agent Acting for a Foreign Principal*

Where an agent contracts for the sale or purchase of goods for a merchant residing abroad, he is presumed to be personally liable (Sec. 230).

2. *The Agent acting for Undisclosed Principal*

Where an agent does not disclose the name of the principal and contracts in his own name, the agent is personally liable for such contracts (Sec. 230).

3. *The Agent Makes himself Expressly Liable*

If an agent, while contracting with a third party, expressly agrees to be personally liable on the contract, he can be held personally liable for any breach of contract.

4. *Principal cannot be Sued*

An agent is presumed to be intended to be personally liable when the principal, though disclosed, cannot be sued, for example, where the principal is a foreign sovereign or a minor (230).

5. *Agency coupled with Interest*

Where the contract with the third party relates to a subject-matter in which the agent has a special interest, agent is personally liable to the extent of his interest because he is really a principal for that extent. An authority coupled with interest is generally irrevocable (Sec. 202).

6. *Usage of Trade*

An agent also incurs personal liability where there is a trade usage or custom to that effect. For example, a jobber may hold a broker personally liable as per the custom of trade in a stock exchange.

7. *Agent Acts beyond his Authority*

When an agent has no authority or acts beyond his authority or exceeds his authority, he can be held personally liable for breach of warranty of authority. He will be liable to compensate for the loss caused by such a false representation.

8. *Pretended Agent*

"A person untruly representing himself to be the authorised agent of another, and thereby inducing a third person to deal with him as such agent, is liable if his alleged employer does not ratify his acts, to make compensation to the other in respect of any loss or damage which he has incurred by so dealing."

9. *Mistake or Fraud*

If the fraud or misrepresentation committed by the agent is for the act beyond the agent's authority, the principal will not be liable : but the agent is personally liable to third parties (Sec. 238).

10. *Agent Appoints sub-agent without Authority*

Where the appointment of sub-agent is without authority, the principal is not bound by the acts of the sub-agent nor is the sub-agent liable to the principal. The agent as the principal of sub-agent is responsible for the acts of the improperly appointed sub-agent, both to the principal and to the third parties (Sec. 193).

11. *Agent Signs a Contract in his Own Name*

Agents signing negotiable instruments will be liable personally unless it is clearly shows that the signature is put in the capacity of agent for and on behalf of the principal.

DELEGATION OF AUTHORITY

Generally, an agent cannot lawfully employ another to perform acts which he has expressly or impliedly undertaken to perform personally. An agent who has the authority from another to do an act must do it himself and cannot delegate his authority to another. Agency arises on the basis of trust and confidence. The agent cannot employ another and entrust the work which he has himself undertaken to do. No such power can be implied because confidence in a particular person is at the root of the contract of agency. This is based on the maxim : *delegatus non potest delegare* (a delegate cannot further delegate). According to Sec. 190. "An agent cannot lawfully employ another to perform acts which he has expressly or impliedly undertaken to perform personally, unless by the ordinary custom of trade a sub-agent may, or from the nature of the agency, a sub-agent must be employed."

But there are certain exceptions where an agent can appoint a sub-agent :

(1) Where the principal has expressly authorised the appointment of a sub-agent.

(2) Where the principal knows that the agent has an intention to appoint a sub-agent, but he does not object to it.

(3) Where sub-agent may be employed by the ordinary custom of trade, for example, architects may generally appoints draftsmen, surveyors etc.
(4) Unforeseen emergencies arising in the course of employment requiring delegation.
(5) Where the nature of work is such that a sub-agent is necessary, for example, manager of a shop may employ sales-assistants.
(6) Where the acts to be done are purely ministerial and do not involve any special care and skill, for example, clerical staff.

SUB-AGENT

According to Sec. 191 of the Act which states that "A sub-agent is a person employed by, and acting under the control of the original agent in the business of the agency." Sub-agent is a person appointed by the original agent to act in the business of agency. The sub-agent works under the control of original agent. The original agent acts as principal for the sub-agent. An agent who employs a sub-agent has the duties and liabilities of a principal to him. Such agent acts under the control of the original agent and the principal is not bound by his acts as there is no privity of contract between a sub-agent and principal.

RELATIONSHIP BETWEEN PRINCIPAL AND SUB-AGENT

The effect of sub-agency is to be seen from two different aspects. (1) A sub-agent may be appointed by the agent properly *i.e.*, in cases in which he is entitled under Sec. 190 to make the appointment, or (2) Improperly *i.e.*, without legal justification for such appointment.

1. *When a Sub-agent is Properly Appointed* (Sec. 192)

Following are the effects of proper appointment of a sub-agent :

(*a*) The principal is bound by and responsible for the acts of a sub-agent.
(*b*) The agent is responsible to the principal for the acts of the sub-agent.
(*c*) The sub-agent is responsible for his acts to the agent, but not to the principal except in case of fraud or wilful wrong.

2. *When a Sub-agent is Improperly Appointed* (Sec. 193)

Following are effects of improper appointment of sub-agent :

(*a*) As between the principal and the third parties, the principal is not represented by or bound by the acts of such sub-agent.
(*b*) The sub-agent is responsible to the agent as if the agent were the principal.
(*c*) The agent is responsible to the principal as well as third parties for the act of the sub-agent.
(*d*) The sub-agent is not responsible to the principal.

SUBSTITUTED AGENT

Section 194 states that "Where an agent, holding an express or implied authority to name another person to act for the principal in the business of the agency has named another person accordingly, such person is not a sub-agent but an agent of the principal for such part of the business of agency as is entrusted to him."

Examples : (1) A directs B, his solicitor to sell his estate by auction, and to employ an auctioneer for the purpose. B named C, auctioneer, to conduct the sale. C is a substituted agent of A. He is A's agent for the purpose of conducting the sale by auction.

(2) A authorises B, a merchant in Calcutta to recover the money due to A from C & Co. B instructs D a solicitor to take legal proceedings against C & Co. for recovery of money. D is not sub-agent, but is a solicitor for A.

Further Section 195 states "In selecting such agent for his principal, an agent is bound to exercise the same amount of discretion as a man of ordinary prudence would exercise in his own case; and if he does this he is not responsible to the principal for the acts or negligence of the agent so selected."

Examples : (1) A instructs B, a merchant to buy a ship for him. B employs a ship surveyor of good reputation to choose a ship for A. The surveyor makes the choice negligently and the ship turns out to be unworthy and is lost. B is not, but the surveyor is, responsible to A.

(2) A consigns goods to B, a merchant for sale. B in due course employs auctioneer in good credit to sell the goods of A, and allows the auctioneer to receive the proceeds of the sale. The auctioneer afterwards becomes insolvent without having accounted for the proceeds. B is not responsible to A for the proceeds.

Difference between a sub-agent and a Substituted Agent

Both, a sub-agent and a substituted agent, are appointed by the agent. However, the following are the points of distinction between the two :

Sub-agent (S. 191, 192, 193)	*Substituted agent (S. 194, 195)*
1. He is appointed by the agent and the sub-agent works under the control of agent. He is the agent of the original agent.	1. He is appointed by the agent. The substituted agent works under the control of principal. Substituted agent is the agent of the principal.
2. There is no privity of contract between the principal and the sub-agent.	2. Privity of contract is established between a principal and substituted agent.
3. The agent is responsible for the acts of his sub-agent.	3. The agent is not liable for the acts of a substituted agent.
4. A sub-agent is appointed by an agent only when he finds it necessary as per the custom of trade or the nature of agency.	4. A substituted agent is appointed by the agent when he has express or implied authority to do so from the principal.
5. Sub-agent is liable to the agent.	5. Substituted agent is liable to the principal.
6. Remuneration or commission to a sub-agent is paid by the agent.	6. Such payments are made by the principal.
7. A principal is not responsible to the third parties for the acts committed by the sub-agent provided he has not been appointed by the consent of the principal.	7. The principal is bound to all the acts of a substituted agent in the same way and extent as he is liable to the acts of his agent.

TERMINATION OF AGENCY

The legal provisions relating to the termination of agency are contained in the Sections 201 to 210 of the Indian Contract Act. According to Section 201 of the Act "An agency is terminated by the principal revoking his authority; or by the agent renouncing the business of the agency; or by the business of the agency being completed, or by either the principal or agent dying or becoming of unsound mind, or by the principal being adjudicated an insolvent under the provisions of any Act for the time being in force for the relief of insolvent debtors." This section, however, is not comprehensive and does not deal with all the modes by which the agency terminates. An agency may be terminated or revoked in any of the following ways :

(*i*) By the act of the parties

(*ii*) By the operation of law

(i) Termination of Agency by the Act of Parties :

1. ***Agreement***

The relation between the principal and agent, like any other agreement, may be terminated at any time, and at any stage by the mutual agreement between the principal and the agent.

2. ***Revocation by the Principal***

A principal has power to revoke the authority of the agent whenever he likes. Revocation may be defined as cancellation. The revocation puts an end to the agency relationship. The revocation may be express or implied.

But, if the authority has been partly exercised, the principal cannot revoke the authority, regarding such acts and obligations as arise from acts already done in the agency (Sec. 204).

Where the agency is a continuous one, notice of its termination to the agent and also to the third parties is essential.

3. ***Renunciation by the Agent***

The agent may renounce the business of agency in the same manner in which the principal has the right of revocation. Reasonable notice must be given of such renunciation otherwise the damage thereby resulting to the principal must be made good by the agent (Sec. 206).

(ii) Termination of Agency by Operation of Law

An agency comes to an end automatically by operation of law in the following cases :

1. ***Completion of Agency Business***

When the business of the agency is completed, agency comes to an end (Sec. 201). That is, where the agency is for a particular object, it is terminated when it is accomplished or its performance becomes impossible. When the agency is for the sale of a house, the agency terminates on the completion of the sale and does not continue until the payment of the price.

2. ***Expiry of Time***

When agency is created for a period of time, the agency is terminated on the expiry of that time, even though the business of the agency may not have been completed.

3. ***Death of Either Party***

An agency is automatically terminated on the death of the principal or the agent. However, the death of the principal cannot operate to bring about an end to the contract of agency until it comes to the knowledge of the agent.

4. ***Insanity of either Party***

An agency is terminated by either principal or agent becoming of unsound mind (Sec. 201).

5. ***Insolvency of the Principal***

According to Section 201, the agency is terminated by the principal being adjudicated as an insolvent under provisions of any Act. This section is silent on the insolvency of the agent, but it is accepted that insolvency of an agent also terminates the agency.

6. *Destruction of the Subject-matter*

An agency which is created to deal with certain subject-matter will be terminated by the destruction of that subject-matter. For example, if an agent is asked to sell a car and the car is destroyed by fire, then the agency comes to end.

7. *Principal or Agent becomes Alien Enemy*

Where the principal or the agent belong to different countries and a war breaks out between the two countries, the contract of agency is terminated.

8. *Dissolution of a Company*

When the company, which is either principal or agent, is wound up, the agency is terminated.

9. *Termination of sub-agent's Authority*

Section 210 of the Act has laid down that termination of the authority of an agent causes the termination of the authority of all sub-agents appointed by him.

IRREVOCABLE AGENCY

Irrevocable agency may be defined as the agency which cannot be revoked. The agency is irrevocable in the following cases

(a) Agency Coupled with Interest

Section 202 of the Act laid down that "Where the agent has himself an interest in the property which forms subject-matter of the agency, the agency cannot, in the absence of an express contract, be terminated to the prejudice of such interest".

> **Example :** A gives authority to B to sell A's land, and to pay himself, out of the proceeds, the debts due to him from A. A cannot revoke this authority, nor can it be terminated by his insanity or death.

Agency is irrevocable during the subsistence of such an interest. An agent is said to have an interest when the agency is created for the purpose of securing some benefit to the agent. In such cases, an agency coupled with interest cannot be terminated even on the death or insanity of the principal. It does not apply where the interest of the agent arises after the creation of the agency.

(b) Agent has Exercised Authority Partly

Section 204 of the Act laid down that "The principal cannot revoke the authority given to his agent after the authority has been partly exercised so far as regards such acts and obligations as arisen from acts already done in the agency."

> **Example :** A authorises B to buy 1,000 bales of cotton on account of A and to pay for it out of A's money remaining in B's hand. B buys 1,000 bales of cotton in his own name so as to make himself personally liable for the price, A cannot revoke B's authority so far as regards payment for the cotton.

(c) Agent is Personally Liable

The principal cannot revoke the agent's authority, if the agent has, in the exercise of his authority, incurred any personal liability. (See the above example).

EFFECTIVENESS OF TERMINATION

Sec. 208 laid down that "The termination of the authority of an agent does not, so far as regards the agent, takes effect before it becomes known to him, or so far as regards third persons, before it becomes known to them." The termination is effective from the time when it comes to the knowledge of the agent or third parties. Even when the agency is terminated automatically by the death, insanity or insolvency of the principal, knowledge of the agent is essential for completing termination as between him and the principal : and knowledge of the third party is essential for making termination effective as between the third party and principal.

Examples : (1) A directs B to sell goods for him, and agrees to give B 5 per cent commission on the price fetched by the goods. A afterwards, by letter, revokes B's authority. B, after the letter is sent, but before he receives it, sell goods for Rs. 100. The sale is binding on A and B is entitled to Rs. 5 as his commission.

(2) A, at Madras, by letter, directs B to sell for him some cotton lying in a warehouse in Bombay, and afterwards, by letter, revokes his authority to sell, and directs B to send the cotton to Madras. B, after receiving the second letter, enters into a contract with C who knows of the first letter, but not of the second, for the sale to him of the cotton. C pays B the money, with which B absconds. C's payment is good as against A.

(3) A directs B, his agent, to pay certain money to C. A dies, and D take out probate to his will. B after A's death, but before hearing of it, pays the money to C. The payment is good as against D, the executor.

Termination of Agency
(By operation of law)

1. Completion of agency business.
2. Expiry of contracted period.
3. Death of the principal or agent.
4. Insanity of the principal or agent.
5. Insolvency of the principal.
6. Destruction of the subject-matter.
7. Principal or agent becoming alien enemy.
8. Dissolution of company.
9. Object of the agency being unlawful.
10. Renunciation of agency by the agent.

THEORETICAL QUESTIONS

1. Define agent. What are the duties of an agent?
2. Briefly explain the various modes by which an agency may be created. *(B.Com. Delhi MS)*
3. Define the term agency. What are the essentials and legal rules for a valid agency?
4. Who is an agent? How does he differ from a servant?
5. Who is an agent? Who may be an agent and who may appoint an agent? *(B.Com. Madurai MS.)*
6. Ratification constitute agency. Discuss. When can an act of agent be ratified? When ratification is not allowed?
7. Classify and explain types of agents.
8. Discuss the nature and extent of the authority of an agent.
9. Who is a sub-agent? When can an agent appoint a sub agent?
10. Distinguish between a sub-agent and substituted agent. *(B.Com., Kerala)*
11. What are the rights and duties of an agent towards his principal? *(B.Com., MS)*
12. What is meant by "Agency by Estoppel' and 'Agency by Necessity'? *(B.Com., Kerala)*
13. When can an agent be held personally liable for the acts done by him on behalf of the principal? *(CA)*
14. Describe the various modes by which an agency may be terminated. *(B.Com., Delhi)*
15. What is an agency coupled with interest? Is such an agency revocable?
16. In what way may a contract of agency be terminated by act of the parties? When is an agency irrevocable? Explain. *(CA)*
17. "Ratification is tantamount to prior authority". Comment. *(B.Com. Madurai MS)*
18. Explain the effect of a contract made by an agent with a third party when he acts for an undisclosed principal. *(B.Com Madurai)*

MULTIPLE CHOICE QUESTIONS

I. Choose correct option for each of the following:

1. **A person appointed to contract on behalf of another person, is known as :**
   (*a*) principal. (*b*) Agent.
   (*c*) Servant. (*d*) contractor.
2. **A mercantile agent to whom the possession of the goods is given for the purpose of selling the same, is known as :**
   (*a*) broker. (*b*) factor.
   (*c*) commission agent. (*d*) insurance agent.
3. **A person appointed by the original agent to act in the business of agency, but under the control of original agent, is known as :**
   (*a*) Agent. (*b*) Del credere agent.
   (*c*) substituted agent. (*d*) sub-agent.
4. **Where one person allows another person to assume an appearance of authority to act on his behalf, such a position is known as :**
   (*a*) express authority. (*b*) Implied authority.
   (*c*) ostensible authority. (*d*) none of these.
5. **Where the agent contracts for a principal who is not competent to contract, in such a case, the agent is :**
   (*a*) personally liable. (*b*) not personally liable.
   (*c*) exceeding authority. (*d*) none of these.
6. **For a valid ratification the principal must have contractual capacity :**
   (*a*) both at the time of the contract and at the time of ratification.
   (*b*) at the time of ratification.
   (*c*) at the time of contract.
   (*d*) at any time.
7. **An agent is personally liable :**
   (*a*) when he acts for an undisclosed principal. (*b*) when He acts for a named principal.
   (*c*) when he acts for a principal not in existence.
8. **If there is no agreement, an agent is :**
   (*a*) not entitled to any remuneration.
   (*b*) entitled to reasonable remuneration.
   (*c*) entitled to remuneration which he thinks reasonable.
   (*d*) entitled to remuneration which the principal thinks reasonable.
9. **For his commission, agent has :**
   (*a*) a general lien. (*b*) no lien at all.
   (*c*) a particular lien.
10. **Agent makes some secret profits out of the business of agency. He loses :**
    (*a*) his remuneration. (*b*) his profits.
    (*c*) not only his profits but also his remuneration.

ANSWERS

1. (*b*) **2.** (*b*) **3.** (*d*) **4.** (*c*) **5.** (*a*) **6.** (*a*) **7.** (*a*) **8.** (*b*) **9.** (*c*) **10.** (*c*)

THE SALE OF GOODS ACT, 1930

CHAPTER

Contract of Sale of Goods

AT A GLANCE

- Introduction
- Scope
- Goods
- Classification of Goods
- Effects of Destruction of Subject-matter
- Contract of Sale
- Essentials of Sale
- Sales and Agreement to sell
- Sales and Hire Purchase
- Sales and Gift of Goods
- Sales and Bailment
- Sales and Mortgage
- Sales and Contract for Work
- Sales and Barter
- Price
- Document to Title to Goods
- Earnest Money
- Theoretical Questions
- Multiple Choice Questions.

INTRODUCTION

The law relating to the sale of goods or movables in India is contained in the Sale of Goods Act 1930. Prior to the enactment of this Act, the law relating to sale of goods was embodied in the Indian Contract Act 1872, in sections 76 to 123. However, as the provisions of the Sections 76 to 123 were found inadequate to meet the complexities of growing mercantile transactions, the said sections were repealed and the Sale of Goods Act 1930 took birth. The (Indian) Sale of Goods Act 1930 is largely based on the (English) Sale of Goods Act 1893. Even today the English authorities on the interpretation of the different sections are followed in India although they are not binding on Indian Courts. It contains 66 Sections and extends to the whole of India except the State Jammu and Kashmir. Law relating to the sale of goods is a branch of Contract Law. The general provisions of the Indian Contract Act continue to be applicable to the contract of sale of goods in so far as they are not inconsistent with the express provisions of the Sale of Goods Act (Sec. 3). Thus, for example, the provisions of the Contract Act relating to capacity of the parties, free consent, agreements in restraint of trade, wagering agreements and measure of damages continue to be applicable to a contract of sale of goods. To constitute a valid contract of sale, consideration for transfer must be money paid or promised. Where there is no money consideration the transaction is not a contract of sale. It is, therefore, necessary that goods should be exchanged for money. If goods are exchanged for goods, the transaction would not become a sale but only a barter. However, if consideration for the transfer of property consists partly of payment of money and partly of goods, the transaction becomes a sale.

SCOPE

The law relating to sale of goods is contained in the Sale of Goods Act 1930, which came into force on 1st July 1930. The sale of Goods Act applies only to movables other than actionable claim and money. That is, the provisions of the Sale of Goods Act are applicable only to those things which can be called 'goods'. Sale of immovable property is governed by the Transfer of Property Act 1882. "Actionable claims" and "money" are excluded from "goods". Actionable claims are defined by the Transfer of Property Act and their transfer is governed by that Act. Actionable claims are claims which can be enforced only by an action or suit, for example, a debt. Money is excluded from the definition of goods for two reasons (*a*) that it constitutes the price for exchange of goods sold and (*b*) that it is governed by a different principles of law due to its being currency. Foreign currency may, however, be bought or sold.

GOODS

Goods form the subject matter of contract of sale. According to Sec. 2 (7) "Goods" means (*i*) every kind of movable property other than actionable claims and money and includes (*ii*) stock and (*iii*) shares, (*iv*) growing crops, grass and (*v*) things attached to or forming part of the land which are agreed to be severed (*i.e.*, separated) before sale or under the contract of sale. Actionable claims and current money have been expressly excluded from the scope of the definition. Actionable claims are things which a person cannot make use of, but which can be claimed by him by means of a legal action, for example, a debt. A debt is not goods because it can only be assigned as per Transfer of Property Act but cannot be sold. Since money is expressly excluded, current money is not goods, because it constitutes the element of price, in transactions of sale. Old coins which are not current money can be treated as goods.

CLASSIFICATION OF GOODS

Goods which from the subject matter of a contract of sale may be divided as under :

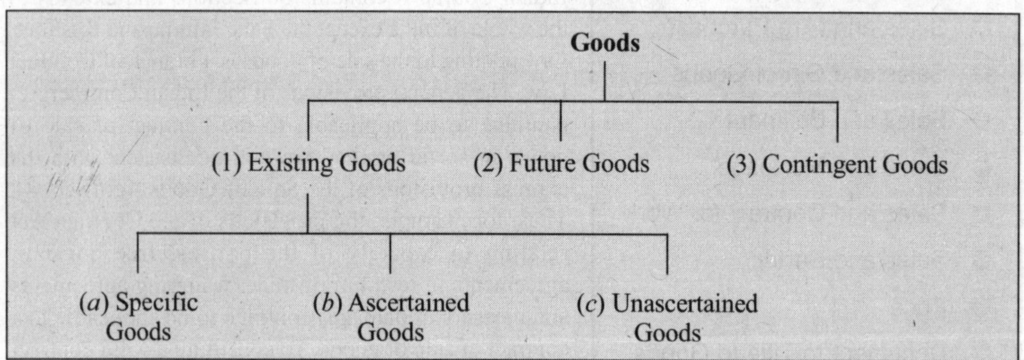

1. *Existing Goods*

Goods owned and possessed by the seller at the time of making the contract of sale are called existing goods. [Sec. 6 (1)]. The existing goods owned by the seller includes also the goods which have been pledged or let on hire, or are in the possession of an agent, or bailee, or servant etc. Sometimes, the seller may be in possession but may not be the owner of the goods. For example, in the case of sale by a mercantile agent or a pledge the goods are possessed but not owned by the seller. The existing goods may be of the following types :

(*a*) *Specific Goods :* Goods identified and agreed upon at the time of the making of the contract of sale are called specific goods. [Sec. 2(14)] Where there is a contract for specific goods, the seller would not fulfil his contract by delivering any goods other than those agreed upon. For example, if A who owns a number of horses, promises to sell one of them, the contract is for unspecified goods. But if the horse that is to be sold has been singled out, the contract is for specific goods.

(*b*) *Ascertained Goods :* 'Ascertained Goods' has not been defined in the Act. These are the goods which are ascertained subsequent to the formation of contract of sale. As contrasted with specific goods which are identified at the time of the sale, ascertained goods mean goods identified in accordance with the agreement after the contract of sale is made. The identification takes place at a later date. For example, if a merchant agrees to supply one bag of sugar from his godown to a buyer, it is a sale of unascertained goods because it is not known which bag will be delivered. As soon as a particular bag is separated out and marked or identified for delivery it becomes specific goods.

(*c*) *Unascertained Goods :* The goods which are not specifically identified at the time of contract of sale, are known as unascertained goods. The expression "unascertained goods", means generic goods, *i.e.*, goods defined by description or even by sample. Unascertained goods are not definite and specific. The seller in the case of a contract for the sale of unascertained goods has the option, rather the right to supply any goods of the kind or the quality contracted for.

2. *Future Goods*

"Future Goods" means goods to be manufactured or produced or acquired by the seller after making the contract of sale" [Sec. 2(6)]. These are the goods which are not in existence at the time of contract of sale. The seller acquires such goods after the making of the contract of sale. When a person purports to make a present sale of the future goods, the contract operates as an agreement to sell and not a sale. It is important to note that the "future goods are neither in existence nor in possession of the seller at the time of contract of sale. Whereas the "unascertained goods" are in existence and in possession of the seller at the time of contract of sale. For example, a contract of sale to sell the crop in advance is a contract to sell and not a sale.

3. *Contingent Goods*

Contingent goods are future goods. According to Sec. 6 (2) "there may be a contract for the sale of goods, the acquisition of which by the seller depends upon a contingency which may or may not happen". A contract for the sale of contingency goods also operates as "an agreement to sell" and not a "sale" so far as the question of passing of property to the buyer is concerned. It is important to note that a contract of sale of contingent goods is enforceable only if the event on the happening of which the performance of the contract is dependent happens, otherwise the contract becomes void. Such contracts give no right of action if the contingency does not happen.

Example : A agrees to sell B a certain paintings provided he is able to purchase it from its present owner. This is an agreement for the sale of contingent goods.

EFFECTS OF DESTRUCTION OF SUBJECT MATTER

Sections 7 and 8 of the Sale of Goods Act 1930 deal with the effect of perishing of goods on the rights and obligations of the parties to a contract of sale. Goods are said to perish when they physically or commercially cease to exist before and after the contract. The effect of perishing of goods may be discussed under the following heads :

1. *Goods Perishing before Making of the Contract* (Sec. 7)

According to Sec. 7 of the Act, "Where there is a contract for the sale of specific goods, the contract is void if the goods without the knowledge of the seller have, at the time when the contract was made perished or become so damaged as no longer to answer to their description in the contract." Where specific goods form the subject matter of a contract of sale and they without the knowledge of the seller perish, at or before the time of the contract, the contract is void. This provision is based on the ground of mutual mistake or impossibility of performance.

Where in a contract for the sale of specific goods, only part of the goods are destroyed or damaged, the effect of perishing will depend upon whether the contract is entire or divisible. If it is entire (indivisible) and part only of the goods has perished, the contract is void. If the contract is divisible, it will not be void and the part available in good condition must be accepted by the buyer.

Example : A agrees to sell B, a specific cargo supposed to be on its way from England to Bombay. It turns out that, before the day of the bargain the ship carrying the cargo has been cast away and the goods lost. Neither party was aware of the facts. The agreement is void.

To make a contract void under this section, the following conditions must be fulfilled :

(1) The contract must be for the sale of specific goods.

(2) The goods must have been perished before the contract is made.

(3) The seller must not have the knowledge of the destruction of the goods.

2. *Goods Perishing before sale but after Agreement to Sell* (Sec. 8)

Sec. 8 of Sale of Goods Act reads as "Where there is an agreement to sell specific goods, and subsequently the goods, without any fault on the part of the seller or buyer, perish or become so damaged as no longer to answer to their description in the agreement before the risk passes to the buyer, the agreement is thereby avoided". In such cases, the contract of sale becomes void if the contract is for the sale of specific goods and the goods are destroyed without any fault of the seller or buyer. This provision is based on the ground of supervening impossibility of performance which makes a contract void.

If only part of the goods agreed to be sold perish, the contract becomes void if it is indivisible. But if it is divisible then the parties are absolved from their obligations only to the extent of perishing of the goods, that is, the contract remains valid as regards the part available in good condition.

However, the following conditions must be satisfied :

(*a*) The contract is an agreement to sell and not an actual sale.

(*b*) The contract should be for specific goods and not for unascertained goods.

(*c*) The goods must have been perished without the fault of seller or buyer.

(*d*) The goods must have perished or damaged before the property or the risk passes to the buyer.

Sometimes, the risk has passed to the buyer at the time of the contract *i.e.*, the buyer has expressly or impliedly undertaken to suffer the loss of the goods. In such cases, the buyer will be liable to pay the damages to the seller for the loss of the goods even if the goods have not been delivered to him.

Sections 7 and 8 apply only to specific goods. If the contract for 'unascertained goods' then the contract shall not become void even if the entire stock of goods is destroyed. And the parties remain liable to fulfil their obligations.

Under Sec. 7, the contract is void *ab initio* and the parties are discharged from their liabilities to perform the contract. On the other hand, Sec. 8 lays down the rule where the goods perish after the agreement to sell but before it becomes sale *i.e.*, before the risk passes to the buyer. Thus, under Sec. 8, the contract is not void *ab initio.* But it becomes void when the goods perish and not before. And the parties are discharged from their liabilities to perform the contract from the time of perishing the goods.

Howell Vs. Coupland (1876)

In this case, the seller agreed to sell to the buyer 200 tons of potatoes to be grown on his land, at £ 2 and 2s a ton. He had sufficient land to grow more than 200 tons. But, without any fault on his part, the crop was attacked by a disease, as a result of which he could deliver only 80 tons. The buyer sued the seller for breach of contract.

Holding that the contract was void, it is observed that "This is not like the case of a contract to deliver so many goods of a particular kind, where no specific goods are to be sold. Here, there was an agreement to sell and buy 200 tons out of a crop to be grown on specific land, so that it is an agreement to sell what will be, and may be, called specific things, therefore, neither party is liable if the performance becomes impossible."

CONTRACT OF SALE

Sec. 4 (1) of the Sale of Goods Act defines a contract of sale of goods as "a contract whereby the seller transfers or agrees to transfer the property in goods to the buyer for a price". Here property means the right of ownership. Further Sec. 4(3) states "where under a contract of sale the property in the goods is transferred from the seller to the buyer, the contract is called a sale, but where the transfer of the property in the goods is to take place at a future time or subject to some condition thereafter to be fulfilled, the contract is called "an agreement to sell". Thus it includes both sale as well as an agreement to sell.

However, in the case of a sale, the property in the goods must be transferred immediately. In the case of an agreement to sell, however, the transfer of property takes place at a future time or subject to some condition thereafter to be fulfilled. An agreement to sell is thus a conditional sale, and hence, an executory contract. It becomes a sale according to Section 4(4), after the lapse of time or fulfillment of the conditions subject to which property in the goods is to be transferred.

Examples : (1) A sells his bike for Rs. 10,000 to B. It is a sale, as the ownership of the bike has been transferred to B by A for a price.

(2) A agrees with B to sell his bike after two months for Rs. 10,000. It is an agreement to sell as the bike is to be transferred on a future date.

Essentials of a Contract of Sale

Sec. 4 of the Sale of Goods Act defines 'sale' as "a contract of sale of goods is a contract whereby the seller transfers or agrees to transfer the property in goods to the buyer for price".

Contract of sale how made ?

"A contract of sale is made by an offer to buy or sell goods for a price and the acceptance of such offer. The contract may provide for the immediate delivery of the goods or immediate payment of the price or both, or for the delivery or payment by installments, or that the delivery or payment or both shall be postponed." Sec. 5 (1).

"Subject to the provisions of any law for the time being in force, a contract of sale may be made in writing or by word of mouth, or partly in writing and partly by word of mouth or may be implied from the conduct of the parties" Sec. 5 (2).

The definition reveals the following essentials of a contract of sales of goods.

(1) *Two Parties*

To constitute a contract of sale, there must be a transfer or agreement to transfer the property in goods by the seller to the buyer. That is, there must be two parties in a contract of sale — seller and buyer. Buyer means a person who buys or agrees to buy goods. Similarly seller is a person who sells or agrees to sell his goods. Sec. 2 (1). The seller and the buyer must be two different persons, for a man cannot purchase his own goods.

Example : *State of Gujrat Vs. Ramlal & Co.* (1965)

A partnership firm was dissolved. The surplus assets including some goods were divided among the partners. The tax officer wanted to tax this as sale. The court observed that "the partners were themselves the joint owners of the goods and they could not be both sellers and buyers. Moreover no money consideration was promised or paid by any partner to the firm as consideration for the goods allotted to him".

(2) *Goods*

The subject matter of the contract of sale must be 'goods'. According to Sec. 2(7), "goods means every kind of movable property other than actionable claims and money; and includes stock and shares, growing crops, grass and things attached to or forming part of the land which are agreed to be severed before sale or under the contract of sale". Goods which form the subject matter of sale may be either existing goods or future goods. Money, actionable claims and immovable property cannot form the subject matter of sale within the meaning of Sec. 2(7).

(3) *Transfer of Property*

'Property' here means 'ownership'. In every contract of sale, the ownership of goods must be transferred by the seller to the buyer, or there should be an agreement by the seller to transfer the ownership to the buyer. According to Sec. 2 (11) "Property means the general property in the goods, and not merely a special property." The property in the goods means the general property *i.e.*, 'all ownership right of the goods. Though passing of the title in the goods is an ingredient of sale, physical delivery of goods is not essential. The term 'property' as used in the Sale of Goods Act means general property in goods as distinguished from special property. For example, If A who owns certain goods pledges them to B, he has general property in the goods, whereas B has special property or interest in the goods to the extent of the amount of advance he has made.

(4) *Price*

The term 'price' is defined in Section 2 (10) as "Price means the money consideration for a sale of goods". Consideration in a contract of sale has necessarily to be money *i.e.*, legal tender. If goods are sold or exchanged for other goods, the transaction is barter and not a sale of goods under this Act. As a matter of fact, the requirement is that the goods must be sold for a definite sum of money and it may be partly in cash and partly in valued up goods. For example, when an old bike is returned to the dealer for a new one and the difference is paid in cash, that would also be a sale. (Aldridge Vs. Johnson 1857).

5. *Contract*

All the essential elements of a contract must be present in a contract of sale. The word contract means an agreement enforceable at law. If any of the essential elements of a valid contract is missing, then the contract of sale will not be valid.

It may be noted that no particular form is necessary for the making of a contract of sale. It may be in any form. A contract of sale may be made (*a*) in writing or (*b*) by words of mouth or (*c*) partly in writing and partly by words of mouth, or (*d*) may be implied from the conduct of the parties. However, if any particular mode is prescribed by any law, then the contract of sale must be made in that particular mode. (Sec. 5 (2)).

Essentials of a Contract of Sale

1. Existence of two persons — buyer and seller.
2. Goods — the subject-matter of contract.
3. Price — the consideration for sale of goods.
4. Transfer of property (ownership).
5. Contracts — all essentials must be present.

SALES AND AGREEMENT TO SELL

Section 4(3) of the Sale of Goods Act, 1930 describes 'sale' in the following words :

Where under a contract of sale, the property (ownership) in the goods is transferred from the seller to the buyer, it is called a sale.

According to Section 4 (3) of the Sale of Goods Act, 'agreement to sell' means :

Where the transfer of the property in the goods is to take place at a future time or subject to some condition thereafter to be fulfilled the contract is called an agreement to sell.

The distinction between sale and an agreement to sell is very necessary to determine the rights and the liabilities of the parties to the contract. The main point of distinction are :

Sale	*Agreement to Sell*
1. *Nature* A sale is an *executed* contract.	An agreement to sell is an *executory* contract.
2. *Transfer of property* The property in the goods passes from the seller to the buyer immediately so that the seller is no more the owner of goods sold.	The transfer of property in the goods is to take place at a future time or subject to certain conditions to be fulfilled.
3. *Risk of Loss* If the goods are destroyed,, the loss falls on the buyers even though they were in the possession of the seller.	If the goods are destroyed, the loss falls on the seller, even through they were in the possession of the buyer.
4. *General and Particular Property* It creates a right in rem, *i.e.*, against the whole world.	It creates a right in personam *i.e.*, against a specified person only.
5. *Performance* Performance of sale is absolute and without any condition.	Performance is conditional and is made in future.
6. *Right of Resale* The property is with the buyer and as such the seller cannot resell the goods. If he does so, the buyer can recover the goods, sometimes, even from third parties.	The property in the goods remains with the seller and he can dispose of the goods as he likes, although he may thereby commit a breach of his contract.
7. *Insolvency of buyer* If the buyer is declared insolvent before making the payment of the price for goods, the seller in the absence of lien over goods, will have to deliver the goods to the official receiver and can claim only the retable dividend.	If the buyer who is declared insolvent, has not paid the price, the seller is not bound to deliver the goods, as the property in goods has not passed to him.
8. *Insolvency of Seller* If the seller is declared insolvent, the buyer is entitled to recover the goods from the official receiver as the buyer has the ownership of the goods sold.	The buyer who has paid the price, cannot claim the title of goods from the seller, if he is declared insolvent. He can only claim a rateable dividend (from the official receiver of the insolvent seller).
9. *Consequences of Breach* If the buyer wrongfully neglects or refuses to pay the price of the goods, the seller can sue for the price, even though the goods are still in his possession.	If the buyer fails to accept and pay for the goods, the seller can only use for damages and not for the price, even though the goods are in the possession of the buyer.

Formalities of Contract of Sale

1. There must be a valid offer to buy or to sell.
2. The offer to buy or sell must be for goods.
3. The sale must be for a price.
4. There must be valid acceptance.
5. There must be payment of price.
6. The contract may be in writing or oral.

SALE DISTINGUISHED FROM OTHER TRANSACTIONS

There are some transactions which bear a close resemblance to a contract of sale, but which are quite different from sale of goods. Therefore, it is necessary to point out the distinguishing features of such transaction.

SALE AND HIRE PURCHASE AGREEMENT

A contract of hire-purchase is entered into mainly with the object of selling goods since it is a development of modern commercial transactions. Under hire purchase agreement the owner of the goods agrees to transfer the property in the goods to the hire-purchaser when a certain fixed number of installments of price are paid by the hirer. Till that time, the hirer remains the bailee and the installments paid by him are regarded as the hire-charges for the use of the goods. If there is a default by the hire-purchaser in paying an instalment, the owner has a right to resume the possession of the goods immediately without refunding the amount received till then, because the ownership still rests with him. Thus, the essence of hire-purchase agreement is that there is no agreement to buy, but there is only a bailment of the goods coupled with an option to purchase them which may or may not be exercised.

The main points of distinction between the sale and hire-purchase are as follows :

Sale	*Hire-purchase*
1. It may be made either orally or in writing.	1. It must be in writing.
2. The ownership of the goods is transferred from the seller to the buyer as soon as the contract is made.	2. The ownership of the goods is transferred from the seller to the hirer only when all the agreed number of instalments are paid.
3. The position of the buyer is that of the owner.	3. The position of the hire-purchaser is that of the bailee.
4. The buyer in a sale can resell the goods.	4. The hire-purchaser cannot resell unless he has paid all the instalments of hire.
5. It is governed by the Sale of Goods Act 1930.	5. It is governed by the Hire purchase Act 1972.
6. The seller takes the risk of any loss resulting from the insolvency of the buyer.	6. The owner takes no such risk,, for if the hirer fails to pay in instalment, the owner has the right to take back the goods.

SALE AND GIFT OF GOODS

Sale and gift involve the transfer of ownership. But the gift is different from a sale as the element of price is missing. Sale is always for a consideration. Gift goods are transferred from the donor to the donee without any consideration.

Sale and Bailment

Bailment is defined by Section 148 of Indian Contract Act 1872 as the "delivery of goods by one person to another for some purpose, upon a contract that they shall, when the purpose is accomplished, be returned or otherwise disposed of according to the directions of the person delivering them."

The following are the main points of difference between the two :

Sale	*Bailment*
1. Ownership in goods is transferred from the seller to the buyer.	1. There is transfer of possession and not of ownership from the bailor to the beilee.
2. The buyer may use the goods in any way he likes.	2. A bailee can use the goods only according to the directions of the bailor.
3. There is no return of goods from the buyer to the seller, unless there is breach.	3. The goods are necessarily returned after the specified time or accomplishment of the purpose.
4. The consideration is the price in terms of money.	4. The consideration is an undertaking to return the goods after the accomplishment of purpose.
5. The question of any charges to be paid by the seller to buyer or vice versa does not arise.	5. The bailor has to repay the charges which the bailee has incurred in keeping the goods safe.

Sale and Mortgage

Sale	*Mortgage*
1. The buyer becomes absolute owner of the goods sold.	1. Ownership of the goods remains vested in the mortgagor.
2. Ownership of the goods as a whole is transferred from the seller to the buyer.	2. Only the possession is transferred and ownership transfer is limited to some interest only.
3. Consideration is the price.	3. Consideration is the advance of the loan and the securing of the debt.

SALE AND CONTRACT FOR WORK AND SKILL

The distinction between sale of goods and contract of work and skill is important in the context of sales tax law in the different states of India. Sales tax is leviable on sale of goods under certain circumstances, whereas it is not leviable on the remuneration received for work and labour rendered. A contract of sale of goods contemplates the delivery of moveable goods; but if in substance the contract is one for the exercise of skill, it is a contract for work and labour. The distinction between the two types of contracts is of importance in England but not in India, except for taxation purposes. The sales of Goods Act does not apply to contracts for work and skill.

Examples : 1. A dentist agreed to make a set of artificial teeth to fit the mouth of a customer. Held, it is contract for the sale of goods. (Lee Vs. Griffin 1861).

2. Again, a contract with an artist who agreed to paint a picture for an agreed sum, on the canvas and with the materials to be supplied by the other party, was held to be a contract for work and skill and not one for sale of goods. (Robinson Vs. Graves 1935).

SALE AND BARTER

A sale is always for a 'price' but in the case of barter, the transfer of ownership of one thing is in return for transfer of another thing. Sale is always made in terms of money while exchange is in terms of kind *i.e.*, exchange of one thing with other.

THE PRICE

According to Sec. 2 (10), "price" means the money consideration for a sale of goods. Price is one of the essential elements of contract of sale as per Sec. 4. It is expressed in terms of money. It is the consideration for transfer or agreement to transfer the property in goods from the seller to the buyer. The price may be money actually paid or promised to be paid depending on whether the agreement is for cash or credit sale. If the price is not fixed and is not capable of being fixed, the whole contract is void *ab initio*. The different modes of fixing the price are contained in Sec. 9 of the Sale of Goods Act which provides as under :

"The price in a contract of sale may be fixed by the contract or may be left to be fixed in a manner thereby agreed or may be determined by the course of dealing between the parties." Sec. 9(1).

"Where the price is not determined in accordance with the foregoing provisions, the buyer shall pay the seller a reasonable price. What is reasonable price is a question of fact dependent on the circumstances of each particular case." Sec. 9 (2).

Sec. 9 provides the following modes of the determination of price :

1. *Price may be Fixed by the Contract.* The parties may fix such price for the goods as they may please. The price may be expressly stated in the contract. Inadequacy of price does not affect a sale.

2. *Price may be fixed in a manner agreed upon.* The contract of sale may provide for some manner in which price is to be fixed. In such cases, the price may be fixed in a manner provided in the contract.

3. *The Fixation of Price by Course of Dealings :* Where the price is not fixed, it can be determined in the course of dealings between the parties or as it is sometimes called the market price of the goods.

4. *Fixation of Reasonable Price :* In the absence of above modes, the buyer shall pay to the seller a reasonable price. What is reasonable price is a question of fact depending upon the circumstances of each case.

Agreement to Sell at Valuation of Third Parties (Sec. 10)

Section 10 (1) provides "where there is an agreement to sell goods on the terms that the price is to be fixed by the valuation of a third party and such third party cannot or does not make such valuation, the agreement is thereby avoided :

"Provided that, if the goods or any part thereof have been delivered to, and appropriated by, the buyer, he shall pay a reasonable price therefor."

Section 10(2) states, that "Where such third party is prevented from making the valuation by the fault of the seller or buyer, the party not in fault may maintain a suit for damages against the party in fault."

Thus the parties may agree to sell and buy goods on the terms that the price shall be fixed by the valuation of a third party. It may, however, be noted that if such third party fails to make the valuation, the contract becomes void. But if the buyer has received the goods and has appropriated them, he becomes bound to pay reasonable price to the seller. Sometime, the third party is influenced or prevented by the buyer or the seller from fixing the price. In such cases, the innocent party may recover damages from the defaulting party.

Document to Title to Goods (Sec. 2(4))

A document of title to goods is a proof of the ownership of the goods. It authorises its holder to receive goods mentioned therein or to further transfer such right to another person by proper endorsement or delivery. According to Sec. 2(4) "Document to title to goods" includes a bill of lading, dock-warrant, warehouse keeper's certificate, wharfinger's certificate, railway receipt, warrant or order for the delivery of goods and any other document used in the ordinary course of business as a proof of the possession or control of goods, or authorizing or purporting to authorize either by endorsement or by delivery, the possessor of the document to transfer or receive goods thereby represented." The Act recognises the following as documents of title to goods :

(*a*) *Bill of lading :* A bill of lading is a receipt given by the ship owner acknowledging the receipt of goods for carriage. It has been defined as a "receipt for goods shipped on board a ship, signed by the person who contracts to carry them, or his agent, and stating the terms on which the goods were delivered to and received by the ship."

(*b*) *Dock warrant :* A dock warrant is document which is issued by a dock owner. It contains the details of the goods; certifying that the goods are held on behalf of the person whose name is appeared in it or his assignee by endorsement. It authorises the person holding it to receive the possession of the goods.

(*c*) *Warehouse keeper's certificate :* Warehouse is a building in which goods are stored. Warehouse keeper's certificate is a document which issued by the warehouse keeper. It is a certificate by the warehouse keeper that the goods specified in the document are in the warehouse, or wharf.

(*d*) *Railway receipt :* A railway receipt is a document which issued by the railway as the acknowledgment of the receipt of goods. It provides that on surrender of the receipt at the destination of the goods by the consignee the goods mentioned therein will be delivered to him.

(*e*) *Delivery Order :* A delivery order is an order which is given by the owner of goods directing a person who holds the goods on his behalf to deliver them to a person named therein.

EARNEST MONEY

The term earnest money may be defined as the money paid by one party, in advance, to another party as a security for the proper performance of his part of the contract. The part payment in advance towards the price of goods may be both advance payment in part and earnest. This depends upon the intention of the parties. When the part payment is made by the buyer in advance as a security for the due performance of the contract of sale by him, it is earnest. When it is not so intended, it is a mere advance payment.

If the contract is properly performed, earnest money is either returned, or adjusted against the price. If the contract is not or cannot be performed because of the fault of the buyer, the earnest money is forfeited by the seller unless otherwise agreed. If the contract is not or cannot be performed because of the fault of none or that of the seller, the buyer may get the earnest money back. If the contract is avoided even because of the fault of the buyer, he may get back the part payment but not the earnest money.

THEORETICAL QUESTIONS

1. Define a contract of sale. What are its essentials?
2. How is a contract of sale made? State briefly the necessary formalities of such a contract with illustrations.
3. Distinguish between sale and agreement to sell. (*CA, B.Com. MS*)
4. Define the term 'goods'. Distinguish between specific and unascertained goods. (*B.Com. Madurai*)
5. How is price fixed in a contract of sale. What are the different modes of determination of price?
6. What is the effect of destruction of specific goods on a contract of sale? (*B.Com. Bombay*)
7. Distinguish between sale and hire purchase.
8. Describe the subject-matter of sale. Distinguish between specific, ascertained and unascertained goods.
9. "Sale is an executed contract but an agreement to sell is an executory contract". Discuss.
10. Define the term 'price'. What are the different modes of determination of price. (*M.Com. Banaras*)
11. What is a "contract for work and skill". Distinguish it from sale. (*B.Com. MS*)
12. Risk 'prima facia' passes with ownership. Discuss. (*B.Com. Madras*)

MULTIPLE CHOICE QUESTIONS

I. Choose correct option for each of the following :

1. **The Sale of Goods Act extends to :**
   (*a*) whole of India.
   (*b*) whole of India except Jammu & Kashmir .
   (*c*) whole of India except Jammu & Kashmir and Dadra and Nagar Haveli.
   (*d*) whole of India except Lakshadweep.
2. **According to Sale of Goods Act, the term "goods" means :**
   (*a*) every kind of movable and immovable property.
   (*b*) every kind of movable property other than actionable claims and currency money.
   (*c*) every kind of movable property and services.
   (*d*) all of the above.
3. **In a contract of sale, price of goods may be paid :**
   (*a*) in cash.
   (*b*) any thing other than cash.
   (*c*) partly in cash and partly in goods valued in terms of money.
   (*d*) either (*a*) or (*c*).
4. **The Sale of Goods Act applies to contracts of :**
   (*a*) sale of goods. (*b*) sale of goods and services.
   (*c*) sale and pledge of goods. (*d*) sale and barter of goods.
5. **In case of sale of goods, the term 'goods' means :**
   (*a*) future goods. (*b*) contingent goods.
   (*c*) ascertained goods. (*d*) both (*a*) and (*b*) above.
6. **The term "goods" includes :**
   (*a*) shares. (*b*) harvested crops.
   (*c*) old coins. (*d*) all of the above.
7. **The Sale of Goods Act came into force :**
   (*a*) July 1, 1930. (*b*) July 1, 1932.
   (*c*) September 1, 1930. (*d*) June 1, 1932.
8. **A contract of sale includes :**
   (*a*) sale. (*b*) sale and agreement to sell.
   (*c*) sale and barter. (*d*) all of the above.

9. A contract of sale may be :

(*a*) conditional. (*b*) absolute.
(*c*) written. (*d*) all of the above.

10. An agreement of hire-purchase includes the agreement of :

(*a*) sale and agreement to sell. (*b*) bailment of goods for hire and agreement to sell.
(*c*) sale and bailment for hire. (*d*) both (*a*) and (*c*).

11. In case of sale of goods :

(*a*) possession of goods must be transferred to the buyer.
(*b*) special property in the goods must be transferred to the buyer.
(*c*) general property in the goods must be transferred to the buyer.
(*d*) both (*a*) and (*b*) above.

12. Following is not the document of title :

(*a*) bill of lading. (*b*) dock warrant.
(*c*) railway receipt. (*d*) none of the above.

13. In agreement to sell, the property (ownership) in the goods passes :

(*a*) immediately. (*b*) at a future date.
(*c*) either immediately or at a future date. (*d*) never.

14. Agreement to sell is :

(*a*) executed contract. (*b*) executory contract.
(*c*) sale. (*d*) implied contract.

15. Sale is :

(*a*) executed contract. (*b*) executory contract.
(*c*) agreement to sell. (*d*) all of the above.

16. According to Sale of Goods Act, the term "Goods' includes :

(*a*) goodwill. (*b*) interest of the partner in a firm.
(*c*) old coins and notes. (*d*) all of the above.

17. A contract of sale of contingent goods is :

(*a*) sale. (*b*) agreement to sell.
(*c*) unlawful. (*d*) all of the above.

18. Where price of goods sold is to be fixed by a third party and the third party refuses to fix the price, the contract becomes :

(*a*) void. (*b*) voidable.
(*c*) illegal. (*d*) void and illegal.

19. Where specific goods are destroyed without any fault of the seller subsequent to the agreement to sell the goods, the agreement :

(*a*) is voidable. (*b*) becomes void.
(*c*) is enforceable. (*d*) is illegal.

20. Where specific goods are destroyed before a contract of sale is made and the seller has no knowledge of the destruction of goods, the contract is :

(*a*) void. (*b*) voidable.
(*c*) illegal. (*d*) enforceable.

21. Under sale of goods Act 1930 the term 'goods' means every kind of movable property and it includes :

(*a*) stock and share. (*b*) growing crops.
(*c*) both (*a*) and (*b*). (*d*) none of the above.

22. The term 'goods' under Sales of Goods Act 1930 does not include :

(*a*) goodwill. (*b*) actional claim.

(*c*) stocks and shares. (*d*) harvested crops

23. The following are goods as per Section 2 (7) of the Sale of goods Act 1930 :

(*a*) trade mark. (*b*) goodwill.

(*c*) patent. (*d*) all of the above.

24. A contract of sale of goods includes :

(*a*) sale only. (*b*) Agreement to sell only.

(*c*) both (*a*) and (*b*). (*d*) barter.

25. Under the sale of goods Act 1930, property means :

(*a*) general property in goods. (*b*) special property in goods.

(*c*) both (*a*) and (*b*). (*d*) none of these.

26. In a sale, the property in goods :

(*a*) is transferred to the buyer. (*b*) yet to be transferred to the buyer.

(*c*) to be transferred at a future time. (*d*) is transferred when goods are delivered.

27. The consideration for the contract of sale can be :

(*a*) in goods. (*b*) in services.

(*c*) partly in money and partly in goods. (*d*) none of these.

28. In case of hire-purchase, the hirers :

(*a*) can pass a goods title to a bonafide purchaser.

(*b*) cannot pass a goods title to a bonafide purchaser.

(*c*) both (*a*) and (*b*).

29. In a sale, if the goods are destroyed, the loss falls on :

(*a*) the buyer. (*b*) the seller.

(*c*) to both - seller and buyer. (*d*) party who is in the possession of goods.

30. The goods are at the risk of a party who has the :

(*a*) ownership of goods. (*b*) possession of goods.

(*c*) Custody of goods. (*d*) both (*b*) and (*c*).

ANSWERS

1. (*b*)	**2.** (*b*)	**3.** (*c*)	**4.** (*a*)	**5.** (*c*)	**6.** (*d*)	**7.** (*a*)	**8.** (*b*)	**9.** (*d*)	**10.** (*b*)
11. (*c*)	**12.** (*d*)	**13.** (*b*)	**14.** (*b*)	**15.** (*a*)	**16.** (*d*)	**17.** (*b*)	**18.** (*a*)	**19.** (*b*)	**20.** (*a*)
21. (*c*)	**22.** (*b*)	**23.** (*d*)	**24.** (*c*)	**25.** (*a*)	**26.** (*a*)	**27.** (*c*)	**28.** (*b*)	**29.** (*a*)	**30.** (*a*)

CHAPTER

Conditions and Warranties

(Sections 11–17)

AT A GLANCE

INTRODUCTION

At the time of selling goods, a seller usually makes certain statements or representations with a view to induce the intending buyer to purchase the goods. Such representations are generally about the nature and quality of the goods, price, mode of its payment, delivery of goods etc. When forming a contract of sale, a party may make a statement with a view to inducing the other party to enter into the contract. Such statements when made before entering into the contract are known as representations. Such representations may be mere expression of opinion or commendation by the seller of his goods — what is often known as a 'puff'. We shall now consider the various terms in a contract of sale and the legal effect of a breach of such terms.

The representations may be a mere expression of the opinion of the seller and may not form a part of the contract. But sometimes these may also form a part of the contract and the intending buyer may rely upon such representations. When these statements or representations do not form a part of the contract of sale, they are not relevant and have no legal effect on the contract. But when these form a part of the contract of sale and the buyer relies upon them, they are relevant and have legal effect on the contract.

CONDITION AND WARRANTY DEFINED

Every contract of sale has a number of stipulations regarding the nature and quality of goods. Such stipulations may be either conditions or warranties. A representation which forms a part of the contract of sale and affects the contract, is called stipulation. However, every stipulation is not of equal importance. A stipulation which is most important for the formation of the contract of sale, is known as a condition. But a stipulation which is of lesser importance for the formation of the contract of sale, is known as a warranty.

According to Sec. 12(1) of the Act, "A stipulation in a contract of sale with reference to goods which are the subject thereof may be a condition or a warranty". Some stipulations may be essential to the contract while some may be collateral or incidental to the contract. A stipulation essential to the contract is called a 'condition'. That which is collateral or incidental to the contract is called a 'warranty'.

What is a Condition? [Sec. 12 (2)]

According to Sec. 12(2), "A condition is a stipulation essential to the main purpose of the contract, the breach of which gives rise to a right to treat the contract as repudiated."

What is Warranty? [Sec. 12(3)]

According to Sec. 12(3), "A warranty is a stipulation collateral to the main purpose of the contract, the breach of which gives rise to a claim for damages but not to a right to reject the goods and treat the contract as repudiated".

In other words, a condition is an important representation by the seller which is essential to the main purpose of the contract. If it proves to be false, the buyer has the right to terminate the contract and to have the refund of the price. Whereas a warranty is a representation by the seller which is not very important factor in the sales of goods. It is only collateral to the main purpose of the contract. And if it proves to be untrue, the buyer cannot put an end to the contract. He can only claim damages from the seller.

Examples : (1) A says to B, "I want a horse which can run at a speed of 40 km/per hour". B, the horse dealer, gives a particular horse. A buys the horse but later on finds that the horse can run only at a speed of 25 km. per hour. This is a breach of condition. Because buyer's stipulation is essential to the main purpose of the contract.

If in the above example, A says to B, "I want a good horse". B, point out a particular horse, says, "This is a good horse and can run at a speed of 40 km. per hour." A buys the horse. A later on finds that the horse can run only 25 km per hour. This is a breach of warranty.

(2) A man buys a particular horse which is warranted quiet to ride and drive. If the horse turns out to be vicious, the buyer's only remedy is to claim damages. But instead of buying a particular horse, a man asks a dealer to supply him with a quiet horse and the dealer supplies him with a vicious one, the stipulation is a condition and the buyer can return the horse and also claim damages for breach of contract. (Hartley Vs. Hymans (1920).

Condition and Warranty — Distinction

Condition	*Warranty*
1. It is a stipulation which is essential to the main purpose of the contract.	1. It is a stipulation which is only subsidiary or collateral to the main purpose of the contract.
2. A contract of sale cannot be fulfilled unless the condition to it, is fulfilled.	2. It is not of vital importance. The main contract can be fulfilled even if the warranty is not fulfilled.
3. **The** breach of condition gives the aggrieved party the right to repudiate the contract and also claim damages.	3. The breach of warranty gives the aggrieved party a right to claim damages only.
4. A breach of condition may be treated as a breach of warranty.	4. A breach of warranty cannot be treated as a breach of condition.

When Condition to be Treated as Warranty (Sec. 13)

A condition is treated to be a warranty and the aggrieved party has the right to claim damages only and not to repudiate the contract under the following circumstances :

(a) Voluntary Waiver of Condition (Sec. 13 (1))

"Where a contract of sale is subject to any condition to be fulfilled by the seller, the buyer may waive the condition or elect to treat the breach of the condition as a breach of warranty and not as ground for treating the contract as repudiated."

The two cases, *i.e.*, (*i*) the buyer waives off the condition or (*ii*) treats its breach as a breach of warranty, are voluntary in nature and depend solely on the will of the buyer. Accordingly, on finding that the seller has committed a breach of a condition, the buyer may repudiate the contract, having a right to do so. If he does not do so, it is presumed that he has waived his right. Having waived the condition, he cannot later insist on its fulfillment by the seller.

Example : A agrees to supply B 10 bags of first quality sugar @ Rs. 1,000 per bag, but supplies only second quality of sugar, the price of which is Rs. 950 per bag. This is a breach of condition. The buyer can reject the goods. But if the buyer elects to accept the goods (treating it as a breach of warranty) and claim for damages @ Rs. 50 per bag.

(b) Acceptance of goods by the Buyer [Sec. 13 (2)]

Under Section 13 (2), "Where a contract of sale is not severable and the buyer has accepted the goods or part thereof, or where the contract is for specific goods, the property in which has passed to the buyer, the breach of any condition to be fulfilled by the seller can only be treated as a breach of warranty and not as a ground for rejecting the goods and treating the contract as repudiated, unless there is a term of the contract, express or implied, to that effect."

Where the buyer has accepted the goods and subsequently he comes to know of the breach of condition, he cannot reject them, but only maintain an action for damages. If the buyer has accepted only part of the goods and the contract is indivisible, he will have to accept the remaining part also. But in case of divisible contracts, he can repudiate as regards remaining goods if he has accepted only part thereof.

Meaning of Acceptance :

According to Sec. 42, the buyer is deemed to have accepted the goods in any of the following cases :

(*i*) When he intimates the seller that he has accepted them,

(*ii*) When the goods have been delivered to him and he does any act in relation to them which is inconsistent with the ownership of the seller, for example, resells or pledges or uses etc.

(*iii*) When, after the lapse of a reasonable time, he retains the goods without intimating the seller that he has rejected them.

(c) By Impossibility

"Nothing in this section shall affect the case of any condition or warranty fulfillment of which is excused by law by reason of impossibility or otherwise" [Sec. 13 (3)].

REMEDIES AVAILABLE TO THE BUYER ON BREACH OF CONDITION

The consequences of breach of condition are discussed below :

1. If the condition is broken, the affected party may repudiate the contract and reject the goods.
2. Elect to treat the breach of condition as breach of warranty and claim damages *i.e.*, monetary compensation.

3. When the affected party treats the breach of condition as breach of warranty, he cannot avoid the contract but he is entitled to recover damage only.
4. No remedy is available when fulfillment of condition is excused by law by reason of impossibility or otherwise [Sec. 13(3)].

Consequences of Breach of Warranty

Following are the consequences of breach of warranty :

1. The breach of warranty gives right to a claim for damages but not to a right to reject the goods and treat the contract as repudiated.
2. The buyer may sue the seller for damages. [Sec. 59 (b)].
3. No remedy is available if the fulfillment of warranty becomes impossible by law. [Sec. 13 (3)].

Express and Implied Conditions and Warranties (Secs. 14 to 17)

In a contract of sale, conditions and warranties may be *express* or *implied*. They are said to be express when at the will of the parties they are inserted in the contract. That is, express conditions and warranties are those which are entered in clear words in the contract.

Conditions and warranties are said to be implied when the law presumes their existence in the contract automatically though they have not been put into it in express words. An implied condition or a warranty may be negatived by an express term to the contrary. It is, however, open to the parties, by virtue of Sec. 62, to vary the implied conditions and warranties expressly agreeing to the contrary.

Example : Mr. A wants to buy a particular TV of a particular model number. Here the model number is an express condition.

Implied Conditions

Unless otherwise agreed, the law incorporates into a contract of sale of goods the following implied conditions :

(*a*) *Condition as to Title* [Sec. 14 (*a*)]

According to Sec. 14 (*a*), "An implied condition on the part of the seller is that, in the case of a sale, he has a right to sell the goods and that, in the case of an agreement to sell, he will have a right to sell the goods at the time when the property is to pass". This is called "condition as to title". It is an important implied condition in every contract of sale. The whole object of the sale is to transfer the property (legal ownership) from one person to another. There can be no sale at all if the seller has no right to sell the goods.

Example : *Rowland Vs. Divall* (1923)

R purchased a second hand car from D who had no title to it. R used the car for 4 months. R was compelled to return the car to the true owner because D obtained the car by theft. R could recover the full price from D. In this case, there was a breach of condition as to title as D had no right to sell the car.

(*b*) *Condition as to Description* (Sec. 15)

Sec. 15 states, "where there is a contract for the sale of goods by description, there is an implied condition that the goods shall correspond with the description;"

It means that in case the description of the article tendered is different in any respect, it is not the article, bargained for, and the other party is not bound to accept it. Where the buyer gives the description of the goods, for example, the buyer gives physical appearance of the goods he requires, or gives brand name, or a particular trade mark etc., it is obvious that the goods supplied should correspond with the description. Breach of this warranty entitles the buyer to reject the goods.

Example : *Beale Vs. Taylor* (1967)

T advertised his car for sale as a "Herald convertible, white, 1961" and the car was bought by B after examination. In fact the car was made of two parts which had been welded together, only one of which was from a 1961 model but the other part was of an earlier model. The court held that the words "1961 Herald" were part of the contractual description and even though the car was fully examined by the buyer, the sale was by description because the buyer had relied in part on a newspaper advertisement issued by the seller. As the car did not correspond with the description, there was a breach of the implied condition and B could reject the car.

(c) Condition as to Sample (Sec. 17)

When under a contract of sale, goods are to be supplied according to a sample agreed upon, the implied conditions are :

(*i*) that the bulk shall correspond with the sample in quality;

(*ii*) that the buyer shall have a reasonable opportunity of comparing the bulk with the sample;

(*iii*) that the goods shall be free from any defect, rendering them unmerchantable, which would not be apparent on reasonable examination of the sample.

Where the contract is severable, the buyer can retain that of the goods which corresponds with the sample and reject the other part. But where the contract is not severable, the buyer may either reject the whole or accept the whole and claim damages for the portion which is inferior to the sample. But he cannot retain one part and reject the other part.

Example : *Lorymer Vs. Smith* (1822)

There was a sale by sample of two parcels of wheat. The buyer went to examine the bulk a week after. One parcel which was lying in the seller's warehouse was shown to him, but the seller refused to show the other parcel which was not there in the warehouse. It was held that the buyer could rescind the contract.

(d) Condition as to Sample as well as Description (Sec. 15)

According to Sec. 15 (second part) "If the sale is by sample as well as by description, it is not sufficient that the bulk of the goods corresponds with the sample if the goods do not also correspond with the description." In such cases, the implied condition is that the goods shall correspond with both, the sample as well as description.

Example : *Nichol Vs. Godts* (1854)

There was a sale of "foreign refined rape oil" warranted only equal to sample. The oil tendered was the same as the sample, but it was not "foreign refined rape oil", being a mixture of it and other oil. It was held that the seller was liable, and the buyer could refuse to accept.

(e) Condition as to Fitness or Quality (Sec. 16)

Sec. 16(1) states "Where the buyer, expressly or by implication, makes known to the seller the particular purpose for which the goods are required, so as to show that the buyer relies on the seller's skill or judgement, and the goods are of a description which it is in the course of the seller's business to supply (whether, he is the manufacturer or producer or not), there is an implied condition that the goods shall reasonably fit for such purposes." In such a case, the rule Caveat

Emptor does not apply. Where an article is fit for one particular purpose alone, and turns out to be unsuitable for that purpose, when used, it is easy to see that condition as to fitness has been broken. But where an article is capable of being applied to a variety of purposes, the buyer must notify the specific purpose, he has in mind, and if this is not shown, the buyer will have no remedy merely because it was unfit for that purpose.

On analysing Sec. 16(1) of the Act, it is revealed that the implied condition as to quality and fitness operates only if the following conditions are satisfied :

(*i*) The buyer requires the goods for a particular purpose, and he lets the seller know about it.

(*ii*) The buyer relies upon the skill and judgement of the seller.

(*iii*) The seller's business is to sell goods of that type.

It is immaterial, whether he is a producer of that type of goods or not.

Examples : (1) *Grant Vs. Australian Knitting Mills* (1936)

Dr. Grant purchased from a retailer two woolen underpants manufactured by the defendant. After wearing one of them, he contracted skin disease which was due to chemical irritant which had negligently omitted to remove in the process of manufacture. It was held that the implied condition of fitness for the buyer's purpose was broken.

(2) *Priest Vs. Last* (1903)

A, who had no knowledge of hot water bottles, went to the shop of a chemist and asked for a hot water bottle. He was shown a bottle which the chemist said will not stand boiling water but was intended to hold hot water. A bought the bottle. After a few days, while using it, it burst and injured his wife. It was found that the bottle was not fit for use as a hot water bottle and, therefore, the chemist was liable for damages.

(f) Condition as to Merchantability [Sec. 16 (2)]

There is always an implied condition in a contract of sale that the goods purchased should be of a merchantable quality. The term 'merchantability' has not been defined in the Act. According to Sec. 16(2), "Where goods are bought by description from a seller who deals in goods of that description (whether he is the manufacturer or producer or not), there is an implied condition that the goods shall be of merchantable quality; provided that, if the buyer has examined the goods, there shall be no implied condition as regards defects which such examination ought to have revealed." In order to apply the implied condition as to merchantability the following requirements must be satisfied, *viz.*,

(*i*) The seller should be a dealer in goods of that description, whether he be the manufacturer or not; and

(*ii*) The buyer must not have any opportunity of examining the goods or there must be some latent defect in the goods which would not be apparent on reasonable examination of the same.

Example : *Morelli Vs. Fitch & Gibbons* (1928)

The plaintiff asked for a bottle of Stone's Ginger wine at the defendant's shop, which was licenced for the sale of wines. While the plaintiff was drawing the cork with a corkscrew, the bottle broke at the neck and injured him. The court held that the sale was one by description and that the bottle was not of merchantable quality, and consequently, the plaintiff was entitled to damages.

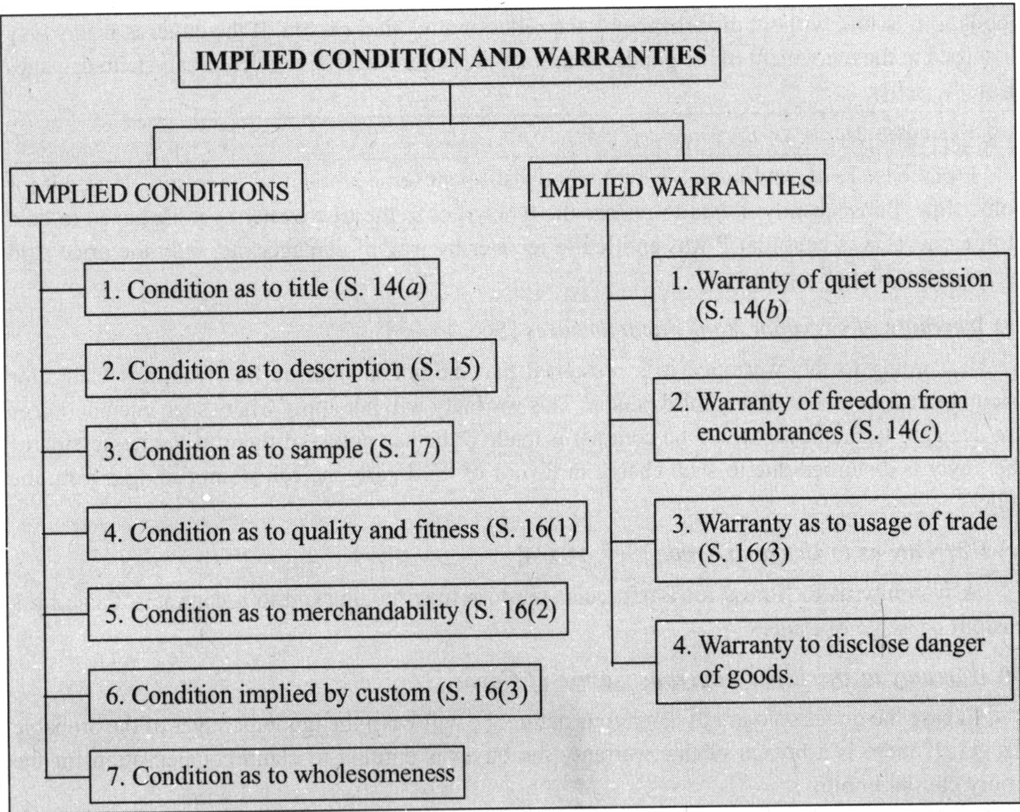

The implied condition as to merchantability is not applicable where the buyer has examined the goods and known the defect which such examination should have revealed. Therefore, in case of patent defects, such examination by a person of ordinary prudence with proper care defeats such implied condition. But there is an implied authority on the part of the seller that the goods are free from latent defects as such defects cannot be found out by such examination.

(g) *Condition Implied by Customs* [Sec. 16 (3)]

According to Sec. 16 (3), "an implied condition as to quality or fitness for a particular purpose may also be as to usage of trade or according to the customs."

(h) *Condition as to Wholesomeness*

This condition is implied only in a contract of sale of eatables and provisions. In such cases the goods supplied must not only answer to description and be merchantable but must also be wholesome. That is, they will be fit for consumption.

> **Example :** *Frost Vs. Avlesbury Dairy Co.* (1905)
>
> F bought milk from AD Co. and the milk contained typhoid germs. F's wife became infected and died. AD Co was liable for damages, because the milk was not fit for human consumption.

Implied Warranties

Unless otherwise agreed, the law also incorporates into a contract of sale of goods, the following implied warranties :

(a) *Warranty of Quiet Possession* [Sec. 14(*b*)]

It is an implied assurance to the buyer that he shall have the possession and enjoyment of the goods sold to him without disturbance by the seller or any other person. If the buyer is in any way disturbed in the enjoyment of the goods because of the seller's defective title, he can claim damages from the seller.

Example : *Mason Vs. Burmingham* (1949)

P purchased a second-hand typewriter and also spent some amount on its repairs. P used it for some time. Subsequently, P had to restore the typewriter to the true owner as it happened to be a stolen one. It was held that P was entitled to recover by way of damages, not only the price paid but also the cost of repairs.

(b) Warranty of Freedom from Encumbrances [Sec. 14 (*c*)]

According to this warranty, it is presumed that the goods shall be free from any charge or encumbrance in favour of any third person. This warranty will not apply where such encumbrances are declared to the buyer when the contract is made or he has notice of them. If the possession of the buyer is disturbed due to such charge in favour of third party, he can claim damages from the seller.

(c) Warranty as to Usage of Trade [Sec. 16 (3)]

A warranty as to fitness for a particular purpose may be annexed to a contract of sale by a custom or usage of trade.

(d) Warranty to Disclose Dangerous Nature of Goods

In case the goods sold are of dangerous nature, he will warn the ignorant buyer of the probable danger. If there is a breach of this warranty the buyer is entitled to claim compensation for the injury caused to him.

Example : *Clark Vs. Army & Navy Cooperative Society* (1963)

C purchases a tin of disinfectant powder from A. A knew that it was likely to be dangerous to C, if it was opened without special care being taken, but tells nothing to C. C opened the tin in the normal way whereupon the disinfectant powder flies into her eyes and causes injury. A is liable in damages to C as he should have warned C of the probable danger.

Exclusion of Implied Conditions and Warranties

Implied conditions or warranties in a contract of sale may be negatived or varied by :

(*a*) express agreement between the parties; or

(*b*) course of dealing between them; or

(*c*) the custom or usage of trade.

CAVEAT EMPTOR

In the case of a sale of goods, there is a fundamental principle of law embodied in the maxim "*Caveat Emptor*", that is, *let the buyer beware*. It is not a part of the seller's duty in a contract of sale to give to the buyer, an article suitable for a particular purpose unless such purpose is made known to the seller. According to the doctrine of Caveat Emptor it is the duty of the buyer to be careful while purchasing goods of his requirement and, in the absence of any enquiry from the buyer, the seller is not bound to disclose every defect in goods of which he may be cognisant. As a matter of fact, it is the buyer's duty to select goods of his requirement. When a person buys some goods, it is his duty to examine them thoroughly. As a general rule, the buyer purchases goods after satisfying himself as to quality and fitness and, therefore, the buyer purchases the goods at his own risk, relying upon his own skill and judgement. If the goods turn out to be defective or do not suit the purpose, or depends upon his own skill and judgement and makes a bad selection he cannot blame anybody except himself. The buyer has to bear the consequences of his wrong selection of goods. Sec. 16 states, "Subject to the provisions of this Act and of any other law for the time being in force, there is no implied warranty or condition as to the quality or fitness for any particular purpose of goods supplied under a contract of sale..."

> **Example :** *Jones Vs. Padgett* (1890)
>
> There was a sale by sample by a woolen manufacturer of cloth to a merchant, who was also a tailor. The fact that the cloth was required for making liveries, was not made known to the seller. Owing to latent defect in the cloth, liveries could not be made out of it. But there was nothing to show that it was unfit for other purposes. It was held that the buyer was without remedy due to non-communication of the purpose for which the cloth was required.

Exceptions of the Doctrine of Caveat Emptor

This principle was originated at the time when goods were mostly sold in the open market. It was presumed that the buyer was in advantageous position to get the opportunity to inspect the goods and to satisfy himself as to its quality and fitness for his purpose. In modern tendency is to narrow the scope of the rule of Caveat Emptor. These days, trade has become international in nature and making difficult for buyers to examine goods before hand, for example, mail order purchases. Thus, it is only the seller, who can assure the quality of the goods and their fitness for buyer's purpose. Because of these reasons, it became necessary to restrict the application of the doctrine of Caveat Emptor, by proving certain exceptions, which are discussed below :

1. *Fitness for Buyer's Purpose* [Sec. 16 (1)]

According to Sec. 16 (1), "where the buyer, expressly or by implication, makes known to the seller the particular purpose for which the goods are required, so as to show that the buyer relies on the seller's skill or judgement, and the goods are of a description which it is in the course of the seller's business to supply (whether he is the manufacturer or producer or not), there is an implied condition that the goods shall be reasonably fit for such purpose". In such cases, the Doctrine of Caveat Emptor does not apply.

2. *Sale under a Patent or Trade Name* [Sec. 16 (1)]

As per proviso to Sec. 16(1), in the case of a contract of sale of a specified article under its patent or other trade name, there is an implied condition that the goods shall be reasonably fit for any particular purpose.

3. *Merchantable Quality* [Sec. 16 (2)]

Where the goods are purchased by description from a seller who deals in such class of goods and they are not of merchantable quality, the doctrine of caveat emptor does not supply. However, the doctrine applies, if the buyer has examined the goods, as regards defects which such examination ought to have revealed.

4. *Custom or Usage of Trade* [Sec. 16 (3)]

An implied warranty or condition as to quality or fitness for a particular purpose may be annexed by the custom or usage of trade. However, custom should not be unreasonable and should not be inconsistent with the express terms of the contract.

5. *Consent by Fraud*

Where the seller makes a false representation amounting to fraud and the buyer relies on it, or where the seller actively conceals a defect in the goods so that the same could not be discovered on reasonable examination, the doctrine of caveat emptor does not apply. A seller, who is guilty of fraud shall have no protection under the doctrine. Such a contract is also voidable at the option of the buyer and the buyer is entitled to avoid the contract and also claim damages for fraud.

6. *Sale by Sample* (Sec. 17)

Where the goods are bought by sample, the doctrine of caveat emptor does not apply if the bulk does not correspond with the sample, or if the buyer is not provided an opportunity to compare the bulk with the sample, or if there is any hidden or latent defect in the goods.

7. *Misrepresentation*

Where the seller has made a false representation relating to the goods and the buyer has relied upon it, the doctrine will not apply. Such a contract being voidable at the option of the innocent party, the buyer has a right to rescind the contract.

8. *Sale of Goods by Description* (Sec. 15)

Where there is a contract for sale of goods by description, there is an implied condition that the goods shall correspond with the description, (Sec. 15). In such cases, the doctrine of Caveat emptor does not apply.

9. *Sale by Sample as well as by description* (Sec. 15)

When goods are sold by sample as well as by description, the buyer need not take care, but it is the seller who is to take care. The tendered goods must correspond with both sample and description; if not, the buyer can reject the goods.

10. *Implied Condition as to Title to Goods* (Sec. 14(*a*)

In a contract of sale, there is an implied condition as to title to goods applies, the seller is bound to deliver the goods to which he has a right to sell at the time when the title is passed to the buyer.

11. *Implied warranty as quiet possession apply* (Sec. 14(*b*)

When in a contract of sale, an implied warranty as to quiet enjoyment and possession of goods applies, the seller is bound to ensure the same. If not, he is liable to pay damages to the buyer.

12. *Implied warranty as to freedom from any charge* (Sec. 14(*c*)

When in a contract of sale, an implied warranty as to freedom from charge or encumbrance applies, the seller is bound to disclose the encumbrance, if any, on the goods. The doctrine of Caveat emptor does not apply in such a case.

All the points, mentioned above, are explained in the beginning of this chapter.

THEORETICAL QUESTIONS

1. Explain the terms 'condition and warranty' under the sale of Goods Act. (*B.Com., MS*)
2. State the difference between condition and warranty. (*B.Com., Bhopal*)
3. When can a condition be treated as a warranty? (*B.Com., MS*)
4. When can a breach of condition be treated as a breach of warranty? (*B.Com., MS*)
5. "A contract of sale of goods is always subject to certain implied conditions, but they can be treated as warranties" Examine.
6. Explain the doctrine of Caveat Emptor with its exceptions. (*B.Com., Chennai*)
7. What are the implied conditions in a contract of sale of goods by sample ? (*B.Com., Madurai*)
8. "In a contract for the sale of goods, there is implied condition or warranty as to the quality of goods or their fitness for any particular purpose." Comment.
9. Explain the implied warranties under the sale of goods Act. (*B.Com., Kerala*)
10. Under what circumstances the rule of caveat emptor is not applicable? (*B.Com., Jabalpur*)

MULTIPLE CHOICE QUESTIONS

I. Choose correct options for each of the following questions :

1. **In a contract of sale of goods, stipulations as to time of payment :**
   (*a*) are deemed to be the essence of contract.
   (*b*) are not deemed to be the essence of contract.
   (*c*) are deemed to be the essence of the contract if such intention appears from the contract.
   (*d*) either (*b*) or (*c*) above.
2. **A buyer may treat the breach of condition as breach of warranty :**
   (*a*) by giving up condition of contract of sale.
   (*b*) by using option to treat the breach of condition as breach of warranty.
   (*c*) by both (*a*) and (*b*).
   (*d*) by either (*a*) or (*b*).
3. **Breach of condition of a contract of sale of goods gives rise to the right to :**
   (*a*) repudiate the contract.
   (*b*) treat the breach of condition as breach of warranty and claim the damages caused due to the breach of condition.
   (*c*) both (*a*) and (*b*).
   (*d*) either (*a*) or (*b*).
4. **In a contract of sale of goods, the implied condition as to fitness of buyer's purpose applies :**
   (*a*) in all the cases.
   (*b*) in the case where the buyer tells his purpose to the seller.
   (*c*) in the case where the buyer relies on seller's skill or judgement to select the goods for his purpose.
   (*d*) in the cases of both (*b*) and (*c*) simultaneously.
5. **In case of breach of a condition, the buyer can :**
   (*a*) claim damage only. (*b*) repudiate the contract.
   (*c*) cannot return the goods. (*d*) refuse to take delivery of goods.
6. **According to Sale of Goods Act, breach of condition gives rise to the right :**
   (*a*) to repudiate the contract. (*b*) to claim damages suffered.
   (*c*) to reject the goods. (*d*) both (*a*) and (*c*) above.
7. **In a contract of sale of goods, the implied condition is :**
   (*a*) that the seller has right to sell the goods at the time of sale.
   (*b*) that the goods shall correspond with the description.
   (*c*) that the goods shall be fit to the buyer's purpose.
   (*d*) both (*a*) and (*b*) above .
8. **In case a buyer uses his option to treat the breach of condition as breach of warranty, he loses :**
   (*a*) right to repudiate the contract. (*b*) right to reject the goods.
   (*c*) right to claim damages. (*d*) both (*a*) and (*b*) above.
9. **Stipulation as time of payment is :**
   (*a*) always deemed to be an essence of a contract of sale.
   (*b*) deemed to be an essence of a contract of sale unless otherwise agreed.
   (*c*) not deemed to be an essence of a contract of sale unless otherwise agreed.
   (*d*) none of these.
10. **In a contract of sale of goods, breach of warranty gives rise to right :**
    (*a*) to claim damages. (*b*) to reject the goods and claim damages.
    (*c*) to reject the goods. (*d*) to treat the contract as repudiated.
11. **In a contract of sale of goods, condition as to merchantable quality of goods applies :**
    (*a*) where goods are bought by description.
    (*b*) where the goods are bought from the person who deals in the goods of that description.
    (*c*) where goods are sold under a trade mark.
    (*d*) in all of the above cases.
12. **In a contract of sale of goods, the implied condition as to wholesomeness of goods applies :**
    (*a*) to clothes. (*b*) soft drinks and milk.
    (*c*) cakes and pastries. (*d*) both in the cases of (*b*) and (*c*) above.

13. Merchantable quality of goods means :
(*a*) that the goods are free from latent defects.
(*b*) that the goods are marketable at their full value.
(*c*) that the goods can be used for the purpose for which they are bought by prudent persons.
(*d*) All of the above.

14. The Sale of Goods Act provides for :
(*a*) an implied condition as to right seller's to sell the goods.
(*b*) an implied warranty that the buyer shall have and enjoy quiet possession of goods.
(*c*) an implied warranty as to freedom from any charge or encumbrance on the goods sold.
(*d*) all of the above cases.

15. According to Sale of Goods Act, a condition is a stipulation :
(*a*) which is essential for the main purpose of contract.
(*b*) which is collateral to the main purpose of the contract.
(*c*) breach of which gives rise to a right to repudiate the contract.
(*d*) both (*a*) and (*c*).

16. In a contract of sale of goods, generally the essence of the contract is :
(*a*) time of delivery of goods.
(*b*) time of payment of price.
(*c*) both (*a*) and (*b*).
(*d*) neither (*a*) nor (*b*).

17. In case of Sale of Goods by sample as well as by description, the implied condition is that the bulk of the goods :
(*a*) shall correspond with the sample.
(*b*) correspond with both the sample and the description.
(*c*) shall correspond with the sample and may or may not correspond with the description.
(*d*) shall correspond with the description and need not correspond with the sample.

18. In a contract of sale, there is :
(*a*) no implied condition as to quality or fitness of goods for a particular purpose.
(*b*) no implied warranty that the goods shall be free from any charge or encumbrance is favour of any third party.
(*c*) an implied warranty as to quality or fitness of goods for a particular purpose if annexed by the usage of trade.
(*d*) above (*a*) and (*b*).

19. In a contract of sale of goods :
(*a*) there are implied conditions and warranties.
(*b*) there may be express conditions and warranties.
(*c*) there are only implied conditions and no implied warranties.
(*d*) both (*a*) and (*b*) above.

20. The doctrine of caveat emptor means that :
(*a*) let the seller beware.
(*b*) let the buyer beware.
(*c*) let the buyer beware and take chance.
(*d*) let the creditor beware.

21. In a contract of sale by description and by sample, the bulk of goods must correspond to :
(*a*) description only.
(*b*) sample only.
(*c*) both description and sample.
(*d*) either description or sample.

22. In case of goods sold by sample, the goods should correspond with the sample, otherwise :
(*a*) buyer can reject the goods.
(*b*) buyer cannot reject the goods.
(*c*) contract is terminated.
(*d*) seller is liable.

23. In a contract of Sale of Goods, there is :
(*a*) an implied condition as to the quality or fitness of goods for any particular purpose of goods.
(*b*) generally no implied condition as to quality or fitness for any particular purpose of goods.
(*c*) no implied condition as to merchantable quality of goods where goods are sold by description.
(*d*) above (*b*) and (*c*).

24. According to Sale of Goods Act, a warranty is a stipulation :
(*a*) breach of which gives rise to a right to repudiate the contract.
(*b*) which is collateral to the main purpose of the contract.
(*c*) breach of which gives rise to a right to claim damages.
(*d*) both (*b*) and (*c*) above.

25. In case of breach of a warranty, the buyer can :
(*a*) refuse to pay the price. (*b*) repudiate the contract.
(*c*) returns the goods. (*d*) claim damages only.

26. The doctrine of Caveat Emptor does not apply, when :
(*a*) the goods are bought by sample. (*b*) the goods are bought by sample and description.
(*c*) the goods purchased under its brand name. (*d*) all of the above.

27. The expression "Caveat Emptor" means :
(*a*) Let Government beware. (*b*) Let the vendor beware.
(*c*) Let the buyer beware. (*d*) Let the creditor beware.

28. A stipulation which is collateral to the main purpose of the contract, and if proves false, gives the buyer only a right to claim damages known as :
(*a*) condition. (*b*) guarantee.
(*c*) warranty. (*d*) none of these.

29. In a sale, there is an implied condition on the part of the seller that he :
(*a*) has a right to sell the goods. (*b*) is in possession of goods.
(*c*) will have the right to sell. (*d*) none of the above.

30. A condition is a stipulation which is :
(*a*) essential to the main purpose of contract of sale.
(*b*) not essential to the main purpose of contract of sale.
(*c*) collateral to the main purpose of contract of sale.
(*d*) none of the above.

ANSWERS

1. (*d*)	**2.** (*b*)	**3.** (*d*)	**4.** (*d*)	**5.** (*b*)	**6.** (*d*)	**7.** (*d*)	**8.** (*d*)	**9.** (*c*)	**10.** (*a*)
11. (*d*)	**12.** (*d*)	**13.** (*d*)	**14.** (*d*)	**15.** (*d*)	**16.** (*a*)	**17.** (*b*)	**18.** (*c*)	**19.** (*d*)	**20.** (*b*)
21. (*c*)	**22.** (*a*)	**23.** (*b*)	**24.** (*d*)	**25.** (*d*)	**26.** (*d*)	**27.** (*c*)	**28.** (*c*)	**29.** (*a*)	**30.** (*a*)

CHAPTER

Transfer of Property in Goods

(Sections 18–30)

AT A GLANCE

- Meaning
- Importance
- Transfer of Property in Goods Sold
- Time when Property Passes
- Specific or Ascertained Goods
- Unascertained Goods
- Reservation of Right of Disposal
- Ownership in Case of Sale on Approval
- Passing of Risk
- Exceptions
- Transfer of Title by Non-owners
- Theoretical Questions
- Objective Type Questions.

MEANING

The phrase 'transfer of property' in goods means transfer of ownership of goods. The term 'property' in the goods may be defined as the legal ownership of the goods. The term 'property in the goods' must be distinguished from the term 'possession of the goods'. The term 'property in the goods' means the ownership of the goods, whereas the term 'possession of the goods' simply mean the custody or physical control over the goods. The expression 'transfer of property' means the transfer of ownership of the goods from seller to the buyer so as to constitute the buyer the owner thereof. Thus, on the transfer of ownership, the seller is no more the owner of the goods. A person may have the possession of the goods but may not be the owner of the same, for example, servant, agent etc. Similarly a person may be the owner of the goods but may not have the possession of the goods. The main purpose of a contract of sale is the transfer of ownership of the goods from a seller to a buyer. When the ownership of the goods is transferred to the buyer, he becomes the owner of the goods, and the seller ceases to be so. The time of transfer of property in the goods decides various rights and liabilities of the seller and the buyer.

IMPORTANCE OF TRANSFER OF PROPERTY

The rights and liabilities of the parties are linked with the transfer of ownership. The following points are significant for the transfer of ownership of the goods :

1. *Risk Follows Ownership*

Sec. 26 provides, "unless otherwise agreed, the goods remain at the seller's risk until the property therein is transferred to the buyer, but when the property therein is transferred to the buyer, the goods are at the buyer's risk whether delivery has been made or not." Risk passes to the buyer as property in the goods passes to him. The risk of destruction or loss of goods sold falls on the buyer and not on the seller though the goods may still be in the possession of seller. If after the contract, the goods are destroyed or damaged, the question, who is to bear the loss is to be decided not on the basis of possession of goods but on the basis of ownership of goods. Because the risk passes with the transfer of ownership.

2. *Action against Third Parties*

When there is danger to the goods being damaged by the action of third parties, it is only the owner who can take action. That is, the right to proceed against a third party for destruction or damage to the goods depends, not on possession but on the transfer of property.

3. *Suit for Price*

The seller can sue for the price, unless otherwise agreed, only if the goods have become the property of the buyer. That is, the transfer of property confers upon the seller the right to sue the buyer for the price.

4. *Insolvency*

When the buyer or seller becomes insolvent, the official assignee is to determine whether the insolvent is the owner of the goods at the time of his becoming insolvent. If he finds that he is the owner of the goods at the time of his insolvency, he can take over the goods and if he finds that he is not the owner at the time of his insolvency he cannot take over it.

TRANSFER OF PROPERTY IN GOODS SOLD

The rules relating to transfer of property as between the seller are discussed in Sections 18 to 25 of the Sale of Goods Act. These basic rules, in brief, are discussed below :

1. *Goods to be Ascertained* (Sec. 18)

According to Sec. 18, "Where there is a contract for the sale of unascertained goods, no property in the goods is transferred to the buyer unless and until the goods are ascertained."

2. *Parties' Intention* [Sec. 19 (1)]

According to Sec. 19 (1), "Where there is a contract for the sale of specific or ascertained goods, the property in them is transferred to the buyer at such time as the parties to the contract intend it to be transferred."

3. *When no Intention is Expressed* (Sec. 19 (3))

According to Sec. 19 (3), "Unless a different intention appears, the rules contained in Sections 20 to 24 of the Sale of Goods Act are rules for ascertaining the intention of the parties as to the time at which the property in the goods is to pass to the buyer."

TIME WHEN PROPERTY PASSES

A sale differs from an agreement to sell by the fact that in the former property is transferred while in the latter it is not transferred. So also if the property has passed to the buyer, the risk of loss, destruction or deterioration of the goods sold, falls on the buyer and not on the seller, even if the goods are remaining in the seller's possession. We shall be studying the rules regarding the transfer of property under the following two heads :

(A) Specific or ascertained goods
(B) Unascertained or future goods

A. Specific or Ascertained Goods (Secs. 20 to 22)

Sec. 18 provides, "Where there is a contract for the sale of unascertained goods, no property in the goods is transferred to the buyer unless and until the goods are ascertained." In case of sale of specific goods, the rules relating to the transfer of ownership are contained in Sections 20 to 22 of the Sale of Goods Act. They are summarised as follows :

1. *When Goods are in Deliverable State* (Sec. 20)

Sec. 20 provides, "Where there is an unconditional contract for the sale of specific goods in a deliverable state, the property in the goods passed to the buyer when the contract is made, and it is immaterial whether the time of payment of the price or the time of delivery of the goods, or both, is postponed." The goods are said to be in a 'deliverable state', when they are in such a state that the buyer would, under the contract, be bound to take delivery of them immediately. The contract must be unconditional, *i.e.*, no condition is imposed regarding the transfer of ownership of goods. The property in the specific goods passes when the contract is made. For example, if a seller has to paint a car to make it acceptable to the buyer, it is not in a deliverable state until it is painted.

> **Example :** *Underwood Vs. BC Cement Syndicate* (1922)
>
> There is a contract for the sale of a machine, weighing 20 tons and embedded in a concrete floor. A part of the machine is destroyed while being removed. The buyer is entitled to refuse to take the machine as it is not in a deliverable state.

2. *When goods have to be Put in Deliverable State* (Sec. 21)

Sec. 21 states, "Where there is a contract for the sale of specific goods and the seller is bound to do something to the goods for the purpose of putting them into deliverable state, the property does not pass until such thing is done and the buyer has notice thereof ". Transfer of property is conditioned by the seller doing something *i.e.*, an act, to put the goods in a deliverable state. The act may be painting, polishing, loading, packing, filling in containers etc. In such cases, the ownership is transferred as soon as the seller has put the goods in a deliverable state and the buyer comes to know about this act of the seller. That is, merely putting the things in a deliverable state would not result in the transfer of property in goods from the seller to the buyer; further the buyer must have notice thereof.

> **Example :** *Rugg Vs. Minnet* (1809)
>
> The contents of a cistern of oil was sold, the oil was to be filled into casks by the seller and then taken away by the buyer. Some of the casks were filled in the presence of the buyer but, before the remainder could be filled, a fire broke out and the entire quantity of oil was destroyed. Held, the buyer must bear the loss of the oil which was put into casks and the seller must bear the loss of the remainder.

3. *When Goods have to be Measured etc. to Ascertain Price* (Sec. 22)

According to Sec. 22, "Where there is a contract for the sale of specific goods in a deliverable state, but the seller is bound to weigh, measure, test or do some other act or thing with reference to the goods for the purpose of ascertaining the price, the property does not pass until such act or thing is done and the buyer has notice thereof." Passing of property is conditional upon the performance of some act with reference to the goods for the purpose of ascertaining the price. Thus, the ownership is transferred to the buyer as soon as the seller has done such act and the buyer comes to know about it.

> **Example :** *Zagury Vs. Furnell* (1809)
>
> The contract was for the sale of 289 bales of goat skins. Each bale marked as containing 5 dozen skins. It was the duty of the seller to count the goat skin in each bale. Before he could count the skins, the bales were destroyed by fire. It was held that the property in the goods had not passed to the buyer as something still remained to be done by the seller for ascertaining the price. As such the loss caused by fire had to be borne by the seller.

B. Unascertained Goods

According to Sec. 18, where there is a contract for the sale of unascertained goods, property in the goods is not transferred to the buyer unless and until the goods are ascertained. Sec. 23(1) states that "where there is a contract for the sale of unascertained or future goods by description and goods of that description and in a deliverable state are unconditionally appropriated to the contract, either by the seller with the assent of the buyer or by the buyer with the assent of the seller, the property in the goods thereupon passes to the buyer. Such assent may be express or implied, and may be given either before or after the appropriation is made. "Until goods are ascertained or appropriated there is merely 'agreement to sell'. Ascertainment means establishing the identity of the goods and appropriation means selection, setting apart or any other act with the intention of using the goods for the performance of the contract. Thus, the 'ascertainment of goods' and their unconditional 'appropriation to be contract' are the two preconditions for the transfer of property from the seller to the buyer, in case of unascertained goods. Ascertainment is the process by which the goods answering the description are identified and set apart. Further, the goods must also be appropriated to the contract. Appropriation is generally made by the seller by putting the goods into boxes or bags with the assent of the buyer. The assent of the buyer may be express or implied.

> **Example :** *Rhode Vs. Thwaites* (1827)
>
> There was a contract for the sale of 20 hogheads of sugar out of a larger quantity. 4 hogheads, which were filled in, were taken away by the buyer. Later, the seller filled 16 more hogheads and informed the buyer asking him to take them away. The buyer says he will take them as soon as he can. But before he could do so, the goods were lost. Held, the property had passed to the buyer at the time of the loss.

Further Sec. 23 (2) states, "Where, in pursuance of the contract, the seller delivers the goods to the buyer or to a carrier of other bailee (where named by the buyer or not) for the purpose of transmission to the buyer, and does not reserve the right of disposal, he is deemed to have unconditionally appropriated the goods to the contract." Thus delivery to a carrier without reserving the right of disposal, is a delivery to the buyer and the property passes at once, at the time of delivery to the carrier. For instance, if goods have been loaded on rail and railway receipt is taken in the name of the buyer and the same is sent to him direct, the ownership is passed immediately on delivery to the railway company. But if the railway receipt is sent to the bank with instruction to deliver it to the buyer on payment of price, the right of disposal is said to have been reserved and no property passes to the buyer on delivery to railway company.

Reservation of Right of Disposal (Sec. 25)

1. According to Sec. 25 (1), "Where there is a contract for the sale of specific goods or where goods are subsequently appropriated to the contract, the seller may, by the terms of the contract or appropriation reserve the right of disposal of the goods until certain conditions are fulfilled. In such case, notwithstanding the delivery of the goods to a buyer, or to a carrier or other bailee for the purpose of transmission to the buyer, the property in the goods does not pass to the buyer until the conditions imposed by the seller are fulfilled." Reservation of the right of disposal means reserving a right to dispose of the goods until conditions, for example price, are fulfilled. The ownership is transferred to the buyer only when the conditions imposed by the seller are fulfilled.

2. According to Sec. 25 (2), "Where goods are shipped and by the bill of lading the goods are deliverable to the order of seller or his agent, the seller is prima facie deemed to reserve the right of disposal." In such cases, the goods are said to be deliverable to the order of the seller or his agent.

3. According to Sec. 25 (3), "Where the seller of goods draws on the buyer for the price, and transmits the bill of exchange and bill of lading to the buyer together, to secure acceptance or payment of the bill of exchange, the buyer is bound to return the bill of lading if he does not honour the bill of exchange and if he wrongfully retains the bill of lading the property in the goods does not pass to him."

Transfer of Ownership in case of Sale on Approval (Sec. 24)

Sec. 24 of the Act lays down, "When goods are delivered to the buyer on approval or "on sale or return" or other similar terms, the property therein passes to the buyer :

(*a*) when he signifies his approval or acceptance to the seller or does any other act adopting the transaction;

(*b*) If he does not signify his approval or acceptance to the seller but retains the goods without giving notice of rejection then, if a time has been fixed for the return of the goods, on the expiration of such time, and, if no time has been fixed, on the expiration of a reasonable time."

The property therein passes to the buyer :

(*a*) When the buyer signifies his approval or acceptance to the seller, or (*b*) When he does any other act adopting the transaction, for instance sells or pledges the goods to third party, or (*c*) If he does not signify his approval or acceptance to the seller but retains the goods, without giving notice of rejection, beyond the time fixed for the return of goods, or if no time has been fixed, beyond a reasonable time.

Passing of Risk (Sec. 26)

Sec. 26 lays down the general rule *the risk prima facie passes with the ownership, i.e.*, the risk and the ownership of the goods go together. This means that in case of loss of the goods, the loss shall be borne by the party who has the ownership of the goods at the time of loss. Sec. 26 lays down, "Unless otherwise agreed, the goods remain at the seller's risk until the property therein is transferred to the buyer, but when the property therein is transferred to the buyer, the goods are at the buyer's risk whether delivery has been made or not."

Exceptions to the above Rule :

1. *Agreement* : The risk and the ownership may be separated by an agreement between the seller and the buyer, as to when the ownership shall be transferred and who shall suffer the loss.
2. *Delay* : Where delivery has been delayed through the fault of the buyer or the seller, the goods are at the risk of the party in fault as regards any loss which might not have occurred but for such fault.
3. *Trade Custom* : We know that the "trade custom" is the customary rule prevalent in a particular trade which is generally followed by the parties, for example, the trade custom may proved that the goods shall be at the risk of the buyer whether or not the ownership has been transferred to him.

Transfer of Titles by Non-owners (Secs. 27 to 30)

General Rule

The general rule is that "no one can give that which one has not got". This general rule is expressed by the maxim, "*nemo dat quod non habet*". This means that "no one can transfer a better title than he himself has." The seller cannot give to the buyer of the goods a better title to the goods than he himself. If the title of the seller is defective, the buyer's title will also be subject to the same defect. If the seller has no title to the goods, the buyer does not acquire any title although he might have acted honestly and might have paid the value of the goods. This is to protect the true owner. If a thief disposes of stolen property, the buyer acquires no title though he may have purchased the goods bonafide for value, and the real owner of the goods is entitled to recover possession of goods without paying anything to the buyer. Section 27 in this regard says that "Subject to the provisions of this Act and of any other law for the time being in force, where goods are sold by a person who is not the owner thereof and who does not sell them under the authority or with the consent of the owner, the buyer acquires no better title to the goods than the seller had, unless the owner of the goods, is by his conduct precluded from denying the seller's authority to sell."

Thus a buyer cannot get a good title to the goods unless he purchases the goods from a person who is the owner thereof or who sells them under the authority or with the consent of the owner.

Examples : (1) A finds a ring of B and sells it to C, who purchases it for value and in good faith. The true owner *i.e.*, B can recover the ring from C, for A having no title could pass none the better.

(2) A was a hirer of certain goods under the hire purchase agreement. He sold the goods to B, who bought them in a good faith. In this case, B will not become the owner of the goods because A was only a hirer and not the owner.

Exceptions to the General Rule : Sale by non-owners

A person, although he is not the owner of the goods, may sell the goods, and pass a better title than he himself has. The following are the various exceptions to the rule :

1. *Sale by Mercantile Agent* (Sec. 27)

Sec. 2 (9) provides that, "Mercantile agent" means a mercantile agent having in the customary course of business as such agent authority either to sell goods, or to consign goods for the purpose of sale or to buy goods, or to raise money on the security of goods. Where a mercantile agent is, with the consent of the owner, in possession of the goods or of documents of title to the goods, any sale made by him when acting in the ordinary course of the business of a mercantile agent shall be binding on the owner and be as valid as if he were expressly authorised by the owner of the goods to make the same provided that : (*i*) the buyer acts in good faith and (*ii*) he has no notice at the time of the contract of sale that the seller has no authority to sell.

Essentials :

1. The agent is in possession of the goods or of the document of title to the goods;
2. He must have the possession in his capacity as a mercantile agent.
3. The mercantile agent sells the goods in the ordinary course of his business as an agent.
4. The buyer acts in good faith. And he should presume that the agent has full authority to sell.

2. *Title by Estoppel* (Sec. 27)

When someone makes another person to believe that a particular thing or fact is true, then afterwards he cannot be allowed to deny the truth of that thing or fact. In a contract of sale, estoppel may arise where the owner by any act or omission leads the buyer to believe that the seller has the right to sell. Thus, when the owner of the goods by his conduct or by statement, wilfully leads the buyer to believe that the seller has the authority to sell, then he is prevented from denying the seller's authority to sell. If a buyer buys goods in such belief, latter on the owner cannot say that the seller had no authority to sell.

> **Example :** *O'Connor Vs. Clark*
>
> M, the owner of a wagon allowed one of his employees K, to have his name painted on it. M did so for the purpose of inducing the public to believe that the wagon belonged to K. C purchased the wagon from K in good faith. C acquires a good title as M is estopped from denying K's authority to sell.

3. ***Sale by a Joint Owner*** (Sec. 28)

Joint owner may be defined as a person who owns the goods jointly with some other persons. Sec. 28 lays down, "If one of several joint owners of goods has the sole possession of them by permission of the co-owners, the property in the goods is transferred to any person who buys them of such joint owner in good faith and has not at the time of the contract of sale notice that the seller has not authority to sell." It is essential to point out that a co-owner can sell his own share even without the application of the provisions of this section. However, according to this section, that the co-owner should be in possession of the same with the consent of the other co-owners and the buyer should act in good faith and without notice that the seller has no authority to sell.

4. ***Sale under a Voidable Contract*** (Sec. 29)

Sec. 29 lays down, "When the seller of goods has obtained possession thereof under a contract voidable under Section 19 or 19(A) of the Indian Contract Act, but the contract has not been rescinded at the time of the sale, the buyer acquires a good title to the goods, provided he buys them in good faith and without notice of the seller's defect of title." A person who has obtained possession of goods under a contract which is voidable on the ground of fraud, misrepresentation, coercion or undue influence, can convey a good title provided the sale takes place before the voidable contract is avoided. However, the buyer gets a valid title only if the following conditions are satisfied :

(*a*) The seller must have obtained the possession of the goods under a voidable contract and not under void contract.

(*b*) The contract must not have been rescinded at the time of sale.

(*c*) The buyer must act in good faith and he should not have any knowledge about seller's defective title.

5. ***Sale by Seller in Possession after Sale*** [Sec. 30 (1)]

Where a seller, having sold goods, continues to be in possession of goods or the documents of title to the goods and sells them either himself or through his mercantile agent to another person, who buys in good faith and without notice of the previous sale, the buyer gets a good title. For the application of this exception it is essential that the possession of the seller must be as seller and not as a hirer or bailee.

6. ***Sale by Buyer in Possession, after Sale*** [Sec. 30(2)]

Where a buyer has agreed to buy the goods and has obtained possession of the same or the documents of title to them with the consent of the seller, resells or pledges the goods either himself or through a mercantile agent, he will convey a good title to the buyer or pledgee provided the person receiving the goods acts in good faith and without notice of any line or other right of the original seller in respect of those goods.

7. ***Resale by Unpaid Seller*** [Sec. 54 (3)]

Section 54 (3) lays down that "Where an unpaid seller who has exercised his right or lien or stoppage in transit resells the goods, the buyer acquires a good title thereto as against the original buyer, notwithstanding that no notice of the re-sale has been given to the original buyer."

8. *Sale in Market Overt*

English law provides an additional exception to the general rule. Market overt is an open, public and legally constituted market. Where a person buys goods in market overt, according to usage of the market, the buyer acquires a good title to the goods. This rule does not apply in India.

9. *Sale by a Finder of goods* (Sec. 169 of Indian Contract Act)

Sometimes, the finder of lost goods sells the goods to a buyer. In such cases, the buyer gets a valid title to the goods if the finder sells the goods under the permitted circumstances :

(*a*) if the owner cannot with reasonable diligence be found, or
(*b*) if found, he refuses to pay lawful charges to the finder, or
(*c*) if the goods are losing the greater part of their value, or
(*d*) if the lawful charges of the finder, in respect of goods found, amount to 2/3rds of their value.

Under Section 176 of the Contract Act, a pawnee of goods has the power to sell the goods pawned under certain conditions and he passes a better title than he himself has. In some cases, a special power of sale is given to officers of court, liquidators of companies, official receivers of insolvent's estate, custom officers etc. All these persons are not owners, yet they sell properties of others and convey a better title to the buyers than they themselves possess.

Sale by Non-owners

1. Sale by Mercantile agent
2. Title by estoppel
3. Sale by joint owner
4. Sale under voidable contract
5. Sale by seller, in possession after sale
6. Sale by buyer, in possession after sale
7. Resale by unpaid seller
8. Sale in market overt
9. Sale by finder of goods
10. Sale by pledgee
11. Sale by official Receiver

THEORETICAL QUESTIONS

1. What do you mean by property in the goods? State the significance of transfer of property and the legal rules relating thereto. (*B.Com., MS*)
2. What is meant by specific and unascertained goods? In a contract of sale, state when the property in the goods passes to the buyer.
3. 'Nemo dat quod non habet' Explain the maxim. (*B.Com., Chennai*)
4. "No seller of goods can give the buyer of goods a better title to those goods than he himself possesses". Examine the statement and mention whether there are any exceptions to this rule.
5. What are rules as to the passing of property from a seller to a buyer in a contract for the sale of unascertained and future goods. (*B.Com., Kerala*)
6. "Risk prima facie passes with property." Comment. (*B.Com., MS*)
7. What are the rules for ascertaining the intention of the parties as to the time when the property in the specific goods is to pass to the buyer. (*B.Com., Madurai*)
8. What is meant by reservation of the right of disposal? (*B.Com., Pune*)
9. State and explain the cases in which a buyer acquires better title over the goods purchased than that of the seller, when the goods are sold by a non-owner. (*B.Com., Chennai*)

MULTIPLE CHOICE QUESTIONS

1. Choose correct option for each of the following :

1. **Passing of property in the goods means :**
   (*a*) passing of possession of the goods.
   (*b*) passing of documents of title to the goods.
   (*c*) passing of absolute legal ownership of the goods.
   (*d*) all of the above.
2. **The property in goods can pass only in case of :**
   (*a*) Ascertained Goods.
   (*b*) Future Goods.
   (*c*) Goods sent on approval or on sale or return basis
   (*d*) Unascertained Goods.
3. **In a contract for the sale of Unascertained goods, the property in goods passes:**
   (*a*) when the contract is made.
   (*b*) when the goods are actually delivered.
   (*c*) when the goods have been unconditionally appropriated by the seller, or buyer without the consent of the other.
   (*d*) none of these.
4. **In a contract of sale of specific or ascertained goods, property in the goods generally passes to the buyer :**
   (*a*) when the parties intend it to pass. (*b*) when the contract is made.
   (*c*) when the price is paid. (*d*) when goods are delivered.
5. **In an unconditional contract for sale of specific goods in a deliverable state, the property in the goods passes :**
   (*a*) when price is paid. (*b*) when contract is made.
   (*c*) when the goods are delivered. (*d*) both (*b*) and (*c*) above.
6. **Where there is a contract for sale of specific goods not in a deliverable state, the property in goods passes when :**
   (*a*) the contract is made.
   (*b*) the goods are actually delivered.
   (*c*) the goods are put into a deliverable state.
   (*d*) the goods are put into a deliverable state and the buyer has notice thereof.
7. **In a contract of sale of specific goods which are yet to be put into deliverable state, the property in the goods passes to the buyer :**
   (*a*) when contract is made.
   (*b*) when parties intend it to pass.
   (*c*) when goods are brought to deliverable state.
   (*d*) when goods are brought to deliverable state and buyer has the notice of it.
8. **In case of sale of unascertained goods, the ownership is transferred to the buyer when the goods are :**
   (*a*) ascertained. (*b*) weighed and measured.
   (*c*) appropriate to the contract. (*d*) both (*a*) and (*c*).
9. **A person who has possession of goods, cannot sell the goods :**
   (*a*) if he is a mercantile agent.
   (*b*) if he possesses goods under voidable contract and the aggrieved party has rescinded the contract.
   (*c*) if he is a servant having custody of the goods.
   (*d*) both (*b*) and (*c*) above.
10. **Where there is an unconditional contract for the sale of specific goods in a deliverable state, the property in the goods passes to the buyer when :**
    (*a*) the goods are delivered to the buyer. (*b*) the price is paid by the buyer.
    (*c*) the contract is made. (*d*) the buyer accepts the goods.

11. Acceptance is deemed to take place when the buyer :
(*a*) Intimates to the seller that he had accepted the goods.
(*b*) Does any act to the goods, which is inconsistent with the ownership of the seller.
(*c*) Retains the goods after the lapse of a reasonable time, without intimating to the seller that he has rejected them.
(*d*) Either (*a*) or (*b*) or (*c*).

12. Where there is a contract for the sale of unascertained goods, the property in goods :
(*a*) passes when the buyer pays the price. (*b*) does not pass until the goods are ascertained.
(*c*) when the contract is entered into. (*d*) when the buyer accepts the goods.

13. In a contract of sale of specific goods in a deliverable state but seller is to do something for the purpose of ascertaining the price, the property in the goods passes to the buyer :
(*a*) when the seller has done all that is required for ascertaining the price.
(*b*) when the seller as well as the buyer have done everything for ascertaining the price.
(*c*) when buyer takes delivery of the goods.
(*d*) both (*b*) and (*c*) above.

14. When goods are sent on "sale or return basis" *i.e.* on approval to a buyer, the property in the goods passes :
(*a*) when the buyer signifies his approval.
(*b*) when the buyer retains the goods after the expiry of time fixed or reasonable time to return the goods.
(*c*) when the buyer pledges the goods without signifying approval.
(*d*) when any of the above stated situations emerges.

15. The property in unascertained goods passes to the buyer :
(*a*) when goods are unconditionally appropriated with the consent of the other party.
(*b*) when goods appropriated are of the same description as given in the contract.
(*c*) when the goods are in a deliverable state.
(*d*) when all of the above conditions satisfied.

16. Essentials involved in appropriation of the goods are :
(*a*) The goods should conform to the description and the quality stated in the contract.
(*b*) The goods must be in a deliverable state.
(*c*) The goods must be unconditionally appropriated to the contract either by delivery to the buyer or to is agent or the carrier.
(*d*) All of the above.

17. In case of sale :
(*a*) Properly in goods does not pass to the buyer.(*b*) Risk in the goods does not pass to the buyer.
(*c*) Both of the above. (*d*) None of the above.

18. Even after appropriation of goods to the contract, the seller is deemed to have reserved the right of disposal of the goods :
(*a*) when goods are deliverable to the order of the seller.
(*b*) when documents of title are sent together with a bill of exchange.
(*c*) when the goods are delivered to the buyer unconditionally.
(*d*) in case of clauses (*a*) or (*b*) above.

19. The following non-owners of goods can transfer a better title than they themselves have :
(*a*) a mercantile agent and a seller having possession of goods sold.
(*b*) an unpaid seller having possession of goods sold.
(*c*) a person having possession of goods under a void agreement.
(*d*) persons under clause (*a*) and (*b*) above.

20. The term "mercantile agent" means an agent who in the customary course of business :
(*a*) has authority to sell the goods.
(*b*) has the authority to buy the goods.

(*c*) has the authority to raise money on the security of goods.
(*d*) has any one of the above authorities.

21. In case of unconditional contract of sale, the property passes to the buyer at the time of making the contract. For this rule to apply, the goods must be :
(*a*) specific.
(*b*) in a deliverable state.
(*c*) physically transferred to buyer.
(*d*) both (*a*) and (*b*).

22. When the goods are sent on sale or return basis, the property in goods does not pass :
(*a*) when the buyer fails to return the goods and the time fixed for the return of goods has not yet expired.
(*b*) when such goods are pledged.
(*c*) when such goods are delivered to a third person on the same basis.
(*d*) none of these.

23. The property in the goods means the :
(*a*) Possession of goods.
(*b*) ownership of goods.
(*c*) custody of goods.
(*d*) both (*a*) and (*b*).

24. In case of sale on approval the ownership is transferred to the buyer when he :
(*a*) accepts the goods.
(*b*) fails to return goods.
(*c*) adopts the transaction.
(*d*) in all the above cases.

25. In case of an agreement to sell, the ownership in the goods remains with :
(*a*) The buyer.
(*b*) Both the buyer and the seller.
(*c*) The Central Government or the State Government, as the case may be.
(*d*) The seller.

26. Appropriation of goods must be :
(*a*) either by buyer or seller.
(*b*) unconditional.
(*c*) with the consent of the other party.
(*d*) as per (*a*), (*b*) and (*c*) above.

27. In case of sale of standing trees, the property passes to the buyer when trees are :
(*a*) felled and ascertained.
(*b*) counted and ascertained.
(*c*) not felled but earmarked.
(*d*) both (*b*) and (*c*).

28. Appropriation of goods to the contract means :
(*a*) separating the goods sold from other goods.
(*b*) by putting the goods sold in suitable receptacles.
(*c*) delivering the goods to the carrier or other bailee for the purpose of transmission to the buyer without reserving the right of disposal.
(*d*) either (*a*) or (*b*) or (*c*).

29. The consent of the seller or buyer as to appropriation of unascertained goods :
(*a*) need not be obtained.
(*b*) must be given before the appropriation is made.
(*c*) must be given after the appropriation is made.
(*d*) may be given before or after the appropriation is made.

30. The main object of a contract of sale is :
(*a*) transfer of possession of goods.
(*b*) transfer of property in goods from seller to buyer.
(*c*) delivery of goods.
(*d*) payment of price.

ANSWERS

1. (*c*)	**2.** (*a*)	**3.** (*d*)	**4.** (*a*)	**5.** (*b*)	**6.** (*d*)	**7.** (*d*)	**8.** (*d*)	**9.** (*d*)	**10.** (*c*)
11. (*d*)	**12.** (*b*)	**13.** (*a*)	**14.** (*d*)	**15.** (*d*)	**16.** (*d*)	**17.** (*d*)	**18.** (*d*)	**19.** (*d*)	**20.** (*d*)
21. (*d*)	**22.** (*a*)	**23.** (*b*)	**24.** (*d*)	**25.** (*d*)	**26.** (*d*)	**27.** (*a*)	**28.** (*d*)	**29.** (*d*)	**30.** (*b*)

CHAPTER

Performance of Contract of Sale

(Sections 31–44)

AT A GLANCE

INTRODUCTION

After the formation of a valid contract of sale, the next stage is its performance. Contract of sale imposes some duties on the seller and the buyer. It also confers some rights to the seller and the buyer. The seller's main duty is to deliver the goods to the buyer. Similarly, the buyer's main duty is to accept the goods and pay the price to the seller as per the terms of the contract. The term "performance of contract of sale" may be defined as the performance of the respective duties of the seller and the buyer as per the terms of the contract. The buyer and the seller are free to provide any terms they like in their contract about the time, place, delivery of goods, payment of the price etc. But when the parties are silent and do not provide any terms and conditions in the contract, then the rules contained in the Sale of Goods Act are applicable.

DELIVERY OF GOODS

According to Sec. 2(2), "delivery means voluntary transfer of possession from one person to another". Delivery is a bilateral act. It requires two parties to act. If transfer of possession of goods is not voluntary *i.e.*, possession is obtained by theft etc., there is no delivery. The performance is mutual and is laid down in Sec. 31 of the Act states that, "It is the duty of the seller to deliver the goods and of the buyer to accept and pay for them, in accordance with the terms of the contract of sale." The primary rule to be followed is that the payment of price and the delivery of goods are to be concurrent. Sec. 32 lays down that "Unless otherwise agreed, delivery of the goods and payment of the price are concurrent conditions, that is to say, the seller shall be ready and willing to give possession of the goods to the buyer in exchange for the price, and the buyer shall be ready and willing to pay the price in exchange for possession of the goods."

MODE OF DELIVERY

Further sec. 33 states that "Delivery of goods sold may be made by doing anything which the parties agree shall be treated as delivery or which has the effect of putting the goods in the possession of the buyer or of any person authorised to hold them on his behalf." Thus delivery need not mean the transfer of physical possession of goods. The essence of delivery is placing the buyer in such a position as to enable him to exercise his rights of ownership over the goods. Therefore, the delivery of goods may be made in any of the following ways :

1. ***Actual Delivery (Physical Delivery)***

Where the goods are actually handed over by the seller to the buyer or his duly authorised agent, it is called actual delivery. Further Sec. 33 states that, delivery of goods may also be made by doing anything which has the effect of putting the goods in the possession of the buyer.

2. ***Symbolic Delivery***

Where a bulk of goods is sold, it is not possible to give actual delivery of the goods. In such case the control over the goods is transferred by delivery of a symbol. For example, the delivery of keys of the godown in which goods are lying, transfer of documents (railway receipt, delivery orders etc.) are the instances of symbolic delivery.

3. ***Constructive Delivery***

Sec. 36 (3) of the Act states that "Where the goods at the time of sale are in the possession of a third person, there is no delivery by seller to buyer unless and until such third person acknowledges to the buyer that he holds the goods on his behalf." Constructive delivery may be defined as the delivery when a third person, in possession of the goods, acknowledges to hold the goods on behalf of the buyers. In such cases, three persons are required — the seller, the person holding the seller's goods and the buyer.

Rules Regarding Delivery of Goods (Sec. 33 to 39)

Following are the provisions relating to the delivery of goods by the seller to the buyer :

1. ***Possession of Goods*** (Sec. 33)

The delivery of goods should be such which enables the buyer to exercise his control over the goods. Thus the delivery of the goods may be either actual or symbolic or constructive. These terms have been explained under the preceding heading.

> **Example :** A sells his horse to B and permits the horse to be removed from A's stable to B's. The removal to B's stable is a delivery.

2. ***Delivery and Payment are concurrent Conditions*** (Sec. 32)

Sec. 32 lays down that "Unless otherwise agreed, delivery of the goods and payment of the price are concurrent conditions, that is to say, the seller shall be ready and willing to give possession of the goods to the buyer in exchange for the price, and the buyer shall be ready and willing to pay the price in exchange for possession of the goods." The delivery of the goods and the payment of their price are the concurrent conditions, *i.e.*, both these conditions should be performed simultaneously, as in the case of cash sales at the counter.

> **Example :** A and B contract that A shall deliver goods to B to be paid for by B on delivery.
>
> **Example :** A need not deliver the goods unless B is ready and willing to pay for the goods on delivery.
>
> **Example :** B need not pay for the goods unless A is ready and willing to deliver them on payment.

3. *Demand for Delivery of Goods* (Sec. 35)

Sec. 35 lays down that "Apart from any express contract, the seller of goods is not bound to deliver them until the buyer applies for delivery." When the goods are subsequently acquired by the seller, he should inform this to the buyer and the buyer should then apply for delivery. The buyer will have no cause of action if he fails to apply for delivery.

4. *Time of Delivery* [Sec. 36(2)]

Sec. 36 (2) lays down that, "Where under the contract of sale the seller is bound to send the goods to the buyer, but no time for sending them is fixed, the seller is bound to send them within a reasonable time." According to the terms of the contract, the seller has to deliver the goods to the buyer and where no time for delivery is fixed, then the delivery of goods must be made within a reasonable time. In commercial dealings, time is the essence of contract. As such it is usual to find a provision in a contract of sale regarding the time of delivery.

5. *Place of Delivery* [Sec. 36(1)]

Sec. 36 (1) lays down that "whether it is for the buyer to take possession of the goods or for the seller to send them to the buyer is a question depending in each on the contract, express or implied, between the parties. Apart from any such contract :

(*a*) goods sold are to be delivered at the place at which they are at the time of the sale; and

(*b*) goods agreed to be sold are to be delivered at the place at which they are at the time of the agreement to sell; or

(*c*) if not then in existence, at the place at which they are manufactured or produced."

6. *Goods in the Possession of Third Person* [Sec. 36 (3)]

Sec. 36 (3) lays down, "Where the goods at the time of sale are in the possession of a third person, there is no delivery by seller to buyer unless and until such third person acknowledges to the buyer that he holds the goods on his behalf." The third person must inform the buyer that he holds the goods on his behalf. When the goods have been sold by the transfer of the document of title to goods, for example, railway receipt or Bill of Lading, the buyer is deemed to be in possession of the goods represented by such document and the assent of the third party is not required.

7. *Effect of Part Delivery* (Sec. 34)

Sec. 34 states that "A delivery of part of goods, in progress of the delivery of the whole, has the same effect, for the purpose of passing the property in such goods, as a delivery of the whole; but a delivery of part of the goods, with an intention of severing it from the whole, does not operate as a delivery of the remainder." Delivery of part of goods sold may amount to delivery of the whole if it is so intended and agreed. But, however, where the part is intended to be severed from the whole, part delivery does not amount to be delivery of the whole.

Example : *Hammond Vs. Anderson* (1803)

Some goods lying at a wharf, were sold and the seller instructed the wharfinger to give delivery to the buyer. The buyer weighed the goods and took away a part of them. There is delivery of the whole. If the part remaining on the wharf is lost, the loss will fall on the buyer.

Example : *Mitchell Reid and Co. Vs. Buldeo Dass* (1888)

X sold 5 bales of certain goods to Y. Y received and paid for one bale and refused to accept the others. This amounts to part delivery.

8. *Expenses of Delivery* [Sec. 36 (5)]

Sec. 36 (5) lays down that "Unless otherwise agreed, the expenses of and incidental to putting the goods into a deliverable state shall be borne by the seller."

9. *Instalment Delivery* (Sec. 38)

Sec. 38 (1) lays down that "Unless otherwise agreed, the buyer of goods is not bound to accept delivery there of by instalments." Unless there is a term in the contract of sale, the seller is not entitled to deliver the goods in instalments and if he does so, the buyer is not bound to accept them.

> **Example :** *Reuter Vs. Sala* (1879)
>
> There was a sale of 25 tons of paper to be shipped in November. The seller shipped 20 tons in November and 5 tons in December. The buyer was entitled to reject the whole 25 tons.

10. *Delivery of Wrong Quantity* (Sec. 37)

The seller is under a duty to comply with the order of the buyer in quality and quantity. Sometimes, the delivery of goods may be of a quantity less than that contracted for, or a quantity larger than agreed, or may be contract goods mixed with goods of a different description. A defective delivery may be either of the following :

(*a*) *Short Delivery* (Sec. 37 (1))

"Where the seller delivers to the buyer a quantity of goods less than he contracted to sell, the buyer may reject them, but if the buyer accepts the goods so delivered he shall pay for them at the contract rate."

> **Example :** A agrees to sell and deliver to B 500 mounds of rice. But only 420 mounds of rice are delivered. B accepts the quantity sent. B must pay for 420 mounds at the contract price. B is entitled to sue for damages on grounds of short delivery.

(*b*) *Excess Delivery* (Sec. 37 (2))

"Where the seller delivers the buyer a quantity of goods larger than he contracted to sell, the buyer may accept the goods included in the contract and reject the rest or he may reject the whole. If the buyer accepts the whole of the goods so delivered, he shall pay for them at the contract rate".

(*c*) *Mixed Delivery* [Sec. 37 (3)]

"Where the seller delivers to the buyer the goods he contracted to sell mixed with goods of a different description not included in the contract, the buyer may accept the goods which are in accordance with the contract and reject the rest, or may reject the whole."

> **Example :** The buyer ordered for supply of certain quality of coal but the seller supplied coal partly according to contract and partly mixed with other quality. The buyer was entitled to reject the whole.
>
> **Example :** A contracts with B to buy 10 tons of cane sugar. B delivers to A 5 tons of cane sugar and 5 tons of beet sugar. A may either (*i*) accept 5 tons of cane sugar which is in accordance with the contract and reject 5 tons of beet sugar which is different description or (*ii*) reject the whole sugar.

11. *Delivery to a Carrier or Wharfinger* (Sec. 39)

Where the seller is required, under the terms of the contract to send the goods to the buyer, delivery to a carrier or wharfinger, whether named by the buyer or not, for the purpose of transmission to the buyer is prima facie delivery to the buyer. However, if the goods are lost in transit and the seller has not made any contract with the carrier on behalf of the buyer, the seller shall be required to bear the loss. (Sec. 39).

> **Example :** *Cooke Vs. Ludlow* (1806)
>
> A buyer ordered goods of the seller to be sent from London by any conveyance for Bristel. The buyer sent the goods to a wharf where he was informed that they would be conveyed to Bristel by the ship "Commerce". He accordingly notified the buyer that they would be sent that ship. As that ship was fully laden, unknown to the seller the goods were sent by another ship and were afterwards lost. The buyer was held liable to pay the price of goods.

12. *Delivery at a Distant Place* (Sec. 40)

Where the seller agrees to deliver goods at his own risk at a place other than that where they are sold, the buyer shall have risk of any natural deterioration in the goods incidental to the transit, unless otherwise agreed between the parties. (Sec. 40).

> **Example :** *Bull Vs. Robinson* (1854)
> Where iron was despatched from Staffordshire to Liverpool in normal conditions but became rusted at the destination, it was held that the buyer could not reject it because rusting and deterioration was necessarily incidental to the course of transit.

ACCEPTANCE OF DELIVERY

1. *Buyer's Right of Examining the Good* (Sec. 41)

Sec. 41 (1) states that, "Where goods are delivered to the buyer which he has not previously examined, he is not deemed to have accepted them unless and until he has had a reasonable opportunity of examining them for the purpose of ascertaining whether they are in conformity with the contract."

Sec. 41(2) states that, "Unless otherwise agreed, when the seller tenders delivery of goods to the buyer, he is bound, on request, to afford the buyer a reasonable opportunity of examining the goods for the purpose of ascertaining whether they are in conformity with the contract."

2. *When Accepted?* (Sec. 42)

Sec. 42 lays down that "the buyer is deemed to have accepted the goods :

(*a*) When he intimates to the seller that he has accepted them;

or (*b*) When he receives delivery of goods, he does any act in relation to them which is inconsistent with the ownership of the seller; (for example : he pledges or resell them)

or (*c*) When after the lapse of a reasonable time, he retains the goods without intimating to the seller that he has rejected them."

> **Example :** *Hardy and Co. Vs. Hillerns and Fowler* (1923)
> Where the buyer took delivery of wheat and sold a part of it and afterwards found that the wheat was not of contract quality and therefore sought to reject it, but it was held that he had lost the right of rejection as he had accepted the wheat by a dealing inconsistent with the rights of the seller in so far as he had sold out a portion of it.

3. *Buyer not Bound to Return the Rejected Goods* (Sec. 43)

Sec. 43 states that "Unless otherwise agreed, where goods are delivered to the buyer and he refuses to accept them, having the right to do so, he is not bound to return them to the seller, but it is sufficient if he intimates to the seller that he refuses to accept them." The goods are then at the seller's risk.

Buyer's Liability for neglecting or Refusing Delivery of Goods (Sec. 44)

Sec. 44 lays down that, "When the seller is ready and willing to deliver the goods and requests the buyer to take delivery, and the buyer does not, within a reasonable time after such request, take delivery of the goods, he is liable to the seller for :

(*a*) any loss occasioned by his neglect or refusal to take delivery, and

(*b*) a reasonable charge for the care and custody of goods".

Sec. 44 also provides that where the neglect or refusal of the buyer to take delivery amount to a repudiation of the contract. The seller may sue for the price or damages.

> **Example :** *Charter Vs. Sullivan* (1957)
>
> C agrees to sell a car to S and he tenders the car to S, who refuses to take delivery. Later on, C sells the car to somebody and incurs a loss. He is entitled to claim damages from S in lieu of breach of contract.

RIGHTS AND DUTIES OF A BUYER

Rights of a Buyer

The following are the rights of the buyer :

1. *Right to have Delivery of Goods* (Sec. 32)

The buyer has the right to take delivery of the goods on payment of price when delivery of goods and payment of price are concurrent conditions in the contract of sale.

2. *Right to Reject the Goods* (Sec. 37)

The buyer is entitled to reject the goods in the following cases :

(*a*) Where the seller delivers lesser quantity than that contracted for;
(*b*) Where the seller delivers larger quantity than that contracted for;
(*c*) Where the seller mixes the contracted goods with goods of a different description.

3. *Right not to Accept Installments* (Sec. 38)

Subject to contract, the buyer is under no obligation to accept delivery of the goods by instalments. He can repudiate the contract in such circumstance. [Sec. 38 (1)].

4. *Right to Examine the Goods* (Sec. 41)

The buyer is not deemed to have accepted the goods unless and until :

(*i*) he has reasonable opportunity to examine the goods;
(*ii*) he is afforded a reasonable opportunity of examining the goods to see whether the goods are in conformity with the contract.

5. *Right not to Return the Rejected Goods* (Sec. 43)

Subject to agreement, the buyer is not liable to return the goods rejected by him rightfully. It is sufficient if he intimates the seller that he refused to accept the goods.

6. *Right to the Notice of Insurance* [Sec. 39 (3)]

It is the duty of the seller to give notice to the buyer to enable him to insure the goods during the sea transit. If he fails to do so, the buyer is not liable for destruction of goods in transit.

Right against the Seller for Breach of Contract

7. *Suit the Seller for non-delivery* (Sec. 57)

Sec. 57 lays down that, "Where the seller wrongfully neglects or refuses to deliver the goods to the buyer, the buyer may sue the seller for damages for non-delivery."

8. *Suit for Specific Performance* (Sec. 58)

The buyer may sue the seller for specific performance of the contract of sale. If the goods are specific or ascertained, the court may order for the specific performance of the contract.

9. *Suit for Breach of Warranty* (Sec. 59)

Section 59 lays down that, "Where there is a breach of warranty, by the seller, or where the buyer elects or is compelled to treat the breach of condition by the seller as a breach of warranty, the buyer may :

(*a*) set up against the seller the breach of warranty in diminution or extinction of the price; or
(*b*) sue the seller for damages for the breach of warranty."

10. *Repudiation of the Contract before due Date* (Sec. 60)

In such a case the buyer has the right for anticipatory breach of contract. Sec. 60 states that where the seller repudiates the contract before the date of delivery, the buyer may either treat the contract as subsisting and wait till the date of delivery or treat the contract as rescinded and sue for damages for breach of contract.

11. *Suit for Interest* [Sec. 61 (2) (b)]

Where there is a breach of contract on the part of the seller and as a result the price is to be refunded to the buyer, the buyer has a right to claim interest on the amount of price.

DUTIES OF THE BUYER

The buyer, in respect to the contract of sale, has to perform the following duties :

1. *Duty to Pay Price and Accept the goods* (Sec. 31)

It is the duty of the buyer to take the delivery of the goods and pay for them in accordance with the terms of the contract.

2. *Duty to Apply for delivery* (Sec. 35)

The seller is not bound to deliver the goods to the buyer until the buyer applies for delivery, in the absence of any contract to the contrary.

3. *Duty to Demand Delivery at a Reasonable Hour* [Sec. 36 (4)]

As per Sec. 36 (4), "Demand or tender of delivery may be treated as ineffectual unless made at a reasonable hour. What is a reasonable hour is a question of fact."

4. *Duty to Accept Instalment Delivery and Pay for It* [Sec. 38 (2)]

Where there is a contract for the sale of goods to be delivered by stated instalments which are to be separately paid for, it is the duty of the buyer to accept the instalment delivery and pay for it.

5. *Duty against Deterioration* (Sec. 40)

Unless otherwise agreed, the buyer has to take the risk of deterioration of the goods incidental to the course of transit.

6. *Duty to Intimate the Seller when Reject the Goods* (Sec. 43)

Unless otherwise agreed, it is the duty of the buyer to inform the seller in case he refuses to accept the goods.

7. *Duty to Take delivery* (Sec. 44)

It is the duty of the buyer to take delivery of the goods within a reasonable time after the tender of delivery. He becomes liable to the seller for any loss occasioned by his neglect or refusal to take delivery.

8. *Duty to Pay Price* (Sec. 55)

Sec. 55 (1) lays down that "Where under a contract of sale the property in the goods has passed to the buyer and the buyer wrongfully neglects or refuses to pay the goods according to the terms of the contract, the seller may sue him for the price of the goods."

9. *Duty to Pay Damages for Non-acceptance* (Sec. 56)

Where the buyer wrongfully neglects or refuses to accept and pay for the goods, the seller may sue him for damages for non-acceptance.

10. *Duty to Pay Increased Tax* (Sec. 64 A)

The buyer is liable to pay so much as will be equivalent to the amount paid or payable in respect of such tax imposed or increase of tax which may be chargeable at the time of sale, in the absence of any contract to contrary.

RIGHTS AND DUTIES OF A SELLER

Rights of a Seller

The rights of seller may be discussed as under :

1. *Right to Claim Compensation* (Sec. 44)

It is the right of the seller to claim compensation for the loss occasioned by the buyer's neglect or refusal to take delivery and also reasonable charges for the care and custody of the goods.

2. *Right to Sue for Price* [Sec. 55 (1)]

Sec. 55 (1) lays down that "Where under a contract of sale the property in the goods has passed to the buyer and the buyer wrongfully neglects or refuses to pay for the goods according to the terms of the contract, the seller may sue him for the price of the goods."

3. *Right to Sue for Price against Contract* [Sec. 55 (2)]

Sec. 55 (2) lays down that, "Where under a contract of sale the price is payable on a certain day irrespective of delivery and the buyer wrongfully neglects or refuses to pay such price, the seller may sue him for the price although the property in the goods has not passed and the goods have not been appropriated to the contract."

4. *Right to Sue for Damages* (Sec. 56)

Sec. 56 lays down that, "Where the buyer wrongfully neglects or refuses to accept and pay for the goods, the seller may sue him for damages for non-acceptance."

5. *Right to Treat the Contract as Subsisting* (Sec. 60)

Sec. 60 states, "Where the buyer repudiates the contract before the date of delivery of goods, seller may either treat the contract as subsisting and wait till the date of delivery, or he may treat the contract as repudiated and sue for damages for the breach."

6. *Right to Interest by Way of Damages* [Sec. 61 (1)]

It is the right of the seller to recover interest or special damages in any case where by law interest or special damages may be recoverable.

7. *Rights of an Unpaid Seller*

(*a*) Right against the goods
(*b*) Right against the buyer personally
(These will be discussed in the next chapter).

Duties of a Seller

The duties and liabilities of the seller may be discussed as follows :

1. ***Duty to Deliver the Goods*** (Sec. 31)

It is the duty of the seller to deliver the buyer goods in accordance with the terms of the contract.

2. ***Duty to Deliver the Goods at the Agreed Place*** [Sec. 36 (1)]

It is the duty of the seller to send the goods to the buyer at the place at which they are contracted to be delivered.

3. ***Duty to Supply the Goods within Specified time*** [Sec. 36 (2)]

It is the duty of the seller to send the goods to the buyer within the fixed time or within reasonable time when no time for sending the goods is fixed.

4. ***Duty to Send the Goods at Reasonable Hour*** [Sec. 36 (4)]

Tender of delivery may be treated as ineffectual unless made at a reasonable hour. What is reasonable hour is a question of fact.

5. ***Duty to Bear the Expenses of Putting the Goods in Deliverable State*** [Sec. 36 (5)]

It is the liability of the seller to bear the expenses of and incidental to putting the goods into a deliverable state.

6. ***Duty to make Contract with Carrier and Wharfinger*** [Sec. 39 (2)]

It is the duty of the seller to make such contract with the carrier or wharfinger on behalf of the buyer as may be reasonable, having regard to the nature of the goods. If he fails to do so he is liable to bear loss if any, incurred in course of transit of the goods.

7. ***Duty to Give Notice to the Buyer*** [Sec. 39 (3)]

Subject to the agreement, it is the duty of the seller to give notice to the buyer to get the goods insured while the goods are sent by a route involving sea transit. If he fails to do so, goods shall be deemed to be at seller's risk during such sea transit.

8. ***Duty to Give Reasonable Opportunity to Examine the Goods*** (Sec. 41)

It is the duty of the seller to afford the buyer a reasonable opportunity of examining the goods for the purpose of ascertaining whether they are in conformity with the contract.

THEORETICAL QUESTIONS

1. Define the term 'Delivery'. Discuss the rules relating to delivery in Sale of Goods Act.
2. When the buyer is deemed to have accepted the goods?
3. 'Delivery does not amount to acceptance of goods' Discuss.
4. 'Delivery of goods and payment of their price are the concurrent conditions' Elucidate.
5. Enumerate the rights and duties of a Seller in respect of the sale of goods.
6. What are the different types of delivery of goods?
7. Discuss the rights and duties of a buyer under Sale of Goods Act.
8. State the rights of a buyer in case of (*a*) short delivery, (*b*) Excess delivery and (*c*) delivery of contract goods mixed with other goods.

MULTIPLE CHOICE QUESTIONS

I. Choose correct option for each of the following :

1. Delivery of goods means voluntary transfer of :

(*a*) ownership of the goods from one person to another.
(*b*) possession of the goods from one person to another.
(*c*) title to the goods from one person to another.
(*d*) both (*a*) and (*c*) above.

2. According to Sale of Goods Act, valid delivery of goods means :
(*a*) delivery of goods in part.
(*b*) part delivery of goods in the process of delivery of whole.
(*c*) delivery of goods in part if the parties so intended.
(*d*) either (*b*) or (*c*) above.

3. In a contract of sale of goods, the delivery of goods is not valid :
(*a*) when it is in accordance with the terms of the contract.
(*b*) when seller is ready but not willing for giving the possession of the goods.
(*c*) when the seller delivers the goods at the place at which they are at time of sale.
(*d*) in all the above cases.

4. Following is not a mode of delivery :
(*a*) quality delivery.
(*b*) constructive delivery.
(*c*) actual delivery.
(*d*) symbolic delivery.

5. Which of the following is symbolic delivery :
(*a*) where the goods are handed over to by a seller to the buyer.
(*b*) where the delivery of goods is effected by delivering a railway receipt to the buyer.
(*c*) where the seller does something which has the effect of putting the goods in the possession of the bailee of the buyer.
(*d*) above (*b*) and (*c*).

6. In a contract of sale, the seller is generally bound to deliver the goods :
(*a*) without the buyer applying for the delivery.
(*b*) at the place at which they are at the time of the sale.
(*c*) at the place at which they are at the time of the agreement to sell.
(*d*) in accordance with (*b*) or (*c*).

7. In a contract of sale, if the seller delivers wrong quantity of goods, the buyer has a right to :
(*a*) reject the whole lot.
(*b*) accept the whole lot.
(*c*) accept the quantity as per the contract and reject the rest.
(*d*) either (*a*) or (*b*) or (*c*).

8. A buyer is deemed to have accepted the delivery of goods :
(*a*) where buyer intimates his acceptance to the seller.
(*b*) where after delivery of goods to the buyer, the buyer does any act in relation to them which is inconsistent with the ownership of the seller.
(*c*) where the buyer retains the goods after the expiry of a reasonable time without intimating that he has rejected the goods.
(*d*) in all the above cases.

9. Under a contract of sale of goods, the delivery of goods may be :
(*a*) actual or symbolic.
(*b*) actual or constructive.
(*c*) actual or structural.
(*d*) any of the (*a*) and (*b*) above.

10. Which of the following is a constructive delivery :
(*a*) where the goods are handed-over by a seller to the buyer personally.
(*b*) where the delivery of goods is effected by delivering a railway receipt to the buyer.
(*c*) where the seller physically delivers the goods to any person authorised by the buyer.
(*d*) where the seller does something which has the effect of putting the goods in the possession of the bailee of the buyer.

ANSWERS

1. (*b*) **2.** (*d*) **3.** (*b*) **4.** (*a*) **5.** (*b*) **6.** (*d*) **7.** (*d*) **8.** (*d*) **9.** (*d*) **10.** (*d*)

XXI CHAPTER

Remedial Measures
(Sections 45–61)

AT A GLANCE

- Who is an unpaid Seller ?
- Rights of an Unpaid Seller against Goods
- Right of Lien
- Rules Relating to Lien
- Loss of Lien
- Right of stoppage in Transit
- Duration of Transit
- When Transit comes to an End
- How Stoppage is Effected
- Distinction between the two
- Effect of Withholding Delivery
- Effect of Sub-sale
- Rights of Unpaid Seller against the Buyer Personally
- Right of Resale
- Remedies for Breach of Contract
- Auction Sales
- Rules for Auction Sale
- Theoretical Questions
- Objective Type Questions.

A contract is comprised of reciprocal promises. In a contract of sale, if seller is under obligation to deliver goods, buyer has to pay for it. In case buyer fails or refuses to pay, the seller is an unpaid seller. The term unpaid seller may be defined as the seller to whom the full price of the goods sold has not been paid.

Who is an Unpaid Seller? (Sec. 45)

Sec. 45 of the Act defines an unpaid seller thus :

"The seller of goods is deemed to be an "unpaid seller" within the meaning of this Act :

(*a*) When the whole of the price has not been paid or tendered;

(*b*) When a bill of exchange or other negotiable instrument has been received as conditional payment, and the condition on which it was received has not been fulfilled by reason of the dishonour of the instrument or otherwise."

Thus a seller is unpaid seller, if :

(*i*) Whole of the price has not been paid or tendered;

(*ii*) When a bill of exchange or other negotiable instrument has been received towards payment and that has been dishonoured.

These are two circumstances in which a seller can be called an unpaid seller. The seller remains unpaid seller so long as any portion of the price, however, small remains unpaid. But if the buyer has tendered the price and the seller wrongfully refuses to accept the tender, he cannot be called an unpaid seller.

The term "seller" includes any person who is in the position of a seller, as, for instance, an agent of the seller to whom the bill of lading has been indorsed, or a consignor or agent who has himself paid, or is directly responsible for the price.

> **Examples :** (1) A sold certain goods to B for Rs. 2,000. B paid Rs. 1,500 and failed to pay the balance. Here, A is in the position of unpaid seller.
>
> (2) A sold goods to B for Rs. 500. B made the payment by cheque. The cheque has been presented to the Banker. But the same was dishonoured. Here, A is in the position of unpaid seller.

RIGHTS OF AN UNPAID SELLER

An unpaid seller has two-fold rights. They are :

(A) Rights against goods

(B) Rights against the buyer personally

A. Rights of an Unpaid Seller Against Goods

This right is studied under the following two heads :

1. Where the ownership of the goods is transferred to the buyer.
2. Where the ownership of the goods is not transferred to the buyer.

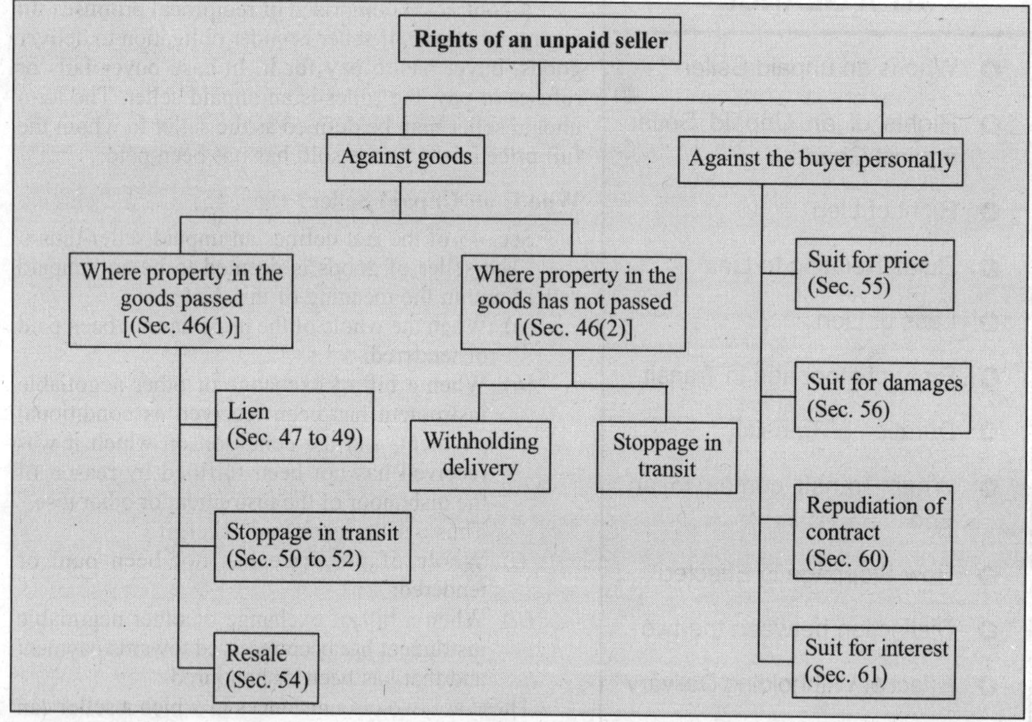

1. *Rights of unpaid Seller where the Ownership of the Goods is Transferred to the Buyer*

According to Sec. 46 of the Act, the unpaid seller has three distincts rights even though property in the goods is transferred to the buyer. These rights are : (*a*) Right of lien, (*b*) Right of stoppage in transit and (*c*) Right of resale.

(*a*) *Right of Lien*

The word 'lien' means 'to retain possession of'. According to Sec. 47 (1) :

"The unpaid seller of goods who is in possession of them is entitled to retain possession of them until payment or tender of the price in the following cases, namely :

(*a*) where the goods have been sold without any stipulation as to credit;

(*b*) where the goods have been sold on credit, but the term of credit has expired;

(*c*) where the buyer becomes insolvent."

The right of lien is one of the unpaid seller's right against the goods, the property in which is transferred to the buyer. It is the unpaid seller's right to retain the goods until the whole of the price is paid or tendered. Lien can be exercised only for non-payment of the price, and not for any other charges due against the buyer. For instance, the seller cannot claim lien for godown charges for storing the goods in exercise of his lien for the price. The lien of an unpaid seller's particular lien, it is a personal right which can be exercised only by him and not by his assignees or his creditors.

The unpaid seller may exercise his lien notwithstanding that he is in possession of the goods as agent or bailee for the buyer. The right of lien is linked with the possession of the goods and not with the title of the goods.

RULES RELATING TO LIEN

(*i*) The seller may exercise his right of lien notwithstanding that he is in possession of the goods as agent or bailee for the buyer.
(*ii*) The lien depends on actual possession of goods and not on title.
(*iii*) Unpaid seller can exercise the lien only for the price and not for any other charges.
(*iv*) Where an unpaid seller has made part delivery of the goods, he may exercise his right of lien on the remainder.
(*v*) The right of lien is not lost, if the seller has obtained a decree for the price of goods (Sec. 49).

LOSS OF LIEN

The right of lien depends only upon the possession of the goods. Thus, the right of lien is lost as soon as the possession of the goods is lost. The circumstances, in which the unpaid seller's lien is lost is discussed under the following cases :

(*a*) Sec. 49 (1) (a) "When he delivers the goods to a carrier or other bailee for the purpose of transmission to the buyer without reserving the right of disposal of the goods :"
(*b*) Sec. 49 (1) (b) "when the buyer or his agent lawfully obtains possession of the goods:"
(*c*) Sec. 49 (1) (c) "by waiver thereof." Waiver may be express or implied. The express waiver is the waiver when the contract of sale provides in express terms that the seller shall not retain the possession of the goods even if the price is not paid. Implied waiver is the waiver where the conduct of the seller shows that he will not exercise his right of lien.
(*d*) Where he assents to a sub-sale by the buyer.

(b) Right of Stoppage in Transit (Sec. 50 to 52)

The right of stoppage in transit means the right of stopping future transit of the goods while they are with a carrier for the purpose of transmission to the buyer, resuming possession of them and retaining possession until payment or tender of the price.

According to Sec. 50, "Subject to the provisions of this Act, when the buyer of the goods becomes insolvent, the unpaid seller who has parted with the possession of the goods, has the right of stopping them in transit, that is to say, he may resume possession of the goods as long as they are in the course of transit, and may retain them until payment or tender of price."

The second right which is available to an unpaid seller is the right to stoppage in transit. This right can be exercised if the following conditions are satisfied :

(*i*) The seller must be unpaid.
(*ii*) The buyer must be insolvent.
(*iii*) Property in the goods must have passed.
(*iv*) Seller has parted with the possession of the goods.
(*v*) Buyer has not got the possession of the goods.

Duration of Transit (Sec. 51)

Sec. 51 lays down, that "Goods are deemed to be in the course of transit from the time when they are delivered to a carrier or other bailee for the purpose of transmission to the buyer, until the buyer or his agent in that behalf takes delivery of them from such carrier or other bailee."

The carrier may hold the goods as :

(*a*) *Seller's agent* : there is no transit because the goods are under the seller's lien.

(*b*) *Buyer's agent* : the seller cannot exercise his right of stoppage in transit because the buyer has acquired possession.

(*c*) *Independent contractor* : The seller has and can exercise the right of stoppage in transit.

When Transit comes to End? (Sec. 51)

The transit is deemed to be at an end and the seller cannot exercise his right of stoppage in the following cases :

1. If the buyer or his agent in that behalf obtains delivery of the goods before their arrival at the appointed destination, the transit is at an end. [Sec. 51(2)].
2. When the goods have arrived at their destination and the carrier acknowledges to the buyer or his agent that he holds the goods or his behalf, the transit is at an end [Sec. 51 (3)].
3. When the carrier wrongfully refuses to deliver the goods to the buyer or his agent, the transit is deemed to be at an end. [51 (6)].
4. If part delivery of the goods has been made with the intention of delivering the whole, transit is terminated even if the remainder is in transit. [Sec. 51(7)].

How Stoppage in Transit is Effected? (Sec. 52)

An unpaid seller may exercise his right of stoppage of goods in transit in any of the following ways :

(*i*) By taking actual possession of the goods; or

(*ii*) By giving notice of his claim to the carrier or other bailee, who possesses the goods.

The notice for such purpose may be given either :

(*a*) to the person who is in actual possession of the goods ; or

(*b*) to his principal.

Such a notice should be given in a manner that it may be effective immediately and the carrier or the other bailee may prevent the delivery to the buyer.

Distinction between Right of Lien and Right of Stoppage in Transit

Lien	*Stoppage in transit*
1. The right of lien can exercised even when the buyer is able to pay but does not pay.	1. The right of stoppage in transit arises when the buyer is insolvent and is unable to pay.
2. This right comes into existence and continues so long as the seller has got possession of the goods.	2. The right comes into operation only after the seller has parted with the possession of the goods.
3. This right comes to an end as soon as the goods go out of the possession of the seller.	3. This right comes to an and as soon as the goods are delivered to the buyer.
4. This right is to retain the possession of the goods.	4. This right is to regain the possession of the goods.
5. This right remains in force till the right of stoppage in transit starts.	5. This right starts when the right of lien comes to an end and remains in force till the delivery of the goods to the buyer.
6. Possession is the test of this right.	6. Test for this right is the non-delivery of the goods to the buyer.

Right off Withholding Delivery [Sec. 46 (2)]

"Where the property in goods has not passed to the buyer, the unpaid seller has, in addition to his other remedies, a right of withholding delivery similar to and co-extensive with his rights of lien and stoppage in transit where the property has passed to the buyer."

Effect of Sub-sale or Pledge by Buyer [Sec. 53]

The unpaid seller's right of lien or stoppage in transit is not affected by any sale or other disposition of the goods which the buyer might have made. Here the sub-purchaser takes the title subject to the rights of the unpaid seller. The seller's lien or right of stoppage in transit is good against a sub-buyer, unless the seller has assented to the sub-sale or pledge of the goods. But a sub-sale by the buyer with the assent of the seller will defeat the seller's lien and right of stoppage.

> **Example :** A sells certain goods to B and delivers them to a carrier for transmission to B. Before the goods reach their destination, A comes to know that B has become insolvent. In the meantime B sells those goods to C. The sale of goods between B and C will not affect the right of A to stop them in transit.

EXCEPTIONS

1. *Seller's consent.* A sub-sale by the buyer with the assent of the seller will defeat the seller's right of lien and the right of stoppage.

2. *Transfer of document of title.* Where a document of title to the goods has been issued, a lawfully transferred to any person as buyer or owner of the goods, and that person transfer the document to a purchaser in good faith and for valuable consideration, the unpaid seller's lien or stoppage in transit is destroyed.

B. Rights of an Unpaid Seller against the Buyer Personally

In addition to his rights against the goods, as discussed above, an unpaid seller has the following rights against the buyer personally:

1. *Suit for Price* (Sec. 55)

On transfer of the ownership of the goods to the buyer, he becomes bound to pay the price to the seller. When he does not pay the price in terms of the contract, legal action can be taken against the buyer by the unpaid seller.

(*a*) Sec. 55 (1) states, "Where under a contract of sale the property in the goods has passed to the buyer and the buyer wrongfully neglects or refuses to pay for the goods according to the terms of the contract, the seller may sue him for the price of the goods."

(*b*) Sec. 55 (2) states, "Where under a contract of sale the price is payable on a certain day irrespective of delivery and the buyer wrongfully neglects or refuses to pay such price, the seller may sue him for the price although the property in the goods has not passed and the goods have not been appropriated to the contract."

2. *Suit for Damages for Non-acceptance* (Sec. 56)

Sec. 56 states, "Where the buyer wrongfully neglects or refuses to accept and pay for the goods, the seller may sue him for damages for non-acceptance."

This section deals with general damages. As such, the seller can recover the estimated loss arising directly and naturally, in the course of events, from the buyer's breach of the contract. Such damages are measured as per provisions contained in Sec. 73 of the Indian Contract Act. They are:

(*i*) Where there is an available market for the goods in question, the difference between the contract price and the market price on the date of breach will be the measure of damages.

(*ii*) Where there is no such market, the measure will be the estimated loss directly or indirectly resulting in the ordinary course of events from such breach.

In the same way, when the seller is ready and requests the buyer to take the delivery of the goods and the buyer wrongfully neglects or refuses to take the delivery within a reasonable time, the seller is entitled to recover from the buyer : (*a*) any loss by the buyer's neglect or refusal to the seller; and (*b*) reasonable charges for the care and custody of goods (Sec. 44).

3. *Suit for Repudiation of the Contract before due Date* (Sec. 60)

Sometimes, the buyer puts an end to the contract before the due date of delivery of goods. Sec. 60 states, "Where either party to a contract of sale repudiates the contract before the date of delivery, the other may either treat the contract as subsisting and wait till the date of delivery, or he may treat the contract as rescinded and sue for damages for the breach." Thus the seller may (*a*) treat the contract as subsisting and wait till the date of delivery or (*b*) treat the contract as rescinded and sue the buyer for damages for breach.

4. *Suit for Interest* (Sec. 61)

Where there is a specific agreement between the parties as to interest on the price of the goods from the date on which the payment becomes due. The seller may recover such interest from the buyer. Further, Sec. 61 (2) states, "In the absence of a contract to the contrary, the Court may award interest at such rate, as it thinks fit, on the amount of price to the seller in a suit by him for the amount of the price, from the date of the tender of the goods or from the date on which the price was payable :"

(c) *Right of Resale* (Sec. 54)

An unpaid seller who has exercised his right of lien and stoppage in transit is also em-powered to effect resale of the goods. This resale right is a valuable right given to an unpaid seller. Section 54 of the Act has given the right of resale to an unpaid seller, in the following circumstances :

1. *Where the goods are Perishable*

Sometimes, the goods are of perishable nature. The unpaid seller, who has exercised the right of lien or stoppage in transit, can resell the goods. The unpaid seller need not give a notice to the buyer of his intention to resell the goods. Perishable goods may include those goods which are apt to deterioration in a mercantile sense.

2. *Where Unpaid Seller gives Notice of his Intention*

When the goods are not of perishable nature and buyer does not pay or tender the price, the seller can resell the goods. However, he should give a notice to the buyer of his intention to resell the goods.

3. *Where the Seller Expressly Reserves his Right of Resale*

Where the seller expressly reserves a right of resale in case the buyer makes default, and, on the buyer making default, resells the goods, the original contract of sale is thereby rescinded. This rescission, however, does not affect the seller's right to claim damages for loss.

The seller is entitled to recover from the original buyer damages caused to him by the resale. But if any profit accrues, such profit shall belong to the seller. However, the seller shall not be entitled to recover damages from the buyer or retain surplus if he fails to give reasonable notice to the buyer. In case of perishable goods, such notice is not necessary.

REMEDIES FOR BREACH OF CONTRACT OF SALE

Remedies available to seller :

1. Suit for price (Sec. 55)
2. Suit for damages for non-acceptance of goods (Sec. 56)

3. Suit for damages for repudiation of contract (Sec. 60)
4. Suit for interest (Sec. 61)

All these remedies have already been discussed.

Remedies available to buyer :

1. Suit for damages for non-delivery of goods (Sec. 57)
2. Suit for damages for repudiation of the contract (Sec. 60)
3. Suit for specific performance (Sec. 58)
4. Suit for breach of warranty (Sec. 59)
5. Suit for interest (Sec. 61)

All these remedies have already been discussed.

Auction Sales (Sec. 64)

Auction sale is a public sale, where goods are offered to be taken by the highest bidder from among the public.

The auction sale is usually organised by giving advertisements about the goods to be sold alongwith other terms and conditions of the auction sale. The auctioneer gives wide publicity for the sale of the goods by auction, and fixes the time and place for it. The intending buyers, known as bidders, can inspect the goods, during the time fixed by the auctioneer, before or at the time of sale.

The offer of the price is known as 'bid' and the person making the bid is known as the 'bidder'. The owner of the goods may himself sell them by auction or appoint a person to sell the goods by auction on his behalf. The person so appointed is known as 'auctioneer'. The relationship between the owner of the goods and the auctioneer is that of the principal and agent.

On the appointed day, time and place, the auctioneer puts up the lots of goods to be sold. Then he invites bids for every lot from the people assembled at the place of auction. He announces every bid made by the people and induces them to make bids of a higher price. When auctioneer finds any bid reasonable and in accordance with the directions of the seller or equal or more than the 'reserve price' if any, he may accept it. He accepts or knocks-down the biggest bid by striking with his hammer or any other approved method. With the 'knock-down' the contract of sale is completed. Before the knock-down, any bidder may retract his bid. Similarly, the auctioneer may reserve a right even to reject the highest bid. It may however be noted that on the fall of the hammer, the ownership does not transfer to the buyer : only the contract of sale is completed.

RULES FOR AUCTION SALE

The rules regarding auction sale are as follows : (Sec. 64)

1. Where goods are put up for sale in lots, each lot is prima facie deemed to be the subject of a separate contract of sale. (Sec. 64(1)).
2. The sale is complete when the auctioneer announces its completion by the fall of hammer or in other customary manner; and until such announcement is made, any bidder may retract his bid. (Sec. 64(2)).
3. A right to bid may be reserved expressly by or on behalf of the seller and where such right is expressly so reserved but not otherwise, the seller or any one person on his behalf may, subject to the provisions hereinafter contained, bid at the auction. (Sec. 64(3)).
4. Where the sale is not notified to be subject to a right of the seller, it shall not be lawful for the seller to bid himself or to employ any person to bid at such sale or for the auctioneer knowingly to take any bid from the seller of any such person; and any sale contravening this rule may be treated as fraudulent by the buyer. (Sec. 64(4)).
5. The sale may be notified to be subject to a reserved or upset price. (Sec. 64(5)).
6. If the seller makes use of pretended bidding to raise the price, the sale is voidable at the option of the buyer. (Sec. 64(6)).

Example : *Dennant Vs. Skinner :* (1948)

D sold a motor car by auction. It was knocked down to K who was only allowed to take it away on giving a cheque for the price and signing an agreement that ownership should not pass until the cheque was cleared. The cheque was not cleared. Meanwhile K sold the car to S. It was held that the property passed on the fall of the hammer and therefore S had a good title to the car. Both sale and sub-sale are valid in favour of K and S respectively.

THEORETICAL QUESTIONS

1. Who is unpaid seller? What are his rights against buyer personally?
2. When and under what circumstances can the seller exercise the right of resale?(*B.Com. Bangalore*)
3. "Right of stoppage in transit begins when the right of lien ends." Comment.
4. Under the Sale of Goods Act, when is a seller of goods deemed to be an unpaid seller? Explain the unpaid seller's right of lien over the goods.
5. What is an unpaid seller's lien? When is it lost? (*B.Com. M.K.*)
6. "The right of stoppage in transit is an extension of the unpaid seller's right of lien" Comment. (*B.Com. Kerala*)
7. Distinguish between an unpaid seller's right of lien and right of stoppage in transit.(*B.Com. Madras*)
8. State the rule regarding sale by auction.
9. Define an unpaid seller. What are the rights of an unpaid seller? (*B.Com. MS*)

MULTIPLE CHOICE QUESTIONS

I. Choose correct option for each of the following :

1. According to the Sale of Goods Act, an unpaid seller is one who has not been paid :

(*a*) part of the price. (*b*) whole of the price.
(*c*) substantial part of the price. (*d*) any one of the above.

2. In a concluded sale, if the goods are destroyed, the loss is to be borne by :

(*a*) The seller. (*b*) Both the seller and buyer.
(*c*) the party who is in possession of goods. (*d*) the buyer.

3. Where the possession of the goods has passed on to the buyer, the rights of an unpaid seller are:

(*a*) rights of lien and resale.
(*b*) right of lien, stoppage in transit and resale the goods.
(*c*) right to sue the buyer for price etc.
(*d*) rights stated in clause (*b*) above and some other rights.

4. A seller is not an unpaid seller :

(*a*) when he sells the goods on credit and the term of credit has not expired.
(*b*) when he refuses to accept valid tender of price.
(*c*) when buyer has validly rejected the goods.
(*d*) in anyone of the above cases.

5. An unpaid seller can exercise his lien :

(*a*) when he is in the possession of goods.
(*b*) when he has delivered the goods to a carrier without reserving the right of disposal.
(*c*) when he has sold the goods on credit.
(*d*) when buyer obtains the possession of the goods.

6. According to Sale of Goods Act, a seller is said to be an unpaid seller :

(*a*) when the buyer's bank fails to honour the cheque.
(*b*) when buyer becomes insolvent before the maturity of the bill.
(*c*) when buyer offers only a part of the price.
(*d*) in anyone of the above cases.

7. When the property in the goods has passed to the buyer, the rights of unpaid seller are :

(a) right of lien on goods.
(*b*) right of stoppage of goods in transit.
(*c*) right of resale of the goods.
(*d*) as stated in clause (*a*), (*b*), and (*c*).

8. An unpaid seller having possession of the goods can exercise the right of lien :

(*a*) when buyer stops the payment of cheque.
(*b*) when buyer becomes insolvent.
(*c*) when he obtains a decree from the Court for the price of the goods.
(*d*) in all the above cases.

9. An unpaid seller can exercise the right of stoppage of goods in transit :

(*a*) when goods are in transit.
(*b*) when the buyer has become insolvent.
(*c*) either in case of (*a*) or (*b*).
(*d*) in both the cases of (*a*) and (*b*).

10. An unpaid seller having possession of the goods can exercise his right of lien :

(*a*) until payment of whole price.
(*b*) until payment of all cost and expenses.
(*c*) until payment of price and expenses.
(*d*) in the cases stated in clauses (*b*) and (*c*) above.

11. The lien of an unpaid seller depends on :

(*a*) possession.
(*b*) ownership.
(*c*) Whether the buyer has paid the price or not.
(*d*) title.

12. Right of stoppage of goods in transit can be exercised :

(*a*) only when the price remains unpaid even on the expiry of credit period allowed and the buyer is solvent.
(*b*) only when the buyer becomes insolvent.
(*c*) even if the carrier holds the goods as seller's agent.
(*d*) even if the carrier holds the goods as buyer's agent.

13. According to the Sale of Goods Act, an unpaid seller can stop the goods in transit :

(*a*) when the buyer has committed some act of insolvency under the law of insolvency.
(*b*) when buyer ceases to pay his debts in the ordinary course of business.
(*c*) when the buyer cannot pay his debts when they become due.
(*d*) in all the above cases.

14. When an unpaid seller has made part delivery of goods :

(*a*) the seller can never exercise the right of lien on the remainder.
(*b*) the seller can not exercise the right of lien on the remainder if it can be shown that part delivery was in the process of delivering the whole.
(*c*) the seller can always exercise the right of lien on the remainder.
(*d*) rights of unpaid seller are unaffected.

15. An unpaid seller can exercise his right of lien :

(*a*) where the goods have been sold on credit and the term of credit has not expired.
(*b*) where the buyer has not become insolvent.
(*c*) for the unpaid price of the goods.
(*d*) for the unpaid price of the goods and other charges.

16. Right of lien can be exercised :

(*a*) only when goods have been sold for cash.
(*b*) only when goods have been sold on credit.
(*c*) only when buyer becomes insolvent.
(*d*) none of these.

17. When the unpaid seller has parted with the goods to a carrier and the buyer has become insolvent he can exercise :

(*a*) right of lien.
(*b*) right of resale.
(*c*) right of stoppage in transit.
(*d*) none of the above.

18. Which of the following right can be exercised by an unpaid seller against the buyer, who is not insolvent :

(*a*) right of lien.
(*b*) right of stoppage in transit.
(*c*) none of the above.
(*d*) both (*a*) and (*b*).

19. Right of stoppage of goods in transit cannot be exercised :

(*a*) If the carrier holds the goods as buyer's agent or as seller's agent.

(*b*) If part delivery is not intended as delivery of the whole.

(*c*) If the buyer has sold the goods without seller's consent.

(*d*) If after the arrival of the goods at the appointed destination, the carrier or other bailee has not acknowledged to the buyer or his agent that he holds the goods on his behalf.

20. Right of stoppage in transit can be exercised :

(*a*) only by taking actual possession of goods.

(*b*) only by giving notice of his claim to the carrier on other bailee who possesses the goods.

(*c*) either of the ways stated in (*a*) and (*b*).

(*d*) none of these.

21. An unpaid seller can exercise his right of stoppage of goods in transit :

(*a*) by giving notice of his claim to the carrier who is in possession of the goods.

(*b*) by taking actual possession of the goods.

(*c*) by notice of his claim to the bailee who is in possession the of goods.

(*d*) either (*a*) or (*b*) or (*c*).

22. Where the transfer of document of title was by way of pledge the unpaid seller's right of lien or stoppage in transit :

(*a*) can be exercised subject to rights of transferor.

(*b*) can be exercised subject to rights of transferee.

(*c*) cannot be exercised at all.

(*d*) none of these.

23. An unpaid seller has :

(*a*) unlimited right to resell the goods.

(*b*) limited right to resell the goods.

(*c*) can expressly reserve the right of resale of the goods in the contract in case of non-payment by the buyer.

(*d*) both (*b*) and (*c*) above.

24. An advertisement to sell the goods by auction is :

(*a*) an offer to sell.

(*b*) an invitation to make an offer to buy.

(*c*) none of these.

25. According to the Sale of Goods Act, the unpaid seller can exercise his right of resale of goods :

(*a*) when goods are of perishable nature.

(*b*) when seller expressly reserves his right of resale.

(*c*) in both the above cases.

(*d*) in the case (*a*) or (*b*).

26. In case of an agreement to sale, if the seller becomes insolvent while the goods are in his possession, the buyer's remedy :

(*a*) Is to claim the goods from the official receiver or assignee.

(*b*) Is to claim dividend from the estate of the seller for the price paid.

(*c*) Is not available.

(*d*) Is to file a suit for damages.

27. Under which circumstances, the right of stoppage can be exercised by the unpaid seller :

(*a*) the buyer has become insolvent.

(*b*) the goods are in transit.

(*c*) the seller must be unpaid.

(*d*) all of the above.

28. Under which circumstances the unpaid seller can exercise right of re-sale :

(*a*) when the goods are of perishable nature.

(*b*) when he gives notice to the buyer.
(*c*) when he gives notice to the buyer of his intention to re-sale and the buyer does not within a reasonable time pay the price.
(*d*) both (*a*) and (*c*).

29. An unpaid seller has not given notice of resale to the buyer. On resale there is a loss :
(*a*) The unpaid seller can recover it from the buyer.
(*b*) The unpaid seller cannot recover it from the buyer.
(*c*) The buyer can recover it from the unpaid seller.
(*d*) The buyer must compensate the unpaid seller.

30. The unpaid seller has right of stoppage of goods in transit only where the buyer :
(*a*) become insolvent. (*b*) acts fraudulently.
(*c*) refuses to pay price. (*d*) all of these.

31. Seller has right to resale where :
(*a*) goods are perishable. (*b*) seller gives notice.
(*c*) seller has reserved such right. (*d*) all of these.

32. In which of the following cases, the unpaid seller loses his right of lien?
(*a*) delivery of goods to buyer. (*b*) tender of price by buyer.
(*c*) delivery of goods to carrier. (*d*) all of these.

33. Under which of the circumstances unpaid seller loses his right of lien :
(*a*) by estoppel.
(*b*) where seller waived the right of lien.
(*c*) where the buyer or his agent lawfully obtains possession of the goods.
(*d*) any of the above.

34. An unpaid seller has not given notice of resale to the buyer. On resale there is a profit. The unpaid seller :
(*a*) is bound to hand it over to the buyer.
(*b*) is not bound to hand it over to the buyer.
(*c*) may dispose it off in any manner he likes.
(*d*) may set it off against a previous loss in similar circumstances.

35. Which of the following is a buyer right against the seller in case of breach of contract ?
(*a*) suit for non-delivery. (*b*) suit for damages for breach of warranty.
(*c*) suit for specific performance. (*d*) all of the above.

36. The bidder at an auction sale can withdraw his bid :
(*a*) any time during auction. (*b*) before payment of price.
(*c*) before fall of hammer. (*d*) none of these.

37. Where in an auction sale, the seller appoints more than one bider, the sale is :
(*a*) void. (*b*) conditional.
(*c*) illegal. (*d*) voidable.

38. An auction sale is complete on the :
(*a*) delivery of goods. (*b*) fall of hammer.
(*c*) payment of price. (*d*) none of the above.

39. In an auction sale, if the seller makes use of pretended bidding to raise the price, then the sale is:
(*a*) valid. (*b*) voidable.
(*c*) void. (*d*) illegal.

40. In an auction sale, the property shall be sold to be :
(*a*) Lowest bidder. (*b*) All biders.
(*c*) Highest bidder. (*d*) none of the above.

41. In case of resale of goods by seller without notice :
(*a*) the new buyer (who buys in resale) will get a good title.
(*b*) the unpaid seller has right to recover the loss on resale.
(*c*) original buyer has no right to recover the profit on resale.
(*d*) none of these.

42. An unpaid seller can exercise the right of stoppage in transit when the carrier hold the goods :
(*a*) as seller's agent. (*b*) as agent of both of them.
(*c*) as buyer's agent. (*d*) in his own name.

43. Notice of Resale by seller must be given :
(*a*) irrespective of the nature of goods.
(*b*) where the seller has expressly reserved the right of resale.
(*c*) where the unpaid seller has exercised his right of lien or stoppage in transit.
(*d*) none of these.

44. An agreement between the bidders not to bid against each other at an auction sale, is known as :
(*a*) knock-out agreement. (*b*) damping agreement.
(*c*) puffers' agreement. (*d*) fraudulent agreement.

45. An unlawful act by which an intending purchaser is prevented from bidding or raising the price at an auction sale, is known as :
(*a*) decoy ducking. (*b*) puffing.
(*c*) damping. (*d*) none of these.

ANSWERS

1. (*d*)	**2.** (*d*)	**3.** (*c*)	**4.** (*d*)	**5.** (*a*)	**6.** (*d*)	**7.** (*d*)	**8.** (*d*)	**9.** (*d*)	**10.** (*a*)
11. (*a*)	**12.** (*b*)	**13.** (*d*)	**14.** (*b*)	**15.** (*c*)	**16.** (*d*)	**17.** (*c*)	**18.** (*a*)	**19.** (*a*)	**20.** (*c*)
21. (*d*)	**22.** (*b*)	**23.** (*d*)	**24.** (*b*)	**25.** (*c*)	**26.** (*b*)	**27.** (*d*)	**28.** (*d*)	**29.** (*b*)	**30.** (*d*)
31. (*d*)	**32.** (*d*)	**33.** (*d*)	**34.** (*d*)	**35.** (*d*)	**36.** (*c*)	**37.** (*d*)	**38.** (*b*)	**39.** (*b*)	**40.** (*c*)
41. (*a*)	**42.** (*d*)	**43.** (*c*)	**44.** (*a*)	**45.** (*c*)					

CHAPTER XXII

Nature of Partnership

AT A GLANCE

INTRODUCTION

The law of partnership is contained in the Indian Partnership Act 1932, which came into force on 1st October 1932, except Section 69 (dealing with the effect of non-registration of firms). The present enactment does not purport to alter in any substantial way the law of partnership, but only to clarify it with a view to avoiding doubts and difficulties, and also for making it uniform with the law in force in England and other parts of Commonwealth. For this purpose the present Act is mainly based on the English Partnership Act 1890, and practically codifies the Indian law of partnership, though, as was to be expected, it expressly provides (Sec. 3) that it is a branch of the general law of contracts and that the rest of the provisions of the Contract Act shall continue to apply to partnerships, except so far as they are inconsistent with the express provisions of this Act.

Sec. 4 of the Indian Partnership Act 1932, defines partnership "Partnership is the relation between persons who have agreed to share the profits of a business carried on by all or any one of them acting for all." The persons who enter into such relationship are individually called 'partners' and collectively as 'firm' and the name under which their business is carried on is called the 'firm name'.

ESSENTIAL ELEMENTS OF PARTNERSHIP

The following are essential elements, which are required under Sec. 4 of the Indian partnership Act, for constituting a valid partnership:

1. Partnership is an *association of two or more persons*.

2. Partnership must be the result of *an agreement* between two or more persons.
3. The agreement must be to carry on some *business*.
4. The agreement must be to *share profits of the business*.
5. Business must be *carried on by all or any one of them acting for all.*

All these above mentioned elements must be present before partnership can be said to come into existence. They are discussed below :

1. *Association of two or more Persons*

There must be a contract between two or more persons. Therefore, unless there are atleast two persons, there cannot be a partnership. Moreover, the persons must be competent to enter into a contract. One person cannot be a partner with himself. When the existing partnership firm, the number of partners is reduced to one, the firm is compulsorily dissolved. As regards maximum number of partners in a partnership firm, Section 11 of the Companies Act 1956, puts the limit at 10 in case of banking business and 20 in case of any other business. Partnership is the result of a contract. It does not arise from status or operation of law or inheritance. Sec. 5 states that "The relation of partnership arises from contract and not from status". In particular the members of a Hindu Undivided family carrying on a family business, as such, are not partners in such business.

2. *An Agreement*

It is another important element of partnership. There must be an agreement between the partners to form the partnership *i.e.*, all the partners must enter into an agreement to constitute a partnership firm. The partnership relation is one of a contractual nature. It arises from contract and not from status (Sec. 5). An agreement among the partners is the basis of such a contract. The agreement may either be express or implied *i.e.*, oral or written. An express agreement is one which is made by words, spoken or written. An implied agreement is one which is inferred from the course of dealing or the conduct of the parties. An agreement of partnership may be for a fixed period, or for an uncertain period or to carry on a particular adventure.

Example : Two brothers were living together with their father. The father, who was a proprietor of a business, dies. The sons inherit the business but do not become partners until there is an agreement, express or implied, to carry on the business as partners.

3. *Business*

The existence of business is essential to form a partnership. Business includes trade, occupation or profession according to the definition given in Sec. 2(b). This element of partnership is very important. Unless there is business, there will be no partnership. The business must be lawful. The idea behind the business is to secure gain. But a society formed for the charitable or religious purpose is not a partnership. In the same way, a voluntary association formed for the purpose of holding a function of a social character is not a partnership. Business is not confined to lengthy operation, but may consist of a single adventure or a single undertaking. Persons may be partners for a single voyage of a ship or for one performance of a play.

Example : *Govind Nair Vs. Maga* (1948)

Two persons jointly purchased a tea shop by contributing equal amount. Further, they spent additional amount to equip the tea shop. Then tea shop was leased out on rent, which was shared by them equally. It was held that they are only co-owners and not partners as they never carried on any business.

To constitute partnership, there must be a business in existence. An agreement to carry on business at a future time does not result in partnership, *i.e.*, the evidence of partnership is business, which is in actual existence. Besides, such business, to be carried on by the firm, should be legal.

4. *Sharing of Profits*

This essential element provides that the agreement to carry on business must be with the object of sharing profits amongst all the partners. Sharing the profits of a business is not only evidence but conclusive evidence of partnership. The partnership must aim to make profit because then only profit may be divided amongst the partners. The term 'profit' means the net profit *i.e.*, surplus money left after providing for all expenses. There must be an agreement among the partners to share the profits of a business. They may share profits in any way they like, *i.e.*, equally or in any other ratio. Where only one partner is entitled to the whole profits, there can be no partnership.

To constitute a partnership it is not essential that the partners should agree to share the losses. Every man who has a share in the profits of a trade, ought also to bear his share of loss. It is open to one or more partners to agree to bear all the losses of the business. Sec. 13 (b), provides that the partners are entitled to share equally in the profits earned, and shall contribute equally to the losses sustained by the firm, unless otherwise agreed. Though sharing in the profits of a business essential, it does not follow that everyone who participates in the profits of a business is necessarily a partner. A manager with a share of profit may claim to be a servant of the firm and not a partner.

5. *Carried on by All or Any of Them* (Mutual agency)

The law of partnership is but an extension of the law of principal and agent. The definition of a partnership provides that the business must be carried on by all the partners or any of them. That is, there must be mutual agency. Thus every partner is both an agent and principal for himself and other partners. A partner is, therefore, an agent in the sense that he can bind the firm and other fellow partners by his acts done in the course of business and he is also a principal of other partners in the sense that he can be bound by the acts of other partners in the ordinary course of business. They are 'agents' for each other and 'principals' for themselves. Their relationship is governed by the 'law of agency'. The partners are largely regulated by the law of 'principal and agent'.

Example : *Cox Vs. Hickman* (1860)

In that case, a debtor transferred his business to trustee with instructions to carry on the business and use the profits for paying his creditors. It was held that the creditors were not partners of the business. It was observed that "The liabilities of one partner for the acts of his copartner is in truth the liabilities of a principal for the acts of his agent. Where two or more persons are engaged as partners in an ordinary trade, each of them has an implied authority from the other to bind all by contracts entered into according to the usual course of business in that trade. Every partner in trade is, for the ordinary purpose of the trade, the agent of his copartners, all are, therefore, liable for the ordinary trade contracts of the other. The public have a right to assume that every partner has authority from his copartners to bind the whole firm in contracts made according to ordinary usage of trade."

TEST OF PARTNERSHIP

The question whether a particular groups of persons constitutes a partnership or not, is often a difficult one to decide. In order to consider whether a group of persons is a partnership or not, the essential elements, mentioned above, should be kept in mind. A partnership is a relation between persons, who have agreed to share the profits of a business carried on by all or any of them acting for all. If there is a specific agreement of partnership between the partners then, there is no difficulty in knowing whether the group is partnership or not. A test of valid partnership is that all the essential element of partnership must be present in a group of persons, to be called as partnership. An association of two or more persons entering into an agreement to share the profits may not necessarily determine partnership, because such an agreement may not carry on business and may be formed for charitable or social objects. Similarly the business may be carried on for profits, but the agreement does not provide for sharing profits, there cannot be a partnership.

Of the essentials of partnership, sharing of profits is an important criterion but is not conclusive (Cox Vs. Hickman). Sec. 6 has categorically laid down that receipt by a person of a share of profits of a business does not of itself make him a partner with persons carrying on the business, and in particular, the receipt of such share or payment :

(*a*) by a lender of money to any persons engaged or about to engage in any business;
(*b*) by a servant or agent as remuneration;
(*c*) by the widow or child of a deceased partner, as annuity; or
(*d*) by a previous owner or part owner of the business, as consideration for the sale of the goodwill or share thereof, does not of itself make the receiver a partner with the persons carrying on the business.

In all the above cases, the element of agency, so necessary to constitute partnership, is absent. Thus, as laid down in Cox Vs. Hickman, the true test of partnership is agency, and not sharing of profits.

The sharing of profit is not a conclusive proof of real relation of partnership. It is a prima facia evidence of partnership. The real relation between the partners is that of mutual agency. Section 6 specifies the following cases where there is *no real relation of partnership* between the group of persons :

(1) Joint owners sharing profits

The joint owners of a property who share the profits or gross returns arising from the property, are not the partners.

Example : X and Y are joint owners of a shop, which they let out at Rs. 5,000 per month, sharing equally by them.

(2) Money lender sharing profits

Money-lender is a person who lends money on interest. Sometimes, a money-lender receives, in addition to or in place of his interest, a portion of the profits of a business. The money-lender is not a partner of the firm.

Example : *Mollow March & Co. Vs. the Court of wards* (1872)

A advanced some money to B and C, two merchants. The merchants agreed to carry on the business subject to the control of A in several respects. A was to receive a commission of 20% on all the profits. It was held that there was no partnership between A and the merchants. The object of the agreement was to give A the maximum security for the repayment of his loan.

(3) Servant or Agent receiving share in profits

A servant or an agent who receives a share of profits as part of his remuneration is not a partner.

Example : *Munshi Abdul Vs. Chanerjee* (1963)

A, a contractor, undertook a contract of loading and unloading railway wagons. He appointed B as his servant to manage the work. It was agreed that the servant would receive 75% of the profits as his remuneration and would bear all the losses, if any. It was held that B was the agent of A and not his partner.

(4) Widow or child of a deceased partner

A widow or child of a deceased partner receiving a share of profits as annuity is not a partner of the firm.

Example : *C.I.T., Vs. Kesharmal* (1968)

A, B, and C were carrying on a business of garments in partnership. A died. After A's death, B and C continued the business. It was agreed to give 10% of the profits of the firm to D, the widow of A, every year. In this case, D is not a partner in the firm.

(5) Seller of Goodwill

If a previous owner of the business shares profit of the firm as consideration for the sale of the goodwill of the business : such a person is not a partner of the firm.

Example : *Rawilson Vs. Clarke* (1846)

A, a surgeon and druggist, sold his practice to B alongwith the name and style under which A was carrying on his practice. It was agreed that A would continue to attend his old profession and to the best efforts introduce B to his patients and to do every reasonable act for promoting B's profession. B allowed a portion of the profits to A. It was held that A and B were not partners in the profession.

Example : *Raghunandan Nanu Vs. Hormasjee Bezonjee* (1927)

In this case, the defendant was admitted as a partner by the plaintiff for one year, subject to the terms that the defendant would get Rs. 500 in lieu of profits but would not be responsible for the losses, no capital to be contributed by him and he would have all the rights of a partner. It was hold that the defendant was a partner.

PARTNERSHIP AND OTHER ASSOCIATIONS

Partnership and Joint Hindu Family

In Hindu law, a business is as heritable as any other property. A Hindu joint family which carries on a trade inherited from its ancestors is called Hindu joint family firm. A person becomes entitled to a share in the family business by birth or adoption. He becomes a joint owner of the business and not a partner. Such joint ownership is created by law and is governed by the Hindu law. The difference between the two are as under :

Partnership	*Joint Hindu Family Firm*
1. *Creation :* Partnership is created by an agreement.	1. Joint Hindu Family firm is created by status (operation of law).
2. *Law :* A partnership is governed by Partnership Act.	2. It is governed by Hindu law.
3. *Registration :* The partnership firm is usually registered.	3. There is no concept of registration.
4. *Number of members :* The number of partners should not exceed ten in case of banking business and twenty in any other business.	4. There is no limit to the maximum number of members.
5. *Admission :* A new partner can be admitted only with the consent of all the existing partners.	5. A person becomes a member only by birth in the family.
6. *Female Members :* A partner may be a male or female.	6. Only the males can be the members of Joint Hindu family firm.
7. *Minor Members :* Under Sec. 30,, a minor, though cannot be a partner, can be taken in a firm for profits only.	7. In a joint Hindu Family firm,, every child of the family is its member since birth.

8. *Law of Agency :* Law of agency applies to a firm as all the partners are the agents of the firm, while the firm is the agent of all the partners.	8. On the other hand, this law does not apply to it, as all the members are not the agents of the family, only the Karta is liable to all.
9. *Liability :* Every partner is liable to unlimited extent for the debts of the firm.	9. Only Karta has unlimited liabilities. Other members or co-parceners are liable to the extent of their share in the joint family business.
10. *Death :* In a partnership, death of a partner dissolves the firm, unless otherwise agreed by the partners.	10. The death of a member of a joint family business has no effect on the firm. The firm continues with other members.
11. *Right to demand Accounts :* A partner has a right to demand and inspect the accounts of the firm.	11. A member has no right to demand the accounts of the past dealings of the family.
12. *Authority :* Partners have authority to borrow and bind other partners.	12. Only manager or Karta of the Joint Hindu family firm has an authority to borrow and bind other members.

Partnership and Co-ownership

The term co-ownership or joint ownership means that a number of persons are having the ownership of some property jointly. The following table gives the comparison between the two :

Partnership	*Co-ownership*
1. *Creation :* A partnership is created by an agreement.	1. Co-ownership may be created either by status or by agreement
2. *Transfer of Interest :* A partner cannot transfer his interest in the partnership without the consent of other partners.	2. Co-owner may transfer his interest in co-ownership without the consent of the other co-owners.
3. *Business :* To carry on business is an essential element of partnership.	3. Co-ownerships may exist without carrying on any business.
4. *Object :* The primary object of partnership is to earn profits.	4. In co-ownership, it is not necessary.
5. *Profits :* An agreement to share profits is an essential element of partnership.	5. The co-ownership may have interest without doing any business and sharing profits does not arise.
6. *Agency :* Partners are agents of one another.	6. One co-owner is not the agent of the other.
7. *Lien :* A partner has a lien on the property of the firm owned in common.	7. Co owner has no lien on the property owned in common.
8. *Number of members :* The number of partners is limited to 20 and banking business to 10.	8. In co-ownership, there is no such limit on the number of co-owners.
9. *Right of Partition :* It is not possible.	9. A co-owner may ask for the partition of the property under co-ownership.

Distinction between a partnership and a company, incorporated under the Companies Act is as follows :

Partnership	*Company*
1. *Registration :* Registration of a firm is not compulsory under the Partnership Act.	1. Registration of a company is compulsory under the Companies Act.
2. *Legal Status :* A partnership firm has no existence apart from its members.	2. A company has a separate legal existence of its own and is considered a separate person from its members.
3. *Membership :* Minimum number of persons is 2 and maximum is limited to 10 in case of banking business and 20 in general business.	3. In the case of public Company minimum members required are 7 and maximum is unlimited. In case of private company minimum is 2 and maximum is limited to 50.
4. *Liability :* Every partner has an unlimited liability : he is also personally liable for all the debts of the firm.	4. Liability of a shareholder is limited to the extent of unpaid amount of shares.
5. *Management :* A partnership firm is managed by the partners themselves.	5. Board of Directors who are elected from among the members of company are only entitled to conduct the business of a company.
6. *Duration :* Partnership has no perpetual existence. It is dissolved on the death or insolvency of any one partner.	6. Company has perpetual existence. It is not dissolved on the death or insolvency of shareholder.
7. *Profit :* Partners get a share of profits out of the profits of the firm.	7. Shareholders of a company get dividend on the shares held by them.
8. *Transfer of Interest :* A partner cannot transfer his interest without consent of all other partners.	8. Shares are freely transferable.
9. *Law of Agency :* Every partner is an agent of the firm and the firm is also an agent of each of its partners.	9. Neither the company is an agent of its members nor any member is the agent of the company.
10. *Contractual Capacity :* Partners can contract with other partners but not with the firm as a whole.	10. The shareholder of a company can enter into contracts with the company.
11. *Property :* Property of the firm is the property of partners. —joint owners.	11. Property belongs to the company. shareholders are not joint owners.
12. *Audit :* The audit of the accounts of the firm is not compulsory.	12. Accounts of a company must be audited by an auditor.
13. *Creditors :* Creditors of the firm are also the creditors of the partners individually.	13. Creditors are only the creditors of the company and not of individual share-holders.
14. *Formation :* A partnership is governed by the partnership Act and the formation of firm is easy.	14. A company is governed by the Companies Act and has to observe a number of legal formalities for its formation.
15. *Dissolution :* A firm may be dissolved at any time by any partner.	15. It comes to an end only when it is wound up according to the provisions of Companies Act.

Partnership and Club

A club is an association of a peculiar nature. The objective of such an organisation is not the acquisition of profits, but the promotion of some beneficial or social objects, such as promotion of health or providing creation for its members. It, therefore, differs from partnership on the following points :

Partnership	*Club*
1. *Number of membership* : There cannot be more than 10 members in case of banking companies and 20 in case of other general business.	1. There is no limit on the number of membership.
2. *Business* : The main object of partnership firm is to carry on business.	2. The club has no object to carry on business.
3. *Liability* : All the partners are severally and jointly liable for the debts of the firm.	3. Members have no such liability for the debts of the club.
4. *Profit* : Partnership is formed to share the profit among the partners.	4. The club is not formed with the object to earn profit and share it among its members.
5. *Management* : All the partners are entitled to participate in the management of partnership business.	5. The management of a club or an association is usually vested in an executive body.
6. *Law* : Partnership is governed by Indian Partnership Act and Indian Contract Act.	6. Club or society is governed by its bye-laws and by the Societies Registration Act 1860.

WHO CAN BE A PARTNER?

1. *Person*

According to Sec. 11 of the Indian Contract Act, every person who is of the age of majority according to law to which he is subject to and who is of sound mind and is not disqualified from contracting by any law to which he is subject, is competent to become a partner. The term 'person' does not include a partnership firm or a limited Company. For instance, a firm A cannot form a partnership with firm B. But all the partners of firm A and all the partners of firm B can form single partnership, subject to the rules regarding the number of partners.

2. *Minor*

A minor cannot be a partner. Sec. 30 (1) lays down that "A person who is a minor according to the law to which he is subject may not be a partner in a firm, but with consent of all the partners for the time being, he may be admitted to the benefits of partnership."

3. *Lunatic*

A person who is of unsound mind cannot become a partner.

4. *Alien Enemy*

An alien enemy cannot enter into a contract of partnership though an alien friend can do so.

5. *Company*

A corporation being an artificial person can neither become a partner nor can it enter into a partnership agreement.

6. *Woman*

A woman, married or unmarried, can be a partner.

7. *Insolvency*

When the partner of a firm is adjudicated an insolvent, he ceases to be a partner from the date on which the order of adjudication was passed by the court.

SOME DEFINITIONS

An act of a firm [Sec. 2 (a)] : This means any act or omission by any or all partners of the firm which gives rise to a right enforceable by or against the firm.

Business [Sec. 2 (b)] : This includes every trade, occupation and profession.

Prescribed [Sec. 2 (c)] : This means prescribed by rules made under this Act.

Third party [Sec. 2 (d)] : means any person who is not a partner in the firm.

Expressions Defined in Indian Contract Act : [Sec. 2(a)] : All the expressions defined in the Indian Contract Act 1872 but not defined in the Indian Partnership Act 1932 have the same meaning in Partnership Act, as have been assigned by the Indian Contract Act 1872.

Firm Name : Persons who have entered into partnership with one another are called collectively 'a firm'. The name under which the partners carry on their business is called the 'firm name'. The partners of a firm may carry on business under any name and style which they please to adopt. The name adopted should not be such as will mislead the public into confusing them with a firm of repute already in existence. Further Sec. 58 (3) provides that a firm name shall contain any of the following words, namely :

"A firm name shall not contain any of the following words, namely, Crown, Emperor, Empire, Imperial, King, Queen, Royal or words expressing or implying the sanction, approval or patronage of Government or the Crown Representative, except when the State Government signifies its consent to the use of such words as part of the firm name by order in writing."

A' firm' is not a separate legal entity distinct from its members. It is merely a collective name of the individuals composing it. As a matter of fact, the assets of the firm are the joint property of the partners. Legal position of a firm is that it has no independent existence apart from its members. A firm as such is not an entity in law and is not 'a person' within the meaning of Section 4 of Indian Partnership Act 1932. A partnership firm cannot be distinguished from its partners. The rights, duties and obligations of a firm are actually the rights, duties and obligations of the persons who own the firm. The legal position of a firm is that it cannot possess property and, therefore, it cannot be a debtor or a creditor.

Partnership Property (Sec. 14)

The term 'Partnership Property' may be defined as the joint property of all the partners as opposed to their personal property. According to Sec. 14, "The property of the firm includes all property and right and interest in property (*i*) originally brought into the stock of the firm, or (*ii*) acquired, by purchase or otherwise, by or for the firm, or for the purposes and in the course of the business of the firm and, includes also (*iii*) the goodwill of the business."

Property of the firm is, therefore, deemed to include :

1. Property originally brought into the firm by the partners and the interest on such assets.
2. Property acquired by the firm subsequent to the formation.
3. Property acquired for the purpose of the business by one or more of the individual partners in the course of the business partnership.
4. Goodwill of the firm.

Further Sec. 14 (para 2) provides that, "Unless the contrary intention appears, property and rights and interests in property acquired with money belonging to the firm are deemed to have been acquired for the firm."

Application of the Property of the Firm (Sec. 15)

Sec. 15 lays down that, "Subject to contract between the partners, the property of the firm shall be held and used by the partners exclusively for the purpose of the business."

The partnership property belongs to all partners, and so a partner cannot directly or indirectly use the property of the firm for his own private purposes, or try to get any advantage because of his connection with the firm, and if any such advantage is derived by him, he must account for the same and pay it to the firm [Sec. 16 (*a*)]

Goodwill

The Act specially provides that goodwill of the firm is partnership property. The term 'goodwill' is not defined in the Partnership Act. Goodwill represents business reputation. It is more commercial term rather than legal term. In general terms "goodwill is the value of the reputation and good connections which a firm has maintained over a period as a result of its honesty, integrity, efficient service to the customers, quality of its products, trade and industry."

In Trego Vs. Hunt (1896), Lord Macnaughten defines goodwill, "the advantage which is acquired by a business, beyond the mere value of its capital, stock, fund and property employed therein, in consequence of the general public patronage and encouragement which it receives from constant and habitual customers."

In Churton Vs. Douglas, goodwill has been defined, "Goodwill, must mean every advantage ... that has been acquired by the old firm in carrying on its business, whether connected with the premises in which the business was previously carried on, or with the name of the late firm, or with any other matter carrying with it the benefit of the business." Goodwill is very important and valuable asset of the firm, even if one cannot touch or see it. It is an intangible asset which results in higher profits due to good reputation of the firm. It is part of the partnership property in which all the partners are jointly interested, and can be sold either separately or alongwith other property of the firm. [Sec. 55(1)].

FORMATION OF PARTNERSHIP

A partnership is based on an agreement. It is created by contract only and not by status or operation of law. The agreement may either be express or implied. The essence of partnership is mutual trust and confidence. There must be free and genuine consent of the parties who must be competent to contract. With a view to carrying on the partnership for long time and to avoid any differences among the partners in future, it is essential that all the terms and conditions of partnership are agreed upon. An oral agreement may be alright till the going is normal : but in times of adversity, there may be dispute among the partners. Therefore, it is in the interest of the partners that the agreement must be in writing. The document in which the respective rights and obligations of the members of a partnership are set forth is called a "Partnership Deed". It should be drafted with care and be signed by all the partners. It must be stamped in accordance with the Indian Stamp Act. Each partner should have a copy of the Deed. The firm should be registered and a copy of the Deed should be filed at the time of registration with the Registrar of Firms because in the absence of such registration partners cannot enforce the conditions laid down in the Deed through a court of law.

PARTNERSHIP DEED

The contents of a partnership deed apply only to the partners of the firm. No other party is supposed to abide by the contents of the deed. It is prepared only with the object of resolving the mutual differences among the partners. Though a partnership deed differs from business to business depending upon its nature. The usual contents of deed of partnership are enumerated below :

1. Date of the agreement;
2. Name and address of the firm;
3. Name and address of the partners;
4. Nature of the business;
5. Duration of partnership;
6. Capital invested by each partner;
7. Ratio to divide profits and loss of the firm;
8. Period of accounting year;
9. Appointment of auditor and his remuneration.;
10. Drawing by partners and interest thereon;
11. Interest on Capital;
12. Salary, commission etc., if any, payable to partners;
13. Duties, functions and powers of partners;
14. Interest on advances made by partners;
15. Rules regarding admission, retirement, death;
16. Method of valuation of goodwill;
17. Restrictions, if any, on partners.
18. Relinquishment of partner from the firm;
19. Circumstance under which the firm will stand dissolved;
20. Arbitration in case of dispute among the partners; etc.

TYPES OF PARTNERSHIPS

Partnerships can be classified as below :

1. *Partnership at Will* (Sec. 7)

Sec. 7 lays down that, "Where no provision is made by contract between the partners for the duration of their partnership, or for the determination of their partnership, the partnership is "partnership at will". It is a partnership for an indefinite period. Thus the following two conditions are to be fulfilled in order that a partnership is at will :

(*a*) Where there is no contract between the partners for the duration of their partnership.

(*b*) Where there is no provision in the contract for the determination of the partnership.

In other words, the partners do not fix any term of partnership and can be put an end at the will of any one of the partners. Such a partnership is terminated by giving notice in writing to all the partners by the one desiring to dissolve the firm. Sec. 43 (1) lays down, "Where the partnership is at will, the firm may be dissolved by any partner giving notice in writing to all the other partners of his intention to dissolve the firm."

Further Sec. 43 (2) lays down that, "The firm is dissolved as from the date mentioned in the notice as the date of dissolution or, if no date is so mentioned, as from the date of the communication of the notice."

2. *Particular Partnership* (Sec. 8)

Sec. 8 lays down that, "A person may become a partner with another person in particular adventures or undertakings." Such a partnership is known as particular partnership. On completion of such an adventure, the partnership comes to an end. It is formed for a particular period or for a specific venture, for instance, construction of particular building dissolved at the expiry of the fixed term or on the completion of the venture [Sec. 42 (*b*)]. If it is continued after the completion of that adventure for which it was entered into, it becomes a partnership at will.

3. *Partnership for a Fixed Term*

It is a type of partnership in which its duration is fixed, *i.e.*, for a fixed period. This type of partnership comes to an end, when the fixed term expires. If the partners carry on the business even after the expiry of the term, it becomes the partnership at will. The partners continue to assume the same rights and duties as they were having before the expiry of the fixed term.

CLASSES OF PARTNERS

Partners of a firm may be of different types. Some important types of partners are given below:

1. *Actual or Active Partner*

A person who becomes a partner by an agreement and is engaged in the actual conduct of the business of the firm, is called the actual or active or ostensible partner. An active partner has authority to bind the firm and the other partners for the acts done by him in the ordinary course of business. And an active partner and all other partners are liable to third parties for all the acts done by him. In case of his retirement, he must give public notice.

2. *Sleeping or Dormant Partner*

A sleeping or inactive partner is one who does not take part in the conduct of business of the firm. He is a partner, who is not known to the outside world. He contributes his share of capital. He enjoys his share of profit out of the profits of the firm and bears share of its losses. He is like an undisclosed principal. He is also liable to third parties for all the acts of the firm. Liability of such partner comes to an end at the time of his retirement. And he is not required to give public notice of his retirement.

3. *Nominal Partners*

A nominal partner is one who has no real interest in the business. He lends his name as one of the partners in the firm. He does not contribute any capital. He does not take part in the conduct of the partnership business. He is known to the public as a partner. He is not entitled to share the profits of the firm. But he is liable to third parties for all the acts of the firm.

4. *Partner in Profits only*

'A partner in profits only' is one who shares the profits of the firm but does not contribute to its losses. Such partner has no interest in the management of the firm. He contributes capital. Like any other type of partner, his liability for the acts of the firm is unlimited.

5. *Sub-partner*

A sub-partner is one who shares the profits of another partner. When a partner agrees to share his profits in a firm with a third person, that third person is called a sub-partner. A sub-partner is not a partner in the original firm. He has no right against the firm. He is not liable for the firm. He can claim agreed share of profits from the contracting partner only.

6. *Partner by Estoppel or Holding Out* (Sec. 28)

A partner by estoppel is one who represents himself to be a partner in the firm, but in reality he is not so. This kind of partner is not a real partner of the firm but "by words spoken or written or by conduct, represents himself, or knowingly permits himself to be represented, to be a partner in a firm." Such a person automatically becomes liable as a partner in that firm to anyone who gives credit to the firm on the faith of such a representation. Sec. 28 lays down that, "Anyone who by words spoken or written or by conduct represents himself or knowingly permits himself to be represented, to be a partner in a firm, is liable as a partner in that firm to anyone who has on the faith of any such representation given credit to the firm, whether the person representing himself or represented to be a partner does or does not know that the representation has reached the person so giving credit." In such cases, he is prevented from denying that he is not a partner. Where a retiring partner does not give a public notice of his retirement and the continuing partners still use his name as a partner, say in letter heads, he will be personally liable on the ground of holding out to third parties. But a deceased partner is an exception to this rule. [Sec. 28 (2)].

POSITION OF A MINOR IN A FIRM

According to Sec. 11 of the Indian Contract Act and the decision of the Privy Council in Mohari bibi Vs Dharamdas Ghose, a minor's agreement is altogether void and unenforceable. The relation of partnership arises from a contract. It follows that a minor cannot make a partnership. However, with the consent of all the partners, a minor may be admitted to the benefits of the partnership.

A partnership firm cannot be formed with only minor persons as partners. There must be atleast two major partners before a minor is admitted into the benefit of partnership. According to Sec. 30 (1), "A person who is a minor according to law to which he is subject may not be a partner in a firm, but, with the consent of all the partners for the time being, he may be admitted to the benefits of partnership." A new partnership cannot be formed with a minor as a partner. A minor can only be admitted to the benefits of an already existing partnership firm.

Rights and Liabilities of a Minor in a Firm

The position of a minor as a partner can be studied in two parts :

(A) *During his Minority i.e.*, position of a minor before attaining the age of majority.

(B) *On attaining Majority i.e.*, position of a minor on attaining the age of majority.

A. *Position of a Minor during his Minority*

Before his attaining majority *i.e.*, during his course of his minority, a minor has the following rights and liabilities :

Rights

1. A minor has the right to receive the agreed share of property and of profits of the firm. [Sec. 30 (2)].
2. A minor partner may have access to and inspect and copy any of the accounts of the firm. [Sec. 30(2)]. He has the right to access to the accounts only, and not to all the books of the firm.
3. Where he is not given the share of profits, he has the right to file a suit for share of the property or profit of the firm. But he can do so only if he wants to sever his connection with the firm [Sec. 30(4)].

Liabilities

1. The liability of the minor partner is confined only to the extent of his share in the profits and property of the firm. He is not personally liable for any act of the firm [Sec. 30(3)].
2. A minor cannot be declared insolvent, but if the firm is declared insolvent, his share in the firm vests in the official receiver or official Assignee.

B. *Position of a Minor on Attaining the Age of Majority*

Option of a Minor : According to Sec. 30 (5), At any time within six months of his attaining majority, or of his obtaining knowledge that he had been admitted to the benefits of partnership, whichever date is later, such person may give public notice that he has elected to become or that he has elected not to become a partner in the firm, and such notice shall determine his position as regard the firm:".

Further, as per Sec. 30, para 2, "Provided that, if he fails to give such notice, he shall become a partner in the firm on the expiry of the said six months."

The rights and liabilities of a minor partner, on attaining the age of majority may be studied under two heads : (*i*) When he elects to become a partner and (*ii*) when he elects not to become a partner.

(i) Rights and Liabilities when a Minor Elects to Become a Partner

Rights

(*i*) His share in the property and profits remains the same as was before becoming a partner.

(*ii*) His rights and liabilities will be similar to those of a full fledged partner.

(*iii*) His rights continue to be the same as they were before, till the date on which he becomes a partner.

Liabilities

(i) His liabilities continue to be the same as they were before till the date on which he becomes a partner.

(*ii*) He becomes personally liable to third parties for all acts of the firm done since he was admitted to the benefits of partnership.

(ii) Rights and Liabilities when a Minor Elects not to become a Partner

Rights

(*i*) His rights will be the same as they were before till the notice is given.

(*ii*) He shall be entitled to sue the partners for his share of property and profits.

Liabilities

(*i*) His liability will be same as it was before, till the notice is given.

(*ii*) His share of property and profits will not be liable for any acts of the firm done after the date of the notice.

Registration of Firms (Sec. 58 to 71)

Prior to the passing of Indian Partnership Act 1932, there was no provision for the registration of partnership firms in India. Registration of firm means the recording of full details of firm in the Register of Firms, kept in the office of the Registrar of Firms. Partnership Act has not made registration of firms compulsory, nor does it seek to impose any penalty for non-registration. It is optional for the firm either to get itself registered or not. The non-registration does not affect the partnership agreement or any transaction between the partners and the third party. However, indirectly the Act introduced certain disabilities which the unregistered firm has to suffer. Sec. 69 of the Act deals with such disabilities, almost every firm finds it necessary to get itself registered. Thus, indirectly partnership Act effectively ensured the registration of firms without making it compulsory. Registration does not create a partnership. This is because partnership comes into existence only by an agreement of two or more persons. Registration provides only a reliable evidence and conclusive proof of the existence of a partnership.

Mode of Registration (Sec. 58)

The procedure of registration of firm is very simple. According to Sec. 58, "The registration of a firm may be effected at any time by sending by post or delivering to the Registrar of the area in which any place of business of the firm is situated or proposed to be situated, a statement in the prescribed form and accompanied by the prescribed fee, stating :

(*a*) the firm name,

(*b*) the place or principal place of business of the firm,
(*c*) the names of any other places where the firm carries on business,
(*d*) the date when each partner joined the firm,
(*e*) the names in full and permanent addresses of the partners, and
(*f*) the duration of the firm."

"The statement shall be signed by all the partners or by their agent specially authorised in this behalf." (Sec. 58 (1)). It shall also be verified by them in the prescribed manner [Sec. 58 (2)].

Further Sec. 59 lays down that, "When the Registrar is satisfied that the provisions of section 58 have been duly complied with, he shall record an entry of the statement in a register called the Register of Firms, and shall file the statement." After this, a certificate of registration will be issued. The submission of completed application form and prescribed fee under Sec. 58 makes the registration effective.

Time of Registration

Registration may take place at any time *i.e.*, at the time of its formation or at any time thereafter. Sec. 69 (2) lays down that, "No suit to enforce a right arising from a contract shall be instituted in any Court by or on behalf of a firm against any third party unless the firm is registered and the persons suing are or have been shown in the Register of Firms as partners in the firm." That is, where the firm intends to institute a suit in a Court of law to enforce rights arising from any contract, registration must be effected before the suit is instituted, otherwise the Court shall not entertain the suit. If a firm files a suit before registration, it must withdraw the suit, get itself registered and then file a fresh suit.

Under Section 70, if any person supplies false or incomplete information, he is punishable with imprisonment extending to three months or with fine or with both.

Effects of Non-registration (Sec. 69)

The consequences of non-registration are as follows :

1. ***Suit between Partners and the Firm*** [Sec. 69 (1)]

In case any dispute arises between a partner and the firm, or among the partners, or between a partner and an ex-partner, or the dispute arises from partnership deed, or upon the rights conferred by partnership Act, a partner of an unregistered firm cannot file a suit.

2. *Suit between the Firm and Third Parties* [Sec. 69 (2)]

No suit can be filed on behalf of an unregistered firm against any third party for the purpose of enforcing a right arising from a contract. However, a suit by a third party against the firm or its partners is not prohibited.

3. *Claim of Set-off* [Sec. 69 (3)]

An unregistered firm cannot claim a set-off in a suit. (Set-off means a claim by the defendant which would reduce the amount of money payable by him to the plaintiff).

Exceptions to Non-registration of Firm

The non-registration of firm does not affect the following rights :

1. The right of the third party to sue the firm or any partner.
2. To enforce a right arising otherwise than out of contract.
3. The rights of firms or partners having no place of business in India.
4. The power of an Official Assignee or Receiver to realise the property of an insolvent partner.

5. The right to sue or claim of set off not exceeding Rs. 100 in value.
6. A partner can bring a suit for damages for misconduct against another partner.
7. Enforcement of any right to sue for the dissolution of firm.
8. Suit for accounts of dissolved firm.
9. Suit for realisation of the property of a dissolved firm.
10. The right of a partner of a firm to refer a dispute to an arbitration.

THEORETICAL QUESTIONS

1. What are the essentials of a partnership? (*B.Com. MS*)
2. What is partnership property? For what purposes can it be used? (*B.Com. Madurai*)
3. "A partnership comes into existence by virtue of an agreement and not by status". Comment.
4. "The law of partnership is but an extension of the law of principal and agent". Comment.
5. State classification of partners and partnership.
6. Explain the procedure for getting a partnership firm registered. When such a registration is treated as complete? What are the effects of non-registration of a firm? (*B.Com. Madurai*)
7. What are the provisions of the Indian Partnership Act with regard to the admission of a minor into the partnership? What will be his rights and liabilities during his minority and after he has attained the majority. (*B.Com. Kerala*)
8. Distinguish between a partnership and joint stock company. (*B.Com. MS*)
9. "Partnership is born out of contract and not status" Explain.
10. What is a partnership Deed? State its main contents. (*B.Com. Chennai*)
11. "The Indian Partnership Act has effectively ensured the registration of firms without making it compulsory". Comment.
12. Distinguish partnership from Joint Hindu Family business and Co-ownership. (*B.Com. Poona*)

MULTIPLE CHOICE QUESTIONS

I. Choose correct option for each of the following :

1. A partnership firm for completing a particular venture is called :
(*a*) fixed term partnership. (*b*) particular partnership.
(*c*) general partnership. (*d*) partnership at will.

2. A partnership for which no duration is fixed is known as :
(*a*) particular partnership. (*b*) partnership at will.
(*c*) fixed term partnership. (*d*) limited partnership.

3. A partner by estoppel or holding out is one :
(*a*) who by his conduct or words presents himself to be a partner of a firm although he is not.
(*b*) who knowingly permits others to represent him as a partner of the firm although he is not.
(*c*) both (*a*) and (*b*).
(*d*) neither of (*a*) and (*b*).

4. In the absence of agreement to the contrary, all the partners of the firm :
(*a*) share profits equally. (*b*) share losses equally.
(*c*) share profits and losses equally. (*d*) do not share profits.

5. The relation between partners arise :
(*a*) from a contract. (*b*) from status.
(*c*) from mutual understanding. (*d*) from legal provisions.

6. The real test of partnership is :
(*a*) business.
(*b*) agreement.
(*c*) sharing of profits.
(*d*) business to be carried on by all or any of them acting for all.

7. The Indian Partnership came into force on :
(*a*) January 1, 1932. (*b*) October 1, 1932.
(*c*) July 1, 1932. (*d*) September 1, 1932.

8. Partnership firm can be formed by :
(*a*) one major and one minor person. (*b*) two major and one minor persons.
(*c*) two or more major persons. (*d*) none of the above.

9. For the purpose of formation of partnership, most essential elements include :
(*a*) agreement and contractual capacity. (*b*) agreement and consideration.
(*c*) agreement and registration. (*d*) contractual capacity and consideration.

10. The provisions regarding maximum number of members in a partnership are given in :
(*a*) The Partnership Act. (*b*) The Companies Act.
(*c*) The Societies Registration Act. (*d*) The Co-operative Societies Act.

11. Most essential element of partnership is :
(*a*) sharing of profits and losses. (*b*) business.
(*c*) mutual agency between the partners. (*d*) contract.

12. The members of a club or association generally :
(*a*) share profits. (*b*) are mutual agents.
(*c*) have unlimited liability. (*d*) are not personally liable.

13. Partner by holding out is :
(*a*) partner of a firm without being partner of the firm for those making contract with the firm on the faith of such misrepresentation.
(*b*) partner of the firm but the outsiders do not know him as such.
(*c*) partner of a partner of a firm.
(*d*) partner of a firm but does not take part in the conduct of the business of the firm.

14. A minor can be :
(*a*) partner of the firm.
(*b*) admitted to the benefits of the partnership by the consent of majority of partners.
(*c*) sleeping partner of the firm.
(*d*) admitted to the profits of the partnership with the consent of all the partners.

15. In joint Hindu family business, all the members of the family are :
(*a*) mutual agents. (*b*) liable to third party.
(*c*) entitled to demand past accounts. (*d*) co-partners.

16. According to the Indian Partnership Act, the business means and includes every :
(*a*) occupation and profession. (*b*) business and profession.
(*c*) trade, occupation and profession. (*d*) trade and business.

17. A partnership at will may be dissolved :
(*a*) by mutual consent of the partners. (*b*) by notice by any partner to all other partners.
(*c*) by completion of the venture. (*d*) by (*a*) and (*b*) above.

18. A partnership firm formed for a fixed period, but the business of the firm is continued even after the expiry of that fixed period, the partnership will be :
(*a*) particular partnership. (*b*) general partnership.
(*c*) further fixed term partnership. (*d*) partnership at will.

19. A sub-partner is :
(*a*) a partner of the partner of a firm. (*b*) an active partner of the firm.
(*c*) a sleeping partner of the firm. (*d*) all of the above.

20. An active partner is one :
(*a*) who is an agent of other co-partners. (*b*) who shares profits of the firm.
(*c*) who is principal of all other co-partners. (*d*) All of the above.

21. A and B co-owners of some inherited firm. Now they agree to continue the business for profits. They are now :

(*a*) partners. (*b*) co-owners.
(*c*) neither (*a*) nor (*b*) above. (*d*) both (*a*) and (*b*) above.

22. A and B jointly own a car which they use for rowing on Sundays and holidays and occasionally let it out on hire and share the earnings equally. It is a —

(*a*) partnership. (*b*) co-ownership.
(*c*) partnership and co-ownership. (*d*) neither (*a*) nor (*b*).

23. A partnership firm is :

(*a*) a separate legal entity from the partners forming it.
(*b*) a collective name of all those individuals who constitute it.
(*c*) a juristic person.
(*d*) both as in clause (*a*) and (*c*).

24. Partners of two computer firms each having 12 partners combine by an agreement into one firm. The new partnership is :

(*a*) void. (*b*) illegal.
(*c*) voidable. (*d*) either (*a*) or (*b*).

25. According to Indian Partnership Act, the registration of firm is :

(*a*) essential. (*b*) compulsory.
(*c*) optional. (*d*) prohibited.

26. A and B agree to divide the profits of a business in equal shares but the loss, if any, is to be borne by A alone. The partnership agreement is :

(*a*) lawful. (*b*) void.
(*c*) illegal. (*d*) voidable.

27. A partnership at will is one :

(*a*) which is to be dissolved after one year. (*b*) which is not registered.
(*c*) where no provision is made by contract for the duration of the partnership.
(*d*) which is other than any of the above.

28. A partner of an unregistered firm can file a suit :

(*a*) against all other partners. (*b*) against the firm.
(*c*) for dissolution of the firm. (*d*) against third parties.

29. A and B, two brothers, buy hundred computer sets agreeing to share the same between them. It is a :

(*a*) partnership. (*b*) co-ownership.
(*c*) joint venture. (*d*) Hindu undivided family business.

30. The application for the registration of the partnership firm should be :

(*a*) signed by all the partners personally.
(*b*) signed by specially authorised agents for this purpose.
(*c*) signed by majority of the partners.
(*d*) signed by persons under clause (*a*) or (*b*).

31. If changes or alterations in the facts of a registered firm are not recorded with the Registrar of Firms :

(*a*) the firm will no more be a registered firm.
(*b*) changes will have effects against third parties.
(*c*) the firm will be treated as unregistered firm for the purpose of instituting a suit.
(*d*) the changes will be ineffective.

32. Any change or alteration in the facts of registered firm must be registered if it relates to :

(*a*) change in the name and address of any of the partners.
(*b*) change in the name address of the firm.
(*c*) admission of a minor to the benefits of the partnership.
(*d*) all of the above.

33. An unregistered firm can file suit :
(*a*) against others to claim set-off of any amount.
(*b*) against others for claims arising out of a contract.
(*c*) against others to enforce statutory rights.
(*d*) against the retired partner.

34. The registration of firm may be effected :
(*a*) at any time during the life of partnership firm.
(*b*) at any time after filing a suit against third party.
(*c*) after agreement by partners for dissolution of the firm.
(*d*) either (*a*) or (*c*).

35. Any application for alteration or changes in a registered firm must be filed with the Registrar of Firms :
(*a*) signed by all the partners.
(*b*) signed by all the partners or by their agents specifically authorised in this behalf.
(*c*) signed by majority of the partners.
(*d*) signed by majority of the authorised agents.

ANSWERS

1. (*b*)	**2.** (*b*)	**3.** (*c*)	**4.** (*c*)	**5.** (*a*)	**6.** (*d*)	**7.** (*b*)	**8.** (*c*)	**9.** (*a*)	**10.** (*b*)
11. (*c*)	**12.** (*d*)	**13.** (*a*)	**14.** (*d*)	**15.** (*d*)	**16.** (*c*)	**17.** (*b*)	**18.** (*d*)	**19.** (*a*)	**20.** (*d*)
21. (*a*)	**22.** (*b*)	**23.** (*b*)	**24.** (*b*)	**25.** (*c*)	**26.** (*a*)	**27.** (*c*)	**28.** (*c*)	**29.** (*b*)	**30.** (*d*)
31. (*d*)	**32.** (*d*)	**33.** (*c*)	**34.** (*a*)	**35.** (*b*)					

CHAPTER

Relation of Partners

AT A GLANCE

RELATION OF PARTNERS TO ONE ANOTHER

(Mutual relation of partners)

The relations of partners are governed by the principle of mutual agency. The essence of partnership is mutual trust and confidence. Every partner is an agent of his other partners for all matters connected with the business. Therefore, one partner has the power to bind all other partners into any amount of liability. The relation of a partnership comes into existence by an agreement between the partners, and such an agreement may provide for mutual rights and duties of the partners. Accordingly the mutual rights and duties of partners amongst themselves are governed by their own contract, which may, either be expressed or implied. The partners are free to make their own rules for the day-to-day conduct of the business of the firm. Sec. 11 lays down that, "Subject to the provisions of this Act, the mutual rights and duties of the partners of a firm may be determined by contract between the partners, and such contract may be expressed or may be implied by a course of dealing."

The partnership Act lays down two general or absolute duties on the partners regarding the conduct of the partners to one another. They are as follows :

A. ***General Duties of Partners*** (Sec. 9)

Sec. 9 lays down that, "Partners are bound to carry on the business of the firm to the greatest common advantage, to be just and faithful to each other, and to render true accounts and full information of all things affecting the firm to any partner or his legal representative." Every partner is bound by law to carry on the business of the firm to the greatest common advantage of the firm. The partners shall be just and faithful to each other and shall, give full information of all thing affecting the firm to any partner or his legal representative. Each partner should be faithful to his other partners. The mutual confidence between the partners is the life blood of the firm. Though partners are not trustees for one another, it has been held in some cases that the relationship between them is of a fiduciary character.

B. *To Indemnify* (Sec. 10)

Sec. 10 lays down that, "Every partner shall indemnify the firm for any loss caused to it by his fraud in the conduct of the business of the firm." The duty imposed by this section is absolute. Since partnership implies utmost good faith, a partner must not act fraudulently against the firm. If he does, he must make up the loss. Thus, this section encourages honesty on the part of the partners. There cannot be any contract to the contrary.

Where there is no specific agreement or the agreement is silent on some specific point, the partnership Act has provided rules in Sections 9 to 17 to govern the mutual relations of partners in regard to their rights and duties. They are as follows :

RIGHTS OF PARTNERS

1. *Right to Take Part in Business* [Sec. 12 (a)]

"Every partner has a right to take part in the conduct of the business". [Sec. 12 (a)]. This right is available to all the partners. It is based on the principle, "partnership is the common business of all the partners." Subject to a contract to the contrary, a partner may abstain from exercising this right.

2. *Right to be Consulted* [Sec. 12 (c)]

It is the right of every partner to be consulted in all matters affecting the business of the firm. Sec. 12 (c) lays down that "Any difference arising as to ordinary matters connected with the business may be decided by a majority of the partners, and every partner shall have the right to express his opinion before the matter is decided, but no change may be made in the nature of the business without the consent of all the partners." Difference of opinion over an ordinary matter may be settled by a majority of the partners. But as to important matters, concerning the nature of the business, no change may be effected without the consent of all the partners.

3. *Right to have Access to Books of Accounts* [Sec. 12 (d)]

"Every partner has a right to have access to and to inspect and copy the books of the firm." (Sec. 12 (d)). Every partner has the right to examine all the records, books and accounts of the firm. But, a minor admitted to the benefits of the partnership has only a right of access to 'accounts' and inspect and copy them, but not to "books".

4. *Right to Share Profits* [Sec. 13 (b)]

"The partners are entitled to share equally in the profits earned and shall contribute equally to the losses sustained by the firm. However, the partners may agree to share the profits in different proportions.

5. *Interest on Capital* [Sec. 13 (c)]

"Where a partner is entitled to interest on the capital subscribed by him such interest be payable only out of profits." 13(c). In the absence of an agreement, no partner is entitled to any interest on capital invested by him in the firm. However, interest which is allowed by an agreement, is payable only out of profits.

6. *Right to Interest on Advance* [Sec. 13 (d)]

"A partner making, for the purposes of the business, any payment of advance beyond the amount of capital he has agreed to subscribe, is entitled to interest thereon at the rate of 6% p.a."

7. *Right to indemnify* [Sec. 13 (e)]

"The firm shall indemnify a partner in respect of payments made and liabilities incurred by him." Every partner is an agent of the firm and as such he is entitled to be indemnified by the firm in respect of (i) payments made, and (ii) liabilities incurred by him in the ordinary and proper conduct of the firm or in emergency to save the firm from losses.

8. *Right to use Partnership Property* (Sec. 14)

Partnership property is the joint property of all the partners. Every partner has a right to see that the property is used for the purpose of partnership business and not for the personal benefit of a partner. If a partner uses the partnership property for his private purpose, he must account to the firm for the profits, which he may have earned.

9. *No New Partner to be Introduced* [Sec. 31 (1)]

"Subject to contract between the partners and to the provisions of Sec. 30, no person shall be introduced as a partner into a firm without the consent of all the existing partners."

10. *Liability before Joining* [Sec. 31 (2)]

An incoming partner will not be liable for any debts or liabilities of the firm before he became a partner, excepting by his own consent.

11. *Right to Retire* [Sec. 32 (1)]

"A partner may retire (*a*) with the consent of all the other partners, (*b*) in accordance with an express agreement by the partners, or (*c*) where the partnership is at will, by giving notice in writing to all the other partners of his intention to retire."

12. *Right not to be Expelled* [Sec. 33 (1)]

"A partner may not be expelled from a firm by any majority of the partners, save in the exercise in good faith of powers conferred by contract between the partners." A partner is entitled to remain in the firm, unless the power to expel him is conferred on the partners by the contract, and unless such power is exercised in good faith by the majority.

13. *Rights to Carry Competing Business* [Sec. 36 (1)]

"An outgoing partner may carry on a business competing with that of the firm and he may advertise such business, but subject to contract to the contrary, he may not (*a*) use the firm name, (*b*) represent himself as carrying on the business of the firm, and (*c*) solicit the custom of persons who were dealing with the firm before he ceased to be a partner."

14. *Right after Retirement* (Sec. 37)

A retired partner or his legal heir, in case, he has not been paid his share out of the estate of the firm, has the right to share the profits earned by the firm or to charge interest at the rate 6% p.a. on his unpaid amount.

DUTIES OF PARTNERS

All the duties of the partners are based on the principle of "good faith". The partners are supposed to act with utmost good faith and mutual understanding. The fundamental duties are in Sec. 9 which reads : "Partners are bound to carry on the business of the firm to the greatest common advantage, to be just and faithful to each other, and to render true accounts and full information of all things affecting the firm to any partner or his legal representative." The other duties are summed up as under :

1. *To Work for Common Advantage* (Sec. 9)

Every partner is bound to carry on the business of the firm to the greatest common advantage. Every partner must use his knowledge and skill for the benefit of the firm and not for his personal gain.

2. *To be Just and Faithful* (Sec. 9)

Every partner should act in good faith and he should be just and faithful in his dealings with the other partners. One should not try to make secret profits, for himself, at the expense of the firm.

3. *To Render True Accounts* (Sec. 9)

Every partner must render true and proper accounts to his copartners. Each partner must be ready to explain the accounts of the firm and produce vouchers in supports of the entries.

4. *Duty to Give Full Information* (Sec. 9)

In a firm all partners are agents of one another. Every partner must give full information of all things affecting the firm to his copartners. Law of agency provides that knowledge to the agent is deemed to be knowledge to the principal.

5. *To Indemnify for Fraud* (Sec. 10)

"Every partner shall indemnify the firm for any loss caused to it by his fraud in the conduct of the business of the firm." A partner can cause loss to the firm by his neglect or want of skill or omission etc., while acting in the ordinary course of business. It is the duty of every partner to make good the loss suffered by the firm due to his fraud.

6. *Duty to Attend diligently* [Sec. 12 (b)]

"Every partner is bound to attend diligently to his duties in the conduct of the business."

7. *Not to Claim Remuneration* [Sec. 13(a)]

"A partner is not entitled to receive remuneration for taking part in the conduct of the business." This is, however, subject to an agreement to the contrary, *i.e.* there may be an agreement to the contrary, *i.e.* there may be an agreement which may provide for remuneration to the partners.

8. *Duty to Share Loss* [Sec. 13 (b)]

"The partners are entitled to share equally in the profits earned, and shall contribute equally to the losses sustained by the firm; Sharing profits necessarily implies sharing of losses also.

9. *To Account for Secret Profit* [Sec. 16 (a)]

"If a partner derived any profit for himself from any transaction of the firm, or from the use of the property or business connection of the firm or the firm name, he shall account for that profit and pay it to the firm." An agent cannot make any profit out of the agency business without the knowledge of his principal. A partner is an agent of the firm.

Example : *Bentley Vs. Craven* (1853)

A and B were partners. B was appointed to buy sugar for the firm. Without the knowledge of A, he supplied his own sugar to the firm at the market price and made a large profits. It was held that the firm was entitled to those profits and A must account to the firm for the profits.

10. *To Account for Profits of Competing Business* [Sec. 16 (b)]

"If a partner carries on any business of the same nature as and competing with that of the firm, he shall account for and pay to the firm all profits made by him in that business."

> **Example :** *Loch Vs. Lynam* (1854)
>
> A and B were partners in a firm. The firm was carrying on business of supplying meat to the Government. Subsequently, it was found that B was also engaged with some other persons in supplying meat to the Government, and thus earned personal profits. It was held that B was bound to account to the firm for profits so made by him.

11. *Duty to Use Partnership Property Exclusively for the Firm* (Sec. 15)

"Subject to contract between the partners, the property of the firm shall be held and used by the partners exclusively for the purposes of the business."

> **Example :** *Gardner Vs. Mccutcheon* (1842)
>
> A and B owned a ship under a partnership. A made considerable personal profits by making various contracts. It was held that A was liable to account for such profits as these were made from the use of partnership property. It is the duty of every partner to use partnership property strictly for the business of the firm. A partner cannot use such property for his own use.

12. *Duty to Act within Authority* [Sec. 19(1)]

Every partner is bound to act within the scope of the actual authority conferred upon him. Where he exceeds his authority, he shall have to compensate the other partners for any ensuing loss, unless they ratify his act.

13. *Not to Assign his Rights* (Sec. 29)

It is the duty of a partner not to assign his rights and interests in the firm to an outsider so as to make him the partner of the firm. He may, however, assign his share in the profits and share in the assets of the firm. But the transferee will not be entitled to take part in the business of the firm, but the share of profits only.

14. *Duty in case of Emergency* (Sec. 21)

"A partner has authority, in an emergency, to do such acts for the purpose of protecting the firm from loss as would be done by a person of ordinary prudence, in his own case, acting under similar circumstances, and such acts and bind the firm."

15. *To be Liable Jointly and Severally* (Sec. 25)

"Every partner is liable, jointly with all the other partners and also severally, for all acts of the firm done while he is a partner."

Rights and Duties of Partners after a Change (Sec. 17)

When a change occurs in the constitution of the firm and yet it carries on business, the partners continuing in the business will, in the eye of law, form a new and different firm. It is called a "reconstituted firm". Section 17 of the Act has laid down the rights and duties of partners in the reconstituted firm as follows :

(*a*) *After a change in the firm :* "Where a change occurs in the constitution of a firm, the mutual rights and duties of the partners in the reconstituted firm remain the same as they were immediately before the change, as far as may be" [Sec. 17 (a)].

(*b*) *After the Expiry of the Term of the Firm :* "Where a firm constituted for a fixed term continues to carry on business after the expiry of that term, the mutual rights and duties of the partners remain the same as they were before the expiry, so far as they may be consistent with the incidents of partnership at will :" [Sec. 17 (b)].

(*c*) *Where Additional Undertaking are Carried Out* : "Where a firm constituted to carry out one or more adventures or undertakings carries out other adventures or undertakings, the mutual rights and duties of the partners in respect of the other adventures or undertaking are the same as those in respect of the original adventures or undertakings." [Sec. 17(c)].

RELATION OF PARTNERS WITH THIRD PARTIES

"Every partner is liable, jointly with all the other partners and also severally, for all acts of the firm done while he is a partner." (Sec. 25). This section is supported by Sec. 43 of the Contract Act which declares that joint promises of every kind create a joint and several obligation in the absence of express agreement to the contrary. Sec. 2(a) defines an "act of a firm" as "any act or omission by any partner or agent of the firm which gives rise to a right enforceable by or against the firm."

Each partner is both a principal and an agent for the other and each is bound by the other's contract in carrying on the trade. Sec. 18 lays down that "Subject to the provisions of this Act, a partner is the agent of the firm for the purpose of the business of the firm." Therefore, even if only one partner acts on behalf of the firm, the third party can make all the partners of the firm liable. Since the firm, not being a legal entity, cannot act by itself, the liability of the firm to third parties is essentially the liability of the partners for the acts done by them, for and on behalf of the firm. A partner can act on behalf of the firm and bind the firm provided: (*a*) he does the act for carrying on, in the usual way, business of the kind, carried on by the firm; and (*b*) the act is done in the name of the firm. One partner can make other partners liable towards the third parties only if he acts within the scope of his express or implied authority.

EXPRESS AUTHORITY OF A PARTNER

When a Partner is expressly authorised by an agreement of all the partners to do certain acts on behalf of the firm, it is called express authority of a partner. The firm is bound by all acts done by a partner by virtue of any express authority given to him.

IMPLIED AUTHORITY OF A PARTNER

This kind of authority may be derived by either of the following : (*a*) usage, (*b*) custom of trade, (*c*) Conduct of the partner and (*d*) statute (Act and rules). An implied authority of a partner can be inferred from the circumstances of the case. Sec. 19 (1) lays down that "Subject to the provisions of Section 22, the act of a partner which is done to carry on, in the usual way, business of the kind carried on by the firm, bind the firm. The authority of a partner to bind the firm conferred by this section is called "Implied authority." The firm will be liable only if the following conditions are fulfilled :

1. The act done by the partner must relate to the normal business of the firm.
2. The act must be such as is done within the scope of the business of the firm in the usual way.
3. The act must be done in the name of the firm or in any other manner expressing or implying an intention to bind the firm.
4. The act done must state that it has been done in the capacity of an agent of other partners.

The implied authority of a partner is linked with the nature of the business and usual manner of carrying it. The business of one partnership differs from that of the other and the requirements in the case of even the same type of business differ. In a trading partnership firm, a partner may carry on, on behalf of the firm, usual commercial activities like, buying and selling of goods, receiving and giving payments, employing servants for the firm, borrowing money etc. But in a non-trading organisation, a partner has no implied power to borrow, pledge etc., though he may sign cheques.

ACTS WITHIN THE IMPLIED AUTHORITY

The following acts of a partner are included within the scope of the implied authority of a partner :

1. To purchase goods of the kind that are used in the business of the firm.
2. To sell the goods on behalf of the firm.
3. To engage servants to perform the business of the firm.
4. To receive payment of the debts due to the firm and give receipts for the same.
5. To settle the accounts with the persons dealing with the firm.
6. To draw, accept, endorse bills of exchange or any other negotiable instruments.
7. Pledging the firm's property as security for loan etc.

(The implied powers have not been mentioned in the Act)

ACTS OUTSIDE THE IMPLIED AUTHORITY

Certain restrictions are imposed on the implied authority of a partner. Sec. 19 (2) lays down the following limitations as regards implied authority of a partner which will not bind the firm. These restrictions are two types : (1) Statutory Restrictions and (2) Restrictions imposed by the Partnership Deed.

1. *Statutory Restrictions* [Sec. 19 (2)]

The following are the subjects for which a partner does not have implied authority :

(*a*) To submit a dispute relating to the business of the firm to arbitration,

(*b*) to open a banking account on behalf of the firm in his own name,

(*c*) to compromise or relinquish any claim or portion of a claim by the firm,

(*d*) to withdraw a suit or proceeding filed on behalf of the firm,

(*e*) to admit any liability in a suit or proceeding against the firm,

(*f*) to acquire immovable property on behalf of the firm,

(*g*) to transfer immovable property belonging to the firm, or

(*h*) to enter into partnership on behalf of the firm.

The firm will not be bound by these restricted acts of a partner whether or not the person dealing with the firm knew about the restrictions.

2. *Restrictions Imposed Partnership Deed*

Sec. 20 lays down that "The partners in a firm may, by contract between the partners, extend or restrict the implied authority on any partner."

Further, second para of Sec. 20 states "Notwithstanding any such restriction, any act done by a partner on behalf of the firm which falls within his implied authority binds the firm, unless the person with whom he is dealing knows of the restriction or does not know or believe that partner to be a partner." When an act is by a partner on behalf of the firm for which his implied authority has been restricted by a contract between the partners, such act binds the firm vis-a-vis third party notwithstanding any such restrictions, unless the third party notwithstanding any such restrictions, unless the third party has the knowledge of the restriction.

Partner's Authority in an Emergency (Sec. 21)

"A partner has authority, in an emergency, to do all such acts for the purpose of protecting the firm from loss as would be done by a person of ordinary prudence, in his own case, acting under similar circumstances, and such acts bind the firm."

Effects of Admission by Partner (Sec. 23)

"An admission or representation made by a partner concerning the affairs of the firm is evidence against the firm, if it is made in the ordinary course of business."

Effect of Notice to Acting Partner (Sec. 24)

"Notice to a partner who habitually acts in the business of the firm of any matter relating to the affairs of the firm operates as notice to the firm, except in the case of a fraud on the firm committed by or with the consent of that partner." Thus a notice to an active partner is the sufficient notice to the firm. Once a notice is served on an acting partner, other partners cannot plead ignorance of the same.

LIABILITY OF PARTNERS TO THIRD PARTIES

The liability of partners to third parties may be divided into three categories :

1. *Liability of a Partner for Acts of the Firm* (Sec. 25)

"Every partner is liable, jointly with all the other partners and also severally, for all acts of the firm done while he is a partner." Liability of all the partners is unlimited. A creditor can sue all partners together or can sue them separately. As between the partners, the liability is adjustable according to the terms of the partnership agreement.

2. *Liability of the Firm for Wrongful Acts of a Partner* (Sec. 26)

"Where, by the wrongful act or omission of a partner acting in the ordinary course of the business of a firm, or with the authority of his partners, loss or injury is caused to any third party, or any penalty is incurred, the firm is liable therefor to the same extent as the partner."

3. *Liability of Firm for Misapplication by Partners* (Sec. 27)

"Where : (*a*) a partner acting within the scope of his apparent authority receives money or property from a third party and misapplied it, or (*b*) a firm in the course of its business receives money or property from a third party, and the money or property is misapplied by any of the partners while it is in the custody of the firm, the firm is liable to make good the loss."

Incoming and Outgoing Partners (Reconstitution of a firm)

Reconstitution of a firm means a readjustment in the relationship between the partners. A firm is a collection of partners. It has no independent legal existence. If there is a change in the number or status of partners, the firm is said to be reconstituted. Whenever, there is change in the constitution, there is necessarily a change in the partnership relation, however, the firm continues as a new firm or a reconstituted firm. A firm may be reconstituted in any of the following ways :

1. Introduction of a new partner [Incoming partner (Sec. 31)]
2. Retirement of a partner [outgoing partner (Sec. 32)]
3. Expulsion of a partner (Sec. 33)
4. Insolvency of a partner (Sec. 34)
5. Death of a partner (Sec. 35)
6. Transfer of a partner's interest (Sec. 29)

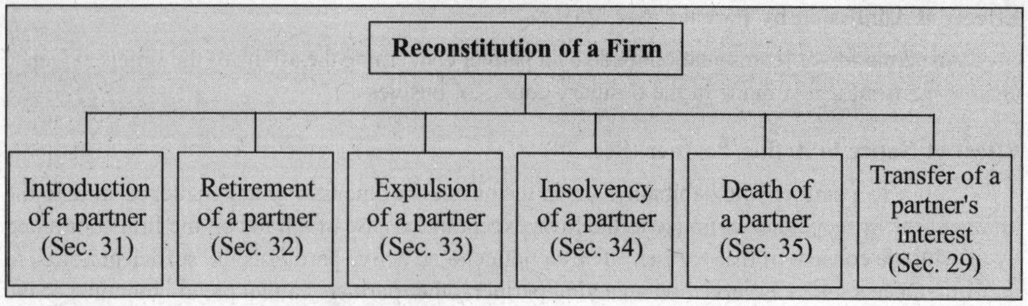

1. *Introduction of a Partner* (Sec. 31)

"No person shall be introduced as a partner into a firm without the consent of all the existing partners." [Sec. 31 (1)]. Mutual confidence and trust among the partners being an essential ingredient of an ideal partnership, it is very much natural that there must be a consent of all the partners to the introduction of a new partner, unless the partners have already agreed otherwise.

LIABILITIES OF INCOMING PARTNER

(*i*) Sec. 31 (2) lays down that, "Subject to the provisions of Sec. 30, a person who is introduced as a partner into a firm does not thereby become liable for any act of the firm done before he became a partner." He cannot be held liable for the acts of the old firm.

(*ii*) The new partner may be made liable for the past liabilities of the firm by mutual agreement. But it does not give right to the creditors of the firm to sue the new partner for the recovery of their debts, because of 'absence of privity of contract'.

(*iii*) He is liable for the acts of the old firm only if :

(*a*) The new firm assumes the liabilities of the old firm, and

(*b*) The creditors accept the new firm as their debtors to discharge the old firm from its liability.

2. *Retirement of a Partner* (Sec. 32)

A partner is said to retire when the surviving partners continue to carry on the business of the firm, and the member retiring ceases to be a partner.

According to Sec. 32 (1), " A partner may retire :

(*a*) with the consent of all the other partners,

(*b*) in accordance with an express agreement by the partners, or

(*c*) where the partnership is at will, by giving notice in writing to all the other partners of his intention to retire."

It is the stage where one partner withdraws from the firm and the other partners continue to carry on the business of the firm without dissolution of partnership between them. Thus retiring partner ceases to be a partner and the firm becomes reconstituted without dissolution.

LIABILITIES OF A RETIRING PARTNER

1. A retiring partner continues to be liable for all the acts of the firm done before his retirement or the acts pending at the time of his retirement unless he is discharged from his liability.
2. A retiring partner with other partners at the time of retirement continues to be liable as partner to the third parties for any act done by any of the partners after retirement until public notice is given of his retirement. [Sec. 32 (3)]. It is based on the principle of Holding Out.

RIGHTS OF A RETIRED PARTNER

1. (Sec. 36) A retired partner may carry on a business competing with that of the firm, but subject to the contrary he may not;
   (*a*) use the name of the firm,
   (*b*) represent himself to carry on the business of the firm, or
   (*c*) solicit the custom of persons who were dealing with the firm before his retirement.
2. Where a partner ceases to be a partner of the firm and there is no final settlement of accounts, the retiring partner is entitled either :
   (*a*) to claim interest at the rate of 6% p.a. on the amount of his share in the property of the firm or
   (*b*) to share profits earned by the firm after retirement as may be attributable to the use of his share of property of the firm.

3. *Expulsion of a Partner* (Sec. 33)

A partner may be expelled from partnership subject to the following conditions :

(*a*) The power of expulsion should be given to the partners by an express contract between the partners.

(*b*) The power of expulsion should be exercised by majority of partners.

(*c*) The power of expulsion should be exercised in absolute good faith [Sec. 33 (1)].

All the above conditions must be satisfied before a partner is expelled from the firm. The power of expulsion of a partner should be exercised in good faith. The test of good faith may be :

(*a*) that expulsion is in the interest of the firm,

(*b*) that the partner to be expelled has been served with a notice, and

(*c*) That he has been given an opportunity of being heard or clarify his position.

The expulsion of a partner done in conformity with the above conditions, would be a regular expulsion. His rights and liabilities would be the same as those of a retiring partner.

Where the expulsion of a partner is done in contravention of the above three conditions, it will be irregular. An irregular expulsion is inoperative. In such case, the expelled partner has any one of the two remedies : (*a*) to claim reinstatement as a partner, or (*b*) to sue for his share of capital and profits in the firm.

4. *Insolvency of a Partner* (Sec. 34)

Sec. 34(1), lays down that, "Where a partner in a firm is adjudicated as insolvent he ceases to be a partner on the date on which the order of adjudication is made, whether or not the firm is thereby dissolved." If a partner is declared insolvent, he is no more a partner in the firm from the date, he is declared insolvent by the court. Whether the firm is thereby dissolved or not depends on the terms of the agreement between the partners. The effects of the insolvency of a partner in the firm are :

(*a*) He ceases to be a partner from the date of the order of adjudicating him insolvent.

(*b*) Though the firm is dissolved on the same date, other partners may decide that the firm shall continue.

(*c*) The estate of the insolvent partner is not liable for the acts of the firm done after the date of the order of adjudication.

(*d*) The firm is also not liable for any act of the insolvent partner after the date of the order as such.

5. *Death of a Partner* (Sec. 35)

Sec. 42 (*c*) lays down that, "Subject to contract between the partners, a firm is dissolved by the death of a partner." However, if the firm continues by virtue of a contract to the contrary, Sec. 35 lays down that the estate of the deceased partner will not be liable for any act of the firm done after his death. (Sec. 35). No public notice of death is required to relieve the deceased partner's estate from future liability.

6. *Transfer of a Partner's Interest* (Sec. 29)

A partner can transfer his interest in a partnership to a stranger. The transfer may be absolute or partial. The transferee, in such cases, has very limited rights over the firm.

(*a*) The transferee does not become a partner of the firm. He cannot interfere in the conduct of the business or require accounts or inspect the books of the firm.

(*b*) The transferee is entitled to receive the share of profits of the transferring partner. The transferee has to accept the account of profits agreed to by the partners.

THEORETICAL QUESTIONS

1. Discuss the rights and duties of partners between themselves. (*B.Com. Chennai*)
2. "A partner may not be expelled from a firm by any majority of the partners" Comment.
3. What is implied authority of a partner, and what its scope? (*B.Com. MS*)
4. How and when may a partner retire? What are the rights and liabilities of a retiring partner?
5. When may a partner be expelled? Discuss the rights and liabilities of an expelled partner. (*B.Com. MS*)
6. State the rights of partners towards one another. (*B.Com. Kerala*)

MULTIPLE CHOICE QUESTIONS

I. Choose correct option for each of the following :

1. In a partnership firm, the decisions can be made by rule of majority when decisions relates to :

(*a*) policy decisions. (*b*) fundamental decisions.
(*c*) ordinary routine matters. (*d*) buying and selling of property.

2. Every partner of the firm has a right to access and to inspect all the books of the firm :

(*a*) personally. (*b*) through his agent.
(*c*) through his legal representative. (*d*) either (*a*) or (*b*) or (*c*) above.

3. Generally, every partner has no implied authority :

(*a*) to borrow money on credit of the firm.
(*b*) to employ servants for the business of the firm.
(*c*) to acquire immovable property for the firm.
(*d*) to issue negotiable instruments on behalf of the firm.

4. Every partner is an agent :

(*a*) of the firm for the purposes of the business of the firm subject to a contract to the contrary.
(*b*) of the other partners for the purposes of business of the firm and other personal matters.
(*c*) of the firm for the purposes of the business and other purposes of the firm.
(*d*) of the firm for the purposes of the business of the firm though he is a sleeping partner of the firm.

5. Subject to a contract to the contrary, every partner of a firm is accountable to the firm for the profits derived for himself :

(*a*) from any transaction of the firm. (*b*) from use of property of the firm.
(*c*) from use of business connection of the firm. (*d*) from all of the above.

6. Every partner advancing money to the firm beyond the amount of capital is entitled to get interest on the amount advanced at the rate of :

(*a*) 9 per cent. (*b*) 6 per cent.
(*c*) 12 per cent. (*d*) 18 per cent.

7. Every partner of a firm generally has no right to :

(*a*) have access to all the books of the firm.

(*b*) receive remuneration for taking part in the conduct of business.
(*c*) share the profits of the firm.
(*d*) interest on advances to the firm beyond capital.

8. Every partner advancing money beyond the amount of capital is entitled to claim interest :
(*a*) out of profits of the firm. (*b*) out of capital of the firm.
(*c*) out of profits and capital of the firm. (*d*) either (*a*) or (*b*).

9. Every partner of a firm is entitled to :
(*a*) share profits and losses equally subject to a contract to the contrary between them.
(*b*) share profits and losses equally if they contribute equal amount of capital to the firm.
(*c*) share profits and losses equally if all partners take active part in the conduct of the business of the firm.
(*d*) share profits only.

10. Where a partner acts beyond his implied authority, partners :
(*a*) can ratify all his acts subsequently. (*b*) can not ratify his acts.
(*c*) can ratify only lawful acts. (*d*) cannot ratify even lawful acts.

11. Any person can be introduced as partner in the firm :
(*a*) if he is a minor.
(*b*) if all the partners give their consent.
(*c*) in accordance with the provisions of the partnership deed.
(*d*) as per clause (*b*) or (*c*) above.

12. A person may be introduced as partner in the firm :
(*a*) with the consent of all the existing partners. (*b*) with the consent of majority of the partners.
(*c*) with the consent of managing partner. (*d*) with the consent of either (*b*) or (*c*) above.

13. A new partner generally shall be liable :
(*a*) for the debts arising from the date of his admission.
(*b*) for the debts existing on the date of his admission.
(*c*) for the existing as well as subsequent debts.
(*d*) for the debts under clause (*a*) or (*c*) above.

14. Generally, all the partners of all kinds of firms have no implied authority :
(*a*) to buy and sell goods.
(*b*) to borrow money for the purposes of the firm.
(*c*) to settle accounts with persons dealing with the firm.
(*d*) to render accounts to the creditors of the firm.

15. Generally, partners have no implied authority :
(*a*) to borrow money, if the firm is a trading firm.
(*b*) to withdraw any suit filed on behalf of the firm.
(*c*) to enter into partnership on behalf of the firm.
(*d*) for both (*b*) and (*c*) above.

16. A notice given to a partner is deemed to be a notice given to the firm when the notice is given to:
(*a*) any active partner. (*b*) any minor partner.
(*c*) sleeping partner. (*d*) any of the partners.

17. When a partner does any act under his implied authority :
(*a*) he binds the firm and all its partners by them.
(*b*) he binds all the partners of the firm except sleeping partner of the firm.
(*c*) he binds partners for profit only.
(*d*) none of the above.

18. A partner of a firm has authority in an emergency :
(*a*) to take any action which he likes.
(*b*) to take any action for protecting the firm from the loss threatened by the emergency.
(*c*) to take any such action which a prudent person would under similar circumstances take.
(*d*) to take both (*b*) and (*c*) above.

19. In order to bind a firm, every partner must do the acts :
(*a*) in the name of managing partner.
(*b*) in the name of the firm.
(*c*) in the name of all the partners of the firm.
(*d*) in the name of active partners of the firm.

20. In the absence of any usage or custom of trade to the contrary, generally partner have no implied authority :
(*a*) to submit a dispute relating to the business of the firm for arbitration.
(*b*) to open a bank account on behalf of the firm in his own name.
(*c*) to settle the accounts with persons dealing with the firm.
(*d*) for (*a*) and (*b*) above.

21. A retired partner continues to be liable to third parties for the acts done by any of the partners after his retirement :
(*a*) if public notice of his retirement is not given.
(*b*) if third parties do not discharge him from his liability.
(*c*) if the other partners do not discharge him from his liability.
(*d*) in case of either (*b*) or (*c*).

22. A partner can retire from a partnership :
(*a*) with the consent of all the partners.
(*b*) in accordance with the express agreement between the partners.
(*c*) by giving notice in writing to all other partners if partnership is not at will.
(*d*) either (*a*) or (*b*).

23. A partner can generally retire from the partnership :
(*a*) with the consent of majority of partners.
(*b*) with the unanimous consent of active partners.
(*c*) by giving notice to all other partners, where the partnership is at will.
(*d*) either (*a*) or (*b*) above.

24. The public notice of retirement of a partner may be given :
(*a*) by public.
(*b*) by the retired partner.
(*c*) by any partner of the reconstituted firm.
(*d*) either by (*b*) or (*c*).

25. A retired partner continues to be liable for any act done by any of the partners until public notice is given :
(*a*) towards all the parties dealing with the firm.
(*b*) towards all the parties dealing with the firm without knowing that retired partner was a partner.
(*c*) towards all the parties who started dealing with the firm after retirement of the partner.
(*d*) towards (*b*) and (*c*) both.

ANSWERS

1. (*c*)	**2.** (*d*)	**3.** (*c*)	**4.** (*a*)	**5.** (*d*)	**6.** (*b*)	**7.** (*b*)	**8.** (*c*)	**9.** (*a*)	**10.** (*c*)
11. (*d*)	**12.** (*a*)	**13.** (*a*)	**14.** (*b*)	**15.** (*d*)	**16.** (*a*)	**17.** (*a*)	**18.** (*d*)	**19.** (*b*)	**20.** (*d*)
21. (*a*)	**22.** (*d*)	**23.** (*c*)	**24.** (*d*)	**25.** (*a*)					

CHAPTER

Dissolution of a Firm

AT A GLANCE

- Mode of Dissolution of Firm
- Consequences of Dissolution
- Rights of Partners
- Liabilities of Partners
- Mode of Settlement of Accounts
- Sale of Goodwill
- Public Notice
- Theoretical Questions
- Objective Type Questions.

Sec. 39 of the partnership Act lays down that, "The dissolution of partnership between all the partners of a firm is called the "dissolution of the firm." Dissolution of firm means a firm ceases to exist. The whole firm is dissolved and the partnership is also terminated. But dissolution of partnership involves a change in the relation of the partners and a new firm is constituted. Thus dissolution of partnership does not end partnership firm. If the partners have agreed that the death, retirement or insolvency of a partner would not dissolve the firm, then on the happening of any of these events, "partnership" would certainly come to an end, although the "firm" may continue under the same firm name.

In case of dissolution of the firm, the business of the firm is closed down, while in case of the dissolution of the partnership, the business of the firm continues, though with a change in the partners. Again, dissolution of firm means complete breakdown or extinction of the relationship of partnership between all the partners of a firm. But, dissolution of partnership involves only a change in the relation of the partners, and the business of the firm continues. So the dissolution of a partnership may or may not include the dissolution of the firm, but dissolution of the firm necessarily means the dissolution of the partnership as well.

MODE OF DISSOLUTION OF FIRM

(Sections 40 to 44)

A partnership firm may be dissolved by any of the following modes :

1. Dissolution by Agreement (Sec. 40)
2. Compulsory Dissolution (Sec. 41)
3. On the happening of certain contingencies (Sec. 42)
4. Dissolution by Notice (Sec. 43)
5. Dissolution by the court (Sec. 44)

1. *Dissolution by Agreement* (Sec. 40)

Sec. 40 lays down that, "A firm may be dissolved with the consent of all the partners or in accordance

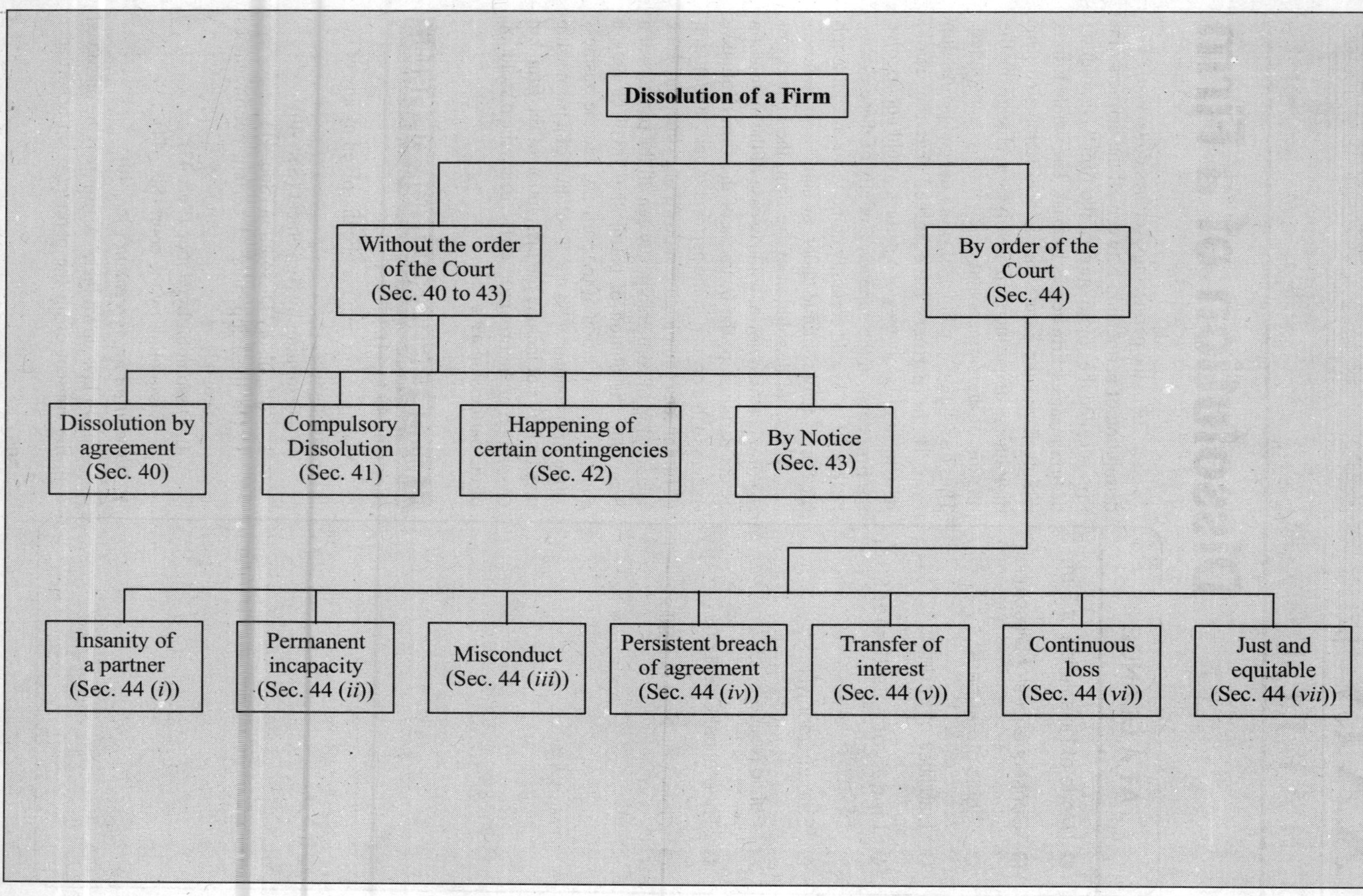
Dissolution of a Firm
Without the order of the Court (Sec. 40 to 43)
By order of the Court (Sec. 44)
Dissolution by agreement (Sec. 40)
Compulsory Dissolution (Sec. 41)
Happening of certain contingencies (Sec. 42)
By Notice (Sec. 43)
Insanity of a partner (Sec. 44 (i))
Permanent incapacity (Sec. 44 (ii))
Misconduct (Sec. 44 (iii))
Persistent breach of agreement (Sec. 44 (iv))
Transfer of interest (Sec. 44 (v))
Continuous loss (Sec. 44 (vi))
Just and equitable (Sec. 44 (vii))

with a contract between the partners." A firm may be dissolved any time with the consent of all the partners of the firm. Partnership is created by contract, it can also be terminated by contract. The contract of dissolution of the firm may be express or implied.

2. *Compulsory Dissolution* (Sec. 41)

A firm is dissolved compulsorily under the following circumstances :

(*a*) When all the partners or all the partners but one, are adjudicated insolvent. It is because of the reason that on being adjudicated insolvent a partner ceases to be the partner of the firm [Sec. 34(1)]; and if all or all but one are insolvent, the firm can no longer exist as there should be atleast two partners.

(*b*) When the business of the firm becomes unlawful due to happening of any such event. Here, it is relevant to mention that where one out of several undertakings or adventures of the firm becomes unlawful, the illegality of one or more of the undertakings or adventures of the firm will not cause the dissolution of the firm.

3. *Dissolution on Happening of Certain Contingencies* (Sec. 42)

Sec. 42 states that "Subject to contract between the partners a firm is dissolved :

(*a*) if constituted for a fixed term, by the expiry of that term;

(*b*) if constituted to carry out one or more adventures or undertakings, by the completion thereof;

(*c*) by the death of a partner; and

(*d*) by the adjudication of a partner as an insolvent."

4. *Dissolution by Notice* (Sec. 43)

Sec. 43 states that, "(1) Where the partnership is at will, the firm may be dissolved by any partner giving notice in writing to all the other partners of his intention to dissolve the firm.

(2) The firm is dissolved as from the date mentioned in the notice as the date of dissolution or, if no date is so mentioned, as from the date of the communication of the notice."

5. *Dissolution by the Court* (Sec. 44)

When there is a difference of opinion between the partners regarding the matter of dissolution, dissolution of firm by the Court is necessitated. Sometimes, a partner wants that the firm should be dissolved while others may not agree to the dissolution. In these circumstances, a partner can go to Court of Law and file a suit for dissolution of the firm. The court has the discretion to pass an order of dissolution *i.e.*, the court may or may not allow the dissolution of the firm. Accordingly, the right of approaching the court can be exercised by every partner. A partner may file a suit for dissolution of the firm on any of the following grounds, and the court may dissolve the firm, if it is satisfied :

(i) Insanity of a Partner [Sec. 44(*i*)]: When a partner becomes insane *i.e.*, unsound mind, the court may allow the dissolution of the firm. The suit for dissolution of the firm may be filed by anyone of the partners other than the partner, who has become insane or by the next friend of the insane partner. Insanity does not itself dissolve the firm. The firm can be dissolved only by an order of the court.

(ii) Permanent Incapacity of a Partner [Sec. 44(*ii*)]: Where a partner becomes permanently incapable of performing his duties as a partner, on a suit being filed by other partner, the court may order a dissolution of the firm. If incapacity is only temporary, the court will not grant dissolution.

(iii) Misconduct of a Partner [Sec. 44(*iii*)]: If a partner is guilty of conduct which is likely to affect prejudicially the carrying on of the business of the firm, the court may order dissolution. Thus, where a partner of a firm of solicitors was convicted of travelling on the railway without a ticket and with intent to defraud, dissolution was granted. The suit in such a case can only be brought by the other partners.

(iv) Persistent Breach of Agreement [Sec. 44(*iv*)]: If a partner wilfully and persistently commits breach of the partnership agreement regarding management, or otherwise conducts himself in such a way that it is not reasonably practicable for the other partners to carry on business in partnership with him, the court may order dissolution. Continuous refusal by a partner to attend to his duties in the partnership business, the fact of hostility between partners which makes cooperation between them impossible, have been held to be sufficient reasons. The suit for dissolution under this ground can be brought by a partner other than the guilty partner.

(v) Transfer of Interest [Sec. 44(*v*)]: If a partner transfers in any way, his whole interest in the partnership to a third party, or allows his share to be charged in execution of a decree against him, or allows the same to be sold for arrears of land revenue or for charges recoverable as land revenue, the court may dissolve the partnership. The transfer of a partner's interest does not by itself dissolve the firm. But the other partners may ask the court to dissolve the firm if such a transfer occurs.

(vi) Continuous Loss [Sec. 44(*vi*)]: The object of partnership is to make profit. But, where the business of a firm cannot be carried on, except at loss, the court may allow the dissolution of the firm.

(vii) Just and Equitable [Sec. 44(*vii*)]: When the court finds any other ground to be just and equitable for the dissolution of the firm, it may order the dissolution of the firm. Such instances may be mismanagement in the firm, deadlock in the management, partners not on speaking terms, quarrels among the partners, lack of cooperation amongst the partners, etc.

CONSEQUENCES OF DISSOLUTION

The rights and liabilities of partners after dissolution of firm are discussed below :

Rights of Partners on Dissolution

1. *Right of Partners to Enforce Winding up* (Sec. 46)

On the dissolution of a firm, each partner is entitled to have the property of the firm sold and proceeds applied :

(*a*) to repay outside debts and liabilities of the firm; and

(*b*) to distribute the surplus, if any, among them, in accordance with their rights.

2. *Rights to have the Debts of the Firm Settled out of the Property of the Firm* (Sec. 49)

Where there are joint debts due from the firm and also separate debts due from any partner, property of the firm shall be applied in the first instance in payment of the debts of the firm, and, if there is any surplus, then the share of each partner shall be applied in payment of his separate debts. The separate property of any partner shall be applied first in the payment of his separate debts and the surplus, if any, in the payment of the debts of the firm.

3. *Rights to Earn Personal Profit by Using Firm's Name* (Sec. 50)

Sometimes, on the dissolution of a firm, a partner buys the goodwill of the firm. In such case, he has the right to use the firm's name and earn personal profits.

4. *Return of Premium on Premature Dissolution* (Sec. 51)

Where a partner has paid a premium on entering into partnership for a fixed term, and the firm is dissolved before the expiration of that term, such a partner shall be entitled to repayment of "rateable amount of premium" for the unexpired period, except where the dissolution has been caused :

(*a*) by the death of a partner;

(*b*) by the misconduct of the partner so admitted; or

(*c*) by mutual agreement of all the partners containing no provision for the return of premium.

5. *Rights where Partnership Contract is Rescinded for Fraud etc.* (Sec. 52)

Where the partnership is rescinded on the ground of fraud or misrepresentation of one of the partners, the partner, entitled to rescind, has the following rights :

(*a*) He has a right of lien on the surplus of the assets of the firm remaining after the debts of the firm have been paid, for any sum paid by him for the purchase of a share in the firm and for capital contribution by him.

(*b*) He is entitled to rank as creditor of the firm in respect of any payment made by him towards the debts of the firm.

(*c*) He has also the right to claim indemnity from the partners guilty of the fraud or misrepresentation against all the debts of the firm.

6. *Right to Restrain from Use of Firm Name or Property* (Sec. 53)

"After a firm is dissolved, every partner or his representative may, in the absence of a contract between the partners to the contrary, restrain any other partner or his representative from carrying on a similar business in the firm name or from using any of the property of the firm for his own benefit, until the affairs of the firm have been completely wound up." But a partner who has purchased the goodwill of the firm, cannot be restrained from using the firm name.

LIABILITIES OF PARTNERS ON DISSOLUTION

1. *Liability for Acts of Partners done after Dissolution* (Sec. 45)

On dissolution of the firm, it becomes necessary to give public notice of the fact of dissolution. Sec. 45 lays down that, "Notwithstanding the dissolution of a firm, the partners continue to be liable as such to third parties for any act done by any of them which have been an act of the firm if done before the dissolution, until public notice is given of the dissolution." The principle does not apply to the case of a deceased partner, insolvent partner and retiring partner: that is, these partners are not liable for the acts done after the dissolution of the firm even if the public notice of dissolution is not given.

2. *Continuing Authority of Partners for the Purpose of Winding up* (Sec. 47)

After the dissolution of the firm the authority of each partner to bind the firm, and other mutual rights and obligations of the partners, continue so far as may be necessary for the following two purposes :

(*a*) to wind up the affairs of the firm, e.g., disposing of the property, realising amount due from debtors and paying to creditors and so on; and

(*b*) to complete transactions begun and unfinished at the time of the dissolution, *e.g.*, taking delivery of the goods ordered before dissolution and paying for them.

After dissolution, a partner cannot bind the firm in any case other than the two cases, mentioned above. A partner who has been adjudicated insolvent cannot bind the firm in any case after the order of adjudication has been passed.

Mode of Settlement of Accounts (Sec. 48)

The settlement of accounts between partners upon dissolution of a firm is to be affected in the manner provided for in the partnership agreement. In the absence of any agreement between the partners regarding the method by which accounts of the partnership are to be settled on its dissolution, the following rules stated in Sec. 48 of Act shall apply :

Sharing Deficiency

The Losses of the firm including the deficiency of capitals shall be paid : [Sec. 48(*a*)]

(*a*) First, out of profits,

(b) Next out of capital, and

(c) Lastly, if necessary, by the partners individually, in the proportion in which they were entitled to share profits.

Application of Assets [Sec. 48 (*b*)]

The assets of the firm including any sums contributed by the partners to make up losses or deficiencies of capital, shall be applied in the following manner and order :

(a) In paying the debts of the firm to the *third parties*;

(b) In paying to each partner rateably, whatever is due to him from the firm for *advances* distinguished from the capital.

(c) In paying to each partner rateably what is due to him on account of *capital*;

(d) The surplus, if any, is divided among the partners in the proportion in which they were entitled to profit. [Sec. 48 (*b*)].

If the assets are enough to pay (*a*) and (*b*) above, but insufficient to repay to each partner, his full capital, the deficiency in the capital is to be borne by the partners in the proportion to which they are entitled to share profits. As per ruling in *Garner Vs. Murray*, the deficiency of capital of the insolvent partner gets distributed among the solvent partners in the ratio of their capitals.

Rule in Garner Vs. Murray (1904)

Garner, Murray and Wilkins were partners in a firm, sharing profits and losses equally. The capital was contributed in unequal shares. There was no partnership Deed. The capital contributed by G being more than the capital contributed by M. W became insolvent. Nothing could be recovered from W. The loss due to *capital deficiency of a partner is to be borne in Capital Ratio and not in profit-sharing ratio.* That is, capital deficiency of an insolvent partner, is a capital loss and is to be shared by solvent partners, in capital ratio.

THE MAIN POINTS IN GARNER VS. MURRAY DECISION

1. Loss due to insolvency is a capital loss.
2. Such loss, due to insolvency, is to be shared by solvent partners in their capital ratio just before dissolution.
3. All solvent partners should bring in their share or realisation loss in cash.
4. If a partner's capital account shows a debit balance, he need not share the capital loss of the insolvent partner.

APPLICATION OF GARNER VS. MURRAY RULE IN INDIA

The rule of Garner Vs. Murray is applicable in India, only if :

(a) There is no agreement to the contrary.

(b) The capitals of partners are not in profit sharing ratio.

(c) There must be capital deficiency in a partner's capital account.

If there is a provision in the partnership deed as to the ratio in which losses or gains including losses arising from capital deficiency of a partner shall be borne, then the solvent partners will bear the insolvent partner's deficiency in that ratio. In the absence of any such agreement, the adjustments shall be made according to the decision in Garner Vs. Murray case. The amount left unsatisfied or unpaid by the insolvent partner has to be transferred to the capital accounts of the other partner in the ratio of their capitals just before dissolution. As regards the cash to be brought in by the solvent partners, it is only a notional entry, actually no cash is brought.

PUBLIC NOTICE

A public notice has to be given :

(1) On the retirement or expulsion of a partner from a registered firm.

(2) On the dissolution of a registered firm.

(3) On the election to become or not to become a partner in a registered firm by a minor on his attaining majority.

(a) In case of registered firms :

The public notice relating to the above matter is given :

(*i*) By notice to the Registrar of Firms under Sec. 63.

(*ii*) By publication in the Official Gazette.

(*iii*) By publication in atleast one vernacular newspaper circulating in the district where the firm to which it relates has its place or principal place of business. (Sec. 72(*a*))

(b) In case of unregistered firms

(*i*) By publication of notice in official gazette.

(*ii*) By publication of notice in atleast one vernacular newspaper. (Sec. 72(*b*))

Sale of Goodwill after Dissolution (Sec. 55)

In settling the accounts of a firm after dissolution, goodwill shall, subject to contract between the partners, be included in the assets, and it may be sold either separately or alongwith other property of the firm.

Where the goodwill of a firm is sold after dissolution, a partner may carry on a business competing with that of the buyer and he may advertise such business, but subject to agreement between him and the buyer, he may not :

(*a*) use the firm name;

(*b*) represent himself as carrying on business of the firm; or

(*c*) solicit the custom of persons who were dealing with the firm before its dissolution.

Any partner may, upon the sale of goodwill of a firm, make an agreement with the buyer that such partner will not carry on any business similar to that of the firm within a specified period or within specified local limits, such agreement shall be valid if the restrictions imposed are reasonable.

THEORETICAL QUESTIONS

1. Discuss the different modes of dissolution of a firm. (*B.Com. MS*)

2. Distinguish between 'dissolution of a firm' and 'dissolution of partnership.

3. State under what circumstances will a court dissolve a firm? (*B.Com. Kerala*)

4. What are the rights and obligations of partners after the dissolution of partnership? (*B.Com. Delhi*)

5. State the mode of settlement of accounts between partners after dissolution of the firm.

6. State the two grounds under which a firm may be compulsorily dissolved. (*B.Com. Nagpur*)

7. What is goodwill? How is it treated on the dissolution of a firm? (*B.Com. Poona*)

MULTIPLE CHOICE QUESTIONS

I. Choose correct option for each of the following :

1. According to Indian Partnership Act, the dissolution of firm means :

(*a*) dissolution of partnership between some of the partners of the firm.

(*b*) dissolution of partnership between majority of partners of the firm.

(*c*) dissolution of partnership between all the partners of the firm.

(*d*) dissolution of partnership between minority partners of the firm.

2. According to Partnership Act, a firm may be compulsorily dissolved :
(*a*) when all but one of the partners are adjudged insolvent.
(*b*) when all the business ventures of the firm but one becomes unlawful.
(*c*) in the case of (*a*) only.
(*d*) in the case of both (*a*) and (*b*).

3. A firm may be dissolved by agreement between the partners and such agreement :
(*a*) may be express.
(*b*) may be implied.
(*c*) may be either express or implied.
(*d*) may be neither express nor implied.

4. In case of dissolution of partnership firm :
(*a*) the business of the firm is closed down.
(*b*) the legal relations between all the partners come to an end.
(*c*) assets are realised and liabilities are paid off of the firm.
(*d*) happens in all the above cases.

5. A partnership firm for a fixed duration may be dissolved :
(*a*) by unanimous consent of the partners.
(*b*) by notice of any of the partners.
(*c*) by majority decision of the partners.
(*d*) by any of the above methods.

6. A partnership firm may be dissolved by notice to all the partners by any partner :
(*a*) if the partnership in for a fixed duration.
(*b*) if the partnership is at will.
(*c*) if the partnership is for a particular venture.
(*d*) if the partnership is for unlimited period.

7. A partnership firm may be dissolved by the order of the Court :
(*a*) when any partner has become of unsound mind.
(*b*) when any partners has become permanently incapable of performing his duties as partner.
(*c*) in case of (*a*) not (*b*).
(*d*) in either of both the cases under clauses (*a*) and (*b*) above.

8. A partner may file a petition for dissolution of the firm if any other partner has transferred his interest :
(*a*) to a third party.
(*b*) to any partner of the firm.
(*c*) to a son of a partner of the firm.
(*d*) in case of (*a*) or (*c*) above.

9. A partnership may be dissolved :
(*a*) on expiry of the term.
(*b*) on completion of the venture.
(*c*) death of a partner.
(*d*) in any of the above contingencies subject to a contract to the contrary.

10. In the case of partnership at will, notice of intention to dissolve the firm may be given :
(*a*) in writing.
(*b*) verbally.
(*c*) on phone.
(*d*) by video conferencing.

ANSWERS

1. (*c*) **2.** (*c*) **3.** (*c*) **4.** (*d*) **5.** (*a*) **6.** (*b*) **7.** (*d*) **8.** (*d*) **9.** (*d*) **10.** (*a*)

CHAPTER

Nature of Negotiable Instruments

AT A GLANCE

- Introduction
- Definition
- Characteristics
- Presumptions
- Promissory Note
- Bill of Exchange
- Pro-note Vs. Bill
- Cheque
- Bills Vs. Cheque
- Crossing of Cheques
- Types of Crossing
- Who may Cross a Cheque
- Classifications
- Bearer and Order Instruments
- Inland and Foreign Instrument
- Time Instrument
- Accommodation Bill
- Fictitious Bill
- Documentary and Clean Bills
- Escrow
- Ambiguous Instruments
- Inchoate Instruments
- Bills in Sets
- Payment in Due Course
- Maturity and Days of Grace
- Calculation of Date of Maturity
- Interest on Bills and Notes
- Theoretical Questions
- Multiple Choice Questions.

INTRODUCTION

The negotiable instruments are the most common credit devices, and are freely used in commercial transactions and monetary dealings. In business dealings, all transactions do not take place in terms of money. It is always not possible for a businessman to carry huge amount of cash in his pocket. Therefore, businessmen adopt a new method of exchanging documents—Bills of Exchange, Cheques etc., in place of actual currency for their day to day transactions. And such documents, which are used as a substitution for money are known as negotiable instruments. The law relating to negotiable instruments is contained in the Negotiable Instruments Act 1881. The Act is based upon the English Common Law relating to promissory notes, bills of exchange and cheques. The Act came into force on Ist March 1882. The Act extends to the whole of India.

> **Note :** Sections referred to in Chapters 25 to 27, unless otherwise stated, are the Sections of the Negotiable Instruments Act 1881.

DEFINITION

The word 'negotiable' means 'transferable by delivery', and the word 'instrument' means 'a written document by which a right is created in favour of some person'. Thus, the term "negotiable instrument" literally means "written document transferable by delivery". According to Sec. 13(1) of the Act defines a negotiable instrument to thus. "A negotiable instrument means a promissory note, bill of exchange or cheque payable either to order or to bearer." The statutory definition seems to be incomplete as it does not throw any light on the nature and characteristics of negotiable instrument. However, the Negotiable Instrument Act expressly recognises only three instruments, *viz.*, promissory note, bill of exchange and cheque as negotiable instruments.

An instrument may be negotiable by statute or by usage. Negotiable Instrument Act mentions only three kinds of negotiable instruments—Promissory Note, Bill of Exchange and Cheque. All these three are negotiable by statute. But it does not mean that there cannot be any other negotiable instruments than these three. As a matter of fact, every other document which fulfills the requirements of a negotiable instrument, is recognised by the usage or customs as negotiable instruments for example, Treasury Bills, Dividend Warrant, Bearer Debenture, Hundis, Railway Receipt, Share Warrant, Government Promissory Note etc. These have acquired the character of negotiability by custom or usage.

Justice Willis defines a negotiable instrument as "A negotiable instrument is one, the property in which is acquired by anyone who takes it bona fide, and for value notwithstanding any defect of title in the person from whom he took it."

According to Willis's definition, the person to whom the negotiable instrument is transferred becomes entitled to get the money mentioned in it. He also has the right to further transfer it to anyone he likes. As a matter of fact, a person who gets a negotiable instrument in good faith and for consideration, becomes its owner and has an unconditional right to receive the money mentioned in it.

According to Thomas, a negotiable instrument is that document, which is, by a legally recognised custom of trade or law, transferable by delivery or endorsement and delivery in such circumstances that :

(*a*) the holder of it for the time being may sue on it in his own name, and

(*b*) the property in it passes free from equities, to a bona fide transferee for value notwithstanding any defect in the title of the transferor.

CHARACTERISTICS OF A NEGOTIABLE INSTRUMENT

A negotiable instrument has the following characteristics :

1. *Freely Transferable*

No legal formalities are necessary to be complied with a transfer. The transfer confers on the transferee not only a right to possession but also right to property. An instrument payable to bearer is transferred by mere delivery. If it is payable on order, the right of ownership passes by indorsement and delivery. Whoever gets possession of the instrument becomes its owner and is entitled to the sum mentioned therein as the holder.

2. *Better Title*

A person taking an instrument bona fide and for value known as holder in due course, gets the instrument free from all defects in the title of the transferor. He is not in any way affected by any defect in the title of the transferor of any prior party. A bona fide holder for value will get a good and an independent title, even though the title of the transferor might be defective. The transferee gets a better title than that of the transferor.

3. *Right to Sue*

In case of a negotiable instrument, the transferee is capable of suing the person liable on the instrument, in his own name without any notice to him, of the notice that he has become the transferee. A holder in due course can recover the full amount on the instrument, in case of dishonour.

4. *Presumptions*

The Act has laid down certain rules of evidence, known as presumptions as to negotiable instruments. Therefore, it is not necessary for the party entitled to receive money on the instrument to prove the validity of his claim. These presumptions (Sections 118 and 119) apply to all negotiable instruments, unless contrary is proved. These presumptions are discussed later in this chapter.

5. *Credit of the Party*

A holder of a negotiable instrument expects its prompt payment because its dishonour means ruins of the credit of all the parties to it. Normally, such instruments will never be dishonoured. Moreover, a negotiable instrument is equivalent to cash as even before the date of its maturity : it can be encashed from a banker on discount.

PRESUMPTIONS OF NEGOTIABLE INSTRUMENTS

Sections 118 and 119 lay down certain presumptions to all negotiable instruments, unless the contrary is proved. In case of any disputes about these presumptions, these need not be proved by the person who holds the negotiable instrument, until contrary is proved. These are rebuttable presumptions. The party liable, proves the non-existence of presumptions, then the burden of proving them shifts to plaintiff. These presumptions, which are also known as special rules of evidence, are the following :

1. *Consideration* [Sec. 118(*a*)]

It is presumed that every negotiable instrument has been made or drawn for the consideration. Moreover, when a negotiable instrument is accepted, indorsed, negotiated or transferred, it is also presumed that it was so accepted, indorsed etc. for a consideration.

2. *Date* [Sec. 118(*b*)]

It is also a presumption under the Act, that every negotiable instrument bearing a date, was made or drawn on such date.

3. *Time of Acceptance* [Sec. 118(*c*)]

It shall be presumed that every accepted bill of exchange was accepted within a reasonable time after its date and before its maturity.

4. *Time of Transfer* [Sec. 118(*d*)]

Until the contrary is proved, it shall be presumed that every transfer of a negotiable instrument was made before its maturity.

5. *Order of Endorsement* [Sec. 118(*e*)]

Until the contrary is proved, it shall be presumed that the indorsement appearing upon a negotiable instrument were made in the order in which they appear thereon.

6. *Stamp* [Sec. 118(*f*)]

Sometimes, a negotiable instrument is lost or destroyed. In such cases it is presumed that it was duly stamped.

7. *Holder in due Course* [Sec. 118(*g*)]

The holder of a negotiable instrument is a holder in due course. But when a negotiable instrument is obtained by a person from its lawful holder by means of an offence or fraud or for unlawful consideration, the holder will have to prove that he is a holder in due course.

For this purpose, he will have to prove :

(*a*) that there was consideration for it;

(*b*) that the defect, if any, in the instrument was not known to him; and

(*c*) that he became its holder before its due date.

8. *Proof of Protest* (Sec. 119)

In a suit upon an instrument, which has been dishonoured, the court on proof of the protest, presumes the fact of dishonour, unless and until such fact is disproved.

PROMISSORY NOTE, BILL OF EXCHANGE AND CHEQUE

Promissory Note

According to Sec. 4, "A promissory note is an instrument in writing (not being a bank note or currency note) containing an unconditional undertaking signed by the maker, to pay a certain sum of money only to, or to the order of, a certain person to the bearer of the instrument."

The person who makes the promise to pay is called the MAKER. He is the debtor and must sign the instrument. The person who will get the money is called PAYEE.

The followings are the illustrations of promissory Note :

A signs instrument in the following terms :

Examples : 1. "I promise to pay B or order Rs. 500."

2. I acknowledge myself to be indebted to B in Rs. 1,000 to be paid on demand, for value received.

But, the following are NOT promissory note :

Examples : 1. Mr. B IOU Rs. 1,000.

2. "I promise to pay B Rs. 500, and all other sums which shall be due to him.

3. I promise to pay B, first deducting thereout any money which he owes me.

4. Promise to pay B Rs. 500," seven days after marriage with C.

5. Promise to pay B Rs. 500, on D's death, provided D leaves me enough to pay that sum.

6. I promise to pay B Rs. 500, and to deliver to him my black horse on Ist January next.

It is also necessary that the promissory note contain an express undertaking to pay. An implied undertaking is insufficient.

Essentials of Promissory Note

Following are the essentials of a valid promissory note :

1. *It must be in Writing*

The writing may, however, be in pencil or in ink, and includes printing or typing or engraving or lithographing.

2. *It must Contain a Promise to Pay*

It must contain an undertaking or promise to pay. A mere acknowledgment of indebtedness not accompanied by promise to pay is not sufficient. However, the use of the word promise is not essential to constitute an instrument as promissory note. It is because the phrase 'payable on demand' necessarily implies a promise to pay at once or immediately.

Example : Where A signs the instrument in the following terms : "I acknowledge myself to be indebted to B in Rs. 1,000, to be paid on demand, for value received." This is a valid promissory note.

3. *The Promise to Pay must be Unconditional*

It must contain definite and an unconditional undertaking to pay. Promise to pay should be unconditional. A conditional instrument is invalid. It must be certain of payment. The promise to pay must contain an unconditional promise to pay. The promise to pay must not depend upon the happening of some uncertain event.

Examples : 1. I promise to pay B Rs. 500 seven days after my marriage with C. It is an uncertain promissory note. Because it is possible that marriage may never take place.

2. I promise to pay B Rs. 500 on C's death, provided C leaves me enough to pay that amount. Here death is sure. But, the payment is conditional and depends on "If C leaves enough to pay". This is uncertain that C may not leave sufficient amount at the time of death.

4. *It must be Signed by the Maker*

The person who promises to pay is known as the maker. The instrument will be complete only when it is signed by the maker. When the maker of pro-note is illiterate, his thumb mark is sufficient.

5. *The Sum Payable must be Certain*

For a valid promissory note it is also essential that the sum of money promised to be payable must be certain and definite. The sum to be paid should be certain and should not include any additions or subtractions.

Example : I promise to pay B Rs. 500 and all other sums which shall be due to him. This is not a promissory note because the amount is uncertain.

6. *Promise to Pay must be Money only*

The promise to pay must be money only. Promise to pay anything other than legal tender, in full or in part, is not a promissory note.

7. *It must Contain Certain Parties*

The maker and payee of the instrument must be certain, definite and different persons. A promissory note cannot be made payable to the bearer. Sec. 31 of the Reserve Bank of India Act provides that no person in India other than the Reserve Bank or the Central Government can make or issue a promissory note payable to bearer.

8. *Other Formalities*

Though the formalities like serial number, date, place, consideration etc., are found on the face of a promissory note, they are not required statutorily. Thus, it will be valid, if the place of its making or the phrase for value received are not written.

Specimen of Promissory Note

Delhi
Rs. 1,000 15th Sept. 2009.

Three months after date I promise to pay Mr. Agarwal or order a sum of Rs. 1,000 (Rs. One thousand only), for value received.

Stamp

Mr. Agarwal Sd-
Delhi Mohanlal

BILL OF EXCHANGE

According to Sec. 5, "A bill of exchange is an instrument in writing containing an unconditional order, signed by the maker, directing a certain person to pay a certain sum of money only to, or to the order of, a certain person or, to the bearer of the instrument."

There must be three parties to the bill of exchange, *i.e.*, Drawer, Drawee and Payee. The maker of a bill of exchange is called the DRAWER. The person who is directed to pay is called the DRAWEE. The person to whom payment is made is called the PAYEE. The drawer or the payee who is in possession of the bill is also called the HOLDER. When the drawee accepts the bill, he is also called the ACCEPTOR. It is the duty of the holder to present the bill to the drawee for his acceptance. Although a bill requires three parties, all the three need not be different entities. The drawer and the payee may be the same person in case a bill is drawn with the words, "pay to me or my order".

Specimen of a Bill of Exchange

Bombay
Rs. 1,000 15th Sept. 2009.

Three months after date pay to X or order the sum of Rs. one thousand only, for value received.

Stamp

To

Accepted
Arun

Arun Sd/-
Delhi Bijoria

Here, Bijoria is the drawer.
Arun is the drawee.
X is the payee.

ESSENTIALS OF A BILL OF EXCHANGE

The definition of a bill is very similar to that of a pro-note and for most purposes the rules which apply to notes are in general applicable to bills. The fundamental requirements and ingredients are the same. However, the requirements of bill of exchange, in brief, are as follows :

(1) It should be in writing
(2) It should be an order to pay to a certain person.
(3) It should contain an unconditional order.
(4) The drawer, drawee and payee must be certain.
(5) It should be signed by the drawer.
(6) The sum payable must be certain.
(7) The bill must contain an order to pay money only.
(8) It should be in the form of an order to the drawee.
(9) It should be properly stamped.
(10) There are certain other formalities, such as number, date, consideration etc. which are usually found in a bill. But they are not essential in law.

From the above, it is clear that there must be Five Certainties in order to have a valid Bill of Exchange. They are :

(*a*) *The drawer must be certain.*
(*b*) *The order must be certain.*
(*c*) *The drawee must be certain.*
(*d*) *The sum payable must be certain.*
(*e*) *The payee must be certain.*

Distinction between a Promissory Note and a Bill of Exchange

Promissory Note	*Bill of Exchange*
1. *Parties* : There are two parties—Maker and Payee.	1. There are three parties—Drawer, Drawee and Payee.
2. *Nature of Payment* : It contains an unconditional promise to pay.	2. It contains an unconditional order to pay.
3. *Payee* : It cannot be made payable to the maker, who is a debtor. The maker and the payee cannot be same person.	3. The drawer and the payee may be the same person. Drawer can order the drawee to pay the money to drawer himself.
4. *Acceptance* : It requires no acceptance as it is signed by the person who is liable to pay.	4. The drawer of a bill of exchange is generally creditor of the drawee and, therefore,, it must be accepted by the drawee before it can be presented for payment.
5. *Liability* : The liability of the maker of a note is primary and absolute.	5. The liability of the drawer (maker) of a bill is secondary and conditional. When the acceptor fails to pay the money he becomes liable.
6. *Notice* : when a pro-note is dishonoured, it is not necessary to give notice of dishonour to the maker.	6. Notice of dishonor must be given by the holder to all the prior parties to the bill.
7. *Payable to bearer* : A pro-note cannot be drawn payable to bearer.	7. It can be so drawn provided it is not drawn 'payable to bearer on demand.'
8. *Protest* : Dishonour of pro-note protest is not necessary.	8. A foreign bill must be protested if such a protest is necessary according to law of the place, where it is drawn.
9. *Sets* : Pro-note cannot be drawn in sets.	9. Bills can be drawn in sets.

CHEQUE

According to Sec. 6, "A cheque is a bill of exchange drawn on a specified banker and not expressed to be payable otherwise than on demand." A cheque is a bill of exchange with the following two distinctive features, which are additional qualifications :

(A) A cheque is always drawn on a specified banker.

(B) A cheque is always payable on demand.

Thus a cheque is a bill of exchange drawn on a bank payable on demand. A cheque, being a species of bill of exchange, must satisfy all requirements of a bill. A cheque has three parties – Drawer, Drawee and Payee. Drawee in case of a cheque is always a banker. A cheque is an unconditional order on the specified banker to pay on demand, a certain sum of money to the bearer of the cheque or to his order. It does not require acceptance. Drawer and the payee may be same person where a person draws a cheque 'payable to self'.

Distinction between a Bill of Exchange and a Cheque

Bill of Exchange	*Cheque*
1. *Drawee :* Anyone can be a drawee.	1. Only banker can be a drawee.
2. *Acceptance :* It needs acceptance.	2. Acceptance is not required.
3. *Payment :* The amount may be payable on demand or after a specified time.	3. The amount is always payable on demand.
4. *Crossing :* It can never be crossed.	4. A cheque may be crossed.
5. *Stamp :* It must be properly stamped.	5. It requires no stamp.
6. *Noting and protesting :* A bill is noted or protested to establish dishonour.	6. A cheque is not to be noted or protested in case of dishonour.
7. *Countermanding payment :* The payment of bill cannot be countermanded.	7. The payment of a cheque may be countermanded by the drawer.
8. *Notice :* Notice of dishonour is necessary to hold the parties liable thereon.	8. Notice of dishonour is not necessary. The parties thereon remain liable even if no notice of dishonour is given.
9. *Grace Days :* A grace of three days is allowed in case time bill.	9. No grace is given.

CROSSING OF CHEQUES

The cheques are of two types—Open (uncrossed) cheques and crossed cheques. Payment of a cheque by the drawee banker depends upon whether the cheque is open or crossed. The payment of open cheque is made at the counter of the banker on its presentation. The open cheque is liable to a great risk in the course of circulation. Since an open cheque is payable to a bearer, it involves a risk of payment to any person, if it is lost. In order to avoid such risk and to protect the interest of the genuine holder, the system of crossing the cheques was introduced.

In case of a crossed cheque, payment can be obtained only through a banker. That is, the payee or the holder, having an account in a bank, has to deposit the crossed cheque for collection, and draw the money when the cheque is collected and the proceeds are credited to his account. It is only with a view to avoiding any such risk of fraud that businessmen introduced the device of crossing. Thus, crossing of a cheque may be defined as, "a direction to the drawee banker to pay the money on a crossed cheque through a banker, so that the party getting the payment of a crossed cheque may be easily traceable."

TYPES OF CROSSING

There are two types of crossing - (*i*) General Crossing and (*ii*) Special Crossing.

General Crossing

A cheque is said to contain a general crossing when two parallel lines are drawn across the face of the cheque. According to Sec. 123. "Where a cheque bears across its face an addition of the words "and company" or any abbreviation thereof, between two parallel transverse lines, or of two parallel transverse lines simply, either with or without the words "not negotiable", that addition shall be deemed a crossing, and the cheque shall be deemed to be crossed generally." A cheque is said to be crossed when two parallel transverse lines, with or without any words, are drawn on the left hand top corner of the cheque. It is relevant to state that such lines are essential for general crossing and may not be drawn in case of special crossing.

Specimen of general crossing

1.

2. & Co

3. Not Negotiable

4. & Co. Not Negotiable

Special Crossing

Sec. 124 of the Act defines special crossing as "Where cheque bears across its face an addition of the name of a banker, either with or without the words "not negotiable" that addition shall be deemed a crossing, and cheque shall be deemed to be crossed specially and to be crossed to that banker." Further, Sec. 126, Para 2 states "Where a cheque is crossed specially the banker on whom it is drawn shall not pay it otherwise than to the banker to whom it is crossed, or his agent, for collection."

Specimens of Special Crossings

Canara Bank

Not Negotiable
Canara Bank

In the case of special crossing the paying banker is to honour the cheque only when it is presented through the bank mentioned in the crossing or an agent of such bank. Further, Sec. 127 states, "Where a cheque is crossed specially to more than one banker, except when crossed to an agent for the purpose of collection, the banker on whom it is drawn shall refuse payment thereof." A special crossing makes the cheque more safer than a general crossing because now a thief will have to search an account-holder of that particular bank only whose name appears in the crossing which may only create more difficulty.

Account Payee (Restrictive crossing)

Although the Act is silent with regard to this form of crossing, it has been recognised by custom amongst businessmen and bankers. The words 'account payee' within a general or a special crossing, are a direction to the collecting banker to collect and credit the payee's account with the proceeds of the cheque. It means that a cheque marked 'account payee only' or A/c Payee' or 'Payee's A/c' have same significance. If the banker goes against this order, he will be guilty of negligence. Hence "account payee only" crossing is not negotiable practically, as banks will collect it on behalf of no person other than the payee.

Not Negotiable Crossing

The words 'Not negotiable' may also be written in both types of crossing–general and special and a crossing with these words is said to be 'Not Negotiable' crossing. Section 130 states that "A person taking a cheque crossed generally or specially, bearing in either case the words "not negotiable" shall not have, and shall not be capable of giving, a better title to the cheque than that which the person from whom he took it had."

The object of 'not negotiable' crossing is to afford protection to the holder or drawer of a cheque, because even if such a cheque goes to wrong hands and from there it is transferred to holder in due course, the true owner will not lose his claim against an indorsee. Thus an indorsee of such a crossed cheque must not accept the cheque unless he knows the indorser very well and is convinced about his having a good title thereto.

WHO MAY CROSS A CHEQUE?

Crossing of an uncrossed cheque does not amount to a material alteration so as to affect the validity of the instrument. Apart from the drawer of a cheque crossing it generally or specially at the time of issue, the holder of a cheque and also the banker may cross it. Section 125 permits the crossing being made even after issue of a cheque in the following ways:

(1) (Sec. 125) "Where a cheque is uncrossed, the holder may cross it generally or specially.

(2) Where a cheque is crossed generally, the holder may cross it specially.

(3) Where a cheque is crossed generally, or specially, the holder may add the word "not negotiable".

(4) Where a cheque is crossed specially, the banker to whom it is crossed may again cross it specially, to another banker, his agent, for collection."

Crossing once made is a material part of the cheque and its alteration except in the above cases will amount to a material alteration. Thus, if a special crossing on a cheque is altered by the holder into a general crossing by striking out the name of the banker, it will be unauthorised. Crossing once made becomes a material part of the cheque and only the drawer of the cheque is entitled to cancel or open the crossing by writing the words "pay cash" and cancelling the crossing alongwith his full signature. Thus, where a cheque is crossed 'account payee' and the holder alters it into a general crossing by striking out the words 'account payee', the alteration is irregular and discharges the instrument.

CLASSIFICATION OF NEGOTIABLE INSTRUMENTS

Bearer and Order Instruments

A promissory note, bill of exchange or cheque may either be bearer or order.

Bearer Instrument

Explanation (*ii*) of Sec. 13(1) states that "A promissory note, bill of exchange or cheque is payable to bearer which is expressed to be so payable or on which the only or last endorsement is an indorsement in blank." The term 'bearer instrument' may be defined as a negotiable instrument the payment of which can be taken by a person who has the possession of the instrument. Thus where an instrument is originally payable to a particular person, but subsequently indorsed in blank, the instrument will become payable to bearer. After the bearer of the instrument is paid, he may be required to acknowledge receipt of the money by signing on the instrument.

Examples : (*i*) Pay to A or bearer.
(*ii*) Pay the bearer.

ORDER INSTRUMENT

Explanation (*i*) of Sec. 13 (1) states that "A promissory note, bill of exchange or cheque is payable to order which is expressed to be payable or which is expressed to be payable to a particular person and does not contain words, prohibiting transfer or indicating an intention that it shall not be transferable."

To negotiate an instrument payable to order, the signature of the holder is necessary.

Examples : (*i*) Pay to A or order.

(*ii*) Pay to the order of A.

(*iii*) Pay to A.

(1) "A promissory note or bill of exchange, in which no time for payment is specified, and a cheque, are payable on demand". (Sec. 19).

(2) A cheque is payable on demand.

(3) A promissory note or a bill of exchange is payable on demand, if it is marked, "At sight" or "On presentment". (Sec. 21).

INLAND AND FOREIGN INSTRUMENTS

Inland Instruments (Sec. 11)

As per Section 11, "A promissory note, bill of exchange or cheque which is (*i*) drawn or made in India and also made payable in India, or (*ii*) drawn or made in India upon any person resident in India, although it may be made payable in a foreign country, is deemed to be an inland instrument".

Examples : (*i*) An instrument drawn and made payable in India.
(*ii*) An instrument drawn in India, upon some person resident in India, though payable in a foreign country.

Foreign Instrument (Sec. 12)

Sec. 12 states that, "Any such instrument not so drawn, made or made payable, shall be deemed to be a foreign instrument." That is, an instrument which is not an inland instrument, is deemed to be a foreign instrument.

Examples : (*i*) Instrument drawn and made payable outside India.
(*ii*) Instrument drawn in India, upon persons resident outside India and payable outside India.

In case of an inland bill only one copy is drawn, while in case of a foreign bill three copies are drawn. In case of dishonour of an inland bill noting is necessary, while noting is not done in a foreign bill.

Instruments Payable on Demand or at Sight

According to Sec. 19, "A promissory note or bill of exchange, in which no time for payment is specified, and a cheque, are payable on demand." A cheque is always payable on demand and it cannot be expressed to be payable otherwise than on demand. (Secs. 6 and 19)

A promissory note or bill of exchange is payable on demand :

(*i*) When it is expressed to be payable 'on demand' or 'at sight' or 'at presentment' (Sec. 21).

(*ii*) When no time for payment is specified in it (Sec. 19).

Further, in a promissory note or a bill of exchange, the expressions 'at sight' and 'on presentment' mean 'on demand'.

Time Instruments

The term 'time instrument' may be defined as the instrument which is payable some time in future. The following are the examples of time instruments :

(*a*) A promissory note or a bill of exchange which is payable after a fixed period, say, 90 days after sight.

(*b*) A promissory note or a bill of exchange which is payable on a specified day, say, 1st March 2011.

(*c*) A promissory note or a bill of exchange which is payable on the happening of an event which is certain to happen, say, on the death of a person.

(*d*) A promissory or bill of exchange which is payable after sight.

Accommodation Bill

A bill may either be a genuine trade bill or an accommodation bill. When a bill is drawn, accepted or endorsed for consideration, it is called a 'genuine trade bill' : but 'an accommodation bill' is drawn, accepted or endorsed without any consideration. That is, a bill which is not backed up by any commercial transaction, is known as an accommodation bill. It is a bill of exchange which is made only to provide financial help to some party. The person who signs (accepts) the bill without any consideration, in order to accommodate some other person, is known as 'accommodating party' (or accommodation party), and the person who has been accommodated, is known as 'accommodated party'.

Example : Mr. A who is in need of Rs. 2,000, draw a bill on B and B accepted the same. A can get the bill discounted with his banker and can get cash. Here, B is the accommodating party.

Since an accommodation bill is drawn for the benefit of the accommodated party, there is an implied agreement between them :

(*a*) The accommodation party is liable to a holder for value of the bill.

(*b*) If the accommodation party has to pay, he can recover the amount paid from the accommodated party.

The obligation of an accommodated party are :

(*a*) He has to undertake the bill on the due date.

(*b*) As an alternative, he must provide the accommodation party with funds to meet the bill on the due date.

(*c*) If the accommodation party has to pay the bill, he must indemnify him for payment duly made by him in respect of the bill.

Further, an accommodation bill can be negotiated after maturity (Sec. 59). Non-presentment of an accommodation bill to the acceptor for payment does not discharge the drawer. (Sec. 98). Failure to give notice of dishonour does not discharge the liability of the prior parties, as it does in the case of other bills. (Sec. 98).

Fictitious Bills

A bill is called a fictitious bill when the name of the drawer or the payee or both are fictitious. The term 'fictitious person' means (*a*) a person who is not in existence or (*b*) a pretended person, *i.e.*, a person who is in existence but never intended by the parties to be drawer or payee of the bill of exchange. Although a fictitious bill is not valid as a negotiable instrument, Sec. 42 of the Act lays down that the acceptor of such a bill is not relieved from liability to any holder in due course, provided the holder in due course can show that the signature of the drawer and the first endorsement on the bill are in the same handwriting. But when the holder in due course known or has reason to believe that the drawer or the payee is a fictitious person, he is not a holder in due course as he has not got the bill in good faith and, therefore, he is not entitled to claim the money.

DOCUMENTARY AND CLEAN BILLS

When documents relating to the goods represented by the bill, *e.g.*, bill of lading or railway receipt, invoice, marine insurance policy etc., are attached to a bill, the bill is called a documentary bill. Such documents are delivered to the buyer only on acceptance or payment of the bill. Such bills are usually used in foreign trade.

Where no such documents are annexed to a bill, it is called a clean bill.

ESCROW

When a bill of exchange is delivered conditionally or for a special purpose as a collateral security or for safe custody only and it is not transferred, it is called escrow. The liability to pay in case of escrow does not arise, if the conditions agreed upon are not fulfilled or the purpose for which the bill was delivered is not satisfied. This, however, does not affect the rights of a holder in due course.

Ambiguous Instruments (Secs. 17 and 18)

An instrument which is vague and cannot be clearly identified either as a promissory note or as a bill of exchange, is an ambiguous instrument. An ambiguous instrument is a faulty instrument. Under Sec. 17, its holder has to elect, whether he wants to treat it as a bill of exchange or a promissory note, once he does so, he is to abide by his choice.

The following are ambiguous instruments :

(*a*) When in a bill, the drawer and the drawee are the same persons :

(*b*) Where the drawee is a fictitious person;

(*c*) Where the drawee is an incompetent person.

If the amount undertaken or ordered to be paid is stated differently in figures and in words, the amount stated in words shall be the amount undertaken or ordered to be paid. (Sec. 18).

Inchoate Instrument (Sec. 20)

An incomplete or blank negotiable instrument properly stamped and signed is termed as an 'inchoate instrument.' Sec. 20 states that, "Where one person signs and delivers to another a paper stamped in accordance with the law relating to negotiable instruments then in force in India, and either wholly blank or having written thereon an incomplete negotiable instrument, he thereby gives prima facie authority to the holder thereof to make or complete, as the case may be, upon it a negotiable instrument, for any amount specified therein and not exceeding the amount covered by the stamp. The person so signing shall be liable upon such instrument, in the capacity in which he signed the same, or to any holder in due course for such amount: provided that no person other than a holder in due course shall recover from the person delivering the instrument anything in excess of the amount intended by him to be paid thereunder."

Rules Regarding Inchoate Instrument

The following rules have been laid down :

(1) The liability of the person signing and delivering an inchoate instrument arises when the person concerned fills in the blank or completes the incomplete instrument.

(2) It is based on the principle of estoppel.

(3) The holder must fill it within a reasonable time.

(4) It is necessary that it should be delivered, otherwise the signer will not be liable for its holder.

(5) The signer cannot escape his liability on the ground of any condition or on the pretext that he asked the holder to make the instrument for a lesser amount.

(6) Instruments which do not require stamps, are not covered by these rules.

Bill in Sets (Secs. 132 and 133)

A bill of exchange is sometimes drawn in parts, specially when it is to be sent from one country to another. When a bill is drawn in sets of three, it is known as drawing the 'bill in sets' When the drawer and the payee of a bill of exchange are in different countries, bills in sets are usually drawn. This is usually done in case of foreign bills because they have to be sent over long distances and there exists possibility of loss or delay. The following are the rules regarding the bill in sets :

(1) A bill drawn in parts, all the parts together make a set and the whole set constitutes one bill only.
(2) Each part of a bill in set should be numbered and must contain a provision that it shall continue payable only so long as the other parts remain unpaid.
(3) If any part of a bill in a set does not mention about other parts, that part will become a separate bill, if it gets into the hands of a holder in due course.
(4) If payment is made on one of the parts of the bill, the whole bill is extinguished.
(5) The drawer must sign each part of the bill and should deliver all the parts. But only one part is required to be stamped and only one part is to be accepted by the drawee.
(6) When more than one part of a set are negotiated to different holders in due course, he who first acquires title to his part, becomes the true owner of the bill and he is entitled to (*a*) have the possession of all other parts; and (*b*) claim the payment of the bill.

Payment in Due Course (Sec. 10)

According to Sec. 10, "Payment in due course, means payment in accordance with the apparent tenor of the instrument in good faith and without negligence to any person in possession thereof under circumstances which do not afford a reasonable ground for believing that he is not entitled to receive payment of the amount therein mentioned." In order to constitute a payment of a negotiable instrument as a 'Payment in due course', the following conditions must be fulfilled :

(1) Payment must be in accordance with the apparent tenor of the instrument. Thus, a payment before maturity is not payment in due course.

> **Example :** If a bill of exchange is paid before the last day of grace and is subsequently endorsed over, it is valid in the hands of a holder in due course and the acceptor will be liable to pay again on the instrument.

(2) Payment must be made in good faith and without negligence. Payment should be made to a person in possession of the instrument under a reasonable belief and without any doubt that he is entitled to receive the amount. If the payment is made negligently, drawee continues to be liable on the bill. If there are suspicious circumstances and the payer fails to make necessary enquiry which may reveal the defects, the payment is not a payment in due course.

(3) The payment must be made to a person in possession of the instrument *i.e.*, the person entitled to receive payment. There should be no suspicion that the possessor is not entitled for payment.

(4) Payment of the instrument must be made in terms of money. Here money means currency or cheque.

(5) The payment must be made by or on behalf of the drawee or acceptor.

MATURITY AND DAYS OF GRACE

The maturity of a bill or note is the date on which it falls due. A bill or note which is payable on demand becomes due immediately on presentation for payment. A bill or note which is not payable on demand becomes mature on the third day after the day on which it is expressed to be payable. The three days are known as the Days of Grace.

Calculation of Date of maturity (Secs. 23 to 25)

The date of maturity of a bill or note is calculated as under :
(1) If a bill or note is payable after a stated number of months after sight or after the happening of a certain event, it will become payable after three days of the corresponding date of the month after the stated number of months.
(2) If the month in which the period terminates has no corresponding day, the period is held to be terminated on the last day of such month.

Example : A bill is payable two months after date and is dated 31st December 2010. It will be payable on 3rd March 2011.

(3) Sec. 24 states that the day on which the bill or note is drawn, or presented for acceptance or sight or the day on which the event happens is excluded.

(4) If the date of maturity of a bill or note is a public holiday, it will be payable on the next business day as provided by Section 25.

The expression "Public Holiday" includes Sundays and any other day declared by the Central Government, by notification in the Official Gazette, to be a public holiday.

Examples : 1. A bill dated 1st January 2011 is made payable four months after date. It falls due on 4th May 2011.

2. A bill dated 1st January 2011 is payable sixty days after date. It falls due on 5th March 2011.

INTEREST ON BILLS AND NOTES

Interest when Rate Specified (Sec. 79)

Sec. 79 states, "When interest at a specified rate is expressly made payable on a promissory note or bill of exchange, interest shall be calculated at the rate specified, on the amount of the principal money due thereon, from the data of the instrument, until tender or realisation of such amount, or until such date after the institution of a suit to recover such amount as the Court directs."

Interest when no Rate Specified (Sec. 80)

Sec. 80 states, "when no rate of interest is specified in the instrument, or when no mention is made of interest at all, interest on the amount due thereon shall, notwithstanding an oral agreement relating to interest between any parties to the instrument, be calculated at the rate of six per cent per annum, from the date at which the same ought to have been paid by the party charged, until tender or realisation of the amount due thereon, or until such date after the institution of a suit to recover such amount as the Court directs."

Explanation to Sec. 80 states that "When the party charged is the endorser of an instrument dishonoured by non-payment, he is liable to pay interest only from the time he receives notice of the dishonour."

THEORETICAL QUESTIONS

1. What are the essential features of Negotiable Instrument? Define Negotiable Instrument. *(B.Com. Andhra)*

2. What is the effect of crossing a cheque with the words—Account Payee only or Not negotiable?

3. Define a Promissory Note. What are its essential elements? *(B.Com. MS)*

4. Defines a cheque. How does it differ from a Bill of Exchange?

5. "A cheque is a specie of a bill of exchange with two additional qualifications." Explain. *(B.Com. Poona)*

6. What do you mean by an accommodation bill? What are the rules regarding the liability of parties and payment of an accommodation bill?

7. "Consideration in a negotiable instrument is presumed". Discuss. *(B.Com. Bhopal)*

8. What is meant by maturity of an instrument? What is meant by instrument payable 'at sight' and 'after sight'?

9. What is meant by 'payment in due course'? *(B.Com. Agra)*

10. When is the payment said to be payment in due course? *(B.Com. Delhi)*

11. Who can cross a cheque? What is the difference between a general crossing and special crossing? *(B.Com. MS)*

12. What are bills in sets? Explain the effect of endorsing the different parts of a bill in favour of different persons. *(B.Com. MS)*

13. Write short notes on : Fictitious Bill, Inchoate Instrument, Escrow, Ambiguous Instrument.

MULTIPLE CHOICE QUESTIONS

Choose correct option for each of the following :

1. **In legal terms, a person who receives a negotiable instrument in good faith and for valuable consideration is known as :**
   (*a*) Holder. (*b*) Holder in due course.
   (*c*) Holder for value. (*d*) None of these.
2. **A negotiable instrument drawn in India on a person residing in India and payable outside India is known as :**
   (*a*) Inland instrument. (*b*) Indo-foreign instrument.
   (*c*) Foreign instrument. (*d*) None of these.
3. **A negotiable instrument in which no time for payment is specified is payable :**
   (*a*) After acceptance. (*b*) After one month.
   (*c*) After sight. (*d*) On demand.
4. **The negotiable instrument Act makes specific mention of three instruments, namely promissory note, bill of exchange and :**
   (*a*) bank draft. (*b*) hundi.
   (*c*) cheque. (*d*) none of those.
5. **A bill of exchange dishonoured due to non-acceptance by the drawee, becomes :**
   (*a*) void. (*b*) invalid.
   (*c*) voidable. (*d*) none of these.
6. **A person who is directed to pay the amount of bill of exchange is known as :**
   (*a*) drawer. (*b*) payee.
   (*c*) drawee. (*d*) Creditor.
7. **A bill of exchange payable to bearer on demand is :**
   (*a*) voidable. (*b*) valid.
   (*c*) invalid. (*d*) conditional.
8. **Which of the following is a valid promissory note ?**
   (*a*) I owe you some amount. (*b*) I owe you Rs. 100.
   (*c*) I promise to pay A or order Rs. 500. (*d*) I promise to pay the bearer Rs. 500.
9. **Which of the following is not an essential of a valid promissory note ?**
   (*a*) A promissory note must be signed by the maker.
   (*b*) It must be in writing.
   (*c*) It must be stamped.
   (*d*) It must be registered.

ANSWERS

1. (*b*) **2.** (*a*) **3.** (*d*) **4.** (*c*) **5.** (*d*) **6.** (*c*) **7.** (*c*) **8.** (*c*) **9.** (*d*)

CHAPTER

Parties to Negotiable Instrument

AT A GLANCE

CAPACITIES OF THE PARTIES

A person, competent to contract, can become a party to Negotiable Instrument. The liability of a party to a negotiable instrument depends upon his contractual capacity. Section 11 of the Indian Contract Act states that "Every person is competent to contract who is of the age of majority according to the law to which he is subject, and who is of sound mind, and is not disqualified from contracting by any law to which he is subject."

Section 26 of the Negotiable Instrument Act declares that "every person capable of contracting according to the law to which he is subject, may bind himself and be bound by the making, drawing, acceptance, endorsement, delivery and negotiation of a promissory note, bill of exchange or cheque." Thus, a person incapable of contracting, cannot bind himself by the negotiable instrument, but may, under circumstances, bind others. An instrument does not become void merely because a minor is a party to it : but remains binding on all the other parties to it.

The following may be the parties which are incompetent to incur a liability for a negotiable instrument as its drawer, maker, acceptor etc.

(1) *Minor* (Sec. 26)

Minor is not competent to contract. Sec. 11 of the Indian Contract Act does not allow a minor to enter into a valid contract. However, Sec. 26 of the Negotiable Instrument Act allows a minor to draw, endorse, deliver and negotiate a negotiable instrument so as to bind all parties except himself. The minor is in a privileged position as in the case of every other contract. Thus, a minor party to a negotiable instrument is not personally liable but the adult parties are.

When there are several joint parties to a negotiable instrument and one or more of them are minors, the minors cannot be sued, but it does not discharge the other major parties from their liability to the instrument. The holder of a negotiable instrument can sue the major parties excluding the minor. Although, he cannot incur liability under a negotiable instrument, he can acquire rights under it. His rights as payee, endorsee or holder are not affected.

A minor can put up his incompetence even against a holder in due course and even the principle of 'estoppel' does not apply on him. A promissory note drawn by a minor even for the supply of necessaries of life to him does not make him liable and does not form consideration of a fresh promissory note made by him on his attaining majority. Only the estate of a minor is liable for necessaries of life supplied to him. Therefore, if a minor gives an instrument for supplying him necessaries of life, his estate will be liable and not he himself.

Thus, it can be concluded that a minor may have rights under a negotiable instrument, but can incur no liability under it. In other words, he can be a payee or promisee, but not a party liable on it.

(2) *Persons of Unsound Mind*

Contracts of idiots, lunatics and drunken persons like those of minors are void. These persons are incompetent to enter into contract. Their position is the same as that of minor. An agreement with a person of unsound mind is void *ab initio* in most of the countries in the world. During the period of soundness such person may draw, indorse, deliver and negotiate such instruments.

(3) *Insolvent*

We know that an insolvent is not competent to enter into a valid contract unless he is discharged by the court. An insolvent is not competent to draw, make, accept or indorse a negotiable instrument so as to bind his estate which now stands vested in the Official Receiver. But if he indorses an instrument, of which he is the payee, to holder in due course, then the holder in due course can recover from all prior parties except the insolvent. The insolvent cannot sue on negotiable instrument.

(4) *Corporation*

Nothing in the Section 26 shall be deemed to empower a corporation to make, indorse or accept such instrument except in cases in which, under the law for the time being in force, they are so empowered. Therefore, a company registered under the Companies Act 1956 cannot draw, accept, make or indorse a bill of exchange, promissory note or cheque unless the company is so empowered by its Memorandum or Articles of Association. A statutory company similarly cannot make, draw, accept or endorse such instruments unless it is so empowered to do by the statute, by which it is formed. A trading company has implied power to bind itself by a negotiable instrument provided that it is not prohibited by its Memorandum or Articles of Association. On the other hand, a non-trading company cannot bind itself by a negotiable instrument, unless it is expressly authorised by its Memorandum or Articles of Association.

(5) *Agent*

According to Sec. 27, "Every person capable of binding himself or of being bound as mentioned in Sec. 26, may so bind himself or be bound by a duly authorised agent acting in his name." But a general authority to transact business and to receive and discharge debts does not confer upon an agent the power of accepting or indorsing bill of exchange so as to bind his principal. The authority of an agent to draw, accept or indorse negotiable instruments must be expressed in clear terms. Then the negotiable instruments can be expressed in clear terms. Then the negotiable instruments can be drawn or accepted by duly authorised agents on behalf of their principals.

According to Sec. 28, "An agent who signs his name to a promissory note, bill of exchange or cheque without indicating thereon that he signs as agent, or that he does not intend thereby to incur personal responsibility, is liable personally on the instrument, except to those who induced him to sign upon the belief that the principal only would be held liable." Thus, an agent may draw, accept or negotiate a negotiable instrument on behalf of the principal so as to bind the latter subject to the following conditions :

(*a*) that the agent has been authorised by the principal to that effect :
(*b*) that the authority has been expressed in clear terms :
(*c*) that the principal is a competent person to enter into a contract.
(*d*) that the agent acts in the name of the principal : and
(*e*) that the agent has not exceeded his authority.

The agent will be personally liable in any of the following cases :

(*a*) if he does not disclose the name of his principal :
(*b*) if he does not indicate that he is an agent.
(*c*) if he executes an instrument without or in excess of his authority.

(6) *Partners and Firm*

In fact, a partnership is a branch of the law of agency. Therefore, in a partnership firm, each partner has authority to bind his copartners for drawing, accepting, making, endorsing, transferring or negotiating a negotiable instrument in the name of and for the firm. But the partners of non-trading firm have no such implied authority. Hence, a partner signing an instrument on behalf of the firm, should do so in the name of the firm.

(7) *Joint Hindu Family*

The karta of a Joint Hindu family represents the family for all transactions with the outsiders. He has an implied authority on behalf of the family to transact its business, to pay debts, to pledge its credit, to borrow money and thus, also to draw, accept, deliver or negotiate an instrument in this regard. The debt is binding on all the members of the family even if they are minors. However, in case of minor members, their share is only liable.

(8) *Legal Representative*

According to Sec. 29, "A legal representative of a deceased person who signs his name to a promissory note, bill of exchange or cheque is liable personally thereon unless he expressly limits his liability to the extent of the assets received by him as such." However, he may escape his personal liability by adding the words to his signature as such "without recourse to me personally" or "without personal liability".

PARTIES TO NEGOTIABLE INSTRUMENTS

Parties to Promissory Note

(1) *Maker :* The person who makes the note promising to pay the amount stated therein is called the Maker.

(2) *Payee :* The person to whom the amount of promissory note is payable.

(3) *Holder :* A person who is either the payee or the indorsee of the promissory note. Holder is a person, who is entitled to the possession of the instrument in his own name and is also entitled to receive the money due on it.

(4) *Endorser/:* The person who indorses (*i.e.*, transfer) the note to another person is called the Indorser.

(5) *Endorsee :* The person to whom the note is indorsed is called the Endorsee.

Parties to Bill of Exchange

(1) *Drawer :* The maker of a bill of exchange is the drawer.

(2) *Drawee :* The person who is directed to pay the bill of exchange by the drawer is called drawee.

(3) *Acceptor :* The person who accepts the bill of exchange is called the acceptor. Generally drawee accepts the bill and on acceptance the drawee becomes the acceptor.

(4) *Payee :* The person named in the instrument, to whom or to whose order the money is, by the instrument, directed to be paid, is called the payee.

(5) *Holder :* As in promissory note.

(6) *Indorser :* As in promissory note.

(7) *Indorsee :* As in promissory note.

(8) *Drawee in case of need :* When in the bill or in any endorsement thereon the name of any person is given in addition to the drawee to be resorted to in case of need, such person is called a "Drawee in case of need."

(9) *Acceptor for honour :* When a bill of exchange has been noted and protested for non-acceptance or for better security, and any person accepts it supra protest for honour of the drawer or of any one of the endorsers, such person is called an acceptor for honour.

Parties to Cheque

(1) *Drawer :* The person who draws a cheque is called the drawer.

(2) *Drawee :* The person who is directed by the cheque to pay is called the drawee. Here drawee must be a banker.

(3) *Payee :* As in promissory note.

(4) *Holder :* As in promissory note.

(5) *Indorser :* As in promissory note.

(6) *Endorsee :* As in promissory note.

HOLDER

According to Sec. 8, "The holder of a promissory note, bill of exchange or cheque means any person entitled in his own name to the possession thereof and to receive or recover the amount due thereon from the parties thereto." The person named in the instrument and to whom or to whose order the amount specified therein is payable, is called the payee. Thus, the payee is one of the original parties to a negotiable instrument. It is his right to retain possession of the instrument and receive money on it, or negotiate the same to any person to whom he owes money. If he negotiates the instrument, the person to whom it is negotiated becomes the holder. In the case of a bearer instrument, however, the bearer himself is the holder, but in the case of an order instrument, the endorsee becomes the holder. If the payee does not negotiate it, he himself will be the holder.

In order to constitute the person a holder of the instrument, it is not necessary that he should be in possession of the instrument. The word 'entitled' used in the section suggests that he must be entitled in his own name to the possession of the instrument. The legal representative of the deceased can claim the instrument as holder by operation of law. The person legally entitled to receive the money due on the instrument, is called the holder. But clerks or servants having the instrument in their custody are not holders except as agents of the holder. A person who obtains possession of the instrument by illegal means, say, theft, is not a holder. Thus, in order to be called a 'holder' a person must satisfy the following two conditions :

(1) He must be entitled to the possession of the instrument in his own name.

(2) He must be entitled to receive or recover the amount due thereon from the parties liable thereto.

Holder in Due Course (Sec. 9)

According to Sec. 9, "Holder in due course" means any person who for consideration became the possessor of a promissory note, bill of exchange or cheque if payable to bearer; or the payee or endorsee thereof, if payable to order, before the amount mentioned in it became payable, and without sufficient cause to believe that any defect existed in the title of the person from whom he derived his title." The analysis of this section reveals that a person becomes a holder in due course of the negotiable instrument if all the following conditions are satisfied.

(1) *He must be Holder :* He must be entitled to the possession of the instrument in his own name under a legal title and to recover the amount thereof from the parties liable thereto.

(2) *He obtained the instrument for valuable consideration.* There must be some consideration to which law attaches value. The consideration, however, need not be adequate. A donee, who acquires title to the instrument by way of gift, is not a holder in due course for want of consideration, although he is a holder. The consideration must also be lawful. It should comply with the essentials of Section 2(*d*) of the Indian Contract Act. It should not fall under any of the provisions of Section 23 of the Indian Contract Act which makes the consideration unlawful.

(3) *He must have become the Holder of the Instrument before Maturity :* The holder who acquires a negotiable instrument after maturity cannot be a holder in due course. In case of instruments payable on demand, he must have taken the instrument within a reasonable time of its issue. After the lapse of reasonable length of time the cheque becomes overdue and any one who takes an over due cheque cannot be a holder in course.

(4) *He must have obtained the instrument in good faith :* He had no cause to believe that any defect existed in the title of the person from whom he derived his title, *i.e.*, he became the holder of the instrument in good faith. Therefore, even if he obtains the instrument from a thief, but without knowledge thereof he obtains a valid title. He must make proper enquiries, and satisfy himself about the title of the transferer. Mere honest belief is not sufficient. He must have taken the instrument bona fide and without any ground for suspicion.

(5) *He must take the instrument complete and regular on the face of it :* If a negotiable instrument is incomplete, for example, blank, undated, not properly stamped, without drawer's name etc. then the holder will not become the holder in due course of such instrument. It was hold that in Arab Bank Vs. Ross (1952) face includes back of the instrument also.

Examples : (*a*) A becomes a possessor of a bill by gift made by his father. A is not holder in due course.

(*b*) A becomes a possessor of a bill payable to bearer before its maturity from B who has no title to it or who has stolen from C. The fact of B's defective title is known to A. A is not holder in due course.
(*c*) A is a payee for valuable consideration of a bill payable to order. He gets this instrument from B without knowledge of any defect in B's title and before its maturity. A is holder in due course.
(*d*) A finds a bill from the street payable to bearer. A is not holder in due course although he gets it before maturity.

Distinction between Holder and Holder in Due Course

Holder	*Holder in due course*
1. The holder cannot have a good title on an instrument if the title of any of the prior parties is defective.	1. The holder in due course may have a good title even if the title of the prior parties is defective,, provided that he had no notice of such defect.
2. It is not necessary that the holder must have received the instrument for some consideration.	2. Consideration is necessary to become a holder in due course.
3. A holder does not enjoy any special privileges.	3. A holder in due course enjoys certain special privileges.
4. A holder means any person entitled in his own name to the possession of the instrument and to recover or receive the amount due thereon from the parties.	4. A holder in due course means a holder who has taken the instrument in good faith and for value, and also before its maturity.

PRIVILEGES OF A HOLDER IN DUE COURSE

Holder in due course acquiring the instrument for consideration and in good faith gets the following rights under the Act :

(1) *Right in Case of Inchoate Instrument* (Sec. 20)

The right of a holder in due course to recover money is not at all affected, even though the instrument was originally an inchoate stamped instrument and the transferor completed the instrument for a sum greater than what was intended by the maker.

(2) *Liability of Prior Parties to Holder in due Course* (Sec. 36)

"Every prior party to a negotiable instrument is liable thereon to a holder in due course until the instrument is duly satisfied." (See 36).

(3) *Acceptor's Liability to the Holder in due Course when Endorsement Forged* (Sec. 42)

An acceptor of a bill of exchange already indorsed is not relieved from liability by reason that such indorsement is forged, if he know or had reason to believe the indorsement to be forged when he accepted the bill.

(4) *Acceptor Bound, although Bill Drawn in Fictitious Name* (Sec. 42)

An acceptor of bill of exchange drawn in fictitious name and payable to the drawer's order is not by reason that such name is fictitious, relieved from liability to any holder in due course claiming under an indorsement by the same hand as the drawer's signature, and purporting to be made by the drawer.

(5) *No Effect of Conditional Delivery* (Sec. 46)

When a negotiable instrument is delivered conditionally or for some special purpose and is negotiated to a holder in due course, it amounts to valid negotiation and he acquires good title to it.

(6) *Instrument Made without Consideration* (Sec. 43)

Under Sec. 25 of the Indian Contract Act, "a contract made without consideration is void." But if a negotiable instrument gets into the hands of holder in due course, he is entitled to recover the amount on it from any of the prior parties thereof.

(7) *Good Title Deriving from Holder in due Course* (Sec. 53)

"A holder of a negotiable instrument who derives title from a holder in due course has the rights thereon of that holder in due course." (Sec. 53).

(8) *Better Title than that of the Transferor* (Sec. 58)

Although the holder of a negotiable instrument does not get a better title than that of the transferor, the position of a holder in due course is different. He gets a better title to the instrument notwithstanding any defect in the title of the transferor.

(9) *Every Holder is a Holder in due Course* (Sec. 118)

The law presumes that holder is a holder in due course, although the presumption is rebuttable.

(10) *Estoppel against Denying Original Validity of Instrument* (Sec. 120)

The drawer of an instrument and the acceptor of a bill, payable to order, cannot, in a suit thereon by a holder in course, deny the validity of the instrument as originally made or drawn.

(11) *Estoppel Denying Capacity of Payee to Endorsee* (Sec. 121)

The drawer of a promissory note for or an acceptor of a bill payable to order, cannot, in a suit thereon by a holder in due course, deny the payee's capacity on the date of the instrument to endorse it.

(12) *Estoppel against Denying Signature or Capacity of Prior Party* (122)

No indorser of a negotiable instrument shall, in a suit thereon by a subsequent holder, be permitted to deny the signature or capacity to contract of any prior party to the instrument.

LIABILITY OF PARTIES

No person can be sued on an instrument unless he appears as a party thereon. The following provisions may be stated in respect of the liabilities of the parties to a negotiable instrument :

(1) *Liability of Drawer* (Sec. 30)

"The drawer of a bill of exchange or cheque is bound, in case of dishonour by the drawee or acceptor thereof, to compensate the holder, provided due notice of dishonour has been given to, or received by, the drawer as hereinafter provided." Before acceptance, the drawer's liability is primary; after acceptance, the drawer's liability is secondary, *i.e.*, he is liable to pay only if the acceptor fails to pay.

(2) *Liability of Drawee of a Cheque* (Sec. 31)

"The drawee of a cheque having sufficient funds of the drawer in his hands, properly applicable to the payment of such cheque must pay the cheque when duly required so to do, and, if default of such payment, must compensate the drawer for any loss of damages caused by such default." (Sec. 31).

(3) *Liability of Maker of Note and Acceptor of Bill* (Sec. 32)

"In the absence of a contract to the contrary, the maker of a promissory note and the acceptor before maturity of a bill of exchange are bound to pay the amount thereof at maturity according to the apparent tenor of the note or acceptance respectively, and the acceptor of a bill of exchange at or after maturity is bound to pay the amount thereof to the holder on demand." (Sec. 32) The maker of a promissory note, and acceptor of a bill, being primarily liable on the instrument, their liability is absolute. As such, they are bound to pay the amount at maturity according to the apparent tenor of the instrument, and the acceptor of a bill at or after maturity, has to pay the amount to the holder on demand.

(4) *Liability of Indorser* (Sec. 35)

"In the absence of a contract to the contrary, whoever indorses and delivers a negotiable instrument before maturity, without, in such endorsement, expressly excluding or making conditional his own liability, is bound thereby to every subsequent holder, in case of dishonour by the drawee, acceptor or maker, to compensate such holder for any loss or damage caused to him by such dishonour, provided due notice of dishonour has been given to, or received by such indorser as hereinafter provided. Every indorser after dishonour is liable as upon an instrument payable on demand." (Sec. 35). The liability, under this section, arises in case of dishonour, to compensate the holder for any loss or damage sustained by him by such dishonour. The liability is subject to a contract to the contrary. This section also states that, after dishonour, every endorser is liable on the instrument, as in the case of an instrument payable on demand.

(5) *Liabilities of Prior Parties* (Sec. 36)

"Every prior party to a negotiable instrument is liable thereon to a holder in due course until the instrument is duly satisfied." (36) The prior parties in relation to the holder in due course include the maker or drawer, the acceptor and all the endorsers. Since according to this section, every prior party is liable until the amount is duly satisfied, the liability of the prior parties is joint and several. As such, the holder in due course may hold all or any of the prior parties liable, in the event of dishonour of the instrument.

Though various parties to a negotiable instrument could be liable thereon but the nature of liability of each one of them is not similar. Some of them are primarily liable like principal debtor while the others are secondarily liable like a surety. According to Sec. 37, "The maker of a promissory note or cheque, the drawer of a bill of exchange until acceptance, and the acceptor are, in the absence of a contract to the contrary, respectively liable thereon as principal debtors, and the other parties thereto are liable thereon as sureties for the maker, drawer or acceptor, as the case may be."

Section 38 of the Act deals with the nature of liability between successive parties. Sec. 38 lays down that "As between the parties so liable as sureties, each prior party is, in the absence of a contract to the contrary, also liable thereon as a principal debtor in respect of each subsequent party."

Example : A draws a bill payable to his own order on B, who accepts. A afterwards endorses the bill to C, C to D, and D to E. As between E and B, B is the principal debtor and A, C and D are his sureties.
As between E and A, A is the principal debtor and C and D are his sureties. As between E and C, C is the principal debtor and D is his surety.

Extent of Liability. Rules regarding compensation (Sec. 117)

According to Sec. 117, "The compensation payable in case of dishonour of a promissory note, bill of exchange or cheque, by any party liable to the holder or any indorsee, shall be determined by the following rules.

(*a*) the holder is entitled to the amount due upon the instrument, together with the expenses properly incurred in presenting, noting and protesting it;

(*b*) when the person charged resides at a place different from that at which the instrument was payable, the holder, is entitled to receive such at the current rate of exchange between the two places;

(*c*) an indorser who, being liable, has paid the amount due on the same is entitled to the amount so paid with interest at 18 per cent per annum from the date of payment until tender or realisation thereof, together with all expenses caused by the dishonour and payment;

(*d*) when the person charged and such indorser resides at different places, the indorser is entitled to receive such sum at the current rate of exchange between the two places.

(*e*) the party entitled to compensation may draw a bill upon the party due to compensate him, payable at sight or on demand, for the amount due to him, together with all expenses properly incurred by him. Such bill must be accompanied by the instrument dishonoured and the protest thereof (if any). If such bill is dishonoured, the party dishonouring the same is liable to make compensation thereof in the manner as in the case of his original bill."

PRESENTMENT AND NEGOTIATION OF INSTRUMENT

What is Presentment?

The process of presenting or placing the instrument before the maker, acceptor or drawee is known as a 'presentment of Negotiable Instrument'. The purpose of presentment of negotiable instrument may, either for acceptance or payment. There are three kinds of presentment :

(1) Presentment of Bills for their acceptance,
(2) Presentment of Promissory Note for sight.
(3) Presentment for payment.

(1) *Presentment of a Bill for Acceptance*

Presentment for acceptance is necessary only in case of Bills of Exchange. The term 'acceptance of a bill' may be defined as the indication by the drawee of his assent to the drawer that he will pay the amount of the bill on due date. After the drawee accepted the bill, he is known as the acceptor.

The liability of the drawee arises only when the bill of exchange is accepted by him. When the drawee of the bill signifies his consent in 'writing' to the drawer's order in the bill, by signing across the face of the bill with or without the word 'accepted' and 'delivers' back the bill to the holder or gives notice of acceptance to the holder, the bill is said to have been accepted.

The following bills need not be presented for acceptance :

(1) A bill payable on demand,

(2) A bill payable on fixed date (say 31st Aug.),

(3) A bill payable on the expiry of certain period (say 3 months).

The following bills, however, must be presented for acceptance in order to charge the parties with liability :

(*a*) A bill payable at a specified period 'after sight'. Such a bill must be presented to the drawee for sight or acceptance in order to fix the maturity of the bill (Sec. 61).

(*b*) A bill in which there is an express stipulation that it shall be presented for acceptance before it is presented for payment.

Essentials of Valid Acceptance

The essentials of a valid acceptance are :

(*a*) The acceptance must appear on the bill itself.

(*b*) The acceptance must be in writing.

(*c*) The acceptance must be signed by the drawee or his authorised agent.

(*d*) The accepted bill must be delivered back to the holder.

Even where the presentation is optional, it is advisable to present the bill to the drawee for his acceptance in order to get :

(1) the additional security of the acceptor's name on the bill, or

(2) an immediate right of recourse against the drawer and the indorsers, if any, in case the bill is dishonoured by non-acceptance.

Kinds of Acceptance

Acceptance may be general or qualified.

General Acceptance

It is also known as absolute acceptance. A general acceptance is according to the apparent tenor of the bill of exchange, *i.e.*, the drawee accepts the bill as originally drawn. In case of general acceptance the drawee makes himself liable to pay the amount due on the bill of exchange without any condition. The mere mention of the name of a bank where a payment is sought to be made does not make acceptance conditional.

Qualified Acceptance (Conditional Acceptance) (Sec. 86)

Where an acceptance is made subject to certain condition or qualification, thereby varying the effect of the bill as drawn, it is a qualified acceptance. For example, if the drawee accepts the bill subject to some condition to be fulfilled or subject to the happening of an event, acceptance is said to be conditional. A qualified acceptance may be :

(*a*) *Conditional :* The payment is made to depend on the fulfillment of some condition or on the happening of some event, for example, "Accepted payable on safe receipt of goods", or "Accepted payable after receiving the railway receipt" etc.

(*b*) *Partial :* An acceptance which undertakes to pay only a part of the amount of the bill is a partial acceptance, for example, a bill drawn for Rs. 5,000 is "accepted for Rs. 4,000 only".

(*c*) *Qualified as to time :* An acceptance which makes the payment of the amount of the bill payable at a time different from that mentioned in the order of the drawer. For example, where a bill is drawn payable 3 months after date and is "accepted, payable six months after date" or "where a bill in which no time is fixed is accepted payable on a particular date is qualified as to time."

(*d*) *Qualified as to place :* It is the acceptance by which the drawee undertakes to pay the amount due on the bill of exchange only at a specified place and not elsewhere, or to pay at a place different from the place mentioned in the bill itself. For example, "Accepted, payable at Canara Bank and not elsewhere", etc.

(*e*) *Acceptance by some of the drawee only :* It is the acceptance by which only one of the several drawees undertakes to pay the amount due on the bill of exchange. Where the drawees are not partners and only one or some of them accept, the acceptance is qualified. But if the drawees are partners, one or more can accept on behalf of all the partners and the acceptance will be general.

(*f*) *Acceptance for payment in instalments :* It is the acceptance by which the drawee undertakes to pay the amount due on the bill of exchange in instalments. For example, a bill drawn for Rs. 1,000 and accepted in words reading as "accepted, payable in monthly instalments of Rs. 500."

Who may accept

A bill can be presented for acceptance to any one of the following :

(1) *Drawee :* The drawee of the bill or his duly authorised agent.

(2) *Joint Drawees of Bill :* Where there are several drawees of a bill who are not partners, each of them can accept it for himself, but none of them can accept it for another without his authority. To make all the drawees liable on the bill, it should be accepted by all of them.

(3) *Legal Representatives of a Drawee :* If the drawee is dead, his legal representatives (*i.e.*, heirs) can accept the bill of exchange.

(4) *Official Receiver :* If the drawee is declared as an insolvent, his official receiver or assignee can accept the bill of exchange.

(5) *The drawee in case of need :* If the original drawee refuses to accept the bill, then the bill should be presented for acceptance to a 'drawee in case of need', if there is any.

(6) *The Agent :* The agent of the acceptor for honour.

(7) *The acceptor for honour :* An acceptor for honour *i.e.*, any person who accepts the bill for the honour of any party already liable on it.

Time and Place for Presentment (Sec. 61)

According to Sec. 61, "A bill of exchange payable after sight must, if no time or place is specified therein for presentment, be presented to the drawee thereof for acceptance, if he can, after reasonable search, be found, by a person entitled to demand acceptance within reasonable time after it is drawn, and in business hours on a business day. In default of such presentment, no party thereto is liable thereon to the person making such default. If the drawee cannot, after reasonable search, be found, the bill is dishonoured."

"If the bill is directed to the drawee at a particular place it must be presented at that place; and if at the due date for presentment he cannot after reasonable search be found there, the bill is dishonoured."

"Where authorised by agreement or usage, a presentment through the post office by means of a registered letter is sufficient."

The rules with regard to time and place of presentment for acceptance are as follows :

(1) Bill must be presented before maturity.

(2) It must be presented by a person entitled to demand acceptance.

(3) It should be presented in business hours on a business day.

(4) If authorised by agreement or usage, presentment through post office by means of a registered letter is sufficient.

(5) Where presentment is obligatory, it must be made within reasonable time or without unreasonable delay.

(6) Where a period for a presentment is specified in a bill, it must be presented within that period.

(7) If the drawee has no particular place of business or a fixed residence, and no place for presentment is specified, presentment can be made wherever the drawee is found.

(8) A bill payable after sight must, if no time is specified therein for presentation, be presented within a reasonable time, after it is drawn.

(9) If, after a reasonable search, the drawee cannot be found, the bill is dishonoured.

(10) If a bill, which requires acceptance, is not presented for acceptance in accordance with rules mentioned above, the drawer and all indorsers are discharged from their liability to the holder.

Drawee time for Deliberation (Sec. 63)

According to Sec. 63, "The holder must, if so required by the drawee of a bill of exchange presented to him for acceptance, allow the drawee forty-eight hours (exclusive of public holidays) to consider whether he will accept it."

Presentment of Acceptance when Excused?

Presentment for acceptance is generally necessary but in following cases, it is excused :

(1) When the drawee cannot be found after reasonable search; (Sec. 61)

(2) When the drawee is a fictitious person; (Sec. 91)

(3) When the drawee is incapable to contract; (Sac. 91)

(4) When acceptance is refused on some other ground.

(5) Where the drawee is dead or insolvent, the instrument may be presented for acceptance to the legal hairs or the assignee. (Sec.75).

When the presentment for acceptance is excused, the bill is treated as dishonoured.

Acceptance for Honour

According to Sec. 7, "When a bill of exchange has been noted or protested for non- acceptance or for better security and any person accepts it supra protest for honour of the drawer or of any one of the indorsers, such person is called as 'acceptor for honour'."

It is a peculiar type of acceptance of a bill of exchange, which is allowed when the original acceptor refuses to accept the bill of exchange. As a general rule, a stranger cannot accept a bill. But when a bill is being dishonoured by non-acceptance, the holder may allow any other person to accept it for the honour of the drawer or any other party thereto.

Conditions for Valid Acceptance for Honour

The analysis of Sections 108 and 109 reveals the following conditions for a valid acceptance for honour are as under :

(1) The acceptance for honour can be made only in case of a bill of exchange which has been noted and protested for non-acceptance or for better security. But before the acceptance for honour, the bill must have been noted or protested for non-acceptance.

(2) It must be made with the consent of the holder.

(3) It must be made only by the person, who is not liable to that bill.

(4) It must be made in writing on the bill and for the whole amount of the bill.

(5) It must be for the honour of any party liable on the bill.

(6) It must indicate that it is an acceptance for honour.

(7) It must be signed by the acceptor for honour.

(8) It must be made before the bill is overdue.

Liability of Acceptor for Honour (Sec. 111)

According to Section 111, "An acceptor for honour binds himself to all parties subsequent to the party for whose honour he accepts to pay the amount of the bill if the drawee do not; and such party and all prior parties are liable in their respective capacities to compensate the acceptor for honour for all loss or damage sustained by him in consequence of such acceptance."

"But an acceptor for honour is not liable to the holder of the bill unless it is presented, or (in case the address given by such acceptor on bill is a place other than the place where the bill is made payable) forwarded for presentment, not later than the day next after the day of its maturity."

2. Presentment for Sight (Sec. 62)

"Presentment for sight" is necessary only in the case of a promissory note which is made payable at a certain period after sight so that the maturity of the note may be ascertained. Sec.62 lays down that "A promissory note, payable at a certain period after sight, must be presented to the maker thereof for sight (if he can, after reasonable search, be found) by a person entitled to demand payment, within a reasonable time after it is made and in business hours on a business day. In default of such presentment, no party thereto is liable thereon to the person making such default."

The rules as laid down in the Act are as follows :

(1) The expression 'after sight' on a note means that the payment is not to be demanded till it has been shown to the maker.

(2) Where a note is made payable after sight, it is necessary to present it for sight in order to fix the maturity of it.

(3) If the maker is not found, after reasonable search, presentment is excused and the instrument is treated to have been dishonoured.

(4) The presentment should be made during business hours on a business day.

(5) In case of default in such presentation, no party thereto is liable thereon to the person making such default.

3. Presentment for Payment (Sec. 64)

According to Sec. 64, "Promissory note, bills of exchange and cheque must be presented for payment to the maker, acceptor or drawee thereof respectively, by or on behalf of the holder as hereinafter provided. In default of such presentment, the other parties thereto are not liable thereon to such holder."

"Where authorised by agreement or usage, a presentment through the post office by means of a registered letter is sufficient."

"Exception—where a promissory note is payable on demand and is not payable at a specified place, no presentment is necessary in order to charge the maker thereof."

Presentment for Payment is Unnecessary (Sec. 76)

Cases in which negotiable instrument need not be presented for payment and still it may be treated as dishonoured. (Sec. 76)

(1) When the presentment is intentionally prevented by the maker, drawee or acceptor.

(2) When business place is closed during the usual business hours.

(3) When there is no person to make payment at the place fixed for payment.

(4) Where the payer is not found even after reasonable search.

(5) When there is a promise to pay without presentation.

(6) Where the payee expressly or impliedly waives his right;

(7) Where the drawer did not suffer any damage by non-payment;

(8) Where the instrument is dishonoured for non-payment.

(9) Where presentment has become impossible.

(10) Where the drawee is a fictitious person.

(11) When drawer and drawee are the same person.

(12) Where a note is payable on demand, but not payable on specified date.

Rules regarding Presentation for Payment (Secs. 64 to 75A)

(1) *Hours for Presentment* (Sec. 65) : presentment for payment must be made during the usual hours of business, and, in case of a cheque during banking hours.

(2) *Presentment for Payment of Instrument Payable after date or Sight* (Sec. 66) : "A promissory note or bill of exchange made payable at a specified period after date or sight thereof must be presented for payment at maturity. "Any delay in presentment, even a day's delay, after maturity discharges all the parties thereof.

(3) *Presentment of Promissory Note Payable in Instalments* (Sec. 67) : "A note payable in installments on the third day after the date fixed for payment of each instalment. If any instalment is not paid on such presentment, it has the same effect as non-payment of the note on maturity."

(4) *Place of Presentment* (Secs. 68 to 71): (*a*) Where a bill is made or accepted at a specified place, it must be presented at that place for payment (Sec. 68).

(*b*) Where the place for payment is specified in the bill, it must be presented for payment at that place (Sec. 69).

(*c*) Where no place is specified for payment, the instrument must be presented at the place of business (if any) or at the usual residence of the maker, drawer or acceptor, as the case may be (Sec. 70).

(*d*) Where the maker, drawee or acceptor has no known place of business or fixed residence and no place is specified in the instrument, Sec. 71 provides that the instrument must be presented, wherever the maker, drawee or acceptor can be found.

(5) *Presentment of cheques* (Secs. 72 and 73) : (*a*) A cheque must be presented at the bank upon which it is drawn before the relation between the drawer and bank is altered to the prejudice of the drawer (Sec. 72).

(*b*) A cheque must, in order to charge any person except the drawer, be presented within a reasonable time after delivery thereof by such person (Sec. 73).

(6) *Presentment of Instrument Payable on Demand* (Sec. 74) : "Subject to the provisions of Section 31, a negotiable instrument payable on demand must be presented for payment within a reasonable time after it is received by the holder 'Sec. (74)'.

(7) *Presentment to Whom* (Sec. 75): As per Section 75, "Presentment for acceptance or payment may be made to the duly authorised agent of the drawee, maker or acceptor, as the case may be, or, where the drawee, maker or acceptor, has died, to his legal representative, or, where he has been declared insolvent, to his assignee (Sec. 75).

(8) *Delay in Presentment* (Sec. 75-A): "Delay in presentment for acceptance or payment is excused if the delay is caused by circumstances beyond the control of the holder, and not imputable to his default, misconduct or negligence. When the cause of delay ceases to operate, presentment must be made within a reasonable time."

(9) *When Presentment Unnecessary* (Sec. 76): In certain cases (given under a separate head) presentment for payment is excused.

(10) *Liability of Banker for Negligence* (Sec. 77) : When a bill discounted from a bank is dishonoured, he must exercise proper care to it and return it to the holder. If he is negligent, he will have to compensate the holder for any loss.

NEGOTIATION

The transfer of a negotiable instrument by one person to another so as to constitute the transferee, the holder of the instrument, is known as negotiation. One of the essential characteristics of a negotiable instrument is that it is freely transferrable from one person to another. Generally, the person who is entitled to receive the payment of a negotiable instrument (*i.e.*, holder) does not retain it till maturity but transfers it to his creditors in payment of his debt, who in turn again transfers it to his creditor and so on the ownership of a negotiable instrument continues to be transferred from one to another. A negotiable instrument can be transferred in two ways :

I. By negotiation under the negotiable Instrument Act.

II. By assignment under the transfer of Property Act.

I. *Negotiation*

According to Sec. 14, "where a promissory note, bill of exchange or cheque is transferred to any person, so as to constitute that person the holder thereof, the instrument is said to be negotiated." Thus, there are two essentials of negotiation :

(*a*) The instrument should be transferred from one person to another, and

(*b*) The transfer should be in such a manner so as to constitute the transferee of the instrument as its holder.

Mode of Negotiation

Transfer by negotiations may be in two ways :

(*i*) Negotiation by delivery

(*ii*) Negotiation by endorsement and delivery

(*i*) Negotiation by Delivery (Sec. 47)

Sec. 47, lays down, "Subject to the provisions of Sec. 58, a promissory note, bill of exchange or cheque payable to bearer is negotiable by delivery thereof.

Explanation : A promissory note, bill of exchange or cheque delivered on condition that it is not to take effect except in a certain event is not negotiable (except in the hand of a holder for value without notice of the condition) unless such event happens." In other words, a negotiable instrument payable to bearer can be transferred by mere delivery and the transferor becomes the holder of the instrument. Thus, where a promissory note, bill of exchange or cheque is payable to the bearer, it may be transferred by simple delivery, and the transferor need not sign his name on the instrument.

The above Section says further that the negotiation of an instrument which is to be affected on a certain event, cannot be affected, unless such event happens.

Examples : (*a*) A, the holder of a negotiable instrument payable to bearer, delivers it to B's agent to keep for B. The instrument has been negotiated.

(*b*) A, the holder of a negotiable instrument payable to bearer, which is in the hands of A's banker, who is at the time the banker of B, directs the banker to transfer the instrument to B's credit in the banker's account with B. The banker does so, and accordingly now possesses the instrument as B's agent. The instrument has been negotiated, and B has become the holder of it.

(*ii*) Negotiation by Endorsement and Delivery (Sec. 48)

According to Sec. 48, "Subject to the provisions of Section 58, a promissory note, bill of exchange or cheque payable to order is negotiable by the holder by indorsement and delivery thereof." This mode of negotiation requires the following two formalities to be complied with :

(*a*) The holder must indorse the negotiable instrument, *i.e.*, he must sign his name on the instrument, and

(*b*) The duly signed instrument must be delivered to the transferee.

Importance of Delivery in Negotiation (Sec. 46)

Section 46 lays down that, "The making acceptance or indorsement of a promissory note, bill of exchange or cheque is completed by delivery, actual or constructives."

"As between parties standing in immediate relation, delivery to be effectual must be made by the party making, accepting or indorsing the instrument, or by a person authorised by him in that behalf."

"As between such parties and of any holder of the instrument other than a holder in due course, it may be shown that the instrument was delivered conditionally or for a special purpose only, and not for the purpose of transferring absolutely the property therein."

"A promissory note, bill of exchange or cheque payable to bearer is negotiable by the delivery thereof."

"A promissory note, bill of exchange or cheque payable to or order is negotiable by the holder of indorsement and delivery thereof."

Negotiable instrument cannot be said to be made, accepted or indorsed unless it is delivered to the proper person. Mere transfer without the intention of passing the property is not sufficient to constitute a complete negotiation.

However, every change of possession need not amount to actual delivery. This is because, delivery to be effective, it is not just sufficient to hand over the instrument by a physical act, but there should also be the intention to transfer property.

Delivery of negotiable instrument may be :

(*a*) *Actual delivery :* Delivery is actual when the instrument is physically handed over by the transferor to the transferee or to someone on his behalf.

(*b*) *Constructive delivery :* It takes place when the instrument is delivered to an agent, clerk or servant of the transferee who holds the instrument on behalf of the transferee.

(*c*) *Conditional delivery :* Where the instrument is delivered with some condition attached, it is called a conditional delivery. In such a case the negotiation is not valid, *i.e.*, the property in the instrument does not pass to the transferee, till the condition in fulfilled. However, if it is subsequently negotiated to a holder in due course, he will get a good title to it and all prior parties shall be liable to him in spite of initial conditional delivery.

INDORSEMENT (ENDORSEMENT)

According to Sec. 15, "Where the maker or holder of a negotiable instrument signs the same, otherwise than as such maker, for the purpose of negotiation, on the back or face thereof or on a slip of paper annexed thereto or so signs for the same purpose a stamped paper intended to be completed as a negotiable instrument, he is said to indorse the same and is called the "Indorser."

Thus, an indorsement consists of the signature of the holder usually made on the back of the negotiable instrument with the object of transferring the instrument. The person making the indorsement is called an 'indorser' and the person to whom the instrument is indorsed is called an 'indorsee'.

ESSENTIALS OF A VALID INDORSEMENT

An endorsement in order to operate as a negotiation must comply with the following conditions :

(1) It should be on the instrument. If there is no space on it, it may be on a separate slip of paper annexed to the instrument called 'allonge'.

(2) The endorser should sign the endorsement in the same style and with the same spellings as written in the instrument.

(3) Signatures should be in ink and not by pencil or rubber stamp.

(4) It should be made by the holder or the maker. It cannot be endorsed by a stranger.

(5) The delivery of the instrument with the intention of passing the property in it to the indorsee is important.

(6) A partial indorsement, *i.e.*, an indorsement which purports to transfer to the endorsee a part only of the amount or which purports to transfer the instrument to two or more endorsees severally does not operate as a negotiation of instrument.

(7) An endorsement may be made in blank or full. It may also be restrictive.

(8) The name of a married woman should be accompanied by the name of her husband.

(9) Mere signature of the holder, without any words, also constitutes endorsement. Any number of endorsements may be made on the instrument.

(10) No particular form of words is necessary to create a contractual relationship between endorser and the endorsee.

An endorsement becomes complete only when :

(*a*) the holder signs on the face or back of the instrument;

(*b*) the instrument is delivered to the endorsee; and

(*c*) it is signed and delivered with the intention of vesting the endorsee with the rights of the holder.

Effect of indorsement (Sec. 50)

According to Sec. 50, "The indorsement of a negotiable instrument followed by delivery transfers to the indorsee the property therein with the right of further negotiation; but the indorsement may, by express words, restrict or exclude such right, or may merely constitute the indorsee an agent to indorse the instrument, or to receive its contents for the indorser, or for some other specified person."

Example : B signs the following indorsements on different negotiable instruments payable to bearer:

(*a*) "Pay the contents to C only".

(*b*) "Pay C for my use."

(*c*) "Pay C or order for the account of B".

(*d*) "The within must be credited to C."

These endorsements exclude the right of further negotiation by C.

(*e*) "Pay C".

(*f*) "Pay C value in account with the Oriental Bank."

(*g*) "Pay the contents to C, being part of the consideration in a certain deed of assignment executed by C to the endorser and others."

These endorsements do not exclude the right of further negotiation by C.

KINDS OF INDORSEMENTS

(1) *Blank or General Endorsement* [Secs. 16(1) and 54]

When the endorser signs his name only on the face or back of the instrument, it is known as blank or general endorsement. A blank endorsement specifies no indorsee and the instrument in consequence becomes payable to bearer even though originally it was payable to order (Sec. 54).

(2) *Full or Special Endorsement* [Sec. 16(1)]

If the indorser, in addition to his signature, also adds a direction to pay the amount mentioned in the instrument to, or to the order of, a specified person, the indorsement is said to be in full. For example, "pay R or order" or "pay to A". etc., followed by the signature of the endorser.

A blank indorsement may be converted into a full endorsement. The provision contained in Sec. 49 of the Act. According to this section, the holder of an instrument indorsed in blank, may convert it into an endorsement in full by writing the name of some person (indorsee) above the signature of the endorser. The advantage of such indorsement is that the holder does not become liable as an indorser though he transfers the instrument.

(3) *Partial Endorsement* (Sec. 56)

It purports to transfer to the endorsee only a part of the amount payable on the instrument. Such an endorsement does not operate as a negotiation of the instrument and is invalid.

> **Example :** A, a holder of a bill for Rs. 1,000, endorses it as "pay Rs. 500 to B or order and "Pay Rs. 500 to C or order. It is invalid. Neither B nor C can sue anybody nor can they endorse the instrument further.

(4) *Restrictive Endorsement* (Sec. 50)

An indorsement is said to be restrictive when the endorser, by express words, restricts the right of further negotiation of the instrument or merely entitles the indorsee of the instrument to receive the contents of the instrument for a specific purpose. For example, "Pay C for my use". "Pay C or order for the account of B."

(5) *Conditional or Qualified Endorsement* (Sec. 52)

An endorsement is conditional or qualified which limits or negatives the liability of the indorser. The endorser limits or excludes his own liability by putting some condition in the instrument. It differs from restrictive indorsement. The restrictive indorsement prohibits further negotiability of the instrument. But the conditional indorsement does not prohibit the negotiability. It simply limits or excludes the liability of the endorser. Such an endorsement is done in any one of the following forms:

(*a*) *Sans Recourse Endorsement*

This endorsement is done in such a way that the endorser does not incur any liability to the endorsee. It is done by adding the words "sans recourse". For example, "Pay to X or order sans recourse."

(*b*) *Facultative Endorsement*

When the endorser increases his liability or abandons some rights against the instrument, it is called a facultative endorsement. For example, "Pay to A or order. Notice of dishonour waived."

(*c*) *Liability Dependent upon a Contingency*

An endorser endorses an instrument in such a way that his liability becomes dependent upon the happening of some specified event, which may or may not happen. For example, "Pay to A or order on his marriage with B".

(*d*) *Sans Frais Endorsement*

Where the endorser does not want the endorsee of any subsequent holder of the instrument to incur any expenses on his account, the endorsement is known as san frais.

Cancellation of Indorsement (Sec. 40)

According to Sec. 40, "Where the holder of a negotiable instrument, without the consent of the indorser, destroys or impairs the indorser's remedy against a prior party, the indorser is discharged from liability to the holder to the same extent as if the instrument had been paid at maturity."

> **Example :** A is the holder of a bill of exchange made payable to the order of B, which contain the following indorsements in blank :
> First indorsement. "B".
> Second indorsement. "Peter Williams".
> Third indorsement. "Wright and Co."
> Fourth indorsement. "John Rozario".
> This bill A puts in suit against John Rozario and strikes out without John Rozario's consent, the indorsement, by Peter William and Wright and Co. A is not entitled to recover anything from John Rozario.

NEGOTIATION BACK

If an endorser, after he has negotiated an indorsement, again becomes its holder before its maturity, the endorsement is called negotiation back. In such a case, all the intermediate parties are absolved of their liability. Even the general rule, that a holder in due course may sue all prior parties to the instrument, does not apply here. Thus, as a result of an instrument being negotiated back to a prior party, restores him to his original position.

Example : A bill is drawn payable to X or order. X endorses it to Y, Y to Z. Z to P, P to Q and Q to X. The endorsement by Q to X is negotiated back. X having come to his original position, cannot sue other parties, *i.e.*, Y, Z, P and Q.

II. ***Assignment***

The term 'assignment' may be defined as the transfer of one's right to recover the payment of a debt. The assignment is the sale of person's right to receive the payment of a debt. The effect of assignment of an instrument as an actionable claim under the Transfer of Property Act also amounts to its transfer from one person to another. In such a case the assignee gets the rights of a holder, but not of a holder in due course, *i.e.*, an assignee gets the rights only as an assignee and not more. The person who transfers his right under the negotiable instrument, is called an assignor. The person to whom such rights are transferred, is called an assignee.

Comparison between negotiation and assignment

The following table gives the comparison between the two

Negotiation	*Assignment*
1. Consideration is presumed.	1. Consideration must be proved.
2. The bonafide holder in due course gets better title than the transferror.	2. The title of the transferee is subject to the same defects as that of transferor.
3. Instruments payable to bearer are negotiated by mere delivery and instruments payable to order are negotiated by endorsement and delivery.	3. Assignment requires a written documents duly signed by the transferor.
4. Notice of transfer to the debtor by the transferee is not necessary.	4. Notice of assignment of a debt, in order to make the assignment complete and effective, must be given by the assignee to the debtor.

Negotiation by Unauthorised Parties (Sec. 58)

(1) ***Lost Negotiable Instrument***

A lost negotiable instrument is one, which has been lost by its holder before it becomes due. According to Sec. 45-A, "Where a bill of exchange has been lost before it is overdue, the person who was the holder of it may apply to the drawer to give him another bill of the same tenor giving security to the drawee, if required, to indemnify him, against all persons whatever in case the bill alleged to have been lost shall be found again." "If the drawer on request as aforesaid refuses to give such duplicate bill, he may be compelled to do so." Thus the following rules are applicable :

(*i*) When a negotiable instrument is lost, the holder should inform all parties liable on it and should also give public notice.

(*ii*) The finder of the lost instruments gets no title to it and cannot sue the party liable thereon for its payment. The rightful holder is entitled to get back the instrument from him.

(*iii*) Where a bill of exchange has been lost before it is overdue, the holder of it may apply to the drawer to give him another bill of the same tenor, giving security to the drawer, if required, to indemnify him against loss.

(*iv*) An acceptor or maker who makes payment in due course on lost bill or note to a finder thereof is discharged from all liability to the rightful owner. But the true owner can recover the money from the finder.

(*v*) Where a bill or note payable to bearer or indorsed in blank is lost and the finder negotiates it to a bona fide transferee for value the latter acquires a valid title to it. He can retain the instrument as against the true owner, and also claim payment from parties liable thereon.

(*vi*) If a negotiable instrument payable to order is indorsed by the finder with a forged signature, the indorsee gets no title even though he might have taken it in good faith and for consideration. Forgery can confer to title.

(2) *Stolen Instrument*

The position in case of a stolen negotiable instrument is almost the same as in the case of lost instrument, with the difference that on being traced the thief is open to criminal prosecution while a finder is not. A thief does not acquire any title to an instrument. If he receives payment on it, the holder can sue him for the recovery of the amount.

(3) *Instrument Obtained by Fraud*

If a person obtains a negotiable instrument by fraud, undue influence or coercion, he is not entitled to enforce its payment as his title is defective. But if such an instrument is transferred to a holder in due course, such a holder will acquire good title to it and the plea of fraud will not be of use against him.

(4) *Instrument Obtained for an Unlawful Consideration*

An instrument obtained for an unlawful consideration is void and does not convey a valid title to the holder as the general rule, as to the legality of object or consideration equally applies to negotiable instruments. A negotiable instrument given for a consideration which is illegal, or opposed to public policy or immoral or specially prohibited statute, is void and creates no obligation between the parties thereto. But if such an instrument passes into the hands of a holder in due course, such holder and any holder deriving title from such holder in due course gets a good title to the instrument.

(5) *Forged Instruments*

A forged instrument is one on which the signature of a drawer, maker or acceptor is forged. A forged indorsement is regarded in law as no indorsement at all. Forged instrument is totally ineffective and its holder cannot recover the amount due on it. A forged signature is altogether inoperative, and a forged instrument is without any title. It cannot confer any right or create any liability. A forged instrument cannot enforce it and if he obtains payment on such instrument, the person making the payment can recover the amount paid him as payment under a mistake.

(6) *Forged Indorsement*

If a negotiable instrument is negotiated through a forged endorsement, a person claiming under such indorsement does not acquire the rights of a holder in due course, even if he has purchased it for value and in good faith. He acquires no title to the instrument. If the party liable to pay on the instrument makes the payment to the indorsee who holds it under a forged indorsement, he shall continue to be liable to the true owner. If in a bearer instrument or in an instrument indorsed in blank, there is a forged indorsement, the holder gets a good title. The reason is that in such instruments the holder derives title by delivery and not through any indorsement. The forged indorsement, is therefore, immaterial.

(7) *Instrument without Consideration*

Unlike ordinary contracts, in the case of negotiable instruments there is a presumption of consideration. Until contrary is proved there shall be a presumption that every negotiable instrument was drawn, made, accepted, indorsed, negotiated or transferred for consideration [118 (*a*)]. Sections 44 and 45 state that when there is a partial absence or failure of consideration, the immediate parties cannot recover more than the consideration, but this rule will not apply to a holder in due course.

THEORETICAL QUESTIONS

1. What do you mean by the capacity of a party to a negotiable instrument? State the extent to which a minor can be a party to a negotiable instrument.
2. Define a holder of bill and distinguish the holder from holder in due course.
3. What is meant by 'acceptance' of a bill of exchange? Describe the essentials of a valid acceptance. Who can be the acceptor of a bill of exchange.
4. What is qualified acceptance? Is the holder bound to acquiescence in such an acceptance and what is the effect of such qualified acceptance?
5. What is the nature of liability of parties to a bill? What is the extent of liability of parties to an instrument?
6. When is a negotiable instrument said to be negotiable? Distinguish between 'Negotiation' and Assignment'.
7. What is the liability of a maker of a promissory note? What is its nature?
8. What is meant by 'presentment of negotiable instruments'?
9. Explain 'presentment for payment' of negotiable instruments. Under what circumstances the presentment for payment is not necessary?
10. State the provisions of the Act relating to time and place of presentment for payment.
11. What is the effect of fraud, forgery and absence of consideration on a negotiable instrument?
12. Define indorsement. What are its essentials, what are its effect and how can it be cancelled? Also discuss the types of endorsement.
13. What is acceptance for honour? How can acceptance for honour be made? What are the liabilities of an acceptor for honour?
14. What is meant by negotiation of a negotiable instrument? State the rights and liabilities of the parties to a negotiable instrument.
15. *Write shorts on :* (*a*) Lost Instrument, (*b*) Stolen instrument, (*c*) Forged instrument, (*d*) Instrument without consideration, (*e*) Forged indorsement. (*f*) Negotiation back, (*g*) Instrument obtained by fraud.

MULTIPLE CHOICE QUESTIONS

Choose correct option for each of the following :

1. A negotiable instrument drawn in favour of a Minor is :
(*o*) void. (*b*) valid.
(*c*) voidable. (*d*) invalid.

2. On acceptance of a bill of exchange by the drawee, he is legally known as :
(*a*) acceptor. (*b*) drawee in case of need.
(*c*) acceptor for honour. (*d*) none of these.

3. Which of the following is not competent to draw a valid negotiable instrument :
(*a*) agent. (*b*) company.
(*c*) partnership firm. (*d*) insolvent.

4. A person becomes a 'holder in due course' of a negotiable instrument if he receives it :
(*a*) in good faith. (*b*) before maturity.
(*c*) for value. (*d*) by satisfying all the above.

5. A holder is a person who is entitle to the instrument in his own name, and the term includes :
(*a*) payee of instrument. (*b*) endorsee of instrument.
(*c*) bearer of instrument. (*d*) all of these.

6. On the acceptance of the bill of exchange by the drawee, the liability of the drawer becomes :
(*a*) primary. (*b*) Conditional.
(*c*) secondary. (*d*) none of these.

7. A negotiable instrument payable to order can be transferred by :
(*a*) simple delivery. (*b*) indorsement and delivery.
(*c*) indorsement. (*d*) registered post.

8. In case, back of a negotiable instrument is full of indorsements, a slip of paper may be attached to the instrument for signing indorsements, which is known as :
(*a*) allonge. (*b*) zickri chit.
(*c*) escrow. (*d*) peth.

9. An indorsement made by an indorser by signing his name and also by writing the name of the indorsee is known as :
(*a*) general endorsement. (*b*) restrictive indorsement.
(*c*) special endorsement. (*d*) none of these.

10. An indorsement by which the indorser excludes his liability by express words, is known as :
(*a*) facultative indorsement. (*b*) sans recourse indorsement.
(*c*) restrictive indorsement. (*d*) contingent indorsement.

11. When during the course of negotiation, the negotiable instrument comes back to the original indorser, it is known as :
(*a*) facultative indorsement. (*b*) reverse indorsement.
(*c*) back recourse indorsement. (*d*) negotiation back.

12. The presentment for acceptance is required in case of a :
(*a*) bill of exchange. (*b*) cheque.
(*c*) promissory note. (*d*) both (*a*) and (*b*).

13. The presentment for acceptance is required in case of a :
(*a*) bill of exchange. (*b*) cheque.
(*c*) promissory note. (*d*) both (*b*) and (*c*).

14. The presentment for sight is required in case of a :
(*a*) bill of exchange. (*b*) cheque.
(*c*) promissory note. (*d*) all of these.

15. A negotiable instrument should be presented for payment to the party who is :
(*a*) primarily liable. (*b*) willing to make payment.
(*c*) secondary liable. (*d*) capable of making payment.

ANSWERS

1. (*b*) **2.** (*a*) **3.** (*d*) **4.** (*d*) **5.** (*d*) **6.** (*c*) **7.** (*b*) **8.** (*a*) **9.** (*c*) **10.** (*b*)
11. (*d*) **12.** (*a*) **13.** (*c*) **14.** (*d*) **15.** (*a*).

CHAPTER

Dishonour and Discharge of Negotiable Instrument

AT A GLANCE

- Introduction
- Dishonour by Non-acceptance
- Dishonour by Non-payment
- Consequences of Dishonour
- Notice of Dishonour, by Whom, to whom, FORM etc.
- Reasonable Time
- Noting and Protest
- Contents – Compensation
- Discharge of Instrument
- Discharge of One or More parties
- Material Alteration, Effect
- International Law
- Hundi
- Theoretical Questions
- Objective Type Questions.

INTRODUCTION

When an instrument on its maturity remains unsatisfied, the instrument is said to be dishonoured. A negotiable instrument may be dishonoured either by (*i*) non-acceptance or (*ii*) non-payment. As presentment for acceptance is required only in case of bill of exchange, it is only the bill of exchange which may be dishonoured by non-acceptance. Thus a negotiable instrument may be dishonoured in either of the following two ways :

(*i*) Due to non-acceptance

(*ii*) Due to non-payment.

A bill of exchange may be dishonoured due to non-acceptance or non-payment because acceptance is required only in case of bill of exchange. A cheque or a promissory note can only be dishonoured due to non-payment as these instruments do not require any acceptance.

Dishonour by Non-acceptance (Sec. 91)

According to Sec. 91, "A bill of exchange is said to be dishonoured by non-acceptance when the drawee, or one of several drawees not being partners, makes default in acceptance upon being duly required to accept the bill, or where presentment is excused and the bill is not accepted."

Thus a bill of exchange is treated as dishonoured due its non-acceptance in any of the following cases :

(1) When the drawee does not accept it within 48 hours from the time of presentment for acceptance;

(2) When presentment for acceptance is excused and it remains unaccepted;

(3) When the drawee is a person incompetent to contract;

(4) When the drawee could not be found after a reasonable search;

(5) Where the acceptance is qualified;

(6) Where one or more of several drawees refuse to accept the bill;

(7) When the drawee is a fictitious person.

Sec. 115 provides that, "if a 'drawee in case of need' is mentioned in a bill, the bill is not deemed to be dishonoured, unless it is dishonoured by such drawee in case of need also".

Dishonour by Non-Payment (Sec. 92)

Sec. 92 provides that, "A promissory note, bill of exchange or cheque is said to be dishonoured by non-payment when the maker of the note, acceptor of the bill or drawee of the cheque makes default in payment upon being duly required to pay the same."

Under Sec. 76, an instrument is also dishonoured by non-payment when its presentment for payment is excused and the instrument remains unpaid even when overdue.

Thus, in brief, the following are the cases of dishonour by non-payment :

(1) when the instrument is duly presented for payment and payment is refused or cannot be obtained;

(2) when presentment for payment is excused, and the instrument remains unpaid at maturity; and

(3) when the instrument which is overdue, remains unpaid.

CONSEQUENCES OF DISHONOUR

As soon as a negotiable instrument is dishonoured, either by non-acceptance or non-payment, the holder takes the following steps :

(1) He becomes entitled to file a suit for the recovery of the amount due from the parties liable to pay.

(2) He must, subject to certain exception, give notice of dishonour to parties against whom he intends to proceed.

(3) He may also have the instrument noted and protested before a notary public.

Notice of Dishonour (Sec. 93)

Notice of dishonour means a formal communication of the fact of dishonour. When a negotiable instrument is dishonoured, the holder must give a notice of dishonour to all the parties to whom he wants to make liable to the instrument. It serves as a warning to the person to whom the notice is given that he could now be made liable. Such notice is necessary irrespective of the nature of the instrument. If he does not give this notice, except in cases when notice of dishonour may be excused, all the prior parties liable thereon are discharged of their liability.

NOTICE OF DISHONOUR, BY WHOM?

(1) The notice of dishonour of the instrument may be given by the holder or any of the parties liable on the instrument to the prior parties (Sec. 93).

(2) According to Sec. 95, the party receiving notice of dishonour, must, in turn give notice of dishonour to the prior party whom he seeks to hold liable. This transmission of notice, as the section itself lays down, should be made within reasonable time.

(3) When an instrument, deposited with an agent for presentment, is dishonoured, the agent will give a notice to his principal and the principal will give such notice (Sec. 96).

NOTICE OF DISHONOUR, TO WHOM?

Notice of dishonour may be given :

(1) to all persons whom the holder seeks to make liable; (Sec. 93) or

(2) to a duly authorised agent of the person to whom it is required to be given; (Sec. 94)

(3) to the legal representative of deceased party; (Sec. 94)
(4) to the assignee of the insolvent (Sec. 94).

When the party to whom notice of dishonour is dispatched, is dead, but the party dispatching the notice is ignorant of his death, the notice is sufficient. (Sec. 97)

Form of notice (Sec. 94)

(1) The notice of dishonour may be oral or in writing.
(2) It may be given even by post.
(3) It may be in any form, but it should inform the party, to whom it is given, that the instrument is dishonoured.
(4) It must be given within a reasonable time.
(5) It must be given at the place of business or residence of the party to whom it is intended.

REASONABLE TIME

A notice of dishonour must be given within a 'reasonable time' of dishonour. The term 'reasonable time will depend upon the nature of the negotiable instrument and the usual course of dealing between the parties with respect to similar instruments.

(1) In calculating the reasonable time, public holidays must be excluded (Sec. 105).
(2) If the holder and the party to whom this notice is to be given carry on business or live in different places, such notice is given within a reasonable time if it is despatched by the next post, or on the day next after the day of dishonour. If they live or carry on business in the same place, the notice should be despatched in time to reach its destination on the day next after the day of dishonour (Sec. 106).
(3) The party receiving the notice must present it within a reasonable time to other parties, *i.e.*, within thc same time as he would have had to give notice if he had been the holder. (Secs. 95 and 107).

When Notice of Dishonour is Unnecessary (Sec. 98)

No notice of dishonour is necessary in the following cases :

(1) When it is dispensed with by the party entitled thereto;
(2) to charge the drawer, when he has countermanded the payment;
(3) when the party charged could not suffer damage for want of notice of dishonour;
(4) when the party entitled to notice, could not be found through reasonable search;
(5) to charge the drawer, when the acceptor is also drawer, *i.e.*, the drawer and the drawee are the same person.
(6) in case of a promissory note, which is not negotiable; and
(7) when the party entitled to notice, knowing the facts, promises unconditionally to pay the amount due on the instrument.

NOTING AND PROTESTING

Noting (Sec. 99)

The term 'noting' may be defined as the recording of the fact of dishonour by a Notary Public upon the negotiable instrument. Where a promissory note or bill of exchange is dishonoured, the holder can, after giving due notice of dishonour, sue the liable parties for the recovery of amount due on the instrument. But before he files such a suit, he needs some authenticated proof of the fact, to be put up before the court, that the bill or note is actually dishonoured. For this the holder takes the bill or note to the Notary Public who makes a demand for acceptance or payment upon the drawee or acceptor or maker formally and on his refusal to do so notes the same on the bill or note. Thus 'noting' means recording the fact of dishonour on the dishonoured instrument or on a paper attached thereto for the purpose. Noting should be done within a reasonable time after dishonour. Noting should specify the following on the instrument :

(*a*) the fact of the instrument being dishonoured;
(*b*) the date of dishonour;
(*c*) the reason, if any, assigned to the dishonour;
(*d*) if the instrument has not been expressly dishonoured, the reason, why it is being treated as dishonoured;
(*e*) the Notary's charges for such noting;
(*f*) a reference to the Notary's register.

Noting is not compulsory under law. If the dishonoured instrument is not 'noted', it does not affect the rights of the holder of the instrument in any way. However, it has certain advantages, for instance, it provides an authentic evidence of dishonour. 'Noting' is authentic and official proof of presentment and dishonour of a negotiable instrument. The question of noting does not arise in the case of a dishonour of a cheque because in such a case the bank, while refusing payment, returns back the cheque giving reasons in writing for the dishonour of the same, and that itself acts as an authentic evidence of the fact of dishonour.

Protesting (Sec. 100)

According to Sec. 100, "when the promissory note or bill of exchange has been dishonoured by non-acceptance or non-payment, the holder may, within a reasonable time, cause such dishonour to be noted and certified by a notary public. Such certificate is called a protest."

Protest for better security : (Sec. 100, para 2) "When the acceptor of a bill of exchange has become insolvent, or his credit has been publicly impeached, before the maturity of the bill, the holder may, within a reasonable time, cause a notary public to demand better security of the acceptor and on its being refused may, within a reasonable time, cause such facts to be noted and certified as aforesaid. Such certificate is called a protest for better security.

Contents of Protest (Sec. 101)

A protest under Section 100 must contain :

(1) The instrument itself or a literal transcript of the instrument and of everything written or printed thereupon.
(2) The name of the person for whom and against whom the instrument has been protested.
(3) The fact and the reasons for dishonour, that is, a statement that payment or acceptance, or better security, as the case may be, was demanded by the notary public from the person concerned and he refused to give it or did not answer, or that he could not be found.
(4) The place and time of dishonour.
(5) The signature of the Notary Public.
(6) In the case of acceptance for honour or payment for honour, the names of the persons by whom and for whom it is accepted or paid.

Notice of Protest (Sec. 102)

"When a promissory note or bill of exchange is required by law to be protested, notice of such protest must be given instead of notice of dishonour, in the same manner and subject to the same conditions; but the notice may be given by the notary public who makes the protest."

Protest of Foreign Bill (Sec. 104)

"Foreign bills of exchange must be protested for dishonour when such protest is required by the law of the place where they are drawn."

The following are the points of distinction between Noting and Protesting :

(1) Noting is merely a record of the fact of dishonour. When the notary public issues a certificate stating the particulars regarding the dishonour, it is called a protest.

(2) Noting is the preliminary step to 'Protesting'.

(3) Noting is made on the negotiable instrument by the notary public by way of memorandum, while a protest is a formal certificate drawn up later on the basis of noting.

Determination of Compensation (Sec. 117)

The compensation for dishonour of a bill or note, payable to the holder is determined as under :

1. ***Compensation to Holder*** [Sec. 117 (*a*) and (*b*)]

The holder of a dishonoured instrument is entitled to receive the following :

(*a*) the amount due upon the instrument;
(*b*) interest on the principal amount at the rate 18% p.a. from the date of payment of the tenor to the date of realization.
(*c*) expenses incurred on its presentment, noting and protesting;
(*d*) when the person charged resides at a different place from that at which the instrument is payable, the holder is entitled to receive the sum at the current rate of exchange between the two places.

2. ***Compensation to endorser*** [Sec. 117 (*c*) and (*d*)]

An endorser, who has paid the amount on the instrument, is entitled to the following :

(*a*) the amount which he has actually paid ;
(*b*) interest at 18% p.a. on the above amount from the date of payment until tender or realization of the instrument;
(*c*) all expenses incurred by him caused by dishonour;
(*d*) any loss caused as a result of difference in the exchange rate of the two countries. As per the Amendment Act of 1988, he will be paid at the current rate of exchange of the two places.

3. ***Re-draft*** [Sec. 117 (*e*)]

Any party entitled to compensation may draw a bill at sight or on demand on any party liable to compensate him. Such a bill is known as a 're-draft'. The redraft must be accompanied by the dishonoured bill and its protest, if any.

DISCHARGE FROM LIABILITY

A negotiable instrument is said to be discharged when the rights and obligations created by it, are extinguished, and the instrument does not give rise to any cause of action. After a negotiable instrument is discharged the rights against all the parties thereto comes to an end, and no party, even a holder in due course, can claim the amount of the instrument from any party thereto. The term' discharge' in relation to negotiable instruments has two meanings, namely, (*i*) the discharge of the instrument, and (*ii*) discharge of one or more parties from liability on the instrument.

Discharge of a negotiable instrument should be distinguished from the discharge of one or more parties liable on it. This is because the discharge of one or more parties thereto does not discharge the other parties liable on it. Thus, the two connotations, *viz*., (*i*) Discharge of the instrument and (*ii*) discharge of one or more parties from liability on the instrument are discussed below :

I. *Discharge of the Instrument*

A negotiable instrument is said to be discharged when it becomes completely useless, that is, no action on that will lie, and it cannot be negotiated further. An instrument is said to be discharged when all rights under it are extinguished, it ceases to be negotiable and even a holder in due course does not acquire any rights under it. Such a discharge of the negotiable instrument would take place when the party who is primarily and ultimately liable on the instrument is discharged from liability. A negotiable instrument may be discharged :

(1) By Payment [Sec. 82 (*c*)]
(2) By acceptor becoming the holder (Sec. 90)
(3) By Renunciation
(4) By cancellation [Sec. 82(*a*)]
(5) By Discharge as a simple contract

(1) *By Payment* [Sec. 82 (*c*)]

When the maker, acceptor or indorser makes payment on an instrument in due course to the person entitled to receive payment in accordance with the apparent tenor of the instrument in good faith and without negligence, discharges the parties to the instrument.

(2) *By Acceptor becoming the Holder* (Sec. 90)

According to Sec. 90, "If a bill of exchange which has been negotiated is, at or after maturity, held by the acceptor in his own right, rights of action thereon are extinguished."

(3) *By Renunciation*

A negotiable instrument is discharged when the holder renounces or gives up his right against all the parties to the instrument. The renunciation must be in writing unless the instrument is also surrendered to the party primarily liable.

(4) *By Cancellation* [Sec. 82 (*a*)]

According to Sec. 82 (*a*), "The maker, acceptor or endorser respectively of a negotiable instrument is discharged from liability thereon to a holder thereof who cancels such acceptor's or indorser's name with intent to discharge him, and to all parties claiming under such holder." This operates as a discharge of the instrument and is known as cancellation.

(5) *By Discharge as a Simple Contract*

A negotiable instrument may be discharged in the same way as any other contract for the payment of money. Thus, a negotiable instrument may be discharged by an agreement of the parties in the form of a novation, or by Rescission or by substitution of another negotiable instrument for the original instrument.

II *Discharge of One or More Parties for their Liability*

A party is said to be discharged from his liability when his liability on the instrument comes to an end. When only some of the parties to a negotiable instrument are discharged, the instrument continues to be negotiable and the undischarged parties remain liable on it. Thus the discharge of one or more parties to an instrument does not discharge the instrument and the rights under it can still be enforced against those parties who continue to be liable thereon.

A party may be discharged in any one of the following ways :

(1) *By Cancellation* [Sec. 82 (*a*)]

When the holder of a negotiable instrument or his agent cancels the name of a party on the instrument with intent to discharge him, such party and all subsequent parties, who have a right of recourse against the party, whose name is cancelled are discharged from the liability to the holder.

[Sec. 82(*a*)]. If the cancellation is done under a mistake, or without the authority of the holder, it would be inoperative and will not discharge any party.

(2) *By Release* [Sec. 82 (*b*)]

If the holder of a negotiable instrument releases any party to the instrument by any method other than cancellation of names, that is, by a separate agreement of waiver, release or remission, the party so released and all parties subsequent to him, who have a right of action against the party so released, are discharged from liability.

(3) *By Allowing Drawee more than 48 Hours* (Sec. 83)

According to Sec. 83, "If the holder of a bill of exchange allows the drawee more than 48 hours, exclusive of public holidays, to consider whether he will accept the same, all previous parties not consenting to such allowance are thereby discharged from liability to such holder".

(4) *By taking Qualified Acceptance* (Sec. 86)

If the holder of a bill takes a qualified acceptance all the previous parties whose consent is not obtained to such acceptance are discharged from liability, unless on notice being given, they assent to such acceptance. (Sec. 86).

(5) *By not giving Notice of Dishonour*

Any party to a negotiable instrument, other than the party primarily liable, to whom notice of dishonour is not sent by the holder is discharged from liability as against the holder, unless the circumstances are such that no notice of dishonour is required to be sent.

(6) *By Non-presentment for Acceptance of a Bill* (Sec. 61)

If the holder of a bill, payable after sight, does not present it to the drawee for acceptance within a reasonable time after it is drawn, the drawer, and all endorsers are discharged from their liability to him.

(7) *By Non-presentment of Cheque*

Where a cheque is not presented for payment within a reasonable time of its issue, and the bank fails and the drawer suffers actual damage through the delay, he is discharged from liability to the holder to the extent to which such drawer is a creditor of the banker, but no more (Sec. 84).

(8) *By Operation of Law*

A negotiable instrument may be discharged by the operation of law as in the case of insolvency of the debtor, or lapse of time, making the debt time-barred under the Limitation Act.

(9) *By Material Alteration* (Sec. 87)

A material alterations of a negotiable instrument renders the same void against persons who were parties thereto before such alteration, unless they have consented to the alteration.

Material Alteration (Secs. 87 to 89)

Any change in an instrument which causes it to speak a different language in legal effect from that which it originally spoke, or which changes the legal identity of the instrument either in its terms or in the relation of the parties to it, is a material alteration. If the material alteration affects the very purpose of the original instrument, that is, if it goes to the root of the instrument, it is a material alteration.

According to Sec. 87, "Any material alteration of a negotiable instrument renders the same void as against any one who is a party thereto at the time of making such alteration and does not consent thereto, unless it was made in order to carry out the common intention of the original parties".

Some alteration is material and some are immaterial. An alteration is material if it alters materially or substantially the operation of the instrument and thereby the rights and liabilities of the parties. "An alteration which alters the business effect of the instrument if used for any business purpose. Any change made in the instrument that causes it to speak a different language from what it originally intended, or which changes the legal identity of the instrument in its terms or in relation to parties thereto is a material alteration."

The following alterations are materials one, viz :

1. alteration in date,
2. alteration in the sum payable,
3 alteration in the time of payment,
4. alteration in the place of payment,
5. addition of place of payment, and
6. addition of rate of interest,
7. tearing an instrument in material part,
8. change of date of indorsement etc.

The Act does not define material alteration. However, a material alteration is one, (*a*) which substantially changes the rights and liabilities of the parties, or any of the parties, to the instruments, or (*b*) which changes the identity and the legal character of the instrument.

Alterations not Vitiating the Instrument

The following alterations do not vitiate the instrument :

(*a*) Conversion of an instrument 'payable to bearer' into an instrument 'payable to order'.

(*b*) Alteration to rectify mistakes;

(*c*) Addition of the words 'on demand' in an instrument, where no time of payment is stated;

(*d*) Alteration made before the issue, delivery or negotiation, that is, completion of the instrument;

(*e*) Alterations made at any time with the consent of the parties;

(*f*) Alterations resulting from an accident;

(*g*) Alteration of any note on the margin of an instrument which is neither a part to it, nor is covered by the signature on it, that is, an alteration which is not material.

Alterations Authorised by the Act

The authorised alterations are those which are permitted by the Negotiable Instruments Act. The following alterations, though material, are permitted by the Act.

(*a*) The filling in of the blanks in an inchoate instrument; (Sec. 20)

(*b*) The conversion of an endorsement in blank into an endorsement in full; (Sec. 49)

(*c*) The qualifying or limiting of an acceptance; (Sec. 86)

(*d*) The crossing of a cheques after it has been issued. (Sec. 125)

Effect of Material Alteration (Sec. 87)

According to Sec. 87, "Any material alteration of a negotiable instrument renders the same void as against anyone who is a party thereto, unless it was made in order to carry out the common interest of the original parties. If any such alteration is made by an endorsee, it discharges his endorsers from all liability to him in respect of the consideration thereof."

The above rule based on Sec. 87 is based on a sound policy and may be defended on two grounds :

(*i*) That nobody should be permitted to take the chance of committing a fraud without running any risk of loss by the event when it is detected; and

(*ii*) That by the alteration, the identity of the instrument is lost, and to hold one of the parties liable under such circumstances would make him liable for something, for which he would never agree.

INTERNATIONAL LAW

A negotiable instrument may be drawn is one country and payable is another country and in such cases, Sections 134 to 137 of the negotiable Instrument Act provide the legal rules, which are discussed below :

(1) *The Law Governing the Liability of the Parties* (Sec. 134)

According to Sec. 134, "In the absence of a contract to contrary, the liability of the maker, or drawer of a foreign promissory note, bill of exchange or cheque is regulated in all essential matters by the law of the place where he made the instrument, and the respective liabilities of the acceptor and indorser by the law of the place where the instrument is made payable."

Example : A bill of exchange was drawn by A in California, where the rate of interest is 25%, and accepted by B, payable in Washington, where the rate of interest is 16%. The bill is indorsed in India and is dishonoured. An action on the bill is brought about against B in India. He is liable to pay interest at the rate of 16% only : but if A is charged as drawer, A is liable to pay interest at the rate of 25%.

(2) *Dishonour of Foreign Instrument* (Sec. 135)

According to Sec. 135, "Where a promissory note, bill of exchange or cheque is made payable in a different place from that in which it is made or indorsed, the law of the place where it is made payable determines what constitutes dishonour and what notice of dishonour is sufficient."

Example : A bill of exchange drawn and indorsed in India, but accepted payable in France, is dishonoured. The indorsee causes it to be protested for such dishonour and gives notice thereof in accordance with the law of France. The notice is sufficient.

(3) *Instrument made out of India but According to Indian Law* (Sec. 136)

Sec. 136 provides that "If a negotiable instrument is made, drawn, accepted or indorsed outside India, but in accordance with the law of India, the circumstance that any agreement evidenced by such instrument is invalid according to the law of the country wherein it was entered into does not invalidate any subsequent acceptance or indorsement made thereon within India."

(4) *Presumption as to Foreign Law* (Sec. 137)

The law of any foreign country regarding promissory notes, bill of exchange and cheques shall be presumed to be the same as that of India, unless and untill the contrary is proved."

HUNDIS

There are many other negotiable instruments recognised by customs. Hundi is one of those instruments. The term 'hundi' is derived from Sanskrit word 'hund' which means to collect. These hundis were, therefore, originally used for collection of debts. Hundis are sometimes drawn in the form of a promissory note but more often they take the form of bill of exchange. A hundi is an indigenous negotiable instrument written in local language of the people. The hundis have been in circulation in India, even before the Negotiable Instruments Act 1881 came into existence and recognised by the customary law as valid and effective negotiable instruments. But Negotiable Instrument Act do not apply to hundis. They are governed by the local usages and customs of the trade where they are intended to be used.

CLASSIFICATION OF HUNDIS

There are mainly two type of hundis–Darshani Hundi and Muddati.

Darshani Hundi

The term 'darshani' means 'at sight'. It is payable at sight. It is similar to demand bill of exchange, that is, which is payable on demand. Darshani hundi sometimes sell at discount and sometimes they sell at a premium. A darshani hundi should be presented for payment within a reasonable time by the holder.

MUDDATI HUNDI

The term 'muddat' or 'miadi hundi' is payable after a specified period of time. It is similar to a time bill of exchange.

Some common type of hundis, which belong to above two classes are as follows;

Shah Jog Hundi

The term 'shah' means a respectable and responsible person, a man of worth, and known in the bazaar. A shah jog hundi is payable only to shah. It is freely transferable from one person to another by mere delivery and no endorsement is required for the same.

Nam Jog Hundi

The term 'nam' means the name of a person. A hundi payable to the specified person is called Nam Jog hundi. It is similar to a shah jog hundi except that in place of the word shah, the name of the payee is written. The nam, jog hundi is payable to the payee or his order, and, therefore, can be negotiable by endorsement and delivery.

Dhani Jog Hundi

The term 'dhani' means holder. Dhani jog hundi is one which is payable to the holder or bearer. It can be negotiated by mere delivery. The words 'dhani jog' are inserted in the hundi.

Firman Jog Hundi

Firman means 'order'. Firman Jog hundi is payable to order. It can be negotiated by endorsement and delivery.

Jawabee Hundi

It is a hundi which is used for remitting money from one place to another. On receipt of the money, the payee has to send an answer to the person remitting the money, that he has received the money. The money is remitted through a banker.

Jokhami Hundi

The term 'jokham' means the risk. Thus, a jokhami hundi is one which is drawn, by the seller on the buyer for the price of the goods sold, and which also covers the risk of loss of goods till they reach the buyer. This is the hundi drawn against goods shipped on the vessel named therein. The drawer of it is the consignor, who draw for the value of goods on the consignee. It is just like a policy of marine insurance and serves two fold purposes (*i*) it puts the drawer of the hundi in funds, as he gets the purchase price, less charges incurred, immediately, and (*ii*) it affects insurance upon the goods. The drawer negotiates the hundi to a broker, who charges a commission for his services.

When the vessel arrives safely, the broker gets the money. If the ship is lost, the broker has to bear the loss. Thus, it protects both the drawer and the drawee.

GENERAL TERMS

Following terms are more commonly used in the negotiation of hundis :

1. *Zickri Chit :* It is a letter of protection, which is given to the holder of the hundi by the drawer or some prior party to the hundi. It is addressed to some respectable person of the area requesting him to pay the amount of the hundi, in case the drawee refuses to accept or pay the amount of the hundi. In such a case, the person addressed therein accepts the hundi and pays it at maturity. Thus, his position is that of the acceptor for honour.

2. *Peth :* It means duplicate of hundi. Sometimes, the original hundi is lost. In such cases, the holder may demand from the drawer a duplicate one. Such a duplicate hundi is called a 'peth'.

3. *Perpeth :* The term 'perpeth' may be defined as the duplicate of the duplicate hundi. Sometimes, a peth is lost. In such cases, the holder may demand another duplicate and each subsequent duplicate is called a perpeth.

4. *Khoka :* A hundi when paid and cancelled is then called a 'khoka'.

5. *Purja :* The term 'purja' may be defined as a request in writing by the borrower to the lender to pay the amount mentioned therein. It bears stamp. It may be noted that 'purja' is not a negotiable instrument. These are commonly used for temporary loans.

THEORETICAL QUESTIONS

1. What is meant by dishonour by non-acceptance and dishonour by non-payment?
2. When a negotiable instrument considered as dishonoured? What are the duties of a holder upon such dishonour? (*B.Com. MS*)
3. When are bills of exchange, promissory note or cheques said to be dishonoured? Who should give notice of dishonour and to whom? (*B.Com. Madurai*)
4. When is a bill of exchange said to be dishonoured? When is notice of dishonour unnecessary?
5. What is understood by protest under the Negotiable Instrument Act? (*B.Com. Kolkata*)
6. What is meant by 'noting; and 'protest' of a dishonoured negotiable instrument?
7. What is the difference between 'discharge of a negotiable instrument' and 'discharge of a party to a negotiable instrument'? When is a negotiable instrument said to be discharged?
8. Explain the meaning of material alteration of a negotiable instrument. What is the effect of such alteration? (*B.Com. Bhopal*)
9. What are the various modes of discharge from liability of parties to a negotiable instrument?
10. "Material alteration of a negotiable instrument makes the instrument void". Explain.(*B.Com. Agra*)
11. Define hundi. Discuss various types of hundis used in India. (*B.Com. Poona*)

MULTIPLE CHOICE QUESTIONS

Choose correct option for each of the following :

1. After the dishonour of a negotiable instrument, the holder may get the fact of dishonour authenticated by a Notary Public. The 'noting' may be done in case of :

(*a*) Promissory note. (*b*) cheque.
(*c*) bill of exchange. (*d*) both (*a*) and (*c*).

2. In case of dishonour of a cheque, the holder's remedy is against the :

(*a*) drawee of a cheque. (*b*) indorsee of a cheque.
(*c*) drawer of cheque. (*d*) both (*a*) and (*c*).

3. A bill of exchange is discharged when its acceptor by negotiation back, becomes its holder :

(*a*) at maturity. (*b*) after maturity.

(*c*) before maturity. (*d*) both (*a*) and (*b*)

4. In which of the following cases of forgery, a banker is discharged from liability by making a payment in due course :

(*a*) payee's indorsement. (*b*) drawer's signatures.

(*c*) both (*a*) and (*b*). (*d*) none of these.

5. The payment of a negotiable instrument becomes due :

(*a*) at maturity. (*b*) after maturity.

(*c*) before maturity. (*d*) on 3rd day of maturity.

6. Which of the following negotiable instrument is not entitled to days of grace :

(*a*) a bill of exchange payable on specified date. (*b*) a promissory note payable on specified date.

(*c*) a pro-note payable after sight. (*d*) a cheque.

7. The negotiable instruments payable on a specified date, are due for payment :

(*a*) from the specified date. (*b*) from the third day after specified date.

(*c*) from the date of issue. (*d*) after presentment for sight.

8. A hundi which is payable 'at sight' is known as :

(*a*) miadi hundi. (*b*) darshani hundi.

(*c*) zikri. (*d*) none of these.

9. A hundi which is payable to the holder or bearer is known as :

(*a*) nam jog hundi. (*b*) firman hundi.

(*c*) jawabi hundi. (*d*) dhani jog hundi.

10. A hundi when paid up and cancelled, is then called :

(*a*) parpeth. (*b*) peth.

(*c*) khoka. (*d*) none of these.

ANSWERS

1. (*d*) **2.** (*c*) **3.** (*d*) **4.** (*a*) **5.** (*a*) **6.** (*d*) **7.** (*b*) **8.** (*b*) **9.** (*d*) **10.** (*c*)

THE CARRIAGE OF GOODS ACT

CHAPTER

Carriage of Goods by Land

AT A GLANCE

- Carriage by Land
- Common Carrier
- Characteristics, Duties, Exceptions
- Rights and Liability
- Private Carrier
- Common Carrier vs. Private Carrier
- Gratuitous Carrier
- Goods
- Railway as Carrier
- Duties
- Liabilities
- Theoretical Questions

Transport plays a vital role in economic development of a country. It facilitates the movement of goods and labour. The role of transport is very important in the development of commerce. Thus, carriage of goods from one place to another within the country or from one country to another plays an important role in commercial life of modern world. Therefore, the study of law relating to 'Contract of Carriage of Goods' is very important.

Goods may be carried by land, sea or air. Therefore, the law relating to carriage of goods may be studied under three heads : (1) Carriage by Land, (2) Carriage by Sea and (3) Carriage by Air. The Indian Statutes relating to the law of carriage are given below:

1. Carriage by Land :
   - (*i*) The Common Carriers Act 1865.
   - (*ii*) The Railway Act 1890.
2. Carriage by Sea :
   - (*i*) The Indian Bills of Lading Act 1856.
   - (*ii*) The Carriage of Goods by Sea Act 1925.
   - (*iii*) The Merchant Shipping Act 1958.
   - (*iv*) The Marine Insurance Act 1963.
3. Carriage by Air :

   Carriage by Air Act 1972.

A contract of carriage may be defined as "a contract under which one person agrees to carry goods or passengers from one place to another for a fixed remuneration. The persons who agree to carry the goods or passengers are called 'carriers'.

CARRIAGE BY LAND

The law relating to carriage of goods by land, including inland navigation, is contained in (*a*) The Carriers Act 1865 and (*b*) The Indian Railways Act 1890.

Classification of Carriers

The carriers are generally classified into (1) Common Carriers (also known as Public Carriers) and (2) Private Carriers. However, there is a third type of carriers known as 'Gratuitous Carriers'. Thus, there are three classes of carriers,

(1) Common or Public Carriers,
(2) Private Carriers, and
(3) Gratuitous Carriers.

1. Common or Public Carriers

A common carrier is one who undertakes for hire to transport from one place to another the goods of anyone willing to employ him either by land, sea or air. The Common Carriers Act 1865 defines a common carrier, as "any individual, firm or company (other than the Government) who transports goods, as a business for money, over land or inland waterways, without discrimination between different consignors."

Characteristics of Common Carrier

According to the definition given above, the characteristics of a common carrier in India are as follows :

(1) The common carrier may be an individual, a firm or company. But the Government is not included in the category. Thus, the post office is not a common carrier, though it may carry goods.

(2) Only the carriers of goods are common carriers, So, carriers of passengers are not included therein.

(3) One who carries goods as his regular business is a common carrier. A person carrying goods occasionally is not a common carrier.

(4) A common carrier is one who is ready to carry the goods of any person without any discrimination. If a carrier reserves to himself the right to reject an offer, he is not a common carrier.

(5) If a carrier offers to carry goods only from one specified place to another or to carry only a particular kind of goods, he is a common carrier.

(6) The term common carrier is restricted to carriage by land and inland waterways only.

(7) Charges for carrying goods are necessarily to be charged. One who carries goods free is not a common carrier.

DUTIES OF A COMMON CARRIER

The Common Carriers Act 1865 lays down the following duties. The English Common Law also apply to matters, not covered by this Act.

(*a*) *Carry for all :* He is bound to receive and carry all goods which he professes to carry for all persons, who agree to pay him proper charges and who choose to employ him for the carriage of their goods.

(*b*) *Carry goods safely :* He is the insurer of goods so takes all reasonable precautions for the safe carriage of the goods and deliver the goods safely.

(*c*) *Delivery within reasonable time :* Upon the completion of the transit, he must deliver the goods as instructed by the consignor at the agreed time or within reasonable time. He should not deviate from customary route and not cause unwanted delay.

(*d*) *Deliver the goods at the place* : He must deliver the goods at the place fixed by the consignor.

(*e*) *Keep the goods in his custody* : Where it is a practice to take delivery of goods at Wharf, the goods must be kept be the Carrier at his own risk in his custody for a reasonable time.

EXCEPTIONS

A common carrier is one who is bound to carry the goods of any person, who chooses to employ him for the purpose, without any discrimination. However, a common carrier cannot be compelled to carry goods under any of the following circumstances :

(1) The vehicle is already full and no room in the vehicle.

(2) The goods are of such nature, which he does not carry.

(3) The goods are of dangerous nature and expense him to extraordinary risk.

(4) The goods are not properly packed.

(5) The goods are not meant to be carried on his customary route.

(6) The consignor is not prepared to pay reasonable amount in advance.

RIGHTS OF COMMON CARRIER

(1) A common carrier is entitled to the agreed remuneration or to a reasonable remuneration for his services. He can demand payment in advance.

(2) He has a right to retain the goods and refuse delivery thereof until his charges for the carriages are paid. He can exercise particular lien over the goods.

(3) A common carrier is not bound to carry goods under certain circumstances (exceptions stated above).

(4) If the consignee refuses to accept delivery of the goods, the carrier is at liberty to take such steps as are reasonable and prudent under the circumstances. He can recover all reasonable expenses incurred by him in this connection.

(5) By entering into a special contract with the consignor, he can limit his liability.

(6) If perishable goods get spoiled on the way, he can sell them, in the absence of any special instructions by the consignor.

(7) He can recover damages from the consignor for loss suffered by him because of dangerous nature of goods not being explained to him by the consignor.

LIABILITY OF COMMON CARRIER

According to the English Common Law, a common carrier of goods is an insurer of goods carried. He is bound to indemnify the owner in full for any loss or damage to the goods, whether caused by his negligence or not, in course of carriage. However, the following are the exceptions to this rule :

(1) *An Act of God* : When damage to the goods is caused by the Act of God, the carrier will not be liable. For example, storm, earthquake, flood, lightening etc. The happening of these things cannot be predicted.

(2) *Enemies of the State* : When damage or loss caused to the goods by the enemies of the state, the carrier will not be liable. This type of loss happens during war with alien enemies with India.

(3) *Inherent Vice in the goods Carried* : A carrier is not liable for any loss arising from inherent vice in the goods carried over. For example, evaporation of liquids, perishing of

fruits, disease in animals, etc., which he can not control and against which he cannot guard.

(4) *Defective packing :* The carrier is not responsible, if the loss is caused due to defective packing of the goods consigned. Glassware, chinaware needs special care, and if the consignor fails to disclose the fact, the carrier is not liable.

(5) *Fault or fraud of the consignor :* If the consignor is guilty of any fraud, the carrier is not liable for any damage or loss.

PRIVATE CARRIER

Private carrier is one who casually or occasionally carries goods for others on special terms mutually agreed upon. He enjoys the discretion of accepting or rejecting any proposal for carriage of goods. He occasionally carries goods for others and that too under special agreement. Thus, he may or may not carry goods for others. He does not make a general offer. The contractor is a private carrier. He negotiates special terms for each service.

A private carrier is not governed by the Carriers Act 1865. His position is that of a bailee. Hence, he is governed by the Indian Contract Act.

COMMON CARRIER VS. PRIVATE CARRIER

(1) A common carrier renders regular services, while private carrier renders casual and non-regular services.

(2) A common carrier generally cannot refuse to carry goods offered to him, while a private carrier keeps this right reserved.

(3) A Common carrier, the terms of carriage are fixed, while private carriers special terms are negotiated.

(4) The liabilities of a common carrier are governed by the Common Carrier Act 1865 while the liabilities of a private carrier are those of a bailee.

GRATUITOUS CARRIER

When a carrier carries goods or passengers without charging anything, he is called a gratuitous carrier.

GOODS

The Carriers Act 1865 divides the goods, for the purpose of carrier's liability into two categories—(1) Scheduled goods and (2) non-scheduled goods. Schedule goods are valuable goods. A list of such goods has been given in the Act, such as gold, silver, precious stones, pearls, jewelry, bills and hundis, coins, title deeds, government securities, articles of ivory, sandalwood etc. Goods, which have not been included in the list are termed as non-scheduled goods.

RAILWAYS AS CARRIERS

Rail transport is regarded as one of the chief means of land transport in the modern world. Railways as carriers of goods, are not governed by the Carriers Act 1865. Railways are owned and operated by the government. The carriage of goods by railways is governed by Indian Railway Act as amended up-to-date. Goods may be transported by railways either in goods trains or in passenger trains. Perishable goods and small packages are generally transported by passenger trains. Sec. 28 of the Railway Act provides as follows :

"A railway administration shall not make or give any undue or unreasonable preference or advantage to, or in favour of, any particular person of railway administration, or any particular description of traffic, in any respect whatsoever, or subject to any particular person or railway administration or any particular description of traffic to any undue or unreasonable prejudice or disadvantage in any respect whatsoever."

The railway administration is bound to carry goods of every person who is prepared to pay necessary freight and observe the regulations concerning packing etc. and to comply with other requirements.

Forwarding Note (Sec. 72)

Every consignor of goods or animals has to execute a note in the form prescribed by the railway administration and approved by the Central Government. The forwarding note contains the description of goods, number of packages, weight, the addresses of consignor and consignee, freight paid or to pay etc. The rules and conditions on which goods are carried are printed on the back of the note.

Railway Receipt (R/R)

On receipt of the forwarding note, the Railway parcel office gives a receipt acknowledging the goods and giving an undertaken to carry them in accordance with the instructions and subject to the terms and conditions, printed on the back. A railway receipt shall be prima facie evidence of the weight and the number of packages. This receipt is referred as the railway receipt and serves as a document of title to the goods. The R/R is sent to the consignee, who must present it to the railway office at the destination to take delivery of goods.

Duties of Railways

(1) The railway administration is bound (like a common carrier) to carry goods of every person who is ready and willing to pay the freight and observes the regulations regarding packing etc. Similarly, railways are bound to carry every passenger who pays the necessary fare. Hence, the railways, as regards duties, are common carriers.

(2) Duty not to give any undue or unreasonable preference or advantage to, or in favour of, any particular person, or any particular description of traffic, in any respect whatsoever, or subject any particular person or any particular description of traffic to any undue or unreasonable prejudice or disadvantage in any respect whatsoever.

LIABILITIES OF RAILWAYS

General Responsibility as Carrier of Goods

(1) With the enactment of the Indian Railways (Amendment) Act 1961, the scope of liability of a railway administration has been much widened and enlarged from that of a bailee. Under amended Sec. 73, railway administration has been held liable for the loss, destruction or deterioration in transit of goods or animals received by it for carriage by rail from all causes except the losses arising from :

(*a*) Act of God,

(*b*) Act of public enemies,

(*c*) Act of war,

(*d*) Arrest, restraint or seizure under legal process,

(*e*) Order by or on behalf of the Central or State Government,

(*f*) Acts of commission or negligence of the consignor or the consignee or their agent,

(*g*) Natural deterioration due to some inherent vice in the goods.

(*h*) Latent defects, or

(*i*) Fire or explosion.

Thus, the liability of a railway administration is the same as that of a common carrier. Further, Sec. 42A of the Railway Act states that a railway administration must not give any unreasonable preference or advantage to any person or to any particular class of traffic.

(2) *Liability during Transit*

Under Sec. 73, the railway administration shall be responsible for the loss, destruction, damages. deterioration or non-delivery in transit of goods and animals to be carried by railways arising from any cause except the causes already stated above.

(3) *Railway Risk and Owner's Risk Rates*

The railway carry goods and animals either at 'railway risk rates' or 'at owner's risk rates'. The former are ordinary rates, while the latter are specially reduced rates. When the goods are carried on owner's risk rate, the railway administration shall not be liable for any loss or damage in transit.

(4) *Delay or Detention in Transit*

If it is proved that the loss or damage has been caused to the goods or animals due to delay or their detention in transit, the railway administration would be liable for it. Under Sec. 76, it can escape from the liability, if it proves that the delay or detention arose without negligence or misconduct on its part or on the part of any of its employees.

(5) *Deviation of Route*

Sometimes loss is caused to the goods or animals because of the deviation of the customary route by the railways. In such a case the railways may be held liable to make good such a loss. If the deviation of route was beyond the control of the railways administration, it can escape from its liability.

(6) *Responsibility for Wrong Delivery*

Where a railway administration delivers the animals or goods in good faith to a person who produces the original railway receipt (R/R), it shall not be responsible on the ground that such person is not legally entitled thereto or the indorsement on the railway receipt is forged or otherwise defective. But if the animals or goods are delivered to a wrong person without the production of a railway receipt the railway administration shall be responsible to the rightful person.

(7) *Liability as a Carrier of Special Value* (Sec. 77)

When any parcel to be carried by railway contains gold, silver, pearls and precious stones, securities etc., the railway administration is not responsible for any loss, destruction or deterioration in the parcel if :

(*a*) Its value exceeds Rs. 500, and

(*b*) The person sending the parcel has not declared its contents and value in writing and has not paid the additional charges, if any.

When such additional freight is paid and the requisite declaration is made, the railway is liable to make good any loss or damage to the article.

(8) *Liability as a Carrier of Animals*

In the case of animals, the railway administration is not liable for loss or damage beyond certain amounts mentioned in the Ist Schedule to the Act. They are as follows : Elephant — Rs. 1,500 per head, horses — Rs. 750 per head, mules, horned cattle and camels — Rs. 200 per head, and in all other cases, including birds — Rs. 30 per head. The railway is not at all responsible if the loss or damage arises from the fright of restiveness of the animals.

(9) *Liability for Passenger Luggage*

The railway administration is responsible for luggage which is booked and handed over to it for carriage in the luggage van. For goods carried by the passenger in his charge, the railway is not responsible unless it is shown that damage was caused by negligence or misconduct on its part or any of its servants. (Sec. 75).

(10) *Liability after Termination of Transit*

The railway administration is not responsible for damage after the wagon is placed at the siding where delivery is to be taken and the owner has been informed in writing. Sec. 76 (C). The railway administration is not responsible in any case for damage etc., after the expiry of seven days after the termination of transit. (Sec. 77).

(11) *Exoneration from Liability*

Under Sec. 78, the railway administration would not be responsible for loss or damage in the following cases :

(*a*) Where the goods have been dispatched with a false description; or

(*b*) Where a fraud has been committed by the consignor or consignee or their agents; or

(*c*) Where the loss or damage is caused by improper loading or unloading of goods, riots, civil commotion, strike, lockout etc.

THEORETICAL QUESTIONS

1. Define the term 'Common Carrier'. Distinguish between a 'Common Carrier' and a 'Private Carrier'.
2. What are the duties of a Common Carrier? (*B.Com. Madurai*)
3. Discuss the duties and liabilities of railway administration as a carrier of animals and goods. (*B.Com. Agra*)
4. State the rights and liabilities of a common carrier. (*B.Com. MS*)

CHAPTER

Carriage by Sea

AT A GLANCE

- Contract of Affreightment
- Implied Warranties
- Charter Party, Kinds, Contents
- Bill of Lading, Characteristics, Kinds
- Bill of Lading vs. Charter Party
- Liability of a Carrier by Sea
- Is Bill of Lading Negotiable?
- Ship-owner's Lien
- Mate's Receipt
- Right of Stoppage in Transit
- Theoretical Questions

The law relating to carriage of goods by sea is contained mainly in (*i*) The Indian Bill of Lading Act 1856 and (*ii*) The carriage of Goods by Sea Act 1925.

CONTRACT OF AFFREIGHTMENT

A contract for the carriage of goods by sea is called 'contract of affreightment'. It may be defined as a contract by which the shipowner undertakes to carry the goods of another (known as shipper) by water, or to furnish a ship for the purpose of so carrying the goods to the destination in return for a price called 'freight'. The consignor and the shipowner are the two parties to the contract. The consideration paid for the carriage is called freight. A contract of affreightment may take either of the two forms, *viz* :

(*a*) A charter party where an entire ship is hired, or

(*b*) A bill of lading where the goods are to be carried in a general ship which is ready and willing to carry goods of any person who intends to use it for that purpose.

IMPLIED WARRANTIES

In a contract for carriage of goods by sea, the following conditions are implied :

(1) The ship is seaworthy and reasonably fit to encounter the 'perils of the sea.'

(2) The ship shall be ready to commence the voyage and shall carry out the same with all reasonable dispatch and diligence.

(3) The ship shall carry out the voyage in the usual and customary manner and shall not deviate from the prescribed or usual course.

(4) The shipper shall not ship dangerous goods.

CHARTER PARTY

A charter Party may be defined as an agreement in writing for the purpose of hiring an entire ship or a substantial part thereof for the purpose of carriage of goods. The person hiring the ship or a part of it, is called the charterer.

The shipowner agrees to place the ship at the disposal of a merchant (called charterer) for the purpose of carrying goods to a particular place for a sum of money which the charterer undertakes to pay as freight for the carriage of the goods. The charterer may hire the ship to carry his own goods or to use the ship as a 'general ship' for carrying the goods of others under bills of lading.

KINDS OF CHARTER PARTY

A contract of charter party may be of any of the following kinds:

(1) *Time Charter*

In this contract, the ship is hired for a specified time irrespective of number of voyages performed by it. Here, the freight is calculated on the basis of the time period for which the ship is hired.

(2) *Voyage Charter*

In this contract, the ship is hired for a particular voyage. Therefore, the freight is calculated on the basis of the distance covered by the voyage and the quantity of the cargo carried. The ownership and control of the ship remain with the owner and are not transferred to the charterer.

(3) *Charter by Demise*

In this contract, the charterer becomes the owner of the ship for the time being and exercises his control over the master and crew of the ship as their employer.

In the case of hiring the whole ship, the terms of the charter party may sometimes amount to a lease or demise of the ship, whereby the possession of the ship comes under the absolute control of the charterer who becomes temporarily the owner of the ship and the captain and the crew become his servants. This is called a 'charter by demise'. Generally, a charter party is without a demise or lease of the ship where, like a simple contract of carriage, the charter only get the right to have his goods conveyed by the ship and the captain and the crew do not become his servants and the possession and control of the ship remain with the shipowner. In such a case it is called a 'charter without demise'.

In the case of a 'charter without demise' or where only a part of the ship is hired, *i.e.*, where the owner of the ship retains to himself the possession and control of the ship and the crew, upon delivering the goods on board the ship, a bill of lading signed by the owner or captain of the ship is given to the charterer as an acknowledgment of the receipt of the goods. It is important to note that a bill of lading issued under a charter party is only a receipt of the goods (the evidence of contract being 'charter party') and is quite different from the bill of lading issued in the case of a 'general ship' where it is the evidence of the contract of carriage.

CONTENTS OR CLAUSES OF CHARTER PARTY

A charter party has no specific form. It differs from trade to trade. It must be signed by the parties and attested by one or more witnesses. The usual clauses of a charter party are as follows :

(1) The name of the ship and its rating in Lloyd's Register.

(2) Names and addresses of the shipowner and the charterer.

(3) The measurement of the ship as indicated by its registered tonnage.

(4) The location of the ship at the date of the charter party.

(5) The shipowner's guarantee that the ship is seaworthy and fit for the contemplated voyage.
(6) The shipowner should bring the ship to the port agreed upon and inform the same to the charterer, its readiness for loading.
(7) The liability of the charterer to pay freight as consideration for the carriage of goods.
(8) Prosecution of the voyage with all convenient speed.
(9) Nature of the duties of the master or the captain of the ship.
(10) The charterer is bound to pay the freight in full whether he utilizes the full capacity or not.
(11) Lay days are the days allowed for loading and unloading the ship. If the charterer does not complete loading within lay days, he is liable to pay damages, called demurrage.
(12) The class of charter party, *i.e.*, whether a 'voyage charter' or a 'time charter', and whether a 'charter by demise' or a 'charter without demise'.
(13) Charterer's liability to cease when the cargo is loaded.
(14) The expected perils for which the shipowner is not liable, if a loss arises due to : (*a*) an act of God, (*b*) state enemies, and (*c*) perils of the sea etc.
(15) The right of charterer to carry the goods of others under bill of lading.
(16) Delivery of the goods in the usual manner when the ship reaches the port of discharge.

BILL OF LADING

Bill of lading is a document which acknowledges the receipt of goods which are delivered to a general ship for carriage. It contains the terms and conditions of the carriage of goods, which have been agreed upon by the parties. The position of a general ship is that of a common carrier. Bill of lading is used even when a ship is chartered and the charterer himself utilizes the whole of the ship. When cargo of different kinds of goods is collected from several merchants by the charterer, the bill of lading is issued to the merchants as receipts of their cargo.

CHARACTERISTICS OF BILL OF LADING

A bill of lading has the following characteristics :
(1) It is an acknowledgment of the receipt of the goods on board the ship.
(2) It is an evidence of the contract of affreightment (where the goods are placed on 'general ship') whereby the shipping company undertakes to carry the goods and to deliver them to the person named therein or his assignees, on payment of freight.
(3) It is a document of title to the goods. It enables the holder to obtain delivery of goods. Its possession is in law equivalent to the possession of goods and, therefore, its transfer is symbolically a transfer of the goods themselves. It can be transferred by endorsement and delivery passing to the endorsee same rights as the endorser, that is, making the endorsee owner of the goods covered thereunder.
(4) It contains the terms and conditions of the carriage of the goods as agreed upon between the parties.

KINDS OF BILL OF LADING

A bill of lading may be of the following kinds :

(1) *Clean Bill of Lading*

When it is stated in the bill of lading that the goods are in good order and condition, the bill is said to be a Clean Bill of Lading. When a clean bill of lading has been issued, the shipowner is estopped from claiming later on that the goods were in a bad condition.

(2) *Dirty Bill of Lading*

A bill of lading is termed as dirty, if it contains a qualified statement, it is termed as 'Dirty', for example, goods shipped in damp condition, packing is loose etc.

(3) *Through Bill of Lading*

Where the goods are to be carried partly by sea and partly by land or partly in this ship and partly in the ship of another shipowner; and if the shipowner has charged for both, the bill of lading is known as 'through Bill of Lading'.

(4) *On Board Bill of Lading*

It is issued when the goods are actually loaded on board the ship and acknowledge accordingly. It is preferred by the importers and the bankers.

(5) *Received Bill of Lading*

It is like a receipt issued by the shipowner that the stated cargo has been delivered to him for shipment in a particular ship. It is the receipt of goods for shipment.

Difference between these two documents

Bill of Lading	*Charter Party*
1. It is an acknowledgment of receipt of goods and a document of title to goods.	1. It is neither an acknowledgement of receipt of goods nor a document of title to goods.
2. It does not amount to a lease of the ship or a part thereof.	2. It may amount to a lease of the ship or a part thereof.
3. It is drawn in sets – two or three.	3. It is not drawn in sets.
4. It is negotiable to some extent and, therefore, considered to be a quasi-negotiable instrument.	4. It is not a negotiable instrument.
5. It is transferable by endorsement and delivery.	5. It is not so.
6. Freight is paid in advance, generally.	6. Freight is paid after safe delivery at port of destination.
7. It is always for a particular destination.	7. It may be for a particular voyage or for a particular period of time.
8. It may or may not be stamped.	8. It is necessarily to be stamped.

LIABILITIES OF A CARRIER BY SEA

The Carriage of Goods by Sea Act 1925 lays down the following rules regarding the liabilities of a carrier of goods by sea from an Indian port :

(1) A carrier of goods by sea, that is, a shipowner is liable only for loss or damage arising or resulting from his negligence, fault or failure in the duties and obligations provided in the Act, and not otherwise.

(2) A shipowner cannot limit his liability arising from his negligence or failure in the duties and any clause in the contract to that effect shall be null and void and inoperative.

(3) The carrier is not responsible for any loss or damage to goods exceeding £ 100 per package or unit or its equivalent unless the nature and value of such goods have been declared by the shipper and inserted in the bill of lading.

(4) The carrier shall not be liable in any event for loss or damage to the goods if the nature or value thereof has been knowingly misstated by the shipper in the bill of lading.

(5) The carrier shall be discharged from all liability for loss unless suit is brought within one year after delivery of the goods.

(6) The carrier is not responsible for loss or damage arising from the act of God, act of war, act of public enemies, seizure under legal process, latent defects in the goods not discoverable, perils of the sea (icebergs, pirates etc.).

IS BILL OF LADING NEGOTIABLE?

Goods shipped under a bill of lading may be made deliverable to a particular person "or to order" or "assigns", in which cases he may transfer such goods to any one he pleases by indorsement and delivery of the bill of lading. Again, the goods shipped under a bill of lading may be made deliverable to a name left blank or "to bearer" in which case the holder is at liberty to fill in the blank and then the bill of lading can change hands by mere delivery.

On account of some points of resemblance between the two kinds of instruments, a bill of lading is also treated as "quasi negotiable" or "as good as negotiable". but in strict sense of the term, a bill of lading is not negotiable instrument, for several reasons :

(1) A bill of lading is governed by the Bills of Lading Act 1856 and it is not included in the definition of negotiable instruments given in Sec. 13 of the Negotiable Instruments Act.

(2) It is to be noted that a bill of lading does not belong to the same category as that of negotiable instruments. The bill is used as a document to represent goods while a negotiable instrument is used in settlement of debts and represents money.

(3) One of the distinctive characteristics of a negotiable instrument is that a transferee of a document may acquire a better title than that of the transferor. But in case of bill of lading, there is no such feature about it. This means that the transferee cannot get any better title than that of the transferor.

THE SHIPOWNER'S LIEN

As a carrier, the shipowner has a lien on the goods carried for the freight and other charges. The lien can be enforced by not parting with the goods until his dues are paid. There is no lien when the freight has been paid in advance or when freight has been agreed to be paid after delivery of the goods.

MATE'S RECEIPT

When goods are delivered to a ship for carriage, a receipt for it, is sometimes given by the Mate, who is an officer of the ship under the captain. The Mate's receipt can be subsequently exchanged for a regular bill of lading.

RIGHT OF STOPPAGE IN TRANSIT

The Indian Bills of Lading Act does not affect the provisions regarding unpaid seller's right of stoppage of goods in transit as given under the Sale of Goods Act. Accordingly, the shipping company is not required to deliver the goods to the holder of bill of lading if the consignor, in exercise of the right of stoppage in transit, gives instructions not to deliver the goods.

THEORETICAL QUESTIONS

1. What is a charter party?
2. Distinguish between a Bill of Lading and Charter Party.
3. What are the implied warranties in a charter party?
4. Is the Bill of Lading a "negotiable instrument"?
5. "A bill of lading is negotiable only in a popular sense and not in technical sense" Explain.

CHAPTER

Carriage by Air

AT A GLANCE

MEANING

The law relating to the carriage by air is contained in the Carriage by Air Act 1972. This Act repeals the Indian Carriage by Air Act 1934. The law relating to carriage by air in India was based upon a draft convention drawn up in the international conference held in Warsaw in 1929. The Warsaw Convention was given effect to in India by the enactment of the Indian Carriage by Air Act 1934. The provisions of that Act were extended to domestic carriage, subject to certain exceptions, adaptations and modifications, issued by a notification on Ist March 1964. A diplomatic conference under the auspices of International Civil Aviation Organisation was held at Hague in September 1955 which adopted a protocol to amend the provisions of the Warsaw Convention. The Hague Protocol was opened for signature on 28th September 1955, and came into force between the ratifying States on Ist August 1963.

The Carriage by Air Act 1972 contains two schedules. Schedule I contains the Warsaw Convention rules which are applicable to international carriage by air of countries which have not yet signed the Hague Protocol. Schedule II contains the amended rules (as amended by the Hague Protocol in 1955) applicable to international carriage by air of countries which have signed the Hague protocol. Fifty seven countries have already ratified the Hague Protocol. The central Government is empowered to make the rules contained in the aforesaid Schedules I and II applicable to the internal carriage by air by a notification in the Official Gazette subject, however, to such exceptions, adaptations and modifications, if any, as may be specified.

DOCUMENTS OF CARRIAGE BY AIR

Chapter II of the second Schedule to the Carriage by Air Act 1972 provides that when goods and passengers are carried by air, the following 'documents of carriage' are to be issued :

(1) *Passenger Ticket*

The carrier must deliver a passenger ticket, in case of carriage of passenger by air and the ticket must contain the following particulars (1) The place and date of issue, (2) The place of departure and of destination, (3) The agreed stopping place, (4) The name and address of carrier or carriers, (5) A statement that the carriage is subject to the rules relating to liability. The carrier may reserve the right to alter the stopping place in case of necessity.

The absence, irregularity or loss of the passenger ticket does not affect the existence or validity of the contract of carriage. But if the carrier accepts a passenger without a passenger ticket, he cannot enjoy the benefit of limiting his liability granted under the Convention.

(2) *Baggage Check (Luggage Ticket)*

The carrier must deliver a luggage ticket for carriage of luggage other than small personal objects of which the passenger takes charge himself.

The luggage ticket is made out in duplicate — one part for the passenger and the other for the carrier. The luggage ticket should have the following information thereon : (1) The place and date of issue, (2) The places of departure and destination, (3) The name and address of the carrier, (4) The number of the passenger ticket, (5) A statement that the delivery of the luggage will be given to the person having the luggage ticket, (6) The number and weight of the packages, (7) The amount of the value declared (8) A statement that the carriage is subject to the rules relating to the liability.

(3) *Air Way Bill (Air Consignment Note)*

Goods carried by air must be covered by an air consignment note. Every carrier of goods has the right to require the consignor to make out and to hand over to him a document called 'Air Consignment Note'. The consignor also has the right to require the carrier to accept the document. Hence it is relevant to mention that the validity of the contract of air carriage is not affected by the absence, irregularity or loss of the air consignment note.

The air way bill must be made out by the consignor in three original parts, a set of three copies. It must be handed over with the goods. The first part is marked for the carrier and must be signed by the consignor. The second part is marked for the consignee : It must be signed by the consignor and by the carrier and must accompany the goods. The third part is signed by the carrier and handed over by him to the consignor after the goods have been accepted.

The carrier of goods has the right to require the consignor to make out separate waybills when there are more than one packages. The air waybills must contain the following particulars: (1) The place and date of its execution, (2) The place of departure and of destination, (3) The agreed stopping places, (4) The name and address of the consignor, (5) The name and address of the first carrier, (6) The name address of the consignee, (7) The nature of goods, (8) The number of the packages, the method of packing and particular marks or numbers on the packages, (9) The weight, the quantity and the volume or dimensions of the goods, (10) The apparent condition of the goods and of the packing, (11) The freight, if it has been agreed upon, the date and place of payment, and the person who is to pay it, (12) If the goods are sent for payment on delivery, the price of the goods, (13) The amount of the value declared, (14) The number of parts of the consignment note, (15) The documents handed to the carrier to accompany the note, (16) The time fixed for the completion of the carriage, and a brief note of the route to be followed. (17) A statement that the carriage is subject to the rules regarding liability.

If the carrier accept goods without an air waybill having been made out, or if the air waybill does not contain the particulars set in (1) to (8) and (17), the carrier shall not be entitled to the benefit of limiting his liability. Further, the consignor must also furnish such information and attach to the air waybill, such documents as are necessary to meet the formalities of customs, octroi etc., before cargo can be delivered to the consignee. The consignor is liable to the carrier for any damage occasioned by the absence, insufficiency or irregularity of any such information or documents.

The consignor is responsible for the correctness of the particulars and statements relating to the cargo which he inserts in the waybill. He will be liable to indemnify the carrier against all damage suffered by him, or by any other person to whom the carrier is liable, by reason of the incorrectness or incompleteness of the particulars and statements furnished by him.

The consignor may withdraw the goods from the custody of the carrier at the place of departure or destination or at any intermediate station. He may change the name of the consignee. He cannot, however, exercise any of these rights in such a way as to prejudice the interests of carrier. The consignor must also pay all necessary expenses.

The consignee is entitled to take delivery of the goods at the place of destination. If the goods are lost or do not arrive at the place of destination within seven days of the date of delivery, he can enforce his rights under the contract of carriage.

The liabilities of the air carrier may be stated as follows :

(1) The carrier is liable for damages in respect of death of or injury caused to a passenger by accident, destruction, damage or loss to any luggage or goods, or delay in carriage.

(2) Subject to contract, the carrier's liability for the death of a passenger limit to 2,50,000 francs.

(3) The carrier's liability in respect of passenger's personal belongings are limited to 5,000 Francs.

(4) Unless the consignor makes a special declaration as to value of goods or luggage, the carrier's liability in respect of registered luggage or goods will be limited to 250 francs per kilogram.

(5) Complaints in respect of the following must be made within the respective periods noted against each of them :
   (*a*) Damage to baggage within 7 days of receipt.
   (*b*) Damage of cargo within 14 days of receipt.
   (*c*) Delay in delivery within 21 days of the date of actual delivery.

THEORETICAL QUESTIONS

1. What is an air consignment note? Who prepares it? What are its contents?
2. Discuss 'passenger ticket' and 'Luggage ticket' as documents of carriage by air.
3. What are the liabilities of the carrier by air for carriage of goods?

The Insolvency Act

CHAPTER

Law of Insolvency

AT A GLANCE

INTRODUCTION

The Law of Insolvency in India is contained in two enactments, namely, (*a*) *the Presidency Towns Insolvency Act 1909, which applies to the Presidency Towns of Calcutta, Madras and Bombay, and (b) the Provincial Insolvency Act 1920, which applies to the whole of India except the Presidency Towns mentioned above.* Most of the provisions of the two Acts are similar. The important points of differences have been noted at appropriate places. However, in brief, the points of differences between the two Acts are given below :

(1) The procedure from the date of presentation of the petition to the date of adjudication.

(2) The duties of the debtor, including his examination.

(3) The person in whom the debtor's property is to be vested.

(4) The doctrine of Relation Back.

(5) The constitution of the courts.

The Indian Acts relating to insolvency are based upon the English statutes on the subject. In English law the terms "bankrupt" and "bankruptcy" are used in the same sense as the terms "insolvent" and "insolvency" in India.

DEFINITION

The Indian Acts do not define the term 'insolvency' and 'insolvent'. According to the popular usage, an 'insolvent is one who is unable to pay his debts. But no man can be called 'insolvent' unless a competent court declares him to be one. Thus an insolvent may be defined as a person against whom an order of adjudication has been passed. An insolvent is called 'bankrupt' in English law.

OBJECT OF INSOLVENCY LAW

Prior to the enactment of insolvency legislation, a debtor who was unable to pay debts was regarded as a sort of criminal or offender and was, in almost every case, sent to jail. During the ancient time no distinction was drawn between honest, but unfortunate, debtors and dishonest debtors. Whether the inability to pay arose from misfortune or was brought about by fraud, they were all committed to prison and remain there at the mercy of their creditors till the debt was repaid. Subsequently, it was felt that any punishment to an insolvent is hardly proper as it neither gives any advantage to the creditors nor provides any relief to the insolvent himself. The present insolvency statutes have adopted a broader outlook and are based on the principle if a person is not in a position to meet out his liabilities at any time, he should be taken out of such a position and be given another chance to improve his financial status. It is done by dividing the property and assets of the insolvent among the creditors in an equitable proportion, and thus, releasing him from future liabilities regarding his past debts and obligations.

The primary object of the Insolvency Laws are stated below :

(1) To give relief to the embarrassed debtor who is unable to discharge his debts and obligations and to protect him from harassment by the creditors and thus, to enable him to make a fresh start, and

(2) To prevent the creditors from getting possession of the assets of the insolvent by fair or foul means.

Blackstone comments, "The laws of bankruptcy are considered as laws calculated for the benefit of trade, and founded on the principles of humanity as well as justice, and to that end they confer some privileges, not only on the creditors, but also on the bankrupt or debtor himself."

INSOLVENCY PROCEDURE

We discuss the whole procedure of insolvency in the following points :

(1) A petition for adjudication as insolvent may be presented either by the debtor himself or by the creditor to the appropriate Insolvency court.

(2) A creditor shall not be entitled to present insolvency petition unless the debt, singly or jointly, is atleast Rs. 500 and the debtor commits an 'act of insolvency'.

(3) When the petition is admitted, the Court fixes a date for hearing the petition.

(4) When the petition is admitted, Court may appoint an Interim Receiver to take immediate possession of the property of the debtor. The appointment of the Interim Receiver is compulsory only when the petition is filed by the debtor himself.

(5) The Interim Receiver functions till the regular officer is appointed.

(6) On the date of hearing the petition, the Court may either dismiss the petition or pass an order of adjudication. If the court is satisfied that the petition is reasonable, it shall make an order of adjudication.

(7) It is only when this order of adjudication is passed that the debtor is said to have been declared insolvent.

(8) As soon as the debtor is thus declared insolvent, all his property vests in an officer, appointed by the Court to conduct the insolvency proceeding. The officer is called "Official Receiver", usually a lawyer under Provincial Insolvency Act or "Official Assignee" under Presidency Towns Insolvency Act.

(9) When the Official Assignee or Receiver takes over the property of the insolvent, it becomes his duty to sell the property with all convenient speed, at reasonable price.

(10) Out of the sale proceeds, the expenses of realisation are met off and then the liabilities of the insolvent debtor are paid off to the possible extent.

(11) A debtor may, at any time after the order of adjudication and within the period specified by the Court, apply to the Court for an order of Discharge.

(12) The court may, if satisfied with the debtor's conduct and the report of the Official Receiver grant or refuse an Order of Discharge.

(13) The Court may pass either an absolute or conditional Order of Discharge. On obtaining the Order of absolute Discharge, the debtor is freed from all his liabilities and can start his life afresh. The Order of Discharge will release the insolvent from all debts and removes the disqualification imposed by the order of adjudication. He is not responsible for any debt which could not have been paid in full during his insolvency proceedings. Again, the debtor becomes a freeman and gets all the rights and privileges of an ordinary citizen of the country.

ACTS OF INSOLVENCY

An 'act of insolvency' is some act of the debtor which shows that he is financially embarrassed. As stated earlier, a person cannot be adjudged insolvent unless : (*a*) he is a debtor within the meaning of Insolvency law, (*b*) he has committed an 'act of insolvency'. The 'acts of insolvency' are laid down by Sec. 9 of the Presidency Towns Insolvency Act, and Sec. 6 of the Provincial Insolvency Act. They are, with certain exceptions, practically the same. According to both the Acts, a debtor commits an 'act of insolvency' in the each of the following cases.

(1) If, in India or elsewhere, he makes a transfer of all or substantially all his property to a third person for the benefit of his creditors generally.

The transfer of the bulk of a person's property for the benefit of creditors is clearly evidence of financial embarrassment and is, therefore, an act of insolvency. Any creditor, who is not a party to the transfer can apply for adjudication on this ground. The intention of the debtor does not matter because the fact of transfer gives jurisdiction to the court. The transfer becomes void if the debtor is adjudged insolvent within three months of the transfer.

(2) If, in India or elsewhere, he makes a transfer of his property, or any part thereof, with the intent to defraud or delay his creditors.

This clause relates to transfer of whole or any part of debtor's property made with the intention of defeating of delaying creditors, and the intention is to be inferred from surrounding circumstances. The transfer becomes void upon the passing of the order of adjudication.

(3) If, in India or elsewhere, he makes any transfer of his property or any part thereof, which would, under this or any other enactment for the time being in force, be void as a fraudulent preference if he were adjudged an insolvent.

A 'fraudulent preference' is a transfer of property or payment made by a debtor to one or more creditors deliberately with a view to giving fraudulent preference to them over the rest of the creditors, though the transfer may be for adequate consideration.

(4) If, with intent to defeat or delay his creditors:

(*i*) he departs from or remains out of India;

(*ii*) he departs from his dwelling house or usual place of business or otherwise absents himself;

(*iii*) he secludes himself so as to deprive his creditors of the means of communicating with him.

Under this clause it is an essential feature of an act of insolvency that the act should be done with the intent to defeat or delay the creditors generally, and not only a particular creditor. The debtor's intention can be inferred from surrounding circumstances.

(5) If any of his property is sold (or under the Presidency Town Insolvency Act, attached for a period of not less than twenty-one days) in execution of the decree of any Court, for the payment

of money. Under the Provincial Insolvency Act, attachment of a debtor's property, for howsoever long a time, is no ground for founding an insolvency petition.

(6) If he petitions to be adjudged an insolvent; even if the petition is subsequently dismissed; any creditor can present an insolvency petition on this ground.

(7) If he has given notice to any of his creditors that he has suspended or is about to suspend payment of his debts. The notice may be oral or in writing, but it must convey a clear impression that the debtor has no intention to pay.

(8) If he is imprisoned in execution of the decree of any court for the payment of money.

(9) If a creditor, who has obtained a money decree against the debtor, has served on him an insolvency notice and he does not comply with that notice within the period specified therein.

Liability of Principal for Agent's Act of Insolvency. Under the explanation to the Secs. 9 and 6 of the Presidency and the Provincial Acts respectively, it has been provided that an 'act of insolvency' committed by an agent of the debtor, amount to an 'act of insolvency' by the debtor himself, even though the agent has no special authority to commit the act.

INSOLVENCY NOTICE

Insolvency notice is a statutory notice which the creditor, who has obtained a decree or order for the payment of money against the debtor, gives in a prescribed from through the Court to his debtor. It requires the debtor to pay, or furnish sufficient security for the payment of, the decretal amount within the time specified therein which shall not be less than one month. On receiving this notice the debtor either :

(*a*) must pay the amount, or

(*b*) must give security for the payment of the amount of the creditor or his agent to their satisfaction, or

(*c*) must prove that he has a counter-claim or set-off against the judgement creditor, which equals or exceeds the decretal amount and which he could not lawfully set-up in the suit in which the decree or order was made against him, or

(*d*) must satisfy the Court that he is entitled to have the decree or order set-aside, or that the decree or order is not executable, under any law proving for the relief of indebtedness.

It must state that non-compliance with the notice would be an act of insolvency on which a petition may be founded. If the insolvency notice mentions a larger amount than what is actually due under the decree or order, the debtor must give notice to the creditor disputing the amount within the time allowed. If the debtor fails to give such notice, the notice will be valid, in spite of the misstatement.

INSOLVENCY COURTS

In the Presidency Towns (*i.e.*, in Calcutta, Madras and Bombay) insolvency matters are dealt with by the High Courts. In other areas, such matters are dealt with by the District Courts. But courts subordinate to the district courts may deal with insolvency matters if they are so empowered by the State Government concerned. Insolvency courts have power to decide all questions relating to the realisation and distribution of the debtor's properties and the determination of all questions relating to priority of claims as between different creditors.

WHO MAY BE ADJUDGED INSOLVENT?

Any person, who is capable of entering into a contract may be adjudged an insolvent provided that (*i*) he is a 'debtor' within the meaning of the insolvency law and (*ii*) he has committed an act of insolvency. If a debtor deals with his property in strange and suspicious manner, which amounts to an "act of insolvency" as per law. Certain special cases are discussed below :

(1) *Minor*

A minor is absolutely incompetent to contract so as to incur any personal liability under any circumstances. Even where necessaries are supplied to a minor, his property and not his person is liable for the payment of the price. Since a minor cannot be a debtor, he cannot be adjudged insolvent.

(2) *Lunatics*

The position of a lunatic is similar to that of a minor. He cannot also be adjudged an insolvent. But he may be adjudged an insolvent, if he has contracted the debt and committed an 'act of insolvency' during a lucid interval of sanity or while he was sane (prior to his lunacy)

(3) *Women*

In India a married or an unmarried woman does not suffer from any contractual incapacity. She can own property and contract debts. Therefore, she can be declared insolvent under appropriate circumstances.

(4) *Foreigner*

A foreigner residing in India can be adjudged insolvent just like an Indian citizen, provided he is a debtor and has committed an act of insolvency. On the other hand, a foreigner, who is a non-resident, cannot be adjudged an insolvent even though he carries on business in India through his agent.

(5) *Joint Debtors*

When money is borrowed by two or more persons jointly, all of them can be declared insolvent on a single petition provided some act of insolvency is committed by each of them or jointly by all.

(6) *Partnership Firm and Partners*

An order of adjudication can be made against a firm in the firm's name, which will be equivalent to the adjudication of all the partners, except minor partners if any, as insolvent, provided each of the partners have committed an 'act of insolvency'. No individual partners can be adjudged insolvent unless he himself has committed an 'act of insolvency'. A single petition may, however, be presented against two or more partners, the liability of each partner being joint and several for any debt due on the firm.

(7) *Joint Hindu Family*

The members of a joint Hindu family may be adjudged insolvent provided they are personally liable on a joint debt and have committed a joint act of insolvency as, for example, a joint transfer of family property in favour of a creditor by way of fraudulent preference. When joint family business is carried on by the Karta, the other members of the family cannot be adjudged insolvent unless they have taken an active part in the conduct of the family business. A minor member of a joint Hindu family can in no case be adjudged insolvent even though he has taken an active part in the conduct of the family business.

(8) *Deceased Persons*

A deceased person cannot be made insolvent on proceedings instituted after his death. His estate may, however, be administered in insolvency. When a debtor dies after the presentation of the petition the proceedings will, unless the Court otherwise orders, be construed as if he were alive.

(9) *Legal Representatives*

A legal representative is not personally liable for the debts of the deceased debtor and, therefore, cannot be adjudged insolvent for the debts of the deceased. The deceased's estate is liable for his debts.

(10) *Incorporated Companies*

A company cannot be declared insolvent. In case of insolvent companies, the proper procedure is winding up.

(11) *Convicts*

A prisoner in the jail can be declared insolvent.

WHO MAY PRESENT PETITION?

An insolvency petition may be presented either by one or more of the creditors (called creditor's petition) or by the debtor himself (called debtor's petition).

CONDITIONS FOR A CREDITOR'S PETITION

A creditor shall be entitled to present an insolvency petition against a debtor only if he satisfies the following conditions :

(1) The debt owing by the debtor to the creditor, or if two or more creditors join in the petition, the aggregate amount of debts owing to such creditors, must amount to Rs. 500 or more.

(2) The debt must be a liquidated sum payable either immediately or at some future time.

(3) The act of insolvency on which the petition is based must have occurred within three months before the presentation of the petition.

4. The debt of the creditor must be in existence both at the time of the alleged act of insolvency, and also at the time of the filing of the petition. It must also continue to exist throughout the hearing of the petition and till the order of adjudication.

SECURED CREDITORS

A secured creditor is one who holds some movable or immovable property of the debtor out of which he can realise his claims, is not ordinarily interested in insolvency proceedings because his dues are safe. But a secured creditor can present an insolvency petition if the following conditions are satisfied :

(*a*) he abandons his security in favour of all the creditors, or

(*b*) the security is insufficient to meet his claims and the insufficiency amounts to atleast Rs. 500. In the latter case he must in his petition mention the valuation of security and show that he satisfies the conditions mentioned above regarding a creditor's petition.

CONDITIONS FOR A DEBTOR'S PETITION

A debtor is entitled to present a petition for the adjudication of himself as an insolvent if any one of the following conditions are fulfilled :

(*a*) his debts amount to Rs. 500, or

(*b*) he has been arrested and imprisoned in execution of the decree of any court for the payment of money, or

(*c*) an order of attachment in execution of a money decree has been made and is subsisting against his property.

Inability to pay his debt is a condition precedent to the presentation of a debtor's petition. The debtor's petition must allege that he is unable to pay his debt and he must furnish a prima facie grounds for his inability to pay. The expression "unable to pay his debt" means that the market value of the realizable assets is less than the total amount of the debts.

PROCEDURE ON ADMISSION OF PETITION

After the insolvency petition is presented to the Court, the procedure laid down in the Code of Civil Procedure 1908 with respect to the admission of plaint is followed (Prov. Sec. 18). Where the insolvency petition is admitted, the Court makes an order fixing the date for hearing the petition. Notice of the order fixing the date is given to the creditors. Where a debtor is not the petitioner, notice of the order fixing the date is also served on him. (Prov. Sec. 19). There are no such corresponding provisions in the Presidency Towns Insolvency Act. Once an insolvency petition, whether presented by a debtor or a creditor, is admitted, it cannot be withdrawn without the leave of the Court. Where two or more insolvency petitions are presented against the same debtor, the Court may consolidate the proceeding on such terms as it thinks fit.

Interim Receiver. Under the Provincial Insolvency Act (Sec. 20), when the Court makes an order admitting the insolvency petition, it may appoint an interim receiver of the property of the debtor or of any part thereof. But where the debtor himself is the petitioner, the Court ordinarily does appoint an interim receiver. Under the Presidency Towns Insolvency Act (Sec. 16), the Court may, if it is shown to be necessary for the protection of the property of the debtor at any time after the presentation of an insolvency petition, and before an order of adjudication is made, appoint the Official Assignee to be the interim receiver of the property of the debtor or of any part thereof. It may direct the interim receiver to take immediate possession of the property of the debtor or any part thereof. The interim receiver is mainly appointed for the protection of the property of the insolvent. The property does not vest in him unless the Court expressly makes an order to that effect.

Dismissal of Petition (Prov. Sec. 25 & Presi. Sec. 13)

Creditor's Petition. The Court shall dismiss a creditor's petition :

(1) Where it is not satisfied with the proof of (*a*) the creditor's right to present the petition, or (*b*) the service on the debtor of the notice of the order admitting the petition, or (*c*) the alleged act of insolvency.

(2) Where it is satisfied by the debtor that he is able to pay his debts or that for other sufficient cause no order ought to be made.

Where a creditor's petition is dismissed, the debtor may apply to the Court for compensation. If the Court is satisfied that the petition was frivolous or vexatious, it may award compensation against such creditor, not exceeding Rs. 1,000. Such amount may be realised as if it were a fine (Prov. Sec. 26).

Debtor's Petition. In the case of a petition presented by a debtor, the court shall dismiss the petition if it is not satisfied of his right to present the petition.

DUTIES OF THE DEBTOR ON ADMISSION OF THE PETITION

On the making of an order by the Court admitting the Insolvency petition and before the passing of the order of adjudication, the debtor must;

(*a*) produce all books of accounts;

(*b*) furnish details regarding his property, creditors and debtors;

(*c*) at any time, thereafter, submit to such examination in respect of his property or creditors, as may be required by the court;

(*d*) attend before the court or interim receiver as and when required; and

(*e*) execute such instruments and to such things to relation to his property as may be required by the Court or Interim Receiver.

If the debtor wilfully fails to perform the above mentioned duties, he shall be punishable on conviction with imprisonment which may extend to one year.

ORDER OF ADJUDICATION

If the Court is satisfied with the proofs and does not dismiss the petition, it shall make an order of adjudication and shall specify in such order that period within which the debtor must apply for his discharge. However, the Court, on sufficient cause being shown, extend the period of the application for discharge. An order of adjudication is an order of the court declaring or adjudging a debtor an insolvent.

Notice of an order of adjudication stating the name, address and description of the insolvent, the date of the presentation of the petition, the date of adjudication, the period within which the debtor shall apply for his discharge, and the Court by which the adjudication is made, shall be published in the Official Gazette and in such other manner as may be prescribed (Presi. Sec. 20 and Prov. Sec. 30).

LEGAL EFFECTS OF AN ORDER OF ADJUDICATION

The order of the Court by which a person is declared insolvent is called the Order of Adjudication. Upon such an order being passed the following consequences ensue;

Under Sec. 17 of the Presidency Towns Insolvency Act and under Sec. 28(2) of the Provincial Insolvency Act, an officer appointed by the Court takes over all the properties of the insolvent. The officer is called the Official Assignee in Presidency Towns and the Official Receiver under the Provincial Act.

(1) *Vesting of Properties of the Insolvent*

As a consequence of the vesting of property in the Official Assignee or Receiver, the insolvent no longer possesses any power to deal with such property in any way and every transaction by the insolvent shall be void as against the Assignee or Receiver. Now it is only the Assignee or the Receiver who can validly deal with respect to the property and give title to a purchaser, file a suit to recover part thereof from a third person or prosecute a suit filed by the insolvent before adjudication.

(2) *Personal Disqualifications*

The insolvent is disqualified from:

(*a*) being appointed or acting as a Magistrate;

(*b*) being selected to any office of a local authority;

(*c*) being elected as a member of local authority.

These disqualifications are, however, removed :

(*a*) if the order of adjudication is annulled; or

(*b*) if he obtains from the court an order of discharge, whether absolute or conditional, with a certificate that his insolvency was caused by misfortune without any misconduct on his part.

(3) *No Fresh Suit by Creditors*

After the Order of Adjudication is passed no creditor can commence any suit or legal proceedings against the insolvent except with the leave of the insolvency court and subject to such terms and conditions as the insolvency court may impose.

(4) *Stay of Pending Suits*

A suit and proceeding already filed, may be stayed but may be continued with the leave of the insolvency court.

(5) *Relation Back*

The insolvency of a person commences, not from the date when the order of adjudication is passed, but from an earlier date. (For details see 'Doctrine of Relation Back).

(6) *Appointment of a Manager*

The Court may, at the time of making an order of adjudication, appoint a special manager, for such period and on such terms as it may consider to be reasonable, to assist the Official Assignee, if in its opinion it is necessary from the point of view of debtor's business or the interest of the creditors in general (Presi. Sec. 19). There is no such specific provision in the Provincial Insolvency Act, but the Court may follow it there also.

(7) *The Protection Order*

The Court may, after passing an order of adjudication, also grant a 'protection order' to the insolvent on his application, prohibiting the arrest or detention of the insolvent debtor in execution of a decree for the payment of money, and, if already arrested, order his release. The protection order may be granted with regard to all debts or some of them and may commence at and take effect for such time as the Court may direct. The Court may also at any time renew or revoke the same. The object of making a 'protection order' is to protect an honest insolvent debtor from the harassment of his creditors after he has officially declared his inability to pay his debts in full. This order is an example of the infusion of humanity into the law. The protection order is just like a privilege granted by the Court to the insolvent. It protect him from being arrested or put into prison. It does not affect the rights of the creditors in any way.

DOCTRINE OF RELATION BACK

An order of adjudication relates back to, and takes effect from, a date earlier than the date of order of adjudication. It means that the commencement of insolvency relates back and, therefore, it is known as the 'Doctrine of Relation Back'.

(*a*) Under Sec. 51 of the Presidency Towns Insolvency Act, the order of adjudication relates back to the date of the first act of insolvency on which such an order is made. In case where there are more acts of insolvency, the order of adjudication will commence from the date of the first act of insolvency within three months preceding the presentation of the insolvency petition.

(*b*) Under Sec. 28(7) of the Provincial Insolvency Act, an order of adjudication relates back to the date of filing of the petition of insolvency on which such an order is passed by the Court.

On the eve of insolvency, generally a debtor may transfer his property and belongings to others with a view to defrauding the creditors. Thus, the creditors may suffer a great deal. It is because of this reason that on the 'Order of Adjudication', the 'Doctrine of Relation Back' applies. Thus the 'Doctrine' provides justice to the creditors. However, there are provisions for the bona fide transaction entered into by the insolvent before the date of adjudication. Thus, the insolvent has been provided with statutory protection.

EFFECT OF INSOLVENCY ON ANTECEDENT TRANSACTIONS

The transactions which are entered into by the insolvent in respect of his property prior to the 'commencement of insolvency' are known as 'antecedent transactions.' The object of such transactions is generally to save some property from the clutches of the Official Receiver or Assignee. Or it may be done to do some favour to one or more of the creditors. It may be recalled that for all practical purposes, insolvency commences not from the date of adjudication but from an earlier date : that is, the 'doctrine of relation back' applies. The effect of such transactions on insolvency is discussed below :

(1) *Execution of a Decree*

When there is some execution of a decree issued by the Court against the property of a debtor, no person is entitled to the benefit of the execution against the Official Receiver or Assignee. However, it is executable on the assets realized during the course of execution by sale or otherwise before the date of admission of the insolvency petition. However, the adjudication does not affect the rights of the secured creditors in respect of property against which the decree is executed.

(2) *Avoidance of Voluntary Transfers*

All voluntary transfers of property by the debtor within two years immediately preceding the 'commencement of insolvency' shall be void against the Official Receiver or Assignee, as the case may be. But the following two types of voluntary transfers are protected and shall not be void : (*a*) Transfer to the wife of the insolvent made before and in consideration of marriage; (*b*) Transfer made in favour of a purchaser or incumbrancer in good faith and for valuable consideration. In order to uphold a transfer under this clause, the transfer must not only be for valuable consideration, but must also have been made in good faith.

(3) *Avoidance of Fraudulent Preferences* (Presi Sec. 56 & Prov. Sec. 54)

A 'fraudulent preference' means a preference given deliberately to some of the creditors in matter of payment or transfer of property to the exclusion of other creditors, though the transfer may be for adequate consideration. The substantial motive of the debtor in making it must be looked at.

Every transfer of property or any other belongings by a debtor is void as a fraudulent preference, if :

(*a*) the debtor on the date of such transfer was unable to pay his debts.
(*b*) the transfer was only to favour any one or more of the creditors;
(*c*) the debtor gave much preference to anyone or more of the creditors over other creditors;
(*d*) the debtor was adjudged insolvent on a petition filed within three months after the date of the transaction.

(4) *Protected Transactions*

"Protected transaction" are those transactions in relation to the insolvent's property which are not invalidated by the insolvency proceedings. All bona fide transactions for valuable consideration entered into by the insolvent shall be valid and binding upon the Official Assignee or Receiver. Such transactions are :

(*a*) Any payment by the insolvent to any of the creditors;
(*b*) Any payment or delivery to the insolvent;
(*c*) Any transfer for valuable consideration; or
(*d*) Any contract or dealing by or with the insolvent for valuable consideration.

But in this regard, it is necessary that :

(*a*) The payment or transaction is bonafide;
(*b*) It is transacted before the date of the order of adjudication;
(*c*) The person making the payment or transaction must have no notice of the insolvency petition having been filed; and
(*d*) It is not a voluntary transfer or a fraudulent preference.

DUTIES OF THE INSOLVENT AFTER ADJUDICATION

(1) ***To Prepare a Schedule of his Assets and Liabilities***

Where an order of adjudication is made against a debtor, he is required to prepare and submit to the Court, a schedule of his assets and liabilities verified by affidavit in the proscribed form within 3 days of the order of adjudication (Presi, Sec. 24). If without any reasonable excuse the insolvent fails to submit a proper and correct schedule, he may be committed to the civil prison by the court. There is no such requirement under the Provincial Insolvency Act. But the Court, through the Official Receiver, is required to prepare a schedule of creditors of the insolvent, as per Sec. 33 of Provincial Insolvency Act.

(2) ***To Attend Meetings of his Creditors***

The insolvent must, unless prevented by sickness or other sufficient cause, attend such meeting of his creditors as the Official Assignee requires him to attend, and disclose before the meeting such information as may be required.

(3) ***To Execute Power of Attorney etc.***

The insolvent must execute such power of attorney, transfers and instruments as may be required by the Official Assignee or Receiver, and must do all such acts and things in relation to his property as may be required by the Assignee or Receiver.

(4) ***To Assist the Official Assignee/Receiver***

The insolvent must assist the Official Assignee or Receiver, to the utmost of his power, in the realisation of his property and the distribution of the proceeds amongst his creditors.

PUBLIC EXAMINATION OF INSOLVENT

After an order of adjudication has been made, the Court fixes the date for holding a Public Examination of the insolvent, under Sec. 27 of the Presidency Towns Insolvency Act. The Public Examination of an insolvent is based on two-fold object : (*i*) to enquire into his conduct, dealings and property; and (*ii*) to find out the causes leading him to insolvency.

It is done to collect a complete information regarding the property and belongings of the insolvent which can be made available for distribution among the creditors. It also covers a thorough search into the affairs of the insolvent and his conduct. The examination is, thus, much extensive as it covers both—all offences relating to the insolvent, and all matters relating to his discharge to be granted by the court.

The Provincial Insolvency Act does not provide for such public examination of the insolvent after the order of adjudication. The Examination is held before such order is passed, *i.e.*, on the hearing of the insolvency petition.

The rules regarding Public Examination of an insolvent, as provided under Secs. 27 and 106 of the Presidency Towns Insolvency Act are :

(1) Before passing the order of adjudication, the Court shall :
   - (*a*) hold the public sitting on a date fixed by the Court;
   - (*b*) give a notice to this effect to all creditors;
   - (*c*) order the insolvent to attend the sitting, to be examined as to his conduct, dealings and property.

(2) Public Examination is conducted as soon as the insolvent files the schedule of his assets and liabilities.

(3) Any creditor or a legal practitioner, on his behalf may question the insolvent regarding his affairs and the causes leading him to insolvency.

(4) Official Assignee may present himself either in person or through his legal practitioner during such examination.

(5) The Court may ask question as it thinks relevant.

(6) The insolvent is to be examined on oath and is bound to answer all such questions put up by the court or allowed by it to be put up to him.

(7) The notes of such examination are taken in writing and read either to or by the insolvent and signed by him.

(8) Such notes are kept as record to be used as evidence against him in any proceedings, either civil or criminal.

(9) Such record is also open for inspection by any of the creditors.

(10) When the court feels that the affairs of the insolvent are properly investigated, it may declare its conclusion.

Public Examination—When dispensed with : Public Examination of the insolvent may be dispensed with when [Presi, Sec. 27 (8)]:

(*a*) He is lunatic or suffers mentally or physically;

(*b*) He is unable to attend the Court because of some disability.

(*c*) When his property is not likely to exceed Rs. 3,000;

(*d*) She is a woman and purdah-nashin.

PRIVATE EXAMINATION OF INSOLVENT

On the application of the Official Assignee or Official Receiver, who has proved his debt, the Court may summon the insolvent. The Court may also summon any person :

(*i*) known or suspected to have in his possession any property of the insolvent; or

(*ii*) supposed to be indebted to the insolvent; or

(*iii*) any person whom the court may deem capable of giving information regarding the insolvent, his dealings, or property.

The Court may require such person to produce any document in his custody, relating to the insolvent, his dealings or property. If such person refuses as such, the Court may issue a warrant to bring him for such examination.

If such person admits before the court during the course of his examination that he has in his possession any property or belonging of the insolvent, the Court may, on the application by the Official Assignee, order him to deliver to the Official Assignee that property on such terms, as it may deem just. On the other hand, the Official Receiver (Presi. Act) will have to file a suit for the recovery of such property from that person.

INTERIM RECEIVER

Interim Receiver means an official appointed by the Court to take possession of the property of the debtor with a view to preserving the same between the time of the admission of the insolvency petition and the making of an order of adjudication.

Under the Provincial Insolvency Act (Sec. 20), when the Court makes an order admitting the insolvency petition, it may appoint an interim receiver of the property of the debtor or of any part thereof. But where the debtor himself is the petitioner, the Court ordinarily does appoint an interim receiver.

Under the Presidency Towns Insolvency Act (Sec. 16), the Court may, if it is shown to be necessary for the protection of the property of the debtor at any time after the presentation of an insolvency petition, and before an order of adjudication is made, appoint the Official Assignee to be the interim receiver of the property of the debtor or of any part thereof. It may direct the interim receiver to take immediate possession of the property of the debtor or any part thereof. The interim receiver is mainly appointed for the protection of the property of the insolvent. The property does not vest in him unless the Court expressly makes an order to that effect. In other words, the appointment of an Interim Receiver has not the effect of divesting a debtor of his property but merely protects it and the debtor continues to be the legal owner of the property. The Official Assignee or Receiver is appointed after the adjudication for the purpose of realisation of the assets of the insolvent and distribution of the proceeds thereof among his creditors, whereas an Interim Receiver is appointed to safeguard the interests of creditors, for example, to check preferential or fraudulent dealings by the debtor or to check harassment of the debtor by some creditor.

THEORETICAL QUESTIONS

1. What are the objects of the Insolvency Law? Discuss in brief the procedure relating to insolvency in India. *(B.Com., Delhi)*
2. Discuss the various acts which are to be considered 'acts of insolvency'. *(B.Com., MS)*
3. What are the significance of an 'act of Insolvency'?
4. Discuss the Doctrine of Relation Back.
5. Discuss the procedure of admitting and hearing of an insolvency petition. Also point out the duties of the debtor on admission of the petition. *(B.Com., Bhopal)*
6. Can the following persons be adjudicated as insolvent—a foreigner, a minor, a lunatic, one of the partners.
7. What are the consequences of the Order of Adjudication? *(B.Com., Madurai)*
8. What is protection order in insolvency?
9. What are the disqualification of a debtor when he is adjudged as insolvent? How can these disqualification he removed?
10. What are the 'acts of insolvency'? *(B.Com., MS)*
11. Write a note public examination.
12. What is the effect of insolvency on antecedent transactions?
13. Explain what is meant by protected transactions.
14. What is an order of adjudication? *(B.Com., MS)*
15. Who is an insolvent? Who (*a*) can and (*b*) cannot be adjudged an insolvent?

CHAPTER

Property and Debts of Insolvent

AT A GLANCE

- Official Assignee
- Official Receiver
- Powers
- Duties
- Superior Title
- Disclaimer of Onerous Property
- Doctrine of Reputed Ownership
- Property
- Committee of Inspection
- Composition and Scheme of Arrangement
- Debts of Insolvent, Provable and not Provable
- Rights of Secured Creditors
- Proof of Debts
- Annulment of Adjudication
- Set off
- Distribution of Property
- Order of Payment of Debt
- Declaration and Distribution of Dividend
- Calculation of Dividend
- Final Dividend
- Small Insolvencies
- Theoretical Questions

OFFICIAL ASSIGNEE AND OFFICIAL RECEIVER

The officer appointed to help the Court to complete the insolvency proceedings, that is, to realise the assets of the insolvent and distribute the same amongst the creditors most fairly, is called the *Official Assignee* under the Presidency Towns Insolvency Act and the *Official Receiver* under the Provincial Insolvency Act.

OFFICIAL ASSIGNEE

The Official Assignee is appointed under the Presidency Towns Insolvency Act 1909, which applies in Bombay, Calcutta and Madras. Rules regarding his appointment are as under :

(*a*) The Official Assignee of Madras presidency town is appointed by the Chief Justice of the High Court at Madras.

(*b*) In the case of Calcutta presidency town, he is appointed by the State Government of West Bengal, after consultation with, and with the concurrence of, the Chief Justice of the High Court at Calcutta.

(*c*) For Bombay presidency town, he is appointed by the State Government of Maharashtra.

An Official Assignee is to give such security and is subject to such rules and is to act in such manner as may be prescribed. He is a corporate body having perpetual succession and a common seal. He may sue and be sued in his corporate name. He has to exercise all acts necessary or expedient to be done to execute his office.

OFFICIAL RECEIVER

The State Government may appoint such persons as it may think fit to be Official Receivers under the

Provincial Act, to act within such limits as may be prescribed. Where such an Official Receiver has been appointed for any local limits, he shall be the receiver for the purpose of every order appointing a receiver or interim receiver made by the Court exercising jurisdiction within those limits, unless the Court for special reasons otherwise directs.

Under the Provincial Insolvency Act 1920, the Court may, at the time of the order of adjudication, or at any time afterwards, appoint a Receiver for the property of the insolvent and such property thereupon vests in such Receiver. The Court may ask him to give any security and shall also fix his remuneration to be paid out of the assets of the insolvent. The Court shall appoint such person as Receiver who is appointed by the State Government as the Official Receiver for that local limit.

POWERS OF OFFICIAL ASSIGNEE OR RECEIVER

Certain powers are conferred upon the Official Assignees or Receiver under both the Acts. He can exercise some of these powers on his own account without the permission of the court, and can exercise some of them with the permission of the court.

Powers without the Permission of the Court : The official Assignee or the Receiver can exercise the following powers without obtaining any prior approval of the Court :

(1) To sell all or any part of the property of the insolvent,

(2) To give receipts for any money received by him,

(3) To distribute the sale proceeds as 'dividend' from time to time, among the creditors proportionately.

Powers with the Permission of the Court : The Official Assignee or the Receiver can also exercise the following powers with the permission of the Court :

(1) To carry on the business of the insolvent, as far as may be necessary, for the beneficial winding up of the same.

(2) To institute, defend or continue any suit or other legal proceeding relating to the property of the insolvent.

(3) To employ a pleader or other agent to take any proceedings or do any business which may be sanctioned by the Court.

(4) To accept as the consideration for the sale of any property of the insolvent, moneys payable at a future date or fully paid-up shares or debentures on such terms as to security as the Court thinks fit.

(5) To mortgage or pledge any part of the property of the insolvent for the purpose of raising money for the payment of his debts or for the purpose of carrying on the business.

(6) To refer any dispute to arbitration, and compromise all debts, claims and liabilities, on such terms as may be agreed upon.

(7) To divide in its existing form amongst the creditors, according to its estimated value, any property which, from its peculiar nature or other special circumstances, cannot readily or advantageously be sold.

DUTIES OF THE OFFICIAL ASSIGNEE OR RECEIVER

The following are the most important duties of an Official Assignee or Receiver :

(1) He must take into custody and control all the books, documents and the assets of the insolvent.

(2) He must realise the property of the insolvent with all convenient speed in most profitable manner.

(3) He must act and function in an honest and impartial manner while distributing the money received by him amongst the creditors because he stands in a fiduciary relationship towards them.

(4) He must maintain proper books and submit his accounts to the Court at such periods and in such form as the Court directs.

(5) He must, from time to time, summon meetings of the creditors and pay due regard to the wishes of the creditors as indicated in such meetings, and must submit schemes of 'Arrangement and Composition', if any, before the creditors.

(6) He must do all such acts as may be required by the Court from time to time, for example, he may be asked to investigate the conduct of the insolvent and make a report to the Court which may guide the Court in making an 'order of discharge.'

SUPERIOR TITLE OF THE OFFICIAL ASSIGNEE OR RECEIVER

The title of the Official Assignee or Receiver is superior to that of the insolvent in respect of the claims arising out of insolvency. Moreover, he has much wider powers than what the insolvent himself has. The superior position of the Official Assignee or Receiver is explained under the following heads :

(1) *Doctrine of Reputed Ownership*

The Doctrine of Reputed Ownership shows the superiority of the Official Assignee or Receiver. Even the true owner cannot claim the goods which are in the possession, order or disposition of the insolvent, but such goods vest in the Official Assignee or Receiver. The insolvent himself cannot claim such goods, if he wants to do so. But the Official Assignee or Receiver can claim these goods as both the Insolvency Acts empower him as such.

(2) *Avoidance of Voluntary Transfers*

All objectionable transfers of property without consideration made by the insolvent within two years preceding the 'commencement of insolvency' are void against the Assignee or Receiver and he can recover the property so transferred. (For more details, refer Chapter 31)

(3) *Avoidance of Fraudulent Preference*

The Official Assignee or Receiver has also a right to set aside every 'fraudulent preference' made by the insolvent within three months preceding the presentation of insolvency petition. It is also a proof of his superior title. (For more details, refer Chapter 31).

(4) *Right to Claim After-acquired Property*

The Official Assignee or Receiver has the right to claim any property acquired by the insolvent after the date of his adjudication and before his discharge. This right also brings him in a superior position than the insolvent.

(5) *Right to Disclaim Onerous Property*

The Official Assignee or Receiver has the right to disclaim onerous property as it creates extra burden upon him. It is also a right maintaining his superiority in rights. (This topic is discussed separately in this chapter).

DISCLAIMER OF ONEROUS PROPERTY

Sections 62-67 of the Presidency Towns Insolvency Act provide for a disclaimer of onerous property by the Official Assignee. 'Onerous property' implies a property which in effect has ceased to be an asset and has become a liability, for instance, unsaleable property, or unprofitable contracts or the land burdened with onerous convenants or partly paid-up shares of an unsuccessful company. Sometimes, some of the property of an insolvent may be burdened with considerable obligations or obligations attached to it may exceed the advantage to be derived from it. In such a case, the retention of that property by the Official Assignee would diminish, rather than increase, the total amount of money available for distribution among the creditors.

For a valid disclaimer of onerous property, it must be made by notice in writing signed by the Official Assignee within 12 months of the date of the order of adjudication or within 12 months of the date on which the Official Assignee came to know of the existence of such property. The Official Assignee is not entitled to disclaim any leasehold property without the leave of the Court.

There are no corresponding provisions as to disclaimer of onerous property in the Provincial Insolvency Act, and such cases falling under it are governed by the ordinary law.

DOCTRINE OF REPUTED OWNERSHIP

Sometimes, an insolvent is in possession of certain property or goods which do not belong to him. If such goods lead other parties to believe that they are the property of the insolvent, they can vest in the Official Assignee or Receiver and be divisible amongst the creditors. Persons who are owners of goods should not leave them with a trader who is in insolvent circumstances. If they do so and the goods are found at the commencement of the insolvency in the possession, order or disposition of the insolvent, in his trade or business, by the consent and permission of the true owner, under such circumstances that he is the reputed owner thereof, such goods are deemed to be the property of the insolvent. The Official Assignee or Receiver can take possession of them for distribution among general body of creditors. This is the 'doctrine of reputed ownership.'

Essentials of the Doctrine of Reputed Ownership

Following are the essentials of the Doctrine of Reputed Ownership :

(1) The insolvent must be a trader.

(2) The property must be goods and movable property.

(3) There must be no mark or other indication showing that the goods belongs to some person other than the insolvent.

(4) The possession order or disposition must be with the consent of the true owner, and not through fraud or mistake.

(5) The goods must be in the sole possession, order or disposition of the insolvent in his trade or business at the commencement of the insolvency.

The Doctrine of Reputed Ownership does not apply in the following cases :

(1) Immovable properties.

(2) Goods taken under hire-purchase agreement.

(3) Goods in the possession of the insolvent as a trustee, bailee, repairer, carrier, factor, agent or pawnee.

PROPERTY OF INSOLVENT

The property or the profits derived out of it, which are disposable by the insolvent himself, is deemed to be the property of the insolvent and it vests in the Official Assignee or Receiver on the adjudication of the debtor as insolvent. According to Sec. 2(*d*) of the Provincial Insolvency Act and Sec. 2 (*e*) of the Presidency Towns Insolvency Act, "the 'property' of an insolvent includes any property over which or over the profits of which he has disposing power, which he may exercise for his benefit."

For the purpose of both the Insolvency Acts, the property of the insolvent may be divided into two categories, *viz*, (*a*) property which is divisible amongst the creditors, and (*b*) Property which is not so divisible amongst the creditors. In both the Acts, the expression 'property of the insolvent' means such of the insolvent's property as is divisible amongst his creditors, and it is such divisible property only which vests in the Official Assignee or Receiver, on the insolvency of the person concerned.

Property not Divisible among Creditors

Following property of an insolvent is not divisible among his creditors :

(1) Property held by the insolvent :

(*a*) on trust,

(*b*) on behalf of other persons,

(*c*) in a fiduciary capacity, for example, property held as a trustee, bailee, factors etc.

(2) (*a*) Under the Presidency Towns Insolvency Act, the tools of his trade (if any), necessary wearing apparel, bedding, cooking utensils and furniture of himself, his wife and children not exceeding in all Rs. 300 in value.

(*b*) Under the Provincial Insolvency Act, properties exempt by the Civil Procedure Code 1908 or by any other enactment for the time being in force, from liability to attachement and sale in execution of a decree, are not distributable as such. Such property includes tools of trade, wearing apparel, bedding, cooking utensils, personal ornaments which a lady has to wear according to religious customs, for example, Mangal Sutra.

(3) The following property is also not divisible among the creditors :

(*i*) Pension

(*ii*) Receipts out of Provident Fund,

(*iii*) Gratuity.

(*iv*) Right of action in respect of a tort. (v) Chance of succession.

(4) A 'spes successionis' *i.e.*, a mere chance of getting some property upon the death of a near relative.

Property Divisible among Creditors

The property of an insolvent which is divisible among his creditors may include the following:

(1) All property which belongs to or vests in him at the commencement of his insolvency.

(2) All property acquired by the insolvent or devolved on him after adjudication and before discharge. Provisions under both the Insolvency Acts, in force, in the country differ in this regard :

(*a*) Under the Provincial Insolvency Act such property vests in the Court or the Official Receiver and is divisible amongst the creditors.

(*b*) Under the Presidency Towns Insolvency Act, it does not vest in the Official Assignee unless he intervenes so as to acquire a right to divide such property amongst the creditors.

(3) Property of which the insolvent is the reputed owner.

(4) Property or the profits derived out of it, over wich he has disposing power or which he may exercise for his own benefit.

(5) Property vested in voluntary transfers made by him.

(6) Property used by him to give fraudulent preferences to any one or more of his creditors.

COMMITTEE OF INSPECTION

Both the Insolvency Acts provide that the Court may, if it so thinks fit, authorise the creditors who have proved their debts to appoint from among themselves a 'Committee of Inspection' for the purpose of superintending the administration of the insolvent's property by the Official Assignee or Receiver. The Committee shall have such powers of control over the proceedings of the Official Assignee or Receiver as may be prescribed.

COMPOSITION AND SCHEME OF ARRANGEMENT

After the insolvency proceedings commence, the debtor can come to an understanding with the creditors regarding the payment of the debts. Such understanding or settlement may be of two types : (*i*) It may be a "composition" of the debts, or (*ii*) It may be a "scheme of arrangement".

A 'composition' is an agreement between the insolvent debtor and all or some of the creditors by which the creditors agree to abandon a part of their claims and accept payment of less than the amount due to them in full satisfaction of their claims. A 'scheme of arrangement' is an agreement between the insolvent debtor and his creditors by which the creditors agree for the gradual realisation of the amount due to them in due course of time, without selling all the debtor's assets.

A debtor cannot settle with his creditors out of the Court after he has been adjudged an insolvent. The Insolvency Acts deal with compositions and schemes entered into after adjudication, which are valid and binding only if approved by the Court. Therefore, an insolvent may at any time after making of an order of adjudication submit proposal for a composition in satisfaction of his debts or a proposal for a scheme of arrangement of his affairs in the prescribed form. A proposal for composition or scheme should be submitted by the debtor only and not by anyone else.

Procedure of Submission of Scheme or Composition

The procedure for composition or sheme of arrangement, under both the Acts is as follows :

(1) An adjudicated insolvent should submit a proposal for composition in satisfaction of his debts, or a scheme of arrangement of his affairs in the prescribed form to the Official Assignee or Receiver.

(2) A copy of such a scheme is sent to each of the creditors by the Official Assignee or Receiver alongwith his report thereon and a meeting of all the creditors is summoned.

(3) Submission of the proposal is a basis of negotiation with the creditors and may be amended at the meeting of the creditors.

(4) Any of the creditors may assent to or dissent from the scheme by a letter addressed to the Official Assignee or Receiver.

(5) If, on the consideration of the proposal in such creditors' meeting, a majority in number and three-fourths in value of all the creditors, whose debts are proved and who are present either in person or by pleader, resolve to accept the proposal, it is put up before the Court for approval.

(6) The Court may hear such an application only when public examination of the insolvent has been concluded except in the case where special leave of the Court is obtained or when an estate is summarily administered.

(7) The Court may approve or reject such an application. Rejection may be on any of the following grounds :

(*a*) Terms of the proposal are not reasonable; or

(*b*) It does not benefit the creditors; or

(*c*) Circumstances require the court to refuse the proposal; or

(*d*) It does not provide for priority in payment of preferential creditors.

(8) If the Court approves the proposal, the terms are embodied in an order of the Court.

(9) The order of adjudication is then annulled and usual proceedings and consequences follow.

(10) Such proposal is binding on all the creditors in regard to their debts due against the insolvent and payable.

DEBTS OF THE INSOLVENT

It is stated earlier that on making an order of adjudication the insolvent's property vests in the Official Assignee or Receiver and the insolvent's creditors can no longer commence any suit against the insolvent. They get only a dividend at a certain rate out of the estate of the insolvent. The debts with reference to which the dividend is calculated are called 'provable debts' and the method by which these debts are established is called 'proof of debts. The creditors are required to prove their claims in insolvency before the Official Assignee (under Presidency Towns Insolvency Act) or the Court (Under Provincial Insolvency Act) and get a pro-rata dividend out of the insolvent's property. The Official Assignee or the Court as the case may be, may at any time call for the production of vouchers or other evidence in support of the claim.

Debts Provable in Insolvency (Under both Acts)

Debts which can be proved and claimed in insolvency proceedings include :

(1) All debts and liabilities, whether present or future, certain or contingent, to which the debtor is subject when adjudicated insolvent.

(2) All debts and liabilities arising before his discharge but before the order of adjudication, by reason of any obligation incurred before the date of such adjudication.

Essentials of provable debts in insolvency are :

(*a*) The debt liability must be liquidated.

(*b*) It must have been incurred before the date of adjudication.

(*c*) The insolvent must be subject to it at any time before his discharge by reason of any obligation incurred before the date of adjudication.

RIGHTS OF SECURED CREDITORS

A secured creditor is one who has lent money to the insolvent on the security of some movable or immovable property. A secured creditor has the right to realise his dues in full out of the security given to him and this right is not affected by the insolvency proceedings. It is, therefore, said that secured creditor stands outside the insolvency. But where the security is not sufficient to meet his claim, he can, if he so desires, come in the insolvency proceedings as an unsecured creditor by relinquishing his security or by deducting the value of the security. Three courses are open to him:

(1) Where a secured creditor realizes his security, he may prove for the balance due to him : his debts minus net amount realized out of the security.

(2) He may prove for the whole debt, if he has relinquished his security for the benefit of general creditors.

(3) He may value his security and state the assessed value in his proof and then prove for the balance that may remain due to him after deducting the assessed value subject to the right of the Court to redeem the security on payment to the creditor of the assessed value.

Where he fails to comply with any of the above alternatives, he is not entitled to any dividend.

Debts not Provable in Insolvency (Under botht the Acts)

The following debts are not provable in insolvency :

(1) Contingent debts and liabilities, the value of which cannot be fairly estimated.

(2) Demands in the nature of unliquidated damages arising otherwise than by reason of a contract or breach of trust.

(3) Time-barred debts at the commencement of insolvency.

(4) Debts contracted after the order of adjudication.

PROOF OF DEBTS

After the making of an order of adjudication every creditor has to lodge the proof of his debt with the Official Assignee (under the Presidency Insolvency Act) and with the Court (under the Provincial Insolvency Act). The proof may be lodged by delivering or sending by post in a registered letter an affidavit verifying the debt. The affidavit must contain a statement of account showing the particulars of the debt. It must also specify the vouchers, if any, by which the debt can be substantiated. The Official Assignee or the Court, as the case may be, may at any time call for the production of the vouchers.

ANNULMENT OF ADJUDICATION

The order of adjudication shall be annulled (cancelled) in the following cases :

(1) Where the order of adjudication was wrongly made, for example, when it is found that the person adjudicated is a minor or lunatic or otherwise outside the jurisdiction of the court etc.

(2) Where it is proved to the satisfaction of the Court that the debts have been paid in full.

(3) Where it is found that the same person has been adjudicated insolvent by more than one Court : insolvency proceedings can be continued in one court only.

(4) Where the insolvent submits a composition or a scheme of arrangement and it is approved by the Court.

(5) Where the adjudication is on a debtor's petition, who did not owe Rs. 500 or more.

The Court may annul an order of adjudication under the following cases :

(1) Where it was made on the petition of a debtor who could not present the petition without the leave of the Court on the ground that on a prior occasion an order of adjudication passed against him was annulled owing to his failure to apply for discharge.

(2) Where the insolvent fails to apply for discharge within the prescribed time, or fails to appear at the hearing of the application for his discharge.

(3) Where an insolvency proceeding is pending simultaneously in two Courts. In such a case, one Court may annul the order of adjudication.

Effect of Annulment of Adjudication

(1) Where an adjudication is annulled, all sales, dispositions of property and payments duly made and all acts done by the Court or Official Assignee or Receiver prior to annulment are valid.

(2) Subject to the dispositions already made, the effect of an annulment is to restore the debtor to his position before his adjudication.

(3) The insolvent's property, on annulment, vests in such person as the court may appoint.

(4) If a debtor is released from a civil prison and the adjudication is annulled, the court may recommit the debtor to jail, if it so thinks fit.

MUTUAL DEALING AND SET-OFF

When there are mutual dealings between the insolvent and a creditor, an account is taken and the creditor is allowed to claim for the balance due, if any. In such accounting the sums paid by one party to the other are set off against sums received by him. But if a creditor who has given credit to the insolvent did so with the knowledge of the presentation of an insolvency petition, he cannot claim the benefit of any set-off.

DISTRIBUTION OF INSOLVENT'S PROPERTY

It is the duty of the Official Assignee or Receiver to take possession of all the property of the insolvent and realise the property with all convenient speed. Out of the sale proceeds of the insolvent's property, the Official Assignee or Receiver retain such sum as are necessary for meeting the cost of administering including his remuneration. The balance is to be distributed among the creditors.

Sec. 49 of the Presidency Towns Insolvency Act and Sec. 61 of the Provincial Insolvency Act deal with payment of debts of the insolvent, particularly as to the order in which they are to be paid and how they are to be paid. There are some debts, which assume priority over other debts in payment and, therefore, are called "Preferential Debts". Then the other debts of the insolvent and partnership debts.

ORDER OF PAYMENT OF DEBTS

(1) *Preferential Debts*

The following debts or claims must be paid in priority to all other debts :

(*a*) All debts due to the Government or any local authority, for example, Income Tax, Land Revenue, Municipal taxes etc.

(*b*) All salary or wages of any clerk, servant or labourer in respect of services rendered to the insolvent during four months before the date of the presentation of the insolvency petition, subject to the following limits :

(*i*) Under the Presidency Towns Insolvency Act :

Rs. 300 in respect of each clerk and

Rs. 100 in respect of each servant or labourer;

(*ii*) Under the Provincial Insolvency Act;

Rs. 20 in respect of each clerk, servant or labourer.

It may be noted that excess of the amount of salary or wages over these limits shall be treated as 'Unsecured debt'.

(c) Rent due to landlord for one month under the Presidency Towns Insolvency Act. Arrears of rent exceeding one month shall be treated as Unsecured debts.

There is no such provision under the Provincial Insolvency Act.

The debts mentioned above rank equally and must be paid in full before any payment can be made for other debts. If the assets are not sufficient, to pay all these debts in full, they are reduced in equal proportion.

(2) *Other Debts*

If any assets are left after paying the preferential claims mentioned above, they are distributed rateably or proportionately among the unsecured creditors who have proved their debts in insolvency (Under the Presidency Towns Insolvency Act) or whose names have been entered in the schedule of creditors (under the Provincial Insolvency Act).

(3) *Payment of Interest*

Where there is any surplus after payment of all the foregoing debts in full, it must be applied in payment of interest, at the rate of 6 per cent per annum, for the period after the order of adjudication until the date of actual payment. If there is still any surplus that must be paid to the insolvent.

(4) *Partnership Debts*

In the case of partners, the partnership property is applicable in the first instance in payment of the partnership debts and the separate property of each partner is applicable in the first instance in payment of his separate debts. Where there is a surplus from the separate property of the partners, it is dealt with as part of the partnership property. Where there is a surplus from the partnership property, it is dealt with as part of the respective separate property of the partner in proportion to the rights and interests of each partner in the partnership property.

DECLARATION AND DISTRIBUTION OF DIVIDEND

The Official Assignee or Receiver is supposed to complete the distribution of the property of the insolvent with convenient speed. Under the Presidency Towns Insolvency Act, the first instalment of the amount of dividend must be declared and paid to the creditors within one year after the adjudication unless the Official Assignees satisfies the Court that there is sufficient reason for postponing the delcaration of dividend to a later date. Subsequent dividends must, in the absence of sufficient reason to the contrary, be declared and paid at intervals of not more than six months. However, it should be done with convenient speed.

Calculation of Dividend (Presi. Sec. 71 & Prov. Sec. 62)

In calculation and distribution of dividends, the Official Assignee or Receiver must retain with him, sufficient assets to meet the following :

(a) The claims of creditors residing at distant places who would not have sufficient time to tender their proofs ;

(b) The claims yet to be determined ;

(c) Disputed claims and proofs;

(d) the expenses likely to be incurred on the administration of the estate or otherwise.

FINAL DIVIDEND

On realizing all the property of the insolvent, the Official Assignee or Receiver declares, with the leave of the Court, a final dividend. Before that he is supposed to give a notice to all those creditors, who have got their claims notified to them, but have not proved them. Such notice states to the creditors that, if they do not prove their claims within the prescribed time mentioned in the notice, he will proceed to final dividend, without any regard to their claims. If the creditors fail to comply with the notice in time, the property of the insolvent is divided among the creditors who have proved their claims without regard to the claims of others, which are not proved.

SMALL INSOLVENCIES

Where the estate of an insolvent is small, both the Insolvency Acts provide for a summary or simplified procedure for the administration of the insolvent's estate with a view to saving expense. The estate of the insolvent is considered to be small if its value is not likely to be Rs. 3,000 under the Presidency Towns Insolvency Act and Rs. 500 under the Provincial Insolvency Act. The insolvencies to be administered in a summary manner are known as 'small insolvencies'. In case of small insolvencies, the provisions of the respective acts apply as usual, subject to certain modifications. They are stated below :

Modifications under the Presidency Towns Insolvency Act

(1) No appeal shall lie from any order of the Court, except with the prior permission of the Court.

(2) No examination of the insolvent shall held, except on the application of a creditor or the official Assignee.

(3) The estate shall, where practicable, be distributed in single dividend.

(4) Such other modification as may be prescribed with a view to saving expense and simplifying procedure.

There can be no modification of the provisions of the Act relating to the discharge of the insolvent.

The Court may at any time, if it thinks fit, revoke an order for the summary administration of an insolvent's estate.

Modifications under the Provincial Insolvency Act

(1) No notice required under the Act shall be published in the official Gazettee, unless the Court otherwise directs.

(2) On the admission of a petition by a debtor, the property of the debtor shall vest in the Court as a receiver.

(3) At the hearing of the petition, the Court shall inquire into the debts and assets of the debtor and determine the same by order in writing, and it shall not be necessary to frame a Schedule of creditors under the provisions of Sec. 33.

(4) The property of the debtor shall realised with all reasonable despatch and thereafter, when practicable, distributed in a single dividend.

(5) The debtor shall apply for his discharge within six months from the date of adjudication.

(6) Such other modifications as may be prescribed with a view to saving expense and simplifying procedure.

The Court may also, if it thinks fit, at any time, revoke the order for the summary administration of the insolvent's estate, and direct for following the ordinary procedure laid down in the Act.

THEORETICAL QUESTIONS

1. Explain briefly the powers and duties of Official Assignee or Receiver. *(B.Com. Madurai)*
2. "In matters arising out of insolvency the Official Assignee or Receiver has a higher title than the insolvent". Comment. *(B.Com. MS)*
3. What property of the insolvent (*a*) is divisible and (*b*) is not divisible among his creditors? *(B.Com. Agra)*
4. "The effect of the 'Doctrine of Reputed Ownership' is to take one's property to pay another's debt." Discuss. *(B.Com. Punjab)*
5. Enumerate the debts payable in insolvency. What is the order in which the creditors are paid.
6. Enumerate the preferential payments in case of insolvency. *(B.Com. Andhra)*
7. What is a 'composition and a scheme of arrangement'? What procedure has been laid down under the Insolvency Acts in relation to them?
8. Write a detailed note on 'Disclaimer of onerous property'. *(B.Com. Kerala)*
9. When can the Insolvency Court annul an order of adjudication? State the effects of an order of annulment of adjudication. *(B.Com. Bhopal)*
10. What do you understand by "small insolvencies"? What special modifications have been made under the two Insolvency Acts relating to them? *(B.Com. MK)*
11. What are the debts provable in insolvency and what are the properties available for their payment? *(B.Com. Delhi)*

CHAPTER

Discharge of Insolvent

AT A GLANCE

The last stage of insolvency proceedings is the discharge of an insolvent. From the date of the order of adjudication to the date from which the Order of Discharge operates, the debtor is an "undischarged insolvent". The intention of the Legislature is that when an insolvent gets a certificate of discharge, he should be a free man again. After the Order of Discharge the term "insolvent" can no longer be applied on him.

The *procedure for discharging an insolvent* is described below :

APPLICATION FOR DISCHARGE

The court does not grant a discharge certificate of its own, but the insolvent is required to apply to the Court for an Order of Discharge. An application for discharge may be made at any time after the order of adjudication as provided under both the Insolvency Acts.

Under Sec. 38 (1) of the Presidency Towns Insolvency Act, the Court does not hear the application for discharge till the public examination of the insolvent has concluded except in those cases where it is dispensed with.

Under Sec. 41 (1) of the Provincial Insolvency Act, an insolvent must, however, apply for discharge within the period specified by the Court for the purpose.

POWERS OF THE COURT

When the Court receives an application for discharge, the Court fixes a day for the hearing of the application. Before passing any order, the Court asks the Official Assignee or Receiver to submit his report regarding the conduct of the insolvent and his dealings with his properties. All creditors are also notified about the date of hearing. The Court hears the insolvent, the creditors and the Official Assignee or Receiver. After hearing the application, the Court may :

(1) grant an absolute discharge; or

(2) refuse the discharge; or
(3) suspend the discharge for a specified time; or
(4) grant conditional discharge as to the insolvent's future earnings, income or after-acquired property; or
(5) require the insolvent, as a condition of his discharge, to consent to a decree being passed against him in favour of the Official Assignee for any part of the balance of the debts proved against him.

EFFECT OF FAILURE TO APPLY FOR DISCHARGE

Where the insolvent neither appears on the day fixed for hearing of his application for discharge nor makes an application for discharge within the time specified in the order of adjudication, the Court shall annul the order of adjudication and the consequences and proceedings on annulment of adjudication will follow.

The annulment of adjudication may be made on the application of :
(*a*) the Official Assignee or Receiver, or
(*b*) a creditor, or
(*c*) the Court on its own motion.

EFFECT OF THE ORDER OF DISCHARGE

The following may be the effect of the order of discharge :
(*a*) It releases the insolvent from all debts provable in insolvency. However, it does not release him from :
  (*i*) any debt due to the Government,
  (*ii*) any debt or liability incurred by means of any fraud or fraudulent breach of trust to which he was a party,
  (*iii*) any debt or liability in respect of which he obtained forbearance by any fraud to which he was a party, or
  (*iv*) any liability to provide maintenance to his wife or legitimate or illegitimate children.
(*b*) It is the conclusive evidence of insolvency and of the validity of proceedings thereto as per the Presidency Towns Insolvency Act.
(*c*) It does not release any person who, at the date of the presentation of the petition, was a partner or co-trustee with the insolvent or any person who was surety for him.
(*d*) It does not affect the criminal liability of an insolvent.

REFUSAL OF ABSOLUTE (UNCONDITIONAL) DISCHARGE

The Court refuses absolute or unconditional order of discharge if it finds proof of any of the following :
(1) When the assets of the insolvent are not of a value of 50 paise in a rupee in the Provincial Insolvency Act and 25 paise in a rupee in the Presidency Towns Insolvency Act, of his unsecured debts, unless the deficiency arose from the circumstances for which he cannot be held responsible.
(2) When he has failed to keep usual and proper books of accounts disclosing his financial position for three years immediately before his insolvency.
(3) When he continues to carry on his business despite being insolvent.
(4) When he has contracted a debt provable in insolvency without any reasonable ground of expectation of being able to repay it.
(5) When he has failed to account satisfactorily for any loss of assets to meet the liabilities.

(6) When he has contributed to his insolvency by rash and hazardous speculation, or by unjust extravagance in living, or by gambling, or by neglect of his business activities.

(7) When he has given undue preference to any of his creditors within three months of the presentation of petition of insolvency.

(8) When he has concealed or removed whole or a part of his property.

(9) When he is guilty of fraud or any other fraudulent breach of trust.

(10) Sec. 39 of the Presidency Towns Insolvency Act Provides two more grounds in this ground, namely :

(*i*) When the insolvent has put any of his creditors to unnecessary expense by a frivolous vexatious defence of any suit brought against him.

(*ii*) When within three months of presentation of petition, he has brought a frivolous or vexatious suit.

(11) Under the Provincial Insolvency Act, when on a previous occasion he has also been adjudged insolvent or has compounded with his creditors.

EFFECT OF REFUSAL OF DISCHARGE

The insolvency proceedings are not terminated until the Order of adjudication is annulled or until the insolvent gets an unconditional discharge. When discharge is refused, the Court does not grant protection to the insolvent and he may be arrested in execution of money decrees.

REMEDIES WHEN DISCHARGE IS REFUSED

When discharge is refused to an insolvent, he may :

(1) apply to the Court for review. The Court may review, rescind or vary any order made by it under its insolvency jurisdiction;

(2) appeal against the order refusing his discharge;

(3) renew his application for discharge if the Court permits him to renew his application (presi. Sec. 42 (1). There is no corresponding provision in the Provincial Insolvency Act but at the same time there is nothing in the Act to suggest that once an application for discharge is refused, it is refused for ever.

THEORETICAL QUESTIONS

1. Discuss the procedure regarding 'discharge' of an insolvent.

2. What are the various circumstances under which the Court must refuse an "absolute order of discharge"?

3. Under what circumstances is an insolvent discharged? What are the effects of such a discharged?

4. When does a Court refuse an unconditional discharge?

5. What are the remedies open to an insolvent whose discharge is refused?

CHAPTER

General Provision of Arbitration Act, 1940

AT A GLANCE

- Arbitration Defined
- Essentials
- Effect of an Arbitration
- Advantages
- Matters which can be Referred to Arbitration
- Matters Which cannot be Referred to Arbitration
- Who Refer Disputes
- Implied Conditions
- Theoretical Questions

The law relating to arbitration is presently contained in the Arbitration Act 1940 which came into force on 1 July 1940. It consists of 49 sections divided into seven chapters. It applies to the whole of India except the State of Jammu and Kashmir.

ARBITRATION DEFINED

In India, reference of disputes to the Panch or the Panchayat is a traditional and widely used method of settling disputes. Arbitration is a method of settling disputes and differences between two or more parties by referring them to a nominated person or persons, who decide the issue after hearing both sides in a quasi-Judicial manner. It is an alternative to a legal action.

According to Sec. 2 (*a*), an arbitration agreement means "a written agreement to submit present or future differences to arbitration, whether an arbitrator is named therein or not."

The arbitration agreement or the arbitration clause in an agreement is sometimes called "submission". An arbitration agreement is also known as "reference". According to Halsbury, "It is agreement made by two or more parties between whom some difference has arise or may thereafter arise whereby they appoint another person to adjudicate upon such dispute and agree to be bound by his decision. The characteristic of arbitration is that it is a private tribunal chosen by the parties." Thus arbitration agreement means an agreement in writing to submit a present dispute or a future difference to arbitration, whether an arbitrator is named or not. Thus, the person, who is appointed to settle the differences or disputes, is called an "arbitrator :" the proceedings before him are called an "arbitration" and his decision is called an "award".

ESSENTIALS OF AN ARBITRATION AGREEMENT

An arbitration agreement, to be valid and binding, should have the following essential elements :

(1) *It must be in Writing*

The arbitration agreement must be in writing. Signatures of the parties are not necessary. What is required is that the terms of the arbitration agreement must be reduced in writing and it must be established that the parties agreed to the settlement of disputes by arbitration. The arbitration agreement may be a clause in a contract or in consignment note or in correspondence between the parties etc.

A formal document signed by the parties is not essentials.

(2) *There must be a Present or Future Dispute*

The existence of a dispute or difference is essential to the validity of a reference to arbitration. Arbitration pre-supposes the existence or the possible existence of a dispute. Dispute means assertion of a right by one party and denial of that right by the other party. If there is no dispute, there can be no right to demand arbitration. If there is no dispute, the arbitration agreement will not operate.

(3) *It must have all Essential Elements of a Valid Contract*

The arbitration agreement must have all the essential elements of a valid contract. The parties must be competent to contract. The terms must be definite and certain. The matter to be referred to arbitration must not be immoral, illegal or opposed to public policy. But if the parties were not *ad-idem*, that is, if there was no contract at all, the arbitration clause is not binding. Where a contract contains an arbitration clause and the contract is rescinded on the ground of fraud or misrepresentation, the arbitration clause remains operative.

ADVANTAGES

The method of settling disputes through arbitration possesses the following advantages, as compared to a law suit.

(1) It is more simple and quicker as regards procedure.
(2) Arbitration is less costly.
(3) Avoidance of publicity is possible.
(4) Generally award, once approved by the Court, is final and no appeal lies from it.
(5) Parties can save unnecessary waste of time.
(6) Secrecy can be maintained.

The above advantages depend upon a competent arbitrator, who acts impartially.

EFFECT OF AN ARBITRATION AGREEMENT

When some persons have entered into an agreement to refer disputes relating to a matter to arbitration they may be presented from agitation the same matter in a court of law. Thus, if a party to an arbitration agreement disregards the agreement and files a suit in a Court of law with respect to the subject matter of such agreement, the other party to the agreement has a right to file an application for *staying the suit* so as to enable arbitration to proceed in terms of the agreement. When some persons have entered into an agreement to refer all disputes between them either existing or future, to arbitration, they cannot institute any suit in a Court of law relating to those matters : otherwise the very purpose of arbitration will be frustrated. If any such civil suit is filed against the arbitration agreement, the Court may grant stay order to the proceedings subject to the following conditions : (Sec. 34).

(1) There must be a valid arbitration agreement in existence.

(2) The subject matter of the suit in question must be within the scope of the arbitration agreement.

(3) It must be shown that the applicant for stay was and is still ready and willing to proceed with the arbitration and do everything necessary for the purpose.

(4) The Court must also be satisfied that there is no sufficient reason why the matter should not be referred to arbitration in accordance with the agreement.

(5) The application for such a stay must be made a party to the arbitration agreement or by some other person claiming under him.

(6) Application for stay must be made during the early stage of proceedings by the arbitration.

(7) The Court must be satisfied that the applicant was ready to abide by the conditions of the arbitration.

MATTERS WHICH CAN BE REFERRED TO ARBITRATION

Unless prohibited by any Act for the time being in force, or by any law, or by public policy, all matters in controversy which can be submitted to a suit in a Civil court can be the subject matter of arbitration.

The following matters may be submitted to arbitration :

(1) Disputes regarding dignity and respect.
(2) Time-barred claims.
(3) Matters of Civil nature, for example, disputes about property and money, dispute arising out of breach of contract, question of law, question of fact etc.
(4) Matters relating to personal rights between parties, for example, a question of marriage, maintenance payable to wife, terms of separation between husband and wife etc.
(5) Question of title to immovable property etc.

MATTERS WHICH CANNOT BE REFERRED TO ARBITRATION

Generally, all matters in dispute, provided they are not of criminal nature, may be referred to arbitration. Consequently, all suits cognizable by a Civil Court, to which the Code of Civil Procedure applies, may be referred. However, the following matters though cognizable by a Civil Court, cannot be referred to arbitration :

(1) Disputes relating to matrimonial relations like a suit for divorce or restitution of conjugal rights.
(2) Insolvency matters, *i.e.*, adjudging a person as an insolvent.
(3) Testamentary matters, for example, the question of genuineness or otherwise of a 'will'.
(4) Guardianship of a minor or lunatics.
(5) Public charities and charitable trusts.
(6) Lunancy proceedings.
(7) Criminal matters.
(8) Illegal transactions etc.

WHO CAN REFER DISPUTES TO ARBITRATION

An arbitration agreement is a contract. Submission of a dispute to an arbitration agreement is like a contract. Therefore, parties to it should be capable of entering into a contract, so that they may be bound by the award given by the arbitration. The capacity of different types of persons to refer a dispute to arbitration are as under :

(1) *Minor :* Because of having no contractual capacity, a minor or a lunatic cannot refer disputes to arbitration. The guardian of a minor can do so, provided it is for the benefit of the minor and is reasonable and proper for the protection of the minor.

(2) *Karta of HUF* : The Karta or manager of a Hindu Undivided Family acting bona fide may enter into an arbitration agreement on behalf of the family so as to bind other co-partners.

(3) *Partner :* A partner can refer disputes relating to the firm to arbitration provided such power is given to him by the partnership deed.

(4) *Agent :* An agent cannot refer a dispute to arbitration unless specifically authorised by his principal.

(5) *Joint Stock Company :* A joint stock company can refer disputes to arbitration subject to its Memorandum and Articles of Association.

(6) *Trustee :* A trustee can refer a dispute to arbitration unless prohibited by the instrument of trust.

(7) *Insolvent :* An Official Assignee or Receiver can make a valid reference with the permission of the Court of a dispute to which the insolvent is a party, so as to bind his estate but an insolvent cannot do so.

(8) *Attorneys and Counsels :* An attorney or counsel has implied authority to refer to arbitration a case of his client, unless restricted by express directions to the contrary.

IMPLIED CONDITIONS OF AN ARBITRATION AGREEMENT

In the absence of a contract to the contrary the Act provides for the implied inclusion of certain provisions in every arbitration agreement. According to Sec. 3 of the Arbitration Act, the following implied conditions as stated in the First Schedule shall apply to every arbitration agreement.

(1) Unless otherwise expressly provided, the reference shall be to a sole arbitrator.

(2) If the reference is to an even number of arbitrators, the arbitrators shall appoint an umpire not later than one month from the latest date of their respective appointments. The term 'umpire' means a third person who is to decide a controversy or questions submitted to arbitrators in case of their disagreement.

(3) The arbitrators shall make their award within four months after entering on the reference or after having been called upon to act by notice in writing from any party to the arbitration agreement or within such extended time as the court may allow.

(4) If the arbitrators have allowed their time to expire without making an award or have delivered to any party to the arbitration agreement or to the umpire a notice in writing stating that they cannot agree, the umpire shall forthwith enter on the reference in lieu of the arbitrators.

(5) The umpire shall make his award within two months of the entering on the reference or within such extended time as the court may allow.

(6) The parties to the reference and all persons claiming under them must, if so required by the arbitrators or the umpire, submit to be examined by them upon oath or affirmation and must produce before them all necessary books, papers and documents and do all other things which, during the reference, the arbitrators or umpire may require.

(7) The award shall be final and binding on the parties and persons claiming under them respectively.

(8) *Costs :* The costs of the reference and award shall be in the discretion of the arbitrators or umpire who may direct to, and by whom, and in what manner, such costs or any part thereof shall be paid. The arbitrators or the umpire may tax or settle the amount of costs to be paid or any part thereof and may award costs to be paid as between legal practitioner and client.

THEORETICAL QUESTIONS

1. Define the term arbitration. What is an arbitration agreement? Discuss the requisites of a valid arbitration agreement? *(B.Com. MS)*
2. Discuss the essential elements of an arbitration agreement. What is the effect of an arbitration.
3. Who may refer disputes to arbitration? What matters can and what matters cannot be referred to arbitration? *(B.Com. Agra)*
4. State the terms which are implied in every arbitration agreement.

CHAPTER

Mode of Arbitration

AT A GLANCE

- Arbitration Without Intervention of the Court
- Arbitration Through the Court when no Suit is Pending
- Arbitration in Suit
- Who is an Arbitrator
- How Arbitrator may be Appointed
- Revocation of Arbitrator's Authority
- Removal of Arbitrator by Court
- Power of Arbitrator
- Duties of Arbitrator
- Arbitrators Remuneration
- Award, Essentials, Filing, Modification, Remission
- Setting Aside an Award
- Power of Court
- Appeal
- Theoretical Questions

The Arbitration Act 1940, has provided the following three types or methods of submission or making reference to an arbitration :

1. Arbitration without the intervention of Court
2. Arbitration through Court when no suit is pending
3. Arbitration in suits.

(1) *Arbitration without the Intervention of Court*

In this case, the parties to an arbitration agreement themselves refer their disputes or differences to arbitration without any assistance of the Court. Certain terms are implied in every arbitration agreement unless a contrary intention is expressed in it. The arbitration proceedings take place outside the Court. Arbitration proceedings proceed upto the stage of making of the award by the arbitrators without intervention of the Court. Sec. 3 states that "an arbitration agreement, unless a different intention is expressed therein, shall be deemed to include the provisions set out in the first schedule to the Arbitration Act in so far as they are applicable to reference." These implied provisions have already been discussed in the previous chapter.

(2) *Arbitration through the Court when no Suit is Pending* (Sec. 20)

Where there is an arbitration agreement, the parties have the option to proceed with the arbitration independently of any Court, in the manner described earlier or apply to the Court under Sec. 20 and proceed with the arbitration under the supervision of the Court. Section 20 of the Arbitration Act lays down the following procedure for having a reference made through Court :

(A) Where any persons have entered into an arbitration agreement before the institution of any suit with respect to the subject matter of the agreement or any part of it, and where a difference has arisen to which agreement applies, they or any of them, instead of proceeding under Chapter II, may apply to a Court having Jurisdiction in the matter to which the agreement relates, that the agreement be filed in Court.

(B) The application shall be in writing and shall be numbered and registered as a suit between one or more of the parties interested or claiming to be interested as plaintiffs and the remainder as defendant or defendants.

(C) On such application being made, the Court shall direct notice thereof to be given to all parties to the agreement other than the applicant, requiring them to show cause within the time specified in the notice why the agreement should not be filed.

(D) Where no sufficient cause is shown, the Court shall order the agreement to be filed, and shall make an order of reference to the arbitrator appointed by the parties, whether in the agreement or otherwise, or where the parties cannot agree upon an arbitrator, to an arbitrator appointed by the Court.

(E) Therefore, the arbitration shall proceed in accordance with, and shall be governed by the other provisions of this Act so far as they can be made applicable.

(3) *Arbitration in Suit* (Secs. 21 to 25)

Where the parties to a suit which is pending in Court, may decide to get it settled by arbitration. In such a case the following procedure is adopted :

(i) Parties to Suit may Apply for Order of Reference (Sec. 21)

Where in a suit all the parties interested agree that any matter in difference between them in the suit may be referred to arbitration, they may at any time before judgement is pronounced, apply in writing to the Court for an order of reference.

(ii) Appointment of Arbitrator (Sec. 22)

The arbitrator, in such a case, is appointed in the manner as may be agreed upon between the parties.

(iii) Order or Reference by the Court (Sec. 23)

The Court, by an order, may refer to the arbitrator, the matter in difference which he is required to determine. It has also to specify the time to make the award.

(iv) Reference to Arbitration by some of the Parties (Sec. 24)

Where only some of the parties to a suit apply to have the matter in difference between them referred to arbitration, the Court may, if it thinks fit, refer such matter to arbitration. But it can be possible only if the matter of difference can be separated from the rest of the subject-matter of the suit. For other matters and to the parties not joined in the said application, the suit shall continue. If the award on such reference made by the arbitrator, it will be binding only on the parties who have joined in the reference.

ARBITRATION WITHOUT THE INTERVENTION OF THE COURT

In arbitration without the intervention of Court, the arbitration proceedings are conducted by the arbitrators without intervention of Court. In this case the arbitration agreement is deemed to include certain provisions, unless a contrary intention is expressed in the arbitration agreement. These implied provisions have already been discussed.

WHO IS AN ARBITRATOR?

Arbitrator is a person who is appointed by mutual consent of the contending parties for the purpose of investigation and settlement of a difference or dispute submitted to him. The law does not prescribe any qualification for an arbitrator. It is opened to the parties to appoint any person of sound mind as an arbitrator. Therefore, any person, who has the capacity to understand and settle such differences or disputes may be appointed as an arbitrator. One of the parties to the dispute may also be appointed as arbitrator provided other party agrees. Sometimes, it is arranged that each party to the dispute shall nominate one or more arbitrators and all such persons shall jointly act as arbitrators. When two or more arbitrators are appointed, the decision of the majority is final, unless a contrary intention appears from the agreement. In case the arbitrators disagree, dispute shall be referred to a third party, who is called an umpire. The decision of the umpire is taken as final. A person is disqualified from acting as an arbitrator in a dispute in relation to which he is a necessary witness.

HOW ARBITRATORS MAY BE APPOINTED?

Any person, corporate bodies, association of persons etc. can be appointed as an arbitrator. Arbitrators may be appointed in any of the following ways :

(1) *Appointment by the Parties*

Generally, parties to the dispute select the arbitrator or arbitrators by mutual consent. Parties can select any person or body of persons, whatever their qualification may be. The name of person or persons who act as arbitrator(s) may or may not be mentioned in the agreement [Sec. 2(*a*)]. If the appointed arbitrator neglects or refuses or is incapable of acting, the parties may, by mutual consent appoint a new arbitrator, in his place.

(2) *Appointment by Third Party* (Sec. 4)

Sec. 4 of the Act provides for appointment of arbitrators by third party or parties. "The parties to an arbitration agreement may agree that any reference thereunder shall be to an arbitrator or arbitrators to be appointed by a person designated in the agreement either by name or as holder for the time being of any office or appointment."

(3) *Power to Party to Appoint New or Sole arbitrator* (Sec. 9)

"Where an arbitration agreement provides that reference shall be to two arbitrators, one to be appointed by each party, then, unless a different intention is expressed in the agreement :

(*a*) if either of the appointed arbitrators neglects or refuses to act, or is incapable of acting, or dies, the party who appointed him may appoint a new arbitrator in his place :

(*b*) if one party fails to appoint an arbitrator, either originally or by way of substitution as aforesaid, for fifteen clear days after the service by the other party of a notice in writing to make the appointment, such other party having appointed his arbitrator before giving the notice, the party who has appointed the arbitrator may appoint that arbitrator to act as sole arbitrator in the reference, and his award shall be binding on both parties as if he had been appointed by consent.

The proviso to this clause provides that the Court may set aside any appointment as sole arbitrator made under clause (*b*) and either, on sufficient cause being shown, allow further time to the defaulting party to appoint an arbitrator or pass such other order as it thinks fit.

The explanation to Sec. 9 provides that, "the fact that an arbitrator or umpire, after a request by either party to enter on and proceed with reference, does not within one month comply with the request may constitute a neglect or refusal to act within the meaning of Secs. 8 and 9."

(4) *Power to Court to Appointment Arbitrator or Umpire* (Sec. 8)

As per Sec. 8, a Court has the power to appoint an arbitrator or umpire in the following cases:

(*a*) Where an arbitration agreement provides that the reference shall be made to one or more arbitrators to be appointed by the consent of the parties, but all the parties do not, after differences have arisen, concur in the appointment or appointments.

(*b*) Where any appointed arbitrator or umpire (*i*) neglects to act, or (*ii*) refuses to act; or (*iii*) is incapable of acting, or (*iv*) dies, and the arbitration agreement does not provide such a vacancy to keep it vacant and parties do not fill it.

(*c*) Where the parties or the arbitrators are required to appoint an umpire and do not appoint him.

Procedure

The following procedure is adopted, when an arbitrator or umpire is to be appointed by the Court :

(1) to serve a written notice to the other parties or arbitrators by any party for such appointment or filling the vacancy;

(2) if such appointment is not made within 15 days of the service of the notice, the party may move to the Court;

(3) the court after issuing the notice to other parties to give them opportunity to be heard, may appoint such an arbitrator or umpire.

(4) such arbitrator or umpire as appointed by the Court will have the power to act in the reference and to make an award as if he is appointed by the consent of all the parties.

Appointment of Three or More Arbitrators (Sec. 10)

Sometimes, an arbitration agreement may provide that a reference shall be made to three arbitrators—one to be appointed by each party and the third by the two appointed arbitrators. In such a case, the award of any two shall prevail.

Where an arbitration agreement provides for more than three arbitrators, the award of the majority or if the arbitrators are equally divided in their opinions, the award of the umpire shall prevail, unless the arbitration agreement otherwise provides.

Revocation of Arbitrator's Authority (Sec. 5)

The authority of an appointed arbitrator of umpire is irrevocable except with the leave of the Court, unless the contrary intention is expressed in the arbitration agreement (Sec. 5).

Arbitrator's authority can be revoked only under the following circumstances :

(1) If there is a provision in the arbitration agreement that the authority of an arbitrator or umpire can be revoked, the authority can accordingly be revoked.

(2) Where all the parties to the dispute mutually agree to revoke the arbitration agreement or the authority of the arbitrator or the umpire.

(3) The Court can, as per Sec. 5, grant leave to revoke :

(*a*) Arbitrator not acting according to the rules of natural justice.

(*b*) Frustration of agreement.

(*c*) Unreasonable delay.

(*d*) Excess or refusal of jurisdiction by the arbitrator.

(*e*) Bias or partiality.

(*f*) Disqualification of the arbitrators.

Effect of death of party : The authority of an arbitrator is not revoked by the death of the party who appointed him. The legal representatives are bound by his award. (Sec. 6).

Effect of insolvency : An arbitration agreement shall not be discharged by the insolvency of any party thereto. It shall be binding on the Official Assignee or Receiver, if he elects to adopt the contract. (Sec. 7).

AUTHORITY REVOKED

The court has the following powers :

(1) Where the Court removes an umpire or one or more arbitrators, the Court on an application of any of the parties to the arbitration agreement, may appoint persons to fill the vacancies. [Sec. 12 (1)].

(2) Where the Court has revoked the authority of an arbitrator or arbitrators or an umpire or the Court removes an umpire who has not entered on the reference or a sole arbitrator or all the arbitrators, it may on the application of any party to the arbitration agreement, either :

(*a*) appoint a person to act as sole arbitrator in the place of the person or persons removed; or

(*b*) order that the arbitration agreement shall cease to have effect with respect to the difference referred : [Sec. 12(2)].

(3) A person appointed under Sec. 12, as an arbitrator or umpire shall have the same power to act in the reference to make an award, as if he had been appointed in accordance with the arbitration agreement.

POWERS OF ARBITRATOR OR UMPIRE

Sec. 13 of the Act points out the powers of an arbitrator or umpire. Such powers are :

(1) to administer oath to the parties and witnesses appearing;

(2) to state a special case for the opinion of the court on any question of law involved or state the award, wholly or in part, in the form of a special case of such question for the opinion of the court;

(3) to make the award conditional or in the alternative;

(4) to correct an award any clerical mistake or error arising from any accidental slip or omission;

(5) to administer any party to the arbitration such interrogatories as may, in the opinion of the arbitrators or umpire, be necessary.

The following powers are usually given to the arbitrators in the arbitration agreement :

(*a*) to award interest upto the date of award;

(*b*) to determine by and to whom the costs of reference and the award shall be paid;

(*c*) when an award of money is given, the arbitrator can fix the instalment thereof and their amount and time.

(*d*) to make interim awards to be followed by a final award;

(*e*) to order for the specific performance of the contract.

DUTIES OF ARBITRATOR OR UMPIRE

(1) Arbitration being a method of settling a dispute between the parties, in a quasi-judicial manner, the arbitrator or umpire must act judicially. The arbitrators or umpire must act within judicial impartiality and free from bias.

(2) He should not consider himself the advocate or agent of the party appointing him. He has more responsibility than a judge, because his award is the final one.

(3) He must give fair hearing to the parties and a reasonable time and opportunity to them to put up their respective claims.

(4) The arbitrators must decide the dispute in accordance with the law. The proceedings before the arbitrators are quasi-judicial and he must conduct the proceedings in accordance with the principle of natural justice.

(5) The arbitrator must give a fair and reasonable opportunity to every party of being heard. If he does not do so, he is guilty of misconduct.

(6) The arbitrator should hear or receive evidence from both sides. He should not bear or receive evidence from one party in the absence of the other party without giving the other party affected by such evidence, the opportunity of answering it.

(7) The arbitrator does not have the power to decide matters on their personal knowledge unless the parties expressly consent to this or the arbitrator is selected for his own personal knowledge.

(8) They must perform all functions personally except those of ministerial character and not to delegate their authority to somebody else.

(9) An arbitrator must not exceed the terms of reference and an award in excess of jurisdiction and determining matters outside the scope of the arbitration agreement is liable to be set aside.

(10) The arbitrator must sign the award. He must make it available to the parties and file it in the court within reasonable time.

ARBITRATOR'S REMUNERATION

The remuneration payable to an arbitrator is generally fixed by agreement between the parties and the arbitrator before the commencement of arbitration proceedings.

In the absence of any such agreement, the arbitrator or the umpire may himself fix the amount of his remuneration and may include it within the award. In such a case, if the parties feel it to be excessive or unjustified, they may move an application to the court (Sec. 38).

The court may order the arbitrator or the umpire to file the award in the court, but before such an order is passed, the applicant will have to deposit the whole amount so demanded. When the remuneration is deposited and the award is filed, the court may pay such amount to the arbitrator as it may feel reasonable. The balance, if any, is returned to the applicant.

AWARD

According to Sec. 2(b) of the Act, "award" means an arbitration award. It is the judgement of the arbitrators on the matters referred to them. It is a final decision of the arbitrators. It is equivalent to a judgement. It is binding on the parties in the same manner, as the decision of a court of law.

ESSENTIALS OF AN AWARD

(1) It must be made in writing and signed by all or majority of the arbitrators.
(2) It must strictly follow the arbitration agreement and must not include the matters not covered by such agreement.
(3) It must be final and complete *i.e.*, including decision on all matters referred to the arbitration.
(4) It must be in conformity with the powers contained in the arbitration agreement.
(5) The award must not be vague. It must be certain. If an award is vague, it is bad and hence void.
(6) After making the award, the arbitrators or the umpire shall give notice in writing to the parties notifying that the award has been made and signed

Filing of Award in Court (Sec. 14)

Sec. 14(1) provides that when the arbitrators or umpire have made their award, they shall sign it and shall give notice in writing to the parties of the making and signing thereof and of the amount of fees and charges payable in respect of the arbitration and award. The notice need not be in a particular form and the requirement of notice is not mandatory. If the notice is not given it does not vitiate the award.

In arbitrations without intervention of the court, the arbitrators or umpire need not necessarily file the award in court to give validity to it. If the award has been acted upon by the parties without filing it in court and obtaining a decree on the basis thereof, it amounts to a settlement of dispute by mutual agreement.

Sec. 14(2) provides that the arbitrators or umpire shall, at the request of any party to the arbitration agreement or any person claiming under such party if so directed by the court and upon payment of the fees and charges due in respect of the arbitration and award and of the costs and charges of filing the award, cause the award or a signed copy of it, together with any depositions and documents which may have been taken and proved before them, to be filed in a court and the court shall thereupon give notice to the parties of the filing of the award.

Sec. 14(3) provides that where the arbitrators, or umpire state a special case, under Sec. 13(b), the court, after giving notice to the parties and hearing them, shall pronounce its opinion thereon and such opinion shall be added to, and form part of the award.

Judgement in Terms of the Award (Sec. 17)

According to Sec. 17, where the Court sees no cause to remit the award or any of the matters referred to arbitration for reconsideration or to set aside the award the Court shall, after the time for making an application to set aside the award has expired, or such application, having been made, after refusing it, proceed to pronounce judgement according to the award, upon the judgement so pronounced a decree shall follow, and no appeal shall lie from such decree except on the ground that it is in excess of, or otherwise in accordance with, the award.

Modification of Award (Sec. 15)

According to Sec. 15, the Court may modify or correct an award :

(*a*) where it appears that a part of the award is upon a matter not referred to arbitration and such part can be separated from the other part and does not affect the decisions on the matter referred; or

(*b*) where the award is imperfect in form, or contains any obvious error which can be amended without affecting such decisions; or

(*c*) where the award contains a clerical mistake or error arising from an accidental slip or omission.

The Court has no power to go into the merits of the dispute and to alter or vary the award so as to convey a different decision from that awarded by the arbitrators. The court can only modify or correct the award under conditions prescribed in clauses (*a*), (*b*) and (*c*) of Sec. 15.

REMISSION OF AWARD

According to Sec. 16(1), the Court may from time to time remit the award or any matter referred to arbitration to the arbitrators or umpire for reconsideration upon such terms as it thinks fit. This can be done in the following cases :

(*a*) Where the award has left undetermined any of the terms referred to arbitration and such matter cannot be separated without affecting the determination of the matters referred, or

(*b*) where the award is so indefinite as to be incapable of execution, or

(*c*) where an objection to the legality of the award is apparent upon the face of it.

The Court can remit the whole award or part thereof : Sometimes the Court may remit the award more than once.

Sec. 16(2) provides that where an award is remitted under Sec. 16(1) and the Court shall fix the time within which the arbitrator or umpire shall submit his decision to the Court. The proviso to this sub-section provides that any time so fixed may be extended by subsequent order of the Court.

Sec. 16(3) provides that an award remitted under Sec. 16(1) shall become void on the failure of the arbitrator or umpire to reconsider it and submit his decision within the time fixed.

When an award has become void or is set aside, the court may, by order, supersede the reference (Sec. 19).

Setting aside an Award (Sec. 30)

Section 30 provides that, "Any award shall not set aside except on one or more of the following grounds. namely :

(*a*) that an arbitrator or umpire has misconducted himself or the proceedings;

(*b*) that an award has been made after his issue of an order by the Court superseding the arbitration or after proceedings have become invalid under Sec. 35;

(*c*) that an award has been improperly procured or is otherwise invalid."

Thus, an award can be set aside on the following grounds :

(1) *If the Arbitrator or Umpire has Misconducted himself* [Sec. 30 (a)]

It may cover the following cases :

(*a*) He is guilty of moral turpitude ;
(*b*) He is guilty of partiality;
(*c*) He acquires an interest in the subject matter unknown to parties;
(*d*) There is a legal misconduct on his part.

(2) *If the Arbitrator has Misconducted the Proceedings* [Sec. 30(a)]

"Misconducted the proceedings" mean such a mishandling of the arbitration as is likely to cause some substantial miscarriage of justice–legal misconduct. Legal misconduct is a valid ground for setting aside an award. For example, showing undue partiality in favour of one party, acting arbitrarily in complete disregard of the principles of natural justice amounts to legal or judicial misconduct. "Any irregularity of action which is not consonant with general principles of equity and good conscience which ought to govern the conduct or arbitrator is legal misconduct."

(3) *If an Award is made after Issue of an Order of Court Superseding the Arbitration* [Sec. 30(b)].

The Court has power to supersede arbitration under Sec. 12(b) and Sec. 19. If an order is made superseding the arbitration the arbitrator becomes *functus officio* and has no power to make an award.

(4) *If the Award is otherwise Invalid*

This covers the following cases, where the award, if made, may set aside by the Court :

(*a*) where the award is made by the arbitrator or umpire not properly appointed;
(*b*) where the arbitration agreement itself is invalid;
(*c*) where the award is in excess of the matters referred to arbitration;
(*d*) where the award is bad not being registered; and
(*e*) where the appointment of arbitrators or umpire is invalid.

(5) *If the Award is Improperly Procured* [Sec. 30 (c)]

When either party having been guilty of fraudulent concealment of any matter, which he ought to have disclosed, or if wilfully misleading or deceiving the arbitrator or umpire, has obtained an award, it shall be set aside. This ground includes corruption, fraud and undue influence. This ground also cover the case where the arbitrator has a secret interest in the subject matter.

(6) *Award with an Apparent Mistake*

If there is a mistake apparent on the face of the award or forms a part of it, the court may also set it aside.

POWERS OF THE COURT

The Act gives various powers to the Court in relation to arbitration proceedings. A brief account of such powers of the court is given below :

(1) The Court can give leave to a party to revoke the authority of the arbitrator appointed by him (Sec. 5).

(2) The Court has power to appoint arbitrator or umpire (Sec. 8).

(3) The Court can remove arbitrators or the umpire and appoint other persons in their place or appoint someone as sole arbitrator [Sec. 11 & 12].

(4) The Court can modify an award (Sec. 15).

(5) The Court remit an award for reconsideration (Sec. 16).

(6) The Court can pass judgement in terms of the award and thereupon a decree is issued which is capable of execution (Sec. 17).

(7) The Court can pass interim orders, wherever necessary (Sec. 18).

(8) The Court can supersede the arbitration agreement where an award has become void or is set aside (Sec. 19).

(9) The Court may order the arbitration agreement to be filled in the Court on the application of the parties or any of them (Sec. 20).

(10) The Court extend the time to make an award (Sec. 28).

(11) The Court can set aside an award (Sec. 30).

(12) The Court can stay any suit or legal proceeding relating to a matter which is covered by valid arbitration. (Sec. 34).

(13) The Court can decide disputes as to arbitrator's remuneration and costs (Sec. 38).

(14) The Court can issue processes for the appearance of witnesses before arbitration. (Sec. 43).

(15) ˜he Court can appoint receiver or any other official for the detention, preservation or ›pection of any property or thing which is the subject matter of the reference. (Schedule II)

Appeals (Sec. 39)

Sec. 39 reads, "(1) An appeal shall lie from the following orders passed under this Act (and from no others) to the Court authorised by law to hear appeals from original decrees of the Court passing the order :

An order :

(*i*) superseding an arbitration;
(*ii*) on an award stated in the form of a special case;
(*iii*) modifying and correcting an award;
(*iv*) filing or refusing to file an arbitration agreement;
(*v*) staying or refusing to stay proceedings where there is arbitration agreement.
(*vi*) staying or refusing to set aside an award.

Provided that the provisions of this Section shall not apply to any order passed by a Small Causes Court."

"(2) No second appeal shall lie from an order passed on appeal under this Section, but nothing in this Section shall affect or take away any right to appeal to the Supreme Court."

THEORETICAL QUESTIONS

1. What are the powers and duties of an arbitrator?
2. Who is an umpire? How he is appointed? What are his powers and duties?
3. When does a Court appoint an arbitrator or umpire? Discuss the procedure for such appointment.
4. How can an award be modified, remitted and set aside?
5. Explain the circumstances under which the Court can remove an arbitrator. *(B.Com. Delhi)*
6. Explain the grounds on which the Court may set aside an award under the Arbitration Act.
7. Define 'legal misconduct' by an arbitrator. What are the consequences of misconduct?
8. Under what circumstances can a court remit an award for reconsideration under the Arbitration Act? Also state when an award becomes void.
9. Who is an arbitrator? What powers does an arbitrator possess? *(B.Com. Kolkata)*
10. Give a brief account of the powers of the court in relation to arbitration agreement.
11. Explain the meaning of award, under arbitration Act. In what cases may the court modify the award? *(B.Com. Agra)*
12. Explain the procedure reference to arbitration with intervention of the court (*i*) where there is no suit pending and (*ii*) where suit is pending.

LAW OF INSURANCE

CHAPTER

Nature and Principles of Insurance

AT A GLANCE

- Introduction
- Insurance Organisation
- Contract of Insurance
- Nature of a Contract of Insurance
- Essentials of a Contract of Insurance
- Classification of Insurance Business
- Fundamental Principles of Insurance Contracts, Premium, Return of Premium
- Days of Grace
- Insurance Policy
- Cover Note
- Re-insurance
- Double Insurance
- Distinction: Re-insurance and Double Insurance
- Theoretical Questions

INTRODUCTION

Risks and uncertainties are incidental to life. In business, as in private life, there are dangers and risks of every kind. Man may meet untimely death. He may suffer from accident. The loss may be of life or property, and may occur due to death, accident, fire, floods, perils of sea, earthquakes etc. All these events, being uncertain, there is always the risk and insecurity to life and property. The risk is uncertain and, therefore, the loss arising from risk is also uncertain. How one can prevent such risks or minimise them? Insurance is a method of eliminating or reducing risk. By insurance, a person can protect himself from loss arising from future uncertain events like fire, accident or early death. With the help of insurance, a person keeps himself protected against the losses which may occur due to the uncertain events. The insurance is a way, by which the loss, likely to be caused by an uncertain event, spread over a large number of persons who are also exposed to the same type of risks and insure themselves against those risks. Insurance may be defined as a cooperative device to spread the loss caused by a particular risk over a number of persons who are exposed to it and who agree to insure themselves against that risk. This means that insurance provides a pool to which the many contribute a certain sum of money called the premium, and out of which the few who suffer losses are compensated by the insurer except life insurance where every policy becomes a claim ultimately.

INSURANCE ORGANISATION

The risks which can be insured have increased in number and extent owing to the growing complexity of the present day economic system. In India, two Corporations are established under separate Acts to deal with the insurance business.

(*I*) The Life Insurance Corporation of India Act 1956, had provided for life insurance legislation for life insurance business conducted by the Life Insurance Corporation of India established under the said Act. It started its functions since 1st September 1956. It owns all the life insurance business (including annuities) in India.

(*II*) The General Insurance Corporation of India established under the General Insurance Corporation of India Act 1972 into four distinct companies which are:

(*a*) The National Insurance Companies Ltd.

(*b*) The New India Insurance Companies Ltd.

(*c*) The Oriental Fire and General Insurance Companies Ltd.

(*d*) The United India Fire and General Insurance Companies Ltd.

Exemptions: Section 36 of the General Insurance Business (Nationalisation) Act 1972, provides exemptions in favour of (1) Calcutta Hospital and Nursing Home Benefits Association Ltd. (2) Export Credit and Guarantee Corporation Ltd. and (3) Deposit Insurance Corporation (established under the Deposit Insurance Corporation Act 1961) which can also carry on the general insurance business in addition to the General Insurance Corporation of India and its four subsidiaries (mentioned above).

CONTRACT OF INSURANCE

Contract of insurance is a contract, under which one party, in consideration of a certain sum of money called premium, undertakes to pay to another person a sum of money or its equivalent on the happening of a specified event: examples, accident or death. In other words, insurance may be defined as a contract between two parties whereby one party called insurer undertakes, in exchange for a fixed sum called premium, to pay the other party called insured a fixed amount of money on the happening of a certain event.

The following terms are commonly used in respect of all insurance contracts:

(*a*) **Insurer:** The person who undertakes to make good the loss is called the **insurer** (assurer or underwriter): such as Life Insurance Corporation of India, an Insurance Company etc.

(*b*) **Insured:** The person, whose loss is to be made good is called the insured (assured). That is, the party to whom this protection is given in exchange of premium is called insured.

(*c*) **Policy:** It is the formal document in writing incorporating the promise made by insurer to cover the insured against risk as also the various terms and conditions of the contract.

(*d*) **Premium:** It is the money consideration given to the insurer for his promise to take up risk to the property of the insured.

The thing or the property insured is called the **subject–matter** of insurance. The interest of the insured in the subject–matter is called **insurable interest**. The amount for which a policy is issued is known as the **insured amount** or **policy amount**.

NATURE OF A CONTRACT OF INSURANCE

As certain element of speculation is present in a contract of insurance, it is called an aleatory contract. A contract of insurance is a type of contingent contract and is a perfectly valid contract. An insurance contract is a device to spread over the risk or loss likely to be caused to the insured due to some uncertainty. It is not gambling or wager. A contingent contract is a contract to do or not to do something, if some event, collateral to such contract, does or does not happen. (Indian Contract Act

Sec. 31) (Refer chapter IX). A wagering agreement is one in which one person promises to pay a certain sum of money to the other on the happening or non–happening of an uncertain event. To quote justice Hawkins "A wagering contract is one by which two persons professing to hold opposite views touching the issue of a future uncertain event mutually agree that, dependent upon the determination of the event, one shall win from the other, and that other shall pay or handover to him, a sum of money or other stake; neither of the contracting parties having any other interest in that contract than the sum of stake he will so win or lose, there being no other real consideration for the making of such contract by either of the parties. "For example: A and B enter into an agreement that if it rains today, A will pay Rs. 100 to B. And if it does not rain today, B will pay Rs. 100 to A. This is a wagering agreement.

A fair amount of uncertainty is also involved in a contract of insurance, as in it the assured has to receive some money on the happening of uncertain event, for examples, accident, fire, death etc. Because of this uncertainty, Lord Mansfield described insurance as a "contract on speculation". Though a contract of insurance resembles to a wagering agreement, but it is not actually wagering agreement or a speculative contract. The contract of insurance is perfectly a valid contract, whereas a wagering agreement is void. In a contract of insurance, the insured person has an insurable interest in the life or property which is to be insured, whereas in a wagering agreement, there is no such insurable interest. (Refer Chapter VIII).

The essence of a contract of insurance is not to win or lose, but to indemnify the assured for the loss suffered by him. Therefore, a contract of insurance is a contract of indemnity. A contract of indemnity is one in which one person promises to indemnify the other for the loss suffered by the latter, that is, where one person promises to make good the loss suffered by the other. This means that in case of loss due to happening of the event insured against, the assured shall be paid the actual amount of loss suffered by him.

It should be noted that all contracts of insurance are contracts of indemnity, except those of life and personal accident insurances where no money payment can indemnify for loss of life or bodily injury. In case of Marine and Fire insurances the insurer undertakes to indemnify the insured for loss or damage resulting from specified perils. Life and personal accident insurances are contingent contracts and not the contracts of indemnity. In these cases, on the happening of the event, (death or accident) the insurer is liable to pay the fixed amount mentioned in the policy.

ESSENTIALS OF A CONTRACT OF INSURANCE

A contract of insurance is a kind of general contract. The general principles of the law of contract apply equally to such a contract. As such to be a valid contract it must fulfil all the essential requirements of a contract as laid down in Sec. 10 of the Indian Contract Act. They are as under:

1. There must be offer and acceptance. The offer is in the form of proposal and acceptance is in the form of policy issued. The canvassing of the agent is an invitation to offer. The offer is made by the insured to the insurer.
2. The parties must be competent to contract, otherwise it will not be valid.
3. The object of the contract must be lawful.
4. Payment of premium and the spreading of risk or loss may be regarded as the consideration of a contract of insurance.
5. The consent of the parties to the contract must be free and genuine.
6. The main document of a contract of insurance is its policy, which should be executed properly.

If the parties are agreed on all material terms – nature, duration, amount to be insured, amount of premium etc., a contract comes into existence.

CLASSIFICATION OF INSURANCE BUSINESS

Risk against the happening of any event may be insured, for example, death, fire, accident, theft, riot etc. However, insurance business is divided into two main branches:

1. Life Insurance business and
2. General Insurance business.

1. *Life Insurance business*

Life insurance is different from other insurances, in the sense that here, the subject–matter of insurance is life of human being. It is the insurance business, which covers the loss and risks of human life. The life insurance business is carried on by and under the control of Life Insurance Corporation of India. This will be discussed in detail in Chapter 37.

2. *General Insurance business.*

It means and includes the following businesses:

(*A*) Fire insurance business,

(*B*) Marine insurance business and

(*C*) Miscellaneous insurance business.

(*A*) *Fire insurance business*

Fire insurance covers risks of fire. It covers the losses caused to the insured due to fire. The insurer undertakes in consideration of the premium paid, to make good any loss or damage caused by fire during a specified period. This will be discussed in detail in Chapter 38.

(*B*) *Marine insurance business*

Such an insurance contract covers the losses incidental to marine adventures. Marine insurance provides protection against loss of marine perils. The marine perils are collision with rock or ship, attack by enemies, fire etc. This will be discussed in detail in Chapter 39.

(*C*) *Miscellaneous business*

All other insurance business except life, fire and marine fall under this category, for examples, motor vehicle insurance, fidelity insurance, personal accident insurance etc. This will be discussed in detail in Chapter 40.

FUNDAMENTAL PRINCIPLES OF INSURANCE CONTRACT

Contracts of insurance are based upon certain fundamental principles or characteristics which are almost common to all types of insurance business. These principles are discussed under the following heads:

1. Utmost good faith
2. Insurable interest
3. Principles of indemnity
4. Doctrine of subrogation
5. Contribution
6. Mitigation of loss
7. Risk must attach
8. Causa proxima
9. Period of insurance

1. Utmost good faith

An insurance contract is a contract of *uberrimae fidei,* that is, of absolute good faith where both parties of the contract must disclose all the material facts truly and fully. It is inherent duty of both parties to a contract of insurance to make full and fair disclosure of all *material facts* relating to the subject–matter of the proposed insurance. This is because insurance shifts risk from one party to another. The general rule of "*Caveat emptor*" (let the buyer beware), which applies to ordinary trade contracts, does not apply to insurance contracts. Non-disclosure of any material fact affects the validity of the contract of insurance. The insured is supposed to disclose all material facts known to him but not known to the insurer. The insured has better or all the means of knowledge about the subject-matter of insurance than the insurer.

L.J. Scrutton observed, "As the underwriter knows nothing and the man who comes to him to ask him to insure knows everything, it is the duty of the assured, the man who desires to have a policy, to make a full disclosure to the underwriters without being asked of all the material circumstances, because the underwriters know nothing and the assured knows everything. This is expressed by saying that it is a contract of utmost good faith — uberrimae fidei." The duty to make a full and true disclosure continues till the contract is concluded, that is, till the proposal of the insured is accepted by the insurer. Any non-disclosure of material facts will amount to constructive fraud under Sec. 17(2) of the Indian Contract Act, which makes silence fraudulent when there is a duty to speak out. The party is under no legal obligation to disclose any fact which may come to his knowledge after the contract of insurance has been concluded. Insured should disclose not only those facts which he honestly believes to be material, but every fact which a reasonable man would have thought to be material. But the non-disclosure of the facts which are not known to the assured himself, does not affect the contract. Besides, he need not disclose the facts which are already known to the insurer. Insurer is also under the legal obligation to observe the same good faith in disclosing the scope of insurance policy, he is prepared to grant

Facts which count materially are those which knowledge influence a party in deciding whether or not to offer or to accept such risk and if the risk is acceptable, on what terms and conditions the risk should be accepted. Thus, these facts have a direct bearing on the degree of risk in relation to the subject-matter of insurance. For example, in case of life insurance, the material facts affecting risk will be age, residence, occupation, health, income etc. In case of property insurance, it would be design, use, owner, situation of the property etc. Since in a contract of insurance, the insured stands in a more advantageous position, he is supposed to disclose all material facts about the subject matter known to him, to the insurer. If the insured fails to disclose such facts, the insurer may avoid the contract. (*Mithoolal Nayak vs. LIC of India*, 1962).

Sec. 19 of the Marine Insurance Act 1963 states that the parties to a marine policy must make full disclosure of all material facts to each other in utmost good faith. This rule applies to all classes of insurance. The insured or assured must disclose all facts which a reasonable man would regard as material. (*Joel vs. Law Union Insurance Co.* 1908) The disclosure of facts must be substantially accurate. Misleading statements amount to a breach of duty. But unimportant misstatements or omissions may be excused. (*Dawsons Ltd. vs. Bonnin* 1922).

The following facts are not required to be disclosed :

(1) Facts which tend to diminish the risk.

(2) Facts which are known or presumed to be known to insurer.

(3) Facts which are waived by the insurer.

(4) Facts of public knowledge.

(5) Facts governed by the conditions of the policy.

As regards the observance of good faith, Sec. 45 of the Insurance Act 1938 makes a special provision in respect of life insurance policy. Accordingly, if a policy of life insurance has run for two years from the data when it was taken, then it cannot be questioned on the ground of non-observance of good faith except when the insurer proves the following two facts:

(*A*) The insured person with a fraudulent intention had concealed or misrepresented the facts material to the contract.

(*B*) The insured person had the knowledge about the falsity of the fact when he stated them to be true.

The burden of proof is on the Corporation if it alleges that insured is guilty of suppressing material facts.

2. Insurable Interest

Insurable interest is necessary to support every contract of insurance otherwise it will be a wagering contract and, thus, void. Insurable interest means the proprietary or pecuniary interest that the insured must have in the subject-matter of insurance. According to Rodda, "Insurable interest may be defined as an interest of such a nature that the occurrence of the event insured against would cause financial loss to the insured." Thus, insurable interest means some pecuniary interest in the subject-matter of insurance. "Insurable interest" is the "risk of loss" to which the assured is likely to be exposed on the happening of the event insured against. The object of insurance is to protect the insurable interest. A person is said to have an insurable interest in the subject-matter insured where he will derive pecuniary benefit from its existence or will suffer pecuniary loss from its destruction. The assured must be in a legally recognised relationship to the subject–matter of insurance in such a way that he will suffer a direct pecuniary loss on the happening of the event insured against. Thus, the insurable interest must be lawful. It must be pecuniary. Love and affection alone cannot constitute insurable interest. A purely sentimental interest or a non-monetary benefit will not cause an insurable interest.

Examples :

(*i*) A person does not have any insurable interest in the house owned by another and therefore cannot get it insured. In case the house is mortgaged to him, he will have insurable interest therein and can get it insured.

(*ii*) *X* borrowed a sum of Rs. one lakh from *Y* and mortgaged his house with *Y* as a security for the repayment of loan. In this case, both *X* and *Y*, has an insurable interest in the house and can insure in order to protect their respective interests.

A man cannot insure the life of a stranger but he can insure the life of himself and of persons in whose life he has a pecuniary interest. It has been held that for the purposes of life insurance, insurable exists in the following cases:

1. Husband has insurable interest in the life of his wife. (*Griffith vs. Fleming* – 1909)
2. Wife has insurable interest in the life of her husband. (*Reed vs. Royal exchange* – 1795)
3. A creditor has insurable interest in the debtors life to the extent of the debt. (*Godsall vs. Boldero* – 1807)
4. A trustee has insurable interest in respect of the interest of which he is a trustee. (*Tidswell vs. Ankerstein* – 1712)
5. A surety has insurable interest in the life of the principal.
6. An employer has insurable interest in the life of his employee.
7. A pledgee has an insurable interest in the goods pledged.
8. The father has interest in the life of the child. etc. etc. (*Howard vs. Friendly Society Ltd.* 1886)

In the case of Life Insurance, the insurable interest must exist at the time of completion of the contract, *i.e.* when the policy is effected. It need not exist at the time of death of the person whose life is insured.

In the case of Fire Insurance, insurable interest must be present both at the time when the insurance is effected and at the time of loss of the subject–matter.

In the case of Marine Insurance, it is not essential for the assured to have an insurable interest at the time of effecting the insurance but he must have insurable interest at the time of loss of the subject-matter insured (Sec. 8 of the Marine Insurance Act 1963).

A contract of insurance is primarily a contract of indemnity except life insurance, personal accident insurance and sickness insurance. Therefore, insurable interest is an essential element of every contract of insurance. This element of insurable interest distinguishes a contract of insurance from a wagering agreement. In the absence of insurable interest the contract of insurance will be void.

3. Principles of Indemnity

A contract of insurance except life insurance, personal accident insurance and sickness insurance, is a contract of indemnity. Indemnity is the controlling principle in case of fire, marine and general insurance contracts. The principle of indemnity does not apply to life insurance.

In this connection, Brett, in *Castellian Vs. Preston* (1883) said, "The very foundation, in my opinion, of every rule which has been applied to insurance law is this, namely, that the contract of insurance contained in the marine or fire policy is a contract of indemnity, and of indemnity only, and this contract means that the assured, in case of loss against which the policy has been made, shall be fully indemnified, but shall never be more than fully indemnified."

Under Sec. 124 of the Contract Act, an indemnity is a promise to compensate against loss, that is indemnity means security against loss. The insurance contract provides that in case of loss, against which the policy has been taken, the assured will be paid the actual amount of loss or the amount of policy, whichever is lower. The idea of compensation payable against losses is important in an insurance contract, for every such contract must prove the existence of insurable interest in the subject–matter of insurance. In case of insurance other than life insurance, it is necessary to show that the insured has this interest not only when the contract is made, but also when the amount is claimed. At the time of making the claim, if this interest cannot be provided, no compensation is payable.

In case of marine and fire insurances the insurer undertakes to indemnify the insured for loss or damage resulting from specified perils. In case of loss the insured can recover from the insurer the actual amount of loss, not exceeding the amount of policy. If there is no loss under the policy, the insurer is under no obligation to indemnify the insured. The object of indemnity is to place the insured after a loss in the position as he occupied immediately before the event. The assured is only indemnified for the loss, he suffers. He is not supposed to make any profit out of it, as it will be against the public policy. In fact, the "principle of indemnity" in a contract of insurance ensures that the purpose of insurance is just to make good the loss caused to the insured. In the absence of this principle, the assured might make efforts in bringing about the event insured against in order to get the policy amount. This would obviously be contrary to the public interest.

Example: A insured his house for Rs. two lakhs. The house was destroyed by fire. It was estimated that it would be restored to its original condition by spending Rs. 50,000. In this case *A* can recover Rs. 50,000 from the insurance company as the actual loss suffered by him is Rs. 50,000.

Under Sec. 31 of the Contract Act, we find, that a contingent contract is a promise to perform certain obligations on the happening or non–happening of a future uncertain event. This definition suits the demands of a life policy, as we have seen above, and it is, therefore, proper to hold that while general insurance is an indemnity, life insurance is a contingent contract.

4. Doctrine of Subrogation

The doctrine of subrogation is a corollary to the principle of indemnity. "Subrogation" may be defined as the substitution of one person for another. In simple meaning, subrogation is a form of substitution. In case of law of insurance, the subrogation means the substitution of the insurance company in place of the assured in respect of all the rights and remedies which the assured has against the third party.

The principle of subrogation is applicable to fire and marine insurance policies. If the assured recovers the full extent of the loss from the insurance company, then the insurance company gets the rights and remedies of the assured, and can proceed against the third party for the recovery of compensation. If the assured also receives the compensation form the third party in respect of the same loss, then he must pay over that amount to the insurance company.

Example: A insures his house with an insurance company. The house is burnt by fire and *A* recovers the loss from the insurance company. *A* subsequently brings an action against neighbour, who was responsible for the fire and recovers damages from the neighbour. Here, the insurance company is entitled to the amount, which *A* recovered from his neighbour. So, *A* must return the amount to the insurance company.

In case a loss has arisen out of tort or mischief by some third party, the insured becomes entitled to proceed against both the insurer as well as the wrongdoer. But since a contract of insurance is a contract of indemnity, the insured cannot be allowed to recover from both and thereby make a profit from his insurance claim. He can make a claim against either the insurer or the wrongdoer. If the insured elects to be indemnified by the insurer, the doctrine of subrogation comes into play and as a result the insurer shall be subrogated to all the rights and remedies of the insured against third parties in respect of the property destroyed or damaged. On paying the amount of policy to the insured, the insurance company steps into the shoes of the assured and become entitled to all the rights of the assured.

The doctrine of subrogation does not apply to personal insurance because the doctrine of indemnity is not applicable to such insurance. The insurers have no right of action against third party in respect of the damages. For example, if an insured dies due to the negligence of a third party, his dependent has right to recover the amount of the loss from the third party alongwith the policy amount. No amount of the policy would be subrogated by the insurer.

In *Castellian Vs. Preston* (1883), Brett said, "the doctrine does not arise upon any terms of the contract of insurance, it is only another proposition which has been adopted for the purpose of carrying out the fundamental rule which I have mentioned and it is a doctrine in favour of the underwriters or insurers in order to prevent the assured from recovering more than full indemnity; it has adopted solely for that reason."

In *Simpson Vs. Thomson* (1877), Lord Cairns defined subrogation thus, "a right founded on the well known principle of law that where one person has agreed to indemnify another he will, on making good the indemnity, be entitled to succeed to all the ways and means by which the person indemnified might have protected himself against or reimbursed himself for the loss".

For example, on a burglary insurance, if compensation has been paid to the insured and then the stolen goods have been recovered, the goods must be hand over to the insurer. If there has been a re-insurance of the policy, the re-insurer will be entitled to proportionate benefits of subrogation.

The principle of subrogation is subject to the following limitations;

1. The insurance company becomes entitled to the rights of the insured only on making good the loss suffered by the insured.

2. The insurer gets only such rights which are available to the insured. He gets no superior rights than the assured.
3. The insurance company is subrogated only to the extent of value insured and no more.
4. The right of the insurer is applicable only when the assured has recovered the full indemnity.
5. The insurance company entitled to the benefit only to the extent of payments made by it.

Examples

1. In *Midland Insurance Vs. Smith* (1881), the wife of the assured set fire to his house and the insurers paid. It was held that the insurers cannot recover the money as the insured has no right of action against his wife.
2. In *Simpson Vs. Thompson* (1877), two ships *A* and *B* belonging to the same owner came into collision. The insurers of the ship *A* indemnified the owner and then sued him as owner of the ship *B* for negligence, claiming the amount they had paid in respect of ship *A*. It was held that it could not recover as there can be no subrogation to those rights which the assured himself does not have. As a person cannot file a suit against himself. Moreover, both the ships were owned by one and the same person.

5. Contribution

The doctrine of contribution applies to contracts of indemnity, *i.e.* to fire and marine insurances. The term "*contribution*" may be defined as the method of distributing the loss among the different insurance companies whose policies attach to the same risk, that is, who are liable for the same risk. Again, where there are more than one insurance on one risk, the principle of contribution applies. There is nothing in law to prevent a person from effecting two or more insurance policies in respect of the same subject–matter. In case of loss, the assured is not entitled to recover more than the full amount of his actual loss, though he may recover the full amount of his actual loss from one insurance company. When the insured recovers the full amount of his actual loss from one insurance company, he will have no right to get further payment from the other insurance companies.

When same property has been insured with more than one insurer at the same time, a double insurance of the property is said to have been effected. The doctrine of contribution is defined in *North British and Mercantile Vs. Liverpool and London Globe* (1877) as follows:

"Contribution exists where the thing is done by the same person against the same loss, and to prevent a man first of all recovering more than the whole loss or if he recovers the whole loss from one which he could have recovered from the other, then to make the parties contribute rateably. But that only applies where there is the person insuring the same interests with more than one office."

This principle aims to distribute the actual amount of loss among the different insurers, who are liable for the same risk under different policies in respect of the same subject-matter. In case of loss, the insured cannot recover from any one or all the insurers more than the amount of actual loss. If any one of the insurers pays whole of the loss to the assured, he is entitled to contributions from his co-insurers in proportion to the amount each insurer has undertaken to pay in case of loss of the same subject–matter.

Example : A insured his house against fire with *X* for Rs. 50,000 and with *Y* for Rs. 75,000. Fire broke out in the building and a loss of Rs. 40,000 occurs. *A* may file a suit against both the insurers or against one only.

The liability of each insurer is determined by applying the following formula:

$$\frac{\text{The sum insured with an insurer}}{\text{The total sum insured with all insurers}} \times \text{Loss}$$

$$\text{Liability of } X = \frac{50{,}000}{1{,}25{,}000} \times 40{,}000 = \text{Rs.}16{,}000$$

$$\text{Liability of } Y = \frac{75{,}000}{1{,}25{,}000} \times 40{,}000 = \text{Rs.}24{,}000$$

It has to be observed that life insurance is a contingent contract and as such this principle of contribution will not apply to life policies. If the same life has been insured more than once, all the different amounts will become payable in full.

The following conditions must be satisfied for the applicability of the principle of contribution:

1. The same subject–matter is insured with more than one insurers.
2. The policies must cover the same peril.
3. The assured must be the same person in all the insurance policies.
4. All the policies must be in force at the time of loss.
5. One insurer has paid to the insured more than his share of loss.

6. Mitigation of Loss

When the event insured against occurs, it is the duty of the assured to use all precautions to minimise or mitigate the loss. The term 'mitigation of loss' may be defined as the minimisation of the loss. For example, in case of a fire insurance policy when the fire occurs, it is the duty of the policy-holder to take steps to mitigate or minimise the loss as if he were uninsured and must do his best for safeguarding the remaining property, otherwise the insurer can avoid the payment of loss attributable to his negligence. The insured must act as a prudent person would do in similar circumstances. In the event of some mishap to the insured property, the assured must take all necessary steps for the purpose of averting or minimising the loss and to save what is left. The insured should not be negligent on the happening of the event merely because the property is insured. If negligence is proved, the insurance company may avoid the payment of loss. However, the insured is not supposed to risk his own life for this purpose.

7. Risk Must Attach

A contract of insurance can be enforced only if the risk has attached. A contract of insurance is made to cover a risk to which the insured person is exposed. Premium is the consideration for the risk run by the insurer and if there is no risk, the question of any premium does not arise. Insurance is a method of eliminating or reducing risk. The insurer receives the premium for running a risk. Thus, the risk must attach to every contract of insurance. The principle of insurance is that for a valid contract of insurance, the risk must attach. If the subject-matter of insurance ceases to exist, for example, the insured ship has already arrived safely or the goods are burnt, at the time the policy is effected, the risk does not attach, and as a result the consideration for the premium has totally failed. Both the parties are ignorant, the risk is not run and thus the contract is void ab–initio. The premium paid can be recovered from the insurers.

8. Causa Proxima

The principle of insurance is that the insurer is liable only for those losses which have been proximately caused by the peril insured against. That is, the insured person can recover the loss from the insurance company only when it is caused by an event insured against, and such event is the proximate cause of loss. *Causa proxima* means proximate cause. The insurer is not liable for any loss caused by remote or indirect cause. The maxim "*causa proxima non remota spectator*" means that proximate and not the remote cause of loss is to be taken into consideration for determining the liability of the insurer.

An assured can recover the loss from the insurer for the damage or destruction of the subject matter only, if it is caused by an event insured against. It is called the rule *Causa Proxima*. If there is only one cause of damage or loss, the liability of the insurer can be fixed easily. But the rule of *causa proxima* applies, when there are so many causes of damage or loss. In such a case, common–sense shall have to be applied. Thus, *causa proxima* is the cause which sets other causes in motion. But when the loss is due to the fault of the assured, the insurer is not liable.

***Example* : 1.** *Pink Vs. Fleming* (1899)

A cargo of oranges in a ship was insured against loss arising on account of collision. The ship collided with another ship during the course of voyage. Because of the collision, the cargo was mishandled. The arrival of the ship was also delayed. Due to mishandling and delay, the oranges became unfit for human consumption. The insurance company refused to pay compensation because the loss was not caused by insured peril. It was held that the insurance company was not liable as the damage of the cargo was not caused due to collision but due to mishandling and delay of the cargo. As such, the assured could not recover the loss.

2. *Hamilton Fraser & Co Vs. Pandrof & Co.* (1887)

In a marine policy, the goods was insured against damage by sea-water. During the voyage, rats made a hole in the zinc pipe which connected the bath room and as a result sea-water got through the hole and damaged the goods. The underwriters contended that as they had not bound to pay. It was held that the proximate cause of damage being sea-water, the insured was entitled to damages: the rats being remote cause.

9. Period of Insurance

A contract of fire insurance is for a fixed duration, usually for one year, and the liability of the insurer automatically comes to an end on the expiry of the period. A contract of marine insurance may be either for a certain period or for a particular voyage. If it is for a certain period, the liability of the insurer comes to an end after the expiry of that period even if the voyage has not yet ended. And if it is for a particular voyage, then the liability of the insurer continues till the voyage has ended even if it takes longer than a year. A contract of life insurance is not a contract for a year only, but is a continuing contract and covers either a specified number of years or the balance of the insured's life. As a contract of life insurance covers a continuing risk, advance payment of premium every year during the whole term of policy is a condition precedent for keeping the policy in force and if the premium due is not paid within the due time plus the grace period, the policy lapses. Life insurance premiums may be paid annually in one lump sum or in installments which may be half-yearly, quarterly or monthly at the option of the assured.

PREMIUM

Premium is the consideration for the insurance. Premium is paid by the insured person to the insurance company for the risk undertaken by it. Usually, premium is paid in cash, but it may also be in kind. Determination of the amount of premium is solely the responsibility of the insurer, who determines it on taking into consideration:

(*a*) the average of losses,

(*b*) the contribution that he receives in the form of premium,

(*c*) special circumstances affecting the risk in particular cases, and

(*d*) margin for overheads, other expenses and profits.

Life insurance premium is fixed on the basis of the average life expectancy or the average rate of mortality.

Premium is payable in monthly, quarterly, half-yearly or annual installments, at the option of the assured. The policy lapses, if the premium is not paid when it falls due and the admissible days of grace are over. The assured or his agent has to pay the premium to the insurer or his agent. In case of life insurance in India, premium is to be deposited at the counter of the concerned office of the Life Insurance Corporation or sent by post at its address.

RETURN OF PREMIUM

In cases where the insurer does not bear any potential risk, he may be asked to return the total premium. Such cases may be the following:

1. Where the consideration for the premium has totally failed, for examples, when the insured subject-matter ceases to exist or the insured ship has already returned safe.
2. Where the contract of insurance is not binding on the parties, for examples, when the policy is void ab–initio or when the contract is ultra vires the insurer.
3. Where the contract of insurance is illegal; in such a case return of premium can be claimed only before the risk comes into existence as loss.
4. Where the assured has no insurable interest at any time during the currency of the risk.
5. Where there is over-insurance or double insurance, bonafide and not knowingly.
6. Where parties are confused about the subject-matter of the insurance – they are not of the same mind, but are misappropriated.
7. Where the contract of insurance is ultra vires the powers of the insurer, for example, when he was not authorised to grant it.
8. Where it is required under the provisions of some law.

The premium is not returnable in the following cases:

1. Where the risk runs even for a very short time.
2. Where the contract of insurance is induced by fraud or misrepresentation on the part of the assured.

DAYS OF GRACE

The days of grace are the days allowed by the insurance company after the expiry of the stipulated period of insurance during which the assured can pay the premium in order to continue or to renew the policy of insurance. In cases where the contract of insurance is for a fixed period, for example, the case of fire insurances the days of grace are allowed to afford to the assured an additional opportunity of renewing the policy and not of continuing it. If before the expiry of the term of an insurance policy, the insurance company gives a notice to the assured that unless the premium is paid, the policy would not be renewed, and if the assured refuses to pay, the insurance company is not liable if the property is destroyed by fire after the expiry of the term of the policy though within the days of grace. In case of life insurances, the policy creates a continuing risk and assured has no option but to continue the policy on the payment of the premium. And if the assured dies during the days of grace without paying the premium, the insurance company remains liable to pay the amount due under the policy.

INSURANCE POLICY

Policy is a written document issued by the insurance company containing the terms and conditions of the contract of insurance. It is stamped and signed by the insurer. Though there is no particular form prescribed by law except in case of marine insurance, where the contract would not be valid unless it is evidenced by a formal marine policy. In other cases existence of a policy is not necessary for the validity of a contract of insurance. In other cases, neither the delivery of the policy to the insured is necessary nor its production is essential on the maturity of the contract of insurance.

COVER NOTE

The insurer may give a written acknowledgment stating that (*a*) the proposal has been accepted, (*b*) the first premium has been received and (*c*) the regular policy will be issued later on. This written acknowledgment is called a "cover Note". It is in the form of an "interim protection note" or a "provisional agrcement", which covers the risk between the date of the contract of insurance and the actual issue of policy. It is neither a policy nor an agreement to issue an insurance policy. It acknowledges the receipt of premium and forms a binding contract of insurance during the interval between the proposal and the final acceptance or rejection of the proposal. However, it has been held that if the cover note is properly stamped, a suit for specific performance of the contract may be founded thereon. If the proposal is rejected and the assured is informed of it, the liability of the insurer under cover note is closed.

RE-INSURANCE

Every insurer has a limit to the risk which he can undertake. Sometimes, it may happen that an insurer accepts an insurance for a sum of money which is beyond his capacity, without giving up the contract. Then in order to safeguard his own interest, he may insure the same risk either wholly or partially with other insurers. Thus, when an insurer passes on a part or whole of the risk to another insurer, so as to reduce his own liability in case of loss, is called re-insurance. Therefore, re-insurance is arranged by the insurer with a view to reducing his risk; thus an insurer distributes the risks with other insurers. Re-insurance is a contract between two insurers and the insured is not a party to it. In such a case, the original insurer is called re-insured and the subsequent insurers are called re-insurers. A policy of re-insurance will lapse with the lapsing of the original policy.

In a contract of re-insurance, an insurer who has accepted to undertake, a higher risk, lays off whole or a part of such risk with another insurer or insurers and thus reduces his own ultimate liability. In this way, in a contract of re-insurance, an insurer insures that very risk which has already been undertaken by another insurer. Since the rate of premium on re-insurance is comparatively lower, the original insurer also gets some profit in re-insurance.

Among the insurers, there is a practice of mutual re-insurance as on one side it spreads over the liability, and on the other, it brings the benefit of reciprocity. However, re-insurance does not supersede the original insurance contract.

Re-insurance can be done by an insurer for all kinds of insurance and all re-insurance contracts are governed by the same rules which apply to the original contracts of insurance. An insurer has an insurable interest in the subject matter insured to the extent of the amount re-insured by him because a contract of re-insurance is also a contract of indemnity. The re-insurer's liability arises only in case when the original insurer has made the payment to the assured.

The re-insurer is, however, not liable to the assured as there is no contract entered into between them. The policy of re-insurance is co-extensive with the original policy and, therefore, it abides by all the terms and conditions of the original policy. The re-insurer is entitled to all the benefits, which the original insurer is entitled to under the policy. If the original policy, for any reason, becomes void or comes to an end, the re-insurance also comes to an end.

The re-insurance contract is also a contract of trust and good faith. Therefore, the insurer must disclose to the re-insurer all material facts known to him. Re-insurer is also entitled to the right of subrogation.

***Example*:** *A* wanted to insure his house against fire for Rs. 10 lakhs. *X*, the insurer found the proposal is profitable and accepted it. However, to minimise the risk of loss, *X* re-insured the house for Rs. 4 lakhs with *Y*, an another insurer. The second insurance between *X* and *Y* is the re-insurance. If the house is totally burnt, *X* will pay Rs. 10 lakhs to *A* and *X* will recover Rs. 4 lakhs from *Y*. Thus *X* can reduce his loss by Rs. 4 lakhs.

DOUBLE INSURANCE

Where the assured insures the same risk with two or more independent insurers, and the total sum assured exceeds the value of the subject-matter, it is called double insurance. It is over-insurance where the total of all the insurances exceeds the total value of the subject-matter insured. If there is no express condition in the policy, both double and over-insurances are allowed.

***Example*:** *X* insured his factory worth Rs. 3 lakhs with *A* for Rs. 2 lakhs and *B* for Rs. 2 lakhs. This is double insurance because the total sum insured (Rs. 4 lakhs) exceeds the value of factory. (Rs. 3 lakhs).

In the above case, if *X* insures with *A* for Rs. 2 lakhs and with *B* for 1 lakh, there is no double insurance.

Rules relating to double insurance are summed up as under:

1. *Life insurance.* There is no question of double insurance. A person can get any number of policies on his life and for any amount as he likes, provided he is ready to pay the premium on all the policies. On maturity, he shall be entitled to claim money under all the policies; whatever the total amount may be.
2. *Property.* (not more than actual loss) A person is free to insure his property with any number of insurers. When a loss occurs he cannot recover more than the actual amount of loss. However, he may claim the loss from the insurers in such order as he likes. He cannot claim the amount in excess of the loss because a contract of insurance is a contract of indemnity. It protects the assured against loss, but does not allow to make any profit out of it.
3. *Trust.* If an insured recovers the amount in excess of actual loss, he holds it as a trustee of the insurers and has to repay them as per their rights when settled.
4. *Contribution.* The insurers are liable to contribute among themselves to the loss in proportion to the amount for which each of them holds liability. If any one of them has paid more than his liability, he is entitled to recover the excess paid by him from his co-insurers, who have paid less than their liability.
5. *No profit.* The insured is never allowed to make a profit out of a fire or any other mischance.

Distinction : Re-Insurance and Double Insurance

1. The re-insurer is liable only to the first insurer. In double insurance, each insurer is liable directly to the policy-holder.
2. Re-insurance is possible in case of all types of insurance but there cannot be any double insurance in case of life insurance.
3. The assured cannot claim any part of his loss from the re-insurer, *i.e.*, second insurance company. In double insurance, the assured can claim his loss from each of the insurance company upto the amount insured with each of them. However, he cannot recover more than the total loss suffered by him.
4. In re-insurance, there is no privity of contract between the insured and the re-insurer. In case of double insurance, it is effected by the same insured person with different insurance companies.

THEORETICAL QUESTIONS

1. Define a contract of insurance. Briefly describe different kinds of contract of insurance. (*B.Com. Madras, Delhi*)
2. "A contract of insurance is a contract of uberrimae fidei". Explain. (*B.Com. Calcutta*)
3. What is meant by insurable interest? (*B.Com. M.S., Madras, Kerala*)
4. What do you understand by "subrogation" in a contract of insurance? Distinguish between subrogation and contribution. (*BA, B.Com, Delhi, Madras, Bombay*)
5. Explain the nature of a contract of insurance. Distinguish between a contract of insurance and wagering agreement. (*B.Com. BBA, Madras, Delhi, MS*)
6. Explain and illustrate the maxim Causa Proxima. (*BA. B.Com. Madras, Madurai*)
7. Explain the fundamental principles of insurance. (*B.Com. M.Com. Kerala, MS, Madurai, Madras*)
8. Define the term "premium". What are the circumstances in which premium is returnable by the insurer? (*B.Com. Madurai, Madras*)
9. "Indemnity is the controlling principle in insurance law, but all insurance contracts are not perfect contracts of indemnity". Illustrate the statement. (*B.Com. MS, Madras*)
10. What is a contract of re-insurance? (*B.Com. Madras*)
11. "Good faith lies at the root of the insurance contracts". Discuss the principles with special reference to fire and marine insurance. (*B.Com. M.Com. Kerala, Madras, Madurai, Delhi*)
12. Discuss re-insurance and double insurance. (*B.Com. Madras*)

CHAPTER

Life Insurance

AT A GLANCE

- Introduction
- Contract of Life Insurance
- Nature of Contract of Life Insurance
- Difference between Life insurance and Property Insurance
- Types of Life Insurance Policies
- Procedure for affecting Life Policies
- Days of Grace
- Surrender Value of Policy, Paid–up Value of Policy
- Revival of Discontinued Policy
- Loan of Life Insurance Policy
- Loss of Policy
- Principles of Life Insurance
- Assignment of Life Policy
- Nomination by Policy–holder
- Legal Position of Nominee
- Comparison between Assignment and Nomination
- Proof of Age
- Proof of Death
- Suicide by the Insured
- Settlement of Claim
- Life Insurance Corporation of India
- Theoretical Questions

INTRODUCTION

The contracts of life insurance business in India are governed by the Insurance Act 1938 and the Life Insurance Corporation of India Act 1956. The life insurance business in India was nationalised in 1956 and the Life Insurance Corporation Act 1956 was passed to carry on the business. Life Insurance Corporation has the monopoly of carrying on this business. Life insurance business is the exclusive domain of the Life Insurance Corporation alone.

CONTRACT OF LIFE INSURANCE

A contract of life insurance is a contract whereby the insurer (Life Insurance Corporation) in consideration of a certain sum of money (premium) undertakes to pay the assured (insured person) or to a person for whose benefit the policy is taken, a stated sum of money on the death of the insured person or on the expiry of certain period, whichever is earlier.

According to Sec. (2) (ii) of the insurance Act 1938, life insurance business means, "the business of affecting contracts upon human life, it includes:

(*a*) any contract whereby the payment of money is assured upon death (except death by accident only) or the happening of any contingency dependent on human life;

(*b*) any contract which is subject to the payment of premiums for a term dependent on human life; and

(*c*) any contract which includes the granting of disability and double or triple accident benefits, the granting of annuities upon human life, and the granting of superannuation allowances."

NATURE OF A CONTRACT OF LIFE INSURANCE

Life insurance is not a contract of indemnity. It stands on a totally different footing from fire and marine insurances. It is a mere contract to pay a certain sum on the death of the assured or on the expiry of the term whichever is earlier. It is not a contract of indemnity as in a life insurance contract, the insurer does not compensate any loss to the assured on death or maturity. Life insurance bears the idea of savings and not at all of indemnity. A contract of life insurance is, therefore, a contingent contract. In a leading case "Dalbey Vs. The India and London life Assurance Co. (1854), Parke observed, "The contract commonly called life assurance when properly considered is a mere contract to pay a certain sum of money on the death of a person, in consideration of the due payment of a certain annuity for his life. This species of insurance in no way resembles a contract of indemnity."

DIFFERENCE BETWEEN LIFE INSURANCE AND PROPERTY INSURANCE

The distinction between life insurance and property (fire and marine) insurance is as under:

1. **Subject-matter:** In life insurance, the subject-matter is *human life* whereas in other forms of insurance, the subject-matter is *goods and property*.
2. **Certainty of Events:** In life insurance the liability of the insurer to pay the sum assured arises upon death of the person concerned or the attainment by him of a certain age. The event upon which the money payable is *certain to occur* but the date of occurrence is uncertain. While in other forms of insurance the peril insured against *may or may not happen* at all.
3. **Indemnity:** Life insurance is a *contingent contract*. The full amount mentioned in the policy must be paid on the happening of the contingency stipulated in the policy. Other forms of insurance are usually *contracts of indemnity* and the insurer is only liable to make good the actual loss suffered.
4. **Valuation of Insurable Interest:** In life insurance, there must be insurable interest *at the time the contract of insurance is entered into*. In fire insurance, the insured must have insurable interest *both at the time when the policy is effected and at the time of loss*. In marine insurance, insurable interest must exist *at the time of loss*.
5. **Duration of Contract:** Life insurance contracts are *long term* contracts, for example, 20 years, 25 years etc. Non-life insurance contracts are entered into *for one year*, subject to renewal at the end of the year.

TYPES OF LIFE INSURANCE POLICIES

Life insurance policies are of various types which are issued to meet the varying needs and tastes of the different classes of people. The life insurance contracts provide elements of protection and investment. After getting insurance, the policyholder feels a sense of protection because he shall be paid a definite sum at the maturity or death, apart from the element of investment. Having different elements in different policies, the policyholders are free to choose the best policies according to their requirements. Under Sec. 49 of Life Insurance Corporation Act 1956, the Life Insurance Corporation is empowered to issue various types of policies. From time to time, Life Insurance Corporation may issue new policies to suit the requirements of the people. There are many types of life insurance policies, with slight differences, issued by the Life Insurance Corporation. The principal types of policies are described below:

1. **The Whole Life Policy:** Under this policy premiums are paid throughout life and the sum insured becomes payable only at the death of the insured. The policy remains in force

throughout the life of the assured and he continues to pay the premium till his death. It is the cheapest policy, because the premium charged under this policy is the lowest. This is also known as Ordinary Life Policy. This policy is suitable to the persons who intend to make provision for financial assistance to their heirs.

2. **Endowment Policy:** This type of policy runs only for a limited period or upto a particular age not exceeding the age of 70 years. The sum assured becomes payable either after a specified number of years or on the death of the assured, whichever is earlier. The premium rate is higher than that of the whole life policy. This type of policy is most popular because it combines the advantage of savings for old age with that of protection of the assured's family in the event of his premature death.
3. **Joint Life Policy:** This types of policy is taken upon the joint lives of two or more persons. The sum assured becomes payable at the end of a specified term of years, or on the first death of either of the lives assured, whichever is earlier, to the survivor or survivors. Premiums are payable throughout the endowment period or till the prior death of any one of the lives assured. The premium is calculated with certain modification according to the age of all insured partners. Paid-up and surrender values are payable on the policy. This policy is suitable to partners of a firm because firm will not discontinue on the outflow of the funds at the death of a partner.
4. **Double Endowment Policy:** Under this policy, the insurer agrees to pay to the assured double the amount of the insured sum if he lives on beyond the date of maturity of the policy. This policy is suitable for persons with physical disability who are otherwise not acceptable for other classes of assurance at the normal tabular rates. Premiums are payable throughout the endowment term or till the prior death of the life insured. The term of the policy is ranging from 10 years to 40 years but no policy is insured to mature at the age exceeding 65 years.
5. **Limited Payment Life Policy:** It is the policy under which the premiums are payable for selected period of years or until death of the insured person if it occurs within this period. Premium under this plan is higher than the premium payable under a whole life plan. The amount of premium depends upon the number of annual premiums stipulated since premiums are payable for a selected period of years or until death if it occurs within this period. The sum insured becomes payable only on the death of the insured. It is suitable policy to meet the family needs.
6. **Participating Policy:** It is also known as "With profit policy". The holders of the participating policies are entitled to share the profit of the insurer. Policy-holders can share the profit and not the loss. Profit, in the form of bonus, declared by the insurance company is added to the value of policy. In such policies, the rate of premium is usually higher as compared to other policies.
7. **Non-participating Policy:** It is also known as "without profit policy". It is the policy under which no profit of the insurance company is added to the value of policy. Premium is lower.
8. **Convertible Whole Life Policy:** This is a whole-life policy which gives its holder an option to get it converted at the end of five years, into an endowment policy. If this option is exercised the policy no longer remains a whole-life policy; if it is not exercised, the policy continues to be a whole-life policy. The object is to provide maximum insurance protection at a minimum cost and at the same time to offer a flexible contract which can be allowed to an endowment policy at the end of five years of policy.

9. **Money Back Policy:** This system provides the payment of policy at regular intervals before the policy matures. For example, for a policy with a term of 12 years. 1/5th of the sum assured becomes payable on the life assured's surviving 4 years, a further 1/5th of the sum assured becomes payable on his surviving 8 years and the balance 3/5th of the sum assured on his surviving to the end of the term of 12 years. And if the insured person dies before the expiry of the term of the policy, the entire policy money becomes payable on death, irrespective of the instalments already paid.
10. **Annuity Policy:** This is a policy under which the amount is payable by the insurer not in one lump-sum, but by monthly, quarterly, half yearly or annual instalments after the assured attains a certain age. The assured may pay the premiums regularly over a certain period or he may pay a single premium at the outset. This type of policy is useful to persons who wish to provide a regular income for themselves and their dependents.
11. **Children Endowment Policy:** These are the policies which are taken to provide funds for the marriage or education of the children. As usual, under these policies also, the assured insures his own life, but the purpose is different, that is, to ensure the education or marriage of children. Under these policies, the premiums are payable for a fixed period. The sum insured becomes payable only at the expiry of fixed period even if the policyholder dies earlier. Under marriage endowment policy, the policy amount is paid in lump-sum and in case of education endowment policy, the policy money is paid in equal half yearly instalments.
12. **Multipurpose Policy:** It is the policy which meets the several needs of a person, for example, provision for self in old age, provision for one's family, provision for education or marriage of children etc. In case of such policies, the premiums are payable during the fixed number of years or till death if it occurs within the fixed period. On the maturity of the policy, the insured person may get the policy money in lump sum or in the form of monthly pension. It gives maximum protection to the beneficiaries in the event of the death of the assured.
13. **Sinking Fund Policy:** This policy is very useful for companies for redeeming their debentures or paying off their loans. A fixed amount is paid as premium annually. It goes on accumulating at a certain rate of interest. At the end of the required period, the amount of the policy is paid to the company. Out of the amount so received, the company redeems its debentures or pays off the loan or replace an asset after a period of time.

With a view to satisfying the needs of the insuring public, in the changing times, the LIC has brought-out new types of policies. LIC has also introduced several non-conventional policies to meet the requirements of the population, for example, policies under LIC Mutual Fund, Jeevan Sathi, Jeevan Mitra etc.

PROCEDURE FOR EFFECTING LIFE POLICY

Anyone who has attained majority can enter into a valid contract with LIC in effecting a policy on self and on those in whom he has insurable interest. A person, who wish to take out a policy on life insurance, has to fill a proposal form supplied by LIC. There are different types of forms for each type of policy. One has to fill up the form with details with regards to the health of the proposer, his family history, age, habits of life, amount, kind and term of policy etc. The proposer must disclose all the material facts truly and fully. There may be medical examination. The proposal form is accompanied by the first premium amount and if the LIC accepts the same unconditionally, they issue the first premium receipt. The risk commences from the date of issuing the receipt, which is more or less an acceptance letter. In due course, LIC sends the insurance policy to the insured. The policy is an evidence of the contract between the insurer and the insured person. Life insurance being a contract of utmost good faith, if the proposal form is false, the insurer can avoid the policy.

DAYS OF GRACE

Days of grace are allowed by LIC, after the expiry of due date for payment of premium. During the period the assured can pay the premium in order to continue the policy. Life Insurance Corporation of India, allow 30 days of grace for payment of yearly, half yearly or quarterly premiums and 15 days for monthly premiums. The days of grace are counted from the next day on which the premium falls due. If death occurs within that period and before payment of the premium then due, the policy will still be valid and the sum assured will be paid after deduction of the said premium. (see previous Chapter for more details).

SURRENDER VALUE OF POLICY

A person usually surrenders the policy when he does not want to continue it. If a policy-holder decides to surrender his policy before its maturity, the insurer agrees to pay some amount to the policyholder. Such an amount is called surrender value. The payment of surrender value brings about the termination of the contract of insurance. Policy acquires a surrender value when it has run for a certain minimum number of years and all the premiums during the said period have been paid in full.

A policy acquires a surrender value only after it has run a specified period. In this regard, LIC provides as under:

(*a*) *In the case of policies completed before 1st April 1973,* the policy will acquire surrender value:

(*i*) after two full years premiums have been paid, when the terms is 20 years or more; or

(*ii*) after 1/10th of the total premiums due have been paid, where the term is 11 to 19 years; or

(*iii*) after more than one year's premium is paid, where the term is 5 to 10 years.

(*b*) *In the case of policies completed on and after 1st April 1973*, the policy will acquire surrender after payment of three full years premiums.

(*c*) *In the case of policies completed on and after 1st January 1976*, the policy will acquire surrender value after payment of five full years premiums or for atleast one-fourth of the total term of the policy, whichever is less, but payment of atleast three full years' premiums is necessary in any case.

(*d*) *In the case of policies completed on or after 1st January 1979*, the policy will acquire the surrender value after the payment of three full years' premiums. This rule is extended retrospectively to all policies.

The surrender value of a policy goes on increasing as more and more premiums are paid.

PAID-UP VALUE OF POLICY

Sometimes, the insured person has paid premiums for a certain minimum number of years and the policy has acquired surrender value, but he does not want to pay the further instalments of premiums and discontinues the same. In such a case, the policyholder becomes entitled to the paid-up value of the policy. Such a value is payable only at the maturity of the policy and thus this value is always higher than the surrender value. Paid-up value is calculated:

$$\text{Paid - up Value} = \frac{\text{No. of premiums actually paid}}{\text{No. of total premiums payable}} \times \text{Sum Assured}$$

The major points of difference between surrender value and paid-up value of a life policy are:

(1) Surrender value accrues after the policy having run for a prescribed period, while paid-up value accrues after two years.

(2) Surrender value is paid during the currency period of the policy, while paid-up value is paid on maturity.

(3) The former is exclusive of bonus while the latter is inclusive of bonus.

(4) Paid-up value is always higher than the surrender value.

REVIVAL OF DISCONTINUED POLICY

When the premium is not paid within the days of grace, the policy lapses, but may be revived during the life-time of the assured, that too within a period of 5 years from the due date of the first unpaid premium and before the date of maturity.

The revival is possible within six months from the due date of the first unpaid premium without evidence of health on payment of the premiums in arrears with interest at the rate of 7.5 per cent per annum compounded half yearly. The revival after the first six months from the due date of the first unpaid premium but before five years from the due date of the first unpaid premium will be effective only on satisfactory production of evidence of health and habits of the assured and no adverse change in personal or family history or occupation.

LOAN ON LIFE INSURANCE POLICY

Where the policy has acquired a surrender value, it also acquires a loan value. The loan value is calculated at 90 per cent of the surrender value in the case of policies which are in force for full sum assured and 85 per cent of surrender value in case of policies which are in paid-up condition. The rate of interest charged at present is 9% p.a. The policy holder enjoys privilege of getting loans on security of his policy. The loan may be repaid as per the terms of the loan agreement. In case the loan is not repaid within the agreed time, it is deducted from the policy amount when it falls due. This is the best way of investments for the insurance companies as there is no danger on money being lost.

LOSS OF POLICY

The insured must inform to the LIC whenever the policy is lost or destroyed. The assured has to execute a bond of indemnity and has to pay fees to the Corporation. Intimation of this loss must also be given in newspapers, if the sum assured is more than Rs. 10,000. Then the Corporation will issue a duplicate copy of the policy.

PRINCIPLES OF LIFE INSURANCE

We have already discussed the fundamental principles of a contract of insurance in general, in Chapter 36. However, the following principles - Insurable Interest and Good Faith, need discussion:

(*A*) *Insurable Interest*

"No insurable interest - no insurance" is a maxim of the law of insurance. Contract of life insurance is void, unless the assured has an insurable interest in the life insured. Insurable interest is the pecuniary interest in the subject-matter of insurance. In case of life insurance, the subject-matter is the life of a person. To be a valid contract of life insurance, a person must have insurable interest in the life sought to be insured. Insurable interest arises out of the pecuniary relationship that exists between the policyholder and the life insured, so that the policyholder stands to lose by the death of the insured and continue to gain by his remaining alive. For example, a wife has an insurable interest in the life of her husband and vice versa. The insurable interest must be real and actual. In life insurance, the assured must have insurable interest in the life upon which insurance is effected at the time when the contract of insurance is entered into. It need not be present at the time of the death of the person insured or when the policy falls due. This is because a contract of insurance is not a contract of indemnity.

In life insurance, insurable interest is presumed to be present in the following cases and no proof for the same is required.

(*a*) One's own life

(*b*) Husband in the life of wife

(*c*) Wife in the life of husband

In all other cases, insurable interest is to be proved, though a person is deemed to have insurable interest in the lives of his dependents.

The rules regarding insurable interest on the lives of others are as under:

1. A person has insurable interest in the life of his relative by whom he is supported. A son has insurable interest on the life of his supporting father but a father does not have insurable interest in the life of his son unless he is dependent on him. Similarly, an elder brother has no insurable interest in the life of his younger brother.
2. A proprietor of a Drama Company has insurable interest on the lives of actors and actresses engaged by him.
3. A creditor has insurable interest in the life of a debtor to the extent of his debt at the time of issue of policy.
4. In the same way, a partner may have insurable interest in the lives of other partners.

(B) Good Faith

The life insurance requires that the principle of utmost good faith should be preserved by both the parties. The utmost good faith says that both the parties, insured and insurer, must be of the same mind at the time of contract because only then the risk may be correctly ascertained. They must make full and true disclosure of the facts materials to the risk. (For more details, see Chapter 36).

ASSIGNMENT OF LIFE POLICY

Assignment is a method by which the interest in a policy of life insurance can be transferred to another. The holder of a life policy can deal with it like any other property and can sell it, transfer it as a security for a loan or give it away as a gift. "*Life insurance policies are marketable commodities which can be validly assigned, with or without consideration to persons who have no interest in the life insured.*" (*Ashely Vs. Ashley* 1829). Assignment has the effect of transferring the rights of the transferor in respect of the policy to the assignee. A life policy being an actionable claim, cannot be transferred by mere delivery. The assignment shall be complete and effectual only on the execution of endorsement either on the policy itself or by a separate deed. Once the assignment is completed, it cannot be revoked by the assignor because he ceases to be the owner of the policy. There is no question whether the assignee has an insurable interest or not. The person (assignee), to whom the policy is assigned, can claim the policy amount on maturity. A valid assignment is irrevocable and cannot be cancelled subsequently.

Sec. 38 of the Insurance Act 1938, contains the following rules regarding assignment of life policies:

1. **Procedure :**
   (*i*) Life policy can be assigned either by an endorsement on the policy itself or by a separate instrument.
   (*ii*) It is immaterial, whether there is consideration or not.
   (*iii*) The endorsement or instrument must be signed by the assignor and the signature be attested by atleast one witness.
2. *Notice:* The assignment will be binding upon the insurer after a notice in writing and endorsement on the instrument.
3. *Priority:* When the assignments are more than one, the priority of claims of the assignees is determined by the order in which the notices have been delivered to the insurers.
4. *Recognition:* From the date of the notice the insurer shall recognise the assignee named in the notice as the only person entitled to benefit under the policy. The assignee can, if necessary, sue without the consent of the assignor.
5. *Acknowledgment:* The insurer is bound to grant a written acknowledgment of the notice on the request of the person by whom the notice was given or of the transferee or assignee on payment of a fee not exceeding rupee one.
6. *Conditional Assignment:* The assignment may be absolute or conditional. Thus, an assignment made in favour of a person subject to the condition that it shall be inoperative or that the interest shall pass to some other person on the happening of specified event during the life time of the insured shall be valid.
7. *Assignment subject to equities:* As soon as the notice of assignment is delivered to the insurer, the assignee becomes entitled to all of its benefits. In the same way, he also becomes liable to all the liabilities and equities for which the assignor was liable on the date of assignment.

NOMINATION BY THE POLICYHOLDER

The holder of a life policy has the right to nominate any person, to whom he wants the insured money to be paid in the event of his death. It can be done either at the time when the policy is taken or any time before the policy matures for payment. The person so nominated is called the 'nominee'. In one policy, there can be more than one nominee. The nominee can claim the policy amount from the insurance company in the event of death of the insured person.

The nomination is valid only if it is made in accordance with the legal rules laid down in Sec. 39 of the Insurance Act 1938. They summed up as under:

(1) *Procedure:* Nomination is usually done on the life policy itself. Besides, it may also be done by an endorsement on the policy provided that it is registered with the insurer and recorded in the records of the policy. The insurer is also supposed to issue an acknowledgment of the nomination being registered.

(2) *Change in Nomination:* The life policyholder may change his nominee at any time before the maturity of the policy by giving a notice in writing to the insurer.

(3) *Cancellation of Nomination:* The life policyholder may cancel his nomination at any time before its maturity by giving a notice in writing to the insurer.

(4) *Automatic Cancellation:* An Assignment of a policy shall automatically cancel a nomination, except an assignment to the insurer to secure a loan which shall affect the rights of the nominee only to the extent of the insurer's interest in the policy.

(5) *Discharge of insurer:* The position of the nominee is that of the heir of the deceased as he gets payment only when the policyholder dies. But if the policy matures for payment during the life time of the insured, the insurer shall pay the money to the policyholder.

LEGAL POSITION OF NOMINEE

A nominee is entitled to receive the money due under the policy if the insured person dies before the policy matures for payment. The nominee has no right to collect the policy amount during the life time of the assured. The nomination simply provides that the policy money is payable to the nominee and the insurer need not look to the legal representatives of the deceased insured. The nominee acquires no beneficial interest under nomination. He is merely an agent to receive the money due under the policy. The policyholder is the owner of the policy and continues to hold interest in it till death. If the policy matures for payment during life time of the policyholder, then benefits arising under the policy shall belong to him and not his nominee. The nominee does not become the owner of the money which he receives under a policy of which he is the nominee. The receipt of money by the nominee merely gives a valid discharge to the insurance company. The money belongs to the legal heirs of the deceased. If a policy is assigned, after a nomination, the nomination is automatically cancelled. The strict legal position of the nominee is that he is entitled to receive and collect the money under the policy only as trustee for the benefit of legal heirs of the deceased.

Comparison between Assignment and Nomination

Assignment	*Nomination*
1. *Meaning:* All the rights of the policyholder pass to the assignee in his own name and for his own benefit, *i.e.* the assignee becomes the owner of the policy.	All the rights of the policyholder does not pass to the nominee. He simply gets the right to collect the policy amount on the death of the insured.
2. *Title:* Assignee gets the title.	Nomince does not get the title.
3. *Consideration:* Assignment of a policy may be with or without consideration.	It is done without consideration.
4. *Procedure:* Assignment can be made on the policy or by a separate deed.	Nomination is done by endorsement on the policy with notice to insurer.
5. *Right of Action:* An assignee can sue the insurer in his own name for his claim.	Nominee does not have such right.
6. *Object:* It is made for the purpose of transferring the rights under the policy.	Here, policy money shall be paid to nominee only if he survives the insured person. It is made for the sake of convenience of the beneficiaries after the death of insured.
7. *Cancellation:* It is irrevocable and cannot be cancelled.	It can be cancelled or changed.
8. *Transfer of Property:* The property in the policy passes to the assignee.	Property in the policy remains at the disposal of the assured.
9. *Payment party:* Payment is made to the assignee.	Nominee gets the payment only in case of death of the assured.

PROOF OF AGE

The rates of premium for most life policies depend on the age of the life assured at the time of effecting the policy. The age of assured is a material fact for the insurer because it has a direct bearing on the risk undertaken by him. Therefore, it is essential that the correct age should be stated in the proposal form. The insurer requires proof of age to be furnished at the time of the proposal itself or at any time after the issue of the policy. The age may be proved with a document, for example, horoscope, birth certificate, School certificate, family record etc. When it is done, the insurer mentions on the policy the words "age admitted". The age so recorded cannot be challenged unless fraud is proved in this regard. If actual age comes to be more than the recorded age, the insurer cannot refuse to pay. However, he can deduct out of the policy amount, the difference of premium between the two ages.

In the following types of cases, the proof of age must invariably accompany the proposal form, as the proposal will not be completed unless the age is proved:

(1) Where the assured has not completed 20 years of age.

(2) Where the assured has completed 50 years of age.

(3) Where the proposal is under "Salary Saving Scheme."

(4) Where the proposal is under "Temporary Assurance Plan" or "Convertible Term Assurance Plan".

(5) Where the proposal is under Immediate annuity, Deferrel annuity or Retirement annuity plan.

(6) Where a supplementary benefits for child is desired under a multi-purpose policy, the proof of age of the beneficiary child.

(7) Where the proposal is under the Children's Deferred Endowment Assurance Plan, the proof in support of (*a*) the age of the life to be insured and (*b*) the age of the proposer, if the premium waiver benefit is desired.

PROOF OF DEATH

Where the policy money is claimed on the death of the insured, the death must be proved. The proof of death may be given by a death certificate from the Municipal authorities on the basis of entries in death register or by oral testimony of the persons who were present at the last rites of the deceased or by presumptive evidence under Sec. 108 of the Indian Evidence Act, that is, the person has not been heard of for seven years by those who would naturally have heard of him if he had been alive. The cause of the death is immaterial for the settlement of insurance claim. On the proof of death of the insured person, the insurance company may pay the policy amount to the persons who are entitled to receive the same.

SUICIDE BY THE INSURED

A contract of life insurance is a contract to pay a certain sum of money on the death of a person or on the expiry of certain period. Thus insurance policy also mature on the death of the life of insured person. The ultimate result of suicide is death. Suicide implies a wilful and intentional taking of one's own life. Suicide means an act to self-destruction. Life policies usually contain a clause that payment will not be made if the assured commits suicide. If a policy has such a clause and the assured commits suicide the insurer is not liable to pay. It is the responsibility of the insurer to prove suicide. Accordingly, if the assured commits suicide within one year of the commencement of the risk, LIC will not be liable for the policy money.

In India, suicide in itself is not a crime but an attempt to commit suicide is a crime. Therefore, a policy in India cannot be avoided on the ground of suicide unless there is a specific clause to that effect in the policy (*Northern India Assurance Co. Vs. Kanhayalal* 1938). However, if the assured validly assigns the policy for valuable consideration, then the assignee can make the LIC liable even if the assured has committed suicide within a year of the issue of policy. But LIC must have been intimated about assignment atleast one month before the date of suicide.

SETTLEMENT OF CLAIM

Claims are payable according to the terms of the contract of insurance. When the policy matures for payment due to the death of the assured or the expiry of the period specified in the policy, the amount of the policy can be claimed from the LIC.

The following steps have to be taken:

(A) *Proof of Title:* The person claiming the money on maturity, must satisfy the insurance that he is entitled to receive the money due under the policy. If the assured is alive on the maturity of policy, he is entitled to claim the policy amount or his assignee, if the policy was assigned. In the event of death of the assured, the assignee or the nominee or the legal representative as the case may be, will have to prove his legal title to the policy amount. Legal representative, in proof of his title, has to furnish "a succession certificate. When there are conflicting claims to the amount due under the policy. LIC pays the amount of claim through the Court. Sec. 47 of the Insurance Act 1938 protects the insurance company.

(B) *Proof of Death:* The death of the assured must be proved. Proof of death may be given by oral testimony or by a death certificate or by presumtive evidence, viz., absence for a period of seven years or more. The insurer may claim the production of a succession certificate. Cause of death is immaterial, that is, whether it is caused by suicide (provided the policy has run for a year) or murder or military operation, it is covered under the policy, unless specified otherwise in the terms of policy.

(C) *Proof of Age:* If the proof of age has not been furnished already, it will have to be submitted at the time of making a claim. Insurance company cannot refuse to pay the claim even if the age turns out to be more than what was given. However, in such cases, it can deduct the amount of difference of premium between the two ages, with interest at 7.5% p.a.

THE LIFE INSURANCE CORPORATION OF INDIA

In India, the life insurance business was nationalised in 1956 and the Life Insurance Corporation Act 1956 was passed to carry on this business. Since then it is carried on by the Life Insurance Corporation of India, which was set up under the provisions of this Act 1956. Sec. 30 of the Act provides that the Corporation shall have the exclusive privilege of carrying on life insurance business in India.

Objects

The main objects of the nationalisation of the life insurance business are:

1. To ensure absolute security to the policyholder.
2. To spread insurance much more widely and in particular to the rural areas.
3. To encourage public savings and to have better utilisation of those savings by investing them under five year plans.
4. To create the insurance habit among the people.
5. To prevent misappropriation of funds and malpractices in the administration of the insurance companies. etc.

Constitution of the Life Insurance Corporation

The Life Insurance Corporation is a body corporate constituted under the special Act - Life Insurance Corporation Act of India. It consists of 16 members. These members are appointed by the Central Government and one of them is appointed as the chairman. While appointing the members of the Corporation, the Central Government shall satisfy itself that the persons to be appointed has no financial or other interest as is likely to prevent him from carrying out the functions of the Corporation independently and to the best interest of the society. (Sec. 4)

Capital of the Corporation

The Life Insurance Corporation has the original total paid up capital of Rs. 5 crores. The entire capital of Rs. 5 crores has been provided by the Central Government. However, on the recommendation of the Corporation, the Central Government may reduce the capital to such an amount as the Government may determine. (Sec. 5)

Functions of the Corporation

The primary and general function of the Corporation is to carry on the life insurance business in India. Subject to the rules, if any, made by the Central Government, it shall be the duty of the Corporation to carry on the life insurance business whether in or outside India, and the Corporation shall so exercise its powers under the Act as to secure that life insurance business is developed to the best advantage of the community (Sec. 6). In the discharge of any of its functions the Corporation shall act so far as may be on business principles. (Sec. 6(1)).

Powers

The powers of the Corporation may be summarised as under:

1. to carry on capital redemption, annuity and reinsurance business;
2. to take such steps as are expedient for the protection or realisation of its investments, including the taking over and administering any property offered as security;
3. to acquire, hold and dispose of any property for the purpose of its business;
4. to transfer the whole or any part of the life insurance business carried on outside India to any other person or persons if it is expedient to do so;
5. to advance or lend money upon the security of movable or immovable property or otherwise;
6. to borrow or raise money in such manner and upon such security as the Corporation may think fit;
7. to carry on either by itself or through any subsidiary any other business in any case where such other business was being carried on by a subsidiary of an insurer whose controlled business has been transferred to and vested in the Corporation under the Act;
8. to carry on any other business which may seem to the Corporation to be capable of being conveniently carried on in connection with its business and calculated directly or indirectly to render profitable the business of the Corporation; and
9. to do also such things as may be incidental or conducive to the proper exercise of any of the powers of the Corporation.

Administration of the Corporation

1. The Corporation may entrust the general superintendence and direction of its affairs and business to an executive committee consisting not more than five of its members and the executive committee may exercise all powers and do all such acts and things as may be delegated to it by the Corporation.

2. The Corporation may also constitute and Investment Committee for the purpose of advising it in matters relating to the investment of its funds, and the Investment Committee shall consist of not more than seven members of whom not less than three shall be members of Corporation and the remaining members shall be person (whether members of the Corporation or not) who have special knowledge and experience in financial matters, particularly matters relating to investment of funds.
3. The Corporation may constitute such other committees as it may think fit for the purpose to discharge such of its functions as may be delegated to them. (Section 19).

The central office of the Corporation is situated at Bombay. It has five zonal offices situated at Mumbai, Kolkata, Chennai, Delhi and Kanpur. There are several Divisional offices, sub-offices, Branch offices and premium collecting centres. (Sec. 18).

Accounts and Audit

The Corporation shall, atleast once in every two years, cause an investigation to be made of actuaries into the financial condition of the business of the Corporation, including a valuation of the liabilities of the Corporation and submit the report of the actuaries to the Central Government.

The amount of the Corporation shall be audited by the professional auditors appointed by the Central Government. The audited annual accounts and annual report shall be submitted to the Central Government which shall place them before both Houses of Parliament. (Sec. 25 and 29).

THEORETICAL QUESTIONS

1. What is life insurance? *(B.Com. M.S.)*
2. Define contract of insurance. State the principles of life insurance with special reference to 'insurable interest' and 'good faith'. *(B.Com. Delhi, Kerala)*
3. Discuss in brief the important types of life insurance policies. *(B.Com. Chennai)*
4. What do you understand by 'assignment' of life insurance policy? State the legal provisions relating to assignment. *(B.Com. M.S.)*
5. What do you understand by nomination by policyholder? State the legal provisions relating to nomination and explain the legal position of a nominee. *(B.Com. M.Com. Chennai, Delhi)*
6. State the comparison between assignment and nomination. *(B.Com, Delhi, Madras)*
7. Write a brief note on Life Insurance Corporation of India. *(B.Com. M.S, Kerala)*
8. What is meant by surrender value of life policy? Distinguish between surrender value and paid-up value of a life policy. *(B.Com. Kerala, Delhi, Madras)*
9. What are the essentials of life insurance contract. How does it differ from fire and marine insurance contracts. *(B.Com. B.A. M.S, Delhi)*
10. "Good faith lies at the root of the insurance contract". Discuss. *(B.Com. Delhi, Bombay, M.S.)*
11. What is meant by insurable interest? Explain insurable interest in connection with life policy. *(B.Com. Kerala, M.S, Bombay)*

CHAPTER

Fire Insurance

AT A GLANCE

INTRODUCTION

The contracts of fire insurance are governed by the Insurance Act 1938 and the General Insurance Business (Nationalisation) Act 1972. Whenever, the law is silent on any point, the principles established by Indian decisions and the English law shall apply. Sec. 2 (6A) of the Insurance Act defines fire insurance as follows: "Fire insurance business means the business of effecting, otherwise than incidentally to some other class of business, contracts of insurance against loss by or incidental to fire or other occurrence customarily included among the risks insured against in fire insurance policies." The term 'contract of fire insurance' may be defined as a contract by which an insurer, in consideration of certain sum of money (premium), undertakes to pay to the assured the amount of his loss, not exceeding a certain specified amount, caused by fire during the specified period. That is, a contract of fire insurance is a contract to indemnify the assured for the loss to his property caused by fire.

NATURE OF CONTRACT OF FIRE INSURANCE

A contract of fire insurance is a contract of indemnity. A contract of indemnity is a contract in which one person promises to indemnify the other for the loss or damage suffered by him. A contract of fire insurance resembles a contract of indemnity. Every contract of insurance except life and personal accidental insurance, is a contract of indemnity. A contract of fire insurance is essentially a contract of indemnity, and not against the accident but against the loss caused by accident. If there is no loss, there is no liability even if there is a fire. The insurer undertakes to pay the amount of the assured's loss not in excess of the maximum amount stated in policy. The insurers undertake to make good the insured's loss by monetary payment or by reinstatement or replacement so that the insured shall be fully indemnified, but this is subject to the sum insured. The law does not sanction any insurance which would enable the insured to profit by the destruction of the thing insured. It will check the temptation to destroy the property insured thereby to secure money. That is, the assured is not allowed to make any profits out of the loss caused by fire.

Example: A building of Rs. 1,00,000 is insured against fire for Rs. 1,50,000. The contract of insurance provided that if the building destroyed by fire within a year, the insurer agreed to pay the loss suffered. It is completely destroyed by fire. The insurer is liable to pay the actual loss, *i.e.* Rs. 1,00,000.

Example: A building of Rs. 1,00,000 is insured against fire for Rs. 75,000 only. The building was burnt by fire within a year. The actual loss was estimated at Rs. 1,00,000. Here, the insurer is liable to pay Rs. 75,000 only as it is the maximum limit.

FIRE AND LOSS BY FIRE

A contract of fire insurance covers the loss caused by fire. 'Fire', within the meaning of fire policy, means fire which has broken bounds and is fortuitous in its nature. There must be actual ignition or burning, whether accidental or otherwise. Heating unaccompanied by ignition is not fire. The term 'fire' may be defined as the production of light and heat by combustion (process of burning). Light and heat alone is not fire unless there is actual ignition (burning by flames). There is fire when something burns. If an actual fire or burning is the proximate cause of the loss, and that fire is accidental or fortuitous in its origin so far as the insured is concerned, then such loss is covered by the fire policy. Damage from lightning is not included in the fire risk but if lightning cause ignition, the loss would be covered by the fire policy. The same is the case with electricity.

Example: *Austin Vs. Drewee* (1816)

Sugar was spoiled by the closing of ventilator due to great heat. Held, insurer was not liable as there is no actual ignition.

All losses which are reasonable and natural consequences of fire are covered by the fire insurance policy. Loss recoverable under fire insurance policy, according to Justice Kelly, is "Any loss resulting from an apparently necessary and bonafide effort to put out a fire, whether it be by spoiling the goods by water or throwing the articles of furniture out of the window, or even by destroying a neighbouring house by explosion for the purpose of checking the progress of the flames, every loss that clearly and proximately results, whether directly or indirectly, from the fire, is within the policy."

Note: Generally, losses by fire resulting from earthquakes, riots, military powers, civil disturbances, rebellion, foreign enemy etc. are not covered by the fire policies. Besides, the losses by theft during or after occurrence of fire are also not covered unless specifically provided for in the policy.

SUBJECT MATTER

The subject-matter of fire insurance may be all kinds of movable and immovable property having monetary value. It includes all types of assets, goods, live-stock, eatables, tools, equipments, and so on. The subject-matter to be insured must be properly described. If a house is insured against fire, it will not include house-hold goods, the horse will not be included with the insurance of a tonga etc.

A fire insurance contract is entered into by the process of an offer and acceptance by the parties. The proposal is made by the insured in writing, that is, filling the printed form and paying the full premium or a part of it to the insurer. On receipt of the proposal with the premium, a cover note is issued by the insurer. Subsequently, the fire policy is issued, if the proposal is accepted by the insurer.

CHARACTERISTICS OF FIRE INSURANCE

The fundamental principles of a contract of insurance have been discussed in Chapter 36. However, the following essentials of a contract of fire insurance are as follows:

1. *It is a contract of indemnity.* The insured, suffering the loss in a fire policy, can only recover to the extent of the actual loss, so far as it does not exceed the sum insured.
2. *The contract is a contract of uberrimae fidei.* The fire insurance is based upon utmost good faith between the parties.
3. *It is a contract from year to year.* The policy is usually for a term of one year, but subject to renewal.
4. Contribution. The principles of and *subrogation* apply to a contract of fire insurance. (Refer Chapter 36 for more details).
5. *Insurable Interest.* In case of fire insurance, the insured must have insurable interest in the subject-matter both, at the time of contract and at the time of loss. Insurable interest in the goods or property means the monetary interest, which the insured has in it.
   Insurable interest in any goods or property may arise either because of:
   (*a*) Ownership
   (*b*) Lawful possession, or
   (*c*) Some contract.
   Thus in view of the above, any of the following persons have insurable interest in the subject-matter of a fire policy:
   (*i*) Owner;
   (*ii*) Pledgee, pawnee, mortgagee;
   (*iii*) Official Receiver or assignee;
   (*iv*) Warehousing man for the goods of customers;
   (*v*) Lawful possessor of goods;
   (*vi*) Carrier;
   (*vii*) Inn-keeper;
   (*viii*) Wharfinger;
   (*ix*) Agent;
   (*x*) Commission agent;
   (*xi*) Trustee;
   (*xii*) Finder of goods etc. (see Chapter 36 for more details).

   Example: *X* borrowed Rs. 50,000 from *Y*, and mortgaged his house with *Y* as a security for the repayment of loan. Here *Y*, the mortgagee acquires an insurable interest in the house to the extent of Rs. 50,000 and *Y* can insure it.

   Example: A consignor delivered some goods to *Y*, a common carrier, for transporting them to consignee. Here, both the consignor and *Y* have insurable interest in the goods. This is because consignor is the owner and *Y*, who is having lawful possession of the goods.

   Example: *X* has found some valuable jewels on the road. He spent Rs. 10,000 in finding the true owner. Here *X* acquires an insurable interest in the jewels to the extent of Rs. 10,000 and can insure it.
6. *Causa Proxima:* The principle of causa proxima applied in fire insurance. (Refer Chapter 36, for more details). If proximate cause of loss or damage is fire, the loss is recoverable. If it is not fire but some other cause remotely connected with fire, the loss is not recoverable unless specifically provided for. Cause of fire is immaterial for a fire insurance claim to be admitted. That is, the origin of cause of fire is immaterial unless it is the deliberate act of the assured himself. Even if it is caused by the negligence of the assured or his servants, the insurer shall continue to be liable. But if the fire is caused by the intentional or deliberate act of the assured, then he is not entitled to recover the money.

The following losses are deemed to have been caused proximately by fire:

(*a*) Loss which is necessarily a consequence of fire, that is, it would not have happened if there had been no fire;

(*b*) Loss which is the reasonable consequence of fire as it happened by fire in the ordinary course of events;

(*c*) Loss caused by water used to extinguish the fire destroying the property.

(*d*) Loss caused by any efforts to arrest or to extinguish the fire;

(*e*) Loss caused in removing the property from the premises affected by fire;

(*f*) Loss by theft during the confusion developed due to fire.

Though the cause of fire is immaterial, it should not be deliberately brought about by the insured. However, it is immaterial if the fire is caused by the negligence of the insured.

Example: *Harris Vs. Poland* (1941)

A women insured her jewels against the risk of fire. Then, the women hid her jewels under the grate (metal frame of a fire place), as a precaution against theft. Later on she forget about the jewels and lit the fire and consequently jewels were damaged. Held, she could recover the loss as the proximate cause of loss was fire. Her act was neither deliberate nor intentional.

Example: *Midland insurance Co. Vs Smith (1881)*

A effected an insurance on his goods against loss or damage by fire. Afterwards *A* and his wife quarrelled and she set fire to and destroyed the goods. Held, *A* was entitled to recover under the fire policy as the wife had set fire to the goods without his connivance. The illegal act was not his but of his wife, and he was covered under the policy against loss caused by an illegal act of another.

(7) Unlike a life insurance policy, a fire policy does not carry any surrender value or paid-up value.

(8) Nothing can be recovered under a fire policy, if the fire is caused by a deliberate act of the policy-holder. In such cases, the policy-holder is liable to criminal prosecution.

Comparison Between Contracts of Life Insurance and Fire Insurance

Life Insurance	*Fire Insurance*
1. Life insurance covers the human life.	Fire insurance covers the property or goods.
2. It is a contract of contingent.	It is a contract of indemnity.
3. A life policy is usually for a fairly long period, say, 10 years, 15 years or 20 years etc.	Fire insurance policies are generally for one year and are renewed from time to time.
4. The claim is certain. Claim is payable either on death or expiry of the period of the policy.	The claim is uncertain, if property is destroyed, there is claim, otherwise no claim.
5. Policy carries a surrender value.	Policy does not carry any surrender value.
6. Whole amount of claim, as fixed in the policy, is payable.	Only the amount of actual loss suffered, subject to the limit mentioned in the policy, is payable.
7. There is a provision for nomination.	There is no provision of nomination.
8. The question of insurable interest arise at the time of completion of the contract.	The question of insurable interest arise both at the time of contract and at the time when the loss takes place.

ASSIGNMENT OF FIRE INSURANCE POLICY

The term 'assignment of fire insurance policy' means passing of the rights and liabilities of the assured under the policy. In English law, policy of fire insurance can be assigned only with the consent of the insurer. In India, such consent is not necessary and the policy can be assigned as a choose-in-action under the Transfer of Property Act 1882. The insurer is bound when notice is given to him. But the assignee cannot recover damages unless he has an insurable interest in the property at the time when the loss occurs. The transfer of the property insured to the assignee is essential because for a valid claim against the insurer, the assignee must have an insurable interest in the property insured at the time of loss. A stranger cannot sue on a fire policy. Under a valid assignment, the assignee becomes entitled to all the benefits under the policy and can sue the insurer, in his own name.

The assignment of the fire policy can be made by an endorsement on the policy itself or by executing a separate document. In both cases a written notice of assignment must be given to the insurer. The consent of the insurer is not required but a notice is required to be given to the insurer. The assured must have insurable interest at the time of assignment and if he parts with or loses his interest in the property insured, an assignment of policy thereafter by him will be of no effect. The policy can only be assigned to a person who has acquired some interest in the property, for example, the purchaser or mortgagee or a bailee etc. Otherwise the assignee will have no insurable interest in the subject-matter at the time of the loss. Thus, it is important to note that a fire policy cannot be assigned without a transfer of the property insured to the assignee.

Thus the following two points are important:

(*i*) The policy cannot be assigned without the transfer of the insured property to the assignee. (Sec. 135 of the Transfer of Property Act 1882), and

(*ii*) Notice of assignment in writing must be given to the insurer. If the insurer pays money to the insured even after such notice, the assignee can also proceed against the assigner in such a case. (Sec. 49 of the Transfer of Property Act 1882).

Note: Under the English Law, a policy of fire insurance can be assigned only with the consent of the insurer. But under the Indian law, the consent of the insurer is not necessary, only a notice in writing to the insurer is sufficient.

TYPES OF FIRE INSURANCE POLICIES

There are various types of fire insurance policies which are issued to meet the varying needs of the individual persons. The principle types are discussed below:

(1) *Valued Policy:* It is a policy in which the amount payable, in case of loss, is fixed at the time of the contract of insurance. In the event of loss, the fixed amount is payable irrespective of the actual amount of loss, without asking for any proof as regards the value of the property. If there is a partial loss, then only the actual loss shall be indemnified. A valued policy is not a contract of indemnity. But it is a contract of contingent. This type of policy is issued for insuring specially pictures, works of art, sculptures, jewelry, rare things etc. Such policies are not common now-a-days.

(2) *Specific Policy:* It is a policy in which the policy amount is less than the actual value of the property. Under such a policy, in case of loss, the insurer is liable to-indemnify actual loss in full, not exceeding the specified sum in the policy, irrespective of under insurance. If the actual loss exceeds the specified sum, the insurance company is liable for the amount specified in the policy.

(3) *Floating Policy:* When one policy covers properties situated at different places or different properties situated at a particular place under one sum and for one premium, it is called a

floating policy. Thus, one single fire policy, under one sum and for one premium, covers the property of the assured lying at different places. Sometimes, the assured is in a position to declare only the total value of the property which is at risk and not the separate values of the property at separate places. The floating policies are always subject to an average clause.

(4) *Average Policy:* Where a property is insured for a sum which is less than its value, the policy may contain a clause that the insurer shall not be liable to pay the full loss but only that proportion of the loss which the amount insured for, bears to the full value of the property. Such a clause is called the average clause and policies containing an average clause are called average policies. Thus, to the extent of under-insurance, the assured is deemed to be a self insurer. For example, if a property worth Rs. 50,000 is insured only for Rs. 40,000 and if the actual loss is assessed at Rs. 20,000, the claim will be settled at Rs. $16{,}000 = \left(\frac{40{,}000}{50{,}000} \times 20{,}000\right)$ and the balance of Rs. 4,000 will be borne by the insured himself.

(5) *Consequential Loss Policy:* (Loss of profit policy) Under this type of policy, the insured is indemnified:

(*a*) For the loss caused by fire, and

(*b*) For the loss of profits which he sustains due to interruption of his business as a result of fire.

In other words, the fire destroys not only the property insured against, but also results in certain consequential losses, such as (*i*) the profits that could have been earned had the property not been destroyed and (*ii*) the payment of standing charges, *i.e.* interest, salaries, taxes etc. (*iii*) increase in the cost of working, for example, taking up of temporary building for the purpose, getting the work done from outside firms at extra cost, etc. Therefore, this type of policy covers all such losses resulting due to fire.

(6) *Reinstatement Policy (Replacement Policy):* In such policies, the insurer undertakes to pay not the value of the property lost, but the cost of replacement of the property destroyed or damaged. The insurer may retain an option to replace the property instead of paying cash. Once the option is selected, it cannot afterwards be changed by the insurance company, for example, if the insurance company offers to replace the property, it cannot later on claim to pay the cost of replacement or vice versa. This policy is also called 'New for Old' policy because the old property is replaced by new properties. Such policies are issued on buildings, plant, machinery etc.

(7) *Comprehensive Policy:* This policy undertakes full protection not only against the risk of fire but combining within the risk against burglary, riot, civil commotion, theft, damage from pest, lightning etc. The policy is also known as 'all insurance' or 'all in one' policy. The insurer can get higher premium and the assured is protected against losses due to several specified perils.

(8) *Declaration Policy:* Under declaration policy, the insured takes out an insurance policy for the maximum amount that he considers would be at risk during the period of policy. On a fixed date of every month or a specified period, the insured furnishes a declaration of the amount. The premium is provisionally paid to 75% of the annual premium amount. The declaration must be made on a specified day or within next 14 days, otherwise the sum insured will be deemed to be the declaration value. This type of policy is advantageous to those businessmen whose stock fluctuate from time to time. This type of policy is issued only to reputed firms because there is scope for fraud.

(9) *Maximum Value with Discount Policy:* A policy is taken for a maximum amount and full premium is paid thereon. At the end of the year, in case of no loss, one-third of the premium paid is returned to the policy-holder. This type of policy is not issued on all types of commodities and is confined only to selected commodities.

(10) *Adjustable Policy:* This type of policy is issued for a definite term on the existing stock. The premium is calculated in the ordinary manner and is paid in full at the inception of the policy. Wherever, there is variation in the stock, the insured informs the insurer. As soon as the information of variation is received, the policy is suitably endorsed and the premium is adjusted on a pro-rata basis.

AVERAGE CLAUSE IN FIRE POLICY

Subject-matter of fire insurance may be over-insured or under-insured, that is, the insurance may be for a higher or lower amount than the actual value of the property insured. The over-insurance is made ineffective because of the fact that, in case of loss, the insurer is liable to pay the actual loss, subject to the maximum of amount for which the policy has been taken. And over-insurance means paying more amount as premium to the insurer.

Generally people under-insure their properties in order to save premium. It is very rare that whole property is destroyed by fire. Normally, the property is partially destroyed. Therefore, in case of partial loss, the assured gets the full amount of loss by paying the small amount of premium. In order to discourage under-insurance, the insurance companies usually insert a special clause, known as the 'average clause' in their fire insurance policies. The purpose of inserting the average clause is to prevent the under-insurance and to induce the assured to take out a fire policy for the correct value of the property.

The effect of average clause is that in case of loss, the assured has to bear a portion of the loss himself. Thus if the subject-matter is under-insured and if the policy contains an average clause, the assured is considered to be his own insurer for the difference in the actual value of the subject-matter and the value for which it is insured. In such a case, if a part of the subject-matter is destroyed, the insurer will suffer a rateable proportion of the loss.

When the fire causes only a partial loss to the property insured, the insured is entitled to the whole loss provided that the amount is covered by the policy. For example, if *A* get his house valuing Rs. 1,00,000 insured against fire for Rs. 40,000 only and suppose, fire damages a part of the house to the extent of Rs. 30,000, he will get the whole loss recovered from the insurer provided that the policy is not covered by the 'average clause'.

If there is no 'average clause' in the fire policy, people get their property for a lesser amount and save the premium and also get the full loss recovered because there are hardly a few chances for the destruction of the whole property. Loss is generally caused partially to the property. Therefore, in order to protect the insurer 'average clause' is inserted in the fire policy. The effect of such a clause is that, if the subject-matter is under-insured, the insured is considered to be his own insurer for the differences in the actual value and the insured value of the subject-matter.

Example: Property worth Rs. 1,00,000 is insured for Rs. 40,000, 40% of the property is burnt by fire. Calculate the Liability of the insurer assuming that the policy has average clause.

Answer:

$$\text{Liability of the insurer} = \frac{\text{Insured Amount}}{\text{Actual value of property}} \times \text{Actual Loss}$$

$$; \quad \frac{\text{Rs.}40{,}000}{\text{Rs.}1{,}00{,}000} \text{''} \; 40{,}000\,(i.e. 40\%) = \text{Rs.}16{,}000$$

If there is no 'average clause', the liability of the insurer would be the whole loss, that is, Rs. 40,000.

It is important to note that average clause applies only if the loss caused by fire is less than the amount insured. Thus, if the loss caused by fire is more than the amount insured then the insurance company is liable for the full amount of the policy in spite of the average clause.

RIGHTS OF INSURER

The rights of an insurer under a fire insurance have been discussed below:

1. *Right to avoid the contract:* Fire insurance contract is a contract of utmost good faith. The fire insurer has the right to avoid the contract, if the insured fails to disclose all material facts or conceals any facts about the subject-matter of fire insurance. Any concealment or mis-statement of facts make the policy voidable.
2. *Right to control over the property:* When the goods are damaged or destroyed, the insurer has an implied right to take the property in his control. Since the insurer has to suffer the loss finally, he can take the property in his control with a view to minimising the loss and also to safeguard his interests.
3. *Right to enter into the property:* On the notice of fire by the insured, the insurer has the right to enter into the premises insured or the premises wherein the insured things are lying. By this right, the insurance company may ascertain the cause and extent of loss and may take steps to minimise the loss.
4. *Right of subrogation:* When the insurer pays the amount of loss to the insured, he steps into the shoes of the insured. He gets all the rights which the insured has against the third parties. He cannot recover more than the actual amount of loss. Therefore, the insurer has the right to receive any benefit or compensation, which the insured gets from a third person for this loss.
5. *Right of salvage:* Salvage is the property or goods saved after fire. When the insurer pays the loss to the insured he gets right over salvage of the things destroyed. He can take the things saved in his possession.
6. *Right of contribution:* When a property is insured with more than one insurer and only one pays the amount of loss as a whole, he has the right to claim contribution from other insurers. All the insurance companies are liable to share the loss proportionately.
7. *Right of reinstatement:* The insurer has the right to replace the property of the insured instead of paying the loss in terms of money. Such right of re-instatement depends upon the option of the insurer. He may insist to re-instate things if:

   (*a*) he has express power to do so under the contract;

   (*b*) he has any suspicion of fraud or arson, and

   (*c*) he is requested to do so by a person having no interest in the contract.

FIRE INSURANCE CLAIM

When the insured property is destroyed by fire, the assured becomes entitled to claim the amount of loss from the insurance company. The following procedure may be followed:

1. *Notice:* On the happening of any destruction or damage due to fire, the insured shall forthwith give notice there of in writing to the insurer. Notice may be given by the insurer or by any other person.
2. *Report to police:* If the loss has been caused by arson, the matter should immediately be reported to the police by the insured and a copy to the insurance company.

3. *Statement of claim:* The insured is required to submit a statement of loss and damage, in detail, to the insurance company within the time specified in the policy.
4. *Evidence:* The insured should submit proof of his claim and the proper evidence to support his claim to the insurance company within a reasonable time.
5. *The assessor:* On receiving the notice, the insurer appoints an assessor to examine the facts of the case and to determine the amount of liability. The assessor is an expert person having the ability and experience in handling claims. The assessor is empowered to act and make necessary arrangement on behalf of the insurer. He goes to the site of fire and personally examines the damaged property and collects all available information. The amount of loss payable by the insurer is usually settled by agreement between the insurer and the insured otherwise the matter has to be referred to arbitration.

If the assured fails to comply with the legal formalities, he may lose his claim altogether. The assured will also lose his claim under the policy if he makes a fraudulent claim to the insurance company. However, the assured is not entitled to recover the loss arising due to his own wilful misconduct.

THEORETICAL QUESTIONS

1. Define a fire insurance contract. What are the characteristics of a fire insurance contract? *(B.Com. Madras)*
2. What is the meaning of fire in fire insurance policy? *(B.Com. Kerala)*
3. Explain the different kinds of fire policies. *(B.Com. Madras, Delhi)*
4. How a fire policy can be assigned? *(B.Com. Bombay, Delhi)*
5. How a claim under fire policy should be made? *(B.Com. Madras)*
6. What is the effect of average clause in fire insurance policies? *(B.Com. Madras, Kerala, Delhi)*
7. Discuss the rights of an insurer under a fire insurance policy. *(B.Com. Madras)*
8. X got his shop insured against fire. He became mad and during madness, he burnt his shop. His son claims the loss from the insurers. Is the insurer liable? (**Ans:** Yes)
9. House of X is insured against fire. He sold it to Y, but did not transfer the policy to Y. Subsequently, the house was destroyed by fire. X claims the loss from insurers. Is he right? (**Ans:** No)
10. During fire whole of the furniture was thrown out of windows and got damaged badly. Is the insurer liable to make good the loss of furniture? (**Ans:** Yes)

XXXIX

CHAPTER

Marine Insurance

AT A GLANCE

- Introduction
- Contract of Marine Insurance
- Nature of Contract of Marine Insurance
- Characteristics of a Marine Insurance
- Elements of Marine Insurance Contract
- Subject Matter of Contract
- Maritime Perils
- Important Definitions
- Procedure to effect Marine Insurance
- The Policy
- Types of Marine Policy
- Form of Marine Policy, Insurable Interest
- Insurable Value
- Warranties
- Disclosure and Representations
- Assignment of Marine Policy
- Premium
- Voyage
- Marine Losses
- Abandonment
- Rights of Insurer
- Theoretical Questions

INTRODUCTION

Marine insurance business is the business of effecting contracts of insurance against the loss by perils of sea. Marine insurance is an agreement between the insurer and insured whereby the insurer undertakes to indemnify the insured in a manner and to the interest thereby agreed, against marine losses incident to marine adventure, in consideration of a premium paid by the insured. The marine insurance business falls under the category of general insurance business. Marine insurance contracts are governed by the Indian Contract Act 1872, the Insurance Act 1938, the General Insurance Business (Nationalisation) Act 1972 and largely by the Marine Insurance Act 1963. The Marine Insurance Act 1963 was specifically passed for marine insurance business.

CONTRACT OF MARINE INSURANCE

Marine insurance is a contract whereby the insurer undertakes to indemnify the assured against losses arising from certain perils or risks to which the ship, merchandise or other interest of the assured may be exposed during a certain voyage or for a certain period of time in consideration of a stipulated sum called premium paid by the assured.

Sec. 3 of the Marine Insurance Act 1963 defines "A contract of marine insurance is an agreement whereby the insurer undertakes to indemnify the assured, in the manner and to the extent thereby agreed, against marine losses, that is, losses incidental to marine adventure."

Sec. 4(1) of the Act, further states that "The contract of marine insurance may, by its express terms or by usage of trade, be extended so as to protect the assured against losses on inland waters or on any land risk which may be incidental to any sea voyage."

It is a contract to compensate the assured for the loss to his vessels, cargoes etc., caused by sea perils. Here, the insurers are known as 'underwriters.'

NATURE OF A CONTRACT OF MARINE INSURANCE

The statutory provisions as contained in Sections 3 and 4(1) of the Marine Insurance Act, make it clear that a contract of marine insurance undertakes to indemnify the losses against marine adventure and marine perils. Thus marine insurance resembles a contract of indemnity. However, a marine insurance contract may be defined as "a contract whereby one party for an agreed consideration, undertakes to indemnify the other against loss arising from certain perils and sea risks to which a shipment merchandised and other interest in a marine adventure may be exposed during a certain voyage or a certain period of time." Thus a contract of marine insurance is a contract of indemnity.

CHARACTERISTICS OF MARINE INSURANCE CONTRACT

The characteristics of a marine insurance contracts are:

(1) It is a *contract of indemnity*. (Refer Chapter 36)

(2) It is a contract based upon the *utmost good faith*. (Refer Chapter 36)

(3) Doctrine of *subrogation and contribution* apply. (Refer Chapter 36)

(4) A Marine policy is invariably subject to *average clause*. (Refer Chapter 38)

(5) All marine insurance contracts are subject to certain *express* and *implied warranties*. (See further in this chapter)

(6) Assured must have *insurable interest* in the subject-matter. (See further in this chapter)

ELEMENTS OF MARINE INSURANCE CONTRACT

The following are the essential features of fundamental principles of marine insurance.

(1) Features of General Contract

(2) Insurable Interest

(3) Utmost Good Faith

(4) Doctrine of Indemnity

(5) Subrogation

(6) Warranties

(7) Proximate Cause

(8) Assignment and Nomination of Policy

(9) Return of Premium (For more details look further in this chapter)

SUBJECT-MATTER OF A CONTRACT OF MARINE INSURANCE

"Every lawful marine adventure may be the subject-matter of a contract of marine insurance." (Sec. 5) Insurance may be effected in relation to all such interests which are exposed to maritime perils.

Sec. 2 (d) states that "there is a marine adventure when:

1. any ship, goods or movable property (*i.e.* insurable property) is exposed to maritime perils;
2. the earning or acquisition, of any freight, passage money, commission, profit or other pecuniary benefit or the security for any advances, loans or disbursements is endangered by the exposure of insurable property to maritime perils;
3. any liability to a third party may be incurred by the owner of, or other person interested in, the insurable property by reasons of maritime perils."

As per Sec. 2(c), "insurable property means any ship, goods or other movables which are exposed to maritime perils."

MARITIME PERILS

Sec. 2(e) of the Marine Insurance Act defines 'maritime perils' as "the perils consequent on, or incidental to, the navigation of the sea. In other words, they mean perils of the sea, fire, war perils, pirates, robbers, thieves, captures, seizures, restraints, and detainments of princes and peoples, jettisons (throwing of goods overboard for saving the residue) and *barratry* (fraudulent practices by the master of the ship) and any other perils which are either of the like kind or may be designated by the policy."

Thus sea perils mean all kinds of perils and misfortunes of a marine character or incidental to a ship, which is covered under the marine insurance contract. These cannot be foreseen as they are not common incidents of voyage.

Perils of the sea cover the following losses:

1. Loss by vessel struck upon a rock.
2. Loss by foundering of a ship.
3. Loss owing to a ship colliding with another ship even when it is due to the negligence of that other ship.
4. Loss due to negligent navigation.
5. Loss due to cargo being destroyed by sea water entering into the ship through a hole created by rats.
6. Loss to the goods destroyed due to heat in the ship.

However, perils do not cover:

1. Loss caused by rats.
2. Loss caused to timber by worms.
3. Loss caused by natural action of salt water of the sea.
4. Death of cattle for want of fodder, voyage being lengthened by the captain of the ship.

SOME IMPORTANT DEFINITIONS

Pirates and rovers mean sea robbers and rioters who attack the ship from the shore.

Barratry means wrongful act wilfully committed by the captain or crew in contravention of their duties, thereby causing prejudice to the owners, for example, intentionally setting fire to ship or running aground the ship.

Jettison refers to throwing a part of the goods overboard with a view to lighten the ship in order to save the ship and residue of the cargoes in an emergency.

Maritime perils mean the perils consequent on, or incidental to, the navigation of the sea, that is to say, perils of the seas, fire, war perils, pirates, rovers, thieves, captures, seizures, restrains and detainment of princes and people, jettison, barratry and any other perils which are either of the like kind or may be designated by the policy.

Marine Insurance means "A contract of marine insurance is an agreement whereby the insurer undertakes to indemnify the assured, in the manner and to the extent thereby agreed, against marine loss, that is to say, losses incidental to marine adventure" (Sec. 3)

Insurable Property means any ship, goods or other movables which are exposed to marine perils.

Bottomry means it is a contract by which the money is borrowed by the master of sea-going ship on the security of the ship or of ship and cargo both, in order to complete voyage. The contract executed into a written document is known as bottomry bond.

Respondentia means it is a contract by which the money is borrowed by the master of sea-going ship on the security of the cargo alone laden or to be laden on board a ship. The contract executed into a written document is known as respondentia bond.

PROCEDURE TO EFFECT MARINE INSURANCE

"A contract of marine insurance is deemed to be concluded when the proposal of the assured is accepted by the insurer, whether the policy be then issued or not; and for the purpose of showing when the proposal was accepted, reference may be made to the slip, covering note or other customary memorandum of the contract, although it be unstamped." (Sec. 23)

The proposer may approach to the insurer directly or through an agent or broker. Generally, the proposal is made through brokers because they are well known of the insurance practices. The broker prepares a slip where material information recorded. This slip is presented to the insurer who will signify his acceptance by initialling the slip and indicating the sum they are prepared to accept. The risk may commence from the date of acceptance or from any other date which is mutually agreed.

Sometimes, the insurer asks additional information from the broker. When the additional information called closing slip has been accepted by the insurer, he may issue policy. Before issuing the policy, open cover is issued to the insured, which becomes inoperative as soon as policy is issued. The document containing the term of the contract is called policy. The assured cannot legally make any claim over the underwriter if the loss occurs before a final policy is issued. The 'open cover' or 'slip' is not legally binding on the insurers. In practice, however, the insurer pays the amount of claim even before the issue of policies. Insurers in marine insurances are generally called "underwriters".

THE POLICY

A contract of marine insurance shall not be admitted in evidence unless it is embodied in a marine policy in accordance with this Act. The policy must be executed and issued either at the time when the contract is concluded or afterwards. (Sec. 24)

A marine policy must specify:

1. The name of the assured, or of some person who effects the insurance on his behalf;
2. The subject-matter insured and the risk insured against;
3. The voyage, or period of time, or both, as the case may be, covered by the insurance;
4. The sum or sums insured;
5. The name or names of the insurer or insurers. (Sec. 25)

A marine policy must be signed by or on behalf of the insurer. Where a policy is subscribed by or on behalf of two or more insurers, each subscription, unless the contrary be expressed, constitutes a distinct contract with the assured. (Sec. 26)

The subject matter insured must be designated in a marine policy with reasonable certainty. The nature and extent of the interest of the assured in the subject-matter insured need not be specified in the policy. (Sec. 28)

TYPES OF MARINE POLICIES

Different classes of policies are issued in marine insurance and they are as follows:

1. *Voyage Policy* [Sec. 27 (1)]
   Voyage policy is a policy of marine insurance against losses incurred during a voyage specified in the policy. The policy may cover the risk 'from a port' or 'at and from a port'. If the policy is 'from a port' it covers the risk only when the ship sails from a particular port. But a policy "at and from a port" protects the subject matter insured both while the ship is at the port of departure and also from the time of the sailing of the ship on voyage.
2. *Time Policy* [Sec. 27 (1)]
   If the contract is to insure the subject-matter for a definite period of time the policy is called a 'time policy'. Generally a time policy cannot be for a period more than a year. The time policy will cover all the risks from the perils of the sea for a stated period of time.
3. *Mixed Policy* (Voyage-cum-time policy) [Sec. 27 (1)]
   This policy is a combination of voyage and time policies and is also known as 'voyage-cum-time policy'. It seeks to insure the subject-matter (for egs. the ship) during a particular voyage for a specified period of time. For example, a ship may be insured for a voyage between Bombay to London for a period of 10 months under a mixed policy.
4. *Valued Policy* (Sec. 29)
   A valued policy is a policy which specifies the agreed value of the subject matter insured. As between the insurer and the assured, the valuation is conclusive, unless there is fraud. Unless the policy otherwise provides, the value fixed by the policy is not conclusive for the purpose of determining whether there has been a constructive total loss.
5. *Unvalued Policy* (Sec. 30)
   Reverse to the valued policy, this policy does not specify the value of the subject matter insured. In such a case, the value of loss is ascertained subsequently, subject to the sum assured, in case when loss occurs.
6. *Floating Policy:* (Sec. 31)
   A floating policy is a policy which describes the insurance in general terms, and leaves the name or names of the ship or ships and other particulars to be defined by subsequent declaration.
   The subsequent declaration or declarations may be made by endorsement on the policy, or in other customary manner.
   Unless the policy otherwise provides, the declarations must be made in the order of dispatch or shipment. They must, in the case of goods, comprise all consignments within the terms of the policy, and the value of the goods or other property must be honestly stated, but an omission or erroneous declaration be rectified even after loss or arrival, provided the omission or declaration was made in good faith.
   Unless the policy otherwise provides, where a declaration of value is not made until after notice of loss or arrival, the policy must be treated as an unvalued policy as regards the subject-matter of that declaration.
7. *Wagering Policy or Honour Policy*

   It is the policy which is issued when the assured has no interest in the subject-matter of insurance. And at the time of contract of insurance, he has no expectation of acquiring any interest in the subject-matter. Thus, a policy containing the words as 'Policy Proof of Interest' (P.P.I.). 'Interest or No Interest' or 'Without Benefit of Salvage to the Insurer' or any other words to that effect, is a wagering policy. Wagering policy is void and cannot be enforced in a Court of Law. Such policies are void, even then, these continue to be common.

In such policies, the existence of insurable interest is not to be proved at the time of loss. Such policies are, no doubt, void, but the insurer meets his liability only as a consideration for honour.

FORM OF MARINE POLICY

Sec. 24 states that a contract of marine insurance must be embodied in a marine policy so as to be admissible in evidence. Its form has been specified in the schedule to the Marine Insurance Act 1963.

The old form of policy is used even to-day. In order to make the standard policy suitable for the different types of contracts, suitable conditions are added to the policy. The conditions are inserted in the policy in the form of clauses. The clause took the standard form with special meanings. They may be pertaining to hull, cargo and freight.

Construction of Marine Policy

Various terms and clauses are used in a marine policy. Some special clauses usually found in marine policy are explained below:

(1) *Lost or not lost clause:* Sometimes, the ship is on a voyage and the parties do not know whether it is still in existence. In such cases, the subject-matter can be insured by incorporating 'lost or not lost' clause in the marine policy. The policy containing this clause is valid even if the goods have already been lost prior to the taking of the policy. And thus, the assured can recover the amount under the policy irrespective of the fact that the goods have already lost prior to the date of policy. However, the assured must observe good faith at the time of taking the policy, that is, he must not be aware of the loss.

(2) *From Clause:* Under this clause, the risk insured commences when the ship starts for its voyage and not while standing in the port.

(3) *At and From Clause:* As per this clause the risk starts when the contract is finalised. Thus, it covers the loss even when the ship is standing in the port. However, the risk will not start, if the ship is not in safety and will start only when it comes into safety.

(4) *F.P.A. Clause:* The term F.P.A. means 'Free from Particular Average'. A policy may exempt the insurer from liability from particular average. The term 'particular average' means partial loss of the subject-matter insured. Sometimes F.A.A., that is, 'free from all average' clause is also there in the marine policy.

(5) *Touch and Stay Clause:* It accords liberty to the vessel to touch and stay at any port, or place whatsoever. In absence of the clause, the liberty to touch and stay at any port or place whatsoever does not authorise the ship to depart from the course of her voyage from the port of departure to the port of destination. Where several ports are specified, the ship may touch or stay at all or any of them.

(6) *Running Down Clause* (Collision Clause): It provides that the underwriter agrees to take upon the liability of the owner of the ship for damage done by his vessel to another vessel on collision to the extent of three-fourths of such liability. The under-writer will be responsible only when this clause is added in the policy. The assured himself has to bear one-fourth of the loss so that he may exercise greater care in the navigation of the vessel.

(7) *Sue and Labour Clause:* Sometimes, the marine policy contains the 'sue and Labour' clause. This clause enables the insurer and the assured to work together with a view to preserve the insured property after the accident. The assured is entitled to recover all expenses incurred by him in mitigation of loss after the casualty has occurred. However, the expenses incurred for averting the occurrence of the peril are not recoverable under this clause.

(8) *The 'Inchmaree' Clause:* Ordinarily the insurer under a marine insurance policy is liable only for loss or damage caused by a sea-peril. The word 'Inchmaree' has been derived from a ship named 'Inchmaree'. And this clause came to be introduced in consequence of the decision of the case in which the ship Inchmaree was involved. *Thames & Mersey Marine Insurance Co. Vs. Hamilton Fraser & Co.* (1887)

Example: The ship 'Inchmaree' was lying at anchor at port and her donkey engine was pumping water into the boilers. The engineer in charge was negligent and kept a valve of the engine closed, whereas it should have been kept open. As a result, water forced into the engine and the pump was broken. The ship-owner claimed compensation from the insurer. It was held that the loss was not due to a sea-peril and so the insurer was not liable. This clause enables the assured to recover the losses caused due to the negligence of the masters, engineers and by bursting of the boilers etc. Thus clause specifically covers the losses caused by:

(*a*) negligence of the master, mariners, engineers, crew etc. during loading and unloading.
(*b*) explosions, bursting of boilers, breakage of shaft etc.
(*c*) latent defect in any machinery.

(9) *All Other Perils Clause:* This clause in marine policy means that the losses arising from other perils which are similar in kind to the perils specifically mentioned in the policy, are also covered by the policy.

(10) *Memorandum or N.B. Clause:* The memorandum or the N.B. clause exempts insurer from liability for partial losses in the case of perishable goods. Lloyd's policy it is usually stated that the insurer will not be liable for losses to goods like sugar, hemp, etc. unless the loss is 5% or more of the value of the goods.

(11) *Barratry Clause:* It includes every wrongful act willfully committed by the master or crew in contravention of their duties, thereby causing prejudice to the owner or charterer and is covered by the policy. Examples of barratry are: wrongfully scuttling a ship, intentionally running her on shore, setting fire to her etc.

INSURABLE INTEREST

Section 7 of the Act defines insurable interest as follows:

"1. Subject to the provisions of the Act, every person has an insurable interest who is interested in marine adventure". Sec. 7 (1)

"2. In particular a person is interested in a marine adventure where he stands in any legal or equitable relation to the adventure or to any insurable property at risk therein, in consequence of which he may benefit by the safety or due arrival of insurable property, or may be prejudiced by its loss, or by damage thereto, or by detention thereof, or may incur liability in respect thereof." Sec. 7(2)

The assured must have "insurable interest" in the subject-matter of the insurance, otherwise the contract of insurance will be a wagering agreement. A person is said to have an insurable interest in the subject-matter when he stands in any legal or equitable relation to the subject-matter in such a way that he may benefit by the safety or due arrival of insurable property, or may be prejudiced by its loss, damage or detention or may incur liability in respect thereof.

Further Section 8 (1) states that "the assured must be interested in the subject matter insured at the time of the loss, though he need not be interested when the insurance is affected."

According to the provisions of the Marine Insurance Act 1963, the following interests are insurable:

1. "The insurer under a contract of marine insurance has an insurable interest in his risk. He may re-insure the said risk to the extent of his interest." (Sec. 11)
2. "The lender of money on bottomry or respondentia bond has an insurable interest in respect of the loan." (Sec. 12)
3. "The master or any member of the crew of a ship has an insurable interest of their wages." (Sec. 13)
4. "In the case of advance freight, the person advancing the freight has an insurable interest, in so far as such freight not repayable in case of loss." (Sec. 14)
5. "The assured has an insurable interest in the charges of any insurance which he may effect." (See. 15)
6. Sec. 16(1) and (2) states that in case of mortgage of the subject matter:
   1. The mortgagor has an insurable interest to the extent of the full value of the property.
   2. The mortgagee has an insurable interest for the sum due or to be due under the mortgage.
7. "A partial interest of any nature is insurable." (Sec. 10)
8. "The owner of insurable property has an insurable interest in respect of the full value thereof, notwithstanding that some third person may have agreed, or be liable to indemnify him in case of loss." (Sec. 16 (3))
9. "A defeasible interest is insurable, as also a contingent interest is insurable." The buyer has an insurable interest in the goods, though he might reject them while selecting the goods as per his choice. (Sec. 9 (1))

INSURABLE VALUE

Insurable value must not be confused with insurable interest. Insurable value is quite different from insurable interest. Section 18 of the Act provides that subject to any express provision of valuation in the policy, the insurable value of the subject matter insured must be ascertained as follows:

1. *Ship:* In insurance on ship, the insurable value at the commencement of risk; of the ship, including her outfit, machinery, fuels, and engine stores etc., plus the charges of insurance upon the whole.
2. *Freight:* In insurance on freight, whether paid in advance or otherwise, the insurable value is the gross amount of the freight at the risk of the assured plus the charges of insurance.
3. *Goods:* In insurance on goods or merchandise, the insurable value is the prime cost of the property insured, plus the expenses of and incidental to shipping and charges of insurance upon the whole.
4. *Any other subject-matter:* In insurance on any other subject-matter, the insurable value is the amount at the risk of the assured when the policy attaches plus the charges of insurance.

WARRANTIES

Though the warranties in marine insurance contracts are different from the warranties in the contracts of sale of goods, the effect of their non-compliance is almost the same. At the time of entering into contract, there are certain undertakings of assurances about the existence or non-existence of certain facts. Warranties are the statements according to which insured promises to do or not to do a particular thing, or to fulfil or not to fulfil a certain condition. A warranty in marine insurance is the same as a condition in any contract and its breach will give right to the party aggrieved to avoid the contract. Thus, the assurances or conditions are known as warranties and form a part of the contract of marine insurance.

According to Sec. 35 (1), a warranty is an undertaking by the assured that some particular thing shall or shall not be done, or that some condition shall be fulfilled, or that a particular state of facts does or does not exist.

Warranty is used to denote certain conditions which are considered essential to the contract of insurance. A warranty is a condition collateral to the contract, breach of which makes the contract void. It must be strictly complied. It is immaterial for what purpose it was introduced and whether it is material to the risk or not.

A warranty in a marine insurance contract may be express or implied. Express warranties are those which are expressly mentioned in the policy of insurance or incorporated in some document referred to in the policy. Implied warranties are stipulations, which are by law, custom or general agreement assumed to be included in the insurance contract although not mentioned in the policy. Thus, warranties may be of the following two types:

(*A*) Express Warranties
(*B*) Implied Warranties

(*A*) *Express Warranties:* (Sec. 37) : Warranties which are expressly stated in the contract of marine insurance are 'express warranties'. They must be included or written upon the policy, or must be contained in some document attached to the policy. Express warranties may be in any form of words from which the intention to warrant is to be informed.

There is no limits to the variety of express warranties. The parties may include any number of express warranties in a marine policy. The following are the express warranties which are commonly included in marine policies:

1. The ship is fit and sea-worthy.
2. The ship will sail on a specified day and proceed to the destination without unnecessary deviation.
3. The ship is neutral and will remain so during the voyage.
4. The ship departs with convoy.
5. The cargo of the ship remains neutral during the voyage.
6. The ship does not enter risky localities or prohibited areas.

There may be other stipulations expressly mentioned.

(*B*) *Implied Warranties:* An implied warranty is one which though not in writing but is assumed to have been included in the marine policy by law, usage, custom, mutual agreements etc. Implied warranties are conditions which are not specifically included in the policy. Such warranties are:

1. *Seaworthiness of the ship:* The ship to be used for voyage must have seaworthiness. It includes:
   (*a*) In a marine policy it is an implied warranty that at the commencement of the voyage, the ship is seaworthy for the purpose of the particular adventure insured. [Sec. 41 (1)]
   (*b*) A ship is deemed seaworthy, when it is reasonably fit in all respects to encounter the ordinary perils of the sea or the adventure insured. It includes that; [Sec. 41 (4)]
      (*i*) the ship is properly constructed;
      (*ii*) it has sufficient and efficient crew and the master;
      (*iii*) its machinery is in perfect working order;
      (*iv*) it is provided with all necessaries of voyage;
      (*v*) it is not over-loaded or badly loaded;
      (*vi*) it is sound as regards its hull;
      (*vii*) it is properly stowed.

(*c*) The warranty of seaworthiness attaches only upto the time of the sailing of the ship. But where the voyage is to be performed in stages, the ship must be seaworthy at the commencement of each stage. [Sec. 41 (3)]

(*d*) Where the marine policy attaches, while the ship is in port, there is an implied warranty that she shall, at the commencement of the risk, be reasonably fit to encounter the ordinary perils of the port. [(Sec. 41 (2)]

(*e*) Where the marine policy is for goods or other movables, there is an implied warranty, that the ship is reasonably fit to carry the goods or other movables to the destination.

2. *Legality of Voyage* (Sec. 43): There is an implied warranty that "the adventure insured is lawful. So far as the assured can control the matter, the adventure shall be carried out in a lawful manner."

3. *Non-deviation:* There is an implied warranty that the ship shall not deviate from its prescribed or usual customary route. If it does, the insurer shall not be liable unless the deviation is lawfully excused.

(4) *No delay in voyage* (Sec. 50): This warranty applies to voyage policies. This warranty implied that there should be no unjustified delay in prosecuting the voyage.

Effects of Breach of warranty: A warranty is a condition which must be exactly complied with, whether it is material to the risk or not. If it be not so complied with, then, subject to any express provision in the policy, the insurer is discharged from the liability as from the date of the breach of warranty, but without prejudice to any liability incurred by him before that date. (Sec. 35 (3)

When Breach of warranty is excused: (Sec. 36): Sec. 36 provides that the following cases breach of warranty is excused:

(*i*) When by reason of change of circumstances, the warranty ceases to be applicable.

(*ii*) When compliance with the warranty is rendered unlawful, by any subsequent change of law.

(*iii*) When the insurer waives the breach.

DISCLOSURE AND REPRESENTATION

"A contract of marine insurance is a contract based upon the utmost good faith and if the utmost good faith is not observed by either party, the contract may be avoided by the other party." (Sec. 19). Thus a contract of marine insurance is a contract of uberrimae fidei.

Duty of Disclosure: Section 20 provides that the assured must disclose to the insurer every material circumstance which is known to the assured. The assured is deemed to know every circumstance which in the ordinary course of business ought to be known to him. The term "circumstance" includes any communication made to or information received by the assured. If the assured fails to make such disclosure the insurer may avoid the contract.

Material Circumstance: Every circumstance is material which would influence the judgement of a prudent insurer in fixing the premium, or determining whether he will take the risk.

In the absence or enquiry the following circumstance need not be disclosed: [Sec.20 (3)]

(*a*) any circumstance which diminishes the risk;

(*b*) any circumstance which is known or presumed to be known to the insurer. The insurer is presumed to know matters of common notoriety or knowledge, and matters which an insurer in the ordinary course of his business as such, ought to know.

(*c*) any circumstance as to which information is waived by the insurer;

(*d*) any circumstance which is superfluous to disclose by reason of any express or implied warranty.

Agent's duty: The agent effecting insurance must also disclose all material circumstance known to him. He need not disclose circumstances which the assured is not bound to disclose. (Sec. 21)

Representations: (Sec. 22) Every material representation made by the assured or his agent to the insurer during the negotiations for the contract, and before the contract, is concluded, must be true. If it be untrue, the insurer may avoid the contract.

A representation is material which would influence the judgement of a prudent insurer in fixing the premium, or determining whether he will take the risk.

A representation may be either as to a matter of fact or as to a matter of expectation of belief.

A representation as to a matter of fact is true, if it be substantially correct, that is to say, if the difference between what is represented and what is actually correct would not be considered material by a prudent insurer. A representation as to a matter of expectation or belief is true if it be made in good faith.

A representation may be withdrawn or corrected before the contract is concluded. Whether a particular representation be material or not is, in each case, a question of fact.

Assignment of Marine Policy (Sections 17, 52 and 53)

Assignment of policy means the passing of the rights and liabilities of the assured under the policy. The procedure and legal provisions for a valid assignment of a marine policy are contained in the sections 17, 52 and 53 of Marine Insurance Act. They are as follows:

1. A marine policy may be transferred by assignment unless such transfer is prohibited by the policy.
2. The assignment of a policy can be made by an endorsement on the policy itself or by any other customary manner.
3. The assignment may be done either before or after the loss occurred.
4. The consent of the under-writer is not necessary for the validity of the assignment, unless the policy imposes such condition.
5. The assignor must possess an insurable interest in the subject-matter insured at the time of assignment. An assured who has parted with or lost his interest in the subject-matter insured cannot make a valid assignment.
6. The assignee must have acquired some interest in the subject-matter insured either as buyer or mortgagee, because for a valid claim against the insurer, the assignee must have an insurable interest in the property insured at the time of loss, for otherwise he cannot be indemnified.

On a valid assignment, the assignee becomes entitled to all the benefits under the policy and he can file a suit against the underwriter on the policy, in his own name.

Premium (Sections 54, 82, 83 and 84)

"Unless otherwise agreed, the duty of the assured or his agent to pay the premium, and the duty of the insurer to issue the policy to the assured or his agent, are concurrent conditions, and the insurer is not bound to issue the policy until payment or tender of the premium." (Sec. 54)

Return of Premium: Sections 82 - 84 of the Marine Insurance Act lays down the circumstances for the return of premium received. They are:

1. Where the policy contains a stipulation for the return of the premium on the happening of a certain event and that event happens. [Sec. 83]
2. Where the consideration for the payment of the premium totally fails and there has been no fraud or illegality on the part of the assured or his agents. [Sec. 84(1)]
3. Where the policy is void or is avoided by the insurer as from the commencement of the risk, provided there has been no fraud or illegality on the part of the assured. [Sec. 84 (3) (*a*)]

4. Where the subject-matter insured, or part thereof, has never been imperilled; but where the subject-matter has been insured 'lost or not lost'; and has arrived in safely at the time when the contract is concluded, the premium is not returnable unless, at such time, the insurer knew of the safe arrival. [Sec. 84(3) (*b*)]
5. Where the assured has no insurable interest throughout currency of the risk. [Sec. 84 (3) (*c*)]

Proportionate part of the premium is returnable in the following cases:

1. Where the policy contains a stipulation for the return of a proportionate part of the premium on the happening of certain event and that event happens. (Sec. 83)
2. Where the consideration for the payment of the premium is apportionable and there is a total failure of any apportionable part of the consideration. (Sec. 84)
3. Where the assured has over-insured under an unvalued policy. [Sec. 84 (3) (*e*)]
4. Where the assured has over-insured by double insurance. [Sec. 84 (3)(*f*)]

VOYAGE

The voyage to be performed by a ship must be properly described and the ship must follow the specified course. Where it is not specified, it must follow the usual and customary course. Sec. 45 states that "Where the place of departure is specified by the policy, and the ship instead of sailing from that place sails from any other place, the risk does not attach." Further Sec. 46 states that "Where the destination is specified in the policy, and the ship, instead of sailing for that destination, sails for any other destination, the risk does not attach."

Deviation of voyage: The deviation of voyage takes place when the ship changes her route of voyage. In case of deviation of voyage, there is neither a change in the port of departure nor in the port of destination.

Deviation occurs under the following circumstances:

1. "Where the course of the voyage is specifically designated by the policy, and that course is departed from:" [Sec. 48 (2) (*a*)]
2. "Where the course of the voyage is not specifically designated by the policy, but the usual and customary course is departed from;" [Sec. 48 (2) (*b*)]
3. Where there are several ports of discharge, the ship must proceed to them in the order designated by the policy; if she does not, there is deviation; [Sec. 49 (1)]
4. "Where the policy only specifies ports of discharge within a given area, the ports must be visited in the geographical order; if the ship does not do so, without any sufficient reason, there is deviation. [Sec. 49 (2)]

Change of voyage: "Where, after the commencement of the risk, the destination of the ship is voluntarily changed from the destination contemplated by the policy, there is said to be change of voyage." [Sec. 47 (1)]

"Unless the policy otherwise provides, where there is a change of voyage, the insurer is discharged from liability as from the time of change, that is to say, as from the time when the determination to change is manifested; and it is immaterial that the ship may not in fact have left course of voyage contemplated by the policy when the loss occurs." [Sec. 47 (2)]

Excuse for Deviation or Delay: Deviation or delay is excused under the following circumstances:

(*a*) where authorised by any special term in the policy; or
(*b*) where caused by circumstances beyond the control of the master and his employer; or
(*c*) where reasonably necessary in order to comply with an express or implied warranty; or
(*d*) where reasonably necessary for the safety of the ship or subject-matter insured; or

(*e*) for the purpose of saving human life or aiding a ship in distress where human life may be in danger; or

(*f*) where reasonably necessary for the purpose of obtaining medical or surgical aid for any person on board the ship; or

(*g*) where caused by the barratrous conduct of the master or crew, if barratry be one of the perils insured against." [Sec. 51 (1)]

"When the cause excusing the deviation or delay ceases to operate the ship must resume her course, and prosecute her voyage with reasonable despatch." [Sec. 51 (2)]

MARINE LOSSES

Losses in marine insurance business are the result of various perils. Only such losses can be recovered by the assured which are caused by the peril insured against and such peril must be the proximate cause of the loss. If the loss takes place on account of any of the perils insured against with the insurer, the insurer will be liable for it and shall have to make good the losses to the assured. The doctrine of Causa Proxima is to be applied while calculating the amount of loss.

Sec. 55 (1) lays down that "unless the policy otherwise provides, the insurer is liable for any loss proximately caused by a peril insured against, but, subject to aforesaid, he is not liable for any loss which is not proximately caused by a peril insured against."

(*a*) "The insurer is not liable for any loss attributable to the *wilful misconduct of the assured*, but, unless the policy otherwise provides, he is liable for any loss proximately caused by a peril insured against even though the loss would not have happened but for misconduct or negligence of the master or crew." [Sec. 55 (2) (*a*)]

(*b*) "unless the policy otherwise provides, the insurer on ship or goods is not liable for any loss proximately caused *by delay*, although the delay be caused by a peril insured against". [Sec. 55 (2) (*b*)]

(*c*) "unless the policy otherwise provides, the insurer is not liable for *ordinary wear and tear*, ordinary leakage and breakage, *inherent vice* or nature of the subject-matter insured, or for any loss proximately caused by rats or vermin, or for any injury to machinery not proximately caused by the marine perils." [Sec. 55 (2) (*c*)]

Kinds of Losses: Broadly speaking, marine losses may be of two types: (1) Total Loss and (2) Partial Loss. [Sec. 56 (1)]

Total Loss: When the subject-matter of insurance,— ship, cargo, freight etc., is totally lost, it is known as 'total loss'. Total Loss may be either (*a*) Actual Total Loss, or (*b*) Constructive Total Loss. (Sec. 56 (2)

(*a*) *Actual Total Loss:* Actual total loss is defined in Sec. 57 (1). It defines "Where the subject-matter insured is destroyed, or so damaged as to cease to be a thing of the kind insured, or where the assured is irretrievably deprived thereof, there is an actual total loss." As per this section, the actual total loss occurs in any one of the following ways:

1. When the subject matter insured is totally destroyed or reduced ashes; or
2. When the subject-matter insured is so damaged that it has completely changed its nature; for example, cement changed into stone by sea-water; or
3. When the assured is deprived of the subject-matter, for example, ship captured by enemies; or
4. When the ship is missing, and after a reasonable time no news of her has been received.

In each of these cases, the underwriter must pay the full insured sum or the actual loss, whichever is lesser, provided that the cause of the loss was one of the perils insured against.

Sec. 57 (2) further states, "In the case of an actual total loss no notice of abandonment need be given to the insurer."

(*b*) *Constructive Total Loss*: Section 60 (1) states "Subject to any express provision in the policy, there is a constructive total loss where the subject-matter insured is reasonably *abandoned* on account of its actual total loss appearing to be unavoidable, or because it could not be preserved from actual total loss without an expenditure which would exceed its value when the expenditure has been incurred." This definition is the general definition of the term 'constructive total loss.

Further Sec. 60 (2) states, "In particular, there is a constructive total loss in the following cases:

1. Where the insured is deprived of the possession of his ship or goods and the cost of recovering the ship or goods would exceed their value when recovered. or
2. Where the ship is so damaged by a peril insured against, that the cost of repairs would exceed the value of the ship if repaired, or
3. In case of damage to goods, the cost of their repairs and forwarding charges will exceed their value.

It is worth-noting the observations of *Justice Maul in Moss Vs. Smith* (1845) in connection with the constructive total loss: "A man may be said to have lost a shilling when he has dropped it into deep water, though it might be possible by some very expensive contrivance to recover it. The shilling exists and it would be recovered at a price, but what man would be foolish enough to spend, say two shillings in order to recover one? The safer course would be to abandon the shilling in the deep water, in which case that shilling would be a constructive total loss."

Partial Loss: Partial loss occurs when the subject-matter of insurance is partially lost. Partial loss may be either (*a*) General Average Loss, or (*b*) Particular Average Loss.

General Average Loss

"A general average loss is a loss caused by or directly consequential on a general average act. It includes a general average expenditure as well as a general average sacrifice." Sec. 66 (1)

Further, Sec. 66 (2) states that "There is a general average act where any extraordinary sacrifice or expenditure is voluntarily and reasonably made or incurred in time of peril for the purpose of preserving the property imperilled in common adventure."

Sec. 66 (3) further states, "Where there is a general average loss, the party on whom it falls is entitled, subject to the conditions imposed by maritime law, to a rateable contribution from other parties interested, and such contribution is called a general average contribution."

Examples of general average loss;

1. Throwing a part of cargo to save the ship and remaining cargo.
2. Damage caused by water used in extinguishing fire in a ship.
3. Money paid to pirates in order to save ship and cargo etc.

The following are the essential features of General Average Loss:

1. The peril must actually exist.
2. The sacrifice or expenditure must be voluntary, and must have been made to avoid a real danger which is common to all interests.
3. Some extraordinary sacrifice or expenditure must be made or incurred.
4. The object of sacrifice or expenditure must be to preserve the property of the common adventure.
5. The danger must be common to all who are called upon to contribute.

Particular Average Loss

"A particular average loss is a partial loss of the subject-matter insured, caused by a peril insured against, and which is not a general average loss." [Sec. 64 (1)]

"Expenses incurred by or on behalf of the assured for the safety or preservation of the subject-matter insured, other than general average and salvage charges are called particular charges. Particular charges are not included in particular average [Sec. 64 (2)]

Wherever damage is caused by accident or otherwise to property in a marine adventure by the perils of the sea and the damage is not one suffered for general benefit, it is called a particular average loss.

It must comply with the following conditions:

1. Only a particular subject-matter must have been destroyed or damaged.
2. The loss must be accidental and not intentional.
3. The loss must be caused by a peril insured against.
4. It must concern solely the owner of the goods and must not be suffered for the general safety of the ship or cargo.
5. The question of contribution from other parties interested in adventure should not arise.

ABANDONMENT

'Abandonment' means surrendering of the insured property, alongwith all proprietary rights, to the insurance company, in order to claim total loss for the same. Where the assured treats the loss as an actual total loss, he must give notice of abandonment to the insurance company. There is no special form of notice of abandonment but it must be worded as to give explicit intimation to the insurer that the assured abandons unconditionally to the underwriter his whole interest in the subject-matter insured. It is usual for the word "abandon" to be used in the notice.

***Notice of Abandonment* (Sec. 62)**

1. "Subject to the provisions of this section, where the assured elects to abandon the subject-matter insured to the insurer, he must give notice of abandonment. If he fails to do so the loss can only be treated as a partial loss."
2. "Notice of abandonment may be given in writing, or by word of mouth, or partly in writing and partly by word of mouth, and may be given in any terms which indicate the intention of the assured to abandon his insured interest in the subject-matter issued unconditionally to the insurer."
3. "Notice of abandonment must be given with reasonable diligence after the receipt of reliable information of the loss, but where the information is of a doubtful character the assured is entitled to a reasonable time to make enquiry."
4. "Where notice of abandonment is properly given, the rights of the assured are not prejudiced by the fact that the insurer refuses to accept the abandonment."
5. "The acceptance of an abandonment may be either express or implied from the conduct of the insurer. The mere silence of the insurer after notice is not an acceptance."
6. "Where notice of abandonment is accepted the abandonment is irrevocable. The acceptance of the notice conclusively admits liability for the loss and the sufficiency of the notice."
7. "Notice of abandonment is unnecessary where at the time when the assured receives information of the loss, there would be no possibility of benefit of the insurer if notice were given to him."
8. "Notice of abandonment may be waived by the insurer."
9. "Where an insurer has reinsured his risk, no notice of abandonment need be given by him."

***Effect of Abandonment*: (Sec. 63)**

1. "Where there is a valid abandonment the insurer is entitled to take over the interest of the assured in whatever may remain of the subject-matter insured and all proprietary rights incidental thereto."

2. "Upon the abandonment of a ship, the insurer thereof is entitled to any freight in course of being earned, and which is earned by her subsequent to the casualty causing the loss, less the expenses of earning it incurred after the casualty, and where the ship is carrying the owner's goods, the insurer is entitled to a reasonable remuneration for the carriage of them subsequent to the casualty causing the loss."

RIGHTS OF INSURER ON PAYMENT

Rights of Subrogation : Sec. 79 (1) "Where the insurer pays for a total loss, either of the whole, or in the case of goods of any apportionable part, of the subject-matter insured, he thereupon becomes entitled to take over the interest of the assured in whatever may remain of the subject-matter so paid for, and he is thereby subrogated to all the rights and remedies of the assured in and in respect of that subject-matter as from the time of the casualty causing the loss."

Sec. 79 (2) "Subject to the foregoing provisions, where the insurer pays for a partial loss, he acquires no title to the subject-matter insured, or such part of it as may remain, but he is thereupon subrogated to all rights and remedies of the assured in and in respect of the subject-matter insured as from the time of the casualty causing the loss, in so far as the assured has been indemnified, according to this Act, by such payment for the loss."

Right of Contribution: Sec. 80 (1) states, "Where the assured is over-insured by double insurance, each insurer is bound, as between himself and the other insurers, to contribute rateably to the loss in proportion to the amount for which he is liable under his contract."

Sec. 80 (2) states, "If any insurer pays more than his proportion of the loss, he is entitled to maintain a suit for contribution against the other insurers, and is entitled to the like remedies as a surety who has paid more than his proportion of the debt."

Effect of Under-insurance: Sec. 81 states, "Where the assured is insured for an amount less than the insurable value, or, in the case of a valued policy, for an amount less than the policy valuation, he is deemed to be his own insurer in respect of the uninsured balance."

THEORETICAL QUESTIONS

1. Define contract of Insurance. What is its nature?

2. What are the essentials of a Marine Policy? State the important terms and clauses of a Marine Policy. (*B.Com. Madras*)

3. Discuss in brief the different types of Marine Policy. (*B.Com. Bombay*)

4. What do you understand by assignment of Marine Policy? State legal provisions relating to assignment. (*B.Com. MS*)

5. Define the term 'warranty' as used in Marine Insurance. What are the different type of warranties? Discuss in detail the implied warranties in a contract of Marine Insurance. (*B.Com., M.Com Kerala*)

6. What is the effect of breach of warranty in marine insurance? State the circumstances in which breach of warranty is excused. (*M.Com. M.S.*)

7. Define the term 'voyage'. What do you understand by "change of voyage" and "deviation of voyage".

8. Discuss different types of losses in Marine Insurance Policy. (*B.Com. Bombay*)

9. What do you understand by 'abandonment' in Marine Insurance? What are the legal rules regarding the notice of abandonment ?

10. What are the rights of an insurer on payment of indemnity under a Marine Policy? (*B.Com. Kerala*)

I

APPENDIX

The Indian Contract Act

(Act. No. IX of 1872)

[*25th April, 1872*]

Whereas it is expedient to define and amend certain parts of the law relating to contracts.

It is hereby enacted as follows :

PRELIMINARY

1. Short title. This Act may be called the Indian Contract Act. 1872.

Extent, Commencement. It extends to the whole of India except the State of Jammu and Kashmir; and it shall come into force on the first day of September, 1872.

Savings. Nothing herein contained shall affect the provisions of any Statute, Act or Regulation, not hereby expressly repealed, nor any usage or custom of trade, nor any incident of any contact, not inconsistent with the provisions of this act.

2. Interpretation clause. In this Act the following words and expressions are used in the following senses, unless a contrary intention appears from the context :

(*a*) "*Proposal*". When one person signifies to another his willingness to do or to abstain from doing anything, with a view to obtaining the assent of that other to such act or abstinence, he is said to make a proposal;

(*b*) "*Promise*". When the person to whom the proposal is made, signifies his assent thereto, the proposal is said to be accepted. A proposal, when accepted, becomes a promise;

(*c*) "*Promisor and promisee*". The person making the proposal is called the "*promisor*", and the person accepting the proposal is called the "*promisee*";

(*d*) "*Consideration*". When at the desire of the promisor, the promisee or any other person has done or abstained from doing, or does or abstains from doing, or promises to do or to abstain from doing something, such act or abstinence or promise is called a *consideration* for the promise;

(*e*) "*Agreement*". Every promise and every set of promises forming the consideration for each other, is an *agreement*;

(*f*) "*Reciprocal Promises*". Promises which form the consideration or part of the consideration for each other are called *reciprocal promises*;

(*g*) "*Void agreement*". An agreement not enforceable by law is said to be void;

(*h*) "*Contract*". An agreement enforceable by law is a *contract*;

(*i*) "*Voidable contract*". An agreement which is enforceable by law at the option of one or more of the parties thereto, but not at the option of the other or others, is a *voidable contract*;

(*j*) "*Void contract*". A contract which ceases to be enforceable by law becomes void when it ceases to be enforceable.

CHAPTER 1

Of The Communication, Acceptance and Revocation of Proposals

3. Communication, acceptance and revocation of proposals. The communication of proposals, the acceptance of proposals, and the revocation of proposals, and acceptances, respectively, are deemed to be made by any act or omission of the party proposing, accepting or revoking, by which he intends to communicate such proposal, acceptance or revocation, or which has the effect of communicating it.

4. Communication when complete. The communication of a proposal is complete when it comes to the knowledge of the person to whom it is made.

The communication of an acceptance is complete,

as against the proposer, when it is put in a course of transmission to him, so as to be out of the power of acceptor;

as against the acceptor, when it comes to the knowledge of the proposer.

The communication of a revocation is complete,

as against the person who makes it, when it is put into a course of transmission to the person to whom it is made, so as to be out of the power of the person who makes it;

as against the person to whom it is made, when it comes to his knowledge.

ILLUSTRATIONS

(*a*) *A* proposes, by letter, to sell a house to *B* at a certain price. The communication of the proposal is complete when *B* receives the letter.

(*b*) *B* accepts *A*'s proposal by a letter sent by post. The communication of the acceptance is complete,—

as against *A*, when the letter is posted;

as against *B*, when the letter is received by *A*.

(*c*) *A* revokes his proposal by telegram. The revocation is complete as against *A* when the telegram is despatched. It is complete as against *B* when *B* receives it.

B revokes his acceptance by telegram, *B*'s revocation is complete as against *B* when the telegram is despatched, and as against *A* when it reaches him.

5. Revocation of proposals and acceptance. A proposal may be revoked at any time before the communication of its acceptance is complete as against the proposer, but not afterwards.

An acceptance may be revoked at any time before the communication of its acceptance is complete as against the acceptor, but not afterwards.

ILLUSTRATION

A proposes, by a letter sent by post, to sell his house to B.

B accepts the proposal by a letter sent by post.

A may revoke his proposal at any time before or at the moment when *B* posts his letter of acceptance, but not afterwards.

B may revoke his acceptance at any time before or at the moment when the letter communicating it reaches *A*, but not afterwards.

6. Revocation how made. A proposal is revoked :

(1) by the communication of notice of revocation by the proposer to the other party;

(2) by the lapse of the time prescribed in such proposal for its acceptance, or, if no time is so prescribed, by the lapse of a reasonable time, without communication of the acceptance;

(3) by the failure of the acceptor to fulfil a condition precedent to acceptance; or

(4) by the death or insanity of the proposer, if the fact of his death or insanity comes to the knowledge of the acceptor before acceptance.

7. Acceptance must be absolute. In order to convert a proposal into a promise, the acceptance must:

(1) be absolute and unqualified;

(2) be expressed in some usual and reasonable manner, unless the proposal prescribes the manner in which it is to be accepted. If the proposal prescribes a manner in which it is to be accepted, and the acceptance is not made in such manner, the proposer may, within a reasonable time after the acceptance is communicated to him, insist that his proposal shall be accepted in the prescribed manner, and not otherwise; but if he fails to do so, he accepts the acceptance.

NOTES

Acceptance of offer to be absolute and unqualified. When certain quantity of a thing was offered to be sold but the other party agrees to buy a lesser quantity of the thing offered, the consent to buy a lesser quantity is neither absolute nor unqualified or unconditional hence no valid acceptance to offer. *M/s Suraj Besan & Rice Mills v. Food Corporation of India.* AIR 1988, Delhi 224.

Duration for acceptance. In absence of fixed duration for the acceptance of offer, acceptance has to be communicated within a reasonable time. *Shree Jaya Mahal Co-operative Housing Society Ltd. v. M/s Zenith Chemical Works Pvt. Ltd.* AIR 1991 Bombay 211.

8. Acceptance by Performing conditions, or receiving consideration. Performance of the conditions of a proposal or the acceptance of any consideration for a reciprocal promise which may be offered with a proposal, is an acceptance of the proposal.

9. Promise, express and implied. In so far as the proposal or acceptance of any promise is made in words, the promise is said to be express. In so far as such proposal or acceptance is made otherwise than in words, the promise is said to be implied.

CHAPTER II

Of Contracts, Voidable Contracts and Void Agreements

10. What agreements are contracts. All agreements are contracts if they are made by the free consent of parties competent to contract, for a lawful consideration and with a lawful object, and are not hereby expressly declared to be void.

Nothing herein contained shall affect any law in force in India, and not hereby expressly repealed, by which any contract is required to be made in writing or in the presence of witnesses, or any law relating to the registration of documents.

11. Who are competent to contract. Every person is competent to contract who is of the age of majority according to the law to which he is subject, and who is of sound mind, and is not disqualified from contracting by any law to which he is subject.

12. What is a sound mind for the purpose of contracting. A person is said to be of sound mind for the purpose of making a contract if, at the time when he makes it, he is capable of understanding it and of forming a rational judgment as to its effect upon his interests.

A person who is usually of unsound mind, but occasionally of sound mind may make a contract when he is of sound mind.

A person who is usually of sound mind, but occasionally of unsound mind, may not make a contract when he is of unsound mind.

ILLUSTRATIONS

(*a*) A patient in a lunatic asylum who is at intervals of sound mind, may contract during those intervals.

(*b*) A sane man, who is delirious from fever, or who is so drunk that he cannot understand the terms of a contract, or form a rational judgment as to its effect on his interests, cannot contract whilst such delirium or drunkenness lasts.

13. "Consent" defined. Two or more persons are said to consent when they agree upon the same thing in the same sense.

14. "Free consent" defined. Consent is said to be free when it is not caused by:

(1) coercion, as defined in Section 15, or

(2) undue influence, as defined in Section 16, or

(3) fraud, as defined in Section 17, or

(4) misrepresentation, as defined in Section 18, or

(5) mistake, subject to the provisions of Sections 20, 21 and 22.

Consent is said to be caused when it would not have been given but for the existence of such coercion, undue influence, fraud, misrepresentation or mistake.

15. "Coercion" defined. "Coercion" is the committing, or threatening to commit, any act forbidden by the Indian Penal Code (XLV of 1860), or the unlawful detaining, or threatening to detain, any property, to the prejudice of any person whatever, with the intention of causing any person to enter into an agreement.

Explanation. It is immaterial whether the Indian Penal Code (XLV of 1860) is or is not in force in the place where the coercion is employed.

ILLUSTRATIONS

A, on board an English ship on the high seas, causes *B* to enter into an agreement by an act amounting to criminal intimidation under the Indian Penal Code (XLV of 1860). *A* afterwards sues *B* for breach of contract at Calcutta.

A has employed coercion, although his act is not an offence by the law of England, and although Section 506 of the Indian Penal Code (XLV of 1860) was not in force at the time when, or place where the act was done.

16. "Undue Influence" defined. (1) A contract is said to be induced by "undue influence" where the relations subsisting between the parties are such that one of the parties is in a position to dominate the will of the other and uses that position to obtain an unfair advantage over the other.

(2) In particular and without prejudice to the generality of the foregoing principle, a person is deemed to be in a position to dominate the will of another :

(*a*) where he holds a real or apparent authority over the other, or where he stands in a fiduciary relation to the other; or

(*b*) where he makes a contract with a person whose mental capacity is temporarily or permanently affected by reason of age, illness, or mental or bodily distress.

(3) Where a person who is in a position to dominate the will of another, enters into a contract with him, and the transaction appears, on the face of it or on the evidence adduced, to be unconscionable, the burden of proving that such contract was not induced by undue influence shall be upon the person in a position to dominate the will of the other.

Nothing in this sub-section shall affect the provisions of Sec. 111 of the Indian Evidence Act 1872 (1 of 1872).

ILLUSTRATIONS

(*a*) *A* having advanced money to his son, *B* during his minority, upon *B*'s coming of age obtains, by misuse of parental influence, a bond from *B* for a greater amount than the sum due in respect of the advance. *A* employs undue influence.

(*b*) *A*, a man enfeebled by disease or age, is induced, by *B*'s influence over him as his medical attendant, to agree to pay *B* an unreasonable sum for his professional services. *B* employs undue influence.

(*c*) *A* being in debt to *B*, the money-lender of his village, contracts a fresh loan on terms which appears to be unconscionable. It lies on *B*, to prove that the contract was not induced by undue influence.

(*d*) *A* applies to a banker for a loan at a time when there is stringency in the money market. The banker declines to make the loan except at an unusually high rate of interest. *A* accepts the loan on these terms. This is a transaction in the ordinary course of business, and the contract is not induced by undue influence.

NOTE

A teacher can be presumed to be in a position to influence the mind and will of his student but a person who gives an incidental assistance in addition to a regular teacher, can not be said to be in a position to influence the student. *Tapan Ranjan Das v. Jolly Das* AIR 1990 Cal. 353.

17. "Fraud" defined. "Fraud" means and includes any of the following acts committed by a party to a contract, or with his connivance, or by his agent, with intent to deceive another party thereto or his agent, or to induce him to enter into the contract :

(1) the suggestion, as a fact, of that which is not true, by one who does not believe it to be true;

(2) the active concealment of a fact by one having knowledge or belief of the fact;

(3) a promise made without any intention of performing it;

(4) any other act fitted to deceive;

(5) any such act or omission as the law specially declares to be fraudulent.

Explanation. Mere silence as to facts likely to affect the willingness of a person to enter into a contract is not fraud, unless the circumstances of the case are such that, regard being had to them, it is the duty of the person keeping silence to speak, or unless his silence is, in itself, equivalent to speech.

ILLUSTRATIONS

(*a*) *A* sells, by auction, to *B*, a horse which *A* knows to be unsound. *A* says nothing to *B* about the horse's unsoundness. This is not fraud in *A*.

(*b*) *B* is *A*'s daughter and has just come to age. Here, the relation between the parties would make it *A*'s duty to tell *B* if the horse is unsound.

(*c*) *B* says to *A*, "If you do not deny it, I shall assume that the horse is sound". *A* says nothing. Here, A's silence is equivalent to speech.

(*d*) *A* and *B* being traders, enter upon a contract. *A* has private information of a change in prices which would affect *B*'s willingness to proceed with the contract. *A* is not bound to inform *B*.

18. "Misrepresentation" defined. "Misrepresentation" means and includes :

(1) the positive assertion, in a manner not warranted by the information of the person making it, of that which is not true, though he believes it to be true;

(2) any breach of duty which, without an intent to deceive, gains an advantage to the person committing it, or any one claiming under him, by misleading another to his prejudice, or to the prejudice of anyone claiming under him:

(3) causing, however innocently, a party to an agreement, to make a mistake as to the substance of the thing which is the subject of the agreement.

19. Voidability of agreements without free consent. When consent to an agreement is caused by coercion, fraud or misrepresentation, the agreement is a contract voidable at the option of the party whose consent was so caused.

A party to contract, whose consent was caused by fraud or misrepresentation, may, if he thinks fit, insist that the contract shall be performed, and that he shall be put in the position in which he would have been if the representation made had been true.

Exception. If such consent was caused by misrepresentation or by silence, fraudulent within the meaning of Sec. 17, the contract nevertheless, is not voidable, if the party whose consent was so caused had the means of discovering the truth with ordinary diligence.

Explanation. A fraud or misrepresentation which did not cause the consent to a contract of the party on whom such fraud was practised, or to whom such misrepresentation was made, does not render a contract voidable.

ILLUSTRATIONS

(*a*) *A*, intending to deceive *B*, falsely represents that five hundred mounds of indigo are made annually at *A*'s factory, and thereby induces *B* to buy the factory. The contract is voidable at the option of *B*.

(*b*) *A*, by a misrepresentation, leads *B* erroneously to believe that five hundred mounds of indigo are made annually at *A*'s factory, *B* examines the accounts of the factory, which shows that only four hundred mounds of indigo have been made. After this *B* buys the factory. The contract is not voidable on account of *A*'s misrepresentation.

(*c*) *A* fraudulently informs *B* that *A*'s estate is free from encumbrance. *B* thereupon buys the estate. The estate is subject to a mortgage. *B* may either avoid the contract, or may insist on its being carried out and mortgage-debt redeemed.

(*d*) *B*, having discovered a vein of ore on the estate of *A*, adopts means to conceal the existence of the ore from *A*. Through *A*'s ignorance *B* is enabled to buy the estate at an under-value. The contact is voidable at the option of *A*.

(*e*) *A* is entitled to succeed to an estate at the death of *B*, *B* dies; *C*, having received intelligence of *B*'s death prevents the intelligence reaching *A*, and thus induces *A* to sell him his interest in the estate. The sale is voidable at the option of *A*.

19-A. Power to set aside contract induced by undue influence. When consent to an agreement is caused by undue influence, the agreement is a contract voidable at the option of the party whose consent was to caused.

Any such contract may be set aside either absolutely, or if the party who was entitled to avoid it has received any benefit thereunder, upon such terms and conditions as to the Court may seem just.

ILLUSTRATIONS

(*a*) *A*'s son has forged *B*'s name to a promissory note. *B* under threat of prosecuting *A*'s son, obtains a bond from *A*, for the amount of the forged note. If *B* sues on this bond, the Court may set the bond aside.

(*b*) *A*, money-leader, advanced Rs. 100 to *B*, an agriculturist, and, by undue influence, induces *B* to execute a bond for Rs. 200 with interest at 6 per cent per month. The Court may set the bond aside, ordering *B* to repay Rs 100 with such interest as may seem just.

20. Agreement void where both parties are under mistake as to matter of fact. Where both the parties to an agreement are under a mistake as to a matter of fact essential to the agreement, the agreement is void.

Explanation. An erroneous opinion as to the value of the thing which forms the subject matter of the agreement, is not to be deemed a mistake as to a matter of fact.

NOTE

Manual mistake is a good ground for avoiding contact. *ITC Ltd. v. George Joseph Fernandes*, AIR 1989 S.C. 839.

ILLUSTRATIONS

(*a*) *A* agrees to sell to *B* a specific cargo of goods supposed to be on its way from England to Bombay. It turns out that, before the day of the bargain, the ship conveying the cargo had been cast away and the goods lost. Neither party was aware of these facts. The agreement is void.

(*b*) A agrees to buy from *B* a certain horse. It turns out that the horse was dead at the time of the bargain, though, neither party was aware of the fact. The agreement is void.

(*c*) *A*, being entitled to an estate for the life of *B*, agrees to sell it to *C*. *B* was dead at the time of the agreement, but both parties were ignorant of the fact. The agreement is void.

21. Effect of mistakes as to law. A contract is not voidable because it was caused by a mistake as to any law in force in India; but a mistake as to a law not in force in India has the same effect as a mistake of fact.

ILLUSTRATION

A and *B* make a contract grounded on the erroneous belief that a particular debt is barred by the Indian Law of Limitation; the contract is not voidable.

22. Contract caused by mistake of one party as to matter of fact. A contract is not voidable merely because it was caused by one of the parties to it being under a mistake as to a matter of fact.

23. What considerations and objects are lawful, and what not. The consideration or object of an agreement is lawful, unless :

it is forbidden by law; or
is of such a nature that, if permitted, it would defeat the provisions of any law; or
is fraudulent; or
involves or implies, injury to the person or property of another; or
the Court regards it as immoral, or opposed to public policy.

In each of these cases, the consideration or object of an agreement is said to be unlawful. Every agreement of which the object or consideration is unlawful is void.

ILLUSTRATIONS

(*a*) *A* agrees to sell his house to *B* for 10,000 rupees. Here *B*'s promise to pay the sum of 10,000 rupees is the consideration for *A*'s promise to sell the house, and *A*'s promise to sell the house is the consideration for *B*'s promise to pay the 10,000 rupees. These are lawful considerations.

(*b*) *A* promises to pay *B* 1,000 rupees at the end of six months, if *C*, who owes that sum to *B*, fails to pay it. *B* promise to grant time to *C* accordingly. Here the promise of each party is the consideration for the promise of the other party and they are lawful considerations.

(*c*) *A* promises, for a certain sum paid to him by *B*, to make good to *B* the value of his ship if it is wrecked on a certain voyage. Here *A*'s promise is the consideration for *B*'s payment, and *B*'s payment is the consideration for *A*'s promise, and these are lawful considerations.

(*d*) *A* promises to maintain *B*'s child, and *B* promises to pay *A* 1,000 rupees yearly for the purpose. Here, the promise of each party is the consideration for the promise of the other party. They are lawful considerations.

(*e*) *A*, *B* and *C* enter into an agreement for the division among them of gains acquired, or to be acquired, by them by fraud. The agreement is void, as its object is unlawful.

(*f*) *A* promises to obtain for *B* an employment in the public service, and *B* promises to pay 1,000 rupees to *A*. The agreement is void as the consideration for it is unlawful.

(*g*) *A*, being agent for a landed proprietor, agrees for money, without the knowledge of his principal, to obtain for *B* a lease of land belonging to his principal. The agreement between *A* and *B* is void, as it implies a fraud by concealment by *A*, on his principal.

(*h*) A promises *B* to drop a prosecution which he has instituted against *B* for robbery, and B promises to restore the value of the things taken. The agreement is void, as its object is unlawful.

(*i*) *A*'s estate is sold for arrears of revenue under the provisions of an Act of the Legislature, by which the defaulter is prohibited from purchasing the estate. *B*, upon an understanding with *A*, becomes the purchaser, and agrees to convey the estate to *A*, upon receiving from him the price which *B* has paid. The agreement is void, as it renders the transaction, in effect, a purchase by the defaulter, and would so defeat the object of the law.

(*j*) *A*, who is *B*'s mukhtar, promises to exercise his influence as such, with *B* in favour of C, and C promises to pay 1,000 rupees to *A*. The agreement is void, because it is immoral.

(*k*) *A* agrees to let her daughter to hire to *B* for concubinage. The agreement is void, because it is immoral, though the letting many not be punishable under the Indian Pental Code (XLV) of 1860.

NOTES

Shifting of prosecution to take the administration of criminal justice out of the hands of judges and place it in own hands by a private person attracts the provisions of section 23. *Union Carbide Corporation v. Union of India*, AIR 1992 S.C. 248. In this case Govt. of India is not a private person hence S. 23 is not attracted.

Marriage Brokerage is opposed to public policy, AIR 1991 M.P. 275.

Public Policy. Connotes some matter which concerns the public good and the public interest. The term public policy is very flexible and changing, this is the reason that court kept on extending the scope of the term. *Central Inland Water Transport Corporation Ltd. v. Brojo Nath Ganguly.* AIR 1986 SC 1571.

VOID AGREEMENTS

24. Agreements void, if considerations and objects unlawful in part. If any part of single consideration for one or more objects, or any one or any part of any one of several considerations for a single object, is unlawful, the agreement is void.

ILLUSTRATION

A promises to superintend, on behalf of *B*, a legal manufacture of indigo, and an illegal traffic in other articles. *B* promises to pay *A* a salary of 10,000 rupees a year. The agreement is void, the object of *A*'s promise and the consideration for B's promise being in part unlawful.

25. Agreement without consideration is void, unless it is in writing and registered, or is a promise to compensate for something done, or is a promise to pay a debt barred by limitation law. An agreement made without considerations is void, unless

(1) it is expressed in writing and registered under the law for the time being in force for the registration of documents and is made on account of natural love and affection between parties standing in a near relation to each other, or unless;

(2) it is a promise to compensate, wholly or in part, a person who has already voluntarily done something for the promisor, or something which the promisor was legally compellable to do; or unless

(3) it is a promise, made in writing and signed by the person to be charged therewith, or by his agent generally or by specifically authorised in that behalf, to pay wholly or in part a debt of which the creditor might have enforced payment but for the law for the limitation of suits.

In any of these cases, such an agreement is a contract.

Explanation. 1. Nothing in this section shall affect the validity, as between the donor and donee, of any gift actually made.

Explanation 2. An agreement to which the consent of the promisor is freely given is not void merely because the consideration is inadequate; but the inadequacy of the consideration may be taken into account by the Court in determining the question whether the consent of the promisor was freely given.

ILLUSTRATIONS

(*a*) *A* promises, for no consideration, to give *B* Rs. 1,000. This is a void agreement.

(*b*) *A*, for natural love and affection, promises to give his son, *B*, Rs 1,000. *A* puts his promise to B, into writing and registers it. This is a contract.

(*c*) *A* finds *B*'s Purse and gives it to him. *B* promises to give *A* Rs. 50. This is a contract.

(*d*) *A* supports *B*'s infant son. *B* promises to pay *A*'s expenses in so doing. This is a contract.

(*e*) *A* owes *B* Rs. 1,000, but the debt is barred by the Limitation Act, *A* signs a written promise to pay *B* Rs. 500, on account of the debt. This is a contract.

(*f*) *A* agrees to sell a horse worth Rs. 1,000 for Rs. 10. *A*'s consent to the agreement was freely given. The agreement is a contract notwithstanding the inadequacy of the consideration.

(*g*) *A* agrees to sell a horse worth Rs. 1,000 for Rs.10. *A* denies that his consent to the agreement was freely given.

The inadequacy of the consideration is a fact which the Court should take into account in considering whether or not *A*'s consent was freely given.

26. Agreement in restraint of marriage, void. Every agreement in restraint of the marriage of any person, other than a minor, is void.

27. Agreement in restraint of trade, void. Every agreement by which any one is restrained from exercising a lawful profession, trade or business of any kind, is to that extent void.

Exception 1. **Saving of agreement not to carry on business of which goodwill is sold.** One who sells the goodwill of a business may agree with the buyer to refrain from carrying on a similar business, within specified local limits, so long as the buyer or any person deriving title to the goodwill from him, carries on a like business therein :

Provided that such limits appear to the Court reasonable, regard being had to the nature of the business.

[Exceptions (2) and (3) are repealed by Partnership Act.]

28. Agreements in restraint of legal proceedings, void.[1] [Every agreement,—

1. Substituted by Act 1 of 1997.
2. The part of Exception I was replaced by the Specific Relief Act, 1877 which is now itself repealed by S.R. Act, 1963.

(*a*) by which any party thereto is restricted absolutely from enforcing his rights under or in respect of any contract, by the usual legal proceedings in the ordinary tribunals, or which limits the time within which he may thus enforce his rights; or

(*b*) which extinguishes the rights of any party thereto, or discharges any party thereto from any liability, under or in respect of any contract on the expiry of a specified period so as to restrict any party from enforcing his rights.

is void to that extent.]

***Exception 1.* Saving of contract to refer to arbitration dispute that may arise.** This section shall not render illegal a contract, by which two or more persons agree that any dispute which may arise between them in respect of any subject or class of subjects shall be referred to arbitration, and that only the amount awarded in such arbitration shall be recoverable in respect of the dispute so referred.

Suits barred by such contract[2] [* * *]

***Exception 2.* Saving of contract to refer questions that have already arisen**—Nor shall this section render illegal any contract in writing, by which two or more persons agree to refer to arbitration any question between them which has already arisen, or affect any provision of any law in force for the time being as to references to arbitration.

29. Agreements void for uncertainty. Agreements, the meaning of which is not certain, or capable of being made certain, are void.

ILLUSTRATIONS

(*a*) *A* agrees to sell to *B* "a hundred tons of oil". There is nothing whatever to show what kind of oil was intended. The agreement is void for uncertainty.

(*b*) *A* agrees to sell to *B* one hundred tons of oil of a specified description, known as an article of commerce. There is no uncertainty here to make the agreement void.

(*c*) *A*, who is dealer of coconut oil only, agrees to sell to *B* "one hundred tons of oil." The nature of *A*'s trade affords an indication of the meaning of the words and *A* has entered into a contract for the sale of one hundred tons of coconut oil.

(*d*) *A* agrees to sell to *B* "all the grains in my granary at Ramnagar". There is no uncertainty here to make the agreement void.

(*e*) *A* agrees to sell to *B* "one thousand mounds of rice at a price to be fixed by *C*". As the price is capable of being made certain, there is no uncertainty here to make the agreement void.

(*f*) *A* agrees to sell to *B* "my white horse for rupees five hundred or rupees one thousand". There is nothing to show which of the two prices was to be given. The agreement is void.

NOTES

Vagueness. Where both parties agree on a term initially either of them can not back out later at the stage of performance of respective part on a pretext that the term was vague and could not be understood *ad-idem. M/s D. Gobindram v. M/s. Shami K. & Co.*, AIR 1961 SC 1285. Mere difficulty in interpretation is not synonymous with Vagueness, *Kedarnath Cine Enterprise (Pvt.) Ltd.* v. *John Philipose.* AIR 1990 Kerala, 198.

30. Agreements by way of wager, void. Agreements by way of wager are void; and no suit shall be brought for recovering anything alleged to be won on any wager or, entrusted to any person to abide the result of any game or other uncertain event on which any wager is made.

Exception in favour of certain prizes for horse-racing. This section shall not be deemed to render unlawful a subscription or contribution, or agreement to subscribe or contribute, made or entered into for or towards any plate, prize or sum of money, of the value or amount of five hundred rupees or upwards, to be awarded to the winner or winners of any horse-race.

Section 294-A of the Indian Penal Code not affected. Nothing in this section shall be deemed to legalize any transaction connected with horse-racing, to which the provisions of section 294-A of the Indian Penal Code (XLV of 1860) apply.

CHAPTER III

Of Contingent Contracts

31. "Contingent contract" defined. A "contingent contract" is a contract to do or not to do something, if some event, collateral to such contract does or does not happen.

ILLUSTRATION

A contracts to pay *B* Rs. 10,000 if *B*'s house is burnt. This is a contingent contract.

32. Enforcement of contracts contingent on an event happening. Contingent contracts to do or not to do anything if an uncertain future event happens cannot be enforced by law unless and until that event has happened.

If the event becomes impossible, such contracts become void.

ILLUSTRATIONS

(*a*) A makes a contract with *B* to buy *B*'s horse if *A* survives *C*. This contract cannot be enforced by law unless and until *C* dies in *A*'s lifetime.

(*b*) *A* makes a contract with *B* to sell a horse to *B* at a specified price, if *C*, to whom the horse has been offered, refuses to buy him. The contract cannot be enforced by law unless and until *C* refuse to buy the horse.

(*c*) *A* contracts to pay *B* a sum of money when *B* marries *C*. *C* dies without being married to *B*. The contract becomes void.

33. Enforcement of contract contingent on an event not happening. Contingent contracts to do or not to do anything if any uncertain future event does not happen, can be enforced when the happening of that event becomes impossible, and not before.

ILLUSTRATION

A agrees to pay *B* a sum of money if a certain ship does not return. The ship is sunk. The contract can be enforced when the ship sinks.

34. When event on which contract is contingent to be deemed impossible, if it is the future conduct of a living person. If the future event on which a contract is contingent is the way in which a person will act at an unspecified time, the event shall be considered to become impossible when such person does anything which renders it impossible that he should so act within any definite time, or otherwise than under further contingencies.

ILLUSTRATION

A agrees to pay *B* a sum of money if *B* marries, *C*. *C* marries *D*. The marriage of *B* to *C* must now be considered impossible, although it is possible that *D* may die and that *C* may afterwards marry *B*.

35. When contracts become void which are contingent on happening of specified event within fixed time. Contingent contracts to do or not to do anything if a specified uncertain event happens within a fixed time, become void if, at the expiration of the time fixed, such event has not happened, or if, before the time fixed, such event becomes impossible.

When contracts may be enforced, which are contingent on specified event not happening within fixed time. Contingent contracts to do or not to do anything, if a specified uncertain event does not happen within a fixed time, may be enforced by law when the time fixed has expired and such event has not happened, or before the time fixed has expired, if it becomes certain that such event will not happen.

ILLUSTRATIONS

(*a*) *A* promises to pay *B* a sum of money if a certain ship returns within a year. The contract may be enforced if the ship returns within the year; and becomes void if the ship is burnt within the year.

(*b*) *A* promises to pay *B* a sum of money if a certain ship does not return within a year. The contract may be enforced if the ship does not return within the year, or is burnt within the year.

36. Agreement contingent on impossible events void. Contingent agreements to do or not to do anything, if an impossible event happens, are void, whether the impossibility of the event is known or not to the parties to the agreement at the time when it is made.

ILLUSTRATIONS

(*a*) *A* agrees to pay *B* 1,000 rupees if two straight lines should enclose a space. The agreement is void.
(*b*) *A* agrees to pay *B* 1,000 rupees if *B* will marry *A*'s daughter *C*. *C* was dead at the time of the agreement. The agreement is void.
[The two last going sections explain themselves.]

CHAPTER IV

OF THE PERFORMANCE OF CONTRACTS

Contracts which must be performed

37. Obligation of parties of contract. The parties to a contract must either perform, or offer to perform, their respective promises, unless such performance is dispensed with or excused under the provisions of this Act, or of any other law.

Promises bind the representatives of the promisors in case of the death of such promisors before performance, unless a contrary intention appears from the contract.

ILLUSTRATIONS

(*a*) *A* promises to deliver goods to *B* on a certain day on payment of Rs. 1,000. *A* dies before that day. *A*'s representatives are bound to deliver the goods to *B* and *B* is bound to pay the Rs. 1,000 to *A*'s representatives.

(*b*) *A* promises to paint a picture for *B* by a certain day, at a certain price. *A* dies before the day. The contract cannot be enforced either by *A*'s representatives or by *B*.

38. Effect of refusal to accept offer of performance. Where a promisor has made an offer of performance to the promisee, and the offer has not been accepted, the promisor is not responsible for the non-performance, nor does he thereby lose his rights under the contract.

Every such offer must fulfil the following conditions :

(1) it must be unconditional;

(2) it must be made at a proper time and place, and under such circumstances that the person to whom it is made may have a reasonable opportunity of ascertaining that the person by whom it is made is able and willing there and then to do the whole of what he is bound by his promise to do;

(3) if the offer is an offer to deliver anything to the promisee, the promisee must have a reasonable opportunity of seeing that the thing offered is the thing which the promisor is bound by his promise to deliver.

An offer to one of several joint promises has the same legal consequences as an offer to all of them.

ILLUSTRATION

A contracts to deliver to *B* at his warehouse, on the 1st March, 1973, 100 bales of cotton of a particular quality. In order to make an offer of performance with the effect stated in this section. *A* must bring the cotton to *B*'s warehouse on the appointed day, under such circumstances that *B* may have a reasonable opportunity of satisfying himself that the thing offered is cotton of the quality contracted for, and that there are 100 bales.

39. Effect of refusal of party to perform promise wholly. When a party to contract has refused to perform, or disabled himself from performing his promise in its entirety, the promisee may put an end to the contract, unless he has signified, by words or conduct, his acquiescence in its continuance.

ILLUSTRATIONS

(*a*) *A*, a singer, enters into a contract with *B*, the manager of a theatre, to sing at his theatre two nights in every week during the next two months, and *B* engages to pay her Rs. 100 for each night's performance. On the sixth night *A* wilfully absents herself from the theatre. *B* is at liberty to put an end to the contract.

(*b*) *A*, a singer, enters into a contract with *B*, the manager of a theatre, to sing at his theatre two nights in every week during next two months, and *B* engages to pay her at the rate of Rs. 100 for each night. On the sixth night *A* wilfully absents herself. With the assent of *B, A* sings on seventh night, *B* has signified his acquiescence of the continuance of the contract, and cannot now put an end to it, but is entitled to compensation for the damage sustained by him through *A*'s failure to sing on the sixth night.

BY WHOM CONTRACTS MUST BE PERFORMED

40. Persons by whom promise is to be performed. If it appears from the nature of the case that it was the intention of the parties to any contract that any promise contained in it should be performed by the promisor himself, such promise must be performed by the promisor. In other cases, the promisor or his representatives may employ a competent person to perform it.

ILLUSTRATIONS

(*a*) *A* promises to pay *B* a sum of money. *A* may perform this promise, either by personally paying the money to *B* or by causing it to be paid to *B* by another, and, if A dies before the time appointed for payment, his representative must perform the promise, or employ some proper person to do so.

(*b*) *A* promises to paint a picture for *B*. *A* must perform this promise personally.

41. Effect of accepting performance from third person. When a promisee accepts performance of the promise from the third person, he cannot afterwards enforce it against the promisor.

42. Devolution of joint liabilities. When two or more persons have made a joint promise, then, unless a contrary intention appears by the contract, all such persons, during their joint lives, and after the death of any of them, his representative jointly with the survivor or survivors, any after the death of the last survivor, the representatives of all jointly, must fulfil the promise.

43. Any one of joint promisors may be compelled to perform. When two or more persons make a joint promise, the promisee may, in the absence of express agreement to the contrary, compel any one or more of such joint promisors to perform the whole of the promise.

Each promisor may compel contribution. Each of two or more joint promisor may compel every joint promisor to contribute equally with himself to the performance of the promise, unless a contrary intention appears from the contract.

Sharing of loss by default in contribution. If any one of two or more joint promisors makes default in such contribution, the remaining joint promisors must bear the loss arising from such default in equal shares.

Explanation. Nothing in this section shall prevent a surety from recovering from his principal, payments made by the surety on behalf of the principal, or entitle the principal to recover anything from the surety on account of payments made by the principal.

ILLUSTRATIONS

(*a*) *A, B* and *C* jointly promise to pay *D* 3,000 rupees. *D* may compel either *A* or *B* or *C* to pay him 3,000 rupees.

(*b*) *A, B* and *C* jointly promise to pay *D* the sum of 3,000 rupees, *C* is entitled to receive the whole. *A* is insolvent but his assets are sufficient to pay one-half of his debts. *C* is entitled to receive 500 rupees from *A*'s estate, and 1,250 rupees from *B*.

(*c*) *A, B* and *C* are under a joint promise to pay *D* 3,000 rupees. *C* is unable to pay anything, and *A* is compelled to pay the whole. *A* is entitled to receive 1,500 rupees from *B*.

(*d*) *A, B* and *C* are under a joint promise to pay *D* 3,000 rupees, *A* and *B* being only sureties for *C*. *C* fails to pay. *A* and *B* are compelled to pay the whole sum. They are entitled to recover it from *C*.

44. Effect of release of one joint promisor. Where two or more persons have made a joint promise, a release of one of such joint promisors by the promisee does not discharge the other joint promisor or joint promisors; neither does it free the joint promisor so released from responsibility to the other joint promisor or joint promisors.

45. Devolution of joint rights. When a person has made a promise to two or more persons jointly, then, unless a contrary intention appears from the contract, the right to claim performance rests, as between him and then with them, during their joint lives, and after the death of any of them, with the representative of such deceased persons jointly with the survivor or survivors, and, after the death of the last survivor, with the representatives of all jointly.

ILLUSTRATION

A, in consideration of 5,000 rupees lent to him by *B* and *C*, promised *B* and *C* jointly to repay them that sum with interest on a day specified, *B* dies. The right to claim performance rests with *B*'s representative jointly with *C* during *C*'s life, and after the death of *C*, with representatives of *B* and *C* jointly.

TIME AND PLACE FOR PERFORMANCE

46. Time for performance of promise, where no application is to be made and no time is specified. Where, by the contract, a promisor is to perform his promise without application by the promisee, and no time for performance is specified, the engagement must be performed within a reasonable time.

Explanation. The question "what is a reasonable time" is, in each particular case, a question of fact.

47. Time and place for performance of promise where time is specified and no application to be made. When a promise is to be performed on a certain day, and the promisor has undertaken to perform it without application by the promisee, the promisor may perform it at any time during the usual hours of business on such day and at the place at which the promise ought to be performed.

ILLUSTRATION

A promises to deliver goods at *B*'s warehouse on the first January. On that day *A* brings the goods to *B*'s warehouse, but after the usual hour of closing it, and they are not received. *A* has not performed his promise.

48. Application for performance on certain day to be at proper time and place. When a promise is to be performed on a certain day, and the promisor has not undertaken to perform it without application by the promisee, it is the duty of the promisee to apply for performance at a proper place and within the usual hours of business.

Explanation. The question "what is a proper time and place" is, in each particular case, a question of fact.

49. Place for performance of promise, where no application to be made and no place fixed for performance. When a promise is to be performed without application by the promisee, and no place is fixed for the performance of it, it is the duty of the promisor to apply to the promisee to appoint a reasonable place for the performance of the promise, and to perform it at such place.

ILLUSTRATION

A undertakes to deliver thousand mounds of jute to *B* on a fixed day. *A* must apply to *B* to appoint a reasonable place for the purpose of receiving it, and must deliver it to him at such place.

50. Performance in manner or at time prescribed or sanctioned by promisee. The performance of any promise may be made in any manner, or at any time which the promisee prescribes or sanctions.

ILLUSTRATIONS

(*a*) *B* owes *A* 2,000 rupees. *A* desires *B* to pay the amount to *A*'s account with *C*, a banker. *B*, who also banks with *C*, orders the amount to be transferred from his account to *A*'s credit, and this is done by *C*. Afterwards, and before *A* knows of the transfer, *C* fails. There has been a good payment by *B*.

(*b*) *A* and *B* are mutually indebted. *A* and *B* settle an account by setting off one item against another, and *B* pays *A* the balance found to be due from him upon such settlement. This amounts to a payment by *A* and *B*, respectively, of the sums which they owed to each other.

(*c*) *A* owes *B* 2,000 rupees, *B* accepts some of *A*'s goods in reduction of the debt. The delivery of the goods operates as a part payment.

(*d*) *A* desires *B*, who owes him Rs. 100, to send him a note for Rs. 100 by post. The debt is discharged as soon as *B* puts into the post a letter containing the note duly addressed to *A*.

PERFORMANCE OF RECIPROCAL PROMISES

51. Promisor not bound to perform, unless reciprocal promisee ready and willing to perform. When a contract consists of reciprocal promises to be simultaneously performed, no promisor need perform his promise unless the promisee is ready and willing to perform his reciprocal promise.

ILLUSTRATIONS

(*a*) *A* and *B* contract that *A* shall deliver goods to *B* to be paid for by *B* on delivery.

A need not deliver the goods, unless *B* is ready and willing to pay for the goods on delivery.

B need not pay for the goods unless *A* is ready and willing to deliver them on payment.

(*b*) *A* and *B* contract that *A* shall deliver goods to *B* at a price to be paid by instalments, the first instalment to be paid on delivery.

A need not deliver, unless *B* is ready and willing to pay the first instalment on delivery.

B need not pay the first instalment unless *A* is ready and willing to deliver the goods on payment of the first instalment.

52. Order of performance of reciprocal promises. Where the order in which reciprocal promises are to be performed is expressly fixed by the contract, they shall be performed in that order; and, where the order is not expressly fixed by the contract, they shall be performed in that order which the nature of the transaction requires.

ILLUSTRATIONS

(*a*) *A* and *B* contract that *A* shall build a house for *B* at a fixed price. *A*'s promise to build the house must be performed before *B*'s promise to pay for it.

(*b*) *A* and *B* contract that *A* shall make over his stock-in-trade to *B* at a fixed price, and *B* promises to give security for the payment of the money. *A*'s promise need not be performed until the security is given, for the nature of the transaction requires that A should have security before he delivers up his stock.

53. Liability of party preventing event on which the contract is to take effect. When a contract contains reciprocal promises, and one party to the contract prevents the other from performing his promise, the contract becomes voidable at the option of the party so prevented; and he is entitled to compensation from the other party for any loss which he may sustain in consequence of the non-performance of the contract.

ILLUSTRATION

A and *B* contract that *B* shall execute certain works for *A* for a thousand rupees, *B* is ready and willing to execute the work accordingly, but *A* prevents him from doing so. The contract is voidable at the option of *B*, and, if he elects to rescind it, he is entitled to recover from *A* compensation for any loss which he has incurred by its non-performance.

54. Effect of default as to that promise which should be first performed, in contract consisting of reciprocal promises. When a contract consists of reciprocal promises, such that one of them cannot be performed or that its performance cannot be claimed till the other has been performed, and the promisor of the promise last mentioned fails to perform it, such promisor cannot claim the performance of the reciprocal promise, and must make compensation to the other party to the contract for any loss which such other party may sustain by the non-performance of the contract.

ILLUSTRATIONS

(*a*) *A* hires *B*'s ship to take in and convery, from Calcutta to Mauritius, a cargo to be provided by *A*. *B* receiving a certain freight for its conveyance. *A* does not provide any cargo for the ship. *A* cannot claim the performance of *B*'s promise, and must make compensation to *B* for the loss which B sustains by the non-performance of the contract.

(*b*) A contracts with *B* to execute certain builder's work for a fixed price, *B* supplying the scaffolding and timber necessary for the work. *B* refuses to furnish and scaffolding or timber, and the work cannot be executed. *A* need not execute the work, and *B* is bound to make compensation to *A* for any loss caused to him by the non-performance of the contract.

(*c*) *A* contracts with *B* to deliver to him, at a specified price, certain merchandise on board a ship which cannot arrive for a month, and *B* engages to pay for the merchandise within a week from the date of the contract. *B* does not pay within the week. *A*'s promise to deliver need not be performed, and *B* must make compensation.

(*d*) *A* promises *B* to sell him one hundred bales of merchandise, to be delivered next day, and *B* promises *A* to pay for them within a month. *A* does not deliver according to his promise, *B*'s promise to pay need not be performed, and *A* must make compensation.

55. Effect of failure to perform at fixed time, in contract in which time is essential. When a party to a contract promises to do a certain thing at or before a specified time, or certain things at or before specified times, and fails to do any such thing at or before the specified time, or contract, or so much of it as has not been performed, becomes voidable at the option of the promisee, if the intention of parties was that time should be of the essence of the contract.

Effect of such failure when time is not essential. If it was not the intention of the parties that time should be of the essence of the contract, the contract does not become voidable by the failure to do such thing at or before the specified time; but the promisee is entitled to compensation from the promisor for any loss occasioned to him by such failure.

Effect of acceptance of performance at time other than that agreed upon. If, in case of a contract voidable on account of the promisor's failure to perform his promise at the time agreed, the promisee accepts performance of such promise at any time other than agreed, the promisee cannot claim compensation for any loss occasioned by the non-performance of the promise at the time agreed, unless, at the time of such acceptance, he gives notice to the promisor of his intention to do so.

56. Agreement to do impossible act. An agreement to do an act impossible in itself is void.

Contract to do act afterwards becoming impossible or unlawful. A contract to do an act which after the contract is made, becomes impossible, or, by reason of some event which the promisor could not prevent, unlawful, becomes void, when the act becomes impossible or unlawful.

Compensation for loss through non-performance of act known to be impossible or unlawful. Where one person has promised to do something, which he knew or with reasonable diligence, might have known, and which the promisee did not know to be impossible or unlawful, such promisor must make compensation to such promisee for any loss which such promisee sustains through the non-performance of the promise.

NOTE

Where change in situation totally upsets the very foundation upon which parties rested their bargain the event is said to have frustrated the Contract. *Easum Engineering Co. Ltd. v. The Fertilizers and Chemicals Travancore Ltd.*, AIR 1991 Mad. 158.

ILLUSTRATIONS

(*a*) *A* agree with *B* to discover treasure by magic. The agreement is void.

(*b*) *A* and *B* contract to marry each other. Before the time fixed for the marriage, *A*, goes mad. The contract becomes void.

(*c*) *A* contracts to marry *B*, being already married to *C*, and being forbidden by the law to which he is subject to practice polygamy. *A* must make compensation to *B* for the loss caused to her by the non-performance of his promise.

(*d*) *A* contracts to take in cargo for *B* at a foreign port, *A*'s Government afterwards declares war against the country in which the port is situated. The contract becomes void when war is declared.

(*e*) *A* contracts to act at a theatre for six months in consideration of a sum paid in advance by *B*. On several occasions *A* is too ill to act. The contract to act on those occasions becomes void.

57. Reciprocal promise to do things legal, and also other things illegal. Where persons reciprocally promise, firstly, to do certain things which are legal, and secondly, under specified circumstance, to do certain other things which are illegal, the first set to promises is a contract, but the second is a void agreement.

ILLUSTRATION

A and *B* agree that *A* shall sell *B* a house for Rs. 10,000 but that, if *B* uses it as a gambling-house, he shall pay *A* rupees 50,000 for it.

The first set of reciprocal promises namely, to sell the house and to pay Rs. 10,000 for it, is a contract.

The second set is for an unlawful object namely, that *B* may use the house as gambling-house, and is a void agreement.

58. Alternative promise, one branch being illegal. In the case of an alternative promise, one branch of which is a legal and the other illegal, the legal branch alone can be enforced.

ILLUSTRATION

A and *B* agree that *A* shall pay *B* Rs. 1,000 for which *B* shall afterwards deliver to *A* either rice or smuggled opium.

This is a valid contract to deliver rice, and a void agreement as to the opium.

APPROPRIATION OF PAYMENTS

59. Application of payment where debt to be discharged is indicated. Where a debtor, owing several distinct debts to one person, makes a payment to him, either with express intimation, or under circumstances implying, that the payment is to be applied to the discharge of some particular debt, the payment, if accepted, must be applied accordingly.

ILLUSTRATIONS

(*a*) *A* owes *B*, among other debts, Rs. 1,000 upon a promissory note, which falls due on the 1st June. He owes *B* no other debt of that amount. On the 1st June *A* pays to *B* Rs. 1,000. The payment is to be applied to the discharge of the promissory note.

(*b*) *A* owes to *B*, among other debts, the sum of Rs. 567. *B* writes to *A* and demands payment of this sum. *A* sends to *B* Rs. 567. This payment is to be applied to the discharge of the debt of which *B* had demanded payment.

60. Application of payment where debt to be discharged is not indicated. Where the debtor has omitted to intimate and there are not other circumstances indicating to which debt the payment is to be applied, the creditor may apply it at his discretion to any lawful debt actually due and payable to him from the debtor, whether its recovery is or is not barred by the law in force for the time being as to the limitation of suits.

61. Application of payment where neither party appropriates. Where neither party makes any appropriation, the payment shall be applied in discharge of the debt in order of time, whether they are or are not barred by the law in force for the time being as to the limitation of suits. If the debts are of equal standing the payment shall be applied in discharge of each proportionately.

CONTRACTS WHICH NEED NOT BE PERFORMED

62. Effect of novation, rescission and alteration of contract. If the parties to a contract agree to substitute a new contract for it, or to rescind or alter it, the original contract need not to be performed.

ILLUSTRATIONS

(*a*) *A* owes moneys to *B* under a contract. It is agreed between *A, B* and *C* that *B* shall thenceforth accept *C* as his debtor instead of *A*. The old debt of *A* to *B* is at an end and a new debt from *C* to *B* has been contracted.

(*b*) *A* owes *B* Rs. 10,000. *A* enters into an agreement with *B* and gives *B* a mortgage of his (*A*'s) estate for Rs 5,000 in place of the debt of Rs. 10,000. This is new contract and extinguishes the old.

(*c*) *A* owes *B* Rs. 1,000 under a contract. *B* owes *C* Rs. 1,000. *B* orders *A* to credit *C* with Rs. 1,000 in his books, but *C* does not assent to the arrangement. *B* still owes *C* Rs. 1,000, and no new contract has been entered into.

NOTES

'Novation'—Ingredients. Material or substantial changes which go to the root of the agreement, replace the old one and constitute a new agreement, this is novation. *Andheri Bridge View Cooperative Housing Society Ltd. v. Krishnakant Anandrao Deo*, AIR 1991, Bombay 129.

63. Promisee may dispense with or remit performance or promise. Every promisee may dispense with or remit, wholly or in part, the performance of the promise made to him, or may extend the time for such performance, or may accept instead of it any satisfaction which he think fit.

ILLUSTRATIONS

(*a*) *A* promises to paint a picture for *B*. *B* afterwards forbids him to do so. *A* is no longer bound to perform the promise.

(*b*) *A* owes *B* 5,000 rupees. *A* pays to *B*, and *B* accepts, in satisfaction of the whole debt, 2,000 rupees paid at the time and place at which the 5,000 rupees were payable. The whole debt is discharged.

(*c*) *A* owes *B* 5,000 rupees. *C* pays to *B* 1,000 rupees, and *B* accepts them in satisfaction of claim on A. This payment is a discharge of the whole claim.

(*d*) *A* owes *B*, under a contract a sum of money, the amount of which has not been ascertained. *A* without ascertaining the amount gives to *B* and *B*, in satisfaction thereof, accepts the sum of 2,000 rupees. This is a discharge of the whole debt, whatever may be its amount.

(*e*) *A* owes *B* 2,000 rupees, and is also indebted to other creditors. *A* makes an arrangement with his creditors, including *B*, to pay them a composition of eight annas in the rupee upon their respective demands. Payment to *B* of 1,000 rupees is a discharge of *B*'s demand.

64. Consequences of rescission of voidable contract. When, a person at whose option a contract is voidable rescinds it, the other party thereto need not perform any promise therein contained in which he is promisor. The party rescinding a voidable contract shall, if he has received any benefit thereunder from another party to such contract, restore such benefit, so far as may be, to person from whom it was received.

65. Obligation of person who has received advantage under void agreement or contract that becomes void. When an agreement is discovered to be void or when a contract becomes void, any person who has received any advantage under such agreement or contract is bound to restore it, or to make compensation for it, to the person from whom he received it.

ILLUSTRATIONS

(*a*) *A* pays *B* 1,000 rupees in consideration of *B*'s promising to marry *C*, *A*'s daughter. *C* is dead at the time of the promise. The agreement is void, but *B* must repay *A* the 1,000 rupees.

(*b*) *A* contracts with *B* to deliver to him 250 mounds of rice before the 1st of May. *A* delivers 130 mounds only before that day, and none after. *B* retains the 130 mounds after the 1st of May. He is bound to pay *A* for them.

(*c*) *A*, a singer, contracts with *B* the manager of a theatre, to sing at his theatre for two nights in every week during the next two months, and *B* engages to pay her a hundred rupees for each night's performance. On the sixth night, *A* wilfully absents herself from the theatre, and *B* in consequence rescinds the contract, *B* must pay *A* for the five nights on which she had sung.

(*d*) A contracts to sing for *B* at a concert for 1,000 rupees, which are paid in advance. *A* is too ill to sing. *A* is not bound to make compensation to *B* for the loss of the profits which *B* would have made if *A* had been able to sing, but must refund to *B* the 1,000 rupees paid in advance.

66. Mode of communication or revoking rescission of voidable contract. The rescission of a voidable contract may be communicated or revoked in the same manner, and subject to the rules, as apply to the communication or revocation of a proposal.

67. Effect of neglect of promisee to afford promisor reasonable facilities for the performance. If any promisee neglect or refuses to afford the promisor reasonable facilities for the performance of his promise, the promisor is excused by such neglect or refusal as to any non-performance caused thereby.

ILLUSTRATIONS

A contracts with *B* to repair *B*'s house.

B neglects or refuses to point out to *A* the places in which his house requires repair.

A is exhausted for the non-performance of the contract, if it is caused by such neglect or refusal.

CHAPTER V

Of certain Relations Resembling those Created by Contract

68. Claim for necessaries supplied to person incapable of contracting, or on his account. If a person, incapable of entering into a contract or anyone whom he is legally bound to support, is supplied by another person with necessaries suited to his condition in life, the person who has furnished such supplies is entitled to be reimbursed from the property of such incapable person.

ILLUSTRATIONS

(*a*) *A* supplies *B*, a lunatic, with necessaries suitable to his condition in life. *A* is entitled to be reimbursed from *B*'s property.

(*b*) *A* supplies the wife and children of *B*, a lunatic, with necessaries suitable to their conditions in life. *A* is entitled to be reimbursed from *B*'s property.

69. Reimbursement of person paying money due by another, in payment of which he is interested. A person who is interested in the payment of money which another is bound by law to pay, and who therefore pays it, is entitled to be reimbursed by the other.

ILLUSTRATION

B holds land in Bengal, on a lease granted by *A*, the Zamindar. The revenue payable by *A* to the Government being in arrear, his land is advertised for sale by the Government. Under the revenue law, the consequence of such sale will be the annulment of *B*'s lease. But to prevent the sale and the consequent annulment of his own lease, pays to the Government the sum due from *A*. *A* is bound to make good to *B* the amount so paid.

70. Obligation of person enjoying benefit of non-gratuitous act. Where a person lawfully does anything for another person, or delivers anything to him not intending to do so gratuitously, and such other person enjoys the benefit thereof, the latter is bound to make compensation to the former in respect of, or to restore, the thing so done or delivered.

ILLUSTRATIONS

(*a*) *A*, a tradesman leaves goods at *B*'s house by mistake. *B* treats the goods as his own. He is bound to pay *A* for them.

(*b*) *A* saves *B*'s property from fire. *A* is not entitled to compensation from *B*, if the circumstances show that he intended to act gratuitously.

71. Responsibility of finder of goods. *A* person who finds goods belonging to another, and takes them into his custody, is subject to the same responsibility as a bailee.

72. Liability of person to whom money is paid, or thing delivered, by mistake or under coercion. A person to whom money has been paid, or anything delivered, by mistake or under coercion, must repay or return it.

ILLUSTRATIONS

(*a*) *A* and *B* jointly owe 100 rupees to *C*. *A* alone pays the amount to *C* and *B*, not knowing this fact, pays 100 rupees over again to *C*. *C* is bound to repay the amount to *B*.

A railway company, refuses to deliver up certain goods to the consignee, except upon the payment of an illegal charge for carriage. The consignee pays the sum charged in order to obtain the goods. He is entitled to recover so much of the charge as was illegally excessive.

NOTE

Doctrine of unjust enrichment is enshrined under Section 72 of Contract Act. *Telco v. The Municipal Corporation of the City of Thane*, AIR 1992 S.C. 645.

CHAPTER VI

Of the Consequences of Breach of Contract

73. Compensation for loss or damage caused by breach of contract. When a contract has been broken, the party who suffers by such breach is entitled to receive from the party who has broken the contract, compensation for any loss or damage caused to him thereby, which naturally arose in the usual course of thing from such breach, or which the parties knew, when they made the contract, to be likely to result from the breach of it.

Such compensation is not to be given for any remote and indirect loss or damage sustained by reason of the breach.

Compensation for failure to discharge obligation resembling those created by contract. When an obligation resembling those created by contract has been incurred and has not been discharged, and person injured by the failure to discharge it is entitled to receive the same compensation from the party in default, as if such person has contracted to discharge it and had broken his contract.

Explanation. In estimating the loss or damage arising from a breach of contract, the means which existed of remedying the inconvenience caused by the non-performance of the contract must be taken into account.

ILLUSTRATIONS

(*a*) *A* contracts to sell and deliver 50 mounds of saltpetre to *B*, at a certain price, to be paid on delivery. *A* breaks his promise. *B* is entitled to receive from A, by way of compensation, the sum, if any, by which the contract price falls short of the price for which *B* might have obtained 50 mounds of saltpetre of like quality at the time when the saltpetre ought to have been delivered.

(*b*) A hires *B* ship to go to Bombay, and there takes on board on the 1st of January, a cargo which *A* is to provide, and to bring it to Calcutta, the freight to be paid when earned. *B*'s ship does not go to Bombay, but *A* has opportunities of procuring suitable conveyance for the cargo upon terms as advantageous as those on which he has chartered the ship. *A* avails himself of those opportunities, but is put to trouble and expense in doing so. *A* is entitled to receive compensation from *B* in respect of such trouble and expense.

(*c*) *A* contracts to buy of *B*, at stated price, 50 mounds of rice, no time being fixed for delivery. *A* afterwards informs *B* that he will not accept the rice if tendered to him. *B* is entitled to receive from *A*, by way of compensation, the amount, if any by which the contract price exceeds that which *B* can obtain for the rice at the time when *A* informs *B* that he will not accept it.

(*d*) *A* contracts to buy *B*'s ship for 60,000 rupees, but breaks his promise. *A* must pay to *B*, by way of compensation, the excess, if any, of the contract price over the price which *B* can obtain for the ship at the time of the breach of promise.

(*e*) *A*, the owner of a boat, contracts with *B* to take a cargo of jute to Mirzapur, for sale at the place starting on a specified day. The boat owing to some unavoidable cause, does not start at the time appointed, whereby the arrival of cargo at Mirzapur is delayed beyond the time when it would have arrived if the boat had sailed according to the contract. After that date, and before the arrival of the cargo, the price of jute falls. The measure of the compensation payable to *B* by *A* is the difference between the price which *B* could have obtained for the cargo at Mirzapur at the time when it would have arrived if forwarded in due course, and its market price at the time when it actually arrived.

(*f*) *A* contracts to repair B's house in a certain manner, and receives payment in advance. *A* repairs the house but not according to contract. *B* is entitled to recover from *A* the cost of making the repairs conform to the contract.

(*g*) *A* contracts to let his ship to *B* for a year, from the 1st of January, for a certain price. Freights rise, and on the 1st of January, the hire obtainable for the ship is higher than the contract price. *A* breaks his promise. He must pay to *B*, by way of compensation, a sum equal to the difference between the contract price and the price for which *B* could hire a similar ship for a year on and from the 1st of January.

(*h*) *A* contracts to supply *B* with a certain quantity of iron at a fixed price, being a higher price than that for which *A* could procure and deliver the iron. *B* wrongfully refuses to receive the iron. *B* must pay to *A*, by way of compensation, the difference between the contract price of the iron and the sum for which *A* could have obtained and delivered it.

(*i*) *A* delivers to *B*, a common carrier, a machine, to be conveyed, without delay, to *A*'s mill, informing *B* that his mill is stopped for want of the machine. *B* unreasonably delays the delivery of the machine, and *A*, in consequence, loses a profitable contract with the Government. *A* is entitled to receive from *B* by way of compensation, the average amount of profit which would have been made by the working of the mill during the time that delivery of it was delayed, but not the loss sustained through the loss of the Government contract.

(*j*) *A*, having contracted with *B*, to supply *B* with 1,000 tons of iron at 100 rupees a ton, to be delivered at a stated time, contracts with *C* for the purchase of 1,000 tons of irons at 80 rupees a ton, telling *C* that he does so for the purpose of performing his contract with *B*. *C* fails to perform his contract with *A*, who cannot procure other iron, and *B*, in consequence rescinds the contact. *C* must pay to A 20,000 rupees, being the profit which *A* would have made by the performance of his contract with *B*.

(*k*) *A* contracts with *B*, to make and deliver to *B*, by a fixed day, for a specified price, a certain piece of machinery. *A* does not deliver the piece of machinery at the time specified, and, in consequence of this *B* is obliged to procure another at a higher price than that which he was to have paid to *A*, and is prevented from performing a contract which *B* had made with a third person at the time of his contract with *A* (but which had not been then communicated to *A*), and is compelled to make compensation for breach of that contract. *A* must pay to *B*, by way of compensation, the difference between the contract price of machinery and the sum paid by *B* for another, but not the sum paid by *B* to the third person by way to compensation.

(*l*) *A*, a builder, contracts to erect and finish a house by the 1st January, in order that *B* may give possession of it at that time to *C*, to whom *B* has contracted to let it. *A* is informed of the contract between *B*, and C. *A* builds the house so badly that, before the first of January, it falls down and has to be rebuilt by *B* who, in consequence, loses the rent which he was to have received from *C*, and is obliged to make compensation to *C* for the breach of his contract. *A* must make compensation to *B* for the cost rebuilding the house, for the rent lost, and for the compensation made to *C*.

(*m*) *A* sells certain merchandise to. *B*, warranting it to be of a particular quality, and *B* in reliance upon this warranty, sells it to *C* with a similar warranty. The goods prove to be not according to the warranty, and *B* becomes liable to pay *C* a sum of money by way of compensation, *B* is entitled to be reimbursed this sum by *A*.

(*n*) *A* contracts to pay a sum of money to *B* on a day specified. *A* does not pay the money on that day. *B* in consequence of not receiving the money on that day, is unable to pay his debts, and is totally ruined. *A* is not liable to make good to *B* anything except the principal sum he contracted to pay, together with interest up to the day of payment.

(*o*) *A* contracts to deliver 50 mounds of saltpetre to *B* on the 1st of January, at a certain price. *B* afterwards, before the 1st of January, contracts to sell the saltpetre to *C* at a price higher than the market price of the 1st of January. *A* breaks his promise. In estimating the compensation payable by *A* to *B*, market price of the 1st January, and not the profit which would have arisen to *B* from the sale to *C* is to be taken into account.

(*p*) *A* contracts to sell and deliver 500 bales of cotton to *B*, on a fixed day. *A* knows nothing of *B*'s mode of conducting his business. *A* breaks his promise, and *B*, having no cotton, is obliged to close his mill. *A* is not responsible to *B* for the loss caused to *B* by the closing of the mill.

(*q*) *A* contracts to sell and deliver to *B*, on the 1st of January, certain cloth which *B* intends to manufacture into caps of a particular kind, for which there is no demand, except at that season. The cloth is not delivered till after the appointed time, and too late to be used that year in making caps. *B* is entitled to receive from *A*, by way of compensation, the difference between the contract price of the cloth and its market price at the time of delivery but not the profits which he expected to obtain by making caps, nor the expenses which he has been put to in making preparation for the manufacture.

(*r*) *A*, a shipowner, contracts with *B* to convey him from Calcutta to Sydney, in *A*'s ship sailing on the first of January, and *B* pays to *A* by way of deposit, one-half of his passage money. The ship does not sail on the 1st of January, and *B*, after being, in consequence, detained in Calcutta for some time, and thereby put to some expense, proceeds to Sydney in another vessel, and in consequence arriving too late in Sydney, looses a sum of money. *A* is liable to repay to *B* his deposit with interest and the expense to which he is put by his detention in Calcutta, and the excess, if any, of the passage money paid for the second ship over that agreed upon for the first, but not the sum of money which B lost by arriving in Sydney too late.

NOTES

In *Karsandas H. Thacker v. M/s The Saran Engineering Co. Ltd.*, AIR 1965 S.C. 1981, reference was made to illustration (k) to Section 73. It is the special feature of Section 73 that it is supported by eighteen illustrations. First of all the controversy is compared to any of these and if similarity is found the case is decided accordingly.

Measure of damages in contract is compensation for the consequence which flows as a natural and capable consequence or which is not remote and could be foreseen. *Devender Singh v. State of U.P.*, AIR 1987 All 306.

74. Compensation for breach of contract where penalty stipulated for. When a contract has been broken, if a sum is named in the contract as the amount to be paid in case of such breach, or if the contract contains any other stipulation by way of penalty, the party complaining of the breach is entitled, whether or not actual damage or loss is proved to have been caused thereby, to receive from the party who has broken the contract reasonable compensation not exceeding the amount so named or, as the case may be, the penalty stipulated for.

Explanation. A stipulation for increased interest, from the date of default may be a stipulation by way of penalty.

Exception. When any person enters into any bail-bond, recognizance or other instrument of the same nature, or, under the provisions of any law, or under the orders of the Central Government or of any State Government, gives any bond for the performance of any public duty or act in which the public are interested, he shall be liable, upon breach of the condition of any such instrument, to pay the whole sum mentioned therein.

Explanation. A person who enters into a contract with Government does not necessarily thereby undertake any public duty, or promise to do an act in which the public are interested.

ILLUSTRATIONS

(*a*) *A* contracts with *B* to pay *B* Rs. 1,000 if he fails to pay *B* Rs. 500 on a given day. *A* fails to pay *B* Rs. 500 on that day. *B* is entitled to recover from *A* such compensation not exceeding Rs. 1,000 as the Court considers reasonable.

(*b*) A contracts with *B* that, if *A* practises as a surgeon within Calcutta, he will pay *B* Rs. 5,000. *A* practises as surgeon in Calcutta. *B* is entitled to such compensation, not exceeding Rs. 5,000, as the Court considers reasonable.

(*c*) *A* gives a recognizance binding him in a penalty of Rs. 500 to appear in Court on a certain day. He forfeits his recognizance. He is liable to pay the whole penalty.

(*d*) *A* gives *B* a bond for the repayment of Rs. 1,000 with interest at 12 per cent at end of six months, with a stipulation that in case of default, interest shall be payable at the rate of 75 per cent from the date of default. This is a stipulation by way of penalty, and *B* is only entitled to recover from *A* such compensation as the Court considers reasonable.

(*e*) *A*, who owes money to *B* a money-lender, undertakes to repay him by delivering to him 10 mounds of grain on a certain date, and stipulates that, in the event of his not delivering the stipulated amount by the stipulated date, he shall be liable to deliver 20 mounds. This is a stipulation by way of penalty, and B is only entitled to reasonable compensation in case of breach.

(*f*) *A* undertakes to repay *B* a loan of Rs. 1,000 by five equal, monthly installments with a stipulation that, in default of payment of any instalment, the whole shall become due. This stipulation is not by way of penalty, and the contact may be enforced according to its terms.

(*g*) A borrows Rs. 100 from *B*, and gives him a bond for Rs. 200 payable by five yearly installments of Rs. 40, with a stipulation that in default of payment of any instalment, the whole shall become due. This is a stipulation by way of penalty.

NOTE

Unless there is a breach of contract recourse to section 74 cannot be taken. It is available only in the cases of concluded contract. *Arvind Coal and Construction Company v. Damodar Vally Corporation*, AIR 1991, Pat. 14.

75. Party rightfully rescinding contract, entitled to compensation. A person who rightly rescinds a contract is entitled to compensation for any damage which he has sustained through the non-fulfillment of the contract.

ILLUSTRATION

A, a singer, contracts with *B* the manager of a theatre, to sing at his theatre for two nights in every week during the next two months, and *B* engages to pay her 100 rupees for each night's performance. On the sixth night *A* wilfully absents herself from the theatre, and *B* in consequence, rescinds the contract. *B* is entitled to claim compensation for the damage which he has sustained through the non-fulfillment of the contract.

CHAPTER VII

Sale of Goods

This chapter of the Act is wholly repealed by the Indian Sale of Goods Act, 1930, (3 of 1930), Sec. 65 but the numbering of the later Chapters and sections is not altered.

CHAPTER VIII

Of Indemnity and Guarantee

124. "Contract of indemnity" defined. A contract by which one party promises to save the other from loss caused to him by the conduct of the promisor himself, or by the conduct of any other person, is called a "contract of indemnity".

ILLUSTRATION

A contracts to indemnity *B* against the consequences of any proceedings which *C* may take against *B* in respect of a certain sum of 200 rupees. This is a contract of indemnity.

125. Rights of indemnity-holder when sued. The promisee in a contract of indemnity, acting within the scope of his authority, is entitled to recover from the promisor :

(1) all damages which he may be compelled to pay in any suit in respect of any matter to which the promise to indemnify applies;

(2) all costs which he may be compelled to pay in any such suit if, in bringing or defending it, he did not contravene the orders of the promisor, and acted as it would have been prudent for him to act in the absence of any contract of indemnity, or if the promisor authorised him to bring or defend the suit;

(3) all sums which he may have paid under the terms of any compromise of any such suit, if the compromise was not contrary to the orders of the promisor, and was one which if would have been prudent for the promisee to make in the absence of any contract of indemnity, or if the promisor authorized him to compromise the suit.

NOTE

Bank guarantees and letters of credit as well as an indemnity given by a bank are covered under the provisions of this Section. *United Commercial Bank v. Bank of India.* AIR 1981 SC 1424 followed by AIR 1986 SC 1924.

126. "Contract of guarantee", "surety", "principal debtor", and "creditor". A "contract of guarantee" is a contract to perform the promise, or discharge the liability, of a third person in case of his default. The person who gives the guarantee is called the "surety", the person in respect of whose default the guarantee is given is called the "principal debtor", and the person to whom the guarantee is given is called the "creditor". A guarantee may be either oral or written.

127. Consideration for guarantee. Anything done, or any promise made for the benefit of the principal debtor may be a sufficient consideration to the surety for giving the guarantee.

ILLUSTRATIONS

(*a*) *B* requests A to sell and deliver to him goods on credit. *A* agrees to do so, provided *C* will guarantee the payment of the price of the goods. *C* promises to guarantee the payment in consideration of *A*'s promise to deliver the goods. This is a sufficient consideration for *C*'s promise;

(*b*) *A* sells and delivers goods to *B*. *C* afterwards, requests *A* to forbear to use B for the debt for a year, and promises that if he does so, *C* will pay for them in default of payment by *B*. *A* agrees to forbear as requested. This is sufficient consideration for *C*'s promise;

(*c*) *A* sell and delivers goods to *B*. *C* afterwards, without consideration, agrees to pay for them in default of *B*. The agreement is void.

128. Surety's liability. The liability of the surety is co-extensive with that of the principal debtor, unless it is otherwise provided by the contract.

ILLUSTRATION

A guarantees to *B* the payment of a bill of exchange by *C*, the acceptor. The bill is dishonoured by *C*. *A* is liable, not only for the amount of the bill, but also for any interest and charge which may have become due on it.

129. "Continuing guarantee". A guarantee which extends to a series of transactions is called a "continuing guarantee".

ILLUSTRATIONS

(*a*) *A*, in consideration that *B* will employ *C* in collecting the rent of *B*'s Zamindari, promises *B* to be responsible, to the amount of 5,000 rupees, for the due collection and payment by *C* of those rents. This is a continuing guarantee.

(*b*) *A* guarantees payment to *B* a tea-dealer, to the amount of £ 100, for any tea he may from time to time supply to *C*. *B* supplies *C* with the tea to the above value of £100 and *C* pays *B* for it. Afterwards *B* supplies C with tea to the above value of £200. *C* fails to pay. The guarantee given by *A* was a continuing guarantee, and he is accordingly liable to *B* to the extent of £100.

(*c*) *A* guarantees payment to *B* of the price of five sacks of flour, to be delivered by *B* to *C* and to be paid for in a month. *B* delivers five sacks to *C*, *C* pays for them. Afterwards *B* delivers four sacks to *C* which *C* does not pay for. The guarantee given by *A* was not a continuing guarantee, and accordingly he is not liable for the price of the four sacks.

NOTE

In the cases of continuing guarantee limitation would only run from the date of breach. *Union Bank of India Ernakulam v. T. J. Stephen* AIR 1990 Ker. 180 (AIR 1979 SC 102 relied upon.)

130. Revocation of continuing guarantee. A continuing guarantee may, at any time be revoked by the surety, as to future transactions by notice to the creditor.

ILLUSTRATIONS

(*a*) *A*, in consideration of *B*'s discounting, at *A*'s request, bills of exchange for *C* guarantees *B*, for twelve months, the due payment of all such bills to the extent of 5,000 rupees. *B* discounts bills for *C* to the extent of 2,000 rupees. Afterwards, at the end of three months, *A* revokes the guarantee. This revocation discharges *A* from all liability to *B*, for any subsequent discount. But *A* is liable to *B* for the 2,000 rupees on default of *C*.

(*b*) *A* guarantees to *B* to the extent of 10,000 rupees, that *C* shall pay all the bills that *B* shall draw upon him. *B* draws upon *C*. *C* accepts the bill. *A* gives notice of revocation. *C* dishonours the bill at maturity. *A* is liable upon his guarantee.

131. Revocation of continuing guarantee by surety's death. The death of the surety operates, in the absence of any contract to the contrary, as revocation of continuing guarantee, so far as regards future transactions.

132. Liability of two persons, primarily liable, not affected by arrangements between them that one shall be surety on other's default. Where two persons contract with a third person to undertake certain liability, and also contract with each other that one of them shall be liable only on the default of the other, the third person not being a party to such contract, the liability of each of such two persons to the third person under the first contract is not affected by the existence of second contract, although such third person may have been aware of its existence.

ILLUSTRATION

A and *B* make a joint and several promissory note to *C*, *A* makes it in fact as surety for *B* and *C* knows this at the time when the note is made. The fact that *A*, to the knowledge of *C* made the note as surely for *B*, is no answer to a suit by *C* against *A* upon the note.

133. Discharge of surety by variance in terms of contract. Any variance, made without surety's consent, in the terms of contract between the principal debtor and the creditor, discharges the surety as to the transactions subsequent to the variance.

ILLUSTRATIONS

(*a*) *A* becomes surety to *C* for *B*'s conduct as a manager in *C*'s bank. Afterwards, *B* and *C* contract, without *A*'s consent, that *B*'s salary shall be raised, and that he shall become liable for one-fourth of the losses on overdrafts. *B* allows a customer to overdraw, and the bank looses a sum of money. *A* is discharged from his suretyship by the variance made without his consent and is liable to make good this loss.

(*b*) *A* guarantees *C* against the misconduct of *B* in an office to which *B* is appointed by *C*, and of which the duties are defined by an Act of the Legislature. By a subsequent Act the nature of the office is materially altered. Afterwards, *B* misconducts himself. *A* is discharged by the change from future liability under his guarantee, though the misconduct of B is in respect of a duty not affected by the later Act.

(*c*) *C* agrees to appoint *B* as his clerk to sell goods at a yearly salary upon *A*'s becoming surety to *C* for *B*'s duty accounting for money received by him as such clerk. Afterwards, without *A*'s knowledge or consent, *C* and *B* agree that *B* should be paid by a commission on the goods sold by him and not by a fixed salary. *A* is not liable for subsequent misconduct of *B*.

(*d*) *A* gives to *C* a continuing guarantee to the extent of 3,000 rupees for any oil supplied by *C* to *B* on credit. Afterwards *B* becomes embarrassed, and without the knowledge of *A, B* and *C* contract that *C* shall continue to supply *B* with oil for ready money, and that the payment shall be applied to the then existing debts between *B* and *C*. *A* is not liable on his guarantee for any goods supplied after this new arrangement.

(*e*) *C* contracts to lend *B* 5,000 rupees on the first March, *A* guarantees repayment. *C* pays the 5,000 rupees to *B* on the 1st January. *A* is discharged from his liability, as the contract has been varied inasmuch as *C* might sue *B* for the money before the 1st of March.

NOTE

Any variance made without the surety's consent in the terms of the contract between the principal debtor and the creditor discharges the surety as to the transactions subsequent to variance AIR 1990 Mad. 115.

134. Discharge of surety by release or discharge of principal debtor. The surety is discharged by any contract between the creditor and the principal debtor, by which the principal debtor is released, or by any act or omission of the creditor, the legal consequence of which is the discharge of the principal debtor.

ILLUSTRATIONS

(*a*) *A* gives a guarantee to *C* for goods to be supplied by *C* to *B*. *C* supplies goods to *B* and afterwards *B* becomes embarrassed and contracts with the creditor (including *C*) to assign to them his property in consideration of their releasing him from their demands. Here *B* is released from his debt by the contract with *C*, and *A* is discharged from the suretyship.

(*b*) *A* contracts with *B* to grow a crop of indigo on *A*'s land and to deliver it to *B* at a fixed rate, and *C* guarantees *A*'s performance of this contract, *B* diverts a stream of water which is necessary for irrigation of *A*'s land, and thereby prevents him from raising the indigo. *C* is no longer liable on his guarantee.

(*c*) *A* contracts with *B* for a fixed price to build a house for *B* within a stipulated time, *B* supplying the necessary timber. *C* guarantees *A*'s performance of the contract. *B* omits to supply the timber, *C* is discharged from his suretyship.

NOTE

Discharge of the debtor by operation of law does not amount to discharge of surely under this section. AIR 1988 Cal. 18 and AIR 1982 S.C. 1497.

135. Discharge of surety when creditor compounds with, gives time to, or agree not to sue principal debtor. A contract between the creditor and the principal debtor, by which the creditor makes a composition with, or promises to give time to, or not to sue, the principal debtor, discharges the surety unless the surety assents to such contract.

136. Surety not discharged when agreement made with third person to give time to principal debtor. Where a contract to give time to the principal debtor is made by the creditor with a third person, and not with the principal debtor, the surety is not discharged.

ILLUSTRATION

C, the holder of an overdue bill of exchange drawn by *A* as surety for *B*, and accepted by *B*, contracts with *M* to give time to *B*, *A* is not discharged.

137. Creditor's forbearance to sue does not discharge surety. Mere forbearance on the part of the creditor to sue the principal debtor or to enforce any other remedy against him does not in the absence of any provision in the guarantee to the contrary, discharge the surety.

ILLUSTRATION

B owes to *C* a debt guaranteed by *A*. The debt becomes payable. *C* does not sue *B* for a year after the debt has become payable. *A* is not discharged from the suretyship.

138. Release of one co-surety does not discharge others. Where there are co-sureties, a release by the creditor of one of them does not discharge the others, neither does it free the surety so released from his responsibility to the other sureties.

139. Discharge of surety by creditor's act or omission impairing surety's eventual remedy. If the creditor does any act which is inconsistent with the rights of the surety, or omits to do any act which his duty to the surety requires him to do, and the eventual remedy of the surety himself against the principal debtor is thereby impaired, the surety is discharged.

ILLUSTRATIONS

(*a*) *B* contracts to build a ship for *C* for a given sum, to be paid by installments as the work reaches certain stages. *A* becomes surety to *C* for *B*'s due performance of the contract. *C*, without the knowledge of *A*, prepays to *B* the two installments. *A* is discharged, by this prepayment.

(*b*) *C* lends money to *B* on the security of a joint and several promissory note made in *C*'s favour by *B*, and by *A*, as surety for *B*, together with a bill of sale of *B*' furniture, which gives power to *C* to sell the furniture, and apply the proceeds in discharge of the note. Subsequently, *C* sells the furniture, but owing to his misconduct and wilful negligence, only a small price is realized. *A* is discharged from liability on the note.

(*c*) *A* puts *M* as apprentice to *B*, and gives a guarantee to *B* for *M*'s fidelity. *B* promises on his part that he will, at least once a month, see *M* make up the cash. *B* omits to see this done, as promised, and *M* embezzles. *A* is not liable to *B* on his guarantee.

140. Rights of surety on payment or performance. Where a guaranteed debt has become due, on default of the principal debtor to perform a guaranteed duty has taken place, the surety, upon payment or performance of all that he is liable for, is invested with all the rights which the creditor had against the principal debtor.

141. Surety's right to benefit of creditor's securities. A surety is entitled to the benefit of every security which the creditor has against the principal debtor at the time when the contract of suretyship is entered into, whether the surety knows of the existence of such security or not; and, if the creditor loses or, without the consent of the surety, parts with such security, the surety is discharged to the extent of the value of the security.

ILLUSTRATIONS

(*a*) *C* advances to *B* his tenant, 2,000 rupees on the guarantee of *A*. *C* has also a further security for the 2,000 rupees by a mortgage of *B*'s furniture. *C* cancels the mortgage. *B* becomes insolvent and *C* sues *A* on his guarantee. *A* is discharged from liability to the amount of the value of the furniture.

(*b*) C, a creditor whose advance to *B* is secured by a decree, receives also guarantee for that advance from *A*, *C* afterwards takes *B*'s goods in execution under the decree, and then, without the knowledge of *A*, withdraws, the execution. *A* is discharged.

(*c*) *A*, as surety for *B*, makes a bond jointly with *B* to *C*, to secure a loan from *C* to *B*. Afterwards, *C* obtains from *B* a further security for the same debt. Subsequently, *C* gives up the further security. *A* is not discharged.

142. Guarantee obtained by misrepresentation invalid. Any guarantee which has been obtained by means of misrepresentation made by creditor, or with his knowledge and assent, concerning a material part of the transaction, in invalid.

143. Guarantee obtained by concealment invalid. Any guarantee which the creditor has obtained by means of keeping silence as to a material circumstance is invalid.

ILLUSTRATIONS

(*a*) *A* engages *B* as clerk to collect money for him. *B* fails to account for some of his receipts, and *A*, in consequence, calls upon him to furnish security for his duly accounting. *C* gives his guarantee for *B*'s duly accounting. *A*, does not acquaint *C* with *B*'s previous conduct. *B* afterwards makes default. The guarantee is invalid.

(*b*) *A* guarantees to *C* payment for iron to be supplied by him to *B* to the amount of 2,000 tons. *B* and *C* have privately agreed that *B* should pay five rupees per ton beyond the market price, such excess to be applied in liquidation of an old debt. This agreement is concealed from *A*. *A* is not liable as a surety.

144. Guarantee on contract that creditor shall not act on it until co-surety joins. Where a person gives a guarantee upon a contract that the creditor shall not act upon it until any person has joined in it as co-surety, the guarantee is not valid if that other person does not join.

145. Implied promise to indemnify surety. In every contract of guarantee there is an implied promise by the principal debtor to indemnify the surety; and the surety is entitled to recover from the principal debtor whatever sum he has rightfully paid under the guarantee, but no sums which he has paid wrongfully.

ILLUSTRATIONS

(*a*) *B* is indebted to *C* and *A* is surety for the debt. *C* demands payment from *A* and on his refusal sues him for the amount. *A* defends the suit, having reasonable grounds for doing so, but is compelled to pay the amount of the debt with cost. He can recover from *B* the amount paid by him for costs, as well as the principal debt.

(*b*) *C* lends *B* a sum of money, and *A* at the request of *B* accepts a bill of exchange drawn by *B* upon *A* to secure the amount. *C*, the holder of the bill, demands payment of it from *A* and, on *A*'s refusal to pay, sues him upon the bill. *A*, not having reasonable grounds for so doing, defends the suit, and has to pay the amount of the bill, and costs. He can recover from *B* the amount of the bill, but not the sum paid for costs, as there was no real ground for defending the action.

(*c*) *A* guarantees to *C*, to the extent of 2,000 rupees, payment for rice to be supplied by *C* to *B*. *C* supplies to *B* rice to a less amount than 2,000 rupees, but obtains from *A* payment of the sum of 2,000 rupees in respect of the rice supplied. *A* cannot recover from *B* more than the price of the rice actually supplied.

146. Co-sureties liable to contribute equally. Where two or more persons are co-sureties for the same debt or duty, either jointly or severally and whether under the same or different contracts, and whether with or without the knowledge of each other, the co-sureties, in the absence of any contract to the contrary, are liable, as between themselves, to pay each an equal share of the whole debt or of that part of it which remains unpaid by the principal debtor.

ILLUSTRATIONS

(*a*) *A*, *B* and *C* are sureties to *D* for the sum of 3,000 rupees lent to *E*, *E* makes default in payment. *A*, *B* and *C* are liable, as between themselves, to pay 1,000 rupees each.

(*b*) *A*, *B* and *C* are sureties to *D* for the sum of 1,000 rupees, lent to *E* and there is a contract between *A*, *B* and *C* that *A* is to be responsible to the extent of one quarter. *B* to the extent of one quarter, and *C* to the extent of one half. *E* makes default in payment. As between the sureties, *A* is liable to pay Rs. 250, *B* Rs. 250 and *C* Rs. 500.

147. Liability of co-sureties bound in different sums. Co-sureties who are bound in different sums are liable to pay equally as far as the limits of their respective obligations permit.

ILLUSTRATIONS

(*a*) *A*, *B* and *C*, as sureties for *D*, enter into three several bonds, each in a different penalty, namely, *A* in the penalty of 10,000 rupees, *B* in that of 20,000 rupees, *C* in that of 40,000 rupees conditioned for *D*'s duly accounting to *E*. *D* makes default to the extent of Rs. 30,000, *A*, *B* and *C* are each liable to pay Rs. 10,000.

(*b*) *A*, *B* and *C*, as sureties for *D* enter into three several bonds, each in a different penalty, namely, *A* in the penalty of Rs. 10,000, *B* in that of Rs. 20,000, *C* in that of 40,000 rupees, conditioned for *D*'s duly accounting to *E*. *D* makes default to the extent of 40,000 rupees. *A* is liable to pay 10,000 rupees and *B* and *C* 15,000 rupees each.

(*c*) *A*, *B* and *C* as sureties for *D*, enter into three several bonds each in a different penalty, namely, *A* in a penalty of Rs. 10,000, *B* in that of Rs. 20,000 *C* in that of 40,000 rupees, conditioned for D's duly accounting to *E*. *D* makes default to the extent of 70,000 rupees. *A*, *B*, and *C* have to pay each the full penalty of his bond.

CHAPTER IX

Of Bailment

148. "Bailment", "bailor" and "bailee" defined. A "bailment" is the delivery of goods by one person to another for some purpose, upon a contract that they shall, when the purpose is accomplished, be returned or otherwise disposed of according to the directions of the person delivering them. The person delivering the goods is called the 'bailor'. The person to whom they are delivered is called the 'bailee'.

Explanation. If person already in possession of the goods of another contracts to hold them as a bailee, he thereby becomes the bailee, and the owner becomes the bailor of such goods although they may not have been delivered by way of bailment.

149. Delivery to bailee, how made. The delivery to the bailee may be made by doing anything which has the effect of putting the goods in the possession of the intended bailee or of any person authorized to hold them on his behalf.

150. Bailor's duty to disclose faults in goods bailed. The bailor is bound to disclose to the bailee faults in the goods bailed, of which the bailor is aware, and which materially interfere with the use of them, or expose the bailee to extraordinary risks; and, if he does not make such disclosure, he is responsible for damage arising to the bailee directly from such faults.

If the goods are bailed for hire, the bailor is responsible for such damage, whether he was or was not aware of the existence of such faults in the goods bailed.

ILLUSTRATIONS

(*a*) *A* lends a horse, which he knows to be vicious, to *B*. He does not disclose the fact that the horse is vicious. The horse runs away, *B* is thrown and injured, *A* is responsible to *B* for damage substained.

(*b*) *A* hires a carriage of *B*. The carriage is unsafe, through *B* is not aware of it, and A is injured, B is responsible to *A* for the injury.

151. Care to be taken by bailee. In all cases of bailment the bailee is bound to take as much care of the goods bailed to him as a man of ordinary prudence would, under similar circumstances, take of his own goods of the same bulk, quality and value as the goods bailed.

152. Bailee when not liable for loss, etc., of thing bailed. The bailee, in the absence of any special contract, is not responsible for the loss, destruction of deterioration of the thing bailed, if he has taken the amount of care of it described in Section 151.

153. Termination of bailment by bailee's act inconsistent with conditions. A contract of bailment is voidable at the option of the bailor, if the bailee does any act with regard to the goods bailed, inconsistent with the conditions of the bailment.

ILLUSTRATION

A lets to *B*, for hire a horse for his own riding, *B* drives the horse in his carriage. This is at the option of *A*, a termination of the bailment.

154. Liability of bailee making unauthorised use of goods bailed. If the bailee makes any use of the goods bailed, which is not according to the conditions of the bailment, he is liable to make compensation to the bailor for any damage arising to the goods from or during such use of them.

ILLUSTRATIONS

(*a*) *A* lends a horse to *B* for his own riding only. *B* allows *C* a member of his family, to ride the horse. *C* rides with care, but the horse accidentally falls and a injured. *B* is liable to make compensation to *A* for the injury done to the horse.

(*b*) *A* hires a horse in Calcutta from *B* expressly to march to Benares. *A* rides with due care, but marches to Cuttack instead. The horse accidently falls and is injured. *A* is liable to make compensation to *B* for the injury to the horse.

155. Effect of mixture, with bailor's consent of his goods with bailee's. If the bailee, with the consent of the bailor, mixes the goods of the bailor with his own goods, the bailor and the bailee shall have an interest, in proportion to their respective shares, in the mixture thus produced.

156. Effect of mixture, without bailor's consent, when the goods can be separated. If the bailee, without the consent of the bailor, mixes the goods of the bailor with his own goods and the goods can be separated or divided, the property in the goods remains in the parties respectively; but the bailee is bound to bear the expense of separation or division, and any damage arising from the mixture.

ILLUSTRATION

A bails, 100 bales of cotton marked with a particular mark to *B*. *B*, without *A*'s consent mixes the 100 bales with other bales of his own, bearing a different mark. *A* is entitled to have his 100 bales returned and *B* is bound to bear all the expenses incurred in the separation of the bales, and any other incidental damage.

157. Effect of mixture, without bailor's consent, when the goods cannot be separated. If the bailee without the consent of the bailor, mixes the goods of the bailor with his own goods, in such a manner that it is impossible to separate the goods bailed from the other goods and deliver them back, the bailor is entitled to be compensated by the bailee for the loss of the goods.

ILLUSTRATION

A bails a barrel of Cape flour worth Rs. 45 to *B*. *B*, without *A*'s consent mixes the flour with country flour of his own, worth only Rs. 25 a barrel. *B* must compensate *A* for the loss of his flour.

158. Repayment by bailor of necessary expenses. Where by the conditions of the bailment, the goods are to be kept or to be carried, or to have work done upon them by the bailee for the bailor, and the bailee is to receive no remuneration, the bailor shall repay to the bailee the necessary expenses incurred by him for the purpose of the bailment.

159. Restoration of goods lent gratuitously. The lender of a thing for use may at any time require its return, if the loan was gratuitous, even though he lent it for a specified time or purpose. But if, on the faith of such loan made for a specified time or purpose, the borrower has acted in such a manner that the return of the thing lent before the time agreed upon would cause him loss exceeding the benefit actually derived by him from the loan, the lender must, if he compels the return, indemnify the borrower for the amount in which the loss so occasioned exceeds the benefit so derived.

160. Return of goods bailed, on expiration of time or accomplishment of purpose. It is the duty of the bailee to return, or deliver according to the bailor's directions, the goods bailed, without demand, as soon as the time for which they were bailed has expired, or the purpose for which they were bailed has been accomplished.

161. Bailee's responsibility when goods are not duly returned. If, by the default of the bailee, the goods are not returned, delivered or tendered at the proper time, he is responsible to the bailor for any loss, destruction or deterioration of the goods from that time.

162. Termination of gratuitous bailment by death. A gratuitous bailment is terminated by the death either of the bailor or of the bailee.

163. Bailor entitled to increase or profit from goods bailed. In the absence of any contract to the contrary, the bailee is bound to deliver to the bailor, or according to his directions, any increase or profit which may have accrued from the goods bailed.

ILLUSTRATION

A leaves a cow in the custody of *B* to be taken care of. The cow has a calf. *B* is bound to deliver the calf as well as the cow to *A*.

164. Bailor's responsibility to bailee. The bailor is responsible to the bailee for any loss which the bailee may sustain by reason that the bailor was not entitled to make the bailment, or to receive back the goods, or to give directions respecting them.

165. Bailment by several joint owners. If several joint owners of goods bail them, the bailee may deliver them back to, or according to the directions of, one joint owner without the consent of all, in the absence of any agreement to the contrary.

166. Bailee not responsible on re-delivery to bailor without title. If the bailor has no title to the goods, and the bailee, in good faith, delivers them back to, or according to the directions of, the bailor, the bailee is not responsible to the owner in respect of such delivery.

167. Right of third person, claiming goods bailed. If a person, other than the bailor, claims goods bailed he may apply to the Court to stop delivery of the goods to the bailor, and to decide the title to the goods.

168. Right of finder of goods : May sue for specific reward offered. The finder of goods has no right to sue the owner for compensation for trouble and expense voluntarily incurred by him to preserve the goods and to find out the owner; but he may retain the goods against the owner until he receives such compensation; and where the owner has offered a specific reward for the return of goods lost, the finder may sue for such reward, and may retain the goods until he receives it.

169. When finder of thing commonly on sale may sell it. When a thing which is commonly the subject of sale is lost, if the owner cannot with reasonable diligence be found, or, if he refuses, upon demand, to pay the lawful charges of the finder, the finder may sell it:

(1) When the thing is in danger of perishing or of losing the greater part of its value, or

(2) When the lawful charges of the finder, in respect of the thing found, amount to two-thirds of its value.

170. Bailee's particular lien. Where the bailee has, in accordance with the purpose of the bailment, rendered any service involving the exercise of labour or skill in respect of the goods bailed, he has, in the absence of a contract to the contrary, a right to retain such goods until he receives due remuneration for the services he has rendered in respect of them.

ILLUSTRATIONS

(*a*) *A* delivers a rough diamond to *B*, a jeweller, to be cut and polished which is accordingly done. *B* is entitled to retain the stone till he is paid for the services he has rendered.

(*b*) *A* gives cloth to *B*, a tailor, to make into a coat. *B* promises *A* to deliver the coat as soon as it is finished, and to give a three months credit for the price. *B* is not entitled to retain the coat until he is paid.

171. General lien of bankers, factors, wharfingers, attorneys and policy-brokers. Bankers, factors, wharfingers, attorneys of a High Court, and policy-brokers may, in the absence of a contract to the contrary, retain as security for a general balance of amount, any goods bailed to them; but no other person have a right to retain, as a security for such balance, goods bailed to them, unless there is an express contract to that effect.

Bailments of Pledges

172. "Pledge", "pawnor" and "pawnee" defined. The bailment of goods as security for payment of a debt or performance of a promise is called, "pledge". The bailor is in this case called the "pawnor". The bailee is called the "pawnee".

173. Pawnee's right of retainer. The pawnee may retain the goods pledged, not only for payment of the debt or the performance of the promise but for the interests of the debt, and all necessary expenses incurred by him in respect of the possession or for the preservation of the goods pledged.

174. Pawnee not to retain for debt or promise other than that for which goods pledged. Presumption in case of subsequent advances. The pawnee shall not in the absence of a contract to that effect, retain the goods pledged for any debt or promise other than the debt or promise for which they are pledged; but such contract, in the absence of anything to the contrary, shall be presumed in regard to subsequent advances made by the pawnee.

175. Pawnee's right as to extraordinary expenses incurred. The pawnee is entitled to receive from the pawnor extraordinary expenses incurred by him for the preservation of the goods pledged.

176. Pawnee's right where pawnor makes default. If the pawnor makes default in payment of the debt, or performance, at the stipulated time or the promise, in respect of which the goods were pledged, the pawnee may bring a suit against the pawnor upon the debt or promise, and retain the goods pledged as a collateral security; or he may sell the thing pledged, on giving the pawnor reasonable notice of the sale.

If the proceeds of such sale are less than the amount due in respect of the debt or promise, the pawnor is still liable to pay the balance. If the proceeds of the sale are greater than the amount so due, the pawnee shall pay over the surplus to the pawnor.

177. Defaulting pawnor's right to redeem. If a time is stipulated for the payment of the debt, or performance of the promise, for which the pledge is made, and the pawnor makes default in payment of the debt or performance of the promise at the stipulated time, he may redeem the goods pledged at any subsequent time before the actual sale of them; but he must, in that case, pay, in addition, any expenses which have arisen from his default.

178. Pledge by mercantile agent. Where a mercantile agent is, with the consent of the owner, in possession of goods or the documents of title to goods, any pledge made by him, when acting in the ordinary course of business of mercantile agent, shall be as valid as if he were expressly authorised by the owner of the goods, to make the same; provided that the pawnee acts in goods faith and has not at the time of the pledge notice that the pawnor has not authority to pledge.

Explanation. In this section the expressions "mercantile agent" and "documents of title" shall have the meaning assigned to them in the Indian Sale of Goods Act, 1930 (3 of 1930).

178-A. Pledge by person in possession under voidable contract. When the pawnor has obtained possession of the goods pledged by him under a contract voidable under Sec. 19 or Sec. 19-A, but the contract has not been rescinded at the time of the pledge, the pawnee acquires a good title to the goods, provided he acts in good faith and without notice of the pawnors defect of title.

179. Pledge where pawnor has only a limited interest. Where a person pledges goods in which he has only a limited interest, the pledge is valid to the extent of that interest.

Suits by Bailees or Bailors against Wrong-doers

180. Suit by bailor or bailee against wrong-doer. If a third person wrongfully deprives the bailee of the use of possession of the goods bailed, or does them any injury, the bailee is entitled to use such remedies as the owner might have used in like case if no bailment had been made; and either the bailor or the bailee may bring a suit against a third person for such deprivation or injury.

181. Apportionment of relief or compensation obtained by such suits. Whatever is obtained by way of relief or compensation in any such suit shall, as between the bailor and the bailee, be dealt with according to their respective interests.

CHAPTER X

Agency

Appointment and Authority of Agents

182. "Agent" and "principal" defined. An "agent" is a person employed to do any act for another, or to represent another in dealing with third persons. The person for whom such act is done, or who is so represented, is called the "principal".

183. Who may employ agent. Any person who is of the age of majority according to the law to which he is subject, and who is of sound mind, may employ an agent.

184. Who may be an agent. As between the principal and third persons, any person may become an agent, but no person who is not of the age of majority and sound mind can become an agent, so as to be responsible to his principal according to the provisions in that behalf herein contained.

185. Consideration not necessary. No consideration is necessary to create an agency.

186. Agent's authority may be expressed or implied. The authority of an agent may be expressed or implied.

187. Definitions of express and implied authority. An authority is said to be express when it is given by words spoken or written. An authority is said to be implied when it is to be inferred from the circumstances of the case; and things spoken or written, or the ordinary course of dealing, may be accounted circumstances of the case.

ILLUSTRATION

A owns a shop in Serampur, living himself in Calcutta, and visiting the shop occasionally. The shop is managed by *B*, and he is in the habit of ordering goods from *C* in the name of *A* for the purposes of the shop, and of paying for them out of *A*'s funds with *A*'s knowledge. *B* has an implied authority from *A* to order goods from *C* in the name of *A* for the purposes of the shop.

188. Extent of agent's authority. An agent, having an authority to do an act, has authority to do every lawful thing which is necessary in order to do such act.

An agent having an authority to carry on a business, has authority to do every lawful thing necessary for the purpose, or usually done in the course of conducting such business.

ILLUSTRATIONS

(*a*) *A* is employed by *B*, residing in London, to recover at Bombay a debt, due to *B*. *A* may adopt any legal process necessary for the purpose of recovering the debt, and may give a valid discharge for the same.

(*b*) *A* constitutes *B*, his agent, to carry on his business of a ship-builder, *B* may purchase timber and other materials, and hire workmen, for the purposes of carrying on the business.

189. Agent's authority in an emergency. An agent has authority, in an emergency, to do all such acts for the purpose of protecting his principal from loss as would be done by a person of ordinary prudence, in his own case, under similar circumstances.

ILLUSTRATIONS

(*a*) An agent for sale may have goods repaired if it be necessary.

(*b*) *A* consigns provisions to *B* at Calcutta, with directions to send them immediately to *C* at Cuttack. *B* may sell the provisions at Calcutta, if they will not bear the journey of Cuttack without spoiling.

Sub-Agents

190. When agent cannot delegate. An agent cannot lawfully employ another to perform acts which he has expressly or impliedly undertaken to perform personally, unless by the ordinary custom of trade a sub-agent may, or, from the nature of the agency, a sub-agent must, be employed.

191. "Sub-agent" defined. A "sub-agent" is a person employed by, and acting under the control of, the original agent in the business of the agency.

192. Representation of principal by sub-agent properly appointed. Where a sub-agent is properly appointed, the principal is, so far as regards third persons, represented by sub-agent, and is bound by and responsible for his acts, as if he were an agent originally appointed by principal.

Agent's responsibility for sub-agent. The agent is responsible to the principal for the acts of the sub-agent.

Sub-agent's responsibility. The sub-agent is responsible for his acts to the agent, but not to the principal, except in cases of fraud or wilful wrong.

193. Agent's responsibility for sub-agent appointed without authority. Where an agent, without having authority to do so, has appointed a person to act as a sub-agent, the agent stands towards such person in the relation of a principal to an agent, and is responsible for his acts both to the principal and to third persons: the principal is not represented by or responsible for the acts of the person so employed, nor is that person responsible to the principal.

194. Relation between principal and person duly appointed by agent to act in business of agency. Where an agent, holding an express or implied authority to name another person to act for the principal in the business of the agency, has named another person accordingly, such person is not a sub-agent, but an agent of the principal for such part of the business of the agency as is entrusted to him.

ILLUSTRATIONS

(*a*) *A* directs *B*, his solicitor to sell his estate by auction, and to employ an auctioneer for the purpose. *B* names *C*, auctioneer, to conduct the sale *C* is not a sub-agent, but is *A*'s agent for the conduct of the sale.

(*b*) *A* authorizes *B*, a merchant in Calcutta, to recover the moneys due to *A* from *C & Co*. *B* instructs *D*, a solicitor, to take legal proceedings against *C* and Co., for the recovery of the money. *D* is not a sub-agent, but is a solicitor for *A*.

195. Agent's duty in naming such person. In selecting such agent for his principal, an agent is bound to exercise the same amount to discretion as a man of ordinary prudence would exercise in his own case; and if he does this, he is not responsible to the principal for the negligence of the agent so selected.

ILLUSTRATIONS

(*a*) *A* instructs *B*, a merchant to buy a ship for him. *B* employs a ship surveyor of good reputation to choose a ship for *A*. The surveyor makes the choice negligently and the ship turns out to be unsea-worthy, and is lost. *B* is not, but the surveyor is, responsible to *A*.

(*b*) *A* consigns goods to *B*, merchant, for sale. *B* in due course, employs auctioneer in good credit to sell the goods of *A*, and allows the auctioneer to receive the proceeds of the sale. The auctioneer afterwards becomes insolvent without having accounted for the proceeds, *B* is not responsible to *A* for the proceeds.

Ratification

196. Right of person as to acts done for him without his authority. Effect of ratification. Where acts are done by one person on behalf of another but without his knowledge or authority, he may elect to ratify or to disown such acts. If he ratify them, the same effects will follow as if they had been performed by his authority.

197. Ratification may be expressed or implied. Ratification may be expressed or may be implied in the conduct of the person on whose behalf the acts are done.

ILLUSTRATIONS

(*a*) *A*, without authority, buys goods for *B*. Afterwards *B* sells them to *C* on his own account; *B*'s conduct implies a ratification of the purchase made for him by *A*.

(*b*) *A*, without *B*'s authority, lends *B*'s money to *C*. Afterwards *B* accepts interest on the money from *C*. *B*'s conduct implies a ratification of the loan.

198. Knowledge requisite for valid ratification. No valid ratification can be made by a person whose knowledge of the facts of the case is materially defective.

199. Effect of ratifying unauthorized act forming part of a transaction. A person ratifying any unauthorized act done on his behalf ratifies the whole of the transaction of which such act formed a part.

200. Ratification of unauthorised act cannot injure third person. An act done by one person on behalf of another, without such other person's authority, which, if done with authority, would have the effect of subjecting a third person to damages, or of terminating any right or interest of a third person, cannot, by ratification, be made to have such effect.

ILLUSTRATIONS

(*a*) *A*, not being authorised thereto by *B*, demands on behalf of *B*, the delivery of a chattel, the property of *B*, from *C* who is in possession of it. This demand cannot be ratified by *B*, so as to make *C* liable for damages for his refusal to deliver.

(*b*) *A* holds a lease from *B*, terminable on three month's notice. *C*, an authorised person, gives notice of termination to *A*. The notice cannot be ratified by *B*, so as to be binding on *A*.

Revocation of Authority

201. Termination of agency. An agency is terminated by the principal revoking his authority; or by the agent renouncing the business of the agency; or by the business of the agency being completed, or by either the principal or agent dying or becoming of unsound mind, or by the principal being adjudicated an insolvent under the provisions of any Act for the time being in force for the relief of insolvent debtors.

202. Termination of agency, where agent has an interest in subject matter. Where the agent has himself an interest in the property which forms the subject matter of the agency, the agency cannot, in the absence of an express contract, be terminated to the prejudice of such interest.

ILLUSTRATIONS

(*a*) *A* gives authority to *B* to sell *A*'s land, and to pay himself, out of the proceeds, the debts due to him from *A*. *A* cannot revoke this authority, nor can it be terminated by his insanity or death.

(*b*) *A* consigns 1,000 bales of cotton to *B*, who has made advances to him on such cotton and desires *B* to sell the cotton, and to repay himself, out of the price, the amount of his own advances. *A* cannot revoke this authority, nor it is terminated by his insanity or death.

203. When principal may revoke agent's authority. The principal may, save as is otherwise provided by the last preceding section, revoke the authority given to his agent at any time before the authority has been exercised so as to bind the principal.

204. Revocation where authority has been partly exercised. The principal cannot revoke the authority given to his agent after the authority has been partly exercised, so far as regards such acts and obligations as arise from acts already done in the agency.

ILLUSTRATIONS

(*a*) *A* authorises *B* to buy 1,000 bales of cotton on account of *A* and to pay for it out of *A*'s money remaining in *B*'s hand. *B* buys 1,000 bales of cotton in his own name, so as to make himself personally liable for the price. *A* cannot revoke *B*'s authority so far as regards payment for the cotton.

(*b*) *A* authorize *B* to buy 1,000 bales of cotton on account of *A* and to pay for it out of *A*'s money remaining in *B*'s hand. *B* buy's 1,000 bales of cotton in *A*'s name and so as not to render himself personally liable for the price. *A* can revoke *B*'s authority to pay for the cotton.

205. Compensation for revocation by principal or renunciation by agent. Where there is an express or implied contract that the agency should be continued for any period of time, the principal must make compensation to the agent, or the agent to the principal, as the case may be. for any previous revocation or renunciation of the agency without sufficient cause.

206. Notice of revocation or renunciation. Reasonable notice must be given of such revocation or renunciation; otherwise the damage thereby resulting to the principal or the agent, as the case may be, must be made good to the one by the other.

207. Revocation and renunciation may be expressed or implied. Revocation and renunciation may be expressed or may be implied in the conduct of the principal or agent respectively.

ILLUSTRATION

A empowers *B* to let *A*'s house. Afterwards *A* lets it himself. This is an implied revocation of *B*'s authority.

208. When termination of agent's authority takes effect as to agent, and as to third persons. The termination of the authority of an agent does not, so far as regards the agent, takes effect before it becomes known to him, or, so far as regards third persons, before it becomes known to them.

ILLUSTRATIONS

(*a*) *A* directs *B* to sell goods for him, and agrees to give *B* 5 per cent, commission on the price fetched by the goods. *A* afterwards, by letter, revokes *B*'s authority, *B*, after the letter is sent, but before he receives it, sell the goods for 100 rupees. The sale is binding on *A*, and *B* is entitled to five rupees as his commission.

(*b*) *A* at Madras, by letter, directs *B* to sell for him some cotton lying in a warehouse in Bombay, and afterwards, by letter, revokes his authority to sell, and directs *B* to send the cotton to Madras. *B*, after receiving the second letter, enters into a contract with *C* who knows of the first letter, but not of the second, for the sale to him of the cotton. *C* pays *B* the money, with which *B* absconds. *C*'s payment is good as against *A*.

(*c*) *A* directs *B*, his agent, to pay certain money to *C*. *A* dies, and *D* takes out probate to his will. *B* after *A*'s death, but before hearing of it, pays the money to *C*. The payment is good as against *D*, the executor.

209. Agent's duty on termination of agency by principal's death or instantly. When an agency is terminated by the principal dying or becoming of unsound mind, the agent is bound to take, on behalf of the representatives of his late principal, all reasonable steps for the protection and preservation of the interests entrusted to him.

210. Termination of sub-agent's authority. The termination of the authority of an agent causes termination (subject to the rules herein contained regarding the termination of the agent's authority) of the authority of all sub-agents appointed by him.

Agent's Duty to Principal

211. Agent's duty in conducting principal's business. An agent is bound to conduct the business of his principal according to the directions given by the principal, or, in the absence of any such directions, according to the custom which prevails, in doing business of the same kind at the place where the agent conducts such business. When the agent acts otherwise, if any loss be sustained, he must make it good to his principal, and, if any profit accrues, he must account for it.

ILLUSTRATIONS

(*a*) *A*, an agent engaged in carrying on for *B* a business, in which it is the custom to invest from time to time, at interest, the moneys which may be in hand, omits to make such investments, *A* must make good to *B* the interest usually obtained by such investments.

(*b*) *B*, a broker, in whose business it is not the custom to sell on credit, sells goods of *A* on credit to *C* whose credit at the time was very high, *C*, before payment, becomes insolvent. *B* must make good the loss to *A*.

212. Skill and diligence required from agent. An agent is bound to conduct the business of the agency with as much skill as is generally possessed by persons engaged in similar business unless the principal has notice of his want of skill. The agent is always bound to act with reasonable diligence, and to use such skill as he possesses; and to make compensation to his principal in respect of the direct consequences of his own neglect, want of skill, or misconduct, but not in respect of loss or damages which are indirectly or remotely caused by such neglect, want of skill, or misconduct.

ILLUSTRATIONS

(*a*) *A*, a merchant in Calcutta, has an agent, *B*, in London, to whom a sum of money is paid on A's account, with orders to remit. *B* retains the money for a considerable time. *A*, in consequence of not receiving the money, becomes insolvent. *B* is liable for the money and interest from the day on which it ought to have been paid, according to the usual rate, and for any further direct loss—as, *e.g.*, by variation of rate of exchange—but not further.

(*b*) *A*, an agent for the sale of goods, having authority to sell on credit, sells to *B*, on credit, without making the proper and usual inquiries as to the solvency of *B*. *B*, at the time of such sale, is insolvent. *A* must make compensation to his principal in respect of any loss thereby sustained.

(*c*) *A*, an insurance broker, employed by *B* to effect an insurance on a ship, omits to see that the usual clauses are inserted in the policy. The ship is afterwards lost. In consequence of the omission of the clauses nothing can be recovered from the under-writers. *A* is bound to make good the loss to *B*.

(*d*) *A*, a merchant in England, directs *B*, his agent, at Bombay, who accepts the agency, to send him 100 bales of cotton by a certain ship. *B*, having it in his power to send the cotton, omits to do so. The ship arrives safely in England. Soon, after her arrival, the price of cotton rises. *B* is bound to make good to *A* the profit which he might have made by the 100 bales of cotton at the time the ship arrived, but not any-profit he might have made by the subsequent rise.

NOTE

Loss incurred to the Principal as a result of misconduct and neglect is to be compensated by the agent. Agent misinformed his principal as to purchase of goods. In reality goods were never purchased. The act falls within the ambit of this section. *Jai Bharti Corporation v. P.N.S.N. Rajshekhara Wadar*, AIR 1992 S.C. 596.

213. Agent's accounts. An agent is bound to render proper account to his principal on demand.

214. Agent's duty to communicate with principal. It is the duty of an agent in the case of difficulty, to use all reasonable diligence in communication with his principal, and in seeking to obtain his instructions.

215. Right of principal when agent deals, on his own account in business of agency without principal's consent. If an agent deals on his own account in the business of the agency without first obtaining the consent of his principal and acquainting him with all material circumstances which have come to his own knowledge on the subject, the principal may repudiate the transaction, if the case shows either that any material fact has been dishonestly concealed from him by the agent, or that the dealings of the agent have been disadvantageous to him.

ILLUSTRATIONS

(*a*) *A* directs *B* to sell *A*'s estate. *B* buys the estate for himself in the name of *C*. *A* on discovering that *B* has bought the estate for himself, may repudiate the sale, if he can show that *B* has dishonestly concealed any material fact, or that the sale has been disadvantageous to him.

(*b*) *A* directs *B* to sell *A*'s estate, *B* on looking over the estate before selling it, finds a mine on the estate which is unknown to *A*, *B* informs *A* that he wishes to buy the estate for himself, but conceals the discovery of the mine. *A* allows to *B* to buy, in ignorance of the existence of the mine. *A*'s on discovering that *B* knew of the mine at the time he bought the estate, may either repudiate or adopt the sale at his option.

216. Principal's right to benefit gained by agent dealing on his own account in business of agency. If an agent, without the knowledge of his principal, deals in the business of the agency on his own account instead of on account of his principal, the principal is entitled to claim from the agent any benefit which may have resulted to him from the transaction.

ILLUSTRATION

A directs *B*, his agent, to buy a certain house for him. *B* tells *A* it cannot be bought, and buys the house for himself. *A* may, on discovering that *B* has bought the house, compel him to sell it to *A* at the price he gave for it.

217. Agent's right of retainer out of sums received on principal's account. An agent may retain, out of any sums received on account of the principal in the business of the agency, all moneys due to himself in respect of advances made or expenses properly incurred by him in conducting such business, and also such remuneration as may be payable to him for acting as agent.

218. Agent's duty to pay sums received for principal. Subject to such deduction, the agent is bound to pay to his principal all sums received on his account.

219. When agent's remuneration becomes due. In the absence of any special contract, payment for the performance of any act is not due to the agent until the completion of such act, but an agent may detain moneys received by him on account of goods sold, although the whole of the goods consigned to him for the sale may not have been sold, or although the sale may not be actually complete.

220. Agent not entitled to remuneration for business misconducted. An agent who is guilty of misconduct in the business of the agency, is not entitled to any remuneration in respect of that part of the business which he has misconducted.

ILLUSTRATIONS

(*a*) *A* employs *B* to recover 1,00,000 rupees from *C*, and to lay it out on good security. *B* recovers 1,00,000 rupees, and lays out 90,000 rupees on good security, but lays out 10,000 rupees on security which he ought to have known to be bad, whereby *A* loses 2,000 rupees. *B* is entitled to remuneration for recovering the 1,00,000 rupees and for investing the 90,000 rupees. He is not entitled to any remuneration for investing, the 10,000 rupees, and he must make good the 2,000 rupees to *B*.

(*b*) *A* employs *B* to recover 1,000 rupees from *C*. Through *B*'s misconduct the money is not recovered. *B* is entitled to no remuneration for his services, and must make good the loss.

221. Agent's lien on principal's property. In the absence of any contract to the contrary, an agent is entitled to retain goods, papers and other property, whether movable or immovable, of the principal received by him, until the amount due to himself for commission, disbursements and services in respect of the same has been paid or accounted for to him.

Principal's duty to agent

222. Agent to be indemnified against consequences of lawful acts. The employer to an agent is bound to indemnify him against the consequences of all lawful acts done by such agent in exercise of the authority conferred upon him.

ILLUSTRATIONS

(*a*) *B*, at Singapur under instructions from *A* of Calcutta, contracts with *C* to deliver certain goods to him. *A* does not send the goods to *B*, and *C* sues *B* for breach of contract. *B* informs *A* of the suit, and *A* authorises him to defend the suit, *B* defend the suit, and is compelled to pay damages, and costs, and incurs expenses. *A* is liable to *B* for such damages, costs and expenses.

(*b*) *B*, a broker at Calcutta, by the orders of *A*, a merchant there, contracts with *C* for the purchase of 10 casks of oil for *A*. Afterwards *A* refuses to receive the oil, and *C* sues *B*. *B* informs *A*, who repudiates the contract altogether. *B* defend, but unsuccessfully, and has to pay damages and costs, and incurs expenses. *A* is liable to *B* for such damages, costs and expenses.

223. Agent to be indemnified against consequences of acts done in good faith. Where one person employs another to do an act, and the agent does the act is good faith, the employer is liable to indemnify the agent against the consequences of that act, though it cause an injury to the rights of third persons.

ILLUSTRATIONS

(*a*) *A*, decree-holder, entitled to execution of *B*'s goods requires the officer of the Court to seize certain goods, representing them to be the goods of *B*. The officer seizes the goods and is used by *C*, the true owner of the goods. *A* is liable to indemnify the officer for the sum which he is compelled to pay to *C* in consequence of obeying *A*'s directions.

(*b*) *B*, at the request of *A*, sells goods in the possession of *A*, but which *A* had no right to dispose of, *B* does not know this, and hands over the proceeds of the sale to *A*. Afterwards, *C* the true owner of the goods, sues *B* and recovers the value of the goods and costs. *A* is liable to indemnify *B* for what he has been compelled to pay *C* and for *B*'s own expenses.

224. Non-liability of employer of agent to do a criminal act. Where any person employs another to do an act which is criminal, the employer is not liable to the agent, either upon an express or an implied promise, to indemnify him against the consequences of that act.

ILLUSTRATIONS

(*a*) *A* employs *B* to beat *C*, and agrees to indemnify him against all consequences of the act, *B* thereupon beats *C* and has to pay damages to *C* for so doing. *A* is not liable to indemnify *B* for those damages.

(*b*) *B*, the proprietor of a newspaper, publishes, at *A*'s request, a libel upon *C* in the paper, and *A* agrees to indemnify *B* against the consequences of the publication, and all costs and damages of any action in respect thereof. *B* is sued by *C* and has to pay damages, and also incurs expenses. *A* is not liable to *B* upon the indemnity.

225. Compensation to agent for injury caused by principal's neglect. The principal must make compensation to his agent in respect of injury caused to such agent by the principal's neglect or want of skill.

ILLUSTRATIONS

A employs *B* as a bricklayer in building a house, and puts up the scaffolding himself. The scaffolding is unskillfully put up, and *B* is in consequence hurt. *A* must make compensation to *B*.

Effect of agency on contracts with third persons

226. Enforcement and consequences of agent's contracts. Contracts entered into through an agent, and obligations arising from acts done by an agent, may be enforced in the same manner, and will have the same legal consequences, as if the contracts had been entered into and the acts done by the principal in person.

ILLUSTRATIONS

(*a*) *A* buys goods from *B*, knowing that he is an agent for their sale, but not knowing who is the principal. *B*'s principal is the person entitled to claim from *A* the price of the goods, and *A* cannot, in a suit by the principal, set-off against that claim a debt due to himself from *B*.

(*b*) *A*, being *B*'s agent, with authority to receive money on his behalf, receives from *C* a sum of money due to *B*. *C* is discharged of his obligation to pay the sum in question to *B*.

227. Principal how far bound, when agent exceeds authority. When an agent does more than he is authorized to do, and when the part of what he does, which is within his authority, can be separated, from the part which is beyond his authority, so much only of what he does as is within his authority is binding as between him and his principal.

ILLUSTRATION

A being owner of a ship and cargo authorizes *B* to procure an insurance for 4,000 rupees on the ship. *B* procures a policy for 4,000 rupees on the ship and another for the like sum on the cargo. *A* is bound to pay the premium for the policy on the ship, but not the premium for policy on the cargo.

228. Principal not bound when excess of agent's authority is not separable. Where an agent does more than he is authorised to do, and what he does beyond the scope of his authority cannot be separated from what is within it, the principal is not bound to recognize the transaction.

ILLUSTRATION

A authorizes *B* to buy 500 sheeps for him. *B* buys 500 sheep and 200 lambs for a sum of 6,000 rupees, *A* may repudiate the whole transaction.

229. Consequences of notice given to agent. Any notice given to or information obtained by the agent, provided it be given or obtained in the course of the business transacted by him for the principal, shall, as between the principal and third parties, have the same legal consequences as if it had been given to or obtained by the principal.

ILLUSTRATIONS

(*a*) *A* is employed by *B* to buy from *C*, certain goods, of which *C* is the apparent owner, and buys them accordingly. In the course of the treaty for the sale, *A* learns that the goods really belonged to *D*, but *B* is ignorant of that fact. *B* is not entitled to set-off a debt owing to him from *C* against the price of the goods.

(*b*) *A* is employed by *B* to buy from *C* goods of which *C* is the apparent owner, *A* was, before he was so employed, a servant of *C*, and then learnt that the goods really belonged to *D*, but *B* is ignorant of that fact. In spite of the knowledge of his agent, *B* may set-off against the price of the goods a debt owing to him from *C*.

230. Agent cannot personally enforce, not be bound by contracts, on behalf of principal. In the absence of any contract to that effect an agent cannot personally enforce contract entered into by him on behalf of his principal, nor is he personally bound by them.

Presumption of contract to contrary. Such a contract shall be presumed to exist in the following cases :

(1) Where the contract is made by an agent for sale or purchase of goods for a merchant resident abroad.

(2) Where the agent does not disclose the name of his principal;

(3) Where the principal, though disclosed, cannot be sued.

231. Rights of parties to a contract made by agent not disclosed. If an agent makes a contract with a person who neither knows, nor has reason to suspect that he is an agent, his principal may require the performance of the contract, but the other contracting party has, as against the principal, the same rights as he would have had against the agent if the agent had been principal.

If the principal discloses himself before the contract is completed, the other contracting party may refuse to fulfil the contract, if he can show that, if he had known who was the principal in the contract, or if he had known that the agent was not a principal, he would not have entered into the contract.

232. Performance of a contract with agent supposed to be principal. Where one man makes a contract with another, neither knowing nor having reasonable ground to suspect that the other is an agent, the principal, if he requires the performance of the contract, can only obtain such performance subject to the rights and obligations subsisting between the agent and the other party to the contract.

ILLUSTRATION

A, who owes 500 rupees to *B* sells 1,000 rupees worth of rice to *B*. *A* is acting as agent for *C* in the transaction, but *B* has no knowledge nor reasonable ground of suspicion that such is the case, *C* cannot compel *B* to take the rice without allowing him to set-off *A*'s debt.

233. Right of person dealing with agent personally liable. In cases where the agent is personally liable, a person dealing with him may hold either him or his principal, or both of them, liable.

ILLUSTRATION

A enters into a contract with *B* to sell him 100 bales of cotton and afterwards discovers that *B* was acting as agent for *C*. *A* may sue either *B* or *C*, or both, for the price of the cotton.

234. Consequence of inducing agent or principal to act on belief that principal or agent will be held exclusively liable. When a person who has made a contract with an agent induces the agent to act upon the belief that the principal only will be held liable, or induces the principal to act upon the belief that the agent only will be held liable, he cannot afterwards, hold liable the agent or principal respectively.

235. Liability of pretended agent. *A* person untruly representing himself to be the authorized agent of another, and thereby inducing a third person to deal with him as such agent, is liable, if his alleged employer does not ratify his acts, to make compensation to the other in respect of any loss or damage which he has incurred by so dealing.

236. Person falsely contracting as agent, not entitled to performance. A person with whom a contract has been entered into in the character of agent is not entitled to require the performance of it, if he was in reality acting, not as agent, but on his own account.

237. Liability of principal inducing belief, that agent's unauthorized acts were authorized. When an agent has, without authority, done acts or incurred obligations to third persons on behalf of his principal, the principal is bound by such acts or obligations, if he has by his words or conduct induced such third persons to believe that such acts and obligations were within the scope of the agent's authority.

ILLUSTRATIONS

(*a*) *A* consigns goods to *B* for sale, and gives him instructions not to sell under a fixed price. *C* being ignorant of *B*'s instructions enters into a contract with *B* to buy the goods at a price lower than the reserved price. *A* is bound by the contract.

(*b*) *A* entrusts *B* with negotiable instruments endorsed in blank. *B* sells them to *C* in violation of private orders from *A*. The sale is good.

238. Effect on agreement, of misrepresentation or fraud by agent. Misrepresentations made, or frauds committed, by agents acting in the course of their business for their principals, have the same effect on agreements made by such agents as if such misrepresentations or frauds had been made or committed by the principals; but misrepresentations made on frauds committed, by agents, in matters which do not fall within their authority, do not affect their principals.

ILLUSTRATIONS

(*a*) *A*, being *B*'s agent for the sale of goods induces *C* to buy them by a misrepresentation, which he was not authorized by *B* to make. The contract is voidable, as between *B* and *C* at the option of *C*.

(*b*) *A*, the captain of *B*'s ship, signs bills of lading without having received on board the goods mentioned therein. The bills of lading are void as between *B* and the pretended consignor.

CHAPTER XI

Of Partnership

Sections 239 to 266 (* * *) Repealed by the Indian Partnership Act, 1932 (IX of 1932), S. 73 and Schedule II.

SCHEDULE

Enactments Repealed

Repealed by S. 3 and Schedule III of the Repealing and Amending Act, 1914 (X of 1914).

II

APPENDIX

The Indian Partnership Act, 1932

[*8th April, 1932*]

An Act to define and demand the law relating to partnership

Whereas it is expedient to define and amend the law relating to partnership; it is hereby enacted as follows :

CHAPTER 1

Preliminary

1. Short title, extent and commencement. (1) This act may be called the Indian Partnership Act, 1932.

[2][(2) It extends to the whole of India [3][except the State of Jammu and Kashmir].]

(3) It shall come into force on the 1st day of October, 1932, except Section 69, which shall come into force on the 1st day of October, 1933.

STATE AMENDMENTS

DADRA AND NAGAR HAVELI. For sub-section (3), substitute the following :

"(3) It shall come into force at once except Section 69, which shall come into force on the 1st day of July, 1966."— Regn. VI of 1963 as amended by Regn. II of 1965.

GOA, DAMAN AND DIU. Same as in Dadra and Nagar Haveli except for the date of enforcement of Section 69 which is January 1, 1965 — Regn. XI of 1963.

LACCADIVE, MINICOY AND AMINDIVI ISLANDS. For sub-section (3), substitute the following :

---

1. For Statement of Objects and Reasons and for Report of Special Committee, see Gazette of India 1931, Part V, p. 31; for report of Select Committee, see ibid, 1932, Part V, p. 1.

   The Act has been applied to Berar by the Berar Laws Act, 1941 (4 of 1941).

   The Act has been extended to Dadra and Nagar Haveli by Reg. 6 of 1963, S. 2 and Schs. 1 and 2 of 1965, to Pondicherry by Reg. 7 of 1963, S. 3 and Sch. 1, to Goa, Daman and Diu by Reg. 11 of 1963, S. 3 and Sch., and to Laccadive, Minicoy and Amindivi Islands by Reg. 8 of 1965, S. 3 and Sch.

   The Act does not apply to partnership of cooperative societies in Maharashtra, vide Mah. Act. 24 of 1961, S. 20 (2).

   The Act has been amended in its application to Madras by Madras Adaptation of Laws (Central Acts) Order, 1950 and by Madras Act 21 of 1959.
2. *Subs.* by A.O. 1950 for the former sub-section.
3. *Subs.* by Act 3 of 1951, S. 3 and Sch., for "except Part B States".

"(3) It shall come into force at once except Section 69, which shall come into force on the expiry of a period of one year from the date of commencement of the rest of this Act."— Regn. VIII of 1965, Section 3 and Schedule I.

PONDICHERRY. Same as in Dadra and Nagar Haveli, except for the date of enforcement of Section 69, which is July 1, 1964 — Regn. VII of 1963, Section 3 and Schedule I.

2. Definitions. In this Act, unless there is anything repugnant in the subject or context,

(*a*) an "act of a firm" means any act or omission by all the partners or by any partner or agent of the firm which gives rise to a right enforceable by or against the firm;

(*b*) "business' includes every trade, occupation and profession;

(*c*) "prescribed" means prescribed by rules made under this Act;

(*d*) "third party" used in relation to a firm or to a partner therein means any person who is not a partner in the firm; and

(*e*) expressions used but not defined in this Act and defined in the Indian Contract Act, 1872 (9 of 1872), shall have the meanings assigned to them in that Act.

STATE AMENDMENTS

MAHARASHTRA. In Section 2 of the Indian Partnership Act, 1932, in its application to the State of Maharashtra after clause (c), the following clause shall be inserted, namely :

"(*C-1*) "Registrar" means the Registrar of Firms appointed under sub-section (1) of Section 57 and includes the Deputy Registrar of Firms and Assistant Registrar of Firms appointed under sub-section (2) of that section;" — Mah. Act 29 of 1984, Section 2 (w.e.f. 1-1-1985).

3. Application of provisions of Act 9 of 1872. The unrepealed provisions of the Indian Contract Act, 1872, save in so far as they are inconsistent with the express provisions of this Act, shall continue to apply to firms.

NOTES

Though the Indian Partnership Act is now an independent Act IX of 1932 but previous to this date, the Law of Partnership was a part (Ch. XI) of the Indian Contract Act of 1872. This present section expressly recognizes that the Law of Partnership is still a branch of the law of the contract and provides that the general provisions of the Indian Contract Act shall continue to govern the partnership transactions in so far as they are not inconsistent with the provisions of this Act.

CHAPTER II

The Nature of Partnership

4. Definition of "partnership", "partner', "firm" and "firm name". "Partnership" is the relation between persons who have agreed to share the profit of a business carried on by all or any of them acting for all.

Persons who have entered into partnership with one another are called individually "partners" and collectively "a firm" and the name under which their business a carried on a called the "firm name".

NOTES

The components of the definition of 'partnership', and therefore of a "firm" consist of (*a*) persons, (*b*) a business carried on by all of them or any of them acting for all and (*c*) an agreement between those persons to carry on such business and to share its profits. It is the relationship between those persons which constitutes the partnership. Dy. C.S.T. v. K. Kelukutty, (1985) 4 SCC 35, 41 : 1985 SCC (Tax) 507.

Whether there was a partnership or not may in certain cases be a mixed question of law and fact, in the sense that whether the ingredients of partnership as embodied in the law of partnership were there or not in a particular case must be judged in the light of the principles applicable to partnership. The following important elements must be there in order to establish partnership (1) there must be an agreement entered into by all parties concerned; (2) the agreement must be to share profits of business; and (3) the business must be carried on by all or any of the persons concerned acting for all. Sharing of profits and contributing to losses were not the only elements in a partnership, existence of agency was essential. *Helper Girdharbhai v. Syed Mohmad Mirasaheb*, (1987) 3 SCC 538.

A firm is not a legal person even though it has some attributes of personality. Partnership is a certain relation between persons, the product of agreement to share profits of a business. 'Firm' is a collective noun, a compendious expression to designate an entity not a person. C.I.T. v. R.M. Chidambaram Pillai, (1977) 1 SCC 431, 433 : 1977 SCC (Tax) 188.

Firm or partnership is not a legal entity separate and distinct from partners and is only compendious description of individuals who compose the firm. *Munshi Ram v. Municipal Committee*, (1979) 3 SCC 83: 1979 SCC (Tax) 205.

A partnership firm is identifiable from the partnership agreement. Same partners may constitute more than one distinct and separate firm but firms have no juristic personality. Dy. C.S.T. v. K. Kelukutty, (1985) 4 SCC 35, 41, 42: 1985 SCC (Tax) 507.

Entrustment of stridhan property to husband does not amount to partnership. *Pratibha Rani v. Suraj Kumar*, (1985) 2 SCC 370 : 1985 SCC (Cri) 180.

5. Partnership not created by status. The relation of partnership arises from contract and not from status;

and, in particular, the members of a Hindu undivided family carrying on a family business as such, or Burmese Buddhist husband and wife carrying on business as such, are not partners in such business.

STATE AMENDMENTS

GOA, DAMAN AND DIU. For the words 'Burmese Buddhist husband and wife carrying on business as such', substitute the words 'a husband and wife under the regime of communion of property carrying on business as such. — Goa, Daman and Diu Act VI of 1966, Section 2 (22-8-1966).

6. Mode of determining existence of partnership. In determining whether a group of persons is or is not a firm, or whether a person is or is not a partner in a firm, regard shall be had to the real relation between the parties, as shown by all relevant facts taken together.

Explanation 1. The sharing of profits or of gross returns arising from property by persons holding a joint or common interest in that property does not of itself make such persons partners.

Explanation 2. The receipt by a person of a share of the profits of a business, or of a payment contingent upon the earning of profits or varying with the profits earned by a business, does not of itself make him a partner with the persons carrying on the business;

and, in particular, the receipt of such share or payment :

(*a*) by a lender of money to persons engaged or about to engage in any business,

(*b*) by a servant or agent as remuneration,

(*c*) by the widow or child of a deceased partner as annuity, or

(*d*) by a previous owner or part owner of the business, as consideration for the sale of the goodwill or share thereof,

does not itself make the receiver a partner with the persons carrying on the business.

7. Partnership at will. Where no provision is made by contract between the partners for the duration of their partnership, or for the determination of their partnership, the partnership is "partnership at will".

NOTES

In income-tax law a firm is a unit of assessment, by special provisions, but is not a full person; which leads to the next step that since a contract of employment requires two distinct persons, viz., the employer and the employee, there cannot be a contract of service, in strict law, between a firm and one of its partners, *C.I.T. v. R.M. Chidambaram Pillai*, (1977) 1 SCC 431, 433 : 1977 SCC (Tax) 188.

8. Particular partnership. A person may become a partner with another person in particular adventures or undertakings.

NOTES

Particular Partnership. Such partnership is limited to a particular transaction or adventure or undertaking. In partnership of this kind the partners incur no responsibility beyond the limits of the particular adventure of undertaking, but the three elements of partnership, namely, agreement, business and mutual agency must exist in this kind of partnership also. For illustration, two solicitors may be partners in so far as a particular case is concerned when they agree to share the profits accruing therefrom, but no further. So also a partner may be limited to the purchase and sale of particular jewels.

CHAPTER III

Relation of Partners to One Another

9. General duties of partners. Partners are bound to carry on the business of the firm to the greatest common advantage, to be just and faithful to each other, and to render true accounts and full information of all things affecting the firm to any partner or his legal representative.

STATE AMENDMENT

MAHARASHTRA. In Section 9 of the principal Act, for the words "or his legal representative" the words, "his heir or legal representative" shall be *substituted.* — Mah. Act 29 of 1984, S. 3 (w.e.f. 1-1-1985).

10. Duty to indemnify for loss caused by fraud. Every partner shall indemnify the firm for any loss caused to it by his fraud in the conduct of the business of the firm.

11. Determination of rights and duties of partners by contract between the partners. (1) Subject to the provisions of this Act, the mutual rights and duties of the partners of a firm may be determined by contract between the partners, and such contract may be expressed or may be implied by a course of dealing.

Such contract may be varied by consent of all the partners, and such consent may be expressed or may be implied by a course of dealing.

Agreement in restraint of trade. (2) Notwithstanding anything contained in Section 27 of the Indian Contract Act, 1872 (9 of 1872), such contract may provide that a partner shall not carry on any business other than that of the firm while he is a partner.

12. The conduct of the business. Subject to contract between the partners:

(*a*) every partner has a right to take part in the conduct of the business;

(*b*) every partner is bound to attend diligently to his duties in the conduct of the business;

(*c*) any difference arising as to ordinary matters connected with the business may be decided by a majority of the partners, and every partner shall have the right to express his opinion before the matter is decided, but no change may be made in the nature of the business without the consent of all the partners; and

(*d*) every partner has a right to have access to and to inspect and copy any of the books of the firm.

STATE AMENDMENTS

MAHARASHTRA. In Section 12 of the principal Act,

(*a*) in clause (*c*), the word "and" appearing at the end shall be deleted;

(*b*) in clause (*d*), for the words "books of the firm", the words "books of the firm; and" shall be *substituted*; (*c*) after clause

(*d*) the following clause shall be added, namely :

(*e*) in the even of the death of a partner, his heirs or legal representatives or their duly authorised agents shall have a right of access to and to inspect and copy any of the books of the firm." Mah. Act 29 of 1984, S. 4 (w.e.f. 1-1-1985).

NOTES

This section deals with the rules determining mutual relations of partners. All these rules are, however, subject to contract between the partners, that is, the rules will govern so far as they are not excluded or varied by agreement between the parties which may be proved by an express declaration to that effect or may be determined from the conduct of the parties.

13. Mutual rights and liabilities. Subject to contract between the partners:

(*a*) a partner is not entitled to receive remuneration for taking part in the conduct of the business;

(*b*) the partners are entitled to share equally in the profits earned, and shall contribute equally to the losses sustained by the firm;

(*c*) where a partner is entitled to interest on the capital subscribed by him, such interest shall be payable only out of profits;

(*d*) a partner making, for the purposes of the business, any payment or advance beyond the amount of capital he has agreed to subscribe, is entitled to interest thereon at the rate of six per cent per annum;

(*e*) the firm shall indemnify a partner in respect of payments made and liabilities incurred by him:

  (*i*) in the ordinary and proper conduct of the business, and

  (*ii*) in doing such act, in an emergency, for the purpose of protecting the firm from loss, as would be done by a person of ordinary prudence, in his own case, under similar circumstances, and

(*f*) a partner shall indemnify the firm for any loss caused to it by his wilful neglect in the conduct of the business of the firm.

NOTES

Scope. This section is one of the most important sections of this Act, which provides important rules relating to the mutual rights, duties and obligations of partners inter se in the absence of a contract to the contrary.

14. The property of the firm. Subject to contract between the partners, the property of the firm includes all property and rights and interests in property originally brought into the stock of the firm, or acquired, by purchase or otherwise, by or for the firm, or for the purposes and in the course of the business of the firm, and includes also the goodwill of the business.

Unless the contrary intention appears, property and rights and interest in property acquired with money belonging to the firm are deemed to have been acquired for the firm.

NOTES

A partner has interest in each and every asset of the firm, including goodwill even during subsistence of the firm, though during subsistence he cannot claim specific share in any particular asset. Partner's interest in the firm's assets in 'property' under S. 2(15) of Estate Duty Act, 1953. On death of a partner, interest in the assets passes to surviving partners, if in terms of partnership deed heir of the decreased partner is not to get any share therein. *Collector of Estate Duty v. Mrudula Nareshchandra*, 1986 Supp SCC 357, 365, 366: 1986 SCC (Tax) 793.

Goodwill is intangible in nature, insubstantial in form and nebulous in character and denotes benefit arising from connection and reputation. It is an asset of the business. *C.I.T. v. B.C. Srinivasa Setty*, (1981) 3 SCC 460: 1981 SCC (Tax) 119.

15. Application of the property of the firm. Subject to contract between the partners, the property of the firm shall be held and used by the partners exclusively for the purposes of the business.

16. Personal profits earned by partners. Subject to contract between the partners,

(*a*) if a partner derives any profit for himself from any transaction of the firm, or from the use of the property or business connection of the firm or the firm-name, he shall account for the profit and pay it to the firm;

(*b*) if a partner carries on any business of the same nature as and competing with that of the firm, he shall account for and pay to the firm all profits made by him in that business.

17. Subject to contract between the partners :

(*a*) **Rights and duties of partners after a change in the firm.** Where a change occurs in the constitution of a firm, the mutual rights and duties of the partners in the reconstituted firm remain the same as they were immediately before the change, as far as may be;

(*b*) **After the expiry of the term of the firm.** Where a firm constituted for a fixed term continues to carry on business after the expiry of that term, the mutual rights and duties of the partners remain the same as they were before the expiry, so far as they may be consistent with the incidents of partnership at will; and

(*c*) **And where additional undertakings are carried out.** Where a firm constituted to carry out one or more adventures or undertakings carries out other adventures or undertakings, the mutual rights and duties of the partners in respect of the other adventures or undertakings are the same as those in respect of the original adventures or undertakings.

CHAPTER IV

Relations of Partners to Third Parties

18. Partner to be agent of the firm. Subject to the provisions of this Act, a partner is the agent of the firm for the purpose of the business of the firm.

NOTES

A conspectus of Sections 18, 12 and 26 of the Partnership Act, shall show where the vehicle belonging to the firm is being driven by a partner, it can be said that it is done with the permission of the owner namely, the firm or with its authority. *Narchinva V. Kamat v. Alfredo Antonio Doe Martins*, (1985) 2 SCC 574, 577, 578.

In common parlance the status of a partner and the firm is different from employees working under the firm, it may be that a partner is being paid some remuneration for any special attention which he devotes but that would not involve any change of status and bring him within the definition of employee. *Regl. Director, E.S.I.C. v. Ramanuja Match industires*, (1985) 1 SCC 218, 221: 1985 SCC (L & S) 213.

19. Implied authority of the partner as agent of the firm. (1) Subject to the provisions of Section 22, the act of a partner which is done to carry on, in the usual way, business of the kind carried on by the firm, binds the firm.

The authority of a partner to bind the firm conferred by this section is called his "implied, authority".

(2) In the absence of any usage of custom of trade to the contrary, the implied authority of a partner does not empower him to:

(*a*) submit a dispute relating to the business of the firm to arbitration,

(*b*) open a banking account on behalf of the firm in his own name,

(*c*) compromise or relinquish any claim or portion of a claim by the firm,

(*d*) withdraw a suit or proceeding filed on behalf of the firm,

(e) admit any liability in a suit or proceeding against the firm,
(f) acquire immovable property on behalf of the firm,
(g) transfer immovable property belonging to the firm, or
(h) enter into partnership on behalf of the firm.

NOTES

Partner undertaking to allow land owned by him for raising cinema hall by the firm for the firm's business with the restriction against alienation of the land during subsistence of the firm—Partnership initially created for a fixed term made at will by a fresh deed — Land sold by such partner not withstanding the restriction not binding on the other partners. *Devi Prasad Rai v. Kanhaiyalal Mukharya*, (1986) 4 SCC 5.

20. Extension and restriction of partner's implied authority. The partners in a firm may, by contract between the partners, extend or restrict the implied authority of any partner.

Notwithstanding any such restriction, any act done by a partner on behalf of the firm which falls within his implied authority binds the firm, unless the person with whom he is dealing knows of the restriction or does not know or believe that partner to be a partner.

21. Partner's authority in an emergency. A partner has authority, in an emergency, to do all such acts for the purpose of protecting the firm from loss as would be done by a person of ordinary prudence, in his own case, acting under similar circumstances, and such acts bind the firm.

22. Mode of doing act to bind firm. In order to bind a firm, an act or instrument done or executed by a partner or other person on behalf of the firm shall be done or executed in the firm name, or in any other manner expressing or implying an intention to bind the firm.

23. Effect of admissions by a partner. An admission or representation made by a partner concerning the affairs of the firm is evidence against the firm, if it is made in the ordinary course of business.

24. Effect of notice to acting partner. Notice to a partner who habitually acts in the business of the firm of any matter relating to the affairs of the firm operates as notice to the firm, except in the case of a fraud on the firm committed by or with consent of the partner.

NOTES

Notice to a partner. The general rule is that a notice to a principal is notice to all his agents; and notice to the agent of matters connected with his agency is notice to the principal. The words 'notice to one partner is notice to all', mean, that a firm cannot, in its character of principal, set up the ignorance of some of its members against the knowledge of others of whose acts it claims the benefit or by whose acts it is bound. It also means that when it is necessary to prove that a firm had notice, all that need be done is to show that notice was given to one of its members who habitually acts in the partnership. The conditions necessary for the application of this section are as follows:

(i) That the partner is one who habitually acts in the business of the firm,

(ii) That the notice to him relates to the affairs of the firm.

(iii) That no fraud is committed by or with the consent of that partner.

25. Liability of a partner for acts of the firm. Every partner is liable, jointly with all the other partners and also severally, for all acts of the firm done while he is a partner.

26. Liability of the firm for wrongful acts of a partner. Where, by the wrongful act or omission of a partner acting in the ordinary course of the business of a firm, or with the authority of his partners, loss or injury is caused to any third party, or any penalty is incurred, the firm is liable therefor to the same extent as the partner.

27. Liability of firm for misapplication by partners. Where:

(a) a partner acting within his apparent authority receives money or property from third party and misapplies it, or

(b) a firm in the course of its business receives money or property from a third party, and the money or property is misapplied by any of the partners while it is in the custody of the firm, the firm is liable to make good the loss.

28. Holding out. (1) Any one who by words spoken or written or by conduct represents himself, or knowingly permits himself to be represented, to be a partner in a firm, is liable as a partner in that firm to any one who has on the faith of any such representation given credit to the firm, whether the person representing himself or represented to be a partner does or does not know that the representation has reached the person so giving credit.

(2) Where after a partner's death the business is continued in the old firm name, the continued use of that name or of the decreased partner's name as a part thereof shall not of itself make his legal representative or his estate liable for any act of the firm done after his death.

29. Rights of transferee of a partners interest. (1) A transfer by a partner of his interest in the firm, either absolute or by mortgage, or by the creation by him of a charge on such interest, does not entitle the transferee, during the continuance of the firm, to interfere in the conduct of the business, or to require accounts, or to inspect the books of the firm, but entitles the transferee only to receive the share of profits of the transferring partner, and the transferee shall accept the account of profits agreed to by the partners.

(2) If the firm is dissolved or if the transferring partner ceases to be a partner, the transferee is entitled against the remaining partners to receive the share of the assets of the firm to which the transferring partner is entitled, and, for the purpose of ascertaining that share, to an account as from the date of the dissolution.

30. Minors admitted to the benefits of partnership. (1) A person who is a minor according to the law to which he is subject may not be a partner in a firm, but, with the consent of all the partners for the time being, he may be admitted to the benefits of partnership.

(2) Such minor has a right to such share of the property and of the profits of the firm as may be agreed upon, and he may have access to and inspect and copy any of the accounts of the firm.

(3) Such minor's share is liable for the acts of the firm, but the minor is not personally liable for any such act.

(4) Such minor may not sue the partners for an account or payment of his share of the property or profits of the firm, save when severing his connection with the firm, and in such case the amount of his share shall be determined by a valuation made as far as possible in accordance with the rules contained in Section 48:

Provided that all the partners acting together or any partner entitled to dissolve the firm upon notice to other partners may elect in such suit to dissolve the firm, and thereupon the Court shall proceed with the suit as one for dissolution and for settling accounts between the partners, and the amount of the share of the minor shall be determined along with the shares of the partners.

(5) At any time within six months of his attaining majority or of his obtaining knowledge that he had been admitted to the benefits of partnership, whichever date is later, such person may give public notice that he has elected to become or that he has elected not to become a partner in the firm, and such notice shall determine his position as regards the firm:

Provided that if he fails to give such notice, he shall become a partner in the firm on the expiry of the said six months.

(6) Where any person has been admitted as a minor to the benefits of partnership in a firm, the burden of proving the fact that such person had no knowledge of such admission until a particular date after the expiry of six months of his attaining majority shall lie on the persons asserting that fact.

(7) When such person becomes a partner

(a) his rights and liabilities as a minor continue up to the date on which he becomes a partner, but he also becomes a partner, but he also becomes personally liable to third parties for all acts of the firm done since he was admitted to the benefits of partnership, and (*b*) his share in the property and profits of the firm shall be the share to which he was entitled as a minor.

(8) Where such person elects not to become a partner,

(*a*) his rights and liabilities shall continue to be those of a minor under this section up- to the date on which he gives public notice,

(*b*) his share shall not be liable for any acts of the firm done after the date of the notice, and

(*c*) he shall be entitled to sue the partners for his share of the property and profits in accordance with sub-section (4).

(9) Nothing in sub-sections (7) and (8) shall affect the provisions of Section 28.

CHAPTER V

Incoming and Outgoing Partners

31. Introduction of a partner. (1) Subject to contract between the partners and to the provisions of Section 30, no person shall be introduced as partner into a firm without the consent of all the existing partners.

(2) Subject to the provisions of Section 30, a person who is introduced as a partner into a firm does not thereby become liable for any act of the firm done before he became a partner.

32. Retirement of a partner. (1) A partner may retire:

(*a*) with a consent of all the other partners,

(*b*) in accordance with an expres agreement by the partners, or

(*c*) where the partnership is at will, by giving notice in writing to all the other partners of his intention to retire.

(2) A retiring partner may be discharged from any liability to any third party for acts of the firm done before his agreement by an agreement made by him with such third party and the partners of the reconstituted firm, and such agreement may be implied by a course of dealing between such third party and the reconstituted firm after he had knowledge of the retirement.

(3) Notwithstanding the retirement of a partner from a firm, he and the partners continue to be liable as partners to third parties for any act done by any of them which would have been an act of the firm if done before the retirement, until public notice is given of the retirement:

Provided that a retired partner is not liable to any third party who deals with firm without knowing that he was a partner.

(4) Notices under sub-section (3) may be given by the retired partner or by any partner of the reconstituted firm.

NOTES

Partner can retire from ongoing partnership without effecting dissolution of the firm, if the partnership agreement provides therefor. Partner's right to retire, therefore, has to be ascertained from the terms of the agreement. Whether the partnership was one at will and whether dissolution was a sought under Section 44, not relevant in this context. *Vishnu Chandra* v. *Chandrika Prasad Agarwal* (1983) 1 SCC 22, 25.

33. Expulsion of a partner. (1) A partner may not be expelled from a firm by any majority of the partners, save in the exercise in good faith of powers conferred by contract between the partners.

(2) The provisions of sub-sections (2), (3) and (4) of Section 32 shall apply to an expelled partner as if he were a retired partner.

34. Insolvency of a partner. (1) Where a partner in a firm is adjudicated an insolvent he ceases to be a partner on the date on which the order of adjudication is made, whether or not the firm is thereby dissolved.

(2) Where under a contract between the partners the firm is not dissolved by the adjudication of a partner as an insolvent, the estate of a partner so adjudicated is not liable for any act of the firm and the firm is not liable for any act of the insolvent, done after the date on which the order of adjudication is made.

35. Liability of estate of deceased partner. Where under a contract between the partners the firm is not dissolved by the death of a partner, the estate of a deceased partner is not liable for any act of the firm done after his death.

36. Rights of outgoing partner to carry on competing business. (1) An outgoing partner may carry on a business competing with that of the firm and he may advertise such business, but, subject to contract to the contrary, he may not:

(*a*) use the firm name,

(*b*) represent himself as carrying on the business of the firm, or

(*c*) solicit the custom of persons who were dealing with the firm before he ceased to be a partner.

Agreements in restraint of trade. (2) A partner may make an agreement with his partners that on ceasing to be a partner he will not carry on a business similar to that of the firm within a specified period or within specified local limits; and notwithstanding anything contained in Section 27 of the Indian Contract Act, 1872 (9 of 1872), such agreement shall be valid if the restrictions imposed are reasonable.

37. Right of outgoing partner in certain cases to share subsequent profits. Where any member of a firm has died or otherwise ceased to be a partner, and the surviving or continuing partners carry on the business of the firm with the property of the firm without any final settlement of accounts as between them and outgoing partner or his estate, then, in the absence of a contract to the contrary, the outgoing partner or his estate is entitled at the option of himself or his representatives to such share of the profits made since he ceased to be a partner as may be attributable to the use of his share of the property of the firm or to interest at the rate of six per cent per annum on the amount of his share in the property of the firm:

Provided that where by contract between the partners an option is given to surviving or continuing partners to purchase the interest of a deceased or outgoing partner, and that option is duly exercised, the estate of the deceased partner, or the outgoing partner, or his estate, as the case may be, is not entitled to any further or other share of profits; but if any partner assuming to act in exercise of the option does not in all material respects comply with the terms thereof, he is liable to account under the foregoing provisions of this section.

38. Revocation of continuing guarantee by change in firm. A continuing guarantee given to a firm, or to a third party in respect of the transactions of the firm, is, in the absence of agreement to the contrary, revoked as to future transactions from the date of any change in the constitution of the firm.

CHAPTER VI

Dissolution of a Firm

39. Dissolution of a firm. The dissolution of partnership between all the partners of a firm is called the "dissolution of the firm".

NOTES

Partnership consisting of eight members - Suit for dissolution of partnership — Maintainable under Partnership Act — Companies Act not applicable. *Vasantrao v. Shyamrao*, (1977) 4 SCC 9.

40. Dissolution by agreement. A firm may be dissolved with the consent of all the partners or in accordance with a contract between the partners.

NOTES

'Dissolution' and 'reconstitution' are two distinct legal concepts, for, a dissolution brings the partnership to an end while a reconstitution means the continuation of the partnership under altered circumstances but in law there would be no difficulty in a dissolution of a firm being followed by the constitution of a new firm by some of the erstwhile partners who may take over the assets and liabilities of the dissolved firm. *C.I.T. v. Pigot Champan & Co.*, (1982) 2 SCC 330 : 1982 SCC (Tax) 97.

Fact that one of the partners retired from partnership with the consent of other partners, sufficient to lead to the conclusion that the firm was dissolved. *Mir Abdul Khaliq v. Abdul Gaffar Sheriff*, (1985) 2 SCC 14.

41. Compulsory dissolution. A firm is dissolved:

(*a*) by the adjudication of all the partners or of all the partners but one as insolvent, or

(*b*) by the happening of any event which makes it unlawful for the business of the firm to be carried on or for the partners to carry it on in partnership:

Provided that, where more than one separate adventure or undertaking is carried on by the firm, the illegality of one or more shall not of itself cause the dissolution of the firm in respect of its lawful adventures and undertakings.

NOTES

Compulsory dissolution by insolvency of partners. This section enumerates the events the occurrence of which compulsorily dissolved when all its partners (or all its partners but one) are adjudicated as insolvents even if there be a contract to contrary. A firm is also dissolved on the adjudication of even one of its members as insolvent unless there is a contract to the contrary.

42. Dissolution on the happening of certain contingencies. Subject to contract between the partners a firm is dissolved:

(*a*) if constituted for a fixed term, by the expiry of the term;

(*b*) if constituted to carry out one or more adventures or undertakings, by the completion thereof;

(*c*) by the death of a partner; and

(*d*) by the adjudication of a partner as an insolvent.

43. Dissolution by notice of partnership at will. Where the partnership is at will, the firm may be dissolved by any partner giving notice in writing to all the other partners of his intention to dissolve the firm.

(2) The firm is dissolved as from the date mentioned in the notice as the date of dissolution or, if no date is so mentioned, as from the date of the communication of the notice.

44. Dissolution by the Court. At the suit of a partner, the Court may dissolve a firm on any of following grounds, namely:

(*a*) that a partner has become of unsound mind, in which case the suit may be brought as well by the next friend of the partner who has become of unsound mind as by any other partner;

(*b*) that a partner, other than the partner suing, has become in any way permanently incapable of performing his duties as partner;

(*c*) that a partner, other than the partner suing, is guilty of conduct which is likely to affect prejudicially the carrying on of the business, regard being had to the nature of the business;

(*d*) that a partner, other than the partner suing, wilfully or persistently commits breach of agreements relating to the management of the affairs of the firm or the conduct of its business, or otherwise so conducts himself in matters relating to the business that it is not reasonably practicable for the other partners to carry on the business in partnership with him;

(*e*) that a partner, other than the partner, suing, has in any way transferred the whole of his interest in the firm to a third party, or has allowed his share to be charged under the provisions of Rule 49 of Order XXI of the First Schedule to the Code of Civil Procedure, 1908 (5 of 1908), or has allowed it to be sold in the recovery of arrears of land revenue or of any dues recoverable as arrears of land revenue due by the partner;

(*f*) that the business of the firm cannot be carried on save at a loss; or

(*g*) on any other ground which renders it just equitable that the firm should be dissolved.

45. Liability for acts of partner done after dissolution. (1) Notwithstanding the dissolution of a firm, the partners continue to be liable as such to third parties for any act done by any of them which would have been an act of the firm if done before the dissolution, until public notice is given of the dissolution:

Provided that the estate of a partner who dies, or who is adjudicated an insolvent, or of a partner who not having been known to the person dealing with the firm to be a partner, retires from the firm, is not liable under this section for acts done after the date on which he ceases to be a partner.

(2) Notices under sub-section (1) may be given by any partner.

46. Right of partners to have business wound up after dissolution. On the dissolution of a firm every partner or his representative is entitled, as against all the other partners or their representatives, to have the property of the firm applied in payment of the debts and liabilities of the firm, and to have the surplus distributed among the partners or their representatives according to their rights.

47. Continuing authority of partners for purposes of winding up. After the dissolution of a firm the authority of each partner to bind the firm, and the other mutual rights and obligations of the partners, continue notwithstanding the dissolution, so far as may be necessary to wind up the affairs of the firm and to complete transactions begun but unfinished at the time of the dissolution, but not otherwise:

Provided that the firm is in no case bound by the acts of a partner who has been adjudicated insolvent; but this proviso does not affect the liability of any person who has after the adjudication represented himself or knowingly permitted himself to be represented as a partner of the insolvent.

48. Mode of settlement of accounts between partners. In settling the accounts of a firm after dissolution, the following rules shall, subject to agreement by the partners, be observed:

(*a*) Losses, including deficiencies of capital, shall be paid first out of profits, next out of capital, and, lastly, if necessary, by the partners individually in the proportions in which they were entitled to share profits.

(*b*) The assets of the firm, including any sums contributed by the partners to make up deficiencies of capital, shall be applied in the following manner and order:

(*i*) in paying the debts of the firm to third parties;

(*ii*) in paying to each partner rateably what is due to him from the firm for advances as distinguished from capital;

(*iii*) in paying to each partner rateably what is due to him on account of capital; and

(*iv*) the residue, if any, shall be divided among the partners in the proportions in which they were entitled to share profits.

49. Payment of firm debts and of separate debts. Where there are joint debts due from the firm, and also separate debts due from any partner, the property of the firm shall be applied in the first instance in payment of the debts of the firm, and, if there is any surplus, then the share of each partner shall be applied in payment of his separate debts or paid to him. The separate property of any partner shall be applied first in the payment of his separate debts, and the surplus (if any) in the payment of the debts of the firm.

50. Personal profits earned after dissolution. Subject to contract between the partners, the provisions of clause (a) of Section 16 shall apply to transactions by any surviving partner or by the representatives of a deceased partner, undertaken after the firm is dissolved on account of the death of a partner and before its affairs have been completely wound up:

Provided that where any partner or his representative has bought the goodwill of the firm, nothing in this section shall affect his right to use the firm name.

NOTES

Section 16 of this Act provides that every partner must, as an agent of the firm, account to the firm for every benefit derived by him from any transaction concerning the partnership or from any use by him of property of the firm name or business connection. This section (i.e., Section 50) merely extends the applications of this rule to the affairs of the partnership even after the dissolution of the firm till they have been finally wound up. In *Clements v. Hall,* where private profits were earned from a renewal of the lease by the surviving partner, it was held that the representatives of the deceased partner were entitled to share such profits. Where a partner retains assets of the firm for his own benefit after dissolution he is liable not only to account for the same but also to pay interest.

51. Return of premium on premature dissolution. Where a partner has paid a premium on entering into partnership for a fixed term and the firm is dissolved before the expiration of that term otherwise than by the death of a partner, he shall be entitled to repayment of the premium or of such part thereof as may be reasonable, regard being had to the terms upon which he became a partner and to the length of time during which he was a partner, unless:

(*a*) the dissolution is mainly due to his own misconduct, or

(*b*) the dissolution is in pursuance of an agreement containing no provision for the return of the premium or any part of it.

52. Rights where partnership contract is rescinded for fraud or misrepresentation. Where a contract creating partnership is rescinded on the ground of the fraud or misrepresentation of any of the parties thereto, the party entitled to rescind is, without prejudice to any other right, entitled:

(*a*) to a lien on, or a right of retention of, the surplus or the assets of the firm remaining after the debts of the firm have been paid, for any sum paid by him for the purchase of a share in the firm and for any capital contributed by him;

(*b*) to rank as a creditor of the firm in respect of any payment made by him towards the debt of the firm; and

(*c*) to be indemnified by the partner or partners guilty of the fraud or misrepresentation against all the debts of the firm.

53. Right to restrain from use of firm name or firm property. After a firm is dissolved, every partner or his representative may in the absence of a contract between the partners to the contrary, restrain any other partner or his representative from carrying on a similar business in the firm name or from using any of the property of the firm for his own benefit, until the affairs of the firm have been completely wound up:

Provided that where any partner or his representative has bought the goodwill of the firm, nothing in this section shall affect his right to use the firm name.

54. Agreements in restraint of trade. Partners may, upon or in anticipation of the dissolution of the firm, make an agreement that some or all of them will not carry on a business similar to that of the firm within a specified period or within specified local limits; and notwithstanding anything contained in Section 27 of the Indian Contract Act, 1872 (9 of 1872), such agreement shall be valid if the restrictions imposed are reasonable.

55. Sale of goodwill after dissolution. (1) In settling the accounts of a firm after dissolution, the goodwill shall, subject to contract between the partners, be included in the assets, and it may be sold either separately or along with other property of the firm.

Rights of buyer and seller of goodwill. (2) Where the goodwill of a firm is sold after dissolution, a partner may carry on a business competing with that of the buyer and he may advertise such business, but, subject to agreement between him and the buyer, he may not:

(*a*) use the firm name,

(*b*) represent himself as carrying on the business of the firm, or

(*c*) solicit the custom of persons who were dealing with the firm before its dissolution.

Agreement in restraint of trade. (3) Any partner may, upon the sale of the goodwill of a firm, make an agreement with the buyer that such partner will not carry on any business similar to that of the firm within a specified period or within specified local limits, and notwithstanding anything contained in Section 27 of the Indian Contract Act, 1872 (9 of 1872), such agreement shall be valid if the restrictions imposed are reasonable.

CHAPTER VII

Registration of Firms

56. Power to exempt from application of the Chapter. The [4][State Government] of any [4][State] may, by notification in the Official Gazette, direct that the provisions of this Chapter shall not apply to [5][the State] or to any part thereof specified in the notification.

57. Appointment of Registrars. (1) The [5a][State Government] may appoint Registrar of Firms for the purposes of this Act, and may define the areas within which they shall exercise their powers and perform their duties.

(2) Every Registrar shall be deemed to be a public servant within the meaning of Section 21 of the Indian Penal Code (45 of 1860).

STATE AMENDMENTS

MAHARASHTRA. For Section 57 of the principal Act, the following section shall be *substituted*, namely:

"57. *Appointment of Registrar of Firms and Deputy and Assistant Registrars of Firms.* (1) The State Government may, by notification in the Official Gazette, appoint a Registrar of Firms who shall exercise, perform and discharge the powers, functions and duties of the Registrar under this Act throughout the State of Maharashtra.

(2) The State Government may likewise appoint one or more Deputy Registrars of Firms and Assistant Registrars of Firms who shall exercise, perform and discharge all or such of the powers, functions and duties of the Registrar and in such areas as the State Government may, by notification in the Official Gazette, specify.

(3) The officers appointed under sub-section (1) and sub-section (2) shall be deemed to be public servants within the meaning of Section 21 of the Indian Penal Code."—Mah. Act. 29 of 1984, S. 5 (w.e.f. 1-1-1985).

UTTAR PRADESH

Substitution of Section 57 of Act IX of 1932. For Section 57 of the Indian Partnership Act, 1932, as applicable to Uttar Pradesh, the following section shall be *substituted*, namely :

"57. *Appointment of Registrar, Deputy Registrars and Assistant Registrars.* (1) The State Government may, by notification, appoint a Registrar of Firms who shall exercise, perform and discharge the powers, functions and duties of the Registrar under this Act throughout Uttar Pradesh.

---

4. *Subs.* by the A.L.O. 1950 for the words "Provincial Government" and "Province" respectively.

5. *Subs.* by A.O. 1937 (1-4-1937) and A.L.O. 1950 (26-1-1950) for "any Province"

5a. *Subs.* by A.L.O. 1950 for the words "Provincial Government".

(2) The State Government may likewise appoint one or more Deputy Registrars of Firms and Assistant Registrars of Firms who exercise, perform and discharge all or such of the powers, functions and duties of the Registrar and in such areas as are notified in the notification.

(3) The officers appointed under sub-section (1) or sub-section (2) shall be deemed to be public servants within the meaning of Section 21 of the Indian Penal Code." (*Vide* U.P. Act 34 of 1979, S. 2, w.e.f. 22-10-1979).

58. Application for registration. (1) The registration of a firm may be effected at any time by sending by post or delivering to the Registrar of the area in which any place of business of the firm is situated or proposed to be situated, a statement in the prescribed form and accompanied by the prescribed fee, stating:

(*a*) the firm name,

(*b*) the place or principal place of business of the firm,

(*c*) the names of any other places where the firm carries on business,

(*d*) the date when each partner joined the firm,

(*e*) the names in full and permanent addresses of the partners, and

(*f*) the duration of the firm.

The statement shall be signed by all the partners, or by their agents specially authorised in this behalf.

(2) Each person signing the statement shall also verify it in the manner prescribed.

(3) A firm name shall not contain any of the following words, namely:

"Crown", "Emperor", "Empress", "Empire", "Imperial", "King", "Queen", "Royal", or words expressing or implying the sanction, approval or patronage of [6][Government], except [7][when the State Government] signifies [8][its] consent to the use of such words as part of the firm name by order in writing[9]***.

STATES AMENDMENTS

GOA, DAMAN AND DIU. IN SECTION 58

(*i*) for sub-section (3), the following shall be substituted, namely: "(3) No firm shall be registered by a name which in the opinion of the Registrar is undesirable.";

(*ii*) after sub-section (3), insert the following:

"(4) Any person aggrieved by an order of the Registrar under sub-section (3) may, within 30 days from the date of communication of such order, appeal to the State Government whose decision shall be final.

(5) A firm's name shall not contain any of the following words, namely, 'Union, State, President, Republic, Governor', or words expressing or implying sanction, approval or patronage of Government unless the Government of Goa, Daman and Diu signifies, by order in writing, its consent to the use of such words as part of the firm's name:

Provided that nothing in this sub-section shall apply to any firm carrying on business under any such name, before the date of the commencement of the Indian Partnership (Goa, Daman and Diu Amendment) Act, 1966.

(6) Any person who contravenes the provisions of sub-section (5) shall be punishable with the fine which may extend to five hundred rupees." — Goa, Daman and Diu Act VI of 1966, Section 3 (22-8-1966).

---

6. The words "the Crown or the Government of India or a Local Government", have been successively adapted by the A.O. 1948 and the A.O. 1950 to read as above.
7. *Subs.* by the A.O. 1937 for "when the G.G. in C."
8. *Subs.* by the A.O. 1937 for "his".
9. The words "under the hand of one of the Secretaries of the Government of India", *omitted by ibid.*

MAHARASHTRA. In Section 58 of the principal Act

(*a*) in sub-section (1),

(*i*) for the words "The registration of a firm" the words, brackets, figure and letter "Subject to the provisions of sub-section (1-A), the registration of a firm" shall be *substituted*;

(*ii*) the words "at any time" shall be deleted;

(*iii*) after the words "prescribed fee' the words "and a true copy of the deed of partnership" shall be *inserted*;

(*iv*) after clause (a), the following clause shall be *inserted*, namely:

(*aa*) the nature of business of the firm;"

(*b*) after sub-section (1), the following sub-section shall be inserted, namely:

"(1-A) The statement under sub-section (1) shall be sent or delivered to the Registrar within a period of one year from the date of constitution of the firm:

Provided that in the case of any firm carrying on business on or before the date of commencement* of the Indian Partnership (Maharashtra Amendment) Act, 1984 (Mah, XXIX of 1984), such statement shall be sent or delivered to the Registrar within a period of one year from such date.";

(*c*) for sub-section (3), the following sub-sections shall be *substituted*, namely:

"(3) A firm shall not have any of the names of emblems specified in the Schedule to the Emblems and Names (Prevention of Improper Use) Act, 1950 (XII of 1950), or any colourable limitation thereof, unless permitted so to do under that Act, or any name which is likely to be associated by the public with the name of any other firm on account of similarly, or any name which, in the opinion of the Registrar, for reasons to be recorded in writing, is undesirable:

Provided that nothing in this sub-section shall apply to any firm registered under any such name before the date of the commencement* of the Indian Partnership (Maharashtra Amendment) Act, 1984 (Mah. XXIX of 1984).

(4) Any person aggrieved by an order of the Registrar under sub-section (3) may, within 30 days from the date of communication of such order, appeal to the officer not below the rank of Deputy Secretary to Government authorised by the State Government in this behalf, in such manner, and on payment of such fee, as may be prescribed. On receipt of any such appeal, the authorised officer shall, after giving an opportunity of being heard to the appellant, decide the appeal, and his decision shall be final." Mah. Act 29 of 1984, S. 6 (w.e.f. 1-1-1985).

PONDICHERRY. For sub-section (3), *substitute* the following sub-sections:

"(3) The Registrar shall refuse to register :

(*a*) a firm under sub-section (1), or

(*b*) an alteration of the firm name,

if the proposed name or alteration of the firm name is identical with the name by which any other existing firm has been registered or in the opinion of the Registrar so nearly resembles such other name as to be likely to deceive or mislead the public or the members of either firm.

(4) Any person who is aggrieved by an order of Registrar under sub-section (3) may file an appeal before such person or authority, in such manner, within such time and on the payment of such fees as may be prescribed, The appeal shall be heard and decided in such manner as may be prescribed." - Pondi, Act VIII of 1969, Section 2 (1-1-1970).

RAJASTHAN. For sub-section (3) of Section 58 *substitute* the following sub-sections:

"(3) No firm shall be registered by a name which, in the opinion of the State Government, is undesirable.

(4) Except with the previous sanction, in writing, of the State Government, no firm shall be registered by a name which contains any of the following words, namely:

* Jan. 1, 1985.

(*a*) 'Union', 'State', 'President', 'Republic' or any word expressing or implying the sanction, approval or partronage of the Central or any State Government; and

(*b*) 'Municipal', 'Chartered' or any word which suggests or is calculated to suggest connection with any municipality or local authority:

Provided that nothing in this sub-section shall apply to any firm registered before the date of commencement of the Indian Partnership (Rajasthan Amendment) Act, 1971." — Raj. Act 10 of 1971, Section 2 (15-9-1971).

TAMIL NADU. For sub-section (3) of Section 58 of the Indian Partnership Act, 1932 (Central Act IX of 1932) (hereinafter referred to as the Principal Act), the following sub-sections shall be *substituted*, namely:

"(3) No firm shall be registered by a name which, in the opinion of the State Government is undesirable.

(4) Except with the previous sanction in writing of the State Government, no firm shall be registered by a name which contains any of the following words, namely:

(*a*) 'Union', 'State', 'President', 'Republic' or any word expressing or implying the sanction, approval or patronage of the Central or any State Government; and

(*b*) 'Municipal', 'Chartered' or any word which suggests or is calculated to suggest connection with any municipality or local authority :

Provided that nothing in this sub-section shall apply to any firm registered before the date of commencement of the Indian Partnership (Madras Amendment) Act, 1965." — (*Vide* Madras Act 35 of 1965, S.2, w.e.f. April 1, 1966).

NOTES

Mode in which registration may be effected. Under this section registration may be effected only of a firm which is in existence. The registration of a firm which has been dissolved is not contemplated by this Act. For registration of a firm together with the prescribed fee a statement on prescribed form should be submitted. The statement should deal with the firm name, the place or principal place of business of the firm, the names of any other place where the firm carries on business, the date when each partner joined the firm, the names in full and permanent addresses of the partners and the duration of the firm. Such statement should be signed by all the partners or by their authorised agents. Substantial compliance with the provisions of the Act would be enough.[9a]

59. Registration. When the Registrar is satisfied that the provisions of Section 58 have been duly complied with, he shall record an entry of the statement in a register called the Register of Firms, and shall file the statement.

STATE AMENDMENTS

MAHARASHTRA. Section 59 of the principal Act shall be renumbered as sub-section (1) of that section, and,—

(*a*) in sub-section (1) as so renumbered, after the words. "file the statement", the words "On the date such entry is recorded and such statement is filed, the firm shall be deemed to be registered," shall be added:

(*b*) after sub-section (1) as so renumbered, the following sub-section shall be added, namely:

"(2) The firm, which is registered, shall use the brackets and word "(Registered)" immediately after its name". Mah. Act 29 of 1984, S. 7 (w.e.f. 1-1-1985).

SECTIONS 59-A, 59A-1 AND 59-B

Andhra Pradesh. After Section 59 of the Indian Partnership Act, 1932 the following section shall be *inserted*, namely:

"59-A. (1) Notwithstanding anything in the Chapter, the Registrar of Firms, Andhra Pradesh, may, by order in writing, amend the register by deleting therefrom the entries relating, to any firm, whose place of business has, by virtue of the provisions contained in the State Reorganization Act, 1956 and the Andhra Pradesh, and Madras (Alteration of Boundaries) Act, 1959, ceased to be in the State of Andhra Pradesh, the Registrar may likewise amend the register by adding thereto the entries relating to any firm included in the register of another State but, whose place of business has, by reason of the said provisions, become included in the State of Andhra Pradesh:

Provided that the Registrar shall, before passing an order under this sub-section, give to the firm concerned an opportunity of making its representation, if any.

(2) The Registrar shall cease to perform the functions of a Registrar under the Act in respect of any firm the entries relating to which the deleted as aforesaid and shall perform the functions of a Registrar under the Act in respect of any firm the entries relating to which are added as aforesaid.

(3) Any person aggrieved by an order under sub-section (1) may appeal to such authority and within such time as may be specified in this behalf by an order made by the Government of Andhra Pradesh and the authority shall pass such order on the appeal as it thinks fit.

(4) An order of the Registrar under sub-section (1) or where an appeal has been preferred against it under sub-section (3) the order of the appellate authority, shall be final." A.P. Act 7 of 1965, S. 2 w.e.f. March 10, 1965).

KERALA. AFTER SECTION 59, *INSERT.*

"59-A. *Amendment of register.* (1) Notwithstanding anything contained in this Chapter, the Registrar of Firms appointed by the State of Kerala may, by order in writing, amend the register by deleting therefrom the entries relating to any firm whose place of business has, by reason of the reorganisation of States ceased to be situated in the State of Kerala.

The Registrar may likewise amend the register by adding thereto the entries relating to any firm included in the register of the State of Madras but whose place of business has, by reason of the said reorganisation of States, become part of the State of Kerala:

Provided that the Registrar shall, before passing an order, make such inquiry as he deems necessary.

(2) After such amendment the Registrar shall cease to perform the functions of a Registrar in respect of any firm the entries relating to which have been deleted as aforesaid and shall perform all the functions of a Registrar in respect of all firms the entries relating to which are added as aforesaid.

(3) Any person aggrieved by an order under sub-section (1) may appeal to such authority and within such time as may be specified in this behalf by the State Government of Kerala and such authority shall pass such order on the appeal as it thinks fit.

(4) An order of the Registrar under sub-section (1), or where an appeal has been preferred against it under sub-section (3), the order of the appellate authority, shall be final.

(5) The provisions of this section shall cease to be in force from such date as the State Government of Kerala may, by notification in the Gazette, appoint." Kerala A.L.O., 1957 (30-10-1957).

MADHYA PRADESH—After Section 59, insert:

"59-A. (1) Notwithstanding anything contained in the Chapter, the Registrar of Firms appointed by the State of Madhya Pradesh may, by order in writing, amend the register by deleting therefrom the entries relating to any firm, whose place of business has, by reason of the reorganization of States, ceased to be situated in the State of Madhya Pradesh.

The Registrar may likewise amend the register by adding thereto the entries relating to any firm included in the register of another State but whose place of business has, by reason of the said reorganization of States, become part of the State of Madhya Pradesh:

9a. In its application to the State of Madras, Section 59-A has been *inserted* by the Madras (Added Territories) Adaptation of Laws Order, 1961.

Provided that the Registrar shall, before passing an order, make such inquiry as he deems necessary.

(2) After such amendment the Registrar shall cease to perform the functions of a Registrar in respect of any firm the entries relating to which have been deleted as aforesaid and shall perform all the functions of a Registrar in respect of all firms the entries relating to which are added as aforesaid.

(3) Any person aggrieved by an order under sub-section (1) may appeal to such authority and within such time as may be specified in this behalf by the State Government of Madhya Pradesh, and such authority shall pass such order on the appeal as it thinks fit.

(4) An order of the Registrar under sub-section (1), or where an appeal has been preferred against it under sub-section (3), the order of the appellate authority shall be final.

(5) The provisions of this section shall cease to be in force from such date as the State Government of Madhya Pradesh may, by notification in the State Gazette, appoint." M.P., Adaptation of Laws (State and Concurrent Subjects) (Third Amendment) Order, 1957 (with retrospective effect from 1-11-1956).

MAHARASHTRA. (1) AFTER SECTION 59, *INSERT*:

"59-A. *Deletion and addition of entries relating to certain firms, by reason of reorganization of States* : (1) Notwithstanding anything contained in this Chapter, a Registrar of Firms appointed for any area by the Government of Bombay may, by order in writing, amend the Register of Firms maintained by him deleting therefrom the entries relating to any firm, whose place of business has, by reason of the reorganization of States under the States Reorganization Act, 1956, ceased to be situated in the State of Bombay. The Registrar may likewise and without any charge or fee, therefore, amend the register by adding thereto the entries relating to any firm included in the register of another State but whose place of business has, by reason of such reorganization, become part of the area within his jurisdiction in the State of Bombay:

Provided that the Registrar shall, before passing any order under this sub-section, make such inquiry as he deems necessary and give notice to the firm and the Registrar of the State concerned.

(2) After such amendment, the Registrar shall cease to perform the functions of a Registrar in respect of any firm the entries relating to which have been deleted as aforesaid and shall perform all the functions of a Registrar in respect of any firm the entries relating to which are added as aforesaid.

(3) Any person aggrieved by an order under sub-section (1) may appeal to such authority, and within such time, as may be specified in this behalf by Government of Bombay by notification in the Official Gazette; and such authority shall pass such order on the appeal as it thinks fit.

(4) An order of a Registrar under sub-section (1), or when an appeal has been preferred against it under sub-section (3), the order of the appellate authority shall be final.

(5) The provisions of this section shall cease to be in force from such date as the Government of Bombay may, by notification in the Official Gazette, appoint." Central Acts on State and Concurrent Subjects (Bombay Adaptation) (Amendment) Order, 1957 (17-10-1957).

(2) After Section 59 of the principal Act, the following section shall be inserted, namely:

"59A-1. *Late registration on payment of penalty*. If the statement in respect of any firm is not sent or delivered to the Registrar within the time specified in sub-section (1-A) of Section 58, then the firm may be registered on payment, to the Registrar, of a penalty of one hundred rupees per year of delay or a part thereof." Mah. Act 29 of 1984, S.8 (w.e.f. 1-1-1985).

(SEE SECTION 59-B BELOW)

MYSORE. In Section 59-A as introduced by Madras Adaptation of Laws (Central Acts) Order, 1957, in sub-section (1), for the words 'by reason of the reorganization of State', the words brackets etc., 'by reason of the addition of the Bellary district to the State of Mysore under the Andhra State Act, 1953 (Central Act XXX of 1953), or of the reorganization of States under the States Reorganization Act, 1956 (Central Act 37 of 1956), shall be *substituted.* Mys. Act XIX of 1961, Section 2 (14-9-1961).

TAMIL NADU. After Section 59, *insert:*

"59-A. *Special provision for amending the register.* (1) Notwithstanding anything contained in this Chapter, the Registrar of Firms appointed by the State Government of Madras may, by order in writing, amend the register by deleting therefrom the entries relating to any firm, the place of business of which has, [by reason of the formation of the State of Andhra or of the addition of the Bellary district to the State of Mysore under the Andhra State Act, 1953 or the reorganization of States under the States Reorganization Act, 1956,] or of the alteration of boundaries under the Andhra Pradesh and Madras (Alteration of Boundaries) Act, 1959, ceased to be located in the State of Madras.

The Registrar may likewise amend the register by adding thereto the entries relating to any firm included in the register of another State but the place of business of which has, by reason of the said reorganization of States or of the said alteration of boundaries, become part of the State of Madras:

Provided that the Registrar, [may], before passing an order, make such inquiry as he deems necessary.

(2) After such amendment the Registrar shall cease to perform the functions of a Registrar in respect of any firm the entries relating to which have been deleted as aforesaid and shall perform all the functions of a Registrar in respect of all firms the entries relating to which are added as aforesaid.

(3) Any person aggrieved by an order under sub-section (1) may appeal to such authority and within such time as may be specified in this behalf by the State Government of Madras; and such authority shall pass such order on the appeal as it thinks fit.

(4) An order of the Registrar under sub-section (1), or where an appellate appeal has been preferred against it under sub-section (3), the order of the authority shall be final.

(5) The provisions of the section shall cease to be in force from such date as the State Government of Madras, by notification in the Official Gazette, appoint." Madras Act 21 of 1959 and Madras Additional Territories A.L.O., 1961 (w.e.f. 1-4-1960).

SECTION 59-B

GUJARAT. AFTER SECTION 59-A, INSERT THE FOLLOWING:

"59-B. *Deletion of entries relating to certain firms by reason of reorganization of Bombay State.* (1) Notwithstanding anything contained in the Chapter, a Registrar of Firms appointed for any area by the Government of Gujarat may, by order in writing, amend the Register of Firms maintained by him by deleting therefrom the entries relating to any firm whose place of business has, by reason of the reorganization of the State of Bombay, by the Bombay Reorganization Act, 1960, ceased to be situated in the State of Gujarat:

Provided that the Registrar shall, before passing any order under this sub-section, make such inquiry as he deems necessary and give notice to the firm and the Registrar of the State of Maharashtra.

(2) After such amendment the Registrar shall cease to perform the functions of a Registrar in respect of any firm the entries relating to which have been deleted as aforesaid.

(3) Any person aggrieved by an order under sub-section (1) may appeal to such authority and within such time as may be specified in this behalf by the Government of Gujarat, by notification in the Official Gazette; and such authority shall pass such order on the appeal as it thinks fit.

(4) An order of a Registrar under sub-section (1), or where an appeal has been preferred against it under sub-section (3), the order of the appellate authority shall be final." Gujarat Adaptation of Laws (State and Concurrent Subjects) (English Amendment) Order, 1961 w.e.f. 1-5-1960."

MAHARASHTRA. After Section 59-A, *insert* the following:

59-B. Same as in Gujarat, except for the corresponding references to Maharashtra—Central Acts on State and Concurrent Subjects (Maharashtra Adaptation) (Amendment) Order, 1961 w.e.f. 1-5-1960.

60. Recording of alterations in firm name and principal place of business. (1) When an alteration is made in the firm name or in the location of the principal place of business of a registered firm, a statement may be sent to the Registrar accompanied by the prescribed fee, specifying the alteration and signed and verified in the manner required under Section 58.

(2) When the Registrar is satisfied that the provisions of sub-section (1) have been duly complied with, he shall amend the entry relating to the firm in the Register of Firms in accordance with the statement, and shall file it along with the statement relating to the firm filed under Section 59.

STATE AMENDMENTS

MAHARASHTRA. In Section 60 of the principal Act:

(*a*) for sub-section (1), the following sub-section shall be *substituted*, namely:

"(1) When an alteration is made in the firm name or in the nature of business of a firm or in the location of the principal place of business of a registered firm, a statement shall be sent to the Registrar, within a period of 90 days from the date of making such alteration, accompanied by the prescribed fee, specifying the alteration and signed and verified in the manner required under Section 58.";

(*b*) in the marginal note, for the words "firm name and the words "firm name, nature of business and" shall be substituted. Mah. Act 29 of 1984, S. 9 (w.e.f. 1-1-1985).

61. Noting of closing and opening of branches. When a registered firm discontinues business at any place or begins to carry on business at any place, such place not being its principal place of business, any partner or agent of the firm may send intimation thereof to the Registrar, who shall make a note of such intimation in the entry relating to the firm in the Register of Firms, and shall file the intimation along with the statement relating to the firm filed under Section 59.

STATE AMENDMENTS

MAHARASHTRA. In Section 61 of the principal Act, for the words "may send intimation thereof the Registrar, who shall" the following shall be *substituted*, namely :

"shall send intimation thereof to the Registrar, within a period of 90 days from the date of such discontinuance or, as the case may be, from the date on which the firm begins to carry on business at such place. The Registrar shall then". Mah. Act 29 of 1984, S. 10 (w.e.f. 1-1-1985).

62. Noting of changes in names and addresses of partners. When any partner in a registered firm alters his name or permanent address, an intimation of the alteration may be sent by any partner or agent of the firm to the Registrar, who shall deal with it in the manner provided in Section 61.

STATE AMENDMENTS

MAHARASHTRA. In Section 62 of the principal Act, of the words "may be sent" the words "shall be sent, within a period of 90 days from the date of making such alteration," shall be *substituted.* Mah. Act 29 of 1984, S. 11 (w.e.f. 1-1-1985).

63. Recording of changes in and dissolution of a firm. (1) When a change occurs in the constitution of a registered firm any incoming, continuing or outgoing partner, and when a registered firm is dissolved any person who was a partner immediately before the dissolution, or the agent of any such partner or person specially authorised in this behalf, may give notice to the Registrar of such change or dissolution, specifying the date thereof, and the Registrar shall make a record of the notice in the entry relating to the firm in the Register of Firms, and shall file the notice along with the statement relating to the firm filed under Section 59.

Recording of withdrawal of a minor. (2) When a minor who has been admitted to the benefits of partnership in a firm attains majority and elects to become or not to become a partner, and the firm is then a registered firm, he, or his agent specially authorised in this behalf, may give notice to the Registrar that he has or has note become a partner, and the Registrar shall deal with the notice in the manner provided in sub-section (1).

STATE AMENDMENTS

MAHARASHTRA. In Section 63 of the principal Act,

(*a*) in sub-section (1),

(*i*) for the word "any", wherever it occurs, the word "every" shall be *substituted*;

(*ii*) for the words "may give notice to the Registrar of such change or dissolution, specifying the date thereof;" the following shall be *substituted*, namely :

"shall, within a period of 90 days from the date of such change or dissolution, give notice to the Registrar of such change or dissolution, specifying the date thereof";

(*b*) after sub-section (1), the following sub-section shall be *added*, namely :

"(1-A) Where a change occurs in the constitution of a registered firm, all persons, who after such change are partners of the firm, shall jointly send an intimation of such change duly signed by them, to the Registrar, within a period of 90 days from the date of occurrence of such change and the Registrar shall deal with it in the manner provided by Section 61."

(*c*) in sub-section (2), for the words "may give notice to the Registrar" the words "shall within a period of 90 days from the date of his election, give notice to the Registrar" shall be *substituted.* Mah. Act 29 of 1984, S. 12 (w.e.f. 1-1-1985).

64. Rectification of mistakes. (1) The Registrar shall have power at all times to rectify any mistake in order to bring the entry in the Register of Firms relating to any firm into conformity with the documents relating to that firm filed under this Chapter.

(2) On application made by all the parties who have signed any document relating to a firm filed under this Chapter, the Registrar may rectify any mistake in such document or in the record or note thereof made in the Register of Firms.

NOTES

This section authorises the Registrar to correct clerical errors whether made by the persons sending statement or notices to the Registrar. It also relates to any mistakes in such statements or notice whether, clerical or otherwise, these can be rectified on an application made by all the parties who have signed the document in question.

65. Amendment of registrar by order of Court. A Court deciding any matter relating to a registered firm may direct that the Registrar shall make any amendment in the entry in the Register of Firms relating to such firm which is consequential upon its decision; and the Registrar shall amend the entry accordingly.

66. Inspection of register and filed documents. (1) The register of Firms shall be open to inspection by any person on payment of such fee as may be prescribed.

(2) All statements, notices and intimations filed under this Chapter shall be open to inspection, subject to such conditions and on payment of such fee as may be prescribed.

67. Grant of copies. The Registrar shall on application furnish to any person, on payment of such fee as may be prescribed, a copy, certified under his hand, of any entry of portion thereof in the Register of Firms.

68. Rules of evidence. (1) Any statement, intimation or notice recorded or noted in the Register of Firms shall, as against any person by whom or on whose behalf such statement, intimation or notice as signed, be conclusive proof of any fact therein stated.

(2) A certified copy of any entry relating to a firm in the Register of Firms may be produced in proof of the fact of the registration of such firm, and of the contents of any statement, intimation or notice recorded or noted therein.

69. Effect of non-registration. (1) No suit to enforce a right arising from a contract or conferred by this Act shall be instituted in any Court by or on behalf of any person suing as a partner in a firm against the firm or any person alleged to be or to have been a partner in the firm unless the firm is registered and the person suing is or has been shown in the Register of Firms as a partner in the firm.

(2) No suits to enforce a right arising from a contract shall be instituted in any Court by or on behalf of a firm against any third party unless the firm is registered and the persons suing are or have been shown in the Register of Firms as partners in the firm.

(3) The provisions of sub-sections (1) and (2) shall apply also to a claim of set-off or other proceeding to enforce a right arising from a contract, but shall not affect:

(*a*) the enforcement of any right to sue for the dissolution of a firm or for accounts of a dissolved firm, or any right or power to realise the property of a dissolved firm; or

(*b*) the powers of an official assignee, receiver or Court under the Presidency-towns Insolvency Act, 1909 (3 of 1909), or the Provincial Insolvency Act, 1920 (5 of 1920), to realise the property of an insolvent partner.

(4) This action shall not apply:

(*a*) to firms or to partners in firms which have no place of business in [10][the territories to which this Act extends], or whose places of business in [11][the said territories] are situated in areas to which, by notification under [12][Section 56], the Chapter does not apply, or

(*b*) to any suit or claim or set-off not exceeding one hundred rupees in value which, in the Presidency-towns, is not of a kind specified in Section 19 of the Presidency Small Cause Courts Act, 1882 (15 of 1882), or outside the Presidency-towns, is not of a kind specified in the Second Schedule to the Provincial Small Cause Courts Act, 1887 (9 of 1887), or to any proceeding in execution or other proceeding incidental to or arising from any such suit or claim.

STATE AMENDMENTS

MAHARASHTRA. In Section 69 of the principal Act,

(*a*) to sub-section (1), the following proviso shall be *added*, namely:

"Provided that the requirement of registration of firm under this sub-section shall not apply to the suits or proceedings instituted by the heirs or legal representatives of the deceased partner of a firm for accounts of the firm or to realise the property of the firm.";

(*b*) after sub-section (2), the following sub-section shall be *inserted*, namely:

"(2-A) No suit to enforce any right for the dissolution of a firm or for accounts of a dissolved firm or any right or power to realise the property of a dissolved firm shall be instituted in any Court by or on behalf of any person suing as a partner in a firm against the firm or any person alleged to be or to have been a partner in the firm, unless the firm is registered and the person suing is or has been shown in the Register of Firms as a partner in the firm:

Provided that the requirement of registration of firm under this sub-section shall not apply to the suits or proceedings instituted by the heirs or legal representative of the deceased partner of a firm for accounts of a dissolved firm or to realise the property of a dissolved firm.";

(*c*) in sub-section (3):

(*i*) for the words, brackets and figures "sub-sections (1) and (2)" the words, brackets, figures and letter "sub-sections (1), (2) and (2-A)" shall be *substituted*;

(*ii*) for clause (*a*), the following clause shall be *substituted*, namely:

"(*a*) the firms constituted for a duration upto six months or with a capital upto two thousand rupees; or". Mah. Act 29 of 1984, S. 13 (w.e.f. 1-1-1985).

SECTION 69-A

MAHARASHTRA. After Section 69 of the principal Act, the following section shall be *inserted*, namely:

"69-A. *Penalty for contravention of Section 60, 61, 62, or 63.* If any statement, intimation or notice under Section 60, 61, 62 or 63 in respect of any registered firm is not sent or given to the Registrar, within the period specified in that section, the Registrar may, after giving notice to the partners of the firm and after giving them a reasonable opportunity of being heard, refuse to make the suitable amendments in the records relating to the firm, until the partners of the firm pay such penalty, not exceeding ten rupees per day, as the Registrar may determine in respect of the period between the date of expiry of the period specified in Section 60, 61, 62,or as the case may be, 63 and the date of making the amendments in the entries relating to the firm." — Mah. Act 29 of 1984, S. 14 (w.e.f. 1-1-1985).

NOTES

Section 69 is mandatory in character and its effect is to render a suit by a plaintiff in respect of a right vested in him or acquired by him under a contract which he entered into as a partner of an unregistered firm, whether existing or dissolved, void. In other words, a partner of an erstwhile unregistered partnership firm cannot bring a suit to enforce a right arising out of a contract falling within the ambit of Section 69 of the Partnership Act. *Seth Loonkaran Sethia v. Ivan E. John.*, (1977) 1 SCC 379, 393.

Suit by partner for money — Fact that partnership was dissolved not mentioned in original plaint — Amendment of plaint to supply omission — Held, permissible, *Ganesh Trading Co. v. Moji Ram*, (1978) 2 SCC 91.

70. Penalty for furnishing false particulars. Any person who signs any statement, amending statement, notice or intimation under this Chapter containing any particulars which he knows to be false or does not believe to be true, or containing particulars which he knows to be incomplete or does not believe to be complete, shall be punishable with imprisonment which may extend to three months, or with fine or with both.

STATE AMENDMENTS

MAHARASHTRA. In Section 70 of the principal Act, for the words "shall be punishable with imprisonment which may extend to three months, or with fine, or with both," the following shall be *substituted*, namely:

"shall on conviction, be punished with imprisonment for a term which may extend to one year, or with fine, or with both:

Provided that in the absence of special and adequate reasons to the contrary to be mentioned in the judgment of the Court, the fine shall not be less than one thousand rupees." — Mah. Act 29 of 1984, S. 15 (w.e.f. 1-1-1985):

---

10. *Subs.* by Act 3 of 1957, S. 3 and Sch. for "Part A States and Part C States"
11. *Subs.* by S.3 and Sch. *ibid*, for "such States".
12. *Subs.* by Act 24 of 1934, Section 2 and Sch. I, for "Section 55."

SECTION 70-A

MAHARASHTRA. After Section 70 of the principal Act, the following section shall be *inserted*, namely :

"70-A. *Maximum fees and power to amend Schedule I.* (1) The fees payable under this Act and the rules made thereunder shall not exceed the maximum fees as specified in Schedule I.

(2) Subject to the provisions of this section, the State Government may, having, regard to the expenditure incurred or to be incurred for carrying out the purposes of this Act. From time to time, by notification in the Official Gazette, vary any of the amounts of maximum fees and other particulars specified in Schedule I, and, thereupon, the said Schedule shall be deemed to be amended accordingly.

(3) Every notification issued under sub-section (2) shall take effect from the date of its publication in the Official Gazette, unless some other date is specified therein for this purpose.

(4) Every notification issued by the State Government under sub-section (2) shall be laid, as soon as may be after it is issued, before each House of the State Legislature, while it is in session, for a total period of thirty days, which may be comprised in one session or in two successive sessions and if, before the expiry of the session in which it is so laid or the session immediately following, both Houses agree in making any modification in the notification or both House agree that the notification should not be issued, and notify such decision in the Official Gazette, the notification shall, from the date of publication of such decision, have effect only in such modified form or be of no effect, as the case may be; so, however, that any such modification or annulment shall be without prejudice to the validity of anything previously done or omitted to be done in pursuance of that notification." Mah. Act 29 of 1984, S. 16 (w.e.f. 1-1-1985).

71. Power to make rules. (1) The [13][State Government] [13a][may by notification in the Official Gazette, make rules] prescribing the fees which shall accompany documents sent to the Registrar of Firms, or which shall be payable for the inspection of documents in the custody of the Registrar of Firms, or for copies from the Register of Firms:

Provided that such fees shall not exceed the maximum fee specified in Schedule I.

(2) The State Government may [14][also] make rules:

(*a*) prescribing the form of statement submitted under Section 58, and of the verification thereof;

(*b*) requiring statements, intimations and notices under Sections 60, 61, 62, and 63 to be in prescribed form, and prescribing the form thereof;

(*c*) prescribing the form of the Register of Firms, and the mode in which entries relating to firms are to be made therein, and the mode in which such entries are to be amended or notes made therein;

(*d*) regulating the procedure of the Registrar when disputes arise;

(*e*) regulating the filing of documents received by the Registrar;

(*f*) prescribing conditions for the inspection of original documents;

(*g*) regulating the grant of copies;

(*h*) regulating the elimination of registers and documents;

(*i*) providing for the maintenance and form of an index to the Register of Firms; and

(*j*) generally, to carry out the purposes of this Chapter.

(3) All rules made under this section shall be subject to the condition of previous publication.

[14a][(4) Every rule made by the State Government under this section shall be laid, as soon as it is made, before the State Legislature.]

STATE AMENDMENTS

MAHARASHTRA. In Section 71 of the principal Act,

(*a*) for sub-section (1), the following sub-section shall be *substituted*, namely :

"(1) Subject to the provisions of Section 70-A, the State Government may, by notification in the Official Gazette, make rules prescribing the fees which shall accompany documents sent to the Registrar or which shall be paid in respect of any intimation, notice or application given to the Registrar or which shall be payable for the inspection of documents in the custody of the Registrar or for copies from the Register of Firms or which shall be paid for supply of any prescribed forms.";

(*b*) in sub-section (2):

(*i*) in clause (a), for the words and figures "under Section 58" the words, brackets and figures "under sub-section (1) of Section 58" shall be *substituted*;

(*ii*) after clause (a), the following clause shall be *inserted*, namely:

"(*aa*) prescribing the manner of filing an appeal under sub-section (4) of Section 58";

(*c*) for sub-section (4), the following sub-section shall be *substituted*, namely:

"(4) Every rule made under this section shall be laid, as soon as may be after it is made, before each House of the State Legislature, while it is in session, for a total period of thirty days, which may be comprised in one session or in two successive sessions, and if, before the expiry of the session in which it is so laid or the session immediately following, both Houses agree in making any modification in the rule or both Houses agree that the rules should not be made, and notify such decision in the Official Gazette, the rule shall, from the date of publication of such decision, have effect only in such modified form or be of no effect, as the case may be; so, however, that any such modification or annulment shall be without prejudice to the validity of anything previously done or omitted to be done in pursuance of that rule." Mah. Act. 29 of 1984, S. 17 (w.e.f. 1-1-1985).

CHAPTER VIII

Supplemental

72. Mode of giving public notice. A public notice under this Act is given:

(*a*) where it relates to the retirement or expulsion of a partner from a registered firm, or to the dissolution of a registered firm, or to the election to become or not to become a partner in a registered firm by a person attaining majority who was admitted as a minor to the benefits of partnership, by notice to the Registrar of Firms under Section 63, and by publication in the Official Gazette and in at least one vernacular newspaper circulating in the district where the firm to which it relates has its place or principal place of business, and

(*b*) in any other case, by publication in the Official Gazette, and in at least one vernacular newspaper circulating in the district where the firm to which it relates has its place or principal place of business.

NOTES

Mode of giving public notice. This section lays down the manner in which the public notice of certain matters relating to partnership firms, may be given. It provides that in all cases, where a public notice is required under this Act, it must be effected by publication in Official Gazette, as well as in at least one vernacular newspaper having circulation in the district in which the firm in question has its place of business.

Public notice relating to registered firm must also be communicated to Registrar of Firms. Such copy of a public notice should be sent to the Registrar of the Firms under Section 63 where the matter relates to:

13. *Subs* by the A.L.O. 1950 for "Provincial Government".

13a. *Subs.* by Act 20 of 1983, S. 2 and Sch. (w.e.f. 15-3-1984).

14. *Ins.* by the A.O. 1937 (1-4-1937).

14a. *Ins.* by Act 20 of 1983, S. 2 and Sch. (w.e.f. 15-3-1984).

(*i*) the retirement or expulsion of partner, or
(*ii*) the dissolution of the firm, or
(*iii*) the election on attaining majority, to become or not to become a partner by a person who as a minor was admitted to the benefits of partnership.

This section may be read with Sections 30, 32, 33, 45, 63 and 69.

73. [*Repeals.*] *Rep. by the Repealing Act, 1938 (1 of 1938), Section 2 and Schedule.*

74. Savings. Nothing in this Act or any repeal effected thereby shall affect or be deemed to affect:

(*a*) any right, title, interest, obligation or liability already acquired, accrued or incurred before the commencement of this Act, or
(*b*) any legal proceeding or remedy in respect of such right, title, interest, obligation or liability,
(*c*) anything done or suffered before the commencement of this Act, or
(*d*) any enactment relating to partnership not expressly repealed by this act, or
(*e*) any rule of insolvency relating to partnership, or
(*f*) any rule of law not inconsistent with this Act.

STATE AMENDMENTS

GOA, DAMAN AND DIU. Section 74 shall be renumbered as sub-section (1) thereof and after it *insert* the following:

"(2) Notwithstanding anything contained in sub-section (1) and other law in force in the Union territory of Goa, Daman and Diu, the provisions of sub-sections (1) and (2) of Section 69 shall apply to all suits instituted in the Union territory of Goa, Daman and Diu after the 1st January, 1965, even if the cause of action with respect to the said suits had arisen before that date." Goa, Daman and Diu Act VI of 1966, Section 4 (22-8-1966).

SCHEDULE 1

Maximum Fees

[See sub-section (1) of Section 71]

Document or act in respect of which the fee is payable	*Maximum fee*
Statement under Section 58	Three rupees
Statement under Section 60	One rupee
Intimation under Section 61	One rupee
Intimation under Section 62	One rupee
Notice under Section 63	One rupee
Application under Section 64	One rupee
Inspection of the Register of Firms under sub-section (1) of Section 66.	Eight annas for inspecting one volume of the Register.
Inspection of documents relating to a firm under sub-section (2) of Section 66.	Eight annas for the inspection of all documents relating to one firm.
Copies from the Register of Firms.	Four annas for each hundred words or part thereof.

STATE AMENDMENTS

ANDHRA PRADESH. For Schedule I to the Indian Partnership Act, 1932, the following new Schedule shall be substituted, namely:

"SCHEDULE I'

Maximum Fees

[See sub-section (1) of Section 71]

S. No.	*Document or act in respect of which the fee is payable*		*Maximum Fee*
			Rs. P.
(1)	Statement under Section 58.		100.00
(2)	Statement under Section 60	... ...	20.00
(3)	Intimation under Section 61	... ...	20.00
(4)	Intimation under Section 62	... ...	20.00
(5)	Notice under Section 63	... ...	20.00
(6)	Application under Section 64	... ...	20.00
(7)	Inspection of the Register of Firms under sub-section (1) of Section 66.	For Inspecting the entry of each firm in the register.	10.00
(8)	Inspection of document relating to a firm under sub-section (2) of Section 66.	For each inspection of all documents relating to one single firm.	10.00"
(9)	Copies from the Register of Firms.	For each hundred words or part thereof. (*Vide* A.P. Act 23 of 1978, Section 2).	10.00

Goa, Daman and Diu. In Sch. I, (*a*) for the words 'eight annas', at both, the places where they occur, *substitute* the words, 'fifty paise'; and (*b*) in entries relating to copies from the Register of Firms, for the words 'four annas', *substitute* the words 'fifty paise'— Goa, Daman and Diu Act VI of 1966, S. 5 (22-8-1966).

Gujarat. *Substitution of Schedules 1 to 9 of 1923.* In the Indian Partnership Act, 1932 (9 of 1932), in its application to the State of Gujarat, for Schedule I, the following Schedule shall be *substituted*, namely:

"SCHEDULE-I

Maximum Fees

(See sub-section (1) of Section 71)

Document or act in respect of which the fee is payable	*Maximum fee*
1	2
Statement under Section 58	Fifty rupees
Statement under Section 60	Twenty-five rupees
Intimation under Section 61	Twenty-five rupees
Intimation under Section 62	Twenty-five rupees
Notice under Section 63	Twenty-five rupees

Application under Section 64	Twenty-five rupees
Inspection of the Register of Firms under sub-section (1) of Section 66.	Ten rupees for inspecting one volume of the Register
Inspection of documents relating to a firm under sub-section (2) of Section 66.	Ten rupees for the inspection of all documents relating to one firm.
Copies from the Register of Firms	Five rupees for each hundred words or part thereof". — Gujarat Act 13 of 1991, S. 2 (published in Guj. Gaz. Extra.,Pt. IV, dt. 16-4-1991).

Kerala. *Substitution of new Schedule for Schedule I.* For Schedule I to the Indian Partnership Act, 1932 (Central Act 9 of 1932), the following Schedule shall be *substituted*, namely :

"SCHEDULE I

Maximum Fees

[See sub-section (1) of Section 71]

Document or act in respect of which the fee is payable	*Maximum fee*
Statement under Section 58	Fifteen rupees.
Statement under Section 60	Five rupees.
Intimation under Section 61	Five rupees.
Intimation under Section 62	Five rupees.
Notice under Section 63	Five rupees.
Application under Section 64	Five rupees.
Inspection of the Register of Firms under sub-section (1) of Section 66.	Two rupees for inspecting one volume of the Register.
Inspection of the documents relating to a firm under sub-section (2) of Section 66.	Two rupees for the inspection of all documents relating to one firm.
Copies from the Register of Firms	Fifty paise for each hundred words or part thereof." (*Vide* Kerala Act 25 of 1973, S. 2).

Madhya Pradesh. *Substitution of Schedule I.* For Schedule I of the Indian Partnership Act, 1932 (IX of 1932), the following Schedule shall be *substituted*, namely:

"SCHEDULE I

Maximum Fees

[See sub-section (1) of Section 71]

Document or act in respect of which the fee is payable	*Maximum fee*
Statement under Section 58	Two hundred rupees
Statement under Section 60	Twenty five rupees
Intimation under Section 61	Twenty five rupees
Intimation under Section 62	Twenty five rupees
Notice under Section 63	Twenty five rupees
Application under Section 64	Twenty five rupees

Inspection of the Register of Firms under sub-section (1) of Section 66.	Ten rupees for inspecting one volume of the Register.
Inspection of documents relating to a firm under sub-section (2) of Section 66.	Ten rupees for the inspection of all documents relating to one firm.
Copies from the Register of Firms.	Two rupees for each hundred words or part thereof." (*Vide* M.P. Act 27 of 1986, S.3).

Maharashtra. For Schedule I appended to the principal Act, the following Schedule shall be *substituted*, namely :

"SCHEDULE I

Maximum Fees

(See Sections 70-A and 71)

Document or act in respect of which the fee is payable	*Maximum fee*
(1)	(2)
(1) Statement under Section 58(1)	Fifty rupees
(2) Memorandum of appeal under Section 58(4)	Twenty-five rupees
(3) Statement under Section 60	Fifteen rupees
(4) Intimation under Section 61	Fifteen rupees
(5) Intimation under Section 62	Fifteen rupees
(6) Notice under Section 63(1)	Fifteen rupees
(7) Intimation under Section 63 (1-A)	Fifteen rupees
(8) Notice under Section 63(2)	Fifteen rupees
(9) Application under Section 64	Fifteen rupees
(10) Inspection of the Register of Firms under sub-section (1) of Section 66,, for inspection of one volume of the Register of Firms.	Seven rupees and fifty paise
(11) Inspection of documents relating to a firm under sub-section (2) of Section 66, for the inspection of all documents relating to one firm.	Seven rupees and fifty paise
(12) Copies from the Register for Firms under Section 67, for each hundred words or part thereof	Two rupees
(13) Price of Forms prescribed under the rules — Mah. Act 29 of 1984,, S. 18 (w.e.f. 1-1-1985).	One rupee per form."

Pondicherry. Column (1) same as the principal Act : for column (2) *substitute* as follows, serially,

Rs. 10.00; Rs. 3.00; Rs. 3.00; Rs. 3.00; Rs. 3.00; Rs. 3.00; Re. 1.00; Re. 1.00; Re. 0.40.

Rajasthan. *Substitution of new Schedule for Schedule I to Central Act IX of 1932.* For Schedule I to the principal Act, the following Schedule shall be *substituted*, namely:

"SCHEDULE I

Maximum Fees

[See sub-section (1) of Section 71]

Document or act in respect of which the fee is payable	*Maximum fee*
1. Statement under Section 58	Fifteen rupees
2. Statement under Section 60	Five rupees
3. Intimation under Section 61	Five rupees
4. Intimation under Section 62	Five rupees
5. Notice under Section 63	Five rupees
6. Application under Section 64	Five rupees
7. Inspection of the Register of Firms under sub-section (1) of Section 66.	Two rupees,, for the inspection of one volume of Register.
8. Inspection of documents relating to a firm under sub-section (2) of Section 66.	Two rupees for the inspection of all documents relating to one firm.
9. Copies from the Register of Firms.	Two rupees for each hundred words or part thereof." (*Vide* Rajasthan Act 10 of 1971, S. 3, w.e.f. 15-9-1971).

Tamil Nadu. *Substitution of new Schedule for Schedule 1 to Central Act IX of 1932.* For Schedule I to the principal Act, the following Schedule shall be *substituted*, namely:

"SCHEDULE I

Maximum Fees

[See sub-section (1) of Section 71]

Document or act in respect of which the fee is payable	*Maximum fee*
1	2
	Rs. P
1. Statement under Section 58	.. 50.00
2. Statement under Section 60	.. 5.00
3. Intimation under Section 61	.. 5.00
4. Intimation under Section 62	.. 5.00
5. Notice under Section 63	.. 5.00
6. Application under Section 64	.. 5.00
7. Inspection of the Register of Firms under sub-section (1) of Section 66.	.. 2.00 for inspecting the entry of each firm in the Register
8. Inspection of documents relating to a firm under sub-section (2) of Section 66.	.. 2.00 for each inspection of all documents relating to one firm.
9. Copies from the Register of Firms.	.. 0.50 for each hundred words or part thereof." (*Vide* T.N. Act 38 of 1982,, S. 2).

Uttar Pradesh. *Substitution of Schedule I to Act IX of 1932.* For Schedule I to the Indian Partnership Act, 1932, the following Schedule shall be *substituted*, namely:

"SCHEDULE I

Maximum Fees

[See sub-section (1) of Section 71]

Document or act in respect of which the fee is payable	*Maximum fee*
(1)	(2)
1. Statement under Section 58 . .	One hundred rupees.
2. Statement under Section 60 . .	Thirty rupees.
3. Intimation under Section 61 . .	Thirty rupees.
4. Intimation under Section 62 . .	Thirty rupees.
5. Notice under Section 63 . .	Thirty rupees.
6. Application under Section 64 . .	Thirty rupees.
7. Inspection of the Register of Firms under sub-section (1) of Section 66. . .	Ten rupees for the inspection of one volume of Register.
8. Inspection of documents relating to a firm under sub-section (2) of Section 66.	Ten rupees for the inspection of all documents relating to one firm.
9. Copies from the Register of Firms. . .	Four rupees for each hundred words or part thereof." (*Vide* U.P. Act 33 of 1974,S. 2 w.e.f. 16-8-1975).

Schedule II. *[Enactments Repealed] Rep. by the Repealing Act, 1938 (1 of 1938) Section 2 and Sch.*

III

APPENDIX

The Sale of Goods Act, 1930

CHAPTER I — PRELIMINARY

1. Short title, extent and commencement. (1) This Act may be called the Sales of Goods Act, 1930.

(2) It extends to the whole of India except the State of Jammu and Kashmir.

(3) It shall come into force on the 1st day of July, 1930.

2. Definitions. In this Act, unless there is anything repugnant in the subject of context,

(1) "buyer" means a person who buys or agrees to buy goods;

(2) "delivery" means voluntary transfer of possession from one person to another;

(3) goods are said to be in a "deliverable state" when they are in such state that the buyer would under the contract be bound to take delivery of them;

(4) "document of title of goods" includes a bill of leading, dock-warrant, warehouse keeper's certificate, wharfinger's certificate, railway receipt, warrant or order for the delivery of goods and any other document used in the ordinary course of business as proof of the possession or control of goods, or authorising of purporting to authorise, either by endorsement or by delivery, the possessor of the document to transfer or receive goods thereby represented;

(5) "fault" means wrongful act or default;

(6) "future goods" means goods to be manufactured or produced or acquired by the seller after the making of the contract of sale;

(7) "goods" means every kind of movable property other than actionable claims and money; and includes stock and shares, growing crops, grass, and things attached to or forming part of the land which are agreed to be severed before sale or under the contract of sale;

(8) A person is said to be "insolvent" who has ceased to pay his debts in the ordinary course of business, or cannot pay his debts as they become due, whether he has committed an act of insolvency or not;

(9) "mercantile agent" means a mercantile agent having in the customary course of business as such agent, authority either to sell goods, or to consign goods for the purposes of sale, or to buy goods, or to raise money on the security of goods;

(10) "price" means the money consideration for a sale of goods;

(11) "property" means the general property in goods, and not merely a special property;

(12) "quality of goods" includes their state or condition;

(13) "seller" means a person who sells or agrees to sell goods;

(14) "specific goods" means goods identified and agreed upon at the time a contract of sale is made; and

(15) expressions used but not defined in this Act and defined in the Indian Contract Act, 1872, have the meaning assigned to them in that Act.

Notes. Delivery. Delivery is of two kinds, (i) actual, and (ii) constructive. When the goods to be delivered or transferred from the hands of the seller or his agent to those of the buyer or his agent, it is actual delivery. Constructive delivery is known as the delivery by attachment.

Goods. Share Certificates are movable property and are, therefore, goods; [AIR 1922 Bom. 303].

Specific Goods. Sub-section (4)—In order that the goods may be specific they must be identified and not merely identifiable. [*Kur Sell* v. *Timber Corpors and Contractors Ltd.*, (1927) 1 KB 314].

3. Application of provisions of Act 9 of 1872. The unrepealed provisions of the Indian Contract Act, 1872, save in so far as they are inconsistent with the express provisions of this Act, shall continue to apply to contracts for the sale of goods.

Note. This section deals with the application of the provisions of the Indian Contract Act of 1872 to contracts for the sale of goods.

CHAPTER II—FORMATION OF THE CONTRACT

CONTRACT OF SALE

4. Sale and agreement to sell. (1) A contract of sale of goods is a contract whereby the seller transfers or agrees to transfer the property in goods to the buyers for a price. There may be a contract of sale between one part-owner and another.

(2) A contract of sale may be absolute or conditional.

(3) Where under a contract of sale the property in the goods is transferred from the seller to the buyer, the contract is called a sale, but where the transfer of the property in the goods is to take place at a future time or subject to some condition thereafter to be fulfilled, the contract is called an agreement to sell.

(4) An agreement to sell becomes a sale when the time elapses or the conditions are fulfilled subject to which the property in the goods is to be transferred.

FORMALITIES OF THE CONTRACT

5. Contract of sale, how made. (1) A contract of sale is made by an offer to buy or sell goods for a price and the acceptance of such offer. The contract may provide for the immediate delivery of the goods or immediate payment of the price or both, or for the delivery or payment by instalments, or that the delivery or payment or both shall be postponed.

(2) Subject to the provisions of any law for the time being in force, a contract of sale may be made in writing or by words of mouth, or partly in writing and partly by word of mouth or may be implied from the conduct of the parties.

Note. A sale is made complete on the purchase-money being agreed to be paid. [21 PR 1875].

SUBJECT MATTER OF CONTRACT

6. Existing or future goods. (1) The goods which form the subject of a contract of sale may be either existing goods, owned or possessed by the seller, or future goods.

(2) There may be a contract for the sale of goods, the acquisition of which by the seller depends upon a contingency which may or may not happen.

(3) Where by a contract of sale the seller purports to effect a present sale of future goods, the contract operates as an agreement to sell the goods.

7. Goods perishing before making of contract. Where there is a contract for the sale of specific goods, the contract is void if the goods without the knowledge of the seller have, at the time when the contract was made, perished or become so damaged as no longer to answer to their description in the contract.

8. Goods perishing before sale but after agreement to sell. Where there is an agreement to sell specific goods, and subsequently the goods without any fault on the part of the seller or buyer perish or become so damaged as no longer to answer to their description in the agreement before the risk passes to the buyer, the agreement is thereby avoided.

THE PRICE

9. Ascertainment of price. (1) The price in a contract of sale may be fixed by the contract or may be left to be fixed in manner thereby agreed or may be determined by the course of dealing between the parties.

(2) Where the price is not determined in accordance with the foregoing provisions, the buyers shall pay the seller a reasonable price. What is a reasonable price is a question of fact dependent on the circumstances of each particular case.

10. Agreement to sell at valuation. (1) Where there is an agreement to sell goods on the terms that the price is to be fixed by the valuation of a third party and such third party cannot or does not make such valuation, the agreement is thereby avoided:

Provided that, if the goods or any part thereof have been delivered to, and appropriated by the buyer, he shall pay a reasonable price therefor.

(2) Where such third party is prevented from making the valuation by the fault of the seller or buyer, the party not in fault may maintain a suit for damages against the party in fault.

CONDITIONS AND WARRANTIES

11. Stipulations as to time. Unless a different intention appears from the terms of the contract, stipulations as to time of payment are not deemed to be of the essence of a contract of sale. Whether any other stipulation as to time is of the essence of the contract or not depends on the terms of the contract.

12. Condition and warranty. (1) A stipulation in a contract of sale with reference to goods which are the subject thereof may be a condition or a warranty.

(2) A condition is a stipulation essential to the main purpose of the contract, the breach of which gives rise to a right to treat the contract as repudiated.

(3) A warranty is a stipulation collateral to the main purpose of the contract, the breach of which gives rise to a claim for damages but not to a right to reject the goods and treat the contract as repudiated.

(4) Whether a stipulation in a contract of sale is a condition or a warranty depends in each case on the construction of the contract. A stipulation may be a condition, though called a warranty in the contract.

13. When condition to be treated as warranty. (1) Where a contract of sale is subject to any condition to be fulfilled by the seller, the buyer may waive the condition or elect to treat the breach of the condition as a breach of warranty and not as a ground for treating the contract as repudiated.

(2) Where a contract of sale is not severable and the buyer has accepted the goods or part thereof, the breach of any condition to be fulfilled by the seller can only be treated as a breach of warranty and not as a ground for rejecting the goods and treating the contract as repudiated, unless there is a term of the contract, express or implied, to that effect.

(3) Nothing in this section shall affect the case of any condition or warranty fulfillment of which is excused by law by reason of impossibility or otherwise.

Note. Waiver of Condition. A party may always waive a stipulation which is for his benefit. [*Hartley v. Hymont*, (1920) 3 K.B. 176].

14. Implied undertaking as to title, etc. In a contract of sale, unless the circumstances of the contract are such as to show a different intention, there is:

(*a*) an implied condition on the part of the seller that, in the case of a sale, he has a right to sell the goods and that, in the case of an agreement to sell, he will have a right to sell the goods at the time when the property is to pass;

(*b*) an implied warranty that the buyer shall have and enjoy quiet possession of the goods;

(*c*) an implied warranty that the goods shall be free from any charge or encumbrance in favour of any third party not declared or known to the buyer before or at the time when the contract is made.

15. Sale by description. Where there is a contract for the sale of goods by description, there is an implied condition that the goods shall correspond with the description; and, if the sale is by sample as well as by description it is not sufficient that the bulk of the goods corresponds with the sample if the goods do not also correspond with the description.

16. Implied conditions as to quality of fitness. Subject to the provisions of this Act and of any other law for the time being in force, there is no implied warranty or condition as to the quality or fitness for any particular purpose of goods supplied under a contract of sale, except as follows:

(1) Where the buyer, expressly or by implication, makes known to the seller the particular purpose for which the goods are required, so as to show that the buyer relies on the seller's skill or judgment, and the goods are of a description which it is in course of the seller's business to supply (whether he is the manufacturer or producer or not), there is an implied condition that the goods shall be reasonably fit for such purpose;

Provided that, in the case of a contract for the sale of a specified article under its patent or other trade name, there is no implied condition as to its fitness for any particular purpose.

(2) Where goods are bought by description from a seller who deals in goods of that description (whether he is the manufacture or producer or not), there is an implied condition that the goods shall be of merchantable quality:

Provided that, if the buyer has examined the goods, there shall be no implied condition as regards defects which such examination ought to have revealed.

(3) An implied warranty or condition as to quality or fitness for a particular purpose may be annexed by the usage or trade.

(4) An express warranty or condition does not negative a warranty or condition implied by this Act unless inconsistent therewith.

Note. This section relates to implied warranty as to quality or fitness of the goods sold.

17. Sale by sample. (1) A contract of sale is a contract for sale by sample where there is a term in the contract, express or implied, to that effect.

(2) In the case of a contract for sale by sample there is an implied condition:

(*a*) that the bulk shall correspond with the sample in quality;

(*b*) that the buyer shall have a reasonable opportunity of comparing the bulk with the sample;

(*c*) that the goods shall be free from any defect, rendering them unmerchantable, which would not be apparent on reasonable examination of the sample.

CHAPTER III — EFFECTS OF THE CONTRACT

TRANSFER OF PROPERTY AS BETWEEN SELLER AND BUYER

18. Goods must be ascertained. Where there is a contract for the sale of unascertained goods, no property in the goods is transferred to the buyer unless and until the goods are ascertained.

19. Property passes when intended to pass. (1) Where there is a contract for the sale of specific or ascertained goods the property in them is transferred to the buyer at such time as the parties to the contract intend it to be transferred.

(2) For the purpose of ascertaining the intention of the parties regard shall be had to the terms of the contract, the conduct of the parties and the circumstances of the case.

(3) Unless a different intention appears, the rules contained in section 20 to 24 are rules for ascertaining the intention of the parties as to the time at which the property in the goods is to pass to the buyer.

20. Specific goods in a deliverable state. Where there is an unconditional contract for the sale of specific goods in a deliverable state, the property in the goods passes to the buyer when the contract is made, and it is immaterial whether the time of payment of the price or the time of delivery of the goods, or both, is postponed.

21. Specific goods to be put into a deliverable state. Where there is contract for the sale of specific goods and the seller is bound to do something to the goods for the purpose of putting them into a deliverable state, the property does not pass until such thing is done and the buyer has notice thereof.

"Specific goods" in this section necessarily means the goods which can be ascertained with certainty.

22. Specific goods in a deliverable state, when the seller has to do anything thereto in order to ascertain price. Where there is a contract for the sale of specific goods in a deliverable state, but the seller is bound to weigh, measure, test or do some other act or thing with reference to the goods for the purpose of ascertaining the price, the property does not pass until such act or thing is done and the buyer has notice thereof.

23. Sale of unascertained goods and appropriation. (1) Where there is a contract for the sale of unascertained or future goods by description and goods of that description and in a deliverable state are unconditionally appropriated to the contract, either by the seller with the assent of the buyer or by the buyer with the assent of the seller, the property in the goods thereupon passes to the buyer. Such assent may be expressed or implied, and may be given either before or after the appropriation is made.

(2) Delivery to Carrier. Where, in pursuance of the contract, the seller delivers the goods to the buyer or to a carrier or other bailee (whether named by the buyer or not) for the purpose of transmission to the buyer, and does not reserve the right of disposal, he is deemed to have unconditionally appropriated the goods to the contract.

24. Goods sent on approval or "on sale or return". When goods are delivered to the buyer on approval or "on sale or return" or other similar terms, the property therein passes to the buyer :

(*a*) when he signifies his approval or acceptance to the seller or does any other act, adopting the transaction;

(*b*) if he does not signify his approval or acceptance to the seller but retains the goods without giving notice of rejection, then, if a time has been fixed for the return of the goods, on the expiration of such time, and, if no time has been fixed, on the expiration of a reasonable time.

25. Reservation of right of disposal. (1) Where there is a contract for the sale of specific goods or where goods are subsequently appropriated to the contract, the seller may, by the terms of the contract or appropriation, reserve the right of disposal of the goods until certain conditions are fulfilled. In such cases, notwithstanding the delivery of the goods to a buyer, or to a carrier or other bailee for the purpose of transmission to the buyer, the property in the goods does not pass to the buyer until the conditions imposed by the seller are fulfilled.

(2) Where goods are shipped or delivered to railway administration for carriage by railway and by the bill of lading or railway receipt, as the case may be, the goods are deliverable to the order of the sellers or his agent, the seller is **prima facie** deemed to reserve the right of disposal.

(3) Where the seller of goods draws on the buyer for the price and transmits to the buyer the bill of exchange together with the bill of lading or, as the case may be, the railway receipt, to secure acceptance or payment of the bill of exchange, the buyer is bound to return the bill of lading or the railway receipt if he does not honour the bill of exchange and if he wrongfully retains the bill of lading or the railway receipt, the property in the goods does not pass to him.

Explanation. In this section, the expressions "railway" and "railway administration" shall have the meanings respectively assigned to them under the Indian Railways Act, 1890 (9 of 1890).

26. Risk prima facie passes with property. Unless otherwise agreed, the goods remain at the seller's risk until the property therein is transferred to the buyer, but when the property therein is transferred to the buyer, the goods are at the buyer's risk whether delivery has been made or not.

Provided that, where delivery has been delayed through the fault of either buyer or seller, the goods are at the risk of the party in fault as regards any loss which might not have occurred but for such fault:

Provided also that nothing in this section shall affect the duties or liabilities of either seller or buyer as a bailee of the goods of the other party.

TRANSFER OF TITLE

27. Sale by person not the owner. Subject to the provisions of this Act and of any other law for the time being in force, where goods are sold by a person who is not the owner thereof and who does not sell them under the authority or with the consent of the owner, the buyer acquires no better title to the goods than the seller had, unless the owner of the goods is by his conduct precluded from denying the seller's authority to sell:

Provided that, where a mercantile agent is, with the consent of the owner, in possession of the goods or of a document of title to the goods, any sale made by him, when acting in the ordinary course of business of a mercantile agent, shall be as valid as if he were expressly authorised by the owner of the goods to make the same : Provided that the buyer acts in good faith and has not at the time of the contract of sale notice that the seller has no authority to sell.

28. Sale by one of joint owner. If one of several joint owners of goods has the sole possession of them by permission of the co-owners, the property in the goods is transferred to any person who buys them of such joint owner in good faith and has not at the time of the contract of sale notice that the seller has no authority to sell.

29. Sale by person in possession under voidable contract. When the seller of goods has obtained possession thereof under a contract voidable under section 19 or 19-A of the Indian Contract Act 1872 (9 of 1872), but the contract has not been rescinded at the time of sale, the buyer acquires a good title to the goods, provided he buys them in good faith and without notice of the seller's defect of title.

30. Seller or buyer in possession after sale. (1) Whether a person, having sold goods, continues or is in possession of the goods or of the documents of title to the goods, the delivery or transfer by that person or by a mercantile agent acting for him, of the goods documents of title under any sale, pledge or other disposition thereof to any person receiving the same in good faith and without notice of the previous sale shall have the same effect as if the person making the delivery or transfer were expressly authorised by the owner of the goods to make the same.

(2) Where a person having bought or agreed to buy goods, obtains, with the consent of the seller, possession of the goods or the documents of title to the goods, the delivery or transfer by that person or by a mercantile agent acting for him, of the goods or documents of title under any sale, pledge or other disposition thereof to any person receiving the same in good faith and without notice of any lien or other right of original seller in respect of the goods shall have effect as if in such lien or right did not exist.

CHAPTER IV — PERFORMANCE OF THE CONTRACT

31. Duties of seller and buyer. It is the duty of the seller to deliver the goods and of the buyer to accept and pay for them, in accordance with the terms of the contract of sale.

32. Payment and delivery are concurrent conditions. Unless otherwise agreed delivery of the goods and payment of the price are concurrent conditions, that is to say, the seller shall be ready and willing to give possession of the goods to the buyer in exchange for the price, and the buyer shall be ready and willing to pay the price in exchange for possession of the goods.

33. Delivery. Delivery of goods sold may be made by doing anything which the parties agree shall be treated as delivery or which has the effect of putting the goods in the possession of the buyer or of any person authorised to hold them on his behalf.

34. Effect of part delivery. A delivery of part of goods, in progress of the delivery of whole, has the same effect, for the purpose of passing the property in such goods, as a delivery of the whole; but a delivery of part of the goods, with an intention of severing it from the whole, does not operate as a delivery of the remainder.

35. Buyer to apply for delivery. Apart from any express contract, the seller of goods not bound to deliver them until the buyer applies for delivery.

36. Rules as to delivery. (1) Whether it is for the buyer to take possession of the goods or for the seller to send them to the buyer is a question depending in each case on the contract, express or implied, between the parties. Apart from any such contract, goods sold are to be delivered at the place at which they are at the time of the sale, and goods agreed to be sold are to be delivered at the place at which they are at the time of the agreement to sell, or, if not then in existence, at the place at which they are manufactured or produced.

(2) Where under the contract of sale the seller is bound to send the goods to the buyer, but no time for sending them is fixed, the seller is bound to send them within a reasonable time.

(3) Where the goods at the time of sale are in the possession of a third person, there is no delivery by seller to buyer unless and until such third person acknowledges to the buyer that he holds the goods on his behalf;

Provided that nothing in this section shall affect the operation of the issue or transfer of any document of title to goods.

(4) Demand or tender of delivery may be treated as ineffectual unless made at a reasonable hour. What is a reasonable hour is a question of fact.

(5) Unless otherwise agreed, the expenses of and incidental to putting the goods into a deliverable state shall be borne by the seller.

37. Delivery of wrong quantity. (1) Where the seller delivers to the buyer a quantity of goods less than he contracted to sell, the buyer may reject them, but if the buyer accepts the goods so delivered he shall pay for them at the contract rate.

(2) Where the seller delivers to the buyer a quantity of goods larger than he contracted to sell, the buyer may accept the goods included in the contract and reject the rest, or he may reject the whole. If the buyer accepts the whole of the goods so delivered, he shall pay for them at the contract rate.

(3) Where the seller delivers to the buyer the goods he contracted to sell mixed with goods of a different description not included in the contract, the buyer may accept the goods which are in accordance with contract are reject the rest, or may reject the whole.

(4) The provisions of this section are subject to any usage of trade, special agreement or course of dealing between the parties.

38. Instalment delivery. (1) Unless otherwise agreed, the buyer of goods is not bound to accept delivery thereof by instalments. (2) Where there is a contract for the sale of goods to be delivered by stated instalments which are to be separately paid for, and the seller makes no delivery or defective delivery in respect of one or more instalments or the buyer neglects or refuses to take delivery of or pay for one or more instalments, it is a question in each case depending on the terms of the contract and the circumstances of the case, whether the breach of contract is a repudiation of the whole contract, or whether it is a severable breach giving rise to a claim for compensation, but not to a right to treat the whole contract as repudiated.

39. Delivery to carrier or wharfinger. (1) Where, in pursuance of a contract of sale, the seller is authorised of required to send the goods to the buyer, delivery of the goods to a carrier, whether named by the buyer or not, for the purpose of a transmission to the buyer, or delivery of the goods to a wharfinger for safe custody, is **prima facie** deemed to be a delivery of the goods to the buyer.

(2) Unless otherwise authorised by the buyer, the seller shall make such contract with the carrier or wharfinger on behalf of the buyer as may be reasonable having regard to the nature of the goods and other circumstances of the case. If the seller omits so to do, and the goods are lost or

damaged in course of transit or whilst in the custody of the wharfinger, the buyer may decline to treat the delivery to the carrier or wharfinger as a delivery to himself, or may hold the seller responsible in damages.

(3) Unless otherwise agreed, where goods are sent by the seller to the buyer by a route involving sea transit, in circumstances in which it is usual to insure, the seller shall give such notice to the buyer as may enable him to insure them during their sea transit, and if the seller fails so to do, the goods shall be deemed to be at his risk during such sea transit.

40. Risk where goods are delivered at a distant place. Where the seller of goods agrees to deliver them at his own risk at a place other than that where they are when sold, the buyer shall, nevertheless, unless otherwise agreed, take any risk of deterioration in the goods necessarily incident to the course of transit.

41. Buyer's right of examining the goods. (1) Where goods are delivered to the buyer which he has not previously examined, he is not deemed to have accepted them unless and until he has had a reasonable opportunity of examining them for the purpose of ascertaining whether they are in conformity with the contract.

(2) Unless otherwise agreed, when the seller tenders delivery of goods to the buyer, he is bound, on request, to afford the buyer a reasonable opportunity of examining the goods for the purpose of ascertaining whether they are in conformity with the contract.

42. Acceptance. The buyer is deemed to have accepted the goods when he intimates to the seller that he has accepted them, or when the goods have been delivered to him and he does any act in relation to them which is inconsistent with the ownership of the seller, or when, after the lapse of a reasonable time, he retained the goods without intimating to the seller that he has rejected them.

43. Buyer not bound to return rejected goods. Unless otherwise agreed, where goods are delivered to the buyer and he refuses to accept them, having the right so to do, he is not bound to return them to the seller, but it is sufficient if he intimates to the seller that he refuses to accept them.

44. Liability of buyer for neglecting or refusing delivery of goods. When the seller is ready and willing to deliver the goods and requests the buyer to take delivery, and the buyer does not within a reasonable time after such request take delivery of the goods, he is liable to the seller for any loss occasioned by his neglect or refusal to take delivery, and also for a reasonable charge for the care and custody of the good:

Provided that nothing in this section shall affect the rights of the seller where the neglect or refusal of the buyer to take delivery amounts to a repudiation of the contract.

CHAPTER V — RIGHTS OF UNPAID SELLER AGAINST THE GOODS

45. "Unpaid seller" defined. (1) The seller of goods is deemed to be an "unpaid seller" within the meaning of this Act:

(a) when the whole of the price has not been paid or tendered;

(b) when a bill of exchange or other negotiable instrument has been received as conditional payment, and the condition on which it was received has not been fulfilled by reason of the dishonour of the instrument or otherwise.

(2) In this Chapter, the term "seller" includes and person who is in the position of a seller as, for instance an agent of the seller to whom the bill of lading has been endorsed, or a consignor or agent who has himself paid, or is directly responsible for the price.

46. Unpaid seller's right. (1) Subject to the provisions of this Act and of any law for the time being in force, notwithstanding that the property in the goods may have passed to the buyer, the unpaid seller of goods as such, has by implication of law:

(a) a lien on the goods for the price while he is in possession of them;

(b) in case of the insolvency of the buyer a right of stopping the goods in transit after he has parted with the possession of them;

(c) A right of re-sale as limited by this Act.

(2) Where the property in goods has not passed to the buyer, the unpaid seller has, in addition to his other remedies, a right of withholding delivery similar to and co-extensive with his rights of lien and stoppage in transit where the property has passed to the buyer.

UNPAID SELLERS'S LIEN

47. Sellers lien. (1) Subject to the provisions of this Act, the unpaid seller of goods who is in possession of them is entitled to retain possession of them until payment or tender of the price in the following cases, namely:

(*a*) where the goods have been sold without any stipulation as to credit;

(*b*) where the goods have been sold on credit, but the term of credit has expired;

(*c*) where the buyer becomes insolvent.

(2) The seller may exercise his right of lien notwithstanding that he is in possession of the goods as agent or bailee for the buyer.

48. Part delivery. Where an unpaid seller has made part delivery of the goods, he may exercise his right of lien on the remainder, unless such part delivery has been made under such circumstances as to show an agreement to waive the lien.

49. Termination of lien. (1) The unpaid seller of goods loses his lien thereon:

(*a*) when he delivers the goods to a carrier or other bailee for the purpose of transmission to the buyer without reserving the right of disposal of the goods;

(*b*) when the buyer or his agent lawfully obtains possession of the goods;

(*c*) by waiver thereof.

(2) The unpaid seller of goods, having a lien thereon, does not lose his lien by reason only that he has obtained a decree for the price of the goods.

STOPPAGE IN TRANSIT

50. Right of stoppage in transit. Subject to the provisions of this Act, when the buyer of goods becomes insolvent, the unpaid seller who has parted with the possession of the goods has the right of stopping them in transit, that is to say, he may resume possession of the goods as long as they are in the course of transit, and may retain them until payment or tender of the price.

51. Duration of transit. (1) Goods are deemed to be in course of transit from the time when they are delivered to a carrier or other bailee for the purpose of transmission to the buyer, until the buyer or his agent on that behalf takes delivery of them from such carrier or other bailee.

(2) If the buyer or his agent in that behalf obtains delivery of the goods before their arrival at the appointed destination, the transit is at an end.

(3) If, after the arrival of goods at the appointed destination, the carrier or other bailee acknowledges to the buyer or his agent that he holds the goods on his behalf and continues in possession of them as bailee for the buyer or his agent, the transit is at an end and it is immaterial that a further destination for the goods may have been indicated by the buyer.

(4) If the goods are rejected by the buyer and the carrier or other bailee continues in possession of them, the transit is not deemed to be at an end, even if the seller has refused to receive them back.

(5) When goods are delivered to a ship chartered by the buyer; it is a question depending on the circumstances of the particular case, whether they are in the possession of the master as a carrier or as agent of the buyer.

(6) Where the carrier or other bailee wrongfully refuses to deliver the goods to the buyer or his agent in that behalf, the transit is deemed to be at an end.

(7) Where part delivery of the goods has been made to the buyer or his agent in that behalf, the remainder of the goods may be stopped in transit, unless such part delivery has been given in such circumstances as to show an agreement to give up possession of the whole of the goods.

52. How stoppage in transit is effected. (1) The unpaid seller may exercise his right of stoppage in transit either by taking actual possession of the goods, or by giving notice of his claim to the carrier or other bailee in whose possession the goods are. Such notice may be given either to the person in actual possession of the goods or to his principal. In the latter case the notice, to be effectual, shall be given at such time and in such circumstances that the principal, by the exercise of reasonable diligence, may communicate it to his servant or agent in time to prevent a delivery to the buyer.

(2) When notice of stoppage in transit is given by the seller to the carrier or other bailee in possession of the goods, he shall re-deliver the goods to, or according to the directions of, the seller. The expenses of such re-delivery shall be borne by the seller.

TRANSFER BY BUYER AND SELLER

53. Effect of sub-sale or pledge by buyer. (1) Subject to the provisions of this Act, the unpaid seller's right of lien or stoppage in transit is not affected by any sale or other disposition of, the goods which the buyer may have made, unless the seller has assented thereto:

Provided that where a document of title to goods has been issued or lawfully transferred to any person as buyer or owner of the goods, and that person transfers the document to a person who takes the document in good faith and for consideration, then, if such last-mentioned transfer was by way of sale, the unpaid seller's right of lien or stoppage in transit is defeated, and, if such last mentioned, transfer was by way of pledge or other disposition for value, the unpaid seller's right of lien or stoppage in transit can only be exercised subject to the rights of the transferee.

(2) Where the transfer is by way of pledge, the unpaid seller may require the pledgee to have the amount secured by pledge satisfied in the first instance, as far as possible, out of any other goods or securities of the buyer in the hands of the pledgee and available against the buyer.

54. Sale not generally rescinded by lien or stoppage in transit. (1) Subject to the provisions of this section, a contract of sale is not rescinded by the mere exercise by an unpaid seller of his right of lien or stoppage in transit.

(2) Where the goods are of a perishable nature, or where the unpaid seller who has exercised his right of lien or stoppage in transit gives notice to the buyer of his intention to re-sell, the unpaid seller may, if the buyer does not within a reasonable time pay or tender the price, re-sell the goods within a reasonable time and recover from the original buyer damages for any loss occasioned by his breach of contract, but the buyer shall not be entitled to any profit which may occur on the re-sale. If such notice is not given the unpaid seller shall not be entitled to recover such damages and the buyer shall be entitled to the profit, if any, on the re-sale.

(3) Where an unpaid seller who has exercised his rights of lien or stoppage in transit re-sells the goods, the buyer acquires a good title thereto as against the original buyer, notwithstanding that no notice of the re-sale has been given to the original buyer.

(4) Where the seller expressly reserves a right of re-sale in case the buyer should make default, and, on the buyer making default, re-sells the goods, the original contract of sale is thereby rescinded, but without prejudice to any claim which the seller may have for damages.

CHAPTER VI—SUITS FOR BREACH OF THE CONTRACT

55. Suit for price. (1) Where under a contract of sale to the property in the goods has passed to the buyer and the buyer wrongfully neglects or refuses to pay for the goods according to the terms of the contract, the seller may sue him for the price of the goods.

(2) Where under a contract of sale the price is payable on a day certain irrespective of delivery and the buyer wrongfully neglects or refuses to pay such price, the seller may sue him for the price although the property in the goods has not passed and the goods have not been appropriated to the contract.

56. Damages for non-acceptance. Where the buyer wrongfully neglects or refuses to accept and pay for the goods, the seller may sue him for damages for non-acceptance.

57. Damages for non-delivery. Where the seller wrongfully neglects or refuses to deliver the goods to the buyer may sue the seller for damages for non-delivery.

58. Specific performance. Subject to the provisions of Chapter II of the specific Relief Act 1877 (1 of 1877) in any suit for breach of contract to deliver specific or ascertained goods, the Court may, if it thinks fit, on the application of the plaintiff, by its decree direct that the contract shall be performed specifically, without giving the defendant the option of retaining the goods on payment of damages. The decree may be unconditional, or upon such terms and conditions as to damages, payment of the price or otherwise, as the Court may deem just, and the application of the plaintiff may be made at any time before the decree.

59. Remedy for breach of warranty. (1) Where there is a breach of warranty by the seller, or where the buyer elects or is compelled to treat any breach of a condition on the part of the seller as breach of warranty, the buyer is not by reason only of such breach of warranty entitled to reject the goods; but he may:

(*a*) set up against the seller the breach of warranty in diminution or extinction of the price; or

(*b*) sue the seller for damages for breach of warranty.

(2) The fact that a buyer has set up a breach of warranty in diminution or extinction of the price does not prevent him from suing for the same breach of warranty if he has suffered further damage.

60. Repudiation of contract before due date. Where either party to a contract of sale, repudiates the contract before the date of delivery, the other may either treat the contract as subsisting and wait till the date of delivery, or he may treat the contract rescinded and sue for damages for the breach.

61. Interest by way of damages and special damages. (1) Nothing in this Act shall affect the right of the seller or the buyer to recover interest or special damages in any case where by law interest or special damages may be recoverable, or to recover the money paid where the consideration for the payment of it has failed.

(2) In the absence of a contract to the contrary, the Court may award interest at such rate as it thinks fit on the amount of the price:

(*a*) to the seller in a suit by him for the amount of the price — from the date of the tender of the goods or from the date on which the price was payable;

(*b*) to the buyer in a suit by him for refund of the price in a case of a breach of the contract on the part of the seller — from the date on which the payment was made.

CHAPTER VII—MISCELLANEOUS

62. Exclusion of implied terms and conditions. Where any right, duty or liability would arise under a contract of sale by implication of law, it may be negatived or varied by express agreement or by the course of dealing between the parties, or by usage, if the usage, is such as to bind both parties to the contract.

63. Reasonable time a question of fact. Where in this Act any reference is made to a reasonable time, the question what is a reasonable time is a question of fact.

64. Auction sale. In the case of a sale by auction:

(1) where goods are put for sale in lots, each lot is **prima facie** deemed to be the subject of a separate contract of sale;

(2) the sale is complete when the auctioneer announces its completion by the fall of the hammer or in other customary manner; and until such announcement is made, any bidder may retract his bid;

(3) a right to bid may be reserved expressly by or on behalf of the seller and, where such right is expressly so reserved, but not otherwise, the seller or any one person on his behalf may, subject to the provisions hereinafter contained, bid at the auction;

(4) where the sale is not notified to be subject to a right to bid on behalf of the seller, it shall not be lawful for the seller to bid himself, or to employ any person to bid at such sale, or for the auctioneer knowingly to take any bid from the seller or any such person; and any sale contravening this rule may be treated as fraudulent by the buyer;

(5) the sale may be notified to be subject to a reserved or upset price;

(6) if the seller makes use of pretended bidding to raise the price, the sale is voidable at the option of the buyer.

64A. In contracts of sale, amount of increased or decreased taxes to be added or deducted. (1) Unless a different intention appears from the terms of the contract, in the event to any tax of the nature described in sub-section (2) being imposed, increased, decreased or remitted in respect of any goods after the making of any contract for the sale of purchase of such goods without stipulation as to the payment of tax where tax was not chargeable at the time of the making of the contract, or for the sale or purchase of such goods tax-paid where tax was chargeable at the time,

(*a*) if such imposition or increase so takes effect that the tax or increased tax, as the case may be, or any part of such tax is paid or is payable, the seller may add so much to the contract price as will be equivalent to the amount paid or payable in respect of such tax or increase of tax, and he shall be entitled to be paid and to sue for and recover such addition; and

(*b*) if such decrease or remission so takes effect that the decreased tax only, or no tax, as the case may be, is paid or is payable, the buyer may deduct so much from the contract price as will be equivalent to the decrease of tax, or remitted tax, and the shall not be liable to pay, or be sued for, or in respect of such deduction.

(2) The provisions of sub-section (1) apply to the following taxes, namely:

(a) any duty of customs or excise on goods;

(b) any tax on the sale or purchase of goods.

65. (Repealed) Rep. by the Repealing Act. 1938 (1 of 1938), S. 2 and Sch.

66. Savings. (1) Nothing in this Act or any repeal effected thereby shall effect or be deemed to effect:

(*a*) any right, title, interest, obligation or liability already acquired, accrued or incurred before the commencement of this Act; or

(*b*) any legal proceedings of remedy in respect of any such right, title, interest, obligation or liability; or

(*c*) anything done or suffered before the commencement of this Act; or

(*d*) any enactment relating to the sale of goods which is not expressly repealed by this Act; or

(*e*) any rule of law not inconsistent with this Act.

(2) The rules of insolvency relating to contracts for the sale of goods shall continue to apply thereto, notwithstanding anything contained in this Act.

(3) The provisions of this Act relating to contracts of sale do not apply to any transaction in the form of a contract of sale which is intended to operate by way of mortage, pledge, charge or other security.

INDEX

A

B

D

E

Q

R

S

T

U

V

W